Dear Colleague,

Thank you for your interest in this new Eighth Edition of *I Never Knew I Had a Choice: Explorations in Personal Growth.* For more than two decades, we have been deeply rewarded by the comments we have received from students who have used the text and gained insight and perspective into their lives—as well as the opportunities life offers them. It is the comments of these students, combined with those of reviewers and our fellow instructors, that have helped us shape this current edition. We thank each of you.

Helping students explore themselves, their lives, and their beliefs and attitudes in a way that is personally empowering is an exciting challenge for all of us who teach, and finding materials that truly encourage students to confront important life issues can sometimes be difficult. Therefore, it is extremely gratifying that over the years so many professors have chosen to use our textbook, *I Never Knew I Had a Choice: Explorations in Personal Growth,* with their students.

Through each edition we have worked to make the book an even more useful and cutting-edge tool for personal growth, and we have made a great effort to help students truly examine their own concerns, decisions, and values—and use that knowledge to exercise healthy options in the present. Throughout the Eighth Edition, we encourage students to be honest with their emotions by doing so ourselves.

Now, the Eighth Edition features increased emphasis on spirituality, the benefits of exercise and self-care, sexuality, holistic health, and ways to manage stress, such as meditation, mindfulness, deep relaxation, massage therapy, time management, money management, and yoga. And, we have connected the book to *InfoTrac® College Edition* and the vast resources available via the Internet in every chapter.

An instructor who used our book in the past told us:

> *". . . I can confidently say that I believe it to be the best possible choice for an in-depth understanding of personality development throughout the lifespan. I believe the easy-to-read format and interactive questions posed at the beginning and end of each chapter allow the reader to not only learn about life stages and theory, but to develop their own person as well."*

With your careful guidance and the new Eighth Edition of our text, it is our hope that your students can embark on a revealing, rewarding journey—one that is not soon forgotten.

Please take a few moments to look through the *Preview* on the following pages, which will tell you about the many new enhancements to the Eighth Edition and its teaching and learning package. And, please send us your thoughts on the book—and encourage your students to do the same! It is only with the input of actual users that we can continue to make this book the best it can be. We look forward to hearing from you!

Sincerely,

Gerald Corey
Marianne Schneider Corey

P.S. Be sure to encourage your students to enter our essay contest, *Choices and Changes: Learning from the Course!* The winner will receive a personal response from us, as well as a $200 prize—and have their work published on the Thomson Brooks/Cole Counseling website! See page 8 of this Preview for more information.

A LETTER FROM THE AUTHORS

THE NEW EIGHTH EDITION

EIGHTH EDITION

I never knew I had a

choice

explorations in personal growth

gerald corey • marianne schneider corey

FROM THE COREY LIBRARY OF TEXTS AND MEDIA

This 'unfinished book' can help your students make the connection between choices and change!

With the help of Jerry and Marianne Corey's *I Never Knew I Had a Choice: Explorations in Personal Growth*, you can help your students begin a personal journey—one that gets them exploring the meaning of life, their own spirituality, healthy relationships, and more. This relevant Eighth Edition is supported by the most current research available, and it explores issues that resonate with today's students. Interactive and highly motivating, *I Never Knew I Had a Choice* allows students to examine and confirm their beliefs, attitudes, and directions in life. And, every step of the way, students have the support of the Coreys, whose warm, inviting tone and personal insights help students realize that they're not alone as they begin to take responsibility for their own growth and independence.

As students fill in their personal reactions to the book's numerous self-inventories, exercises, and activities, they complete the text and thus make the book their own. Soon, students begin to see that the choices they make can inspire real and lasting change in significant dimensions of their life. And, with the Coreys' encouragement, students quickly feel empowered to make these life-changing decisions with more confidence.

Healthy sexuality . . . spirituality . . . holistic health . . .
New coverage of today's topics help students
learn to make informed decisions
regarding their well being

Every chapter of this life-changing, empowering Eighth Edition features new research and insights that help students enhance their physical, emotional, and interpersonal well being.

304 CHAPTER NINE

Intimacy can be conceived of as a close emotional relationship characterized by a deep level of caring for another person and is a basic component of all loving relationships.

Listening to Our Bodies

Television and e-mail commercials promoting Viagra have given men another way to ensure sexual responsiveness. **Erectile dysfunction (ED)**, sometimes referred to as impotence, is the consistent inability to achieve and maintain a penile erection required for adequate sexual relations. Most men are unable to achieve or maintain an erection on occasion for any number of reasons: fatigue, stress, or alcohol or drug abuse (Hales, 2005). Sometimes there is a physical reason, and sometimes this is due to the side effects of certain prescription drugs. In addition, ED is frequently due to psychological factors such as feelings of guilt, prolonged depression, hostility or resentment, anxiety about personal adequacy, fear of pregnancy, or a generally low level of self-esteem. Men who experience erectile dysfunction might ask themselves, "What is my body telling me?"

When we are unable to be sexually responsive, our bodies are often sending us an important message about our emotional health or possibly about our

This edition presents a positive view of sexuality, and includes new material on such sexuality-related issues as boundaries, sexual values and behavior, the HIV/AIDS crisis, and communication and sexual intimacy, consistently encouraging students to make informed decisions.

170 CHAPTER FIVE

Yoga is a path to health and wellness.

YOGA

Over the past three decades yoga has become quite popular throughout the Western world, and it appeals to a wide range of people, from children to the elderly, with all levels of abilities. This brief section on yoga consists of a summary of a few of the points Feuerstein and Bodian (1993) make about the practice of yoga in their book *Living Yoga: A Comprehensive Guide for Daily Life.* **Yoga** is not simply a form of calisthenics, a system of meditation, or a religion. However, like meditation and mindfulness, yoga is a way of life. Yoga is

In the Eighth Edition, the Coreys offer a deeper discussion of religion, spirituality, and discovering meaning in life, and they explore spirituality as a factor in health and wellness. Additionally, an expanded and updated section on wellness and life choices investigates sound health practices and discusses meditation and yoga, the benefits of exercise, and a holistic approach to health.

"…provides a strong foundation of psychology with a wise consideration of how these concepts can lead to better personal choices. I am impressed with how the book continues to evolve, remain fresh, and relevant with each new edition. I hope this text continues to have great longevity because it has had a tremendous impact on students that I worked with over the years."

Troy Smith
North Shore Community College

With the Coreys' guidance, students explore the latest issues and their own beliefs—and aim toward positive changes

Choice Theory Approach to Personal Growth

Although this book is based largely on the humanistic approach in psychology, we draw from other psychological schools in exploring key topics. One of these approaches is **reality therapy,** which is based on a cognitive-behavioral model. Reality therapy teaches people how to make effective choices and satisfy their basic needs. Choice theory underlies the practice of reality therapy, which was founded by the psychiatrist William Glasser. **Choice theory** posits that everything we do can be explained in terms of our attempts to satisfy our basic needs: *survival, love and belonging, power or achievement, freedom or independence,* and *fun.* Each of us has all five needs, but they vary in strength. For example, we all have a need for love and belonging, but some of us need more love than others. Choice theory is based on the premise that because we are by nature social creatures we need to both receive and give love. Glasser (1998, 2000) believes

The Eighth Edition now covers the choice theory approach to personal growth. This new material helps readers evaluate their own behavior as it illustrates how to create action plans designed for change.

The book's extensively revised and expanded discussion of diversity now addresses ways to appreciate and respect diversity and covers such issues as white privilege and discrimination against gays and lesbians.

Prejudice and Discrimination Against Lesbians and Gay Men

In the past many people felt ashamed and abnormal because they had homosexual feelings. Heterosexuals frequently categorized gay and lesbian people as deviants and as sick or immoral. Pardess (2005) points out that negative views of homosexuals and opposition to homosexuality have been part of the culture of many religious traditions (Christianity, Judaism, and Islam), and in most religious settings homosexuality is considered to be morally wrong and a sin. According to Pardess, antigay prejudices are not limited to any specific cultural, social, or educational group. These prejudices exist across religions, professions, institutions, and cultures. For these and other reasons, many gay, lesbian, and bisexual individuals conceal their sexual identity, perhaps even from themselves. Furthermore, they are frequently confronted with heterosexism, interpersonal discrimination, verbal harassment, physical assault, and institutional discrimination (Matlin, 2004).

Today, the gay liberation movement is actively challenging the social stigma attached to sexual orientation, and those with same-sex partners are increasingly asserting their rights to live as they choose, without discrimination.

sense of mistrust toward human relationships. Although neither orientation is fixed in an infant's personality for life, it is clear that well-nurtured infants are in a more favorable position with respect to future personal growth than are their more neglected peers.

Daniel Goleman (1995) believes infancy is the beginning point for establishing emotional intelligence. He identifies the most crucial factor in teaching emotional competence as timing, especially in our family of origin and in our culture of origin during infancy. He adds that childhood and adolescence expand on the foundation for learning a range of human competencies. Later development offers critical *windows of opportunity* for acquiring the basic emotional patterns that will govern the rest of our lives.

John Bowlby (1969, 1973, 1980, 1988) studied the importance of attachment, separation, and loss in human development and developed **attachment theory,** an extension of psychoanalytic theory. **Attachment** involves an emotional bonding with another who is perceived as a source of security (Pistole & Arricale, 2003). Bowlby (1988) emphasizes the relationships that the infant has with others, especially the mother (or another "attachment figure"), and proposes that the maintenance of affectional bonds is essential for human survival. Infant attachment relationships can be broadly classified as secure or insecure. The quality of care an infant receives is related to the quality of relationships in later life (Peluso, Peluso, White, & Kern, 2004).

Ainsworth, Blehar, Waters, and Wall (1978) designed an experiment to observe the attachment behavior of young children, and based on these observations, they defined three patterns of attachment: secure, anxious-avoidant, and anxious-ambivalent. According to Bowlby (1969, 1973) and Ainsworth et al.

A fuller exploration of childhood and adolescent development includes new examinations of attachment theory during infancy, racial identity development in adolescence, and the challenges faced by adolescents.

Compelling and revealing exercises in every chapter help students see the choices they can make—and help them experience true personal growth

KEVIN'S STORY

*W*hen I reached middle age, I began to question how I wanted to continue living. My father suffered a series of heart attacks. I watched my father decline physically, and this jolted me into the realization that both my father's time and my own time were limited. I finally went for a long-overdue physical examination and discovered that I had high blood pressure, that my cholesterol level was abnormally high, and that I was at relatively high risk of having a heart attack. I also learned that several of my relatives had died of heart attacks. I decided that I wanted to reverse what I saw as a self-destructive path. After talking with a physician, I decided to change my patterns of living in several ways. I was overeating, my diet was not balanced, I was consuming a great deal of alcohol to relax, I didn't get enough sleep, and I didn't do any physical exercise. My new de cision involved making contacts with friends. I learned to enjoy playing tennis and racquetball on a regular basis. I took up jogging. If I didn't run in the morning, I felt somewhat sluggish during the day. I radically changed my diet in line with suggestio from my physician. As a result, I lowered both my cholesterol level and my blood pre sure without the use of medication; I also lost 20 pounds and worked myself into exc lent physical shape. Getting into personal counseling was extremely helpful, because my sessions with a counselor helped me make some basic changes in the way I approach life and also helped me put things into perspective.

Personal Stories offer first-person accounts of how others have dealt with their own struggles and the choices they have made in response to their challenges.

20 CHAPTER ONE

_____ I generally think and choose for myself.
_____ I usually like myself.
_____ I know what I want.
_____ I am able to ask for what I want.
_____ I feel a sense of personal power.
_____ I am open to change.
_____ I feel equal to others.
_____ I am sensitive to the needs of others.
_____ I care about others.
_____ I can act in accordance with my own judgment without feeling guilty if others disapprove of me.
_____ I do not expect others to make me feel good about myself.
_____ I can accept responsibility for my own actions.
_____ I am able to accept compliments.
_____ I can give affection.
_____ I can receive affection.
_____ I am not so security-bound that I will not explore new things.
_____ I am generally accepted by others.
_____ I can give myself credit for what I do well.
_____ I am able to enjoy my own company.
_____ I am capable of forming meaningful relationships.
_____ I live in the here and now and am not preoccupied with the past or the future.
_____ I feel a sense of significance.
_____ I am not diminished when I am with those I respect.
_____ I believe in my ability to succeed in projects that are meaningful to me.

Take Time to Reflect sections pose reflective questions that prompt students to think critically about how the material affects them.

Where Can I Go From Here?

1. Write an account in your journal of the first 6 years of your life. Although you may think that you cannot remember much about this time, you can learn more by following these guidelines:
    a. Write down a few key questions that you would like answered about your early years.
    b. Seek out your relatives, and ask them some questions about your early years.
    c. Collect any reminders of your early years, particularly pictures.
    d. Visit the place or places where you lived and went to school.

2. When you reflect on your childhood and adolescent years, how did your ability to cope with experiences influence the way you cope with present life situations? What healthy coping mechanisms did you adopt? What maladaptive coping mechanisms did you adopt?

3. From among the many exercises in this chapter chose those that you are willin self-help program during your What things are you willing t some of the changes you want

4. Pictures often say more abo What do your pictures tell abou

Each chapter begins with *Where Am I Now?* inventories and ends with *Where Can I Go From Here?*, a section filled with exercises and questions, as well as *Resources for Future Study*, a section that lists websites, **InfoTrac® College Edition** key words, and print resources dedicated to the chapter topic. The Coreys specifically designed and selected these features to help students deepen and personalize their understanding of the chapter material.

Where Am I Now?

Use this scale to respond to these statements:

3 = This statement is true of me *most* of the time.
2 = This statement is true of me *some* of the time.
1 = This statement is true of me *almost none* of the time.

___ 1. I am capable of looking at my past decisions and then making new decisions that will significantly change the course of my life.
___ 2. "Shoulds" and "oughts" often get in the way of my living my life the way I want.
___ 3. To a large degree I have been shaped by the events of my childhood and adolescent years.
___ 4. When I think of my early childhood years, I remember feeling secure, accepted, and loved.

___ 5. As a child, I was taught that it was acceptable to express feelings such as anger, fear, and jealousy.
___ 6. I had desirable models to pattern my behavior after when I was growing up.
___ 7. In looking back at my early school-age years, I had a positive self-concept and experienced more successes than failures.
___ 8. I went through a stage of rebellion during my adolescent years.
___ 9. My adolescent years were lonely ones.
___ 10. I was greatly influenced by peer group pressure during my adolescence.

5

ONLINE RESOURCES

Book Companion Website
Accessible through
http://counseling.wadsworth.com/coreychoice/
This updated Book Companion Website includes online text-specific resources created especially for this Eighth Edition of *I Never Knew I Had a Choice*. Your students can access a variety of chapter-by-chapter resources, including flashcards, **InfoTrac® College Edition** exercises, cases, and chapter-by-chapter online quizzing.

InfoTrac® College Edition . . . now with InfoMarks™
NOT SOLD SEPARATELY.
FREE four-month access to **InfoTrac® College Edition**'s online database of more than 18 million reliable, full-length articles from 5,000 academic journals and periodicals (including *Counselor Education and Supervision, Journal of Counseling and Development,* and *Journal of Multicultural Counseling and Development*) includes access to **InfoMarks**—stable URLs that can be linked to articles, journals, and searches. **InfoMarks** allow you to use a simple "copy and paste" technique to create instant and continually updated online readers, content services, bibliographies, electronic "reserve" readings, and current topic sites. And, incorporating **InfoTrac College Edition** into your course is easy—references to this virtual library are built into the Coreys' text. And to help students use the research they gather, their free four-month subscription to **InfoTrac College Edition** includes access to **InfoWrite,** a complete set of online critical thinking and paper writing tools. To take a quick tour of **InfoTrac College Edition**, visit http://www.infotrac-college.com/ and select the "User Demo." *(Journals subject to change. Certain restrictions may apply. For additional information, please consult your local Thomson representative.)*

Opposing Viewpoints Resource Center
The text packaged with access to Opposing Viewpoints Resource Center:
0-495-04314-1
Newly available from Thomson Brooks/Cole, this online center allows you to expose your students to all sides of today's compelling issues, such as racism, poverty, drug abuse, prejudice, abortion, health care reform, and civil rights. This online resource center draws on the acclaimed social issues series published by Greenhaven Press, as well as core reference content from other Gale and Macmillan Reference USA sources. This site also includes a built-in research guide and paper writing tips.

Coming Summer 2005!
Counseling Curriculum Connector:
http://counseling.wadsworth.com/connector

Social Work Curriculum Connector:
http://socialwork.wadsworth.com/connector
These unique, easy-to-navigate websites—tailored to the needs of both Counseling and Social Work courses—allow you to explore Brooks/Cole's online resources—including glossaries, flash cards, web links, quizzes and exams, *InfoTrac College Edition* research exercises, and videos—by curriculum area, by system size addressed in the material, and by fields of practice to which the material is relevant.

Also available!
Student Guide for Helping Professions Curriculum Connector
0-495-00112-0
Packaged with the text
0-495-04313-3

Instructor's Guide for Helping Professions Curriculum Connector
0-495-00110-4

Instructor's Resource Manual
0-534-60790-X

This updated and expanded *Instructor's Manual* includes guidelines for using the book and teaching the course, as well as: chapter objectives, chapter outlines, web links, and a glossary (with definitions for each chapter's key terms); a student study guide; approximately 25 multiple-choice and essay test items for every chapter; transparency masters; a list of suggested readings; questions for thought and discussion; numerous activities and exercises for classroom participation; examples of various formats of personal-growth classes; guidelines for maximizing personal learning and for reviewing and integrating the course; and a student evaluation instrument to assess the impact of the course on readers.

Brooks/Cole Annual Clips for Coursework Video for the Helping Professions
2005 Edition 0-534-53347-7
2006 Edition—*Coming Summer 2005* 0-534-53382-5

The 2005 edition of this exclusive video contains clips of social problems such as school violence and substance abuse; clips of counselors and social workers in action, including interviews with children and families; counseling work with victims of school violence; and clips of outcomes and social welfare strategies, policies, and practices in the past and present. A new customized video is available yearly. Instructors: please contact your Thomson representative for details.

Films for the Humanities
A list of films available to qualifying adopters of the Coreys' text can be obtained from your local Thomson Wadsworth sales representative.

ExamView®
Computerized Testing
Cross-Platform CD-ROM for Windows® and Macintosh® 0-534-60787-X

Professors can create, deliver, and customize tests and study guides (both print and online) in minutes with this easy-to-use assessment and tutorial system. **ExamView** offers both a Quick Test Wizard and an Online Test Wizard that guide the user step-by-step through the process of creating tests.

Now, it's YOUR choice! Create a custom workbook with the interactive exercises from this text and your own materials! Ask your local sales representative how you can craft a workbook tailored to the specific needs of your students. Exercises and special features can include: *Where Am I Now?*, *Take Time to Reflect*, *Where Can I Go From Here?*, *Rogers Indicator of Multiple Intelligences*, and the *Quick Discrimination Index*—plus your own materials and resources. Visit http://www.textchoice2.com for details.

RESOURCES FOR INSTRUCTORS

Listen to what student users of the text have to say about their learning experience with the Coreys

"Never before have I felt that nearly every sentence had so much importance as when I read this book. This book will be kept as part of my personal reference library to reinforce my problem solving skills." —Student, Prospect Hall College's Psychology and Success class

"This book was very enlightening. It made me realize characteristics and motivations underlying my behavior and choices. I realized that I have more control over my life than I thought I did." —Student, CSU San Bernardino's Personal and Social Adjustment class

"This was the most interesting textbook I have ever read. It is the first textbook I have ever read cover to cover without skipping any pages. The book dealt with real topics and was written in a way that kept my attention. The Take Time to Reflect *sections really made me think about the chapters and what they meant to me as an individual."* —Student, New Hampshire College's Psychology of Individual Adjustment class

"I liked this whole book. It showed me that I do have a choice." —Student, Mayville State University's Mental Hygiene class

"It made me think about my own life and how I can change my thinking. It gives a clear in-depth understanding of psychology, and helps you gain power to make a choice." —Student, Art Institute of Ft. Lauderdale's Psychology of Learning class

"The Take Time to Reflect *sections helped to make me apply the information to my life and to make me aware of how to make my life better."* —Student, Vincennes University, Applied Psychology

Encourage your students to enter our
Choices and Changes: Learning from the Course Essay Contest

The winner will be awarded a cash prize of $200 and a personal response from Jerry and Marianne Corey!

As your students progress through your course and the new edition of **Choice,** encourage them to enter our new **Choices and Changes: Learning from the Course** essay contest. The goal? To get students to describe, in writing, a personal behavior, the choices they had at the start of the course, and the changes they have made as a result.

Each essay will be read and judged by our contest panel. A winner will be announced each semester. The winning essays will be posted on our *I Never Knew I Had a Choice* website and winning students will receive a $200 cash prize as well as a personal response from the authors.

For entry forms, rules and details, deadlines, and other information, visit **http://counseling.wadsworth.com**

I Never Knew
I Had a Choice

EXPLORATIONS IN PERSONAL GROWTH

Eighth Edition

Gerald Corey

California State University, Fullerton
Diplomate in Counseling Psychology
American Board of Professional Psychology

Marianne Schneider Corey

Private Practice/Consultant

THOMSON

BROOKS/COLE

Australia • Canada • Mexico • Singapore • Spain
United Kingdom • United States

THOMSON
BROOKS/COLE

Executive Editor: Lisa Gebo
Acquisitions Editor: Marquita Flemming
Assistant Editor: Monica Arvin
Editorial Assistant: Christine Northup
Technology Project Manager: Barry Connolly
Marketing Manager: Caroline Concilla
Marketing Assistant: Mary Ho
Marketing Communications Manager: Tami Strang
Project Manager, Editorial Production: Matt Ballantyne
Art Director: Vernon Boes
Print Buyer: Doreen Suruki
Permissions Editor: Joohee Lee

Production Service: The Cooper Company
Text Designer: Lisa Delgado
Art Editor: Vernon Boes
Photo Researchers: Stephen Forsling, Heidi Jo Corey
Copy Editor: Kay Mikel
Illustrator: Interactive Composition Corporation
Cover Designer: Andy Norris
Cover Image: Ulf Sjostedt/Getty Images
Cover Printer: Phoenix Color Corp
Compositor: Interactive Composition Corporation
Printer: Courier-Westford

For more information about our products, contact us at:
Thomson Learning Academic Resource Center
1-800-423-0563
For permission to use material from this text or product, submit a request online at **http://www.thomsonrights.com.**
Any additional questions about permissions can be submitted by e-mail to **thomsonrights@thomson.com.**

Library of Congress Control Number: 2004114816

ISBN 0-534-60786-1

Instructor's Edition: ISBN 0-534-60788-8

Thomson Higher Education
10 Davis Drive
Belmont, CA 94002-3098
USA

Asia (including India)
Thomson Learning
5 Shenton Way
#01-01 UIC Building
Singapore 068808

Australia/New Zealand
Thomson Learning Australia
102 Dodds Street
Southbank, Victoria 3006
Australia

Canada
Thomson Nelson
1120 Birchmount Road
Toronto, Ontario M1K 5G4
Canada

UK/Europe/Middle East/Africa
Thomson Learning
High Holborn House
50/51 Bedford Row
London WC1R 4LR
United Kingdom

Latin America
Thomson Learning
Seneca, 53
Colonia Polanco
11560 Mexico
D.F. Mexico

Spain (including Portugal)
Thomson Paraninfo
Calle Magallanes, 25
28015 Madrid, Spain

In memory of our friend Jim Morelock,

a searcher who lived and died with dignity

and self-respect, who struggled and questioned,

who made the choice to live his days fully

until time ran out on him at age 25.

Brief Contents

Contents

Preface

Never Knew I Had a Choice is intended for college students of any age and for all others who wish to expand their self-awareness and explore the choices available to them in significant areas of their lives. It is also used by counselors in private practice settings and in public and private mental health organizations for workshops and groups. The topics discussed include choosing a personal style of learning; reviewing childhood and adolescence and the effects of these experiences on current behavior and choices; meeting the challenges of adulthood and autonomy; maintaining a healthy body and wellness; managing stress; appreciating the significance of love, intimate relationships, gender roles, and sexuality; work and recreation; dealing creatively with loneliness and solitude; understanding and accepting death and loss; choosing one's values and meaning in life; embracing diversity; and pathways to personal growth.

This is a personal book because we encourage readers to examine the choices they have made and how these choices affect their present level of satisfaction . . . and because we describe our own experiences and values with regard to many of the issues we raise. Each chapter begins with a self-inventory (Where Am I Now?) that gives readers the opportunity to focus on their present beliefs and attitudes. Within the chapters, Take Time to Reflect exercises offer an opportunity to pause and reflect on the issues raised. Additional activities and exercises (Where Can I Go From Here?) are suggested at the end of each chapter for use in the classroom or outside of class. We wish to stress that this is an unfinished book; readers are encouraged to become coauthors by writing about their own reactions in the book and in their journals.

Although the themes underlying this edition of the book are basically the same as previous editions, whenever possible we have updated material to reflect current thinking. The introductory chapter addresses the importance of self-exploration and invites students to consider the value in learning about oneself, others, and personal growth. Social concerns must balance self-interests, however, and we maintain that self-fulfillment can occur only if individuals have a sense of social consciousness. To improve the book and to keep current with developments in the field, the eighth edition includes some new topics and provides expanded discussions of other topics. In addition, key terms are now boldfaced in the text and are accompanied by their definition. Finally, the references list has been updated.

Chapter 1 presents different models of personal growth. We have added a section on the choice theory approach to personal growth, including a discussion of how to evaluate behavior and how to make action plans designed for change. We have streamlined the discussions of multiple intelligences and multiple learning styles, as well as the section on how to get the most from this book and the course.

Chapter 2 contains an updated the treatment of development during childhood and adolescence. This chapter features Erikson's psychosocial model and the self-in-context theories as they deal with development throughout the life span. There are new discussions of attachment theory during infancy, racial identity development in adolescence, and the challenges faced by adolescents.

In Chapter 3 we continue the discussion of the life-span perspective by focusing on the psychosocial theory and the self-in-context perspective. This edition also contains a fuller discussion of the stereotypes common to late adulthood.

Chapter 4 has an expanded section on wellness and life choices. We have revised our discussions on maintaining sound health practices, the benefits of exercise, a holistic approach to health, and diet and developing sensible eating habits. Increased attention has been given to spirituality as a key factor in health and wellness.

Chapter 5 examines the impact of stress on the body, causes of stress, destructive and constructive reactions to stress, and stress and the healthy personality. Expanded coverage has been given to how stress can lead to physical illness. The sections on the use of humor, meditation, and mindfulness as ways to deal effectively with stress have been revised and expanded. Other topics of discussion include time management, money management, yoga, deep relaxation, and massage therapy.

Chapter 6 deals with the many facets of love, the meaning of love, and our fears of loving and being loved. Major organizational and content changes have been made in this chapter.

Chapter 7 contains guidelines for meaningful interpersonal relationships, including friendships, couple relationships (including gay and lesbian relationships), and family relationships. The discussion of meaningful relationships has been revised, and the section on gay and lesbian relationships has been expanded.

Although the organization of topics on gender roles in Chapter 8 is much the same as in the previous edition, there has been considerable revision for this edition. Many new resources have been included, particularly with regard to male roles, female roles, women in the world of work, and challenging traditional gender roles. There is new material on masculinity as it pertains to the African American, Latino, and Asian American cultures. This chapter continues with a developmental theme but focuses on how life experiences influence beliefs about gender identity.

Chapter 9 contains revised material on the boundaries in sexuality, sexual abstinence as an option, sexual values and behavior, and the HIV/AIDS crisis and its effects on sexual behavior, along with practical guidelines to reduce the risks of infection. There is new material on communication and sexual intimacy. Sexual abuse, incest, date and acquaintance rape, and sexual harassment on the campus and in the workplace are also discussed.

Chapter 10 benefits from some of the newer sources on the role of work and recreation in our lives. This chapter contains revised sections on factors in career decision making and an expanded discussion of retirement.

Chapter 11 discusses the creative dimensions of solitude, with an expanded section on loneliness and young adulthood, and loneliness of the immigrant experience.

Chapter 12 deals with fears of death, the interdependence of life and death, the importance of grieving, and suicide. The expanded discussion of suicide includes more of the myths and misconceptions surrounding suicide along with coverage on physician-assisted suicide. The information on hospice, grief work, and the stages of dying has also been revised with increased coverage on the tasks facing both the dying and those who are grieving losses.

The meaning of life is the central subject of Chapter 13, and a new section on religion/spirituality and meaning in life is included. The section on diversity has been extensively revised and greatly expanded. Some new topics include a discussion of White privilege, appreciating and respecting diversity, and ways that we are both alike and different.

Chapter 14 encourages students to think about where they will choose to go from here. Readers are reminded that their journey toward personal growth is only beginning. This chapter offers a variety of avenues for growth that readers may wish to pursue now and in the future.

Fundamentally, our approach in *I Never Knew I Had a Choice* is humanistic and personal; that is, we stress the healthy and effective personality and the common struggles most of us experience in becoming autonomous. We especially emphasize accepting personal responsibility for the choices we make and consciously deciding whether and how we want to change our lives. There are multiple approaches to the study of personal adjustment and growth. We emphasize the existential and humanistic approach because to us it best sheds light on the role of choice and responsibility in creating a meaningful life for ourselves. We also include other theoretical perspectives in many of the chapters, such as choice theory and reality therapy, transactional analysis, cognitive-behavior therapy, feminist theory, self-in-relation theory, and the psychosocial approach to development.

Although our own approach can be broadly characterized as humanistic and existential, our aim has been to challenge readers to recognize and assess their own choices, beliefs, and values rather than to convert them to a particular point of view. Our basic premise is that a commitment to self-exploration can create new potentials for choice. Many of the college students and counseling clients with whom we work are relatively well-functioning people who desire more from life and who want to recognize and remove blocks to their personal creativity and freedom. Most of them are looking for a practical course that deals with real issues in everyday living and that will provide an impetus for their own personal growth. It is for people like these that we have written this book.

The experiences of those who have read and used the earlier editions of *I Never Knew I Had a Choice* reveal that the themes explored have application to individuals of all ages and backgrounds. Readers who have taken the time to write us about their reactions say that the book encouraged them to take an honest look at their lives and to challenge themselves to make certain changes. Many readers who have used this book for a college course have told us that they have shared it with friends and relatives.

I Never Knew I Had a Choice was developed for a variety of self-exploration courses, including Introduction to Counseling, Therapeutic Group, Psychology of Personal Growth, Personal Development, Personal Growth and Development, Personality and Adjustment, Introduction to Human Behavior, Life Processes, Personal and Interpersonal Effectiveness, Character and Conflict, Values of the Helping Professions, Human Potential Seminar, Psychology of Personal Well-Being and Adjustment, and Applied Psychology. *Choice* has also been adopted in courses ranging from the psychology of personal growth on the undergraduate level to graduate courses for training teachers and counselors. It is also used in group counseling courses as a catalyst for small group interaction and for workshops in training group leaders. Courses that make use of an interactive approach will find *Choice* a useful tool for discussion.

We have written this book to facilitate interaction—between student and instructor, among the students within a class, between students and significant people in their lives, between the reader and us as authors—but most important of all our aim is to provide the reader with an avenue for reflection. This is not a book that can be read passively; it is designed to provoke thoughtful reflection.

Readers are encouraged to look at the direction of their lives to see if they like where they are heading. Our experience has been that active, open, and personal participation in these courses can lead to expanded self-awareness and greater autonomy in living.

An updated and expanded *Instructor's Resource Manual* accompanies this textbook. It includes about 40 test items, both multiple-choice and essay, for each chapter; a student study guide covering all chapters; suggested readings; questions for thought and discussion; numerous activities and exercises for classroom participation; guidelines for using the book and teaching the course; examples of various formats of personal-growth classes; guidelines for maximizing personal learning and for reviewing and integrating the course; glossary of key terms; transparency masters; additional Web sites and InfoTrac College Edition suggestions; and a student evaluation instrument to assess the impact of the course on readers.

Acknowledgments

We would like to express our deep appreciation for the insightful suggestions given to us by friends, associates, reviewers, students, and readers. The following people, many of whom had used *I Never Knew I Had a Choice* in earlier editions, reviewed the entire manuscript and provided useful suggestions that were incorporated into this edition.

Pre-revision reviewers include John Johnson, Penn State at DuBois; Troy Smith, North Shore Community College; Richard Kandus, Mt. San Jacinto College, California; Eva Glahn Atkinson, Brescia University; Leslie Ann Moore, University of Texas at Austin; Patrick Callanan, California State University, Fullerton; Juan Kenigstein, Breyer State University; Mildred Similton, Pfeiffer University; and Doris Van Auken, Holy Cross College.

Expert reviewers for selected chapters for the 8th edition include Charles A. Corr, Southern Illinois University (Chapter 12); Stephen J. Freeman, Texas A&M University (Chapter 12); Linda S. Krajewski, California State University, San Bernardino (Chapters 2 and 3); Wolfgang Linden, University of British Columbia (Chapters 4 and 5); Leslie Ann Moore, University of Texas at Austin (Chapters 2 and 3); Michael Moulton, Northwestern State University (Chapter 9); Roberta Nutt, Texas Women's College (Chapter 8); Debra S. Osborn, University of South Florida (Chapter 10); Kristi Perryman, Ozark Psychological Associates, Springfield, MO (Chapters 2 and 3); Fredric E. Rabinowitz, University of Redlands (Chapter 8); and Patricia E. Stowers, Indiana University (Chapters 7 and 9).

We want to recognize the following people who offered ideas for revision of this edition: Patrick Callanan, Cindy Corey, and J. Michael Russell. We also appreciate the selection of photographs by Heidi Jo Corey.

Finally, as is true of all our books, *I Never Knew I Had a Choice* continues to develop as a result of a team effort, which includes the combined talents of a number of people. Special recognition is due to those individuals with whom we worked closely on the production of this book. These people include Marquita Flemming, editor of counseling and human services, who works closely with us on all our projects; Matthew Ballantyne, production project manager; Cecile Joyner, production editor; and Kay Mikel, manuscript editor, whose insight and creative editorial skills kept this book reader friendly. Recognition goes to Vernon Boes, art director, for overseeing the design of the book, and to Lisa Delgado, who designed the interior pages. Our thanks go to Madeleine Clarke for her work in compiling the index. We are grateful to all of these people who continue to devote extra time and effort to ensure the quality of our books.

Gerald Corey
Marianne Schneider Corey

I Never Knew I Had a Choice

EXPLORATIONS IN PERSONAL GROWTH

Eighth Edition

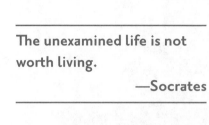

1

The unexamined life is not
worth living.

—Socrates

Invitation to Personal Learning and Growth

© PhotoDisc/Getty Images

Where Am I Now?

Each chapter begins with a self-inventory designed to assess your attitudes and beliefs regarding a particular topic. Think carefully about each question. By answering these questions as honestly as you can, you will increase your awareness and clarify your personal views on a range of subjects.

Use this scale to respond to these statements:

> 3 = This statement is true of me *most* of the time.
>
> 2 = This statement is true of me *some* of the time.
>
> 1 = This statement is true of me *almost none* of the time.

1. I believe I influence the course of my life through my choices.

2. I have a good sense of the areas in my life that I can change and those aspects that I cannot change.

3. Generally, I have been willing to pay the price for taking the personal risks involved in choosing for myself.

4. It is within my power to change even if others around me do not change.

5. Happiness and success are largely related to a sense of belonging and to social connectedness.

6. My present personality is determined both by who and what I have been and by the person I hope to become.

7. At their deepest core, people are good and can be trusted to move forward in a positive way.

8. I am an active learner.

9. I am looking forward to getting fully involved in this course.

10. I am willing to challenge myself to examine my life in an honest way.

T o make changes in your life, you need to first assess where you are today. Is your life typically satisfying? Are you getting what you want out of life? Do you feel a sense of encouragement that you can make changes in your daily life? Do you have an understanding of how your actions affect others? As you read this book, it is our hope that you will increase your awareness about who you are and how you relate to the world, and that you will feel inspired to make the changes that will result in a more satisfying life.

CHOICE AND CHANGE

We Do Have Choices!

It is exciting for us when our students and clients discover that they can be more in charge of their own lives than they ever dreamed possible. As one counseling client put it: "One thing I can see now that I didn't see before is that I can change my life if I want to. *I never knew I had a choice!*" This remark captures the central message of this book: We can make choices, and we do have the power to re-create ourselves through our choices.

Reflect on the quality of your life and decide for yourself how you want to change. Challenge your fears rather than being stopped by them. Socrates, in his wisdom, said, "The unexamined life is not worth living." Examine your values and your behavior. What crises have you faced? How did these crises affect your life? Did they represent a significant turning point for you? The Chinese symbol for crisis represents both *danger* and *opportunity*. As you engage yourself in this book, consider ways to use any challenging life situations as opportunities for discovering choices and feeling empowered to make changes.

Are You Ready to Change?

Deciding to change is not a simple matter. You may wonder if you need to change or if the cost of changing would be worth it. You may have entertained some of these thoughts when you contemplated making a change in your life:

- I don't know if I want to rock the boat.
- Things aren't all that bad in my life.
- I'm fairly secure, and I don't want to take the chance of losing this security.
- I'm afraid that if I start to think too much about myself I might be overwhelmed.

It is common for people to have doubts and fears about making changes. In fact, it is a mark of courage to acknowledge your hesitations to change and your anxiety over accepting greater responsibility for your life.

It is no easy matter to take an honest look at your life and begin to live differently. Those who are close to you may not approve of or like your changes, and they may put up barriers to your efforts. Your cultural background may make it more difficult for you to assume a new role and to modify certain values. These factors are likely to increase your anxiety as you contemplate making your own choices rather than allowing others to choose for you.

If you desire change in a certain area of your life, what is the best way to bring about this change? The process of change begins when you are able to recognize and accept certain facets of yourself, even though you may not want to acknowledge some personal characteristic. Sometimes it is not possible to make a desired change, but even in these cases you have power over your attitude. You can choose how you perceive, interpret, and react to your situation. The Serenity Prayer* outlines the sphere of our responsibility:

> GOD, GRANT ME the serenity to accept the things I cannot change, courage to change the things I can, and wisdom to know the difference.

The **paradoxical theory of change** holds that personal change tends to occur when we become aware of *what we are* as opposed to trying to become *what we are not* (Beisser, 1970). The more we attempt to deny some aspect of our being, the more we remain the same. Thus, if you desire change in some area of your life, you first need to accept who and what you are. If you live in denial, it is difficult to make changes. Recognizing who you are at the present time is the starting point for the path you might choose to take.

Change is not facilitated by being critical of yourself or by guilting yourself over all that you are not. Change occurs when you are able to view yourself as you are and treat yourself kindly and respectfully. Once you are able to identify and acknowledge those aspects of yourself that you tend to deny, you increase your choices and open yourself to possibilities for changing. Take small steps in

---

*Attributed to Friedrich Oetinger (1702–1782) and Reinhold Niebuhr, "The Serenity Prayer" (1934).

the direction you want to move. It may help to remember that perfection is a direction, not a goal that you arrive at once and for all. Wanting to be different is the beginning of a new direction.

Self-exploration, being honest with yourself and others, thinking for yourself, and making a commitment to live by your choices, requires concerted effort. Taking charge of your life involves a price. A degree of discomfort and even fear may be associated with discovering more about yourself. When you are considering making life changes, ask yourself this question: What is the cost, and is it worth the price? Change is a proactive process, and only you can decide what you are willing to risk and how much change is right for you.

What About Other People?

Making choices for yourself and being in control of your life is important, but you cannot ignore the reality that you are a social being and that many of your decisions will be influenced by your relationships with significant people in your life. Philip Hwang (2000) asserts that happiness entails possessing a healthy balance of both self-esteem and other-esteem. Rather than searching for ways to enhance self-esteem, Hwang makes a strong case for promoting personal and social responsibility. **Other-esteem** involves respect, acceptance, caring, valuing, and promoting others, without reservation. We need to strive to understand others who may think, feel, and act differently from us. American culture stresses the self, independence, and self-sufficiency. Hwang suggests that our challenge is to learn to see the world anew by reexamining our attitudes, values, and beliefs and developing a balance between caring for self and showing high esteem for others.

In *Habits of the Heart,* the authors assert that the goal of most Americans is to become one's own person, almost to give birth to oneself (Bellah, Madsen, Sullivan, Swidler, & Tipton, 1985). But in their many interviews, a common theme emerged: the notion that the good life cannot be lived alone, that we do not find ourselves in isolation, and that connectedness to others in love, work, and community is absolutely essential to our self-esteem and happiness.

> WE FIND OURSELVES not independently of other people and institutions but through them. We never get to the bottom of ourselves on our own. We discover who we are face to face and side by side with others in work, love, and learning. (p. 84)

Making a commitment to examine your life does not mean becoming wrapped up in yourself to the exclusion of everyone else. Unless you know and care about yourself, however, you will not be able to develop good connections with others.

MODELS FOR PERSONAL GROWTH

One of the obvious benefits of choosing to change your life is that you will grow by exposing yourself to new experiences. But just what does personal growth entail? In this section we contrast the idea of growth with that of adjustment and offer a humanistic model of what ideal growth can be. We also discuss some divergent perspectives on what constitutes the ideal standard of personal growth.

Adjustment or Growth?

Although this book deals with topics in what is often called "the psychology of adjustment," we are not fond of this common phrase. The term **adjustment** is frequently taken to mean that some ideal norm exists by which people should be measured. This notion raises many questions: What is the desired norm of adjustment? Who determines the standards of "good" adjustment? Is it possible that the same person could be considered well adjusted in our culture and poorly adjusted in some other culture? Do we expect people who live in chaotic and destructive environments to adjust to their life situations?

The notion of adjustment suggests a single standard of measurement that identifies universal qualities of the well-adjusted or psychologically healthy person. Within the limits imposed by genetic and environmental factors, we see the possibilities for creating our own vision of who we want to become rather than conforming to a single standard. In forming this vision, cultural values and norms play a crucial role. For example, if you are in your 20s and still live with your parents, some would view this as dependent behavior on your part and think that you should be living apart from your family of origin. From another cultural perspective, however, it might be inappropriate for you to be living on your own.

Instead of talking about adjustment, we tend to talk about **growth.** The notion of personal growth involves the individual in defining and assessing growth for him- or herself. Personal growth is best viewed as a lifelong process rather than as a fixed point at which you arrive. You will face numerous crises at various stages of your life. These crises can be seen as challenges to change, giving your life new meaning. Growth also encompasses your relationship with significant others, your community, and your world. You do not grow in a vacuum but through your engagement with other people. To continue to grow, you have to be willing to let go of some of your old ways of thinking and acting so new dimensions can develop. During your reading and studying, think about the ways you may have restricted your choices and the degree to which you are willing to exercise new choices and take action to bring about change. Ask yourself these questions:

- What do I want for myself, for others, and from others?
- What do I like about my life?
- What about my life am I having difficulty with?
- How would I like to be different?
- What are possible consequences if I do or do not change?
- How will my changes affect others in my life?
- What range of choices is open to me at this time in my life?
- How has my culture influenced the choices I have made? How might my cultural values either enhance or inhibit my ability to make changes?

A Humanistic Approach to Personal Growth

I Never Knew I Had a Choice is based on a humanistic view of people. A central concept of this approach to personal growth is **self-actualization.** Striving for self-actualization means working toward fulfilling our potential, toward becoming all that we are capable of becoming. **Humanistic psychology** is based on the premise that this striving for growth exists but is not an automatic process. Because growth often involves some pain and considerable turmoil, many of us experience a constant struggle between our desire for security, or dependence, and our desire to experience the delights of growth.

Although other people have made significant contributions to humanistic psychology, we have chosen to focus on four key people who devoted much of their professional careers to the promotion of psychological growth and the self-actualization process: Alfred Adler, Carl Jung, Carl Rogers, and especially Abraham Maslow and his extensive investigation of the process of self-actualization. It is particularly interesting to note the close parallels between the struggles of these men in early childhood and the focus of their adult investigations. Based on a set of life experiences, each of these men made a choice that influenced the development of his theory.

Alfred Adler (1958, 1964, 1969) made major contributions during Sigmund Freud's era and was a forerunner of the humanistic movement in psychology. In opposition to Freud's deterministic views of the person, Adler's theory stresses self-determination. Adler's early childhood experiences were characterized by a struggle to overcome weaknesses and feelings of inferiority, and the basic concepts of his theory grew out of his willingness to deal with his personal problems. Adler is a good example of a person who shaped his own life as opposed to having it determined by fate.

Adler's idea that feelings of inferiority are the wellsprings of creativity has real meaning to me (Jerry), for I believe that our striving for superiority (a sense of personal competence) grows out of our feelings of inferiority. My own fear of failing and feelings of inadequacy have been my best teachers. I have learned that failure isn't fatal, that much can be gained from reflecting on mistakes, and how essential it is to have a personal vision. I encourage my students to dare to dream what may seem like impossible dreams, to believe in themselves in spite of their self-doubts, and then to work hard to make their dreams reality.

Adlerian psychologists contend that we are not the victims of fate but are creative, active, choice-making beings whose every action has purpose and meaning. Adler's approach is basically a growth model that rejects the idea of "psychological sickness." Instead, Adlerians talk of people being discouraged. Adlerian therapists view their work as providing encouragement so people can grow to become what they were meant to be. They teach people better ways to meet the challenges of life tasks, provide direction, help people change unrealistic assumptions and beliefs, and offer encouragement to those who are discouraged.

One of Adler's basic concepts is **social interest,** an individual's attitudes in dealing with other people in the world, which includes striving for a better future. Adler equates social interest with identification and empathy with others. For him, our happiness and success are largely related to a sense of belonging and a social connectedness. As social beings, we need to be of use to others and to establish meaningful relationships in a community. Adler asserted that only when we feel united with others can we act with courage in facing and dealing with life's problems. Because we are embedded in a society, we cannot be understood in isolation from our social context. Self-actualization is thus not an individual matter; it is only within the group that we can actualize our potential. Adler maintained that the degree to which we successfully share with others and are concerned with their welfare is a measure of our maturity. Social interest becomes the standard by which to judge psychological health.

The Western concept of social interest is grounded in **individualism,** which affirms the uniqueness, autonomy, freedom, and intrinsic worth of the individual and emphasizes personal responsibility for our behavior and well-being. The ultimate aim of this orientation is the self-actualization of the individual becoming all that he or she can be. By contrast, the Eastern concept of social interest rests on **collectivism,** which affirms the value of preserving and enhancing the well-being of the group as the main principle guiding social action. This collective orientation emphasizes unity, unification, integration, and fusion. It does not view self-actualization as the ultimate good. Instead, it emphasizes cooperation, harmony, interdependence, achievement of socially oriented and group goals, and collective responsibility.

Carl Jung (1961), who was a contemporary of Adler, made a monumental contribution to the depth of understanding of the human personality. His pioneering work sheds light on human development, particularly during middle age. Jung's personal life paved the way for the expansion of his theoretical notions. His loneliness as a child is reflected in his personality theory, which focuses on the inner world of the individual. Jung's emotional distance from his parents contributed to his feeling of being cut off from the external world of conscious reality. Largely as a way of escaping the difficulties of his childhood, Jung turned inward and became preoccupied with pursuing his unconscious experiences as reflected in his dreams, visions, and fantasies. At age 81 he wrote about his recollections in his autobiography, *Memories, Dreams, Reflections* (1961). He made a choice to focus on the unconscious realm in his personal life, which also influenced the development of his theory of personality.

According to Jung, humans are not merely shaped by past events but strive for growth as well. Our present personality is determined both by who and what we have been and also by the person we hope to become. The process of self-actualization is oriented toward the future. Jung's theory is based on the assumption that humans tend to move toward the fulfillment or realization of all their capabilities. Achieving **individuation**—a fully harmonious and integrated personality—is a primary goal. To reach this goal, we must become aware of and accept the full range of our being. The public self we present is only a small part of who and what we are. For Jung, both constructive and destructive forces coexist in the human psyche, and to become integrated we must accept the **shadow** side of our nature with our primitive impulses such as selfishness and greed. Acceptance of our shadow does not mean being dominated by this dimension of our being but simply recognizing that this is a part of our nature.

According to Carl Jung, humans are not merely shaped by past events, but they strive for growth as well.

Courtesy of Janice and Michael Holmes-Short

Carl Rogers (1980), a major figure in the development of humanistic psychology, focused on the importance of nonjudgmental listening and acceptance as a condition for people to feel free enough to change. Rogers's emphasis on the value of autonomy seems to have grown, in part, out of his own struggles to become independent from his parents. Rogers grew up fearing his mother's critical judgment. In an interview, Rogers mentioned that he could not imagine talking to his mother about anything of significance because he was sure she would have some negative judgment. He also grew up in a home where strict religious standards governed behavior. In his early years, while at a seminary studying to be a minister, Rogers made a critical choice that influenced his personal life and the focus of his theory. Realizing that he could no longer go along with the religious thinking of his parents, Rogers questioned the religious dogma he was being taught, which led to his emancipation and his psychological independence. As a college student, he took the risk of writing a letter to his parents telling them that his views were changing from fundamentalist to liberal and that he was developing his own philosophy of life. Even though he knew that his departure from the values of his parents would be difficult for them, he felt that such a move was necessary for his own intellectual and psychological freedom.

Rogers built his entire theory and practice of psychotherapy on the concept of the **fully functioning person.** Fully functioning people tend to reflect and ask basic questions: Who am I? How can I discover my real self? How can I become what I deeply wish to become? How can I get out from behind my facade and become myself? Rogers maintained that when people give up their facade and accept themselves they move in the direction of being open to experience (that is, they begin to see reality without distorting it). They trust themselves and look to themselves for the answers to their problems, and they no longer attempt to become fixed entities or products, realizing instead that growth is a continual process. Such fully functioning people, Rogers wrote, are in a fluid process of challenging and revisiting their perceptions and beliefs as they open themselves to new experiences.

In contrast to those who assume that we are by nature irrational and destructive unless we are socialized, Rogers exhibited a deep faith in human beings. In his view people are naturally social and forward-moving, strive to function fully, and have at their deepest core a positive goodness. In short, people are to be trusted, and because they are basically cooperative and constructive, there is no need to control their aggressive impulses.

Abraham Maslow was one of the most influential psychologists contributing to our understanding of self-actualizing individuals. He built on Adler's and Jung's works in some significant ways, yet he distinguished himself in discovering a psychology of health. Maslow was concerned with taking care of basic survival needs, and his theory stresses a hierarchy of needs, with satisfaction of physiological and safety needs prerequisite to being concerned about actualizing one's potentials. Self-actualization became the central theme of the work of Abraham Maslow (1968, 1970, 1971). Maslow uses the phrase "the psychopathology of the average" to highlight his contention that merely "normal" people may never extend themselves to become what they are capable of becoming. Further, he criticized Freudian psychology for what he saw as its preoccupation with the sick and negative side of human nature. If our findings are based on observations of a sick population, Maslow reasoned, a sick psychology will emerge. Maslow believed that too much research was being conducted on anxiety, hostility, and neuroses and too little into joy, creativity, and self-fulfillment.

In his quest to create a humanistic psychology that would focus on our potential, Maslow studied what he called self-actualizing people and found that they differed in important ways from so-called normals. Some of the characteristics Maslow found in these people included a capacity to tolerate and even welcome uncertainty in their lives, acceptance of themselves and others, spontaneity and creativity, a need for privacy and solitude, autonomy, a capacity for deep and intense interpersonal relationships, a genuine caring for others, a sense of humor, an inner-directedness (as opposed to the tendency to live by others' expectations), and the absence of artificial dichotomies within themselves (such as work/play, love/hate, and weak/strong). Maslow's theory of self-actualization, along with the implications for the humanistic approach to psychology, is presented next.

Overview of Maslow's Self-Actualization Theory

Maslow postulated a **hierarchy of needs** as a source of motivation. The most basic are the physiological needs. If we are hungry and thirsty, our attention is riveted on meeting these basic needs. Next are the safety needs, which include a sense of security and stability. Once our physical and safety needs are fulfilled, we become concerned with meeting our needs for belonging and love, followed by working on our need for esteem, both from self and others. We are able to strive toward self-actualization only after these four basic needs are met: physiological, safety, love, and esteem. Maslow emphasized that people are not motivated by all five needs at the same time. The key factor determining which need is dominant at a given time is the degree to which those below it are satisfied. Some people come to the erroneous conclusion that if they were "bright" enough or "good" enough they would be further down the road of self-actualization. The truth may be that in their particular cultural, environmental, and societal circumstances these people are motivated to work toward physical and psychological survival, which keeps them functioning at the lower end of the hierarchy. Keep in mind that an individual is not much concerned with actualization, nor is a society focused on the development of culture, if the basic needs are not met.

We can summarize some of the basic ideas of the humanistic approach by means of Maslow's model of the self-actualizing person (Figure 1.1). He describes self-actualization in *Motivation and Personality* (1970), and he also treats this concept in his other books (1968, 1971). Some core characteristics of self-actualizing people are self-awareness, freedom, basic honesty and caring, and trust and autonomy.

Self-Awareness Self-actualizing people are more aware of themselves, of others, and of reality than are nonactualizing people. Specifically, they demonstrate the following behavior and traits:

1. *Efficient perception of reality*
   a. Self-actualizing people see reality as it is.
   b. They have an ability to detect phoniness.
   c. They avoid seeing things in preconceived categories.
2. *Ethical awareness*
   a. Self-actualizing people display a knowledge of what is right and wrong for them.
   b. They have a sense of inner direction.
   c. They avoid being pressured by others and living by others' standards.
3. *Freshness of appreciation*. Like children, self-actualizing people have an ability to perceive life in a fresh way.
4. *Peak moments*
   a. Self-actualizing people experience times of being one with the universe; they experience moments of joy.
   b. They have the ability to be changed by such moments.

Figure 1.1
Maslow's Hierarchy
of Needs

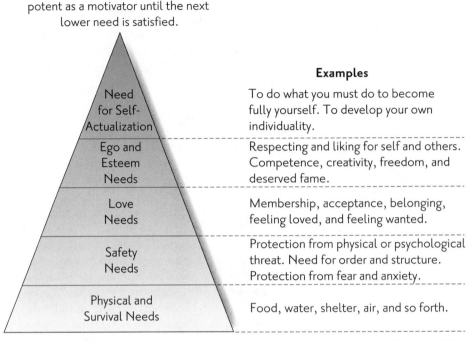

Each higher need does not become
potent as a motivator until the next
lower need is satisfied.

Examples

Need for Self-Actualization	To do what you must do to become fully yourself. To develop your own individuality.
Ego and Esteem Needs	Respecting and liking for self and others. Competence, creativity, freedom, and deserved fame.
Love Needs	Membership, acceptance, belonging, feeling loved, and feeling wanted.
Safety Needs	Protection from physical or psychological threat. Need for order and structure. Protection from fear and anxiety.
Physical and Survival Needs	Food, water, shelter, air, and so forth.

From *Motivation and Personality* by Abraham H. Maslow. Copyright © 1987. Reprinted by permission of Prentice-Hall, Inc.,
Upper Saddle River, N.J.

Freedom Self-actualizing people are willing to make choices for themselves, and they are free to reach their potential. This freedom entails a sense of detachment and a need for privacy, creativity and spontaneity, and an ability to accept responsibility for choices.

1. *Detachment*
    a. For self-actualizing people, the need for privacy is crucial.
    b. They have a need for solitude to put things in perspective.
2. *Creativity*
    a. Creativity is a universal characteristic of self-actualizing people.
    b. Creativity may be expressed in any area of life; it shows itself as inventiveness.
3. *Spontaneity*
    a. Self-actualizing people do not need to show off.
    b. They display a naturalness and lack of pretentiousness.
    c. They act with ease and grace.

Basic Honesty and Caring Self-actualizing people show a deep caring for and honesty with themselves and others. These qualities are reflected in their interest in humankind and in their interpersonal relationships.

1. *Sense of social interest*
   a. Self-actualizing people have a concern for the welfare of others.
   b. They have a sense of communality with all other people.
   c. They have an interest in bettering the world.

2. *Interpersonal relationships*
   a. Self-actualizing people have a capacity for real love and fusion with another.
   b. They are able to love and respect themselves.
   c. They are able to go outside themselves in a mature love.
   d. They are motivated by the urge to grow in their relationships.

3. *Sense of humor*
   a. Self-actualizing people can laugh at themselves.
   b. They can laugh at the human condition.
   c. Their humor is not hostile.

Trust and Autonomy Self-actualizing people exhibit faith in themselves and others; they are independent; they accept themselves as valuable persons; and their lives have meaning.

1. *Search for purpose and meaning*
   a. Self-actualizing people have a sense of mission, of a calling in which their potential can be fulfilled.
   b. They are engaged in a search for identity, often through work that is a deeply significant part of their lives.

2. *Autonomy and independence*
   a. Self-actualizing people have the ability to be independent.
   b. They resist blind conformity.
   c. They are not tradition-bound in making decisions.

3. *Acceptance of self and others*
   a. Self-actualizing people avoid fighting reality.
   b. They accept nature as it is.
   c. They are comfortable with the world.*

This profile is best thought of as an ideal rather than a final state that we reach once and for all. Thus it is more appropriate to speak about the self-actualizing process rather than becoming a self-actualized person.

---

*From *Motivation and Personality* by Abraham H. Maslow. Copyright © 1987. Reprinted by permission of Prentice-Hall, Inc., Upper Saddle River, N.J.

MAYA ANGELOU
An Example of a Self-Actualizing Person

A person we consider to be on the path of self-actualizing is Maya Angelou, a well-known writer and poet. She has written many books that continue to have an impact on her readers, and she is a frequent speaker to various groups. You may recall that she delivered one of her poems at the second inaugural ceremony for President Clinton. Angelou embodies many of the characteristics Maslow describes. In *Maya Angelou: The Poetry of Living*, Margaret Courtney-Clarke (1999) uses ten words to describe Maya Angelou: joy, giving, learning, perseverance, creativity, courage, self-respect, spirituality, love, and taking risks. Various contributors expanded on these themes and gave brief personal reactions to this woman whom they view as very special.

JOY: Maya's message to young children is: "Laugh as much as you can! Take every opportunity to rejoice. Find the humor in life at every opportunity." (Defoy Glenn, p. 19)

GIVING: "You cannot give what you don't have. Maya has this reservoir of love for people and that's why they love her, because it's like a mirror image." (Louise Meriwether, p. 28)

LEARNING: "She has an absolute rapacious desire to know; she really wants to know about everything . . . ." (Connie Sutton, p. 40)

PERSEVERANCE: "Maya has come to believe that troubles are a blessing. They force you to change, to believe." (Andrew Young, p. 62)

CREATIVITY: "The human brain is capable of more things than we can imagine, and if one dreams it—and believes it—one certainly should try it. As Maya says, 'The human mind is a vast storehouse, there is no limit to it.'" (Defoy Glenn, p. 69)

COURAGE: "Maya speaks with courage all the time. She talks about courage as a virtue. In most of her presentations she uses this. She has the courage to say, 'We are more alike than we are unalike.'" (Velma Gibson Watts, p. 76)

SELF-RESPECT: "Maya often says, 'I am a human being and nothing human can be alien to me, and if a human did it, I can do it. I possess the capacity to do it.'" (Defoy Glenn, p. 90)

SPIRITUALITY: "A phenomenal woman! She embraces us with her great love, informs us with her profound wisdom, and inspires us with her poetic and artistic genius. A person of uncommon dignity, rare courage, undaunted faith, dogged determination, grace, integrity, and finally, matchless generosity—Maya Angelou is an international treasure." (Coretta Scott King, p. 108)

LOVE: "If you want to see a miracle in the twentieth century look at Maya Angelou. The spirit is always moving. It moves to far ends of the earth. A spirit of love, of care, of liberation. . . . Maya Angelou's spirit liberates." (Rev. Cecil Williams, p. 110)

TAKING RISKS: "The process of decay starts the moment things are created. So, to hold on too tightly prevents one from getting things, because one's hands are so full one cannot take on anything else." (Defoy Glenn, p. 126)

What are some ways you can engage yourself in the self-actualizing process? The activities at the end of each chapter and the Take Time to Reflect sections scattered throughout the book can help you begin this lifelong quest. As you read about the struggles you are likely to encounter in trying to become all you are capable of becoming, we hope you will begin to see some options for living a fuller life.

Choice Theory Approach to Personal Growth

Although this book is based largely on the humanistic approach in psychology, we draw from other psychological schools in exploring key topics. One of these approaches is **reality therapy,** which is based on a cognitive-behavioral model. Reality therapy teaches people how to make effective choices and satisfy their basic needs. Choice theory underlies the practice of reality therapy, which was founded by the psychiatrist William Glasser. **Choice theory** posits that everything we do can be explained in terms of our attempts to satisfy our basic needs: *survival, love and belonging, power or achievement, freedom or independence,* and *fun.* Each of us has all five needs, but they vary in strength. For example, we all have a need for love and belonging, but some of us need more love than others. Choice theory is based on the premise that because we are by nature social creatures we need to both receive and give love. Glasser (1998, 2000) believes the need to *love and to belong* is the primary need because we need people to satisfy the other needs. It is also the most difficult need to satisfy because we must have a cooperative person to help us meet it.

Choice theory explains that our "total behavior" is always our best attempt to get what we want to satisfy our needs. **Total behavior** teaches that all behavior is made up of four inseparable but distinct components—*acting, thinking, feeling,* and *physiology*—that necessarily accompany all of our actions, thoughts, and feelings. Behavior is purposeful because it is designed to close the gap between what we want and what we perceive we are getting. Specific behaviors are always generated from this discrepancy. Our behaviors come from the inside, and thus we choose our destiny.

Robert Wubbolding (2000), a reality therapist, describes the key procedures used in the practice of reality therapy using an acronym, **WDEP.** Each of the letters refers to a cluster of strategies: W = wants and needs; D = direction and doing; E = self-evaluation; and P = planning. These strategies are designed to promote change, which we will return to as we discuss many of the topics in remaining chapters. Let's look at each of these strategies in more detail.

Wants (Exploring Wants, Needs, and Perceptions)   A critical question that we frequently raise in this book is, "What do you want?" Here are some useful questions to help you answer this question:

- If you were the person that you wish you were, what kind of person would you be?
- What would you be doing if you were living as you want to?
- What is it you want that you don't seem to be getting from life?
- What do you think stops you from making the changes you would like?

Direction and Doing   Reality therapy stresses current behavior and is concerned with past events only insofar as they influence how clients are behaving now. Even though problems may be rooted in the past, we need to learn how to deal with them in the present by learning better ways of getting what we want. The key question is, "What are you doing?"

Evaluation   The core of reality therapy is to invite individuals to make the following self-evaluation: "Does your present behavior have a reasonable chance of getting you what you want now, and will it take you in the direction you want to go?" Ultimately, it is up to you to evaluate your present actions and the direction this is taking you. You are not likely to change until you first decide that a change is advantageous. Making this choice hinges on first making an honest self-assessment. Wubbolding (2000) suggests questions like these:

- Is what you are doing helping or hurting you?
- Is what you are doing now what you want to be doing?
- Is your behavior working for you?
- Is what you want realistic or attainable?
- After you examine what you want carefully, does it appear to be in your best interests and in the best interest of others?

Planning and Action   Making behavioral changes involves identifying specific ways to fulfill your wants and needs. Once you determine what you want to change, the next step is to formulate an action plan. A plan gives you a starting point, but plans can be modified as needed.

Wubbolding (2000) discusses the central role of planning and commitment in the change process. He uses the acronym SAMIC[3] to capture the essence of a good plan: simple, attainable, measurable, immediate, involved, controlled by the planner, committed to, and continuously done. You will gain more effective control over your life with plans that have the following characteristics:

- The plan is within your limits and capacities. It is important that your plan is realistic, for if your expectations are too high you are setting yourself up for failure. A question to ask is, "What plans could you make now that would result in a more satisfying life?"

- Good plans are simple and easy to understand. Although they need to be specific, concrete, and measurable, plans should be flexible and open to revision as clients gain a deeper understanding of the specific behaviors they want to change.

- The plan involves a positive course of action, and it is stated in terms of what you are willing to do. Even small plans can help you take significant steps toward your desired changes.

- Develop plans that you can carry out independently of what others do.

- Effective plans are repetitive and, ideally, are performed daily.

- Plans are carried out as soon as possible. Ask yourself, "What are you willing to do today to begin to change your life?"

- Before you carry out your plan, it is a good idea for you to evaluate it with someone you trust to determine if it is realistic and attainable and if it relates to what you need and want. It is essential that you make a commitment to implement your plan. After the plan has been carried out in real life, it is useful to evaluate it again and make any revisions that may be necessary.

In *The Art of Happiness*, the Dalai Lama and Howard Cutler (1998) point out that bringing about genuine inner transformation and change is a gradual process that involves a sustained effort. They write:

> IT TAKES A LONG TIME TO DEVELOP the behavior and habits of mind that contribute to our problems. It takes an equally long time to establish the new habits that bring happiness. There is no getting around these essential ingredients: determination, effort, and time. These are the real secrets to happiness (p. 231).

As you study the topics in this book, think about areas of your life you want to change, develop an action plan, and find ways to commit to implementing your plan.

Take Time to Reflect   These sections in this book provide an opportunity for you to pause and reflect on your own experiences as they relate to the topic being discussed. Unlike most quizzes and tests you have taken, these inventories do not emphasize "right" and "wrong" answers but rather answers that make sense to you and have personal meaning. Taking these inventories will probably be a different experience for you, and you may have to make a conscious effort to look within yourself for the response or answer that makes sense to you rather than searching for the expected response that is external to you.

I. To what degree do you have a healthy and positive view of yourself? Are you able to appreciate yourself, or do you discount your own worth? Respond to these statements using the following code:

3 = This statement is true of me *most* of the time.
2 = This statement is true of me *some* of the time.
1 = This statement is true of me *almost none* of the time.

_____ I generally think and choose for myself.

_____ I usually like myself.

_____ I know what I want.

_____ I am able to ask for what I want.

_____ I feel a sense of personal power.

_____ I am open to change.

_____ I feel equal to others.

_____ I am sensitive to the needs of others.

_____ I care about others.

_____ I can act in accordance with my own judgment without feeling guilty if others disapprove of me.

_____ I do not expect others to make me feel good about myself.

_____ I can accept responsibility for my own actions.

_____ I am able to accept compliments.

_____ I can give affection.

_____ I can receive affection.

_____ I am not so security-bound that I will not explore new things.

_____ I am generally accepted by others.

_____ I can give myself credit for what I do well.

_____ I am able to enjoy my own company.

_____ I am capable of forming meaningful relationships.

_____ I live in the here and now and am not preoccupied with the past or the future.

_____ I feel a sense of significance.

_____ I am not diminished when I am with those I respect.

_____ I believe in my ability to succeed in projects that are meaningful to me.

Now go back over this inventory and identify not more than five areas that keep you from being as self-accepting as you might be. What can you do to increase your awareness of situations in which you do not fully accept yourself? For example, if you have trouble giving yourself credit for things you do well, how can you become aware of times when you discount yourself? When you do become conscious of situations in which you put yourself down, think of alternatives.

2. Take a few minutes to review Maslow's theory of self-actualization and then consider these questions as they apply to you:
   - Which of these qualities do you find most appealing? Why?
   - Which would you like to cultivate in yourself?
   - Which of Maslow's ideal qualities do you most associate with living a full and meaningful life?
   - Who in your life comes closest to meeting Maslow's criteria for self-actualizing people?

3. We recommend that later in the course you review your answers to this exercise and take this inventory again. Compare your answers and note any changes that you may have made in your thinking or behavior.

ARE YOU AN ACTIVE LEARNER?

The self-actualization process of growth implies that you will be an **active learner:** that is, you assume responsibility for your education, you question what is presented to you, and you apply what you learn in a personally meaningful way. Your schooling experiences may not have encouraged you to learn actively. Review your school experiences and assess whether you are an active learner.

What do you want out of college or out of life in general? Identifying, clarifying, and reaching goals must be an active process related to your values. Getting a clear sense of your values is no easy task. Many people have trouble deciding what they really want. If this is true for you, a first step you can take in sorting out what you want from college is to ask yourself these questions:

- Is what I am doing now what I want to be doing?
- Does it reflect my values?
- Do I believe I have the right to make my own choices?
- Am I finding meaning in what I am doing?
- What would I rather be doing?

Use the idea of what you would rather be doing as a catalyst for changing. What will it take for you to say "I am doing what I really want to be doing right now"? Many of your values may be redefined at various points in your college career and in life. But your goals will be much more meaningful if you define them for yourself rather than allow others to set goals for you. It is unrealistic to expect all of your time in college to be exciting, but there is a lot you can do to create interest, especially when you have a goal.

Take Time to Reflect

1. How would you evaluate your experience in elementary school?

_____

_____

2. How would you evaluate your high school experience?

_____

_____

3. How do you evaluate your present college experience up to this point?

_____

_____

4. To what degree have you been a questioner?

_____

_____

5. To what degree have you been motivated externally or internally?

_____

_____

6. To what degree are you a confident learner?

_____

_____

7. To what degree has your learning been meaningful?

_____

_____

8. What important things (both positive and negative) did you learn about yourself as a result of your schooling?

_____

_____

9. If you do not like the kind of learner you have been up until now, what can you do about it? What changes would you like to make?

_____

_____

MULTIPLE INTELLIGENCES AND MULTIPLE LEARNING STYLES

People differ in how they learn best and in what kinds of knowledge they tend to learn most easily. For example, auditory learners tend to understand and retain ideas better from hearing them spoken, whereas visual learners tend to learn more effectively when they can literally see what they are learning. We encourage you to take and score your results on the Rogers Indicator of Multiple Intelligences (RIMI), found on pages 33 to 38, as a way to identify your learning style.

Behind differences in learning styles may lie basic differences in **intelligence.** Intelligence itself is not one single, easily measured ability but a group of abilities. Howard Gardner (1983), a professor of education at Harvard University, has discovered that we are capable of at least seven different types of intelligence and learning:

- Verbal-linguistic
- Musical-rhythmic
- Logical-mathematical
- Visual-spatial
- Bodily-kinesthetic
- Intrapersonal
- Interpersonal

To this list, Daniel Goleman (1995) adds emotional intelligence as a critical aspect of intelligence with definite implications for personal learning. **Emotional intelligence** pertains to the ability to control impulses, empathize with others, form responsible interpersonal relationships, and develop intimate relationships.

Traditional approaches to schooling—teaching methods, class assignments, and tests—have been geared to and measure the growth of verbal-linguistic and logical-mathematical abilities, what we generally refer to as IQ. Yet several, if not all, of the other forms of intelligence and learning are equally vital to success in life. Emotional intelligence is certainly basic to learning interpersonal skills, yet this domain tends not to be emphasized in the educational programs of our schools and colleges.

Intelligence is not a singular entity. It is complex and multidimensional, and you may find that you have strengths in several different areas. The model of **multiple intelligences** is best used as a tool to help you identify areas you may want to pursue. As you will see in Chapter 10, other factors besides ability (or intelligence) need to be considered in deciding on a field of study or a career.

Let's examine the specific characteristics of each of these kinds of intellectual abilities and then consider the implications for college learning.

- If you are a **verbal-linguistic learner,** you have highly developed auditory skills, enjoy reading and writing, like to play word games, and have a good

There are multiple intelligences and multiple learning styles.

memory for names, dates, and places; you like to tell stories; and you are good at getting your point across. You learn best by saying and hearing words. Your learning is facilitated by opportunities to listen and to speak. You prefer to learn by listening to lectures or audiotapes, and by discussing what you have heard. You will probably profit more from reading after you have heard about the material you are to read. You may learn best by taping lectures and listening to them again or by listening to your textbook on audiotape. Reciting information and teaching others what you know are useful ways for you to learn. People whose dominant intelligence is in the verbal-linguistic area include poets, authors, speakers, attorneys, politicians, lecturers, and teachers.

• If you are a **musical-rhythmic learner,** you are sensitive to the sounds in your environment, enjoy music, and prefer listening to music when you study or read. You appreciate pitch and rhythm. You probably like singing to yourself. You learn best through melody and music. Musical intelligence is obviously demonstrated by singers, conductors, and composers, but also by those who enjoy, understand, and use various elements of music.

• If you are more a **logical-mathematical learner,** you probably like to explore patterns and relationships, and you enjoy doing activities in sequential order. You are likely to enjoy mathematics, and you like to experiment with things you do not understand. You like to work with numbers, ask questions, and explore patterns and relationships. You may find it challenging to solve problems and to use logical reasoning. You learn best by classifying information, engaging in abstract thinking, and looking for common basic principles. People with well-developed logical-mathematical abilities include mathematicians, biologists, medical technologists, geologists, engineers, physicists, researchers, and other scientists.

- If you are a **visual-spatial learner,** you prefer to learn by reading, watching videotapes, and observing demonstrations. You will learn better by seeing pictures and graphically mapping out material to learn rather than relying mainly on listening to lectures. You tend to think in images and pictures. You are likely to get more from a lecture *after* you have read the material. Besides the printed word, you may learn well by seeing pictures and forming images of what is to be learned. You learn by looking at pictures, watching movies, and seeing slides. You may rely on word processors, books, and other visual devices for learning and recall. People with well-developed visual-spatial abilities are found in professions such as sculpting, painting, surgery, and engineering.

- If you are a **bodily-kinesthetic learner,** you process knowledge through bodily sensations and use your body in skilled ways. You have good balance and coordination; you are good with your hands. You need opportunities to move and act things out. You tend to respond best in classrooms that provide physical activities and hands-on learning experiences. You prefer to learn by doing, by getting physically involved through movement and action. You tend to learn best by experimenting and figuring out ways of solving a problem. People who have highly developed bodily-kinesthetic abilities include carpenters, television and stereo repairpersons, mechanics, dancers, gymnasts, swimmers, and jugglers.

- If you are an **intrapersonal learner,** you prefer your own inner world, you like to be alone, and you are aware of your own strengths, weaknesses, and feelings. You tend to be a creative and independent thinker; you like to reflect on ideas. You probably possess independence, self-confidence, determination, and are highly motivated. You may respond with strong opinions when controversial topics are discussed. You learn best by engaging in independent study projects rather than working on group projects. Pacing your own instruction is important to you. People with intrapersonal abilities include entrepreneurs, philosophers, and psychologists.

- If you are an **interpersonal learner,** you enjoy being around people, like talking to people, have many friends, and engage in social activities. You learn best by relating, sharing, and participating in cooperative group environments. People with strong interpersonal abilities are found in sales, consulting, community organizing, counseling, teaching, or one of the helping professions.

- If you are an **emotional learner,** you have competence in the emotional realm: empathy, concern for others, curiosity, self-control, cooperation, the ability to resolve conflicts, the ability to listen well, communication skills, and relatedness to others. You are interested in cultivating matters of your heart as much as those of your head, and you are interested in the interdependence of people at least as much as you are in developing your own independence. You are able to express and control a range of your emotions; you are accepting of the emotions of others; you strive for connections with others; and you have an interest in increasing both your self- and other-esteem (Hwang, 2000). According to Goleman (1995), academic performance is related to the emotional and social area as much as it hinges on other facets of intelligence. When emotional competencies are lacking, Goleman believes this results in disconnection, which, in turn, leads to prejudice, self-involvement, aggressive behavior, depression, addictive behavior, and an inability to manage emotions. Emotional learners promote cooperative and collaborative learning, reach out to others, and apply what they know to making the world a better place to live.

Although you may have a preference for one of these ways of learning, remain open to incorporating elements from the other styles as well. In a course such as this, it can benefit you if you look for ways to blend the emotional domain with the other forms of intelligence and learning styles. You are likely to find that you learn best by integrating many pathways rather than by depending exclusively on one avenue in your educational journey. The more you can view college as a place to use all your talents and improve your learning abilities in all respects, the more meaningful and successful your college journey will be.

Taking Responsibility for Learning

At the beginning of a new semester some college students are overwhelmed by how much they are expected to do in all their courses while maintaining a life outside of school. One reaction to this feeling of being swamped is to put things off, which results in getting behind with your assignments, which typically leads to discouragement.

If you take responsibility for your own learning, you are much more likely to succeed. Students who fail to see their own role in the learning process often blame others for their failures. If you are dissatisfied with your education, first take a look at yourself and see how much you are willing to invest in making it more vital.

We think you will get a great deal more from your college education if you spend time now reflecting on your past experiences. Think about how your present values and beliefs are related to your experiences in school. Recall a particularly positive school experience. How might it be affecting you today? Consider your educational experiences up to this point and think about your attitudes and behaviors as a student. What kinds of experiences have you had as a student so far, and how might these experiences influence the kind of learner you are today? If you like the kind of learner you are now, or if you have had mostly good experiences with school, you can build on that positive framework as you approach this course. You can continue to find ways to involve yourself with the material you will read, study, and discuss. If you feel cheated by a negative educational experience, you can begin to change it now. In what ways do you want to become a different learner now than you have been in the past? We challenge you to find ways to bring meaning to your learning by being active in the process. You can get the most out of your courses if you develop a style of learning in which you raise questions and search for answers within yourself.

You can make the choice to be actively engaged or only marginally involved in applying the themes in this book in your life. You can make this class different by applying some of the ideas discussed in this chapter. Once you become aware of those aspects of your education that you do not like, you can decide to change your style of learning.

It is also essential that you develop effective study habits and learn basic time management skills. Although acquiring these skills alone does not guarantee successful learning, knowing how to organize your time and how to study can contribute significantly to assuming an active and effective style of learning. One aid to learning, found in the Where Can I Go From Here? section at the end of this chapter, is the Rogers Indicator of Multiple Intelligences (RIMI) self-evaluation, which can help you understand how you learn best.

One way to begin to become an active learner is to think about your reasons for taking this course and your expectations concerning what you will learn. This Take Time to Reflect exercise will help you focus on these issues.

Take Time to Reflect

I. What are your main reasons for taking this course?

_____

2. What do you expect this course to be like? Check all the comments that fit you.

_____ I expect to talk openly about issues that matter to me.
_____ I expect to get answers to certain problems in my life.
_____ I hope I will become a more fulfilled person.
_____ I hope I will have less fear of expressing my feelings and ideas.
_____ I expect to be challenged on why I am the way I am.
_____ I expect to learn more about how other people function.
_____ I expect to better understand myself by the end of the course.

3. What do you most want to accomplish in this course?

_____

_____

4. What are you willing to do to become actively involved in your learning? Check the appropriate comments.

_____ I am willing to participate in class discussions.

_____ I am willing to read the material and think about how it applies to me.

_____ I am willing to question my assumptions and look at my values.

_____ I am willing to spend some time most days reflecting on the issues raised in this course.

_____ I am willing to keep a journal, recording my reactions to what I read and experience and assessing my progress on meeting my goals and commitments.

Other commitments to become an active learner include:

_____

_____

GETTING THE MOST FROM THIS BOOK: SUGGESTIONS FOR PERSONAL LEARNING

Throughout this book, both of us write in a personal style and openly share with you how we arrived at our beliefs and values. We hope that knowing our assumptions, biases, and struggles will help you evaluate your own position more clearly. We are not suggesting that you adopt our philosophy of life but that you use the material in this book as a catalyst for your own reflection. There are no simple answers to complex life issues, and each person's life is unique. Although self-help books provide insights and useful information for many people, we have concerns about the kinds of books that give an abundance of advice or attempt to offer easy answers. The same can be said of television talk shows or therapists who offer counsel on the radio to callers with personal problems. Information and even suggestions can be useful at the right time, but rarely can an individual's problems be resolved by uncritically accepting others' advice or directives. Advice-giving differs from counseling. Although giving advice may be of benefit in the short term, it often does not teach people how to deal with future problems, and it can promote dependency. Counseling is aimed at helping people learn coping strategies that they can apply to a range of present and future problems they may face, which tends to promote self-direction.

In the chapters that follow, we offer a great deal of information for you to reflect on and to use as a basis for making better choices. Our aim is to raise questions that lead to thoughtful reflection on your part and to meaningful dialogue with others. We encourage you to develop the practice of examining questions that engage you and have meaning in your life. Instead of looking for simple solutions to your problems, consider making time for personal reflection as a way to clarify your options in many areas of your life. Listen to others and consider what they say, but even more important, learn to look inside yourself for direction. Listen to your inner voice. This book can become a personal companion; use it to enhance your reflection on questions that are personally significant to you.

This course is likely to be different from many of the courses you have taken. Few courses deal primarily with you as the subject matter. Most college courses challenge you intellectually, but this book is geared toward integrating intellectual and personal learning. To a large degree, what you get from this course will depend on what you are willing to invest of yourself. It is important that you clarify your goals and the steps you can take to reach them. The following guidelines will help you become active and involved in personal learning as you read the book and participate in your class.

1. **Preparing.** Read this book for your personal benefit, and make use of the Take Time to Reflect sections and the Where Can I Go From Here? exercises at the end of each chapter, which can help you apply the material to your own life. Many of the exercises, questions, and suggested activities will appeal differently to different readers. Considerations such as your age, life experiences, and cultural background will have a bearing on the meaning and importance of certain topics to you. We have written this book from our own cultural framework, but the topics we address are common to all of us. In our work with people from various cultures, we continue to find that these human themes transcend culture and unite us in our life struggles.

2. **Dealing with fears.** It is natural to experience some fear about participating personally and actively in the class. How you deal with your fears is more important than trying to eliminate your anxieties about getting involved in a personal way. Facing your fears takes courage and a genuine desire to increase your self-awareness, but by doing so you take a first big step toward expanding the range of your choices.

3. **Establishing trust.** You can choose to take the initiative in establishing the trust necessary for you to participate in this course in a meaningful way, or you can wait for others to create a climate of trust. One way to establish trust is to talk with your instructor outside of class.

4. **Practicing self-disclosure.** Disclosing yourself to others is one way to come to know yourself more fully. Sometimes participants in self-awareness courses or experiential groups fear that they must give up their privacy to be active participants. However, you can be open and at the same time retain your privacy by deciding how much you will disclose and when it is appropriate to do so.

5. **Being direct.** Adopt a direct style in your communication. Make "I" statements. For example, instead of saying "You can't trust people with what you

feel because they will let you down if you make yourself vulnerable," try instead, "I can't trust people with what I feel because they will let me down if I make myself vulnerable."

6. **Listening.** Work on developing the skill of really listening to what others are saying without thinking of what you will say in reply. Active listening (really hearing the full message another is sending) requires remaining open and carefully considering what others say instead of too quickly giving reasons and explanations.

7. **Avoiding self-fulfilling prophecies.** You can increase your ability to change by letting go of ways you have categorized yourself or been categorized by others. If you start off with the assumption that you are stupid, helpless, or boring, you will probably convince others as well. Your negative beliefs about yourself will certainly get in the way of being the person you would like to be.

8. **Practicing outside of class.** One important way to get the maximum benefit from a class dealing with personal learning is to think about ways of applying what you learn in class to your everyday life. You can make specific contracts with yourself (as part of your action plan) detailing what you are willing to do to experiment with new behavior and to work toward desired changes.

9. **Keeping a journal.** In one sense this is an *unfinished* book. You are invited to become a coauthor by completing the writing of this book in ways that are meaningful to you. Throughout the book we suggest that you keep a journal. It is important that you decide what to put in it and how to use it. Reviewing your journal will help you identify some of your critical choices and areas of conflict. Consider writing about some of these topics:

- What I learned about others and myself through today's class session
- The topics that were of most interest to me (and why)
- The topics that held the least interest for me (and why)
- The topics I wanted to talk about
- The topics I avoided talking about
- Particular sections (or issues) in the chapter that had the greatest impact on me (and why)
- Some things I am learning about myself by reading the book
- Some specific things I am doing in everyday life as a result of this class
- Some concrete changes in my attitudes, values, and behavior that I find myself most wanting to make
- What I am willing to do to make these changes
- Some barriers I encounter in making the changes I want to make

It is best to write what first comes to mind. Spontaneous reactions tend to tell you more about yourself than well-thought-out comments.

10. **Organizing your reading.** There is no perfect organization or sequencing of chapters in this kind of book. Generally, we had some rationale for the order of the chapters, but each of the 14 chapters can be read separately, as each was written to stand alone. We do have some suggestions, however, about reading parts of certain chapters early during the course. Chapter 14 contains a list of specific suggestions of how to continue the self-exploration process once you complete the course. We suggest that you read this early in the course to determine whether specific ideas mentioned can be incorporated in your daily practice. Chapter 13 contains a detailed discussion of formulating your philosophy of life, and some instructors assign some type of philosophy of life paper as a course project.

SUMMARY

We do not have to live by the plans that others have designed for us. With awareness we can begin to design our own blueprints and to make significant choices. Taking a stand in life by making choices can result in both gains and losses. Changing long-standing patterns is not easy, and there are many obstacles to overcome. Yet a free life has many rewards. One of these benefits is personal growth. Growth is a lifelong process of expanding self-awareness and accepting new challenges. It does not mean disregard for others but rather implies fulfilling more of our potential, including our ability to care for others. Four scholars who have made significant contributions to the concept of personal growth in a framework of humanistic psychology are Alfred Adler, Carl Jung, Carl Rogers, and Abraham Maslow. Perhaps the best way to conceptualize personal growth is by considering Maslow's ideal of self-actualization. William Glasser's reality therapy, which is based on choice theory, is a useful model in understanding how our behavior is aimed at satisfying our needs. Keep in mind that until our basic needs have been met we are not really much concerned about becoming fully functioning persons. If you are hungry or are living on the streets, you are not likely to reflect on the meaning of becoming an actualized individual. Remember also that self-actualization is not something that we do in isolation; rather, it is through meaningful relationships with others and through social interest that we discover and become the persons we are capable of becoming. Paradoxically, we find ourselves when we are secure enough to go beyond a preoccupation with our self-interests and become involved in the world with selected people.

Striving for self-actualization does not cease at a particular age but is an ongoing process. Rather than speaking of self-actualization as a product we attain, it is best to consider the process of becoming a self-actualizing person. Four basic characteristics of self-actualizing people are self-awareness, freedom, basic honesty and caring, and trust and autonomy. This course can be a first step on the journey toward achieving your personal goals and living a self-actualizing existence while at the same time contributing to making the world a better place.

People differ in how they learn best and the kind of knowledge they tend to learn most easily. Understanding the various learning styles will enable you to approach learning in a personal and meaningful way. Intelligence is not a singular entity; rather, it is complex and multidimensional. Discovering your dominant forms of intelligence can help you identify areas for study or career options.

A major purpose of this chapter is to encourage you to examine your responsibility for making your learning meaningful. Even if your earlier educational experiences have taught you to be a passive learner and to avoid risks in your classes, being aware of this influence gives you the power to change your learning style. We invite you to decide how personal you want your learning to be in the course you are about to experience.

Where Can I Go From Here?

At the end of each chapter are additional activities and exercises that we suggest you practice, both in class and out of class. Ultimately you will be the one to decide which activities you are willing to do. You may find some of the suggested exercises too threatening to do in a class, yet exploring the same activities in a small group in your class could be easier. If small discussion groups are not part of the structure of your class, consider doing the exercises alone or sharing them with a friend. Do not feel compelled to complete all the activities; select those that have the most meaning for you at this time in your life.

1. These are exercises you can do at home. They are intended to help you focus on specific ways in which you behave. We have drawn the examples from typical fears and concerns often expressed by college students. Study the situations by putting yourself in each one and deciding how you might typically respond. Then keep an account in your journal of actual instances you encounter in your classes.

Situation A: You would like to ask a question in class, but you are afraid that your question will sound dumb and that others will laugh.

Issues: Will you simply refrain from asking questions? If so, is this a pattern you care to continue? Are you willing to practice asking questions, even though you might experience some anxiety? What do you imagine will happen if you ask questions? What would you like to have happen?

Situation B: You feel that you have a problem concerning authority figures. You feel intimidated, afraid to venture your opinions, and even more afraid to register a point of view opposed to your instructor's.

Issues: Does this description fit you? If it does, do you want to change? Do you ever examine where you picked up your attitudes toward yourself in relation to authority? Do you think they are still appropriate for you?

Situation C: Your instructor seems genuinely interested in the students and the course, and she has extended herself by inviting you to come to her office if you have any problems with the course. You are having real difficulty grasping the material, and you are falling behind and doing poorly on the tests and assignments. Nevertheless, you keep putting off going to see the instructor to talk about your problems in the class.

Issues: Have you been in this situation before? If so, what kept you from talking with your instructor? If you find yourself in this kind of situation, are you willing to seek help before it is too late?

2. Review Maslow's characteristics of self-actualizing people, and consider the following questions:

a. To what degree are these characteristics a part of your personality?

b. Do you think Maslow's ideal of self-actualization fits for individuals of all cultural and ethnic groups? Are any characteristics inappropriate for certain cultures?

3. The *Rogers Indicator of Multiple Intelligences* (RIMI) is a self-inventory created by Dr. Keith Rogers, a professor at Brigham Young University. By taking this inventory, you can pinpoint your dominate intelligences. It should take you approximately 15 minutes to complete the inventory. Use the grid at the end of the RIMI to interpret each of your scores on the seven kinds of intelligences, indicating low intensity, moderate intensity, and high intensity areas.

The Rogers Indicator of Multiple Intelligences*

DIRECTIONS: For each statement, mark a box for your most accurate response according to descriptors above the boxes. Think carefully about your knowledge, beliefs, preferences, behavior, and experience. Decide quickly and move on. There is no right or wrong, no good or bad, no expected or desirable response. Use your heart as well as your head. Focus on the way you really are, not on the way you "ought to be" for someone else.

	Rarely 1	Occasionally 2	Sometimes 3	Usually 4	Almost always 5
1. I am careful about the direct and implied meanings of the words I choose.	❑	❑	❑	❑	❑
2. I appreciate a wide variety of music.	❑	❑	❑	❑	❑
3. People come to me when they need help with math problems or any calculations.	❑	❑	❑	❑	❑
4. In my mind, I can visualize clear, precise, sharp images.	❑	❑	❑	❑	❑
5. I am physically well-coordinated.	❑	❑	❑	❑	❑

*Reprinted by permission from the Rogers Indicator of Multiple Intelligences © 1995 by J. Keith Rogers, Ph.D.

The Rogers Indicator of Multiple Intelligences *(continued)*

	Rarely 1	Occasionally 2	Sometimes 3	Usually 4	Almost always 5
6. I understand why I believe and behave the way I do.	❑	❑	❑	❑	❑
7. I understand the moods, temperaments, values, and intentions of others.	❑	❑	❑	❑	❑
8. I confidently express myself well in words, written or spoken.	❑	❑	❑	❑	❑
9. I understand the basic precepts of music such as harmony, chords, and keys.	❑	❑	❑	❑	❑
10. When I have a problem, I use a logical, analytical, step-by-step process to arrive at a solution.	❑	❑	❑	❑	❑
11. I have a good sense of direction.	❑	❑	❑	❑	❑
12. I have skill in handling objects such as scissors, balls, hammers, scalpels, paintbrushes, knitting needles, pliers, etc.	❑	❑	❑	❑	❑
13. My self-understanding helps me to make wise decisions for my life.	❑	❑	❑	❑	❑
14. I am able to influence other individuals to believe and/or behave in response to my own beliefs, preferences, and desires.	❑	❑	❑	❑	❑
15. I am grammatically accurate.	❑	❑	❑	❑	❑
16. I like to compose or create music.	❑	❑	❑	❑	❑
17. I am rigorous and skeptical in accepting facts, reasons, and principles.	❑	❑	❑	❑	❑
18. I am good at putting together jigsaw puzzles, and reading instructions, patterns, or blueprints.	❑	❑	❑	❑	❑
19. I excel in physical activities such as dance, sports, or games.	❑	❑	❑	❑	❑
20. My ability to understand my own emotions helps me to decide whether or how to be involved in certain situations.	❑	❑	❑	❑	❑

The Rogers Indicator of Multiple Intelligences *(continued)*

	Rarely 1	Occasionally 2	Sometimes 3	Usually 4	Almost always 5
21. I would like to be involved in helping professions such as teaching, therapy, or counseling, or to do work such as political or religious leadership.	❑	❑	❑	❑	❑
22. I am able to use spoken or written words to influence or persuade others.	❑	❑	❑	❑	❑
23. I enjoy performing music, such as singing or playing a musical instrument for an audience.	❑	❑	❑	❑	❑
24. I require scientific explanations of physical realities.	❑	❑	❑	❑	❑
25. I can read maps easily and accurately.	❑	❑	❑	❑	❑
26. I work well with my hands as would an electrician, seamstress, plumber, tailor, mechanic, carpenter, assembler, etc.	❑	❑	❑	❑	❑
27. I am aware of the complexity of my own feelings, emotions, and beliefs in various circumstances.	❑	❑	❑	❑	❑
28. I am able to work as an effective intermediary in helping other individuals and groups to solve their problems.	❑	❑	❑	❑	❑
29. I am sensitive to the sounds, rhythms, inflections, and meters of words, especially as found in poetry.	❑	❑	❑	❑	❑
30. I have a good sense of musical rhythm.	❑	❑	❑	❑	❑
31. I would like to do the work of people such as chemists, engineers, physicists, astronomers, or mathematicians.	❑	❑	❑	❑	❑
32. I am able to produce graphic depictions of the spatial world as in drawing, painting, sculpting, drafting, or map-making.	❑	❑	❑	❑	❑
33. I relieve stress or find fulfillment in physical activities.	❑	❑	❑	❑	❑

The Rogers Indicator of Multiple Intelligences *(continued)*

	Rarely 1	Occasionally 2	Sometimes 3	Usually 4	Almost always 5
34. My inner self is my ultimate source of strength and renewal.	❑	❑	❑	❑	❑
35. I understand what motivates others even when they are trying to hide their motivations.	❑	❑	❑	❑	❑
36. I enjoy reading frequently and widely.	❑	❑	❑	❑	❑
37. I have a good sense of musical pitch.	❑	❑	❑	❑	❑
38. I find satisfaction in dealing with numbers.	❑	❑	❑	❑	❑
39. I like the hands-on approach to learning when I can experience personally the objects that I'm learning about.	❑	❑	❑	❑	❑
40. I have quick and accurate physical reflexes and responses.	❑	❑	❑	❑	❑
41. I am confident in my own opinions and am not easily swayed by others.	❑	❑	❑	❑	❑
42. I am comfortable and confident with groups of people.	❑	❑	❑	❑	❑
43. I use writing as a vital method of communication.	❑	❑	❑	❑	❑
44. I am affected both emotionally and intellectually by music.	❑	❑	❑	❑	❑
45. I prefer questions that have definite "right" and "wrong" answers.	❑	❑	❑	❑	❑
46. I can accurately estimate distances and other measurements.	❑	❑	❑	❑	❑
47. I have accurate aim when throwing balls or in archery, shooting, golf, etc.	❑	❑	❑	❑	❑
48. My feelings, beliefs, attitudes, and emotions are my own responsibility.	❑	❑	❑	❑	❑
49. I have a large circle of close associates.	❑	❑	❑	❑	❑

The Rogers Indicator of Multiple Intelligences *(continued)*

DIRECTIONS: In the chart below, the box numbers are the same as the statement numbers in the survey. You made a rating judgment for each statement. Now, place the numbers that correspond to your ratings in the numbered boxes below. Then add down the columns and write the totals at the bottom to determine your score in each of the seven intelligence categories. Then, for the meanings of the scores, consult the interpretations that follow the chart.

	Verbal/ Linguistic	Musical/ Rhythmic	Logical/ Mathematical	Visual/ Spatial	Bodily/ Kinesthetic	Intrapersonal	Interpersonal
	1	2	3	4	55	6	7
	8	9	10	11	12	13	14
	15	16	17	18	19	20	21
	22	23	24	25	26	27	28
	29	30	31	32	33	34	35
	36	37	38	39	40	41	42
	43	44	45	46	47	48	49
Totals							
Interpretations of knowledge, belief, behavior							

The Rogers Indicator of Multiple Intelligences *(continued)*

To some degree we possess all of these intelligences, and all can be enhanced. We are each a unique blend of all seven; however, we all differ in the degree to which we prefer and have the competence to use each of the intelligences. Here are interpretations for the scores in the three ranges of low, moderate, and high.

Score	Intensity of Preference and/or Competence
7–15 (3)	Low Intensity: You tend to "avoid" it, and are probably uncomfortable when required to use it. Tertiary preference (3). This intelligence probably is not one of your favorites. In most circumstances, you lack confidence and will go out of your way to avoid situations involving intensive exercise of this intelligence. Your competence is probably relatively low. Unless you are unusually motivated, gaining expertise might be frustrating and likely would require great effort. All intelligences, including this one, can be enhanced throughout your lifetime.
16–26 (2)	Moderate Intensity: You tend to "accept" it, or use it with some comfort and ease. Secondary preference (2). You could take or leave the application or use of this intelligence. Though you accept it, you do not necessarily prefer to employ it. But, on the other hand, you would not necessarily avoid using it. This may be because you have not developed your ability, or because you have a moderate preference for this intelligence. Your competence is probably moderate also. Gaining expertise would be satisfying, but probably would require considerable effort.
27–35 (1)	High Intensity: You tend to "prefer" it, and use it often with comfort and facility. Primary preference (1). You enjoy using this intelligence. Applying it is fun. You are excited and challenged by it, perhaps even fascinated. You prefer this intelligence. Given the opportunity, you will usually select it. Everyone knows you love it. Your competence is probably relatively high if you have had opportunities to develop it. Becoming an expert should be rewarding and fulfilling, and will probably require little effort compared to a moderate or low preference.

NOTE: After you have scored the RIMI, ask yourself: Do the scores I received on the RIMI correspond to what I know about myself? Based on this inventory, what are the implications of my style of learning? How might I want to change the way I approach learning? How can I best learn?

Resources for Future Study

Web Site Resources

WADSWORTH, THE COMPLETE PSYCHOLOGY PUBLISHER
http://psychology.wadsworth.com/

This is a resource for both students and faculty alike that provides numerous resources in the field of psychology. It offers a continuously updated professional association conference calendar, links to current research through journal sites and professional associations, and a Faculty Lounge (password required) with resources for instructors.

MENTAL HELP NET
http://www.mentalhelp.net/

Mental Help Net is an excellent site that explores all aspects of mental health. It "has become the most comprehensive source of online mental health information, news, and resources available today." This site includes items such as HealthScout, which offers daily updated news articles, online support forums, books, and so on. With links to more than 8,000 resources, whatever you are looking for about mental health is probably here.

AMERICAN SELF-HELP CLEARINGHOUSE SOURCE BOOK
http://www.cmhc.com/

This site provides contact information for more than 800 self-help groups and organizations across the United States.

AMERICAN COUNSELING ASSOCIATION (ACA)
http://www.counseling.org

ACA is a major organization of counselors that puts out a resource catalog that provides information on the various aspects of the counseling profession. The site provides information about membership, journals, books, home-study programs, videotapes, and audiotapes.

AMERICAN PSYCHOLOGICAL ASSOCIATION (APA)
http://www.apa.org/

This is the major professional organization of psychologists. This resource provides leads for current research and literature on many of the topics in this book.

 InfoTrac College Edition Resources

For additional readings, explore INFOTRAC COLLEGE EDITION, our online library:
http://www.infotrac.college.com/wadsworth

Hint: Enter these search terms:

personal growth	humanistic psychology
active learning	Adlerian psychology
multiple intelligence	Jungian psychology
learning style	self-actualization
personal adjustment	self-awareness

Print Resources

Goleman, D. (1995). *Emotional intelligence.* New York: Bantam Books.

Hwang, P. O. (2000). *Other-esteem: Meaningful life in a multicultural society.* Philadelphia, PA: Accelerated Development (Taylor & Francis).

Miller, T. (1995). *How to want what you have: Discovering the magic and grandeur of ordinary existence.* New York: Avon.

Peck, M. S. (1987). *The different drum: Community making and peace.* New York: Simon & Schuster (Touchstone).

Seligman, M. E. P. (1993). *What you can change and what you can't.* New York: Fawcett (Columbine).

2

What we resist persists.

Reviewing Your Childhood and Adolescence

© PhotoDisc/Getty Images

Where Am I Now?

Use this scale to respond to these statements:

    3 = This statement is true of me *most* of the time.

    2 = This statement is true of me *some* of the time.

    1 = This statement is true of me *almost none* of the time.

1. I am capable of looking at my past decisions and then making new decisions that will significantly change the course of my life.

2. "Shoulds" and "oughts" often get in the way of my living my life the way I want.

3. To a large degree I have been shaped by the events of my childhood and adolescent years.

4. When I think of my early childhood years, I remember feeling secure, accepted, and loved.

5. As a child, I was taught that it was acceptable to express feelings such as anger, fear, and jealousy.

6. I had desirable models to pattern my behavior after when I was growing up.

7. In looking back at my early school-age years, I had a positive self-concept and experienced more successes than failures.

8. I went through a stage of rebellion during my adolescent years.

9. My adolescent years were lonely ones.

10. I was greatly influenced by peer group pressure during my adolescence.

T his chapter and the next one lay the groundwork for much of the rest of the book by focusing on our lifelong struggle to achieve psychological emancipation, or **autonomy.** The term *autonomy* refers to mature independence and interdependence. As you will recall from the previous chapter, becoming a fully functioning person occurs in the context of relationships with others and with concern for the welfare of others. If you are an autonomous person, you are able to function without constant approval and reassurance, are sensitive to the needs of others, can effectively meet the demands of daily living, are willing to ask for help when it is needed, and can provide support to others. In essence, you have the ability both to stand alone and to stand by another person. You are in harmony with both your inner world and your outer world. Although you are concerned with meeting your needs, you do not do so at the expense of those around you. You are aware of the impact your behavior may have on others, and you consider the welfare of others as well as your own self-development. Self-development that occurs at the expense of others will almost inevitably backfire because harm you bring to others will generally result in harm being returned to you. Concern for others is not simply an obligation that requires self-sacrifice. Healthy relationships involve self-enhancement and attention to the welfare of others.

Achieving personal autonomy is a continuing process of growth and learning. Your attitudes toward gender-role identity, work, your body, love, intimacy, sexuality, loneliness, death, and meaning—themes we discuss in later chapters— were originally influenced by your family of origin and your cultural context and by the decisions you made during your early years. Personality development is a process that occurs throughout the life span. Each stage of life has its own challenges, and you continue to develop and change throughout your life. In this chapter we describe the stages from infancy through adolescence; in Chapter 3 we take up early, middle, and late adulthood.

STAGES OF PERSONALITY DEVELOPMENT: A PREVIEW

Each of the developmental theorists has a somewhat different conceptualization of the stages from infancy to old age. By getting a picture of the challenges at each period of life, you will be able to understand how earlier stages of personality development influence the choices you make later in life. These stages are not precise categories that people fall into neatly, and different theories have slightly different conceptualizations of how long people remain in a given stage of life. In reality there is great variability among individuals within a given developmental phase. Your family of origin, culture, race, gender, and socioeconomic status are some factors that have a great deal to do with the manner in which you experience the developmental process. Some people at age 70 are truly old in their appearance, way of thinking, and general health. Yet others at 70 may still retain a great deal of vitality and truly be young. Chronological age is not the only index in considering physical, emotional, and social age.

There are many theoretical approaches to understanding human development. These theories provide a road map to understanding how people develop in all areas of personal functioning. We cannot address all of these models in this book, but we can establish a foundation from which you will be able to reflect on turning points in your childhood and adolescent years. As you read the detailed descriptions of the life cycle, think about how what is written either fits or does not fit for you. Reflecting on your life experiences will bring enhanced meaning to the discussion of these life stages.

In much of this chapter we describe a model that draws on Erik Erikson's (1963, 1982) theory of human development. We also highlight some major ideas about development from the **self-in-context** approach, which emphasizes the individual life cycle in a systemic perspective (see McGoldrick & Carter, 2005, for more on this). The **systemic perspective** is grounded on the assumption that how we develop can best be understood through learning about our role and place in our family of origin. The systemic view is that individuals cannot really be understood apart from the family system of which they are a part. We also draw on some basic concepts of Freudian psychoanalytic theory of personality.

Sigmund Freud, the father of **psychoanalysis,** developed one of the most comprehensive theories of personality in the early 1900s. He pioneered new techniques for understanding human behavior, and his efforts resulted in the most comprehensive theory of personality and psychotherapy ever developed. Freud emphasized unconscious psychological processes and stressed the importance of early childhood experiences. According to his viewpoint, our sexual and social development is largely based on the first 6 years of life. During this time, Freud maintained, we go through distinct stages of development. Our later personality development hinges on how well we resolve the demands and conflicts of each stage. Most of the problems people wrestle with in adulthood have some connection with unresolved conflicts dating from early childhood.

Erikson built on and extended Freud's ideas, stressing the psychosocial aspects of development and carrying his own developmental theory beyond childhood. Erikson is often credited with bringing an emphasis on social factors to contemporary psychoanalysis. Although intellectually indebted to Freud, Erikson suggested that we should view human development in a more positive light, focusing on health and growth. Erikson's **psychosocial theory** focuses on the emergence of the self and the ways in which the self develops through our interactions with our social and cultural environment. Later in this chapter we will return to a more detailed discussion about development and protection of the self.

Erikson believes that we face the task of establishing an equilibrium between ourselves and our social world at each stage of life. Psychosocial theory stresses integration of the biological, psychological, and social aspects of development. This model provides a conceptual framework for understanding trends in development; major developmental tasks at each stage of life; critical needs and their satisfaction or frustration; potentials for choice at each stage of life; critical turning points or developmental crises; and the origins of faulty personality development, which lead to later personality conflicts.

Erikson described human development over the entire life span in terms of eight stages, each marked by a particular crisis to be resolved. For Erikson, a **crisis** is a turning point in life, a moment of transition characterized by the potential to go either forward or backward in development. Levinson (1996) writes that a developmental crisis occurs when an individual has great difficulty meeting the tasks of the current period and that the individual often experiences moderate to severe crises during these transitional periods. The crisis revolves around being caught between the ending of one phase of life and the beginning of another era in one's development. Individuals may not know which way to turn. They can move neither forward nor backward, and there is a sense of imminent danger of the loss of a future. Indeed, as was mentioned in Chapter 1, a crisis offers both dangers and opportunities. At these critical turning points we can achieve successful resolution of our conflicts and move ahead, or we can fail to resolve the conflicts and remain fixated at a transitional period. To a large extent, our lives are the result of the choices we make at each stage of life.

McGoldrick and Carter (2005) have criticized Erikson's theory of individual development for underplaying the importance of the interpersonal realm and connection to others. Contextual factors have a critical bearing on our ability to formulate a clear identity as an individual and also to be able to connect to others. The self-in-context perspective, as described by McGoldrick and Carter, takes into account race, socioeconomic class, gender, ethnicity, and culture as central factors that influence the course of development throughout the individual's life cycle.

The **feminist perspective,** a systemic approach that emphasizes the social context of behavior and how gender affects behavior, is also critical of the Freudian psychoanalytic approach and Erikson's focus on the individual. During the late 1960s and the early 1970s, feminist writers began to focus on the limitations of traditional psychoanalytic theories and techniques that neglected or misunderstood many aspects of women's experiencing. Feminists began to develop conceptual models and ways of practicing that emphasized human connections (Miller & Stiver, 1997). Feminist thought provides a unique perspective on developmental concerns of both women and men and broadens the psychodynamic approach and the psychosocial model of Erikson. Not limited to individual development and autonomy, the focus is on going beyond the self and establishing connections with others. In *The Healing Connection: How Women Form Relationships in Therapy and in Life,* Jean Baker Miller and Irene Pierce Stiver (1997) develop this theme, explaining how we create connections with others and how disconnections derail us throughout our lives.

Our approach has been to combine Erikson's psychosocial theory and the self-in-context theory, integrating their separate strengths to provide a

A child's basic task in the first year of life is to develop a sense of trust in self, others, and the environment.

meaningful framework for understanding key factors influencing our development throughout the life cycle. The life-span perspective presented in these two chapters relies heavily on concepts borrowed from Erikson's model and the self-in-context theories (especially McGoldrick & Carter, 2005). We also rely on the feminist perspective of personality development (see Miller & Stiver, 1997) as this approach applies to the various life stages. In addition, we are indebted to a number of other writers, including Berne (1975), Borysenko (1996), Elkind (1984), Gould (1978), Goleman (1995), Mary and Robert Goulding (1978, 1979), Jordan, Kaplan, Miller, Stiver, and Surrey (1991), Levinson (1996), Sheehy (1976, 1981, 1995), and Steiner (1975). Table 2.1 provides an overview of the major turning points in the life-span perspective of human development from infancy through adolescence.

INFANCY

From birth to age 2 infants are becoming acquainted with their world. Developmental psychologists contend that a child's basic task in the first year of life is to develop a sense of trust in self, others, and the environment. Infants need to count on others; they need to sense that they are cared for and that the world is a secure place. They learn this sense of trust by being held, caressed, and loved.

Table 2.1   Overview of Developmental Stages From Infancy Through Adolescence

Life Stage	Self-in-Context View	Erikson's Psychosocial View	Potential Problems
Infancy (birth to age 2)	This is a time for the development of empathy and emotional attunement. Some specific tasks include learning to talk, making needs known, developing coordination, recognizing self as a separate person, and trusting others. Infants learn how to sit, stand, walk, run, manipulate objects, and feed themselves. They communicate both frustration and happiness.	*Infancy.* Basic task is to develop a sense of trust in self, others, and the environment. Infants need a sense of being cared for and loved. Absence of a sense of security may lead to suspiciousness and a general sense of mistrust toward human relationships. Core struggle: *trust* versus *mistrust.* Theme: hope.	Later personality problems that stem from infancy can include greediness and acquisitiveness, the development of a view of the world based on mistrust, fear of reaching out to others, rejection of affection, fear of loving and trusting, low self-esteem, isolation and withdrawal, and inability to form or maintain intimate relationships.
Early childhood (ages 2–6)	The theme of this phase is a growing understanding of interdependence. Great strides in language and motor development are made. A key task is to develop emotional competence, which involves being able to delay gratification. This stage ushers in the awareness of "otherness" in terms of gender, race, and disability. Other tasks include learning cooperative play, being able to share, developing peer relationships, becoming aware of self in relation to the world around us, and increasing our ability to trust others.	*Early childhood.* A time for developing autonomy. Failure to master self-control tasks may lead to shame and doubt about oneself and one's adequacy. Core struggle: *self-reliance* versus *self-doubt.* Theme: will. *Preschool age.* Characterized by play and by anticipation of roles; a time to establish a sense of competence and initiative. Children who are not allowed to make decisions tend to develop a sense of guilt. Core struggle: *initiative* versus *guilt.* Theme: purpose.	Children experience many negative feelings such as hostility, rage, destructiveness, anger, and hatred. If these feelings are not accepted, individuals may not be able to accept their feelings later on. Parental attitudes can be communicated verbally and nonverbally. Negative learning experiences tend to lead to feelings of guilt about natural impulses. Strict parental indoctrination can lead to rigidity, severe conflicts, remorse, and self-condemnation.
Middle childhood (ages 6–12)	This is a time when children learn to read, write, and do math. They increase their understanding of self in terms of gender, race, culture, and abilities. There is an increased understanding of self in relation to family, peers, and community. A key task is developing empathy, or being able to take the perspective of others.	*School age.* Central task is to achieve a sense of industry; failure to do so results in a sense of inadequacy. Child needs to expand understanding of the world and continue to develop appropriate gender-role identity. Learning basic skills is essential for school success. Core struggle: *industry* versus *inferiority.* Theme: competence.	Problems that can originate during middle childhood include negative self-concept, feelings of inferiority in establishing social relationships, conflicts over values, confused gender-role identity, dependency, fear of new challenges, and lack of initiative.

Table 2.1	Overview of Developmental Stages From Infancy Through Adolescence *(continued)*		
Life Stage	*Self-in-Context View*	*Erikson's Psychosocial View*	*Potential Problems*
Pubescence (ages 11–13 for girls) (ages 12–14 for boys)	A time of finding one's own voice and the beginning of developing a sense of autonomy. Some specific developmental tasks include asserting oneself, developing emotional competence, increasing capacity for moral understanding, coping with dramatic bodily changes, increasing ability to deal with social relationships and work collaboratively, and developing awareness of own and others' sexuality. This is a time of expanded sense of self in relation to peers, family, and community.		
Adolescence (ages 13–20)	The theme of this period is searching for an identity, continuing to find one's voice, and balancing caring of self with caring about others. Key developmental themes include dealing with rapid body changes and body image issues, learning self-management, developing one's sexual identity, developing a philosophy of life and a spiritual identity, learning to deal with intimate relationships, and an expanded understanding of self in relation to others.	*Adolescence.* A critical time for forming a personal identity. Major conflicts center on clarification of self-identity, life goals, and life's meaning. Struggle is over integrating physical and social changes. Pressures include succeeding in school, choosing a job, forming relationships, and preparing for future. Core struggle: *identity* versus *role confusion.* Theme: fidelity.	A time when an individual may anticipate an *identity crisis.* Caught in the midst of pressures, demands, and turmoil, adolescents often lose a sense of self. If *role confusion* results, the individual may lack sense of purpose in later years. Absence of a stable set of values can prevent mature development of a philosophy to guide one's life.

Infants form a basic conception of the social world during this time, and Erikson saw their core struggle as **trust versus mistrust.** If the significant other persons in an infant's life provide the needed warmth, cuddling, and attention, the child develops a sense of trust. When these conditions are not present, the child becomes suspicious about interacting with others and acquires a general sense of mistrust toward human relationships. Although neither orientation is fixed in an infant's personality for life, it is clear that well-nurtured infants are in a more favorable position with respect to future personal growth than are their more neglected peers.

Daniel Goleman (1995) believes infancy is the beginning point for establishing emotional intelligence. He identifies the most crucial factor in teaching emotional competence as timing, especially in our family of origin and in our culture of origin during infancy. He adds that childhood and adolescence expand on the foundation for learning a range of human competencies. Later development offers critical *windows of opportunity* for acquiring the basic emotional patterns that will govern the rest of our lives.

John Bowlby (1969, 1973, 1980, 1988) studied the importance of attachment, separation, and loss in human development and developed **attachment theory,** an extension of psychoanalytic theory. **Attachment** involves an emotional bonding with another who is perceived as a source of security (Pistole & Arricale, 2003). Bowlby (1988) emphasizes the relationships that the infant has with others, especially the mother (or another "attachment figure"), and proposes that the maintenance of affectional bonds is essential for human survival. Infant attachment relationships can be broadly classified as secure or insecure. The quality of care an infant receives is related to the quality of relationships in later life (Peluso, Peluso, White, & Kern, 2004).

Ainsworth, Blehar, Waters, and Wall (1978) designed an experiment to observe the attachment behavior of young children, and based on these observations, they defined three patterns of attachment: secure, anxious-avoidant, and anxious-ambivalent. According to Bowlby (1969, 1973) and Ainsworth et al. (1978), a **secure pattern** is characterized by feelings of intimacy, emotional security, and physical safety when the infant is in the presence of an attachment figure. These infants relate well with others in their world. Infants exhibiting the **anxious-avoidant pattern** experience an insecure attachment relationship because their attachment figures consistently reject them. These infants tend to use some form of disconnection or avoidance as a defense (Bowlby, 1980). Their sense of self is distorted, and their relationships in later life may be impaired. Infants using the **anxious-ambivalent pattern** exhibit intense distress at their caretaker's departure and an inability to be comforted upon return of the caretaker. Some of the effects of rejection in infancy include tendencies in later childhood to be fearful, insecure, jealous, aggressive, hostile, or isolated. This disconnection with self and others inhibits learning the essential emotional habits that will enable them to care about others, to be compassionate, and to form meaningful connections with others. Both the anxious-avoidant and the anxious-ambivalent patterns of attachment support Bowlby's (1980) contention that children form some style of attachment regardless of the lack of emotional responsiveness from the caregiver.

And what happens beyond infancy? These early experiences with an attachment figure become internalized by the child, and these patterns serve as the blueprint for future relationships with others (Peluso et al., 2004). Ainsworth et al. (1978) have related different kinds of insecure attachments to the caretaker to later childhood and adolescent behavior, which tends to involve emotional detachment, a sense of being alone, uncertainty, and problems in interpersonal relationships. According to Pistole and Arricale (2003), in later relationships secure attachments are characterized by a positive self-image and a positive view of the partner. Adults with secure attachments appropriately rely on the partner as a safe haven and a base for exploration, and they experience satisfying relationships.

A sense of being loved during infancy is the best safeguard against fear, insecurity, and inadequacy. Children who receive love from parents or other attachment figures generally have little difficulty accepting themselves, whereas children who feel unloved and rejected may find it very difficult to accept themselves. In addition, rejected children learn to mistrust the world and to view it primarily in terms of its ability to do them harm.

At times parents may be unduly anxious about wanting to be the perfect mother and father. They spend time worrying about "doing the right thing at the right time." This chronic anxiety can be the very thing that causes difficulties as their sons and daughters will soon sense that they must be "perfect children." Children can and do survive the "mistakes" that all parents make, but chronic neglect or overprotection can have negative long-term effects. Sally's story illustrates the possible effects of severe deprivation during the early developmental years.

SALLY'S STORY

I was released for adoption by my biological parents and spent the first decade of my life in orphanages and foster homes. I pleaded to stay with one set of foster parents who had kept me for over a year and then said I had to go. I spent many years thinking that something was wrong with me. If my own parents didn't want me, who could? I tried to figure out what I had done wrong and why so many people sent me away. As an adult, I still yearn for what I missed during infancy and childhood. I don't get close to anyone now because if I do they might leave me. I had to isolate myself emotionally to survive when I was a child, and I still operate on the assumptions I had as a child.

I am so fearful of being deserted that I won't venture out and take even minimal risks. I am 40 years old now, but I still feel like a child.

Sally is not unusual. We have worked with a number of individuals who suffer from the effects of early psychological deprivation, and we have observed that in most cases such deprivation has lingering adverse effects on a person's level of self-love and the ability to form meaningful relationships later in life. Many people, of all ages, struggle with the issue of trusting others in a loving relationship. They are unable to trust that another can or will love them, they fear being rejected, and they fear even more the possibility of closeness and being accepted and loved. Many of these people do not trust themselves or others sufficiently to make themselves vulnerable enough to experience love. We have all heard about children who were adopted, perhaps as infants, who are now striving to find their natural parents. Even if they love their adopted parents and view them as having done a splendid parenting job, these adult children often feel a void and wonder about the circumstances of their adoption. These adult children may feel that their biological mother and father did not want them or that in some way they were at fault for what happened. Many people reexperience their childhood feelings of hurt and rejection during the process of counseling; in this way they come to understand that even though they did not feel loved by their parents this does not mean that others find them unlovable now.

At this point, pause and ask yourself these questions:

- Am I able to trust others? Myself?
- Am I willing to make myself known to a few selected people in my life?
- Do I basically accept myself as being OK, or do I seek confirmation outside of myself?
- How far will I go in my attempt to be liked? Do I need to be liked and approved of by everyone?
- Am I in any way like Sally? Do I know of anyone who has had experiences similar to hers?
- How much do I really know about my early years? What have I heard from my parents and extended family about my infancy and early childhood?

EARLY CHILDHOOD

The tasks children must master in **early childhood** (ages 2–6) include learning independence, accepting personal power, and learning to cope with impulsive and aggressive reactions and behavior. The critical task is to begin the journey toward autonomy by progressing from being taken care of by others to meeting some of their own physical needs.

Erikson identified the core struggle of early childhood, which for him ranges from ages 1 to 3, as the conflict of **autonomy versus shame and doubt.**

Children who fail to master the task of establishing some control over themselves and coping with the world around them develop a sense of shame, and they doubt their capabilities. Erikson emphasized that during this time children become aware of their emerging skills and have a drive to try them out. To illustrate this point, I (Marianne) remember when I was feeding one of our daughters during her infancy. Heidi had been a very agreeable child who swallowed all of the food I put into her mouth. One day, much to my surprise, she spit it right back at me! No matter how much I wanted her to continue eating, she refused. This was one way in which Heidi began asserting herself with me. As my children were growing up, I strove to establish a good balance between having them develop their own identity and at the same time providing them with guidance and appropriate limits.

During early childhood, great strides in language and motor development are made. This is a time for the beginning of an increased understanding of what it means to be interdependent. Goleman (1995) points to the importance of developing emotional competence, especially learning to regulate and control emotions and impulses, and also to delay gratification. Peer relationships are particularly critical at this time, and children need to acquire a cooperative spirit and the ability to share. This is a time when children begin to become aware of themselves in relation to the world around them. They also become aware of "otherness" in terms of gender, race, and disability (McGoldrick & Carter, 2005).

Erikson identified the preschool years (ages 3–6) as being characterized by play and by anticipation of roles. During this time, children try to find out how much they can do. They imitate others; they begin to develop a sense of right and wrong; they widen their circle of significant persons; they take more initiative; they learn to give and receive love and affection; they identify with their own gender; they begin to learn more complex social skills; they learn basic attitudes regarding sexuality; and they increase their capacity to understand and use language.

According to Erikson, the basic task of these preschool years is to establish a sense of competence and initiative. The core struggle is between **initiative and guilt.** Preschool children begin to initiate many of their own activities as they become physically and psychologically ready to engage in pursuits of their own choosing. If they are allowed realistic freedom to make some of their own decisions, they tend to develop a positive orientation characterized by confidence in their ability to initiate and follow through. If they are unduly restricted or if their choices are ridiculed, however, they tend to experience a sense of guilt and ultimately to withdraw from taking an active stance. One middle-aged woman we talked with still finds herself extremely vulnerable to being seen as foolish. She recalls that during her childhood family members laughed at her attempts to perform certain tasks. She incorporated certain messages she received from her family, and these messages greatly influenced her attitudes and actions. Even now she vividly carries these pictures in her head, and to some extent these messages continue to control her life.

In the preschool years, children widen their circle of significant persons and learn more complex social skills.

© Barbara Rios/Photo Researchers, Inc.

Parents who squelch any emerging individuality and who do too much for their children hamper their development. They are saying, however indirectly, "Let us do this for you, because you're too clumsy, too slow, or too inept to do things for yourself." Young children need to experiment; they need to be allowed to make mistakes and still feel that they are basically worthwhile. If parents insist on keeping their children dependent on them, the children will begin to doubt their own abilities. If parents do not respect and support their children's efforts, the children may feel ashamed of themselves or become insecure and fearful.

Sometimes children may want to do more than they are capable of doing. For example, the 5-year-old son of a friend of ours went on a hike with his father. At one point the boy asked his father to let him carry a heavy backpack the way the "big people" do. Without saying a word, the father took his backpack off and handed it to his son, who immediately discovered that it was too heavy for him to carry. The boy simply exclaimed, "Dad, it's too heavy for me." He then went happily on his way up the trail. In a safe way the father had allowed his son to discover experientially that he was, indeed, too small. He had also avoided a potential argument with his son.

Young children also must learn to accept the full range of their feelings. They will surely experience anger, and it is important that they know and feel that anger is permissible. They need to feel loved and accepted with all of their feelings, otherwise they will tend to stifle their anger so as not to lose the love of their parents. When anger cannot be acknowledged or expressed, it becomes toxic and finds expression in indirect ways. One of the results of denying anger is that children begin to numb all of their feelings, including joy.

As adults, many of us have difficulty acknowledging our anger, even when it is fully justified. We may swallow our anger and rationalize away other feelings because we learned when we were very young that we were unacceptable when we had such feelings. As children we might have shouted at our parents: "I hate you! I never want to see you again!" Then we may have heard an upset parent reply: "How dare you say such a thing—after all I've done for you! I don't ever want to hear that from you again!" We soon take these messages to mean, "Don't be angry! Never be angry with those you love! Keep control of yourself!" And we do just that, keeping many of our feelings to ourselves, stuffing them in the pit of our stomach and pretending we do not experience them. It is not surprising that so many of us suffer from migraine headaches, peptic ulcers, hypertension, and heart disease.

Pause and reflect on some of your own current struggles with these issues:

- Am I able to recognize my own feelings, particularly if they are "unacceptable" to others?

- How was anger expressed in my family?

- How do I express my anger to those I love?

- How was love expressed in my family?

- Have I established a good balance between depending on others and relying on myself?

- Am I able to let others know what I want? Can I be assertive without being aggressive?

- What positive or negative messages did I receive from my parents? Which of these messages did I accept, which did I reject?

IMPACT OF THE FIRST 6 YEARS OF LIFE

You may be asking yourself why we are emphasizing the events of this period. In working with clients we continue to realize the influence of these early years on their levels of integration and functioning as adults. Sometimes people ask, "Why look back into my past? I don't see any point in dredging up that painful period, especially since I've worked so hard to get that part of my life under control."

Many of these childhood experiences have a profound impact on both the present and the future. If you reached faulty conclusions based on your early life experience, you are likely to still be operating on the basis of them. If you told yourself as a child, "I can never do enough for my father," then as an adult you may feel that you can never do enough (or be enough) to meet the expectations of those who are significant in your life. Not only is our current

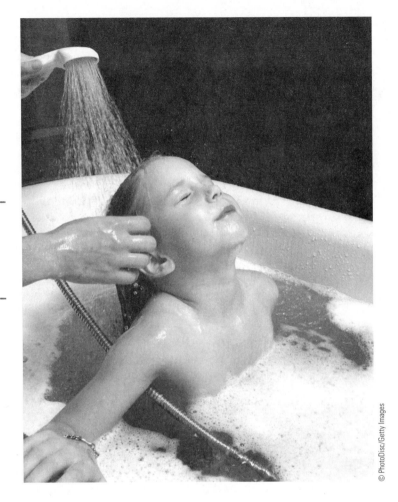

A sense of being loved during the early years is the best safeguard against insecurity and inadequacy.

© PhotoDisc/Getty Images

functioning influenced by early interpretations, but our future is too. Our goals and purposes have some connection with the way we dealt with emerging issues during the first 6 years of life.

In working in counseling groups with relatively well-functioning adults who have "normal" developmental issues, we find that a new understanding of their early years often entails a certain degree of emotional pain. Yet by understanding these painful events, they have a basis for transcending them and avoiding replaying these old self-defeating themes throughout their lifetime. We do not think healthy people are ever really "cured" of their vulnerabilities. For example, during your preschool years, if you felt abandoned by the divorce of your parents, you are still likely to have vestiges of doubts and fears when forming close relationships. Yet you do not have to surrender to these traces of mistrust. Instead, you can gain control of your fears of loving and trusting.

In reviewing your childhood, you may find some aspects that you like and do not want to change. You may also find a certain continuity in your life that is meaningful to you. At the same time, if you are honest with yourself, you are likely to become aware of certain revisions you would like to make. This awareness is the first critical step toward changing.

Typical problems and conflicts we encounter among people in our therapeutic groups include an inability to trust oneself and others; an inability to freely accept and give love; difficulty recognizing and expressing the full range of one's feelings; guilt over feelings of anger toward those one loves; difficulty in accepting oneself as a woman or a man; and problems concerning a lack of meaning or purpose in life or a clear sense of personal identity and aspirations. Notice that most of these adult problems are directly related to the turning points and tasks of the early developmental years. The effects of early learning are reversible in most cases, but these experiences, whether favorable or unfavorable, clearly influence how we interpret both present and future critical periods in our lives.

Some people learn new values, come to accept new feelings and attitudes, and overcome much of their past negative conditioning. Other people steadfastly hang on to the past as an excuse for not taking any action to change in the present. We cannot change in a positive direction unless we stop blaming others for the way we are now. Statements that begin "If it hadn't been for . . ." are too often used to justify an immobile position. Blaming others for our present struggles ultimately keeps us trapped, waiting for "them out there" to change before we can change. When we become aware of pointing an accusing finger at someone else, it is a good idea to look at our other fingers—pointing back at us! Once we are able to see in ourselves the very traits that we accuse others of, and once we quit blaming others, we make it possible to take charge of our own life.

We may experience anger and hurt for having been cheated in the past. However, it is imperative that we eventually reclaim the power we have given to others. When we do not recognize and exercise the power we now have, we restrict our choices to move in new directions.

Take Time to Reflect

1. Close your eyes and reflect for a moment on your memories of your first 6 years. Attempt to identify your earliest concrete single memory—something you actually remember that happened to you, not something you were told about. Spend a few minutes recalling the details and reexperiencing the feelings associated with this early event.

   • Write down your earliest recollection.

   _____

   _____

- What is your main memory of your father? Mother? Siblings?

_____

_____

2. Reflect on the events that most stand out for you during your first 6 years of life. In particular, think about your place in your family, your family's reaction to you, and your reactions to each person in your family. What connections do you see between how it felt to be in your family as a child and how you now feel in various social situations? What speculations do you have concerning the impact your family had then and the effect that these experiences continue to have on your current personality?

_____

_____

3. Take the following self-inventory. Respond quickly, marking "T" if you believe the statement is more true than false for you as a young child and "F" if it tends not to fit your early childhood experiences.

_____ As a young child, I felt loved and accepted.
_____ I basically trusted the world.
_____ I felt that I was an acceptable and valuable person.
_____ I felt I needed to work for others' approval.
_____ I experienced a great deal of shame and self-doubt as a child.
_____ I felt that it was not OK for me to express anger.
_____ My parents trusted my ability to do things for myself.
_____ I believe I developed a natural and healthy concept of my body and my gender-role identity.
_____ I had very few friends as a young child.
_____ I felt that I could talk to my parents about my problems.

   Look over your responses. What do they tell you about the person you now are? If you could live your childhood over again, how would you like it to be? Record some of your impressions in your journal.

MIDDLE CHILDHOOD

During **middle childhood** (ages 6–12), children face these key developmental tasks: engage in social activities; expand their knowledge and understanding of the physical and social worlds; continue to learn and expand their concepts of an appropriate feminine or masculine role; develop a sense of values; learn new communication skills; learn how to read, write, and calculate; learn to give and take; learn how to accept people who are culturally different; learn to tolerate ambiguity; and learn physical skills. McGoldrick and Carter (2005) point out that during middle childhood there is an increased understanding of self in terms of gender, race, culture, and abilities; of self in relationship to family, peers, and community; and an increase in the capacity for empathy. These authors add that by ages 9 to 12 children begin to form an identification with causes, aspirations, and privileges of groups they belong to, which provides the motivation for them to think and act in certain ways. A key social ability in children is empathy, which involves understanding the feelings of others, being able to take others' perspective, and respecting differences in how people feel about things (Goleman, 1995). This empathy includes being able to understand distress beyond an immediate situation and to feel for the plight of an entire group such as those who are oppressed or live in poverty. Goleman gives a clearer picture of the role relationships play in the development of children:

> RELATIONSHIPS ARE A MAJOR FOCUS, including learning to be a good listener and question-asker; distinguishing between what someone says or does and your own reactions and judgments; being assertive rather than angry or passive; and learning the arts of cooperation, conflict resolution, and negotiating compromise. (p. 268)

According to Erikson, the major struggle of middle childhood is between **industry and inferiority.** The central task of this period is to achieve a sense of industry; failure to do so results in a sense of inadequacy and inferiority. Development of a sense of industry includes focusing on creating and producing and on attaining goals. Of course, starting school is a critical event of this time. The first 4 years of school are vital to successful completion of a healthy outcome of this stage. The child's self-concept is especially fragile before the fourth grade; if teachers are critical of a child's performance, this could have a lasting impact. Children who encounter failure during the early grades may experience severe handicaps later on. A child with early learning problems may begin to feel worthless as a person. Such a feeling may, in turn, drastically affect his or her relationships with peers, which are also vital at this time. Helen's story illustrates some of the common conflicts of the elementary school years.

HELEN'S STORY

I started kindergarten a bit too early and was smaller than most of the other children. I had looked forward to beginning school, but I soon felt overwhelmed. I began to fail at many of the tasks other children were enjoying and mastering. Gradually, I began to avoid even simple tasks and to find excuses for my failures. I became increasingly afraid of making mistakes, and I thought that everything I did had to be perfect.

My teachers thought I was sensitive and needed a lot of encouragement and direction, but I continued to quit too soon because I didn't think my work was "good enough." When I was in the third grade, I was at least a grade level behind in reading, despite having repeated kindergarten. I began to feel stupid and embarrassed because I couldn't read as well as the other children, and I did not want to read aloud. Eventually, I received instruction in remedial reading. I liked this attention, but then they gave me some reading tests and I didn't do well. I hate taking tests, and I always think I will fail.

I might have given up on school a long time ago, but many people helped me continue in spite of my fears. I am in college now, and I am still anxious about taking tests. I am learning to control my feelings of inadequacy and self-doubt, and I am arguing back to those old voices that say I am basically inadequate.

Helen's case indicates that the first few years of school can have a powerful impact on a child's life and future adjustment to school. Her school experiences colored her view of her self-worth and affected her relationships with other children.

At this point ask yourself these questions:

- Can I identify in any ways with Helen's feelings?
- What struggles did I experience in forming my self-concept?
- Does Helen remind me of anyone I know?

Forming a self-concept is a major task of middle childhood. Let's take a closer look at what this entails.

Developing a Self-Concept

The term **self-concept** refers to your awareness about yourself. It is your picture of yourself that includes your perceptions about the kind of person you are. This picture includes your view of your worth, value, and possibilities; the way you see yourself in relation to others; the way you ideally would like to be; and the degree to which you accept yourself as you are. From ages 6 to 12 the view you have of yourself is influenced greatly by the quality of your school experiences, by contact with your peer group and with teachers, and by your interactions with your family. To a large extent, your self-concept is formed by what others tell you about yourself, especially during the formative years of childhood. Whether you develop a positive or negative outlook on yourself has a good deal to do with what people close to you have expected of you.

This view of yourself influences how you present yourself to others and how you act and feel when you are with them. For example, you may feel inadequate around authority figures. Perhaps you tell yourself that you have nothing to say or that whatever you might say would be stupid. More often than not, others will see and respond to you in the way you "tell" them you are, both verbally and nonverbally. Monitor the messages you are sending to others about yourself, and become aware of the patterns you might be perpetuating. It is difficult for those who are close to you to treat you in a positive way when you consistently discount yourself. Why should others treat you better than you treat yourself? In contrast, people with a positive self-concept are likely to behave confidently, which causes others to react to them positively.

Once we have established our self-concept, a variety of strategies are available to help us maintain and protect it from outside threats. Next we discuss how these various ego defenses are aimed at coping with anxiety.

Protecting the Self: Ego-Defense Mechanisms

Ego-defense mechanisms are psychological strategies we use to protect our self-concept from unpleasant emotions. We use these protective devices at various stages of life to soften the blows of harsh reality. Ego defenses typically originate during the early and middle childhood years, and later experiences during adolescence and adulthood reinforce some of these self-defense styles. We often carry these habitual responses into adulthood as a way to cope with anxiety. We will use Helen's story to illustrate the nature and functioning of some of these ego defenses. For the most part Helen made poor adjustments to her school and social life during her childhood years. Other children stayed away from her because of her aggressive and unfriendly behavior. She did not like her elementary school experience, and her teachers were not overly fond of her. Helen's behavioral style in coping with the pressures of school included blaming the outside world for her difficulties. In the face of these failures in life, she might have made use of any one or a combination of the following ego-defense mechanisms.

Repression The mechanism of repression is one of the most important processes in psychoanalytic theory, and it is the basis of many other ego defenses. By pushing threatening or painful thoughts and feelings from awareness, we sometimes manage the anxiety that grows out of situations involving guilt and conflict. Repression may block out stressful experiences that could be met by realistically facing and working through a situation. Helen was unaware of her dependence/independence struggles with her parents; she was also unaware of how her painful experiences of failure were contributing to her feelings of inferiority and insecurity. Helen had unconsciously excluded most of her failures and had not allowed them to come to the surface of awareness.

Denial Denial plays a defensive role similar to that of repression, but it generally operates at a preconscious or conscious level. In denial there is a conscious effort to suppress unpleasant reality. It is a way of distorting what the individual thinks, feels, or perceives to be a stressful situation. Helen simply "closed her eyes" to her failures in school. Even though she had evidence that she was not performing well academically, she refused to acknowledge this reality.

Displacement Displacement involves redirecting emotional impulses (usually hostility) from the real object to a substitute person or object. In essence, anxiety is coped with by discharging impulses onto a "safer target." For example, Helen's sister Joan was baffled by the hostility she received from Helen. Joan did not understand why Helen was so critical of her every action. Helen used Joan as the target of her aggression because Joan did exceptionally well at school and was very popular with her peers.

Projection Another mechanism of self-deception is projection, which consists of attributing to others our own unacceptable desires and impulses. We are able to clearly see in others the very traits that we disown in ourselves, which serves the purpose of keeping a certain view of ourselves intact. Typically, projection involves seeing clearly in others actions that would lead to guilt feelings in ourselves. Helen tended to blame everyone but herself for her difficulties in school and in social relationships. She complained that her teachers were unfairly picking on her, that she could never do anything right for them, and that other children were mean to her.

Reaction Formation One defense against a threatening impulse is to actively express the opposite impulse. This involves behaving in a manner that is contrary to one's real feelings. A characteristic of this defense is the excessive quality of a particular attitude or behavior. For example, Helen bristled when her teachers or parents offered to give her help. She was convinced that she did not need anyone's help. Accepting their offers would have indicated that she really was stupid.

Rationalization Rationalization involves manufacturing a false but "good" excuse to justify unacceptable behavior and explain away failures or losses. Such excuses help restore a bruised ego. Helen was quick to find many reasons for the difficulties she encountered, a few of which included sickness, which caused her to fall behind in her classes; teachers who went over the lessons too fast; other children who did not let her play with them; and siblings who kept her awake at night.

Compensation Another defense reaction is compensation, which consists of masking perceived weaknesses or developing certain positive traits to make up for limitations. The adjustive value in this mechanism lies in keeping one's self-esteem intact by excelling in one area to distract attention from an area in which the person is inferior. The more Helen experienced difficulties at school and with her peers, the more she withdrew from others and became absorbed in artwork that she did by herself at home.

Regression Faced with stress, some people revert to a form of immature behavior that they have outgrown. In regression, they attempt to cope with their anxiety by clinging to such inappropriate behaviors. Faced with failure in both her social and school life, Helen had a tendency to engage in emotional tirades, crying a lot, storming into her room, and refusing to come out for hours.

Fantasy Fantasy involves gratifying frustrated desires by imaginary achievements. When achievement in the real world seems remote, some people resort to screening out unpleasant aspects of reality and living in their world of dreams. During her childhood, Helen developed a rich fantasy in which she imagined herself to be an actress. She played with her dolls for hours and talked to herself. In her daydreams she saw herself in the movies, surrounded by famous people.

Although ego-defense mechanisms have some adaptive value, their overuse can be problematic. Self-deception can soften harsh reality, but the fact is that reality does not change through the process of distorting those aspects of it that produce anxiety. When these defensive strategies do not work, the long-term result is an even greater degree of anxiety. Overreliance on these defenses leads to a vicious circle—as the defenses lose their value in holding anxiety in check, people step up the use of other defenses.

All defenses are not self-defeating, however, and there is a proper place for them, especially when stresses are great. In the face of certain crises, for example, defenses can enable people to cope at least temporarily until they can build up other resources, both from their environment and from within themselves.

Take Time to Reflect Spend some time reflecting on the defense mechanisms you used during your childhood years.

1. Do you see any analogies between the defenses you employed as a child and those you sometimes use at this time in your life?

_____

_____

2. List some of the defenses you use, and examine how they might serve you better.

_____

_____

3. Imagine how your life might be different if you gave up all your defenses. Write about this life in your journal.

_____

_____

PUBESCENCE

The years from about 11 to 14 constitute a stage of transition between childhood and adolescence. For girls, **pubescence** generally occurs between the ages of 11 and 13; for boys it is between the ages of 12 and 14. During this phase, boys and girls experience major physical, psychological, and sexual changes. Most people find the pubescent period particularly difficult. It is a paradoxical time. Preadolescents are not treated as mature adults, yet they are often expected to act as though they had gained complete maturity. Continually testing the limits, young people have a strong urge to break away from dependent ties that restrict their freedom. It is not uncommon for preadolescents to be frightened and lonely, but they may mask their fears with rebellion and cover up their need to be dependent by exaggerating their independence. They are typically finding they have a voice and are willing to use it. Much of preadolescent rebellion is an attempt to declare their uniqueness and establish a separate identity. This is the time when individuals assert who and what they want to be.

As infants we must learn to trust ourselves and others; as preadolescents we need to find a meaning in life and adult role models in whom we believe. As toddlers we begin to assert our rights as independent people by struggling for autonomy; as preadolescents we make choices that will shape our future. As preschoolers we try to achieve a sense of competence; as preadolescents and as adolescents we explore choices about what we want from life, what we can succeed in, what kind of education we want, and what career may suit us.

ADOLESCENCE

Adolescence spans the period from about age 13 for girls and age 14 or 15 for boys until the late teens or to about age 20. Adolescence is a critical period in the development of personal identity. For Erikson, the major developmental conflicts of adolescence center on clarification of who they are, where they are going, and how they are going to get there. He sees the core struggle of adolescence as **identity versus role confusion.** Failure to achieve a sense of identity results in role confusion. Adolescents may feel overwhelmed by the pressures placed on them and find the development of a clear identity a difficult task. They may feel pressured to make an occupational choice, to compete in the job market or in college, to become financially independent, or to commit themselves to physically and emotionally intimate relationships. In addition, they may feel pressured to live up to the standards of their peer group. Peer group pressure is a powerful force, and some adolescents lose a sense of themselves by conforming to the expectations of their friends. If the need to be accepted and liked is stronger than the need for being true to one's values, adolescents will most likely find themselves behaving in inauthentic ways and increasingly looking to others to tell them what and who they should be.

© PhotoDisc/Getty Images

Adolescents have a need for self-expression and establishing a separate identity.

Adolescence is a time when young people evolve their sexual and gender identities, learn to form intimate relationships, and learn to function in an increasingly independent manner. Adolescents renegotiate their identity and relationship with their parents, acquire a range of new attitudes and skills, develop an ethical and spiritual sense, and continue the process of defining their gender-role identity.

A crucial part of the identity-formation process is *individuation,* separating from our family system and establishing an identity based on our own experiences. This process of psychological separation from parental ties is the most agonizing part of the adolescent struggle and lays the foundation for future development. Although achieving psychological separation from one's family is a common theme in Western cultures, in some other cultures the wishes of parents continue to have a major influence on the behavior of adult children. Furthermore, becoming psychologically separate from one's family may not be seen as a guiding value. Instead, the collective good is given far more weight than individual fulfillment. In many countries there is no adolescent phase. At puberty boys and girls are initiated into adult roles for which they have long been prepared. The cultural conflict can be enormous when families emigrate to the West and their children want to assimilate into the mainstream culture.

Feminist therapists view the early adolescent period as one of expanding relationships with parents—not "getting rid" of parents (Miller & Stiver, 1997). More than needing "separation" from their parents, both preadolescents and adolescents need to *change* their relationship with their parents. If adolescents are able to maintain trustworthy connections with parents, they will be better able to undertake other changes they need to make.

Adolescents confront dilemmas similar to those faced by older people in our society. Both age groups need to find a meaning in life and must cope with feelings of uselessness. Older people may be forced to retire and may encounter difficulty replacing work activities; young people have not completed their education or acquired the skills necessary for many occupations. Instead, they are in a constant process of preparation for the future. Even in their families adolescents may feel unneeded. Although they may be given chores to do, many adolescents do not experience much opportunity to be productive.

The question of options is made even more urgent by the myth that the choices we make during adolescence bind us for the rest of our lives. Adolescents who believe this myth will be hesitant to experiment and test out many options. Too many young people yield to pressures to decide too early what they will be and what serious commitments they will make. Thus they may never realize the range of possibilities open to them. To deal with this problem, Erikson suggested a **psychological moratorium**—a period during which society would give permission to adolescents to experiment with different roles and values so they could sample life before making major commitments.

Forming a philosophy of life is a central task of adolescence. Sexual, religious, spiritual, and racial issues take on a new perspective and are subject to new understanding and revision (McGoldrick & Carter, 2005). Many adolescents experiment with alcohol, drugs, and sex. Although some experimentation is healthy, some of these practices can have dire consequences for adolescents. Adolescents are faced with choosing the beliefs and values that will guide their actions as adults. In meeting this challenge, young people need adequate models because a sense of moral living is largely learned by example. Adolescents are especially sensitive to duplicity and are quick to spot phony people who tell them how they ought to live while themselves living in very different ways. They learn values by observing and interacting with adults who are positive examples rather than by being preached to. Of course, not all role models are positive. In some cases adolescents adopt drug dealers or other criminals as role models. Many adolescents look for an identity by affiliation with a gang, and they may find role models within this group.

Today's adolescents also have to cope with violence at school. It is not uncommon for adolescents, and even children, to bring guns or knives to school. News reports of an adolescent injuring fellow classmates or a teacher are all too common. Not only do today's teens have to contend with peer pressure, parental pressure, and the confusion and pain that accompanies finding their identities, they also have to worry about being shot by a schoolmate or being the victim of some other form of violence or intimidation.

Adolescents who belong to certain racial groups are the targets of racism, and they encounter discrimination and oppression both at school and in society at large. Beverly Daniel Tatum (1999) writes about racial identity development in adolescence and raises the question, "Why are all the Black kids sitting together in the cafeteria?" In addition to raising questions such as "Who am I?" and "Who can I be?" Black youth are also considering questions such as "Who am I ethnically and racially?" and "What does it mean to be Black?" During adolescence, race becomes personally salient for Black youth as they search for answers to questions such as: "What does it mean to be a young Black person? How should I act? What should I do?" In her discussion of understanding racial identity development, Tatum states that Black youths absorb many of the beliefs and values of the dominant society. As a function of growing up in a Eurocentric culture, Black adolescents may come to value the role models and lifestyles that are portrayed by the dominant group more highly than those of their own cultural group. As a result of their heightened awareness of the significance of race, Black youths often grapple with what it means to be targeted by racism. In response to their growing awareness of the systematic exclusion of Black people from full participation in the dominant society, many Black youths experience anger and resentment. This often leads to the development of an oppositional social identity, which protects Black individuals from the psychological assault of racism and keeps the dominant group at bay.

When a group of Black teens sit together in the cafeteria, school administrators want to understand why this is so and how this can be prevented. Tatum's (1999) response is that such a racial grouping is a developmental process in response to the environmental stressor of racism. She adds: "Joining with one's peers for support in the face of stress is a positive coping strategy. What is problematic is that the young people are operating with a very limited definition of what it means to be Black, based largely on cultural stereotypes" (p. 62).

Our childhood experiences have a direct influence on how we approach the adolescent years, and how well we master the tasks of adolescence has a bearing on our ability to cope with the critical turning points of adulthood. If we do not develop a clear sense of identity during adolescence, finding meaning in adult life becomes extremely difficult. As we progress from one stage of life to the next, we at times meet with roadblocks and detours and may experience anxiety, depression, or alienation. These barriers are often the result of having failed to master basic psychological competencies at an earlier period. When we encounter such obstacles, we can accept them as signposts and continue down the same path or use them as opportunities for growth. Miller and Stiver (1997) contend that these roadblocks can be turned to pathways of connection between people, which leads to the development of healthy individuals.

In sum, for most people adolescence is a difficult period, characterized by paradoxes: they strive for closeness, yet they also fear intimacy and often avoid it; they rebel against control, yet they want direction and structure; although they push and test limits imposed on them, they see some limits as a sign of caring; they are not given complete autonomy, yet they are often expected to act as though they were mature adults; they are typically highly self-centered, self-conscious, and preoccupied with their own world, yet they are expected to cope with societal demands to go outside themselves by expanding their horizons; they are asked to face and accept reality, and at the same time they are tempted by many avenues of escape; and they are exhorted to think of the future, yet they have strong urges to live for the moment and to enjoy life.

Adolescence is typically a turbulent and fast-moving period of life, often marked by feelings of powerlessness, confusion, and loneliness. It is a time for making critical choices, even the ultimate choice of living fully or bringing about one's own death. Decisions are being made in almost every area of life, and these decisions to a large extent define our identity. The following Take Time To Reflect is a chance for you to identify some of the choices you made during your adolescent years and to clarify the impact these experiences continue to exert on you today.

Take Time to Reflect Review the choices open to adolescents, and especially think of the choices you remember having made at this time in your life. How do you think those choices have influenced the person you are today?

1. What major choices did you struggle with during your adolescent years?

_____

_____

2. How do you think your adolescence affected the person you are today?

_____

_____

SUMMARY

A road map of the developmental tasks of the life span reveals that each stage presents certain dangers and offers particular opportunities. Crises can be seen as challenges to be met rather than as catastrophic events that happen to us. The Chinese symbol for crisis encompasses both danger and opportunity.

In normal development, critical turning points and choices appear at each developmental stage. Our early experiences influence the choices we make at later stages in our development. Developmental stages are not discrete but blend into one another. We all experience each period of life in our own unique ways.

The struggle toward autonomy, or psychological independence, begins in early childhood, takes on major proportions during adolescence and young adulthood, and extends into later adulthood. The process of individuation and the values attached to it are greatly influenced by culture. Actualizing our full potential as a person and learning to stand alone in life, as well as to stand beside others, is a task that is never really finished. Although major life events during childhood and adolescence have an impact on the way that we think, feel, and behave in adult life, we are not hopelessly determined by such events. Instead, we can choose to change our attitude toward these events, which in turn will affect how we behave today.

Critical turning points face us during each transition in our lives. At these points we can either successfully resolve the basic conflict or get stuck on the road to development. The basic task of infancy is to develop a sense of trust in others and our environment so we can trust ourselves. Attachment theory, an extension of psychoanalytic theory, emphasizes the relationships the infant has with another who is perceived as a source of security. This theory proposes that the maintenance of affectional bonds is essential for human survival. Infant attachment can be broadly classified as secure or insecure. Later personality problems that can stem from a failure to develop trust include fearing intimate relationships, low self-esteem, and isolation. Early childhood presents the challenge of beginning to function independently and acquiring a sense of self-control. If we do not master this task, becoming autonomous is extremely difficult. During this phase of life, we are forming our gender-role identity, and ideally we experience a sense of competence that comes with making some decisions for ourselves. Parental attitudes during this period are very powerful, and these attitudes are communicated both verbally and nonverbally. Our school experiences during middle childhood play a significant role in our socialization. At this time the world is opening up to us, and we are expanding our interests outside of the home. Problems that typically begin at this phase include a negative self-concept, conflicts over values, confused gender-role identity, a fear of new challenges, and disturbed interpersonal relationships. Adolescence is the period when we are forming an identity as well as establishing goals and values that give our lives meaning. A danger of this time of life is that we can follow others out of a fear of being rejected and fail to discover what it is that we want for ourselves.

Each of these developmental stages helps lay the foundation on which we build our adult personality. As you will see in the next chapter, mastery of these earlier challenges is essential if we are to cope with the problems of adult living.

Where Can I Go From Here?

1. Write an account in your journal of the first 6 years of your life. Although you may think that you cannot remember much about this time, you can learn more by following these guidelines:

   a. Write down a few key questions that you would like answered about your early years.

   b. Seek out your relatives, and ask them some questions about your early years.

   c. Collect any reminders of your early years, particularly pictures.

   d. Visit the place or places where you lived and went to school.

2. When you reflect on your childhood and adolescent years, how did your ability to cope with experiences influence the way you cope with present life situations? What healthy coping mechanisms did you adopt? What maladaptive coping mechanisms did you adopt?

3. From among the many exercises in this chapter, chose those that you are willing to integrate into a self-help program during your time in this course. What things are you willing to do to bring about some of the changes you want in your life?

4. Pictures often say more about you than words. What do your pictures tell about you? Look through any pictures of yourself as a child and as an adolescent, and see if there are any themes. What do most of your pictures reveal about the way you felt about yourself? Bring some of these pictures to class. Have other members look at them and tell you what they think you were like then. Pictures can also be used to tap forgotten memories.

Resources for Future Study

Web Site Resources

ADOLESCENT DIRECTORY ONLINE
http://education.indiana.edu/cas/adol/adol.html

This site offers resources about adolescents that cover a range of health, mental health, and parenting issues.

InfoTrac College Edition Resources

For additional readings, explore InfoTrac College Edition, our online library:
http://www.infotrac.college.com/wadsworth

Hint: Enter these search terms:

human development AND psychosocial

life span AND development

human development AND stages

developmental crisis

feminist AND development

infancy

early childhood

middle childhood

ego defense mechanism

Print Resources

Bloomfield, H. H., with Felder, L. (1985). *Making peace with yourself: Transforming your weaknesses into strengths.* New York: Ballantine.

Borysenko, J. (1996). *A woman's book of life: The biology, psychology and spirituality of the feminine life cycle.* New York: Riverhead Books.

Covey, S. R. (1990). *The seven habits of highly effective people.* New York: Simon & Schuster (Fireside Books).

Edelman, M. W. (1992). *The measure of our success: A letter to my children and yours.* Boston: Beacon Press.

Erikson, E. (1963). *Childhood and society* (2nd ed.). New York: Norton.

Erikson, E. (1982). *The life cycle completed.* New York: Norton.

Goleman, D. (1995). *Emotional intelligence.* New York: Bantam Books.

McGoldrick, M., & Carter, B. (2005). Self in context: The individual life cycle in systemic perspective.

In B. Carter & M. McGoldrick (Eds.), *The expanded family life cycle: Individual, family, and social perspectives* (3rd ed., pp. 27–46).

Miller, J. B., & Stiver, I. P. (1997). *The healing connection: How women form relationships in therapy and in life.* Boston: Beacon Press.

Tatum, B. D. (1999). *Why are all the Black kids sitting together in the cafeteria?* New York: Basic Books.

Independence means not being
lonely even when you are alone.
—Bernie Siegel

Adulthood
and Autonomy

Where Am I Now?

Use this scale to respond to these statements:

    3 = This statement is true of me *most* of the time.

    2 = This statement is true of me *some* of the time.

    1 = This statement is true of me *almost none* of the time.

_____ 1. My family of origin has greatly influenced my values and beliefs.

_____ 2. I'm an independent person more than I am a dependent person.

_____ 3. I think about early messages I received from my parents.

_____ 4. I am psychologically separated from my parents and have become my own parent.

_____ 5. As I get older, I feel an urgency about living.

_____ 6. Much of my life is spent doing things that I do not enjoy.

_____ 7. I look forward with optimism and enthusiasm to the challenges that lie ahead of me.

_____ 8. I expect to experience a meaningful and rich life when I reach old age.

_____ 9. There are many things I cannot do now that I expect to do when I retire.

_____ 10. I have fears of aging.

I n this chapter we continue our discussion of the life-span perspective by focusing on the transitions and turning points in adulthood. Our childhood and adolescent experiences provide the foundation for our ability to meet the developmental challenges of the various phases of adulthood. But throughout adulthood many choices remain open to us. Before taking up early, middle, and late adulthood, we examine how you can become more autonomous. One facet of the struggle toward autonomy involves recognizing the early life decisions you made and realizing that you can change them if they are no longer appropriate or useful. This change entails questioning some of the messages you received and accepted during your early childhood. You can also learn to argue with your self-defeating thoughts and beliefs and acquire a more positive and constructive set of beliefs.

We describe some typical developmental patterns, but everybody does not go through these stages in the same way at the same time. We are not trying to lock you into categories of what is "normal" at each of the stages of development. There is a range of variability at each of these stages, and you will need to determine what meaning your experiences have for you and how you have dealt with the tasks of the various stages of life.

Your family and your culture influence the manner in which you deal with developmental tasks. It is important that you understand the ways your culture and family-of-origin experiences have contributed to influencing the person you are. Your passage through adulthood is characterized by the choices you make in response to the demands made on you; look for a pattern of choices in your life. You may see that you are primarily adapting yourself to others, or you may discover a pattern of choosing the path of security rather than risking new adventures. You may be pleased with many of the decisions you have made, or you may wish you had decided differently. As you think about these choices at critical turning points in your adulthood, look for a unifying theme beginning in childhood. Once you become aware of patterns in your life, you can work to change those patterns that you determine are not serving you well. When you understand your earlier experiences and any self-defeating decisions that have influenced you, you can begin to revise these decisions and create a different future.

If you are a young adult, you may wonder why you should be concerned about middle age and later life. You can expand the range of your choices by looking at the choices you are making now that will have a direct influence on the quality of your later adulthood. As you read this chapter, reflect on what you hope to be able to say about your life when you reach later adulthood.

THE PATH TOWARD AUTONOMY AND INTERDEPENDENCE

As we leave adolescence and enter young adulthood, our central task is to assume increased responsibility and independence. Although most of us have moved away physically from our parents, our extended family, and often our community, not all of us have done so psychologically. To a greater or lesser degree, the people who have been significant in your early years will have a continuing influence on your life. For this reason it is essential that you gain awareness of how you are presently influenced and determine whether these forces are enhancing your life or restricting your development as a mature adult. Many people may have had a significant influence during your childhood and adolescent years, but in this chapter we emphasize the role parents (or caretakers) had. In later chapters we discuss in detail relationships other than parental relationships.

Autonomy, or **maturity,** entails that you accept responsibility for the consequences of your choices rather than hold others accountable if you are not satisfied with the way your life is going. Finding your own identity is not something you do at a given time once and for all. The struggle toward autonomy begins in early childhood and continues throughout life.

Maturity is not necessarily equal to independence and self-sufficiency. In writing about genuine maturity from the self-in-context perspective, McGoldrick and Carter (2005) remind us that the ultimate goal is to develop a mature, interdependent self. We must establish a solid sense of our unique self in the context of our connection to others. This systemic perspective is based on the assumption that maturity requires the ability to empathize, communicate, collaborate, connect, trust, and respect others. McGoldrick and Carter maintain that the degree to which we are able to form meaningful connections with people who differ from us in gender, class, race, and culture "will depend on how these differences and connections were dealt with within our family of origin, within our communities, within our culture of origin, and within our society as a whole" (p. 28).

The feminist approach to psychological development stresses connections and disconnections in relationships. Miller and Stiver (1997) use the word **connection** to mean "an interaction between two or more people that is mutually empathic and mutually empowering" (p. 26). They use the term **disconnection** to mean "an encounter that works against mutual empathy and mutual empowerment" (p. 26). Miller and Stiver believe the source of psychological problems is disconnection, or the "psychological experience of rupture that occurs whenever a child or adult is prevented from participating in a mutually empathic and mutually empowering interaction" (p. 65). The goal is to learn to be an authentic individual who finds meaningful connections or relationships with others. Optimum mental health involves creating relationships based on caring

It is important that you understand the ways your culture and your family-of-origin experiences have contributed to influencing the person you are.

for others, or a sense of mutual empathy. Mutually empowering relationships are characterized by both parties in the relationship fulfilling their needs and feeling good about each other. In contrast, a relationship in which one person gains power at the expense of the other is characterized as a disconnection.

Cultural factors play a significant role in determining the kinds of relationships that govern our lives. For example, some cultures value cooperation and a spirit of interdependence over independence. In some cultures parents, extended family, and the community continue to have a significant influence on individuals throughout the life cycle. Respect and honor for parents and extended family members may be values that are extolled above individual freedom by these adult children.

Regardless of your cultural background, your parents had some influence on your decisions and behavior throughout your childhood and adolescent years. In your move toward autonomy and connection with others, it is probably wise to evaluate your past decisions to determine how well these decisions are working for you today. You very well may share many of your parents' values, but striving for maturity implies a degree of self-direction and self-determination. However, rebellion against whatever your parents stand for is not a sign of being autonomous. The self-in-relation theory stresses the interdependence of people rather than independence, and Jordon and her colleagues (1991) put this matter nicely:

> THUS, THE SELF DEVELOPS in the context of relationships, rather than as an isolated or separate autonomous individual. We are emphasizing the importance of a two-way interaction model, where it becomes as important to understand and to be understood, to empower as well as to be empowered. (p. 59)

Making decisions about the quality of life you want for yourself and affirming these choices is partly what autonomy is about. Another part of autonomy is the quality of relationships with people who are significant in your life. To be able to relate to others in a meaningful way—to form connections—you first need self-knowledge and a mature sense of yourself. Autonomy includes far more than being a separate self; our conception of autonomy includes *self-in-relation* and *self-in-context.*

Becoming your own person is not "doing your own thing" irrespective of your impact on those with whom you come in contact. Instead, being autonomous implies that you have questioned the values you live by and made them your own; part of this process includes concern for the welfare of those people you love and associate with. At this point, consider how you would answer these questions:

- To what degree do you think you can live by your own standards and still be sensitive to the needs and wants of others?
- To what degree do you want to become more autonomous, even though this involves some risk?

Recognizing Early Learning and Decisions

Transactional analysis (TA) offers a useful framework for understanding how our learning during childhood extends into adulthood. TA is a theory of personality and a method of counseling that was originally developed by Eric Berne (1975) and later extended by practitioners such as Claude Steiner (1975) and Mary and Robert Goulding (1978, 1979). The theory is built on the assumption that adults make decisions based on past premises—premises that were at one time appropriate to their survival needs but may no longer be valid. It stresses the capacity of the person to change early decisions and is oriented toward increasing awareness, with the goal of enabling people to alter the course of their lives. Through TA people learn how their current behavior is affected by the rules and regulations they received and incorporated as children and how they can identify the "life script," and also the family script, that determines their actions. These scripts are almost like plots that unfold. Individuals are able to realize that they can now change what is not working while retaining that which serves them well.

The Life Script The concept of the life script is an important contribution of TA. A **life script** is made up of both parental teachings and the early decisions we make as children. Often, we continue to follow our scripts as adults.

Scripting begins in infancy with subtle, nonverbal messages from our parents. During our earliest years, we learn much about our worth as a person and our place in life. Later, scripting occurs in both subtle and direct ways. Some of the messages we might "hear" include: "Always listen to authority." "Don't act like a child." "We know you can perform well, and we expect the best from you, so be sure you don't let us down." "Never trust people; rely on yourself." "You're really stupid, and we're convinced that you'll never amount to much." These messages are often sent in disguised ways. For example, our parents may never have told us directly that sexual feelings are bad or that touching is inappropriate. However, their behavior with each other and with us may have taught us to think in this way. Moreover, what parents do not say or do is just as important as what they say directly. If no mention is ever made of sexuality, for instance, that very fact communicates significant attitudes.

On a broader level than the messages we receive from our parents are the life scripts that are part of our cultural context. Cultural values are transmitted in many ways in the family circle. Here are a few examples of cultural messages pertaining to the family:

- Older people are to be revered and respected.
- Don't bring shame to the family.
- Don't talk about family matters outside the family circle.
- Don't demonstrate affection in public.
- Always obey your parents and grandparents.
- The mother is the heart of the family.
- The father is the head of the family.
- Avoid conflict and strive for harmony within the family.
- Work hard for the good of the entire family.

Our life script, including the messages from both our family of origin and our culture, forms the core of our personal identity. Our experiences may lead us to conclusions such as these: "I really don't have any right to exist." "I can only be loved if I'm productive and successful." "I'd better not trust my feelings because they'll only get me in trouble." These basic themes running through our lives tend to determine our behavior, and very often they are difficult to unlearn. In many subtle ways these early decisions about ourselves can come back to haunt us in later life. Our beliefs about ourselves can even influence how long and how well we live. After his liver transplant, the late Mickey Mantle looked back on his life with a number of regrets. He thought he would die very young because both his father and grandfather died at an early age, leading to his famous line: "If I had known I was going to live so long, I'd have taken better care of myself."

A personal example may help clarify how early messages and the decisions we make about them influence us in day-to-day living. In my (Jerry's) own case, even though I now experience myself as successful, for many years I felt unsuccessful and unworthy. I have not erased my old script completely, and I still experience self-doubts and struggle with insecurities. I do not think I can change such long-lasting feelings by simply telling myself "OK, now that I'm meeting with success, I'm the person I was meant to be." I continue to reflect on the meaning of my life and explore how what I am doing relates to my life's purpose. To some extent, my striving for success is one way of coping with feelings of inadequacy.

I am convinced that part of my motivational force toward success is linked to the acceptance I wanted from my parents, especially from my father. In many important ways my father did not feel successful, and I believe on some level that my own strivings to prove my worth are entangled with a desire to make up for some of the successes that could have been his. Even though my father died 37 years ago, on a psychological plane I am still making some attempt to win his acceptance and make him proud of my accomplishments. Also, I feel some responsibility to make more of my talents in my life than he did in his life. Although my external reality has certainly changed from the time I was a child to now, I realize that my connection with my father is revealed in underlying patterns associated with my work. For me this does not mean that I need to put an end to my projects, but I do want to be aware of the driving force in my life.

In short, although I believe I can change some of my basic attitudes about myself, I cannot get rid of all vestiges of the effects of my early learning and decisions. We need not be determined by our early decisions, but it is wise to be continually aware of manifestations of our old ways that interfere with our attempts to develop new ways of thinking and being.

Injunctions Let's look more closely at the nature of the early messages, or **injunctions,** that we incorporate in our lives. First of all, these injunctions are not just planted in our heads while we sit by passively. By making decisions in response to real or imagined injunctions, we assume some of the responsibility for indoctrinating ourselves. Thus, if we hope to free ourselves, we must become aware of what these "oughts" and "shoulds" are and of how we allow them to operate in our lives. Here are some common injunctions and some possible decisions that could be made in response to them (Goulding & Goulding, 1978, 1979).

1. *"Don't make mistakes."* Children who hear and accept this message often fear taking risks that may make them look stupid. They tend to equate making mistakes with being a failure.
   - *Possible decisions:* "I'm scared of making the wrong decision, so I simply won't decide." "Because I made a dumb choice, I won't decide on anything important again!" "I'd better be perfect if I hope to be accepted."

© Myrleen Ferguson/PhotoEdit

Childhood injunctions can affect our entire lives. This girl may have received the family message "don't belong" and could be a loner as an adult.

2. *"Don't be."* This lethal message is often given nonverbally by the way parents hold (or do not hold) the child. The basic message is "I wish you hadn't been born."
   - *Possible decisions:* "I'll keep trying until I get you to love me."

3. *"Don't be close."* Related to this injunction are the messages "Don't trust" and "Don't love."
   - *Possible decisions:* "I let myself love once, and it backfired. Never again!" "Because it's scary to get close, I'll keep myself distant."

4. *"Don't be important."* If you are constantly discounted when you speak, you are likely to believe you are unimportant.
   - *Possible decisions:* "If, by chance, I ever do become important, I'll play down my accomplishments."

5. *"Don't be a child."* This message says: "Always act adult!" "Don't be childish." "Keep control of yourself."

- *Possible decisions:* "I'll take care of others and won't ask for much myself." "I won't let myself have fun."

6. *"Don't grow."* This message is given by the frightened parent who discourages the child from growing up in many ways.
   - *Possible decisions:* "I'll stay a child, and that way I'll get my parents to approve of me." "I won't be sexual, and that way my father won't push me away."

7. *"Don't succeed."* If children are positively reinforced for failing, they may accept the message not to seek success.
   - *Possible decisions:* "I'll never do anything perfect enough, so why try?" "I'll succeed, no matter what it takes." "If I don't succeed, then I'll not have to live up to high expectations others have of me."

8. *"Don't be you."* This involves suggesting to children that they are the wrong sex, shape, size, color, or have ideas or feelings that are unacceptable to parental figures.
   - *Possible decisions:* "They'd love me only if I were a boy (girl), so it's impossible to get their love." "I'll pretend I'm a boy (girl)."

9. *"Don't be sane"* and *"Don't be well."* Some children get attention only when they are physically sick or acting crazy.
   - *Possible decisions:* "I'll get sick, and then I'll be included." "I am crazy."

10. *"Don't belong."* This injunction may indicate that the family feels that the child does not belong anywhere.
    - *Possible decisions:* "I'll be a loner forever." "I'll never belong anywhere."

Overcoming Injunctions   I (Marianne) want to share some messages I heard growing up, as a personal example of a struggle with listening to injunctions from both parents and society. I was born and spent my childhood and adolescence in a farming village in Germany. Some of the messages I received, though they were not typically verbalized, were "You can't do anything about it." "Things could be worse, so don't talk so much about how bad things are." "Accept what you have, and don't complain about what you don't have." "Don't be different. Fit in with the community. Do what everybody else does." "Be satisfied with your life."

Although my childhood was very good in many respects and I was satisfied with part of my life, I still wanted more than I felt I could get by remaining in the village and becoming what was expected of me. It was a continuing struggle not to surrender to these expectations, but having some adult role models who themselves had challenged such injunctions inspired me to resist these messages. As early as age 8 I felt a sense of daring to be different and hoping someday to go to the United States. Although I doubted myself at times, I still began saving every penny I could lay my hands on. Finally, at the age of 19 I asked my father for permission to take a ship to the United States and surprised him when I told him that I had saved enough money to buy a ticket.

Even though there were many obstacles, I seemed to be driven to follow a dream and a decision that I made when I was only 8 years old. When I did come to the United States, I eventually fulfilled another dream, and consequently challenged another injunction, by furthering my education. The theme of my struggles during my earlier years is that I was not willing to surrender to obstacles. I argued with myself about simply accepting what seemed like limited choices for a life's design, and in doing so I began writing a new life script for myself. It was important to me not to feel like a victim of circumstances. I was willing to do what was necessary to challenge barriers to what I wanted and to pursue my dreams and goals. Although I fought against these injunctions at an early age, they have not gone away forever. I continue to have to be aware of them and not allow them to control me as an adult.

Think about some of the childhood decisions you made about yourself and about life. It is certainly a challenge for you to identify and challenge self-defeating assumptions and to learn new and constructive ones in their place. This is one reason for learning how to critically evaluate these questions:

- What messages have I listened to and "bought"?
- How valid are the sources of these messages?
- In what ways do I now continue to say self-defeating sentences to myself?
- How can I challenge some of the decisions I made about myself and make new ones that will lead to a positive orientation?

Learning to Dispute Self-Defeating Thinking

As children and adolescents, we uncritically incorporate certain assumptions about life and about our worth as a person. **Rational emotive behavior therapy** and other cognitive-behavioral therapies are based on the premise that emotional and behavioral problems are originally learned from significant others during childhood. Others gave us faulty beliefs, which we accept unthinkingly. We actively keep alive false beliefs by the processes of self-suggestion and self-repetition (Ellis, 2001). It is largely our own repetition of early-indoctrinated faulty beliefs that keeps dysfunctional attitudes operational within us. Self-defeating beliefs are supported and maintained by negative and dysfunctional statements that we make to ourselves over and over again: "If I don't win universal love and approval, then I have no chance of being happy." "If I make a mistake, that would prove that I am a failure."

Albert Ellis (2001), who developed rational emotive behavior therapy (REBT), describes some of the most common ways people make themselves miserable by remaining wedded to their irrational beliefs. Ellis has devised an **A-B-C theory of personality** that explains how people develop negative evaluations of themselves.

He holds that it is our faulty thinking, not actual life events, that creates emotional upsets and leads to our misery. He contends that we have the power to control our emotional destiny and suggests that when we are upset it is a good idea to look to our hidden dogmatic "musts," "oughts," and absolutistic "shoulds." For Ellis, practically all human misery and serious emotional turmoil is unnecessary.

An example will clarify this A-B-C concept. Assume that Sally's parents abandoned her when she was a child (A, the activating event). Sally's emotional reaction may be feelings of depression, worthlessness, rejection, and unlovability (C, the emotional consequence). However, Ellis asserts, it is not A (her parents' abandonment of her) that caused her feelings of rejection and unlovability; rather, it is her belief system (B) that is causing her low self-esteem. She made her mistake when she told herself that there must have been something terrible about herself for her parents not to want her. Her faulty beliefs are reflected through self-talk such as this: "I am to blame for what my parents did." "If I were more lovable, they would have wanted to keep me." The A-B-C theory of disturbance holds that when dysfunctional emotional reactions occur there are usually several core irrational beliefs, which include *absolutistic musts and shoulds, awfulizing, I-can't-stand-it-itis,* and *damning oneself and others.* This kind of thinking is what gets us into psychological trouble and results in much of our misery (Ellis, 2001).

REBT is designed to teach people how to dispute faulty beliefs that get in the way of effective living. Let's apply REBT to our example. Sally does not need to continue believing she is basically unlovable. Instead of clinging to the belief that something must have been wrong with her for her parents to have rejected her, Sally can begin to dispute this self-defeating statement and think along different lines: "It hurts that my parents didn't want me, but perhaps they had problems that kept them from being good parents." "Maybe my parents didn't love me, but that doesn't mean that nobody could love me." "It's unfortunate that I didn't have parents in growing up, but it's not devastating, and I no longer have to be a little girl waiting for their protection." One member of a therapeutic group of ours had major struggles in believing he was a worthwhile person. Joaquin learned how to pay attention to his internal dialogue and realized how his thoughts influenced what he did and how he felt about himself. Joaquin reported the following about how his self-talk got in his way.

JOAQUIN'S STORY

What I am noticing and changing are my internal dialogues that I carry on within myself. I see how I have always judged myself critically. I have somehow made a major breakthrough on giving myself a break from the negative chatter that has always gone on in my thoughts. It finally dawned on me that I am my own worst critic.

I seem to finally be in the process of forgiving myself and getting down to some more reasonable expectations for myself. I am attempting to allow myself the many small failures in my life. The part that is different is that I am asking myself what I could do different next time. I want to focus on the lesson that allows me to learn, not the mistakes.

Joaquin is a good example of a person who can change his life by challenging and changing his self-destructive beliefs about himself. Ellis stresses that your feelings about yourself are largely the result of the way you think. Thus, if you hope to change a negative self-image, it is essential to learn how to dispute the illogical sentences you now continue to feed yourself and to challenge faulty premises that you have accepted uncritically. Further, you also need to work and practice replacing these self-sabotaging beliefs with constructive ones. If you wish to learn how to combat the negative self-indoctrination process, we recommend *Overcoming Destructive Beliefs, Feelings, and Behaviors* (Ellis, 2001). Other useful books in this area are *Feeling Good: The New Mood Therapy* (Burns, 1981) and *How to Want What You Have: Discovering the Magic and Grandeur of Ordinary Existence* (Miller, 1995).

Learning to Challenge Your Inner Parent and Your Inner Critic

We would like to expand a bit on the general concepts of transactional analysis and rational emotive behavior therapy and discuss some related ideas about challenging early messages and working toward autonomy. The term **inner parent** refers to the attitudes and beliefs we have about ourselves and others that are a direct result of things we learned from our parents or parental substitutes. As we move through life, we tend to internalize messages we received from parents and authority figures. The willingness to question and challenge the critical voices we have internalized is one of the marks of autonomy.

Many of the qualities we incorporated from our parents may be healthy standards for guiding our behavior. No doubt our past has contributed in many respects to the good qualities we possess, and many of the things we like about ourselves may be largely due to the influence of the people who were important to us in our early years. However, part of maturity entails looking for the subtle ways we have acquired our values, perhaps without making a deliberate choice about certain values.

How do we learn to recognize the continuing influence of early messages? One way to begin is by thinking about where we acquired our values and beliefs about ourselves. It is likely to help by beginning to notice things you do and avoid doing, and ask yourself why. For instance, suppose you avoid enrolling in a college course because you long ago categorized yourself as "not bright enough." You may tell yourself that you would never be able to pass the class, so why even try? In this case an early decision you made about your

When you become aware of negative self-talk, it is useful to challenge your critical voices.

© PhotoDisc/Getty Images

intellectual capabilities prevents you from branching out to new endeavors. Rather than stopping at this first obstacle, however, you could challenge yourself by asking, "Who says I'm dumb? Even if my teachers have told me that I'm slow, is it really true? Why have I accepted this view of myself uncritically? Let me check it out and see for myself." In carrying out this kind of dialogue, we can talk to the different selves we have within us. You may be struggling to open yourself to people and to trust them, for example, while at the same time you hear the inner injunction "Never trust anybody." In this case you can carry on a two-way discussion between your trusting side and your suspicious side. The important point is that we do not have to uncritically accept as truth the messages we learned when we were children. As adults we can now put these messages to the test.

Hal and Sidra Stone (1993) have developed a therapeutic process aimed at transforming this "inner critic" from a crippling adversary to a productive ally. The Stones claim that the **inner critic** is our inner voice that criticizes us and makes constant judgments about our worth. This aspect of our personality develops early in our lives and absorbs these judgments of people in our environment. The inner critic checks our thoughts, controls our behavior, kills our spontaneity and creativity, and leads to feelings of shame, anxiety, depression, exhaustion, and low self-esteem. Developed as a way to protect us from the pain and shame of being discovered as being less than we should be, this inner voice reflects the concerns of our parents, church, and significant others from our early years. Here are some of the characteristics of this inner critic:

- It constricts your ability to be creative.
- It prevents you from taking risks.
- It makes you particularly vulnerable to fearing mistakes and failure.
- It warns you never to look foolish.
- It takes the fun out of life.
- It makes you susceptible to the judgments of others.

The content of the inner critic may vary from culture to culture, according to the value system of each particular culture, but this critical voice is universal and seems to have the power to cripple people and render them less effective than they might be. The Stones explain how to minimize the negative impact of this self-destructive internal dialogue and how to transform this negative force by developing an internal source of support very much like an internal parent who protects you and your creative process. You do not conquer your inner critic by attempting to destroy it, but paradoxically, you lessen its negative impact by "embracing your inner critic" (Stone & Stone, 1993).

In *Making Peace With Your Parents*, psychiatrist Harold Bloomfield (1983) points out that many of us suffer from psychological wounds as a result of unfinished business with our parents. We often keep the past alive by insisting on blaming them for all our problems. Instead of pointing the blaming finger at our parents, as adults we can give to ourselves some of the things we may still expect or hope for from our parents. If we do not get beyond blaming our parents, we end up resenting them. As long as we cling to our resentments, expect our parents to be different than they are, or wait for their approval, we are keeping painful memories and experiences alive. If we harbor grudges against our parents and focus all our energies on changing them, we have little constructive energy left over to assume control of our own lives. Borysenko (1988) emphasizes that it is by letting go of resentments and regrets that we are able to free ourselves from the past. We are only able to savor the present when our energy is available in the moment rather than being bound up in the threads of unfinished business.

If you want a closer relationship with your father and insist that he talk to you more and approve of you, for example, you are likely to be disappointed. He may not behave the way you want him to, and if you make changing him your central goal, you are keeping yourself helpless in many respects. You do not have the power to control your father's attitudes or behavior, yet you do have choices with respect to how you will relate to your father. As long as you are stuck in a blaming mode, you will not be able to recognize the power you have within you to change the influence that you allow your father to have in your life. You can learn to ask yourself before you act, "Will doing or saying what I am about to do or say bring us closer together? If it won't, then I won't do or say it." If you make some significant changes in the way you talk to your father and in the way you treat him, you may be greatly surprised at how he might change. You will increase your chances of success if you do what you want him to do.

To be at peace with yourself, you need to let go of festering resentments, to work through unresolved anger, and to cease blaming others. These factors not only poison relationships but also take a toll on the way you feel about yourself. It is only when you find a sense of inner peace that you can hope to make peace with the significant people in your life. You do have a choice. Even though your family situation may have been far from ideal, you now can choose the attitude you take toward your past circumstances. If you choose to assume responsibility for the person you are now, you are moving in the direction of becoming your own parent.

Take Time to Reflect   This self-inventory is designed to increase your awareness of the injunctions you have incorporated and to help you challenge the validity of messages you may not have critically examined.

1. Place a check (✓) in the space provided for each of these "don't" injunctions that you think applies to you.

    _____ Don't be you.   _____ Don't fail.

    _____ Don't think.   _____ Don't be foolish.

    _____ Don't feel.   _____ Don't be important.

    _____ Don't be close.   _____ Don't brag.

    _____ Don't trust.   _____ Don't let us down.

    _____ Don't be sexy.   _____ Don't change.

List any other injunctions you can think of that apply to you:

_____

_____

2. Check the ways you sometimes badger yourself with "do" messages.

    _____ Be perfect.   _____ Be practical at all times.

    _____ Say only nice things.   _____ Listen to authority figures.

    _____ Be more than you are.   _____ Always put your best foot forward.

    _____ Be obedient.   _____ Put others before yourself.

    _____ Work up to your potential. _____ Be seen but not heard.

List any other injunctions you can think of that apply to you:

_____

_____

3. What messages have you received concerning

   your self-worth? _____

   your ability to succeed? _____

   your gender role? _____

   your intelligence? _____

   your trust in yourself? _____

   trusting others? _____

   making yourself vulnerable? _____

   your security? _____

   your aliveness as a person? _____

   your creativity? _____

   your ability to be loved? _____

   your capacity to give love? _____

4. Because your view of yourself has a great influence on the quality of your interpersonal relationships, we invite you to look carefully at some of the views you have of yourself and also to consider how you arrived at these views. To do this, reflect on these questions:

   a. How do you see yourself now? To what degree do you see yourself as confident? Secure? Worthwhile? Accomplished? Caring? Open? Accepting?

   _____

   _____

b. Do others generally see you as you see yourself? What are some ways others view you differently from how you view yourself?

_____

_____

c. Who in your life has been most influential in shaping your self-concept? How did this person do this?

_____

_____

5. Review your responses to these exercises and identify areas where you would like to change. Ask yourself, "Is this a person with whom I would like to have a relationship?" In your journal list some of your ideas about how you can begin the process of detecting the messages you now give yourself. Write about some of the areas you most want to change.

STAGES OF ADULTHOOD

Some developmental theorists reject the notion of well-defined stages of adulthood, contending that adult development is highly individualized. Other researchers conceptualize the life cycle in general periods of development. We will continue to discuss the developmental process from the point of view of Erikson's psychosocial stages and the self-in-context perspective, concentrating on the core struggles and choices from early adulthood through late adulthood (see Table 3.1). Levinson (1996) conducted in-depth interviews with 45 women and found that women go through the same sequence of seasons as men, and at the same ages, making a case for the underlying order in the course of human development. However, Levinson emphasizes that although there is a single human life cycle there are myriad variations related to gender, class, race, culture, historical epoch, specific circumstances, and genetics. In short, there are wide variations between and within genders as well as in the specific ways individuals traverse each season of life. It is best to keep this variation in mind as we examine the stages of adulthood.

Table 3.1	Overview of Developmental Stages From Early Adulthood to Late Adulthood		
Life Stage	**Self-in-Context View**	**Erikson's Psychosocial View**	**Potential Problems**
Early adulthood (ages 21–34)	The major aim of this period of life is being able to engage in intimate relationships and find satisfying work. Some developmental issues include caring for self and others, focusing on long-range goals, nurturing others physically and emotionally, finding a meaning in life, and developing a tolerance for delayed gratification to meet long-range goals.	*Young adulthood.* Sense of identity is again tested by the challenge of achieving intimacy. Ability to form close relationships depends on having a clear sense of self. Core struggle: *intimacy* versus *isolation.* Theme: love.	The challenge of this period is to maintain one's separateness while becoming attached to others. Failing to strike a balance leads to self-centeredness or to an exclusive focus on the needs of others. Failure to achieve intimacy can lead to alienation and isolation.
Middle adulthood (ages 35–49)	A time for "going outside oneself." This period sees the reassessment of one's work satisfactions, of involvement in the community, and of accepting choices made in life. A time for solidifying one's philosophy of life. Tasks include nurturing and supporting one's children, partner, and older family members. One challenge is to recognize accomplishments and accept limitations.	*Middle age.* Individuals become more aware of their eventual death and begin to question whether they are living well. The crossroads of life; a time for reevaluation. Core struggle: *generativity* versus *stagnation.* Theme: care.	Failure to achieve a sense of productivity can lead to stagnation. Pain can result when individuals recognize the gap between their dreams and what they have achieved.
Late middle age (ages 50–64)	This is the beginning of the wisdom years, in which key themes are helping others, serving the community, and passing along one's values and experiences. A few critical tasks of this period include dealing with declining physical and intellectual abilities, coming to terms with the choices one has made in life, planning for work transitions and retirement, defining one's senior roles in work and community, and dealing with the death of parents.		

| Table 3.1 | Overview of Developmental Stages From Early Adulthood to Late Adulthood *(continued)* | | |

Life Stage	Self-in-Context View	Erikson's Psychosocial View	Potential Problems
Late adulthood (age 65 onward)	Themes of this final stage of life are grief, loss, resiliency, retrospection, and growth. This is a time to find new levels of meaning in life and to appreciate what one has accomplished. Some tasks of this period are responding to loss and change, remaining connected to others, coming to terms with death, focusing on what else one can do for others and oneself, engaging in a life review, accepting increased dependence on others, accepting death of a spouse or loved ones, and dealing with diminished control of one's life.	*Later life.* Ego integrity is achieved by those who have few regrets, who see themselves as living a productive life, and who have coped with both successes and failures. Key tasks are to adjust to losses, death of others, maintaining outside interests, and adjusting to retirement. Core struggle: *integrity* versus *despair.* Theme: wisdom.	Failure to achieve ego integrity often leads to feelings of hopelessness, guilt, resentment, and self-rejection. Unfinished business from earlier years can lead to fears of death stemming from a sense that life has been wasted.

In *New Passages*, Gail Sheehy (1995) describes a new map for the stages of adult life. Contending that we need new markers for life transitions, she states that "the old demarcation points we may still carry around—an adulthood that begins at 21 and ends at 65—are hopelessly out of date" (p. 7). People who are today in their 20s, 30s, and early 40s are confronted with a different set of conditions than was the case 20 years ago. Today, people at 50 are dealing with transitions that were characteristic of people at 40 just a couple of decades ago. Sheehy's research, based on a collection of life histories of people facing the challenges of "second adulthood" (age 45 and beyond), leads her to one overriding conclusion: "There is no longer a standard life cycle. People are increasingly able to customize their life cycles" (p. 16).

EARLY ADULTHOOD

Early adulthood encompasses ages 21 through 34. There are many changes during this stage of adulthood, and the decisions made here will have far-reaching effects.

Provisional Adulthood

According to Sheehy (1995), contemporary young adults live at an accelerated pace, even though many of the responsibilities of full adulthood are delayed. This is a time when we begin detaching from the family and searching for a personal identity. Some of the tasks of this period involve locating ourselves in a peer group role, establishing a gender identity, finding an occupation, separating from our family of origin, and developing a personal worldview. From the perspective of the Levinsons (1996), this period of life is necessarily provisional in that it is an initial attempt to make a place for ourselves in a new world and a new generation. According to Erikson (1963, 1968), we enter adulthood after we master the adolescent conflicts over identity versus role confusion. Our sense of identity is tested anew in adulthood, however, by the challenge of **intimacy versus isolation.**

One characteristic of the psychologically mature person is the ability to form intimate relationships. Before we can form such relationships, we must have a clear sense of our own identity. Intimacy involves sharing, giving of ourselves, and relating to another out of strength and a desire to grow with the other person. Failure to achieve intimacy can result in isolation from others and a sense of alienation. If we attempt to escape isolation by clinging to another person, however, we rarely find success in the relationship.

The self-in-context theory of McGoldrick and Carter (2005) places the early adulthood period from ages 21 to 35. At this stage the major aim is development of the ability to engage in intense relationships committed to mutual growth and in satisfying work. McGoldrick and Carter acknowledge the differences in the pathways at this phase, depending on the person's culture, race, gender, class, and sexual orientation. In general, they view this phase as one of generativity in terms of partnering, working, and rearing children, but barriers to healthy development can derail potentially productive people. Racism and poverty can make it extremely difficult to escape from the underclass, especially as the life cycle continues. Gay and lesbian young adults also may have difficulties at this stage because of the social stigma attached to their partnering and parenting or to the necessity of keeping their identity a secret. Haldeman (2001) indicates that social stigma affects people powerfully, especially when it is part of their early life experiences. Gay, lesbian, and bisexual parents frequently encounter the misconception that same-sex parents influence a child's gender role identity, conformity, and sexual orientation. However, a number of reviews indicate that there are no grounds for concerns as to a child's gender role identity if he or she has same-sex parents (Haldeman, 2001).

Emerging Adulthood

The late teens and the early 20s can no longer be considered a brief period of transition from adolescence into adult roles. This distinct period in the life cycle is characterized by change and exploration of possible life directions. Arnett (2000) proposes a new theory of human development focusing on the period from roughly ages 18 to 25 that he calls the period of **emerging adulthood.** The term *emerging* captures the dynamic, rich, complex, changeable, and fluid quality of this period of life.

> HAVING LEFT THE DEPENDENCY of childhood and adolescence, and having not yet entered the enduring responsibilities that are normative in adulthood, emerging adults often explore a variety of possible life directions in love, work, and worldviews. Emerging adulthood is a time of life when many different directions remain possible, when little about the future has been decided for certain, when the scope of independent exploration of life's possibilities is greater for most people than it will be at any other period of the life course. (p. 469)

The traditional notions of what it means to attain adulthood—completing an education, establishing a career, getting married and becoming a parent, and moving out on one's own—are ranked at the bottom in importance by these young adults. What matters most to emerging adults are three individualistic qualities: accepting responsibility for one's self, making independent decisions, and becoming financially independent. This notion of becoming a self-sufficient person is similar to the concept of autonomy described earlier in this chapter.

Arnett (2000) characterizes emerging adulthood as a time of change and exploration for most young people in industrialized societies—a time when they examine life's choices regarding love, work, and worldview:

- *Love.* Explorations in love during emerging adulthood generally involve a deeper level of intimacy than in adolescence. The emerging adult considers the kind of person he or she is and questions what kind of person he or she wishes to have as a partner through life.

- *Work.* Emerging adults consider how their work experiences are apt to set the foundation for the jobs they may have throughout adulthood. Identity issues are closely related to the exploration of work possibilities. Questions typically raised include: "What kind of work will best fit the person that I am?" "What kind of work will be satisfying in the long term?" "What are the chances of securing a job in the field that seems to best suit me?"

- *Worldview.* Emerging adults often find themselves questioning the worldview they were exposed to during childhood and adolescence. Many young people go through a process of reexamining the religious beliefs and values they learned as children. This explanation sometimes results in forming a different value system, but oftentimes it leads to rejecting an earlier belief system without constructing a new set of values.

Emerging adulthood must be understood within a cultural context, for this period exists only in cultures that allow young people a prolonged period of independent exploration during their late teens and 20s. This is a time when personal freedom and exploration are higher for most people than at any other time in life.

Entering the 20s

During their 20s, young adults are faced with a variety of profound choices. They move away from the safe shelter of the family and confront insecurity about the future as they attempt to establish independence. This time is often characterized by considerable agitation and change.

If you are in this age group, you are no doubt facing decisions about how you will live. Your choices probably include questions such as: "Will I choose the security of staying at home, or will I struggle financially and psychologically to live on my own?" "Will I stay single, or will I get involved in some committed relationship?" "Will I stay in college full time, or will I begin a career?" "What are some of my dreams, and how might I make them become reality?" "What do I most want to do with my life at this time, and how might I find meaning?" Add your own questions to this list.

Choices pertaining to work, education, marriage, family life, and lifestyle are complex and deeply personal, and it is common to struggle over what it is we really want. There is the temptation to let others decide for us or to be overly influenced by the standards of others. But if we choose that path, we remain psychological adolescents at best. We have the choice of living by parental rules or leaving home psychologically and deciding for ourselves what our future will be. Steve and Amanda are both struggling with concerns commonly faced by emerging adults.

STEVE'S STORY

I want to live on my own, but it's very difficult to support myself and go to college at the same time. The support and approval of my parents is surely something I want, yet I am working hard at finding a balance between how much I am willing to do to get their approval and how much I will live by my values. I love my parents, yet at the same time I resent them for the hold they have on me.

AMANDA'S STORY

I want to be in a close relationship with a man, but I know that I am also afraid of getting involved. I wonder if I want to spend the rest of my life with the same person. At other times I'm afraid I'll never find someone I can love who really loves me. I don't want to give up my freedom, nor do I want to be dependent on someone.

Transition From the 20s to the 30s

The transition from the late 20s to the early 30s is a time of changing values and beliefs for most people. Inner turmoil often increases during this period, and commitments to relationships and careers are often made. Others may defer these responsibilities for various reasons, and couples may delay having children until their late 30s.

During this transition, people often take another look at their long-term dreams, and they may reevaluate their life plans and make significant shifts. Some become aware that their dreams may not materialize. This recognition often brings anxiety, but it can be the catalyst for making new plans and working hard to attain them. Consider Pam's evolution in her process of striving to make her dreams turn to reality.

PAM'S STORY

When I was growing up, a college education was not considered essential for a female. The belief in my family was that as a female I would grow up, get married, have children, and be financially supported by my husband.

When I turned 17 I attended college for a couple of years, but I did not take my studies seriously. I got married and very soon my husband and I had marital problems, and we eventually divorced. Reality turned out to be very different from the dreams I had while growing up.

In my late 20s I began taking inventory of my life. I realized that I wanted a career that I found meaningful, one that I felt would make a difference. I wanted financial security and a nice home in which to raise my children. Although I had remarried by this time, I did not want to make the same mistake again of depending on someone else to fulfill my goals and secure my future. For me, education seemed to be the key to achieve these goals. At 30, I returned to college and completed my last 2 years with a 4.0 grade point average. What I learned and what I am continuing to learn is that you don't achieve goals by dreaming about them, wishing for them, or depending on someone else to fulfill them. Instead, dreams become reality by working hard. I did not understand the value of an education and how having a college education could change my life and help me achieve my goals. I see things very differently now. I see how life is not about luck. Life is about choices, personal responsibility, and hard work.

Take Time to Reflect

1. Think about a few of the major turning points in your young adulthood. Write down two significant turning points, and then state how you think they were important in your life. What difference did your decisions at these critical times make in your life?

   Turning point: _____

   Impact of the decision on my life: _____

   _____

   Turning point: _____

   Impact of the decision on my life: _____

   _____

2. Complete the following sentences by giving the first response that comes to mind:

   a. To me, being an independent person means _____

   b. The things I received from my parents that I most value are _____

   c. The things I received from my parents that I least like and most want to change are

   _____

   d. If I could change one thing about my past, it would be _____

   e. My fears of being independent are _____

   f. One thing I most want for my children is _____

   g. I find it difficult to be my own person when _____

   h. I feel the freest when _____

3. What has been the greatest surprise for you between what you were taught and led to believe and your actual experience of living as an adult in the world?

   _____

   _____

MIDDLE ADULTHOOD

The period of life between the ages of 35 and the late 40s is characterized by a "going outside of ourselves." **Middle adulthood** is a time when people are likely to engage in a philosophical reexamination of their lives and, based on this evaluation, may reinvent themselves in their work and their involvement in the community (McGoldrick & Carter, 2005). Levinson (1978) states that middle adulthood is characterized by a fluctuation between periods of stability and transition. At this time, individuals reexamine life decisions they made earlier and make choices about what changes they want to make in their life now. This period involves a time for learning how to live creatively with ourselves and with others, and it can be the time of greatest productivity in our lives. In middle age we reach the top of the mountain yet at the same time realize that we eventually will begin the downhill journey. In addition, we may painfully experience the discrepancy between the dreams of our 20s and 30s and the hard reality of what we have achieved.

The Late 30s

People in their 30s often experience doubts and reevaluate significant aspects of their lives, and it is not uncommon for them to experience a crisis. These crises center on doubts about their earlier commitments and on concerns over getting locked into choices that make it difficult for them to move in new directions. During this period of unrest, disillusionment, and questioning, people often modify the rules and standards that govern their lives. They also realize that their dreams do not materialize if they simply wish for things to happen, but that they need to actively work at attaining their goals.

At this stage of life, even if our life choices have served us well to date, we often find that we are ready for some changes. This is a time for making new choices and perhaps for modifying or deepening old commitments. We are likely to review our commitments to career, marriage, children, friends, and life's priorities. Because we realize that time is passing, we make a major reappraisal of how we are spending our time and energy. We are awakened to the reality that we do not have forever to reach our goals.

This process of self-examination may involve considerable turmoil and crisis. We may find ourselves asking: "Is this all there is to life?" "What do I want for the rest of my life?" "What is missing from my life now?" A woman who has primarily been engaged in a career may now want to spend more time at home and with the children. A woman who has devoted most of her life to being a homemaker may want to begin a new career outside the home. Men may do a lot of questioning about their work and wonder how they can make it more meaningful. It is likely that they will struggle with defining the meaning of success. They may be exteriorly focused in measuring success, which puts the source of the meaning of life on quicksand. They are likely to begin to question the price of success. Single people may consider finding a partner, and those who are married may experience a crisis in their marriage, which may be a sign that they are ready to revise old patterns.

Life During the 40s

Sheehy (1995) claims that it is a mistake to view the early 40s as a time when people decline. Although many people believe their time is running out when they reach 40, others often find ways to avoid the restrictive identity that used to define middle age. We may find that we are retaining some of our youth for a longer period of time. Sheehy's (1995) research revealed a new theme of rebirths permeating the stories of people in middle life. The second half of life enlarges the boundaries of vital living, and it offers new opportunities for growth and change.

Sheehy's views on middle life are supported by Erikson's psychosocial developmental theory. For Erikson, the stimulus for continued growth in middle age is the core struggle between **generativity and stagnation.** Generativity includes being productive in a broad sense—for example, through creative pursuits in a career, in leisure-time activities, in teaching or caring for others, or in some meaningful volunteer work. Two basic qualities of the productive adult are the ability to love well and the ability to work well. Adults who fail to achieve a sense of productivity begin to experience a form of psychological death.

When we reach middle age, we come to a crossroads. During our late 30s and into our mid-40s, we are likely to question what we want to do with the rest of our lives. We face both dangers and opportunities—the danger of slipping into predictable routines and the opportunity to choose to rework the narrow identity of the first half of our life.

Adults at midlife face many new physical, psychological, social, and spiritual challenges, regardless of their racial/cultural identity. This time of life is characterized by bodily changes, increasing responsibilities, continuing career concerns, and increasing involvement in the community (Tatum, 1999). In writing about racial/cultural identity that African American people may experience throughout the life cycle, Thomas Parham (1989) contends that middle adulthood may represent the most difficult struggle with racial identity because of the increased responsibilities and increased potential for opportunities. In her discussion of racial identity in adulthood, Tatum (1999) points out that the process of reexamining one's racial identity is a work in progress that continues into late adulthood. Racial identity, like gender identity, unfolds over the life span.

During middle age we realize the uncertainty of life, and we discover more clearly that we are alone. We stumble on masculine and feminine aspects of ourselves that had been masked. We may also go through a grieving process, because many parts of our old self are dying, and we may reevaluate and reintegrate an

© Nancy Ney/DKStock/Getty Images

The second half of life enlarges the boundaries of vital living.

emerging identity that is not the sum of others' expectations. Here are a few of the events that might contribute to a midlife transformation:

- We may come to realize that some of our youthful dreams will never materialize.
- We may begin to experience the pressure of time, realizing that now is the time to accomplish our goals.
- We recognize our accomplishments and accept our limitations.
- We may realize that life is not necessarily just and fair and that we often do not get what we had expected.
- There are marital crises and challenges to old patterns. A spouse may have an affair or seek a divorce.

- Coping with getting older is difficult for many; the loss of some of our youthful physical qualities can be hard to face.
- Our children grow up and leave home at this time. People who have lived largely for their children now may face emptiness.
- We may be confronted with taking care of our elderly parents when taking care of our children is just coming to an end.
- The death of our parents drives home a truth that is difficult for many to accept; ultimately, we are alone in this life.
- We may lose a job or be demoted, or we may become increasingly disenchanted with our work.

Along with these factors that can precipitate a crisis, new choices are available to us at this time:

- We may decide to go back for further schooling and prepare for a new career.
- We might deepen our friendships.
- We can choose to develop new talents and embark on novel hobbies.
- We may look increasingly inward to find out what we most want to do with the rest of our life and begin doing what we say we want to do.
- This is a time to make choices about solidifying our philosophy of life and deepening our spirituality.

Carl Jung was the first modern voice to address the possibility of adult personality development (see Schultz & Schultz, 2005, for an in-depth look at Jung's influence). He took the position that personality development simply cannot progress very far by the end of adolescence and young adulthood. According to Jung, we are confronted with major changes and possibilities for transformation when we begin the second half of life between 35 and 40. Jung's therapy clients consistently revealed signs of experiencing a pivotal middle-age life crisis. Although they may have achieved worldly success, they typically were challenged with finding meaning in projects that had lost meaning. Many of his clients struggled to overcome feelings of emptiness and flatness in life.

Jung believed major life transformations are an inevitable and universal part of the human condition at this juncture in life. He maintained that when the zest for living sags it can be a catalyst for necessary and beneficial changes. To undergo such a transformation requires the death of some aspect of our psychological being, so new growth can occur that will open us to far deeper and richer ranges of existence. To strive for what Jung called individuation—integration of the unconscious with the conscious and psychological balance—people during their middle-age years must be willing to let go of preconceived notions and patterns that have dominated the first part of their lives. Their task now is to be open to the unconscious forces that have influenced them and to deepen the meaning of their lives.

For Jung, people can bring unconscious material into awareness by paying attention to their dreams and fantasies and by expressing themselves through poetry, writing, music, and art. Individuals need to recognize that the rational thought patterns that drove them during the first half of life represent merely one way of being. At this time in life, you must be willing to be guided by the spontaneous flow of the unconscious if you hope to achieve an integration of all facets of your being, which is part of psychological health (Schultz & Schultz, 2005).

You may be some distance away from middle age right now, but you can reflect on the way your life is shaping up and think about the person you would like to be when you reach middle age. To help you in making this projection, consider the lives of people you know who are over 40. Do you have any models available in determining what direction you will pursue? Are there some ways you would not want to live?

Some of the issues facing middle-aged people are illustrated in the stories that follow. For example, Manuel says it is difficult to always be striving for success, and he shares some of his loneliness.

MANUEL'S STORY

*S*o much of my life has been bound up in becoming a success. While I am successful, I continually demand more of myself. I'm never quite satisfied with anything I accomplish, and I continually look ahead and see what has to be done. It's lonely when I think of always swimming against the tide, and I fear getting dragged into deep water that I can't get out of. At the same time, I don't seem to be able to slow down.

A 49-year-old reentry student described going back to college as "a wonderful adventure that has opened new doors for me, and created a few obstacles." Although Linda had self-doubts and was intimidated over even the thought of becoming a student again, she cast her doubts aside and pursued her dream of attending a university. She challenged the expectations of remaining in old roles and made choices to do something different with her life.

LINDA'S STORY

*A*s a young woman I tried too hard to be superwife, mother, daughter, and friend. I had the role of peacemaker, was very quiet, stayed in the background, and desired to help a star to shine. I had always been there for others, sometimes to the neglect of my own needs and wants. I put too much effort into doing and little into just being. As a result of my personal therapy and other learning, I knew I wanted to change. I started to embrace being genuine and took more risks. I became more verbal and enjoyed participating in class. I began to notice where I could shine. I let go of the self-talk that kept me feeling stupid. I saw hope.

LATE MIDDLE AGE

The time between the ages of the early 50s and the mid-60s can be considered **late middle age** blending into early aging. This is also a time when many adults are beginning to consider retirement, pursue new interests, and think more about what they want to do with the rest of their lives. This time in the life cycle is often characterized by the beginning of wisdom or the reclaiming of the wisdom of interdependence. This tends to be a time when serving others and passing along experiences becomes manifest.

The 50s

People begin the process of preparing for older age in their 50s. Many are at their peak in terms of status and personal power, and this can be a satisfying time of life. They do not have to work as hard as they did in the past, nor do they have to meet others' expectations. They can enjoy the benefits of their long struggle and dedication rather than striving to continually prove themselves. It is likely that rearing children and work are moving toward a culmination. Adults at this stage often do a lot of reflecting, contemplating, refocusing, and evaluating, so they can continue to discover new directions.

Rather than focusing on the 50s as a time of decline, we can enhance our lives by looking for what is going right for us. Instead of concentrating on retirement, widowhood, meaninglessness, and impoverishment, Sheehy (1995) suggests that we look at the positive and creative dimensions of middle life—sources of love, meaning, fun, spiritual companionship, sexuality, and sustained well-being. Sheehy reports that this is an exciting time for women: "As family obligations fade away, many become motivated to stretch their independence, learn new skills, return to school, plunge into new careers, rediscover the creativity and adventurousness of their youth, and, at last, listen to their own needs" (p. 140). Although many women may experience this as an exciting time, they are often challenged to cope with both the physical and psychological adjustments surrounding menopause. Some women, fearing that menopause means losing their youthful looks, sink into depression. For many, menopause represents a crisis. In *The Silent Passage,* Gail Sheehy (1992) tells us that far from being a marker that signifies the beginning of the end, menopause is better seen as a gateway to a second adulthood. Sheehy's book breaks the silence of menopause that is caused by shame, fear, misinformation, and the stigma of aging in a youth-obsessed society.

For men, the 50s can be a time to awaken their creative side. Instead of being consumed with achievement strivings, many men reveal human facets of themselves beyond rational thinking that can result in a richer existence. But men, too, are challenged to find new meaning in their lives. Projects that once were highly satisfying may now lack luster. Some men become depressed when they realize that they have been pursuing empty dreams. They may have met goals they set for themselves only to find that they are still longing for a different kind of life. For both women and men in their 50s, examining priorities often leads to new decisions about how they want to spend their time.

The 60s

During what Sheehy (1995) refers to as the "age of integrity," our central developmental tasks include adjusting to decreased physical and sensory capacities, adjusting to retirement, finding a meaning in life, being able to relate to the past without regrets, adjusting to the death of a spouse or friends, accepting inevitable losses, maintaining outside interests, and enjoying grandchildren. Moving into the aging phase brings a call for reflection and integration. Many physical and psychological changes occur as we approach old age. How we adapt to these changes is influenced by our past experiences, coping skills, beliefs about changing, and personality traits. At this time, work, leisure, and family relationships are major dimensions of life.

The vast majority of people in their 60s are quite able, both physically and mentally, to function independently. Most have reached a stage where maximum freedom coexists with a minimum of physical limitations. Indeed, only 10% of Americans 65 and over have a chronic health problem that interferes with their daily living (Sheehy, 1995, pp. 350–352).

A challenge during this phase of the life cycle is coming to terms with the reality that not everything could be done. People must let go of some of their dreams, accept their limitations, stop dwelling on what they cannot do, and focus on what they *can* do (McGoldrick & Carter, 2005).

Take Time to Reflect If you have reached middle age, write down your reactions to a few of these questions that have the most meaning for you. If you have not reached middle age, think about how you would like to be able to answer these questions when you reach that stage in your life. What do you need to do now to meet your expectations? Do you know a middle-aged person who serves as a role model for you?

- Is this a time of "generativity" or of "stagnation" for you? Think about some of the things you have done during this time of life that you feel the best about.

- Do you feel productive? If so, in what ways?

- Are there some things that you would definitely like to change in your life right now? What prevents you from making these changes?

- What questions have you raised about your life during this time?
- Have you experienced a midlife crisis? If so, how has it affected you?
- What losses have you experienced?
- What are some of the most important decisions you have made during this time of your life?
- What do you look forward to in your remaining years?
- If you were to review the major successes of your life to this point, what would they be?

LATE ADULTHOOD

In many countries those age 70 and older are the fastest growing portion of the population. America is aging, yet it is just one of many countries whose populations are growing older. Although **late adulthood** spans the period of the mid-60s onward, it is imprecise to define late adulthood strictly in terms of chronological age. As is the case for each of these developmental stages, there is a great deal of individual variation at this final stage of life. Many 70-year-old people have the energy of middle-aged people. Consider Philip Rabinowitz as an example of a person who does not let age stop him. At age 100, he sprinted in a race with other men and looks forward to competing again in a race (KCAL News, July 5, 2004). How people look and feel during late adulthood is more than a matter of physical age; it is largely a matter of attitude. To a great degree, vitality is influenced by a state of mind more than by the actual years lived.

Themes During Late Adulthood

The death of parents and the loss of friends and relatives confront us with the reality of preparing ourselves for our own death. A basic task of late adulthood is to complete a life review in which we put our life in perspective and come to accept who we are and what we have done. This is also a time in life when spirituality may take on a new meaning and provide us with a sense of purpose, even as we face an increasing dependence on others (McGoldrick & Carter, 2005).

Prevalent themes for people during late adulthood include loss; loneliness and social isolation; feelings of rejection; finding meaning in life; dependency; feelings of uselessness, hopelessness, and despair; fears of death and dying; grief over others' deaths; sadness over physical and mental deterioration; and regrets over past events. Today, many of these themes characterize people in their mid-80s more than people in their 60s and even 70s.

According to Erikson, the central issue of this age period is **integrity versus despair.** Those who succeed in achieving ego integrity feel that their lives have been productive and worthwhile and that they have managed to cope with failures as well as successes. They can accept the course of their lives and are not obsessed with thoughts of what might have been and what they could or should have done. They can look back without resentment and regret and can see their lives in a perspective of completeness and satisfaction. They accept themselves for who and what they are, and they also accept others as they are. They believe that who they are and what they have become are to a great extent the result of their choices. They approach the final stage of life with a sense of integration, balance, and wholeness. They can view death as natural, even while living rich and meaningful lives until the day they die.

Unfortunately, some elderly people fail to achieve ego integration. Typically, such people fear death. They may develop a sense of hopelessness and feelings of self-disgust. They approach the final stage of their lives with a sense of personal fragmentation. They often feel that they have little control over what happens to them. They cannot accept their life's cycle, for they see whatever they have done as "not enough" and feel that they have a lot of unfinished business. They yearn for another chance, even though they realize that they cannot have it. They feel inadequate and have a hard time accepting themselves, for they think that they have wasted their lives and let valuable time slip by. These are the people who die unhappy and unfulfilled.

Stereotypes of Late Adulthood

It is truly a challenge for us to change the image of late adulthood and the assumptions often made about an aging society, which are based on myths and stereotypes (Deets, 2000). What gets in the way of understanding elderly people as individuals with this capacity for great variation are the common stereotypes many people hold about the elderly.

Ageism refers to prejudice toward or stereotyping of people simply because they are perceived as being "old" (American Psychological Association, 2004). Ageism predisposes us to discriminate against old people by avoiding them or in some way victimizing them primarily because of their age. Here are some of the stereotypes associated with older people that need to be challenged:

- All elderly eventually become senile.
- Old people are nonproductive and cannot contribute to society.
- Retirement is just a step away from death.
- It is disgraceful for an old person to remarry.
- Old people are not creative.
- Growing old always entails having a host of serious physical and emotional problems.
- Older people are set in their ways, stuck on following rigid patterns of thinking and behaving, and are not open to change.

Stereotypes of older people need to be challenged.

© Ron Dahlquist/Stone/Getty Images

- When people grow old, they are no longer capable of learning or contributing.
- Old people are no longer beautiful.
- An elderly person will die soon after his or her mate dies.
- Most elderly persons are socially isolated.
- Old people are no longer interested in sex or intimacy.
- Most old people live in institutional settings.
- Older adults have increased rates of mental illness.
- Depression is a natural consequence of aging.
- Preoccupation with death and dying is typical of older adults.

These negative perceptions and stereotypes of older people are common in our society. The attitudes older people have about aging are extremely important.

Like adolescents, older adults may feel a sense of uselessness because of how others view them. It is easy to accept the myths of others and turn them into self-fulfilling prophecies. Older people themselves can harbor ageist attitudes and stereotypes (American Psychological Association, 2004), and they can be rendered helpless if they accept such erroneous beliefs.

Challenging the Stereotypes

Old age does not have to be something we look toward with horror or resignation; nor must it be associated with bitterness. However, many elderly people in our society do feel resentment, and we have generally neglected this population, treating them as an undesirable minority that is merely tolerated. Their loss is doubly sad, because the elderly can make definite contributions to society.

Elderly people have a wealth of life experiences and coping skills, and they are likely to share this wisdom if they sense that others have a genuine interest in them. Many elderly persons are still very capable, yet the prejudice of younger adults often keeps us from acknowledging the value of the contributions the elderly offer us. Perhaps because we are afraid of aging and confronting our own mortality, we "put away" the elderly so that they will not remind us of our future.

Do you know some older people who are living testimony that growing old does not mean that life is over? Do you know anyone in late adulthood who is blowing the stereotypes of aging? Here are some older people whose lives are evidence that aging is more than simply a chronological process. It has a lot to do with one's attitude and state of mind.

Aunt Mary We often imagine that people in their 80s and 90s live in rest homes and convalescent hospitals. We forget that many people of advanced age live by themselves and take care of themselves quite well. For instance, I (Marianne) occasionally visited with one of Jerry's aunts who lived to be 101 years old. We always had good discussions about the past as well as the present. Aunt Mary had an incredible memory and showed interest in what was happening in the world. Until a few years before her death, she was active through gardening, sewing, and taking care of her household. At times she resisted fully accepting her limitations, but eventually she was willing to receive the help needed to make her life more comfortable. For example, at one time she fought her family when they wanted to give her a lifeline system (a system the elderly use to signal a need for help). Eventually she did accept the offer, and she explained to me how the system worked. She had a deep religious faith, which gave her the strength to cope with many of the hardships she had to endure. Another source of vitality was her involvement with her children, grandchildren, and great grandchildren. I always walked away from my visits with Aunt Mary feeling uplifted, positive about aging, and saying to myself "I hope I will feel as positive about life should I be fortunate enough to reach beyond 100."

Billie Just turning 90, Billie was given a party in her honor by her friends, children, and grandchildren. Billie took care of her husband, who was paralyzed, for more than 25 years. She lived in another state, and she surprised her family by telling them that she was selling her home and moving to where her family lives. Billie recently made a number of new moves in her life. She bought a new home, joined a new church, enrolled in a swimming class, found herself a new hairdresser, bought herself a satellite dish so that she could watch sports events with her newfound friends, and plays bridge. She recently passed her driver's test and got her license renewed, and she still drives all over town. Billie manages fine living on her own, and she delights over the routine visits with family members. She recently had a bout with pneumonia, which she recovered from exceptionally well in her own home.

Art Art was widowed several years ago. No one would guess that he is 90 by looking at him. A few years ago he moved 200 miles from the home he and his wife resided in for 30 years to make a new home with some of his family. His occupation was carpentry, and although he has been retired for many years, he is actively engaged in a number of building projects for others and for himself. Just recently he began to teach at-risk youth and ex-gang members the art of carpentry. In addition to learning carpentry from Art, one youth acknowledged that he also benefits from Art's wisdom on life. Art is still spry, is able to laugh and cry, and just 4 years ago he remarried.

George Dawson At age 102 George Dawson became an author—4 years after learning to read (Kinosian, 2000). With the help of Seattle school teacher Richard Glaubman, Dawson wrote *Life Is So Good* (Dawson, 2000), a first-person narrative chronicling Dawson's journey as an African American man growing up and living in the South. Dawson explains his healthy and long life this way: "I never worry. Ever. What is there to worry about? That's just trying to control other people and things that happen to you" (Kinosian, 2000). This case is an excellent illustration of the point we made earlier that vitality is influenced by a state of mind more than by chronological years lived.

Bob and Betty A couple in their late 80s who have been married for 65 years, Bob and Betty still enjoy each other's company. In addition to what they have as a couple, they are also blessed as individuals. They enjoy good health, live independently in their own home, are involved with a large extended family, enjoy many grandchildren and great grandchildren, and assume leadership roles in their church. They spend many hours doing volunteer work. Routinely, they make trips to Mexico where they serve as missionaries, providing assistance to an orphanage and a local church. Those who know them marvel at their ability to handle the strain connected with devoting countless hours to missionary work. What is most notable about them is their love for their family and their strong religious faith. Betty's quiet strength and gentleness blend nicely with Bob's incredible sharp wit and humor.

The Delany Sisters In their inspirational book, *Having Our Say* (Delany & Delany, 1993), Bessie and Sarah Delany show us, even at the ripe ages of 102 and 104, that it is possible to maintain an interest in the world about them. The two women illustrate a wonderful example of aging with integrity. Both of them, of African American descent, were professional women, one a teacher and the other a dentist. The two sisters reflect on their long life and give us some insight about what led to their longevity. Although surprised at their longevity, they continued to live a healthy lifestyle that included exercise and a good diet. The sisters depended on each other as well as on family to care for them, yet they were able to retain a degree of independence. They gave a flavor of the challenge of growing old in their own words:

> BUT IT'S HARD BEING OLD, because you can't always do everything you want, exactly as *you* want it done. When you get as old as we are, you have to struggle to hang on to your freedom, your independence. We have a lot of family and friends keeping an eye on us, but we try not to be dependent on any one person. (p. 238)

Most people who have read their book or listened to their interviews are surprised by their incredible interest and definite opinions on a range of current affairs. The Delany sisters offer us a good illustration of remaining vital in spite of living more than 100 years.

Many very elderly people lead exemplary lives. Willard Scott, a national weatherman, often recognizes people on the morning news who have reached age 100 or above. Many of these individuals are described as living an active life, which shows us that aging is partially a state of mind. The Delany sisters, and others who have lived long and rich lives, frequently cite a host of elements that contributed to their advanced age:

- Being fortunate to have good genes
- Work that has provided meaning and fulfillment
- Involvement with family and friends
- An interest in doing good for others
- Staying involved in life and not retiring from life
- Having strong religious convictions
- A sense of humor
- The ability to grieve losses
- The willingness to forgive and not to be bitter
- Expressing rather than holding onto irritations
- A sense of pride in self
- Regular physical exercise
- Practicing good nutritional habits

Mary Cunningham The evening news (KTLA, August 11, 2002) reported on a 95-year-old woman who certainly is challenging stereotypes about aging. Mary decided that it would be fun to sky dive, so she jumped from an airplane at 13,000 feet and soared through the air at a speed of over 100 miles per hour before her parachute opened. The report showed her jumping and landing. This was not her first experience with sky diving. Since she was 91 she has done this four times!

The people briefly described here do not fit the stereotypes of the elderly. They are living proof that one can age and at the same time live a full and rich life. There is no formula for growing old with grace and dignity. One of the ways to increase the chances of reaching an active old age is to make choices at earlier ages that will provide the foundation for these later years. Although you may not have reached old age, we hope you won't brush aside thinking about your eventual aging. Your observations of the old people you know can provide you with insights about what it is like to grow older. From these observations you can begin to formulate a picture of the life you would like to have as you get older.

Take Time to Reflect Imagine yourself being old. Think about your fears and about what you would like to be able to say about your life—your joys, your accomplishments, and your regrets. To facilitate this reflection, consider these questions:

- What do you most hope to accomplish by the time you reach old age?
- What are some of your greatest fears of getting old?
- What kind of old age do you expect? What are you doing now that might have an effect on the kind of person you will be as you grow older?
- Do you know some elderly person who is a role model for you?
- What are some things you hope to do during the later years of your life? How do you expect that you will adjust to retirement?
- How would you like to be able to respond to your body's aging? How do you think you will respond to failing health or to physical limitations on your lifestyle?
- Assume that you will have enough money to live comfortably and to do many of the things that you have not had time for earlier. What do you think you would most like to do and with whom?
- What would you most want to be able to say about yourself and your life when you are elderly?

In your journal write down some impressions of the kind of old age you hope for as well as the fears you have about your aging.

SUMMARY

Adulthood involves the struggle for autonomy, which means that we know ourselves and that we are able to form meaningful connections with others. Our quest for autonomy and maturity is truly a lifelong endeavor. Each stage of adulthood presents us with different tasks. Meeting the developmental tasks of later life hinges on successfully working through earlier issues. One part of this quest is learning to evaluate our early decisions and how these decisions currently influence us.

Transactional analysis can help us recognize early learning and decisions. Our life script is made up of both parental messages and decisions we make in response to these injunctions. The events of childhood and, to some extent, adolescence contribute to the formation of our life script, which we tend to follow into adulthood. By becoming increasingly aware of our life script, we are in a position to revise it. Instead of being hopelessly "scripted" by childhood influences, we can use our past to change our future. In short, we can shape our destiny rather than being passively shaped by earlier events.

During early adulthood, it is important to learn how to form intimate relationships. To develop intimacy, we must move beyond the self-preoccupation that is characteristic of adolescence. This is also a time when we are at our peak in terms of physical and psychological powers and can direct these resources to establish ourselves in all dimensions of life. Choices that we make pertaining to education, work, and lifestyle will have a profound impact later in life.

As we approach middle age, we come to a crossroads. Midlife is filled with a potential for danger and for new opportunities. At this phase we can assume a stance that "it's too late to change," or we can make significant revisions. There are opportunities to change careers, to find new ways to spend leisure time, and to find other ways of making a new life.

Later life can be a time of real enjoyment, or it can be a time of looking back in regret to all that we have not accomplished and experienced. It is important to recognize that the quality of life in later years often depends on the choices we made at earlier turning points in life.

Now that you have studied each stage of life, reflect on the meaning of these stages to you. If you have not yet arrived at a particular stage, think about what you can do at this time to assure the quality of life you would like in a future phase.

The experiences and events that occur during each developmental stage are crucial in helping to determine our attitudes, beliefs, values, and actions regarding the important areas of our lives that will be discussed in the chapters to come: gender-role identity, work, the body, love, sexuality, intimate relationships, loneliness and solitude, death and loss, and meaning and values. For this reason we have devoted considerable attention to the foundations of life choices. Understanding how we got where we are now is a critical first step in deciding where we want to go from here.

Where Can I Go From Here?

1. Do you believe you are able to make new decisions? Do you think you are in control of your destiny? In your journal write down some examples of new decisions—or renewals of old decisions—that have made a significant difference in your life.

2. Mention some critical turning points in your life. Draw a chart in your journal showing the age periods you have experienced so far and indicate your key successes, failures, conflicts, and memories for each stage.

3. After you have described some of the significant events in your life, list some of the decisions you have made in response to these events. How were you affected by these milestones in your life? Think about what you have learned about yourself from doing these exercises. What does all of this tell you about the person you are today?

4. Many students readily assert that they are psychologically independent. If this applies to you, think about some specific examples that show that you have questioned and challenged your parents' values and that you have modified your own value system.

5. To broaden your perspective on human development in various cultural or ethnic groups, talk to someone you know who grew up in a very different environment from the one you knew as a child. Find out how his or her life experiences have differed from yours by sharing some aspects of your own life. Try to discover whether there are significant differences in values that seem to be related to the differences in your life experiences. This could help you reassess many of your own values.

6. Talk with some people who are significantly older than you. For instance, if you are in your 20s, interview a middle-aged person and an elderly person. Try to get them to take the lead and tell you about their lives. What do they like about their lives? What have been some key turning points for them? What do they most remember of the past?

You might even suggest that they read the section of the chapter that pertains to their present age group and react to the ideas presented there.

Resources for Future Study

Web Site Resources

ERIKSON TUTORIAL HOME PAGE
http://snycorva.cortland.edu/~ANDERSMD/ ERIK/WELCOME.HTML

This site provides handy information about Erik Erikson's eight stages of psychosocial development, including a summary chart of key facts for each stage, an introduction to each stage, and other links to information on Erikson and psychosocial development.

SENIORNET
http://www.seniornet.com/

SeniorNet seeks to provide access and education about computer technology and the Internet to those who are 50+ years old. The site offers links, information, and discussion groups on a wide variety of topics of interest to seniors. If you are interested in learning about computers and the Internet, you can look up their learning centers online here or call them at 415-495-4990 for the location nearest you.

ADULT DEVELOPMENT AND AGING: APA DIVISION 20
http://www.iog.wayne.edu/apadiv20/ apadiv20.htm

Division 20 of the American Psychological Association is devoted to the study of the psychology of adult development and aging. Here you will find information on instructional resources for teachers, resources for students, and links for publications, conferences, and other related Web sites.

InfoTrac College Edition Resources

For additional readings, explore INFOTRAC COLLEGE EDITION, our online library:
http://www.infotrac.college.com/wadsworth

Hint: Enter these search terms:

transactional analysis

rational emotive behavior therapy (REBT)

cognitive therapy

early adulthood

middle adulthood

midlife crisis

late adulthood

multicultural aspects of development

Print Resources

Bloomfield, H. H., with Felder, L. (1983). *Making peace with your parents.* New York: Ballantine.

Ellis, A. (2001). *Overcoming destructive beliefs, feelings, and behaviors.* Amherst, New York: Prometheus Books.

Goleman, D. (1995). *Emotional intelligence.* New York: Bantam Books.

Goulding, M., & Goulding, R. (1979). *Changing lives through redecision therapy.* New York: Brunner/Mazel.

Goulding, R., & Goulding, M. (1978). *The power is in the patient.* San Francisco: TA Press.

Levinson, D. J., in collaboration with Levinson, J. D. (1996). *The seasons of a woman's life.* New York: Ballantine Books.

McGoldrick, M., & Carter, B. (2005). Self in context: The individual life cycle in systemic perspective. In B. Carter & M. McGoldrick (Eds.) *The expanded family life cycle: Individual, family, and social perspectives* (3rd ed., pp. 27–46). Boston: Allyn & Bacon.

Miller, J. B., & Stiver, I. P. (1997). *The healing connection: How women form relationships in therapy and in life.* Boston: Beacon Press.

Miller, T. (1995). *How to want what you have: Discovering the magic and grandeur of ordinary existence.* New York: Avon.

Sheehy, G. (1995). *New passages: Mapping your life across time.* New York: Random House.

Stone, H., & Stone, S. (1993). *Embracing your inner critic: Turning self-criticism into a creative asset.* San Francisco: Harper.

Tatum, B. D. (1999). *Why are all the Black kids sitting together in the cafeteria?* New York: Basic Books.

4

Wellness stresses positive health rather than merely the absence of disabling symptoms.

Your Body and Wellness

© PhotoDisc/Getty Images

Where Am I Now?

Use this scale to respond to the following statements:

    3 = This statement is true of me *most* of the time.

    2 = This statement is true of me *some* of the time.

    1 = This statement is true of me *almost none* of the time.

1. Making changes in my lifestyle to improve my health is not something I often think about.

2. The way I treat my body expresses the way I feel about myself.

3. When I look in the mirror, I feel comfortable with my physical appearance.

4. When something ails me, I want a quick fix.

5. I like to give hugs and receive hugs.

6. My diet consists mainly of fast food.

7. Exercise is a priority in my life.

8. I am motivated to take better care of myself in all respects.

9. I set aside sufficient time for rest and sleep.

10. I take care of my physical and emotional needs.

In this chapter we begin by exploring the topic of our general state of wellness. We take a holistic approach to wellness, which involves considering all aspects of our being. We look at the ways self-image is influenced by people's perceptions of their body. We also address how bodily identity, which includes the way people experience themselves and express themselves through their body, affects their beliefs, decisions, and feelings about themselves.

As you read, think about these questions: Do you take care of the physical you? How comfortable are you with your body? How do your feelings and attitudes about your body affect your self-worth, sexuality, and love? How aware are you of the impact your emotional state has on your physical state? How does the quality of your relationships affect your physical health?

We also explore the goal of wellness as a lifestyle choice that enhances body and mind, which includes making decisions about diet, exercise, and rest and learning to accept responsibility for our health. Although most of us would readily say that we desire the state of wellness as a personal goal, many of us have experienced frustrations and discouragement in attaining this goal. Wellness is not something that merely happens to us. It is the result of a conscious commitment to our physical and psychological well-being and being faithful to this commitment. Wellness is more than the absence of illness. In many ways the medical model ignores wellness and focuses on the removal of symptoms, which results in a limited view of health. Too often physicians do not explore with their patients aspects of their lifestyle that may contribute to their health problems.

An honest examination of the choices you are making about your body and your overall wellness reveals a great deal about how you feel about your life. We believe that we are in charge of our general health, and the way we lead our life affects our physical and psychological well-being. This includes accepting responsibility for what we eat and drink, how we exercise, and the stresses we experience. (Stress and approaches to managing stress are the subjects of Chapter 5.)

Our body gives us critical information. We can choose to listen to this information, ignore it, or deny it. If you listen to your body, you will be able to make life-enhancing choices. We invite you to think about these questions as you read this chapter: At this time in your life, what priority do you place on your own wellness? If you are not taking care of your body, what beliefs and assumptions may be getting in the way? What resources do you require to begin modifying those parts of your lifestyle that affect your bodily well-being?

Rest and sleep, exercise, diet and nutrition, and spirituality are all aspects of well-being. As you read this chapter, we encourage you to think about what you want for yourself in the long term. A main challenge many of us face is "What can I do to discontinue any habitual, unhealthy choices and replace them with new patterns of living?" We hope you will reflect on the full range of choices available to you to help you stay healthy.

WELLNESS AND LIFE CHOICES

Traditional medicine focuses on identifying symptoms of illness and curing disease. By contrast, **holistic health** focuses on all facets of human functioning:

> AUTHENTIC HOLISTIC MEDICINE is a medicine of the heart, of caring for the whole patient in a co-creative manner in which both physician and patient share responsibility in health and illness. (Brenner, 2002, p. 110).

The **holistic approach** is based on the assumption that the mind and the body are an integral unit that cannot be separated. It emphasizes the intimate relationship between our body and all the other aspects of our self—psychological, social, intellectual, and spiritual. As Brenner puts it: "Holistic medicine claims not only to care about mind/body/spirit but also to cure them" (p. 109).

Wellness is an active process consisting of conscious choices we make in fashioning a healthy lifestyle. Hales (2005) captures the essence of wellness when she writes: "Wellness can be defined as purposeful, enjoyable living or, more specifically, a deliberate lifestyle choice characterized by personal responsibility and optimal enhancement of physical, mental, and spiritual health" (p. 4). Wellness is not simply the absence of disease and disabling symptoms; rather, positive health is a self-created state of being (Brenner, 2002). Wellness involves taking steps to prevent illness, which leads to a more balanced and satisfying life (Hales, 2005). Just as there are many degrees of being ill, there are degrees of wellness.

There are many rewards for adopting a wellness lifestyle. Donatelle, Snow-Harter, and Wilcox (1995) list these important long-term benefits:

- Improved cardiovascular efficiency
- Increased muscular tone, strength, flexibility, and endurance
- Reduced risk for injuries
- Improved sense of self-control, self-efficacy, and self-esteem
- Improved management and control of stress
- Improved outlook on life
- Improved interpersonal relationships
- Decreased mortality (death) and morbidity (illness) from infections and chronic diseases

Wellness is a lifestyle choice rather than a one-time decision. The wellness process involves identifying personal goals, prioritizing your goals and values, identifying any barriers that might prevent you from reaching your goals, making an action plan, and then committing yourself to following through on your plans to reach your goals. This may seem a rather simple pathway to wellness, but simplicity is not to be confused with ease of doing. Many people who desire general wellness are reluctant to put what they know into an action plan designed to bring about the changes they say they want.

In the *Wellness Workbook*, Travis and Ryan (1994) describe wellness as a bridge supported by two piers: self-responsibility and love. They write that self-responsibility and love flow from the appreciation that we are not merely separate individuals, nor are we simply the sum of separate parts. For them, health is best conceived on an illness–wellness continuum that ranges from premature death on one end to high-level wellness on the other end. The essence of wellness is captured in these brief statements of Travis and Ryan:

> WELLNESS IS A CHOICE; a way of life; a process; an efficient channeling of energy; an integration of body, mind, and spirit; and the loving acceptance of yourself. (p. xiv)

Wellness as an Active Choice

Wellness entails a lifelong process of taking care of our needs on all levels of functioning. Well people are committed to creating a lifestyle that contributes to taking care of their physical selves, challenging themselves intellectually, expressing the full range of their emotions, finding rewarding interpersonal relationships, and searching for a meaning that will give direction to their lives. In *An Invitation to Health*, Dianne Hales (2005) emphasizes the importance of taking charge of your health:

> YOU HAVE MORE CONTROL over your life and well-being than does anything or anyone else. Through the decisions you make and the habits you develop, you can influence how well—and perhaps, how long—you will live. (p. 1)

Unfortunately, many of us know *what* to do, yet we do not accept the personal responsibility that is required to be well. Some of us deny our part in our level of wellness. We may think of getting sick as something that is always beyond our control. Although we have a great deal of information on wellness, many of us are hesitant to use this knowledge in living a healthy lifestyle. We all know that smoking, excessive use of alcohol or drugs, poor diet, and lack of exercise are not conducive to good health. The challenge for most of us is to understand our addictions and to forgo some short-term pleasures for longer-term benefits as a route to better health. Achieving wellness is a process of conscious choice and effort, and the results are often slow. It takes consistent commitment to create a healthy lifestyle.

Speaking at the Evolution of Psychotherapy Conference, Herbert Benson (2000) explained that health and well-being are akin to a three-legged stool: one leg is pharmaceuticals, the second leg is surgery, and the third leg is self-care. Although the first two legs are awesome in their efficacy, they are not effective in treating 60% to 90% of the problems brought to health care professionals. According to Benson, visits to physicians are related to stress and other mind–body interactions, and the solutions to these problems lie in self-care. Learning the relaxation response (see Benson 1976, 1984), understanding our core beliefs, and embracing our spirituality are crucial to taking care of ourselves and fostering our sense of well-being.

A combination of factors contributes to our sense of well-being, and a holistic approach pays attention to specific aspects of our lifestyle: how we work and play, how we relax, how and what we eat, how we think and feel, how we keep physically fit, our relationships with others, our values and beliefs, and our spiritual needs and practices. A personal friend, Ron Coley, uses an acronym—**REDS (rest, exercise, diet, and spirituality)**—to capture the essence of living a balanced life as a key to health. When something is amiss in our lives, we are generally failing to take proper care of one of these basic human dimensions. Maintaining a balanced life involves attending to our physical, emotional, social, mental, and spiritual needs.

Bernie Siegel (1988), a psychologically and spiritually oriented physician, believes illness serves a function and makes sense if we look at what is going on with people who become physically sick. He investigates the quality of their psychological and spiritual lives as the key to understanding the mystery of illness and fostering health. From Siegel's perspective, when we are not meeting our emotional and spiritual needs, we are setting ourselves up for physical illness. In his work with cancer patients, Siegel finds that one of the most common precursors of cancer is a traumatic loss or a feeling of emptiness in one's life. He also finds that depressed people—those "going on strike from life"—are at much greater risk for contracting cancer. As a physician, Siegel views his role not simply as finding the right treatments for a disease but also as helping his patients resolve emotional conflicts, find an inner reason for living, and release the healing resources within.

The popularity of Siegel's works point to the power within us to keep ourselves well and heal ourselves. Scores of self-help books and home videos address the subjects of stress management, exercise, meditation, diet, nutrition, weight control, control of smoking and drinking, and wellness medicine. We are beginning to realize the value of preventive medicine, and wellness clinics, nutrition centers, and exercise clubs are becoming increasingly popular. We encourage you to think about the priority you are placing on physical and psychological well-being and invite you to consider whether promoting wellness is high on your agenda.

One Man's Wellness Program

Kevin was in one of our therapeutic groups, and when we first met him, Kevin struck us as being closed off emotionally, rigid, stoic, and defensive. For many years he had thrown himself completely into his work as an attorney. Although his family life was marked by tension and bickering with his wife, he attempted to block out the stress at home by burying himself in his law cases and by excelling in his career. Kevin's story underscores the truth that many of us are not motivated to change until we have faced a serious health concern. Here is his own account of his life.

KEVIN'S STORY

When I reached middle age, I began to question how I wanted to continue living. My father suffered a series of heart attacks. I watched my father decline physically, and this jolted me into the realization that both my father's time and my own time were limited. I finally went for a long-overdue physical examination and discovered that I had high blood pressure, that my cholesterol level was abnormally high, and that I was at relatively high risk of having a heart attack. I also learned that several of my relatives had died of heart attacks. I decided that I wanted to reverse what I saw as a self-destructive path. After talking with a physician, I decided to change my patterns of living in several ways. I was overeating, my diet was not balanced, I was consuming a great deal of alcohol to relax, I didn't get enough sleep, and I didn't do any physical exercise. My new decision involved making contacts with friends. I learned to enjoy playing tennis and racquetball on a regular basis. I took up jogging. If I didn't run in the morning, I felt somewhat sluggish during the day. I radically changed my diet in line with suggestions from my physician. As a result, I lowered both my cholesterol level and my blood pressure without the use of medication; I also lost 20 pounds and worked myself into excellent physical shape. Getting into personal counseling was extremely helpful, because my sessions with a counselor helped me make some basic changes in the way I approach life and also helped me put things into perspective.

Let's underscore a few key points in Kevin's case. First of all, he took the time to seriously reflect on the direction he was going in life. He did not engage in self-deception; rather, he admitted that the way he was living was not healthy. On finding out that heart disease was a part of his family history, he did not assume an indifferent attitude. Instead, he made a decision to take an active part in changing his life on many levels.

With the help of counseling, Kevin realized the high price he was paying for bottling up emotions of hurt, sadness, anger, guilt, and joy. Although he did not give up his logical and analytical dimensions, he added to his range as a person by allowing himself to express what he was feeling. He learned that unexpressed emotions would find expression in some form of physical illness or symptom. He continued to question the value of living exclusively by logic and calculation, in both his professional and personal life. As a consequence, he cultivated friendships and let others who were significant to him know that he wanted to be closer to them. Kevin was challenged to review his life to determine what steps he could take to get more from the time he had to live. Perhaps his experience will inspire you to review your own life and the choices you are currently making that affect your wellness.

Accepting Responsibility for Your Body

The American public is becoming increasingly informed about exercise programs, dietary habits, and ways to manage stress. More health insurance companies are paying for preventive medicine as well as remediation, and some are asking clients to complete lifestyle surveys to identify positive and negative habits that affect their overall health. Many communities provide a wide variety of programs aimed at helping people improve the quality of their lives by finding a form of exercise that suits them.

Physicians report that it is not uncommon for patients to be more interested in getting pills and in removing their symptoms than in changing a stressful lifestyle. Some of these patients see themselves as victims of their ailments rather than as being responsible for them. However, with increased attention being paid to the possible side effects of drugs and medications, many patients are taking steps to educate themselves about prescription drugs and to question their physicians about the medications they prescribe. Some people still prefer to give authority for health care to their physicians, but others are taking a more active role and assuming more responsibility in their health care.

Some physicians resist prescribing pills to alleviate the symptoms of what they see as a problematic lifestyle. Psychologically oriented physicians emphasize the role of *choice* and *responsibility* as critical determinants of our physical and psychological well-being. They challenge patients to look at what they are doing to their bodies through lack of exercise, the substances they take in, and other damaging behavior. Although they may prescribe medication to lower a person's extremely high blood pressure, they inform the patient that medications can do only so much and that what is needed is a change in lifestyle. The patient is encouraged to share with the physician the responsibility for maintaining wellness.

Many popular books on natural methods of healing are on the market today, but "natural" remedies are not necessarily superior to synthetic prescription drugs. Herbal remedies often share the same active ingredients as prescription drugs, but in unknown concentrations, and there may be side effects with herbal substances. These substances are not regulated by the FDA, and their effectiveness and contraindications are not well-documented. It is a mistake to conclude that anything "natural" is automatically good for us.

Whether you see yourself as helpless or as an active agent in maintaining your health makes a world of difference. If you believe you simply catch colds or are ill-fated enough to get sick, and if you do not see what you can do to prevent bodily illnesses, your body is not getting your support. But if you recognize that the way you lead your life has a direct bearing on your physical and psychological well-being, you can be more in control of your health. Psychological factors play a key role in enhancing physical well-being and preventing illness. Likewise, most physical illnesses affect us psychologically (Hales, 2005). The following Take Time to Reflect exercise can help you answer the question, "Who is in charge of my body and my health?"

Take Time to Reflect

1. Here are some common rationalizations people use for not changing patterns of behavior that affect their bodies. Look over these statements and decide which ones, if any, fit you.

_____ I don't have time to exercise every day.
_____ No matter how I try to lose weight, nothing seems to work.
_____ I sabotage myself, and others sabotage me, in my attempts to lose weight.
_____ I'll stop smoking soon.
_____ When I have a vacation, I'll relax.
_____ Even though I drink a lot (or use drugs), it calms me down and has never interfered with my life.
_____ I need a drink or a smoke to relax.
_____ Food isn't important to me.
_____ I simply don't have time to eat three balanced meals a day.
_____ If I stop smoking, I'll surely gain weight.
_____ I simply cannot function without several cups of coffee.
_____ If I don't stop smoking, I might get lung cancer or die a little sooner, but we all have to go sometime.

What other statements do you sometimes use that you could add to this list?

_____

_____

2. Complete the following sentences with the first word or phrase that comes to mind:

a. One way I take care of my body is _____.

b. One way I neglect my body is _____.

c. When people notice my physical appearance, I think that _____.

d. When I look at my body in the mirror, I _____.

e. I could be healthier if _____.

f. One way to cut down the stress in my life is to _____.

g. If I could change one aspect of my body, it would be my _____.

h. One way that I relax is _____.

i. I'd describe my diet as _____.

j. For me, exercising is _____.

3. As you review your responses to this exercise, what changes, if any, do you want to make? What steps can you take at this time to bring about these changes?

_____

_____

MAINTAINING SOUND HEALTH PRACTICES

Earlier we described REDS (rest, exercise, diet, and spirituality) as a formula for wellness. Developing sound habits pertaining to sleeping, exercising, eating, and cultivating our spirituality is basic to any wellness program.

Rest and Sleep

Sleep is a fundamental aspect of being healthy. Rest is restorative. During sleep our physical body is regenerated, and dreaming enables us to explore our unconscious (George, 1998). Sleep helps us recover from the stresses we experience during the day, and it provides us with energy to cope effectively with challenges we will face tomorrow. If we sleep between 6 and 9 hours each night, we are in the normal range. George (1998) reminds us that many of us disturb our sleeping cycle from taking its natural course by staying up longer to get more done and by jarring ourselves out of sleep with an alarm clock. George tells us that restful sleep is vital for relaxation and that we need to discover our personal sleeping cycle. He adds: "The key to quality sleep is being able to identify our natural sleeping pattern and then adhere to the required quota as much as possible" (p. 58). Experts in sleep tell us that the quality of sleep matters more than the quantity. The amount of sleep that is normal for different individuals can vary. What is important is to pay attention to our body and to adjust our sleeping habits based on what we need.

Sleep deprivation leads to increased vulnerability to emotional upset and leaves us susceptible to the negative consequences of stress. Some of the signs that you may not be getting adequate sleep include moodiness, continuing

Getting proper sleep is a
fundamental aspect of
being healthy.

© PhotoDisc/Getty Images

tiredness, tiredness on waking up, difficulty concentrating, and falling asleep in
class or when trying to study. Sleep disturbances or insufficient sleep tend to result in increased irritability, difficulty concentrating, memory loss, increased
physical and emotional tension, and being overly sensitive to criticism. Insomnia can be caused by stress and is often the result of not being able to "turn off
thinking" when you are trying to sleep. If you are interested in sleeping well, do
what you can to take your mind off your problems. Ruminating about your difficulties is one of the key factors contributing to insomnia.

Not getting adequate sleep is one matter, but it is also possible to get more
sleep than you need, which may have negative results. Sleeping more than 9 or
10 hours can have a number of side effects. Your overall metabolic rate may

lower, making it difficult to maintain your ideal weight; muscle tone may drop, which can reduce the ease with which you can exercise; and mental performance may suffer due to lethargy (Rice, 1999).

It is a good idea to monitor how well and how often you get the sleep and rest you require to function optimally. Of course, most of us experience occasional insomnia, mild sleep disorders, and difficulty falling asleep. If this becomes a chronic problem, it certainly deserves attention. If you find that you have serious problems getting adequate sleep, you may want to consult your physician, your campus health center, or a sleep disorder specialist. One effective approach is cognitive-behavior training, which combines cognitive therapy with specific strategies to improve sleep habits (Hales, 2005).

Exercise

A sedentary lifestyle is more common than a physically active lifestyle. About 75% of adults in the United States do not follow a regular exercise program (Brannon & Feist, 2004). A sedentary lifestyle is a hazard to health, for it increases all causes of mortality. Sedentary living doubles the risk of cardiovascular diseases, diabetes, and obesity; it increases the risk of colon cancer, high blood pressure, osteoporosis, depression, and anxiety (Hales, 2005).

A central component to maintaining wellness is regular exercise. Exercise is a natural means of reducing the negative effects of stress, it helps prevent disease, and it can prolong and enhance our life. Research supports the value of physical activity for both cardiovascular health and improved psychological functioning (Brannon & Feist, 2004). Exercise has a number of benefits, some of which are described by Hales (2005):

- Increases respiratory capacity
- Improves digestion and fat metabolism
- Strengthens bones and increases joint flexibility
- Improves circulation
- Improves mood and reduces psychological symptoms
- Reduces the risk of heart disease
- Lowers body fat and reduces weight
- Increases muscle strength and tone

Other benefits to regular physical activity include:

- Slowing down the aging process
- Releasing anger, tension, and anxiety
- Increasing feelings of well-being, self-esteem, and improved self-concept
- Preventing hypertension
- Providing a buffer against stress
- Improving work efficiency

Brisk walking for 20 to 30 minutes several times a week is an easy way to get regular exercise and keep fit.

© David Young-Wolff/PhotoEdit

- Decreasing negative thinking
- Alleviating and preventing anxiety and depression
- Improving sleeping
- Providing a source of enjoyment

Although there are many benefits to keeping physically fit, there are some risks involved with exercise. Hazards associated with physical activity include exercise addiction, exercise-related injuries, becoming obsessed with body image, and sudden death while exercising (Brannon & Feist, 2004). Some people approach exercise in a driven manner, which may undo some of its potential benefits. We may get inspired to exercise only to discover that we are overly ambitious in our goals and become discouraged. It is good to keep in mind that the experts tell us that even moderate exercise is beneficial. There are some hazards to jogging, especially the risk of muscular and skeletal injuries. Moderation is a good course to follow. Before embarking on a rigorous physical fitness program, it is important to discuss your proposed exercise program with your physician. An exercise program needs to be planned with care to minimize the risks and maximize the gains to your overall wellness.

Psychological fitness is every bit as important as physical fitness. George (1998) poetically captures this notion: "For true, holistic well-being, the health of the inner self must be given as much attention as our physical condition. If we neglect the mind's welfare, we become tense and pale, even seriously unwell. There is little point in maintaining the temple if the sanctuary inside is in ruins" (p. 63). George's words are a reminder to us to avoid thrashing our bodies to the limit to reap the rewards of fitness. Consider ways to exercise that bring the body and the mind together.

How much exercise is enough? Allan Abbott, M.D. (personal communication, July 25, 2004) questions the advice of some physicians to exercise for 20 to 30 minutes, 3 times a week. Based on his review of experts in this field who assessed the scientific evidence, Abbott suggests that every adult should accumulate 30 to 40 minutes or more of moderate physical activity on 5 to 7 days per week. For most people this moderate physical activity can be accomplished by brisk walking (about 3 to 4 miles an hour). Even short periods of intermittent activity accumulated over a day have value. Consider walking rather than driving short distances, and take the stairs rather than the elevator. The total amount of regularly performed physical activity seems to be more important than the manner in which the specific activity is performed. Almost any amount of exercise is better than no exercise.

Various studies have confirmed the substantial benefits of walking. Regular walking helps your heart, lungs, and circulatory system and controls body weight. The positive effects of walking are similar to those of running, without the stressful wear and tear on your knees, joints, and shins. A consistent walking program can also relieve stress and invigorate your mind and body, and it is an excellent way to prevent a host of illnesses such as high blood pressure, diabetes, and osteoporosis.

Designing an adequate and enjoyable program of physical activity is difficult for many people. If you are not physically fit, your initial attempts can be painful and discouraging. It is tempting to give up. If you are just starting out, consider exercising for 10 to 15 minutes and gradually increase the time. The secret to developing and maintaining a successful exercise program is to select a form of exercise that you enjoy. Create healthy goals for your exercise program. It is a good idea to gradually increase your participation in your program. If you complete a goal that you set for yourself, reward yourself for sticking to your plan. Appreciate what you have done and avoid chastising yourself for what you cannot yet do. Although it is important to engage in your exercise program regularly, be careful not to overdo it. More is not always better. If you approach exercise compulsively, it might become another demand on you, which may increase the stress in your life. Exercise, like rest, can be a break from the grind of work and can refresh you.

In our own lives, both of us place a high priority on regular exercise. Each of us is involved in some type of physical exercise daily. We have chosen activities we enjoy, which makes it easier to be consistent. Because we are involved in a great deal of mental activity, physical activity is welcomed and creates a healthy balance for us.

Diet and Nutrition

There is a lot of truth in the axiom "You are what you eat." Your daily diet affects your long-term health more than any other factor within your control. Brenner (2002) writes: "Diet, like health, is a state of mind. Diet is a relationship between yourself and the food you choose to eat. And perhaps most importantly, it's what you think and feel about the food you eat" (p. 113).

If your primary diet is poor, you will not have the energy you need to meet the demands of everyday life. Irregular and inconsistent eating patterns are a

© PhotoDisc/Getty Images

Your diet is the relationship between yourself
and the food you choose
to eat.

key nutritional problem for many. We often hear students make the claim that
eating healthy is too time consuming. It is difficult to develop sound diet and
nutrition practices when the consequences of not doing so may not be immediate. Healthy eating does not have to take an abundance of time, especially when
new patterns are developed and a varied diet becomes part of your daily life.
Most nutritional experts suggest a varied diet, and the specifics can be found in
the voluminous literature that is available.

By learning how to eat wisely and well, how to manage your weight, and
how to become physically fit, you can begin a lifelong process toward wellness.
Making healthy choices about diet and nutrition entails having specific knowledge about what you eat, so it is well for you to become a smart nutrition consumer. Besides eating to live, eating can bring increased satisfaction to living.

Eating for health and eating for pleasure are not incompatible. From Andrew
Weil's (2000) perspective, *eating well* means using food to influence health and
well-being and, at the same time, to satisfy your senses and to provide pleasure
and comfort. It is possible to eat in ways that best serve our body while also getting the enjoyment we expect from food. Weil believes *what* and *how* we eat are
critical determinants of how we feel and how we age. He also believes food can
function as medicine to influence a variety of common ailments.

At the University of Arizona's Program in Integrative Medicine, Weil teaches
physicians and other health professionals lifestyle medicine, which is oriented
toward prevention of diseases. He encourages people to change their lifestyle

habits before disease appears. Eating well is one aspect of lifestyle, which is only one set of variables in the mix accounting for healthy living. Weil contends that there are multiple determinants of health, starting with genetics and including a great many environmental, psychosocial, and spiritual factors. But diet is one of the lifestyle factors over which we have a large degree of control. We cannot change our genes. We cannot always control the quality of air we breathe, and we cannot completely avoid the stresses of everyday life. But we can decide what to eat and what not to eat: "My conclusion is that diet is an important influence on health, one that you can control to a greater extent than other factors, and that eating a good diet does not excuse you from attending to other aspects of lifestyle if you want to enjoy optimum health" (Weil, 2000, p. 22).

Spirituality

Spirituality is another key ingredient in a balanced life. Hales (2005) believes that spirituality is an important facet of wellness and health. She states: "Spiritually healthy individuals identify their own basic purpose in life; learn how to experience love, joy, peace, and fulfillment; and help themselves and others achieve their full potential" (p. 6).

Spirituality has many meanings and plays greater or lesser roles in different people's lives. For us, **spirituality** encompasses our relationship to the universe and is an avenue for finding meaning and purpose in living. It is an experience beyond the merely physical realm that helps us discover unity in the universe. One definition of spirituality is the practice of letting go of external noise and connecting with your inner self. Religion may be a vital aspect of your spirituality, but many people perceive themselves as being deeply spiritual, but not religious, beings. **Religion** refers to a set of beliefs that connect us to a higher power or a God. For many people, affiliation with a church is an organized means by which they express their religion. It encompasses three loves: love of God, love of neighbor, and love of self. In addition to formal prayer and religious practices, meditation, mindfulness, and living in the moment are some of the paths that can lead you to a greater sense of spirituality. At this point consider your definition of spirituality.

His Holiness the Dalai Lama is the spiritual leader of the Tibetan people. In his book, *Ethics for the New Millennium* (1999), he makes what he considers to be an important distinction between religion and spirituality. He views religion as being concerned with some form of faith tradition that involves acceptance of a supernatural reality, including perhaps the belief in a heaven or nirvana. A part of religion includes dogma, ritual, and prayer. The Dalai Lama sees spirituality as being concerned with qualities of the human spirit, which include love and compassion, patience, tolerance, forgiveness, contentment, a sense of responsibility, and a sense of harmony. Spiritual acts presume concern for others' well-being.

We appreciate Walt Schafer's (2000) personal guiding philosophy, which balances self-care with social responsibility. For him, true wellness involves being concerned about the well-being of others and having a commitment to the common good. He invites his readers to reflect on his four-part philosophy:

1. Continually have visions and dreams, some of which have social significance— that will benefit others.
2. Work hard, at least partly with others, to bring these dreams and visions to reality.
3. Balance this hard work with play, care of body and spirit, intimacy, friendship, and healthy pleasures.
4. Enjoy the process (pp. 482–483).

From our perspective, having a guiding personal philosophy is the core of wellness. Finding meaning and purpose in your life is a never-ending spiritual process. Feeding your soul may be as important as feeding your body for your overall health. There are many ways to nourish your spirit, some of which include spending some time in quiet reflection, appreciating natural beauty in silence, lying on the ground and watching the clouds go by, visiting a sick person, planting some seeds or flowers in a garden, engaging in volunteer work, attending a church service, kissing or hugging someone you love, writing a letter to someone you have not seen in a long time, reading something inspirational or spiritual, praying for yourself and others, writing in your journal, or watching an inspirational movie. Recall the last time you did something to nourish your spirit, or the spirit of someone else. What did you do? What was it like for you to participate in a spiritual experience? How important is spirituality for you? We will return to the topic of spirituality and meaning in life in Chapter 13.

Reflect on the balance in your life. Are there some aspects of your daily living that you want to modify? The following Take Time to Reflect will help you identify how the REDS formula is functioning in your life.

Take Time to Reflect

1. What are your sleeping patterns? Are they adequate? What changes, if any, might you want to make?

_____

_____

2. What kind of physical activity do you enjoy most? Are there any patterns you are interested in changing?

_____

_____

3. Are there any changes in your diet, nutrition, and eating habits you may want to make?

_____

_____

4. How do you define spirituality for yourself?

_____

_____

5. What are your thoughts about balancing self-care with a sense of social commitment? To what extent is personal wellness dependent upon having a concern for the welfare of others?

_____

_____

6. As you consider the balance involved in the REDS (rest, exercise, diet, and spirituality) formula, how do you see each dimension affecting your life? Identify one goal for each of these areas as a target for making changes in your life. What can you do to increase the chances of committing yourself to a plan aimed at making real changes in your health practices?

_____

_____

YOUR BODILY IDENTITY

We are limited in how much we can actually change our body, but there is much we can do to work with the material we have. First, however, we must pay attention to what we are expressing about ourselves through our body, so we can determine whether we *want* to change our bodily identity. This involves increasing our awareness of how we experience our body through touch and movement.

As you read this section, reflect on how well you know your body and how comfortable you are with it. Then you can decide about changing your body image, if you so desire.

Experiencing and Expressing Yourself Through Your Body

For some of us the body is simply a vehicle that carries us around. If someone asks us what we are thinking, we are likely to come up with a quick answer. If asked what we are experiencing and sensing in our body, however, we may be at a loss for words. Yet our body can be eloquent in its expression of who we are. Much of our life history is revealed through our bodies. We can see evidence of stress and strain in people's faces. Some people speak with a tightened jaw as if they were literally trying to choke off their feelings. Others walk with a slouch and shuffle their feet, as if expressing their hesitation in presenting themselves to the world. Their bodies may be communicating more than their speech. What story does your body tell about you? Here are some ways that your body can express your inner self:

- Your eyes can express excitement or emptiness.
- Your mouth can be tight or at ease.
- Your neck can hold back your anger or tears and can also hold your tensions.
- Your chest can develop armor that inhibits your ability to freely express your crying, laughing, or breathing.
- Your diaphragm can block the expression of anger and pain.
- Your abdomen can develop armor that is related to fear of attack.

Unexpressed emotions do not simply disappear. The chronic practice of "swallowing" emotions can take a physical toll on the body and manifest itself in physical symptoms such as severe headaches, ulcers, digestive problems, and a range of other bodily dysfunctions. In counseling clients, we often see a direct relationship between a person's physical constipation and his or her emotional constipation. When people are successful in expressing feelings of hurt and anger, they often comment that they are finally no longer physically constipated. If people seal off certain emotions, such as grief and anger, they also keep themselves from experiencing intense joy. Let's take a closer look at what it means to experience yourself through your body.

Experiencing Your Body One way of experiencing your own body is by paying attention to your senses of touch, taste, smell, seeing, and hearing. Simply pausing and taking a few moments to be aware of how your body is interacting with the environment is a helpful way of learning to make better contact. For example, how often do you allow yourself to really taste and smell your food? How often are you aware of the tension in your body? How many times do you pause to smell and touch a flower? How often do you listen to the chirping of birds or the other sounds of nature?

Enjoying our physical selves is something we often fail at. Treating ourselves to a massage, for example, can be not only exhilarating but can give us clues as to how alive we are physically. Singing and dancing are yet other avenues through which we enjoy our physical selves and express ourselves spontaneously. Dance is a popular way to teach people to "own" all parts of their bodies and to express themselves more harmoniously. Engaging in sports and other forms of physical exercise can also be approached with the same playful attitude as dancing and singing. These are a few ways to become more of a friend and less of a stranger to your body. You can express your feelings through your body if you allow yourself to be in tune with your physical being.

The Importance of Touch Some people are very comfortable with touching themselves, with touching others, and with being touched by others. They require a degree of touching to maintain a sense of physical and emotional well-being. Other people show a great deal of discomfort in touching themselves or allowing others to be physical with them. They may stiffen and quickly move away if they are touched accidentally. If such a person is embraced by another, he or she is likely to become rigid and unresponsive. For instance, in Jerry's family of origin there was very little touching among members. He found that he had to recondition himself to feel comfortable being touched by others and touching others. In contrast, Marianne grew up in a German family characterized by much more spontaneous touching.

Some time ago I (Marianne) was teaching in Hong Kong and became friends with a college counselor. One day while we were walking she spontaneously interlocked her arm with mine. Then she quickly pulled it back, looked embarrassed, and apologized profusely. Her apology went something like this: "I am very sorry. I know that you in America do not touch like this." I let her know that I, too, came from a culture where touching between females was acceptable and that I had felt very comfortable with her touching me. We discovered that we had had similar experiences of fearing rejection by American women who misunderstood our spontaneous touching.

In many cultures touching is a natural mode of expression; in others, touching is minimal and is regulated by clearly defined boundaries. Some cultures have taboos against touching strangers, against touching people of the same sex, against touching people of the opposite sex, or against touching in certain social situations. In spite of these individual and cultural differences, studies have demonstrated that physical contact is essential for the healthy development of body and mind.

Harlow and Harlow (1966) studied the effects of maternal deprivation on monkeys. In these experiments the monkeys were separated from their mothers at birth and raised in isolation with artificial mothers. When young monkeys were raised under conditions of relatively complete social deprivation, they manifested a range of symptoms of disturbed behavior. Infant monkeys reared in isolation during the first 6 months after birth showed serious inadequacies in their social and sexual behavior later in life. There are critical periods in development when physical stimulation is essential for normal development. Touching is important for developing in healthy ways physically, psychologically, socially, and intellectually.

People are bombarded by unrealistic models of what constitutes an ideal body.

© Andreas Kuehn/Stone/Getty Images

Body Image

Body image involves more than size. A healthy body and a positive image of your body gives you pleasure and helps you do what you want to physically. You might ask yourself if your body keeps you from doing what you would like to do. If so, then you might explore what you are willing to do to change it. Judging yourself and blaming yourself are not effective ways to bring about change. Accepting the body you have and deciding what you can and will do to enhance that body is the beginning of change.

We rarely come across people who are really satisfied with their physical appearance. However, there is a significant difference between the model who says, "I don't like the way my body looks," and the man who continually struggles to keep his weight under control. The task of understanding the body is not simple. Judging yourself, telling yourself that you are hopeless, and being impatient with your rate of progress are not helpful means of understanding your body. Once you reach these kinds of judgments about yourself, you limit the kind of feedback you are open to. Any feedback that does not support that self-perception will be enjoyed for a few moments, but will not last. The most important component in effecting change in your bodily image is your own perception. This is where any program of change begins.

Your view of your body and the decisions you have made about it have much to do with the choices you will make in other areas of your life. In our view people are affected in a very fundamental way by how they perceive their body and how they think others perceive it. Some people feel they are unattractive, unappealing, or physically inferior, and these self-perceptions are likely to have a powerful effect on other areas of their life. For example, you may be very critical of some of your physical characteristics; you may think your nose is unattractive, that you are too short or too tall, or that you are not muscular enough. Or you may have some of these common self-defeating thoughts:

- If I had a better body, then I'd be happy.
- If I were physically more attractive, people would like me.
- I never look good enough.
- It's too much work to change the things I dislike about my body.

Perhaps some part of you believes that others will not want to approach you because of your appearance. If you feel that you are basically unattractive, you may tell yourself that others will see your defects and will not want to be with you. In this way you contribute to the reactions others have toward you by the messages you send them. You may be perceived by others as aloof, distant, or judgmental. Even though you may want to get close to people, you may also be frightened of the possibility of meeting with their rejection.

You may say that there is little you can do to change certain aspects of your physical being such as your height or basic build. Yet you *can* look at the attitudes you have formed about these physical characteristics. How important are they to who you are? How has your culture influenced your beliefs about what constitutes the ideal body? We are also prone to develop feelings of shame if we unquestioningly accept certain cultural messages about our bodies. Sometimes the sense of shame remains with people into adulthood. The following brief descriptions represent some typical difficulties:

- Donna painfully recalls that during her preadolescence she was much taller and more physically developed than her peers. She was often the butt of jokes by both boys and girls in her class. Although she is no longer taller than most people around her, she still walks stoop-shouldered, for she still feels self-conscious and embarrassed over her body.

- Herbert, a physically attractive young man, is highly self-conscious about his body, much to the surprise of those who know him. He seems to be in good physical condition, yet he gets very anxious when he gains even a pound. As a child he was overweight, and he developed a self-concept of being the "fat kid." Even though he changed his physique years ago, the fear of being considered fat still lurks around the corner.

Consider whether you, too, made some decisions about your body early in life or during adolescence that still affect you. Did you feel embarrassed about certain of your physical characteristics? Today you may still be living by old perceptions and feelings. Even though others may think of you as an attractive person, you may react with suspicion and disbelief. If you continue to tell yourself that you are in some way inferior, your struggle to change your self-concept may be similar to that of Donna or Herbert.

Weight and Your Body Image

From years of experience reading student journals and counseling clients, we have concluded that many people are preoccupied with maintaining their "ideal weight." Although some people view themselves as too skinny and strive to gain weight, many more are looking for effective ways to lose weight. Young people are bombarded by unrealistic models of what constitutes an ideal body. In a recent television report, young college women were objecting to the unrealistic portrayal of ideal bodies by the use of models who did not look like them. These women took issue with the unrealistic standard of what it means to be physically fit and attractive. They refused to accept the image presented. They wanted models in advertisements to be more inclusive of the general population.

You may be one of those people who struggle with societal standards as to what makes a body attractive. You may find that your weight significantly affects the way you feel about your body. Do these statements sound familiar to you?

- I've tried every diet program there is, and I just can't seem to stick to one.
- I'm too occupied with school to think about losing weight.
- I love to eat, and I hate to exercise.

In our travels to Germany and Norway we have noticed how the ideal weight differs from culture to culture. The same thin person who is viewed as attractive in the United States might well be seen as undernourished in Germany. A person with a certain amount of weight is generally considered attractive and healthy looking in Germany. One young American woman who struggled with her weight and body image told us that when she spent some time in Norway she did not think of herself as being physically unattractive. There many people commented about her vitality. However, when she returned to her home in the United States, she was much more conscious of her appearance.

It may also help to examine how unrealistic societal standards regarding the ideal body can lead to the perpetual feeling that you are never physically adequate. For example, our society places tremendous pressure on women to be thin. Messages from the media reveal that thinness and beauty are often equated. For the many women who accept these cultural norms, the price they often pay is depression and loss of self-esteem.

Hirschmann and Munter (1995) describe a brief exercise on self-image in their book, *When Women Stop Hating Their Bodies: Freeing Yourself From Food and Weight Obsession.* Both men and women can benefit from these self-reflection questions. As you read these questions, pause long enough to form your own answers: Did you have a bad body thought today? As you got up this morning and looked in the mirror, what did you see and what did you tell yourself? As you were choosing what you would wear today, what thoughts and feelings did you have? If you watched television and saw an advertisement or a model, did this leave you with the feeling that you are somehow deficient? Did you step on the scale to check your weight and use this scale as a barometer for how good you would feel about yourself for the rest of the day? Did you have an interaction with someone that left you feeling self-conscious about your body? If you do this, how much energy does it take from your life? For the next few minutes, imagine that your body type somehow becomes the cultural ideal. Every magazine that you open has models in it who are built exactly like you rather than more than 20% thinner than the average person. How would you do things differently in your life? How would you dress? What would you eat? How would you feel when you looked in the mirror? What would you do with all the energy you used to expend on wishing you looked different?

Certainly, the topic of body image applies to both men and women. However, in this society women are subject to greater pressures to live up to the ideal size, which results in their preoccupation with weight and body image. In some ways, keeping women focused on achieving a "perfect" body is a form of oppression. Many eating problems that women face have to do with their internalized hatred of not being thin. Consider the case of Kate, who writes about her personal experience with weight problems and her body image.

KATE'S STORY

*A*lthough I have overcome a large degree of my body hatred, I continue to struggle with accepting and living with my body as it is. My last relationship ended with my partner justifying his disinterest with a critique of my body size. His words will probably sting me as long as I live.

Although part of me agrees with the negative comments people have made about my size, another part of me knows that their words are a form of oppression taught to them by our society. This does not excuse their behavior, but it helps me to understand that all of us are victims of our sexist standards. As a woman, I have worn my bad body image like a suit of armor. In many ways it protects me from having to examine other parts of my life.

The challenge in overcoming eating problems is multifold. Those of us who struggle with these issues need to continue to be brave and to ask ourselves if we can stand the thought of accepting ourselves for who we are. In recent months I have come to realize that my bad body image is not only a result of sociocultural factors but is also a form of self-preservation. I am used to being dismissed and rejected because of my body size. In an ironic way it has become a safe way to feel my pain. The challenge has been and continues to be for me to face those feelings within myself that have nothing to do with the size or shape of my legs, thighs, and stomach.

Kate's story illustrates a woman's struggle to accept her body, but other people are driven to meet societal standards of an attractive and "perfect" body. In its extreme form, this striving can lead to eating disorders. Anorexia and bulimia are frequently linked to the internalization of unrealistic standards that lead to negative self-perceptions and negative body images. Michelle's description of her struggle with anorexia nervosa illustrates how self-destructive striving for psychological and physical perfection can be.

MICHELLE'S STORY

When I was around 11 years old, I gradually began to lose weight for reasons that were a mystery even to me. I knew I was not slimming down to win the approval and acceptance of my peers at school, and I was not losing weight to feel fit and healthy. On the contrary, when my parents finally took me to the doctor to be examined for my weight loss, I was secretly hoping I would be diagnosed with some strange disease so I would receive everyone's attention and concern. I was consumed with guilt over the fact that I wanted my parents to worry about me, yet I continued to shed pounds. I vividly recall the moment my doctor explained that I had a disorder called anorexia nervosa. It was relatively unheard of at that time. I was sick, and just as a physical pain is the body's way of alerting one to a more serious problem, my anorexia was my psyche's way of alerting me to my deep emotional pain.

For most of my life I felt completely empty and emotionally dead inside. In retrospect I am certain that the loss of my birthmother (who gave me up for adoption when I was an infant) laid the foundation for subsequent losses in my life to be internalized very deeply. I must have justified my mother's departure with the excruciating message that "I was not enough." This theme of loss and abandonment in my life undoubtedly contributed to my emotional emptiness. I proceeded through life feeling grossly inadequate as a human being and attempted to remedy this by transforming myself into a "perfect" child—a parent's dream come true!

I strived to excel in virtually everything I attempted to ensure that I would be acceptable in the eyes of my parents. I couldn't risk losing my parents' affection and love, and my self-esteem was then so low that I believed I had to accomplish extraordinary feats to be deemed as worthy as the average child.

At a very basic level I felt emotionally and spiritually bankrupt, and my starved, emaciated body was truly a reflection of my starved, malnourished soul. I had such a deflated sense of myself that my anorexia gave me an identity; it gave me someone to be and it gave me one more "label" to wear.

I started to make the most progress in my recovery when I could finally let go of the false security of these labels I had clung to for so many years. After a great deal of work in therapy, I was able to let go of some control and allow myself to experience just being an ordinary person. I have accomplished a lot of things in my life that I am extremely proud of, but the one thing I am most proud of is that I have learned to be comfortable making mistakes and to simply be human.

It is easy to get trapped in self-destructive patterns of critical self-judgment. Being and feeling healthy—and choosing what that entails for you—are the real challenges to wellness.

Although weight is a significant health factor, nutritional and exercise habits are also crucial to your overall well-being. Rather than too quickly deciding that you need to either gain or lose weight or to change your nutritional habits, it is a good idea to consult your physician or one of the nutrition centers in your area. If you decide you want to change your weight, there are many excellent support groups and self-help programs designed for this purpose. The counseling centers at many colleges offer groups for weight control and for people with eating disorders.

A basic change in attitude and lifestyle is important in successfully dealing with a weight problem. People with weight problems do not eat simply because they are hungry. They are typically more responsive to external cues in their environment. One of these is the acquiescence of well-meaning friends, who may joke with them by saying, "Oh, don't worry about those extra pounds. What's life without the enjoyment of eating? Besides, there's more of you to love this way!" This kind of "friendship" can make it even more difficult to discipline ourselves and to watch what and how much we eat.

In our counseling groups we often encourage people who view themselves as having a weight problem to begin to pay more attention to their body and to increase their awareness about what their body communicates to them and to others. A useful exercise has been to ask them, "If your body had a voice, what would it be saying?" Here are some examples of what their bodies might communicate:

- I don't like myself.
- My weight will keep me at a distance.
- I'm making myself ill.
- I'm burdened.

- I don't get around much anymore!
- I'm self-indulging.
- I work very hard, and I don't have time to take care of myself.

If you do not like what your body is saying, it is up to you to decide what, if anything, you want to change. Should you decide that you do not want to change, you need not be defensive about it. There is no injunction that you must change.

If you have not liked your physical being for some time but have not been able to change it, there may be some genetic or physical reasons that make it extremely difficult for you to manage your weight. Some people's medical history prevents them from having a great deal of choice regarding their weight, in spite of exercise and healthy nutrition.

In *What You Can Change and What You Can't,* Seligman (1993) tells us that in 1990 Americans spent more than $30 billion on the weight-loss industry. Seligman believes dieting is a cruel hoax and that it does not work. In fact, he believes dieting might work against overweight people and that it may be bad for health. Furthermore, dieting may result in eating disorders such as bulimia and anorexia.

According to Seligman's findings, although there are some health risks to being overweight, there are also serious health risks from losing weight and regaining it. He suspects that the weight-fluctuation hazard may be greater than the risk of remaining overweight. It is clear that Seligman does not view dieting as the answer to being overweight. Here are a few of the points he emphasizes:

- Weight is generally regained after dieting.
- There are some destructive side effects to dieting such as repeated failure, eating disorders, depression, and fatigue.
- Losing and regaining weight itself presents a health risk comparable to the risk of being overweight.
- Achieving fitness is a more sensible approach than fighting fatness.

Being overweight is a complex problem, and these thoughts on dieting are worth considering. Before you embark on any fitness or weight-loss program, consider your own situation carefully and talk with your physician about alternatives.

Many of us get stuck because we focus on what society dictates as being the ideal weight and body image. We hope you are able to raise your awareness about the societal messages you have operated under, and we encourage you to challenge these cultural messages. The Take Time to Reflect exercise is designed to assist you in clarifying your attitudes about your perception of your body. Ask yourself: "How satisfied am I with the body I have? How can I move toward increased self-acceptance?"

Take Time to Reflect

1. What are your attitudes toward your body? Take some time to study your body and become aware of how you look to yourself and what your body feels like to you. Try standing in front of a good-sized mirror, and reflect on these questions:

   • Look at your face. What is it telling you?

   • What are your eyes conveying to you?

   • Can you see yourself smiling?

   • Is your body generally tight or relaxed? Where do you feel your tension?

   • Which parts, if any, of your body do you feel ashamed of or try to hide?

   • What about your body would you most like to change? What do you like the most? The least?

2. Each time you complete the exercise just described, record your impressions or keep an extended account of your reactions in your journal.

3. If you consider yourself to be overweight, is your weight a barrier and a burden? Try to understand what your weight is doing for you. Is it trying to keep people away from you?

4. Imagine yourself looking more the way you would like to. Let yourself think about how you might be different, as well as how your life would be different.

5. As a result of reading this chapter and doing these exercises, what actions are you willing to take to become more invested in taking care of yourself?

SUMMARY

The purpose of this chapter has been to encourage you to think about how you are treating your body and how you can take control of your physical and psychological well-being. Even if you are not presently concerned with health problems, you may have discovered that you hold some self-defeating attitudes about your body. A theme of this chapter has been to examine what might be keeping you from really caring about your body or acting on the caring that you say you have. It is not a matter of smoking or not smoking, of exercising or not exercising; the basic choice concerns how you feel about yourself and about your life. When you accept responsibility for the feelings and attitudes you have developed about your body and your life, you begin to free yourself from feeling victimized by your body.

Getting adequate rest and sleep is a key element to overall health; if you are rested, you will be less prone to the negative impact of stress. Exercise not only makes you look and feel better, it is essential for cardiovascular fitness. Exercise can enable you to stay both physically and psychologically fit. Making healthy nutritional choices provides you with the necessary fuel to meet the challenges of life and is essential to physical well-being. Spiritual practices may be as important to your overall well-being as eating and exercising. A comprehensive view of health includes nourishing both your body and your spirit.

You can enhance your experience of the world around you by seeing, hearing, smelling, tasting, and touching. You can become less of a stranger to your body through relaxation, dance, and movement. Touch is particularly important. For healthy physical and emotional development, you need both physical and psychological contact.

Your body presents an image to you and to others of how you view yourself. Your attitudes about your body are acquired in the context of your culture, and you can challenge these attitudes, especially if they are self-critical. Think about how your perceptions of your body affect other areas of your life. What are some of the changes you are most invested in making regarding self-care? Your ability to love others, to form nourishing sexual and emotional relationships with others, to work well, to play with joy, and to fully savor each day depends a great deal on both your physical and psychological health. You may be keeping yourself imprisoned if you are unwilling to initiate positive contact with other people simply because you assume they won't like the way you look. Allow your body to express your feelings of tenderness, anger, and enthusiasm. If you tend to be rigid and under control, imagine how it would feel to be free of these restraints.

Remember that you are a whole being, composed of physical, emotional, social, intellectual, and spiritual dimensions. If you neglect any one of these aspects of yourself, you will feel the impact on the other dimensions of your being. Take a moment to think again about how well you are taking care of yourself physically. How committed are you to a wellness perspective? Consider the value you place on taking good care of yourself through practices such as meditation, relaxation exercises, paying attention to your spiritual life, participating in meaningful religious activities, maintaining good nutritional habits, getting adequate sleep and rest, and participating in a regular exercise program. Ask yourself whether your daily behavior shows that you value your physical and psychological health. Once you have made this assessment, decide on a few areas you would like to improve. Then begin working on a plan to change one aspect at a time.

Where Can I Go From Here?

I. Wellness means different things to different people. When you think of wellness, what aspects of your life do you most think of? Look at what you are doing to maintain a general state of wellness. How much of a priority do you place on wellness?

2. If you sometimes have trouble sleeping, try some of the suggestions listed in this chapter to see if they might work for you. If you do not get adequate rest and sleep, what steps can you take to make changes?

3. Assess how exercise (or the lack of exercise) is affecting how you feel physically and psychologically and how it influences your ability to deal with stress. If you are interested in engaging in some form of regular physical activity, decide on some exercise that you would enjoy doing. Start small so you don't get overwhelmed, but stick with your physical activity for at least 2 to 4 weeks to see if you begin to feel a difference.

4. In your journal record for a week all of your activities that are healthy for your body as well as those that are unhealthy. You may want to list what you eat, whether you smoke or drink, your sleep patterns, and what you do for exercise and relaxation. Then look over your list and choose one or more areas that you would be willing to work on during the next few months.

Resources for Future Study

Web Site Resources

GO ASK ALICE!
http://www.goaskalice.columbia.edu/

Columbia University's Health Education Program has created a widely used Web site designed for undergraduate students. Alice! offers answers to questions about relationships, sexuality, sexual health, emotional health, fitness and nutrition, alcohol, nicotine and other drugs, and general health. If you cannot find an answer to what you are looking for, you can "Ask Alice!" yourself.

CENTERS FOR DISEASE CONTROL AND PREVENTION
http://www.cdc.gov/

The Centers for Disease Control and Prevention (CDC) offers news, fact sheets on disease information and health information, articles, statistics, and links regarding health and illness in the United States (also offered in Spanish).

MAYO CLINIC HEALTH OASIS
http://www.mayohealth.org/mayo/common/htm/index.htm

This site offers "reliable information for a healthier life" and provides news items, highlights, and specific health category centers for information and resources on various diseases, medications, and general health.

EATING DISORDERS SHARED AWARENESS
http://www.eating-disorder.com/

This site is dedicated to helping others through awareness, education, support, and friendship. It also provides links to other sites such as Mirror-Mirror (Canada) and Something Fishy (New York), which have a multitude of links and information on a wide variety of topics related to eating disorders.

NATIONAL ASSOCIATION FOR HEALTH AND FITNESS
http://www.physicalfitness.org

This is a network of state and governors' councils that promotes physical fitness for persons of all ages and abilities.

NATIONAL CENTER ON PHYSICAL ACTIVITY
AND DISABILITY
http://www.ncpad.org

This site promotes the "substantial health benefits that can be gained from participating in regular physical activity" and "provides information and resources that can enable people with disabilities to become as physically active as they choose to be."

SHAPE UP AMERICA!
http://www.shapeup.org

Shape Up America is a nonprofit organization dedicated to helping you achieve a healthy weight for life.

InfoTrac College Edition Resources

For additional readings, explore INFOTRAC COLLEGE EDITION, our online library:
http://www.infotrac.college.com/wadsworth

Hint: Enter these search terms:

wellness

holistic health

holistic medicine

sleep deprivation

physical exercise

physical fitness

integrative medicine

spirituality

body image

eating disorder

Print Resources

Benson, H. (1976). *The relaxation response.* New York: Avon Books.

Benson, H. (1984). *Beyond the relaxation response.* New York: Berkeley Books.

Brannon, L, & Feist, J. (2004). *Health psychology: An introduction to behavior and health* (5th ed.). Belmont, CA: Wadsworth/Thomson Learning.

Brenner, P. (2002). *Buddha in the waiting room: Simple truths about health, illness, and healing.* Hillsboro, OR: Beyond Words.

Dalai Lama. (1999). *Ethics for the new millennium.* New York: Riverhead Books.

Fontana, D. (1997). *Teach yourself to dream: A practical guide.* San Francisco: Chronicle Books.

Fontana, D. (1999). *Learn to meditate: A practical guide to self-discovery and fulfillment.* San Francisco: Chronicle Books.

George, M. (1998). *Learn to relax: A practical guide to easing tension and conquering stress.* San Francisco: Chronicle Books.

Hales, D. (1987). *How to sleep like a baby.* New York: Ballantine.

Hales, D. (2005). *An invitation to health* (11th ed.). Belmont, CA: Wadsworth/Thomson Learning.

Hales, D. (with Zartman, Thomas C.). (2001). *An invitation to fitness and wellness.* Belmont, CA: Wadsworth/Thomson Learning.

Hirschmann, J. R., & Munter, C. H. (1995). *When women stop hating their bodies: Freeing yourself from food and weight obsession.* New York: Fawcett Columbine.

Kottler, J. A. (2001). *Making changes last.* Philadelphia, PA: Brunner-Routledge (Taylor & Francis Group).

Seligman, M. E. P. (1990). *Learned optimism: How to change your mind and your life.* New York: Pocket Books.

Seligman, M. E. P. (1993). *What you can change and what you can't.* New York: Fawcett Columbine.

Schafer, W. (2000). *Stress management for wellness* (4th ed.). Belmont, CA: Wadsworth.

Siegel, B. (1988). *Love, medicine, and miracles.* New York: Harper & Row (Perennial Library).

Siegel, B. (1989). *Peace, love, and healing. Bodymind communication and the path to self-healing: An exploration.* New York: Harper & Row.

Siegel, B. (1993). *How to live between office visits: A guide to life, love, and health.* New York: HarperCollins.

Travis, J. W., & Ryan, R. S. (1994). *Wellness workbook* (3rd ed.). Berkeley, CA: Ten Speed Press.

Weil, A. (2000). *Eating well for optimum health: The essential guide to food, diet, and nutrition.* New York: Alfred A. Knopf.

5

Either you control your stress,
or stress controls you.

Managing
Stress

Where Am I Now?

Use this scale to respond to these statements:

    3 = This statement is true of me *most* of the time.

    2 = This statement is true of me *some* of the time.

    1 = This statement is true of me *almost none* of the time.

    1. My lifestyle is generally stressful.

    2. I have relied on drugs or alcohol to help me through difficult times, but I do not abuse these substances.

    3. It is relatively easy for me to fully relax.

    4. The way I live, I sometimes worry about having a heart attack.

    5. I am able to recognize how my thoughts contribute to my stress.

    6. Stress has sometimes made me physically ill.

    7. If I do not control stress, I believe it will control me.

    8. I meditate to reduce my stress.

    9. Burnout is a real concern of mine.

    10. I feel a need to learn more stress management techniques.

Stress is an event or series of events that leads to strain, which often results in physical and psychological health problems. Stress has both positive and negative effects. It is important to differentiate between eustress (pronounced "you-stress") and distress. **Eustress,** or good stress, provides us with the necessary motivation to strive for the best. A certain amount of stress can be a challenge and can help us draw attention to our reserves in finding creative solutions to the problems of everyday living. **Distress** refers to the negative effects of stress that can deplete us and fragment us. Distress leads to negative physical and psychological states.

Everyday living involves dealing with frustrations, conflicts, pressures, and change. Moreover, at certain times in our lives most of us are confronted with severely stressful situations that are difficult to cope with—the death of a family member or a close friend, a national crisis, a natural disaster, the loss of a job, a personal failure, or an injury. Even changes that we perceive to be positive, such as getting a promotion or moving to a new location, can be stressful and often require a period of adjustment.

If stress is severe enough, it takes its toll on us physically and psychologically. In *Learn to Relax*, Mike George (1998) identifies a range of physiological and psychological symptoms that serve as signs for us to reevaluate our priorities. Our body or state of mind may be telling us that something in our life needs to change. Some of these signs include loneliness, insecurity, loss of concentration and memory, fatigue and sleeping difficulties, mood swings, impatience, restlessness, obsessive working, loss of appetite, and fear of silence. These signs often serve as an invitation to examine what we are doing and to create better ways of dealing with life's demands. It is clear that learning to cope with stress is essential if we hope to maintain a sense of wellness. Managing stress is not something we do once and for all; it is a process of meeting challenges with calm and determination.

Siegel (1988) indicates that our level of stress is largely determined by cultural factors. Cultures that emphasize competition and individualism produce the most stress. Cultures that place a high value on cooperation and collectivism produce the least stress and also have the lowest rates of cancer. In collectivist cultures, supportive relationships are the norm, the elderly are respected and given an active role, and religious faith is valued. Siegel is convinced that chronic patterns of intense stress lower the efficiency of the body's disease-fighting cells. His work with cancer patients has taught him that stresses resulting from traumatic loss and major life changes are in the background of most of those who get cancer. He adds, however, that not everyone who suffers stressful changes in lifestyle develops an illness. The deciding factor seems to be how people cope with the problems and stresses they face. It seems to be particularly important to be able to express your feelings about situations rather than denying that your feelings exist or swallowing them.

In most places in the modern world, stress is an inevitable part of life. We cannot eliminate stress, but we can learn how to monitor its physical and psychological impact—we can manage stress. Recognizing ineffective or destructive reactions to stress is an essential step in dealing with stress. In discussing how to manage stress in a challenging world, Schafer (2000) identifies a strong sense of internal control as the most important personal quality for effectively dealing with external stressors. The opposite of internal control is helplessness, or a sense that life is controlled entirely by external forces. Schafer asserts, "The best path for confidence for turning adversity into challenges is the belief that you can make things happen, that you control your own destiny" (p. 481).

Although many sources of stress are external, how we perceive and react to stress is subjective and internal. By interpreting the events in our lives, we define what is and is not stressful—we determine our level of stress. Therefore, the real challenge is learning how to recognize and respond constructively to the sources of stress rather than trying to eliminate them. Some constructive paths to stress management addressed in this chapter include learning time management and money management practices, challenging self-defeating thinking and negative self-talk, developing a sense of humor, acquiring mindfulness, practicing meditation and other centering activities, and learning how to relax.

SOURCES OF STRESS

Stress of one kind or another is present in each of the stages in the life cycle (Chapters 2 and 3). As we discovered in Chapter 4, wellness is a central buffer against stress, and stress frequently accelerates the development of illnesses. Because stress tends to be self-imposed, we have more control over stress than we typically realize. Before we can exert control, however, we must identify the source of our stress. Two major sources of stress are environmental and psychological factors.

Environmental Sources of Stress

Many of the stresses of daily life come from external sources. Consider some of the environmentally related stresses you face at the beginning of a semester. You are likely to encounter problems finding a parking place on campus. You may stand in long lines and have to cope with many other delays and frustrations. Some of the courses you need may be closed; simply putting together a decent schedule of classes may be next to impossible. You may have difficulty arranging your work schedule to fit your school schedule, and this can be compounded by the external demands of friends and family and other social commitments. Loneliness can influence your psychological and physical well-being, and extreme

Many of the stresses of daily life come from external sources.

© PhotoDisc/Getty Images

loneliness is often a stressor. Financial problems and the pressure to work to support yourself (and perhaps your family too) make being a student a demanding task. Test anxiety and attempting to fit too many things into one day can add needless stress to the many new pressures college students face. Typically, college is a time when many critical choices are made that will shape an individual's career goals and professional identity (Rice, 1999).

Our minds and bodies are also profoundly affected by more direct physiological sources of stress. Illness, exposure to environmental pollutants, improper diet, lack of exercise, poor sleeping habits, and abusing our bodies in any number of other ways all take a toll on us. Racism, oppression, and discrimination are major stresses in the environment that many individuals are subjected to.

Discrimination on the basis of race, age, gender, or sexual orientation creates stress in the lives of many people. Listening to news reports of the ravages of war and violence are other stressors that take a toll on us psychologically and physically.

Psychological Sources of Stress

Any set of circumstances that we perceive as being threatening to our well-being puts a strain on our coping abilities. Stress is in the mind of the beholder, and our appraisals of stressful events are highly subjective. How we label, interpret, think about, and react to events in our lives has a lot to do with determining whether those events are stressful. Weiten and Lloyd (2003) identify frustration, conflict, change, and pressure as four key elements of psychological stress. As we consider each of these sources of stress, think about how they apply to you and your situation.

Frustration results from something blocking attainment of your needs and goals. External sources of frustration (all of which have psychological components) include failures, losses, job discrimination, accidents, delays, traffic jams, hurtful interpersonal relationships, loneliness, and isolation. Additionally, internal factors can hinder you in attaining your goals. These include a lack of basic skills, physical handicaps, a lack of belief in yourself, and any self-imposed barriers you may create that block the pursuit of your goals. What are some of the major frustrations you experience, and how do you typically deal with them?

Conflict, another source of stress, occurs when two or more incompatible motivations or behavioral impulses compete for expression. Conflicts can be classified as approach-approach, avoidance-avoidance, and approach-avoidance (Weiten & Lloyd, 2003).

- **Approach-approach conflicts** occur when a choice must be made between two or more attractive or desirable alternatives. Such conflicts are inevitable because we have a limited amount of time to do all the things we would like to do and be all the places we would like to be. An example of this type of conflict is being forced to choose between two job offers, both of which have attractive features.

- **Avoidance-avoidance conflicts** arise when a choice must be made between two or more unattractive or undesirable goals. These conflicts are the most unpleasant and the most stressful. You may have to choose between being unemployed and accepting a job you do not like, neither of which appeals to you.

- **Approach-avoidance conflicts** are produced when a choice must be made between two or more goals, each of which has attractive and unattractive elements. For example, you may be offered a challenging job that appeals to you but that entails much traveling, which you consider a real drawback.

How many times have you been faced with two or more desirable choices and forced to choose one path? And how many times have you had to choose between unpleasant realities? Perhaps your major conflicts involve your choice of a lifestyle. For example, have you wrestled with the issue of being independent or letting others make choices for you? What about living a self-directed life or living by what others expect of you? Consider for a few minutes some of the major conflicts you have recently faced. How have these conflicts affected you? How do you typically deal with the stress you experience over value conflicts?

Change can exacerbate stress, especially life changes that involve readjustment in our living circumstances. Holmes and Rahe's (1967) classic study on the relationship between stressful life events and physical illness found that changes in personal relationships, career changes, and financial changes are often stressful, even if these changes are positive. Thus, within a relatively short period of time, you may get married, move into a new house, and begin a family. Any one of these changes can be stressful, but the combined effect of these changes often increases the intensity of stress you experience. However, the demands for adjustment to these life changes are more important than the type of life changes alone.

Pressure, which involves expectations and demands for behaving in certain ways, is part of the "hurry sickness" of modern living. Also, we continually place internally created pressures on ourselves. Many people are extremely demanding of themselves, driving themselves and never quite feeling satisfied that they have done all they could or should have. Striving to live up to the expectations of others, coupled with self-imposed perfectionist demands, is a certain route to stress. If you find yourself in this situation, consider some of the faulty and unrealistic beliefs you hold. Are you overloading your circuits and heading for certain burnout? In what ways do you push yourself to perform, and for whom? How do you experience and deal with pressure in your daily life?

EFFECTS OF STRESS

Stress produces adverse physical effects. In our attempt to cope with everyday living, our bodies experience what is known as the **fight-or-flight response.** Our bodies go on constant alert status, ready for aggressive action to combat the many "enemies" we face. If we subject ourselves to too many stresses, the biochemical changes that occur during the fight-or-flight response may lead to chronic stress and anxiety. This causes bodily wear and tear, which can lead to a variety of what are known as psychosomatic or psychophysiological disorders. These are not a product of one's imagination. They are real bodily disorders manifested in disabling physical symptoms that are caused by emotional factors and the prolonged effects of stress. These symptoms range from minor discomfort to life-threatening conditions.

Hales (2005) reports that an increasing number of studies over the past 20 years have shown that stress contributes to approximately 80% of all major physical illnesses, some of which include cardiovascular disease, cancer, endocrine and metabolic disease, skin rashes, peptic ulcers, migraine and tension headaches, emotional disorders, musculoskeletal disease, infectious illnesses, and premenstrual syndrome. Other symptoms that often are stress-related are asthma and other respiratory disorders, high blood pressure, skin disorders, arthritis, digestive disorders, disturbed sleeping patterns, poor circulation, strokes, and heart disease. According to Hales, as many as 75% to 90% of visits to physicians are related to stress. Explore how your physical symptoms may actually serve a purpose. Ask yourself how your life might be different if you were not ill.

Allan Abbott (a family-practice doctor) and Colony Abbott (a nurse) are two friends of ours who spent some time treating indigenous people in Peru. This experience stimulated their interest in the ways in which stress affects the body. The Abbotts became especially interested in coronary-prone behavior, which is so characteristic of the North American way of life. The leading causes of death in North America are cardiovascular diseases and cancer (diseases the Abbotts relate to stress), but these diseases rarely cause the death of Peruvian Indians, whose lives are relatively stress free.

In the Abbotts' view our bodies are paying a high price for the materialistic and stressful manner in which we live. Allan Abbott estimates that about 75% of the physical ailments he treats are psychologically and behaviorally related to stress, and he asserts that most of what he does as a physician that makes a significant difference is psychological in nature rather than medical. According to Abbott, belief in the doctor and in the process and procedures a doctor employs has a great deal to do with curing patients. Taking a blood test, having an X ray done, getting a shot, and simple conversation with the physician all appear to help patients improve. Indeed, faith healers work on this very principle, embracing the role of belief and its effect on the body.

A **psychosomatic illness** is a real physical illness that is caused by emotional factors. William Glasser (1998), a psychiatrist and founder of reality therapy, maintains that a psychosomatic (or psychophysiological) illness is a creative process. In a chronic illness for which there is no known physical cause, our bodies are involved in a creative struggle to satisfy our needs. Because there is no specific medical treatment for these psychosomatic disorders, Glasser advises that the best course of action is to attempt to regain effective control over whatever is out of control in your life. Rather than accepting passive statements such as "I am depressed," Glasser helps clients realize their active role in *depressing, angering, headaching,* or *anxietying* themselves. He emphasizes that people choose these behaviors in an attempt to meet their needs and wants, and people have some control over what they continue to choose to do. Although it may be difficult to directly control your feelings and thoughts, Glasser maintains that you do have control over what you are *doing.* If you change what you are doing, you increase the chances that your feelings and thoughts will also change. For instance, if you are depressing over failing an exam, it may be difficult to directly control your feelings of disappointment. You could spend much energy berating yourself; however, you could also use that same energy to reflect on ways to prevent this situation for occurring in the future. By engaging in a new way of thinking and behaving, it is likely that you will eventually begin to feel differently about this situation.

In *Joy's Way*, Brugh Joy (1979) describes how a life-threatening illness was the catalyst for him to call an end to a prosperous and growing private practice as a physician and a position as a clinical professor of medicine. He dropped a role that had brought him a great deal of success and security but that had also sickened him in some key respects. After giving up traditional medicine, Joy traveled through Europe, Egypt, India, and Nepal for 9 months on his own pilgrimage toward spiritual reawakening, which led to his physical and psychological healing. Along with Bernie Siegel and other physicians, Joy believes we become sick because of the stresses associated with psychological and spiritual anomalies. From Joy's perspective, people generally become sick for one of two reasons: either because their life is too restricted for the person they potentially could become or because their life is too expansive and exceeds their potential.

An intimate connection exists between the body and the mind, and that emotional restriction can lead to sickness. However, Brenner (2002) believes it is simplistic to view all illness as caused by ourselves and rejects the idea of self-induced disease. He says: "Responsibility does not mean there is a direct causal relationship between you and your illness, nor does responsibility involve judgment, censure, or blame" (p. 25). Although it may be helpful to assume that we have a part to play in our illness, we need to reject taking blame for our illness.

In our work as counselors, we see evidence of this connection between stress and psychosomatic ailments. We often encounter people who deal with their emotions by denying or repressing them or finding some other indirect channel of expression. Consider Lou's situation. He is a young man who suffered from occasional asthmatic attacks. He discovered during the process of therapy that he became asthmatic whenever he was under emotional stress or was anxious. To his surprise, Lou found that he could control his symptoms when he began to express his feelings and talk about what was upsetting him. While continuing to receive medical supervision for his asthma, he improved his physical condition as he learned to more fully explore his emotional difficulties. As Lou let out his anger, fear, and pain, he was able to breathe freely again.

Other examples can be found that illustrate how our bodies pay the price for not coping with stress adequately. Consider Arista's account of how the stress of her perfectionist strivings resulted in severe headaches.

ARISTA'S STORY

I describe myself as a perfectionist, yet this word implies that I am constantly striving for something I never reach. This is not accurate as I almost always reach my goals. So I redefine myself as driven, ambitious, and focused. In today's world, these are assets associated with the highest powered executives in the United States.

As a graduate student in a counseling program, I have had my share of stress and pressure. Over the past three semesters, I noticed that my monthly headaches were increasing in frequency and duration. At first I believed it was stress. But the headaches would wake me up from a deep sleep, my head pounding and hammering, and the hypochondriac in me sought medical attention, which was to no avail. There was no blood clot in my brain, nor did I suffer from any other terminal illness.

So I pushed on, each semester getting closer and closer to graduating with a degree that would bring me my dream of counseling and teaching. I began to systematically record the time and date of each headache. When the last day of the semester arrived, I eagerly began my summer vacation. Weeks went by without so much as a twinge of pain in my head.

As the fall semester approaches, I am certain that my headaches will begin again. In anticipation, I have begun meditating and will try to learn to work with my pain, instead of against it, which often makes it worse. I hope to learn to play and relax. Praising the side of me that works so hard by taking time for myself to meditate, watch soaps, shop, or lie in the sun is a goal I have for myself. Life will inevitably feel out of control at times, and my body will cry out for a break when I push too hard.

Stories such as Arista's are not uncommon. Physical symptoms often decrease or disappear when we learn to identify and appropriately express our feelings or challenge unrealistic goals of perfectionism.

Some people seem especially resilient, coping with stress with little apparent disruption in their lives. Suzanne Ouellette (Kobasa, 1979a, 1979b, 1984) provides evidence that personality plays a significant role in helping people resist stress-related illnesses. Her studies addressed the question of who stays well and why. Ouellette identified a personality pattern she labeled "hardiness," which distinguishes people who succeed in coping with change without becoming ill. **Hardiness** is characterized by an appetite for challenge, a sense of commitment, and a strong sense of being in control of one's life. Individuals who possess a high level of hardiness tend to have a clearly defined sense of self and purpose. They perceive change as stimulating and as providing them with options for growth.

Not only do hardy personalities seem to be able to survive stress and life changes, but they actually appear to thrive under conditions of rapid and clustered changes. Based on her study of high-stress executives who remained healthy, Ouellette (Kobasa 1979b, 1984) identified these personality traits:

• **A liking for challenge.** Hardy executives tend to seek out and actively confront challenges. They thrive under conditions of challenge, difficulty, and adversity. Rather than viewing difficult situations as being catastrophic, they perceive them as an opportunity for growing and learning. For them, change is the norm of life. They view change as stimulating and as providing them with opportunities for growth. Instead of being riveted to the past, they welcome change and see it as a stimulus for creativity. Less hardy executives tend to view change as threatening.

• **A strong sense of commitment.** People who are committed have high self-esteem, a clearly defined sense of self, a zest for life, and a meaning for living. Stress-resistant executives display a clear sense of values, well-defined goals, and a commitment to putting forth the maximum effort to achieve their goals. In contrast, less hardy executives lack direction and do not have a commitment to a value system.

• **An internal locus of control.** Individuals with an internal locus of control believe they can influence events and their reactions to events. Such individuals accept responsibility for their actions. They believe their successes and failures are determined by internal factors, such as their abilities and the actions they take. People with an external locus of control believe what happens to them is determined by factors external to themselves such as luck, fate, and chance. Hardy individuals tend to exhibit an internal locus of control, whereas less stress-resistant individuals feel powerless over events that happen to them.

Ouellette's work has been a catalyst for research on the way personality affects health and the ability to tolerate stress, and hardiness traits have shown up in many other studies. Her studies demonstrate that hardiness is a buffer against distress and illness in coping with the stresses associated with change (Ouellette, 1993).

Take Time to Reflect

1. What things cause you the most stress in your life?

_____

_____

2. What have you tried to do to manage these stressors?

_____

_____

3. What are some other steps you could take to more effectively manage your stress?

_____

_____

4. In this chapter we encourage you to assume personal responsibility for the way stress affects your body. For example, instead of saying "I have a headache," you are asked to say "I am headaching." How might your life be different if you accepted responsibility for your bodily symptoms (such as stomachaches, headaches, and muscular tension)?

_____

_____

5. Having a "hardy personality" can help you stay healthy as you cope with change and stress. What personality characteristics do you have that either help or hinder you in dealing with stressful situations?

_____

_____

DESTRUCTIVE REACTIONS TO STRESS

Reactions to stress can be viewed on a continuum from being effective and adaptive, on one end, to being ineffective and maladaptive, on the other. If our reactions to stress are ineffective over a long period of time, physical and psychological harm is likely. Ineffective ways of dealing with stress include defensive behavior and abusing drugs or alcohol. Burnout is a common outcome of ineffectively coping with stress.

Defensive Behavior

If we experience stress associated with failure in school or work, we may defend our self-concept by denying or distorting reality. Although defensive behavior does at times have adjustive value and can result in reducing the impact of stress, such behavior actually increases levels of stress in the long run. If we are more concerned with defending our bruised ego than with coping with reality, we are not taking the steps necessary to reduce the source of stress. In essence, we are denying that a problem situation exists or we are minimizing an unpleasant reality. One problem with relying too heavily on defensive behavior is that the more we use defense mechanisms the more we increase our anxiety. When this happens, our defenses become entrenched. This leads to a vicious cycle that is difficult to break and ultimately makes coping with stress more difficult. We suggest that you take time to review the discussion on ego-defense mechanisms in Chapter 2 and reflect on the degree to which you use defense mechanisms to cope with the stresses in your life.

Drugs and Alcohol

Many people are conditioned to take an aspirin for a headache or a tranquilizer when they are anxious, to rely on stimulants to keep them up all night at the end of a term, and to use a variety of drugs to reduce other physical symptoms and emotional stresses. Some time back, I (Jerry) took a vigorous bike ride on rough mountain trails. I returned home with a headache, a condition that afflicts me only occasionally. Instead of recognizing that I had overexerted myself and needed to take a rest, my immediate reaction was to take aspirin and proceed with my usual work for the day. My body was sending me an important signal, which I was ready to ignore by numbing. Perhaps many of you can identify with this tendency to quickly eliminate symptoms rather than recognize them as a sign of the need to change certain behaviors. Too many of us rely heavily on drugs to alleviate symptoms of stress rather than looking at the lifestyle that produces this stress.

Many of us use drugs or alcohol in some form or another. We are especially vulnerable to relying on drugs when we feel out of control, for drugs offer the promise of helping us gain control. Consider some of the ways we attempt to control problems by relying on both legal and illegal drugs. If we are troubled with shyness, boredom, anxiety, depression, or stress, we may become chemically dependent to relieve these symptoms. A drawback to depending on these substances to gain control is that through them we numb ourselves physically and psychologically. Instead of paying attention to our bodily signals that all is not well, we deceive ourselves into believing we are something we are not.

When drugs or alcohol are used excessively to escape painful reality, the "solution" to a problem becomes another problem. As tolerance is built up for these substances, we tend to become increasingly dependent on them to anesthetize both physical and psychological pain, and addiction can result. Alcohol is perhaps the most widely used and abused drug of all. It is legal, accessible, and socially acceptable. Alcohol abuse is dangerous and debilitating, and often its effects are not immediately noticeable.

Once the effects of the drugs or alcohol wear off, we are still confronted by the painful reality we sought to avoid. Although drugs and alcohol can distort reality, at the same time these substances prevent us from finding direct and effective means of coping with stress. The problem here is that stress is now controlling us instead of our controlling stress.

Burnout as a Result of Continual Stress

Burnout is a state of physical, emotional, intellectual, and spiritual exhaustion characterized by feelings of helplessness and hopelessness. It is the result of repeated pressures, often associated with intense involvement with people over long periods of time. Striving for unrealistically high goals can lead to a chronic state of feeling frustrated and let down. People who are burned out have depleted themselves on all levels of human functioning. Although they have been willing to give of themselves to others, they have forgotten to take care of themselves and generally feel negative about themselves and others.

Burnout is a concern for many students, and they say that burnout often catches them by surprise. Frequently they do not recognize their hurried lifestyle, nor do they always notice the warning signs that they have pushed themselves to the breaking point. Many students devote the majority of their time to school and work while neglecting their friendships, not making quality time for their family, and not taking time for their own leisure pursuits. Semester after semester they crowd in too many credits, convincing themselves that they must push themselves to graduate so they can start their career. They become apathetic and wait for the semester to end. They are physically and emotionally exhausted and often feel socially cut off.

What can we do at those times when we feel psychologically and physically exhausted? Once we recognize our state and seriously want to change it, the situation does not have to be hopeless. Instead of working harder, we can "work smarter," which means changing the way we approach our jobs so we suffer less stress (see Chapter 10). Setting realistic goals is another coping skill. We can also work at conquering feelings of helplessness because such feelings lead to frustration and anger, which in turn result in our becoming exhausted and cynical. We can learn to relax, even if such breaks are short. Instead of taking personally all the problems we encounter, we can condition ourselves to assume a more objective perspective. Most important, we can learn that caring for ourselves is every bit as important as caring for others.

Although learning coping skills to deal with the effects of burnout is helpful, our energies are best directed toward preventing this condition. The real challenge is to learn ways to structure our lives so we can avoid burnout. Prevention is much easier than attempting to cure a condition of severe physical and psychological depletion. Prevention includes becoming sensitive to the first signs of burnout creeping up on us and finding ways to energize ourselves. Learning how to use leisure to nurture ourselves is important. Each of us will find a different path to staying alive personally, but we must slow down and monitor the way we are living to discover that path.

CONSTRUCTIVE RESPONSES TO STRESS

To cope with stress effectively, you first need to face up to the causes of your problems, including your own part in creating them. Instead of adopting destructive reactions to stress, you can employ task-oriented constructive approaches aimed at realistically coping with stressful events. Let us emphasize that although there are many useful approaches to dealing with stress, most of these are not adequate measures and are not sufficient to bring about long-lasting change. Feuerstein and Bodian (1993) point out how essential it is that we understand the basic causes of stress reactions. Deeper levels of stress management must involve insights and self-discovery if we hope to manage stress in a profound, life-altering manner. If we do not address the emotional and mental origins of stress, then using coping techniques is like putting out a fire— only to come back and find it burning again. With this deeper understanding, it is possible for us to alter some of these basic causes and at the same time utilize a range of constructive coping strategies.

Weiten and Lloyd (2003) describe constructive coping as behavioral reactions to stress that are relatively healthy and recommend these coping strategies:

- Confront the problem directly.
- Accurately and realistically appraise a stressful situation rather than distorting reality.
- Learn to recognize and manage potentially disruptive emotional reactions to stress.
- Learn to exert behavioral self-control in the face of stress.

In addition to these characteristics, three other strategies for constructively coping with stress are modifying your self-talk, learning to laugh and enjoy humor, and turning stress into strengths. Later in this chapter we discuss other healthy approaches to managing stress, but let's examine these three ideas in more detail now.

Changing Self-Defeating Thoughts and Messages

Your thoughts and what you tell yourself can contribute to your experience of stress. For example, these thoughts about using time often bring about stress: "When I take time for fun, I feel guilty." "I'm constantly feeling rushed, telling

© PhotoDisc/Getty Images

Learning how to use leisure to nurture ourselves is important.

myself that I ought to be doing more and that I should be working faster." "If there were more hours in a day, I'd find more things to do in a day and feel even more stressed."

In Chapter 3 we discussed ways to challenge parental injunctions, cultural messages, and early decisions. Those same principles can be effectively applied to coping with the negative impact of stress. Most stress results from beliefs about the way life is or should be. For example, the pressures you might experience to perform and to conform to external standards are greatly exacerbated by self-talk such as "I must do this job perfectly." You can use the cognitive techniques described in Chapter 3 to deal with certain faulty beliefs based on "shoulds," "oughts," and "musts." If you can change your self-defeating beliefs about living up to external expectations, you are in a position to behave in ways that produce less stress. Even if it is not always possible to change a difficult situation, you can modify your beliefs about the situation. Doing so can result in decreasing the stress you experience. By monitoring your self-talk, you can identify beliefs that create stress. From a personal perspective I (Jerry) know how difficult it is to change certain internalized messages.

JERRY'S STORY

I often listen to messages pertaining to doing more and making full use of my time. People who know me well see the following behavior patterns: being wedded to work, impatience, doing several things at once, getting overly involved in projects, meeting self-imposed deadlines, and a desire to control the universe! Over the years I have realized that I cannot cram my life with activities all year, fragmenting myself with many stressful situations, and then expect a "day off" to rejuvenate my system. Even though I am a somewhat slow learner in this respect, a few years ago I recognized the need to find ways of reducing situations that cause stress and to deal differently with the stresses that are inevitable. It has been useful for me to identify my individual patterns, beliefs, and expectations that lead to stress. Furthermore, I am increasingly making conscious choices about my ways of behaving—recognizing that my choices can result in either stress or inner peace. I continue to learn that changing my thinking and behavior is an ongoing process of self-monitoring and making choices. One more thing—some say that I don't have much stress in my personal life, rather, I just cause it for others!

Acquiring a Sense of Humor

Too many of us take ourselves far too seriously and have a difficult time learning how to enjoy ourselves. If we are overly serious, there is very little room for expressing the joy within us. Laughing at our own folly, our own inconsistencies, and at some of our pretentious ways can be highly therapeutic. Of course, humor should never be directed at belittling others. If we can laugh *with* others this can enhance our relationships. Taking time for play and laughter can be the very medicine we need to combat the negative forces of stress. If we learn to "lighten up," the stresses that impinge upon us can seem far less pressing. Laughter is a healing force; humor can be a powerful antidote to physical illness and stress.

Humor not only acts as a buffer against stress but also provides an outlet for frustration and anger. Humor can allow us to express our fears and a range of feelings without causing distress to ourselves or others (Hales, 2005). Studies exploring the physiological changes caused by laughter show that laughter can release endorphins, stimulate the heart, lower blood pressure, stimulate respiratory activity and oxygen exchange, alter brain wave patterns and breathing rhythms, reduce perceptions of pain, decrease stress-related hormones, and strengthen the immune system (Hales, 2005; Vergeer, 1995). Vergeer states that humor can be considered a transformative agent of healing and an approach for putting stressful situations into a new perspective. John Gottman, who conducts residential workshops with couples, contends that couples who have a sense of humor are more likely to deal successfully with differences, disappointments, and conflicts than those who lack a sense of humor (see Gottman & Silver, 1999).

Tips for Managing Stress

Stress does not have to be a liability. You can transform stress into strength by taking steps to creatively cope with your stress. Although many strategies for stress reduction are based on simple commonsense principles, actually putting them into action is more challenging. As you examine these strategies, identify the ones you are interested in remembering and putting into daily practice.

- Find ways to simplify your life.
- Become more aware of the demands you place on yourself and on others.
- Make the time each day to do something that you enjoy.
- Practice consciously doing one thing at a time.
- When you feel stressed, pause to take a few deep breaths.
- Regularly practice one or more relaxation techniques.
- Strive to live in the present. If you become aware of regretting past actions or worrying about the future, tell yourself that this moment is what counts.
- Practice being kind to yourself and to others.
- Ask others to help you learn to deal effectively with stress.

Even if it is not always possible to change a difficult office situation, you can modify your beliefs about the situation.

To put these techniques into practice, write your favorite tips on a small card that you can look at throughout the day. Simply remembering to stop what you are doing at different times during the day to ask yourself what you are experiencing is a good beginning to significantly reduce your stress level. At these times you can identify your self-talk and learn to give yourself new and more constructive thoughts. Look for the humor in life and remember to smile and laugh more.

A wide variety of stress reduction strategies can be helpful to you in managing the stress in your life. The following sections focus in more detail on a variety of stress buffers that are positive ways to deal with stress.

TIME MANAGEMENT

You can learn to manage your time so you get what you want from your life. There is no one best way to budget your time; you have to find the system that works for you. **Time management** is not an end in itself. If your time management program begins to control you, this is probably a sign that it is best to reevaluate and reset your priorities. Although learning to manage time is essential, too many of us become overly fixated on clock time. In writing about relaxing with time, George (1998) makes this thoughtful statement:

> INCREASINGLY, OUR LIVES ARE RULED by the clock, but clock time is a human invention made to serve us. We must not allow the measurement of time to dominate our thinking, or we will sabotage ourselves in a self-fulfilling cycle of anxiety undermining success. (p. 120)

George admits that many aspects of our lives are necessarily clock-bound, but he suggests that we look for periods when we can pay more attention to the natural inclinations of our body clock rather than a mechanical clock. How many of us have a meal when we are hungry or go to bed when we are tired?

We all have the same amount of time: 24 hours a day, 168 hours a week, and 8,760 hours a year. How people use time varies greatly from individual to individual. Consider time as a valuable resource that enables you to do what you want in your life. The way you choose to use your time is a good indicator of what you value. If you are interested in making better use of your time, a good place to begin is by monitoring your time. Once you have identified how you spend your time, you will be able to make conscious choices of where you want to allocate your limited time.

Using time wisely is related to living a balanced life and is thus a part of wellness. Ask yourself these questions:

• Am I making the time to eat properly, get adequate sleep, and maintain a regular exercise program?

- Do I know where I want to go in the next few months and years?

- Am I generally accomplishing what I have set out to do each day? Is it what I *wanted* to do?

- Do I take the time to balance fun with work? Do I tell myself I do not have time for fun?

- Am I feeling rushed?

- Do I make time for nurturing my significant relationships? If I tell myself that I do not have time for my friends, what is the message here?

- Is there time in my day for meeting my spiritual needs? Do I allow time for quiet reflection of my priorities in life?

- Do I generally like the way I am spending my time? What would I like to be doing more of? What would I like to reduce or cut out in my daily activities?

- How would I like to use time differently than I did yesterday? Last week? Last month?

Time management is a key strategy in managing stress. Indeed, much of the daily stress we experience is probably due to our taking on too many projects at once, not using our time effectively, or procrastinating. Putting things off, especially if they need immediate attention, is a direct route to stress. Although there are some short-term gains to procrastination, in the long run it tends to lead to disappointment, feelings of failure, anxiety, and increased stress. Ask yourself if procrastination has sometimes gotten you into trouble. If you want to change a pattern, ask yourself if the tasks you are putting off are of value to you. If certain tasks are not meaningful to you, it may be best to consider dropping them.

If we are not in control of where our time is going, then time is in control of us. Here are some suggestions for positive actions you can take to remain in charge of your time:

- Reflect on your long-range goals, prioritizing the steps you will take in reaching them. Establish clear and attainable goals. Set goals and reevaluate them periodically.

- Break down long-range goals into smaller goals. Develop a plan of action for reaching subgoals. It will help to break down a project into smaller elements that you are willing to complete at a specific time.

- Be realistic in deciding what you can accomplish in a given period of time.

- Before accepting new projects, think about how realistic it is to fit one more thing into your schedule. Put yourself in the driver's seat, and do not allow others to overload your circuits.

- Make use of a schedule book or a planner so that you can organize your time efficiently. Create a schedule that helps you get done what you want to accomplish. Make use of daily, weekly, monthly, and yearly planners. Make a daily "to do" list to keep yourself from becoming overwhelmed.

- Do not try to do everything yourself. Ask for help from others and learn to delegate.

- Be comfortable with what you accomplish. You cannot be productive every moment. Make time in your schedule for fun, exercise, journal writing, meditation, socializing, and leisure.

- If you do too many things at once, you increase your stress level. Concentrate on doing one thing at a time as well as you can.

- Strive to live in the present moment and experience what is going on now as fully as possible. Avoid ruminating about what you could have done in the past or endlessly planning about the future. Living in the past or in the future makes it difficult to savor present experiences and tends to escalate stress.

As you are learning how to organize your time, you will surely meet with obstacles. You may underestimate how long a project will take, unexpected demands may chew up time you had blocked off for studying, or other external factors may throw off your plans. Be patient with yourself and tolerate some setbacks. Skills in time management take time to acquire. You may hear old voices in your head telling you that you never get done what is important to you. Learn to dispute those internal voices that stand between you and your goals.

MONEY MANAGEMENT

Financial pressures are consistently mentioned by students as a major stressor. Money, like time, is a limited resource that must be spent wisely, and many of the time management tips presented previously can be applied to money management as well. In learning to manage your time, the first step was to track where you spent your time. Likewise, the initial step in managing your financial resources is to discover where your money goes. To do this, we suggest that you monitor all of your expenses for at least one month. Fixed expenses, such as rent and tuition, can be recorded directly on your expense record. Keeping a complete expense record is an important step toward increasing your awareness of how you are spending money. Examine this month-long record and decide the degree to which you are satisfied with your spending habits. You are likely to be surprised at how much you spent in some categories.

The next step in managing your finances is to determine all the sources of income at your disposal. This will allow you to plan a budget. Evaluate whether the way you are spending your money fits your goals and values. Look at each category of expenses and ask yourself if the amount you are spending reflects your goals. One general guideline in budgeting is not to spend more money than you make. If you need help developing your personal budget, courses and workshops in managing personal finances are available through the extended education programs at most colleges.

Credit card spending can also be a real source of stress. This is especially the case if you do not pay off your charges within a reasonable time. The general guideline for good money management is simple: if you don't have it, don't spend it! Preparing a realistic budget and sticking to it is bound to decrease your level of stress. Effective money management can go a long way toward helping you reach your goals.

MEDITATION

Meditation is a process of directing our attention to a single, unchanging, or repetitive stimulus. Meditation may include repetition of a word, sound, phrase, or prayer, but its main purpose is to eliminate mental distractions and relax the body. Fontana (1999) says: "Put simply, meditation is the experience of the limitless nature of the mind when it ceases to be dominated by its usual chatter" (p. 16).

Meditation sharpens our concentration and our thinking power and is aimed at personal transformation. During much of our waking time, we are thinking and engaging in some form of verbalization or inner dialogue. In fact, many of us find it difficult to quiet the internal chatter that typically goes on inside our heads. We are not used to attending to one thing at a time or to fully concentrating on a single action. Oftentimes we miss the present moment by thinking about what we did yesterday or what we will do tomorrow or next year. Meditation is a tool to increase awareness, become centered, and achieve an internal focus. In meditation our attention is focused, and we engage in a single behavior. The process of meditation keeps our attention anchored in the present moment. Our attention is cleansed of preconceptions and distracting input so that we can perceive reality more freshly. Through its ability to help us navigate the mind, meditation restores our capacity for inner listening, allowing us to make the best choices (Borysenko, 1988). Although we narrow our focus of attention when we meditate, the result is an enlarged sense of being.

One answer to our fragmented existence is to practice **mindfulness,** or "bringing the mind home" through meditation (Rinpoche, 1994). George (1998) uses the analogy of the mind being like a desktop—piled high with so much information that we are unable to function effectively. Our minds sometimes become cluttered with worries, regrets, negative self-images, memories, reactions, hopes, and fears, which leads to our true self getting buried deeper and deeper. Meditation is a way to sort out the confusion and to bring about tranquility, enabling us to focus on constructive thoughts and to discover positive images of ourselves. In George's words: "By relaxing our minds through meditation, we can clear our desks and experience a renewed sense of self. This will bring with it identity, clarity and freedom in a cascade of revolutionary thinking" (p. 125).

Meditation is effective in creating a deep state of relaxation in a fairly short time. The meditative state not only induces profound relaxation but also reduces physical and psychological fatigue. Its beneficial effects are numerous, and it has been shown to relieve anxiety and stress-related disease. People who consistently practice meditation show a substantial reduction in the frequency of stress-related symptoms. Some of the physical benefits that can result from the regular practice of meditation include relief from insomnia, lower blood pressure, improved posture, increased energy, and better management of pain (Fontana, 1999). There are also mental benefits of meditation, such as improved tranquility, patience, concentration and memory, and enhanced understanding and empathy for others. Notice how many of the benefits of meditation are strikingly similar to the benefits of regular exercise discussed in Chapter 4.

There are as many different ways to meditate as there are meditators. Some people allow an hour each morning for silence and internal centering. Others find that they can enter a meditative state while walking, jogging, bike riding, or doing T'ai Chi. You do not have to wear exotic garb and sit in a lotus position to meditate. Sitting quietly and letting your mind wander or looking within can be a simple form of meditation.

Some of us may be convinced that we do not have time for morning meditation. However, if we do not carve out time for this centering activity, it is likely that we will be bounced around by events that happen to us throughout the day. To make meditation part of our daily pattern, concerted effort and consistent practice are required. Many writers on meditation recommend a 20- to 30-minute session in the morning. For many of us, this might seem unrealistic. However, if we modify this recommendation to fit our situation, we might discover that devoting some time to centering is beneficial.

It is better to assume a sitting position for meditating rather than lying in bed, and meditating on an empty stomach is recommended for achieving deep meditative states. These exercises must be practiced for at least a month for meditation's more profound effects to be experienced. Several excellent guides to meditation include *Meditation* (Easwaran, 1991), *Going to Pieces Without Falling Apart* (Epstein, 1998), *Learn to Meditate* (Fontana, 1999), *Wherever You Go, There You Are* (Kabat-Zinn, 1994), and *Meditation* (Rinpoche, 1994).

MINDFULNESS

Living by the values of accomplishing and producing, we sometimes forget the importance of experiencing the precious moment unfolding before us. By emphasizing *doing*, we forget the importance of *being*. The idea of mindfulness is that we experience each moment fully. Thich Nhat Hanh (1991) reminds us that we do a good job of *preparing* to live, but that "we have difficulty remembering that we are alive in the present moment, the only moment there is for us to be alive. Every breath we take, every step we make, can be filled with peace, joy, and serenity. We need only to be awake, alive in the present moment" (p. 5). Nhat Hanh (1992) teaches that life is a miracle, which entails appreciating the peace and beauty that surrounds us and is within each of us. He suggests that we can begin the practice of mindfulness by simply paying attention to our breathing. We can then extend this to other facets of our daily life, such as walking.

Mindfulness has the aim of keeping us in the here and now, focusing on *what is* rather than on *what if*. If you are living in the present moment, you are not ruminating about the past or worrying about the future. Living in the present allows you to gain full awareness of whatever actions you are engaged in and to be fully present when you are with another person. This is the essence of living mindfully. Nhat Hanh (1992) teaches that we can transform this moment into a wonderful moment if only we stop running into the future, stop fretting about the past, and stop being focused on accumulating things. It is important to realize that living mindfully in the present does not imply getting rid of the past or the future. Nhat Hanh (1992) captures this idea nicely: "As you touch the present moment, you realize that the present is made of the past and is creating the future. Touching the present, you touch the past and the future at the same time" (p. 123).

Mindfulness is like meditation in that the aim is to clear our mind and calm our body. Mindfulness helps us to slow down and experience what we are doing. It is a state of active attention that involves focusing on here-and-now awareness. Mindfulness is "meditation in action" involving being present to our experience (Borysenko, 1988). Easwaran (1991) encourages us to slow down if we hope to acquire a mindful approach to living. If we are driven by a hectic and hurried pace, we become robotlike with little freedom and no choices. Easwaran believes that if we want freedom of action, good relations with others, health and vitality, and a calm and clear mind, it is essential that we make strides in slowing down. He teaches that as we acquire the skills of mindfulness, our senses become keener, our thinking patterns become more lucid, and we increase our sensitivity to the needs of others.

The ability to observe our physical, emotional, and mental activities with a degree of nonjudgmental detachment enables us to become increasingly aware of what we do and say. George (1998) reminds us that

> WE ALL HAVE A CHOICE. We can live life in the "fast lane," pushing ourselves hard from one experience to the next, until one day we can push ourselves no more; or we can turn off the superhighway to follow the quieter, slower roads that encourage our driving skills, rather than our driving speed. Ultimately, we may reach the same destination. However, the different routes by which we travel there will determine the state of our mind and body on arrival. (p. 11)

Jon Kabat-Zinn (1990) describes some basic attitudes necessary to the practice of mindfulness:

- Do not judge. Become aware of automatic judging thoughts that pass through your mind.
- Be open to each moment, realizing that some things cannot be hurried.
- See everything as if you are looking at it for the first time.
- Learn to trust your intuitions.
- Rather than striving for results, focus on accepting things as they are.
- Develop an accepting attitude.
- Let go. Turn your mind off and simply let go of thoughts.

Mindfulness is not limited to periods of formal practice; rather, it is meant to become a way of life and something that we can practice throughout our daily existence.

Two useful books on the subject of mindfulness by Jon Kabat-Zinn are *Full Catastrophe Living* (1990) and *Wherever You Go, There You Are* (1994).

DEEP RELAXATION

You don't have to settle for a range of psychophysiological problems such as indigestion, backaches, insomnia, and headaches as part of your life. If you can genuinely learn to relax and take care of yourself in positive and nurturing ways, you will enhance your life and the lives of the people close to you.

One of the best ways to stop our frantic pace is by learning and practicing breathing. Breathing is an effective way to control unhappiness, agitation, fear, anxiety, and anger (Nhat Hanh, 1992). Take a few moments right now to become aware of your breathing. Breathing is our most natural instinct, but many of us have forgotten how to breathe. Relearning the correct way to breathe can have a significant impact on our well-being and can contribute to our ability to relax. If we are not able to breathe properly, we cannot fully relax our body and our mind (George, 1998).

Now devote a few moments to reflecting on how you relax. Do you engage in certain forms of relaxation on a regular basis? Are you able to stop and incorporate relaxation into your everyday routines? What do you consider to be relaxing? What would you be doing if you increased the quantity and quality of your relaxation time?

Williams and Knight (1994) describe a **progressive muscular relaxation** technique that they recommend be practiced for 10 to 20 minutes. This form of deep relaxation involves these steps:

- Get comfortable, be quiet, and close your eyes.
- Pay attention to your breathing. Breathe in slowly through your nose. Exhale slowly through your mouth.

- Clench and release your muscles. Tense and relax each part of your body two or more times. Clench while inhaling; release while exhaling.
- Tense and relax, proceeding through each muscle group.

Herbert Benson (1976, 1984), a Harvard cardiologist, described a simple meditative technique that has helped many people cope with stress. Benson's experiments revealed how it is possible to learn to control blood pressure, body temperature, respiration rate, heart rate, and oxygen consumption through the use of what he called the **relaxation response.** Benson's work demonstrates that it is possible to make use of self-regulatory, noninvasive techniques in the prevention of stress-related illnesses. In his studies participants achieved a state of deep relaxation by repeating a mantra (a word used to focus attention, such as *om*). He described the following three factors as crucial to inducing this state:

- Find a quiet place with a minimum of external distractions. The quiet environment contributes to the effectiveness of the repeated word or phrase by making it easier to eliminate distracting thoughts.
- Find an object or mantra to focus your attention on and let thoughts simply pass by. What is important is to concentrate on one thing only and learn to eliminate internal mental distractions as well as external ones.
- Adopt a passive attitude, which includes letting go of thoughts and distractions and simply returning to the object you are dwelling on. A passive attitude implies a willingness to let go of evaluating yourself and to avoid the usual thinking and planning.

In writing about choosing a suitable relaxation technique, Feuerstein and Bodian (1993) make it clear that there is no perfect technique that will miraculously make stress disappear. All methods of deep relaxation require the individual to assume a great deal of responsibility. For most of us, it has taken years to build up tension patterns. It stands to reason that it will take effort and perseverance to overcome years of negative mental and physical conditioning. Feuerstein and Bodian provide this encouragement:

> IF YOU HAVE NEVER ENGAGED in regular psychophysical discipline, you may be surprised at how long it can take you to develop the ability to relax deeply. In any case, don't lose heart. The importance of relaxation techniques in reducing stress and increasing immune system function has been well documented, so your patience will be well rewarded. (p. 117)

In the complex society most of us live in, you will inevitably encounter obstacles to fully relaxing. Even if you take a few moments in a busy schedule to unwind, your mind may be reeling with thoughts of past or future events. Another problem is simply finding a quiet and private place where you can relax and a time free from interruptions. Learn how to let go for even a few minutes so you can unwind while waiting in a line or riding on a bus. Deep relaxation is a powerful positive response to stress.

Yoga is a path to health
and wellness.

YOGA

Over the past three decades yoga has become quite popular throughout the
Western world, and it appeals to a wide range of people, from children to the elderly, with all levels of abilities. This brief section on yoga consists of a summary
of a few of the points Feuerstein and Bodian (1993) make about the practice of
yoga in their book *Living Yoga: A Comprehensive Guide for Daily Life.*

Yoga is not simply a form of calisthenics, a system of meditation, or a religion. However, like meditation and mindfulness, yoga is a way of life. Yoga is

about doing the best you can at that day or time, without comparing yourself to others. As a noncompetitive activity, yoga enables you to see the strengths you already have and to build on those strengths. Those who practice yoga have a personal goal. Some of the goals that motivate people to engage in yoga are to reduce stress, expand awareness, deepen spirituality, or provide greater flexibility. It is important to know your goals so you can choose a form of yoga that fits your needs.

In addition to managing stress, yoga provides numerous health benefits in both prevention and treatment of illnesses. For years Eastern health practitioners have known of the health value of practicing yoga, and now Western doctors are acknowledging the significant health benefits of yoga. Some of these benefits include lowering blood pressure and cholesterol levels and decreasing problems associated with chronic illnesses such as arthritis, rheumatism, back pain, digestive disorders, insomnia, diabetes, migraines and headaches, varicose veins, and obesity (Choudhury, 1978). Specific types of yoga can work on both internal and external organs as well as on the muscular and skeletal systems. If this is a practice you would like to develop, the chances are that you will find yoga classes in your area.

THERAPEUTIC MASSAGE

In many European countries, and in Eastern cultures as well, massage is a well-known way to enhance health. In fact, physicians often prescribe therapeutic massage and mineral baths to counter the negative effects of stress. Massage is a legitimate route to maintaining wellness and coping with stress, but use caution in selecting a reputable practitioner.

Earlier we talked of the need for touch to maintain the well-being of the body and mind, and we also mentioned how the body tells the truth. Massage is one way of meeting the need for touch; it is also a way to discover where and how you are holding onto the tension produced by stressful situations. Practitioners who have studied physical therapy and therapeutic massage say that the body is the place where changes need to be made if long-lasting psychological changes are to result.

Massage therapy has been popularized recently as a part of alternative medicine. The benefits of massage therapy include facilitating growth, reducing pain, increasing alertness, reducing depression, and enhancing immune function (Field, 1998). Therapeutic massage is an excellent way to develop awareness of the difference between tension and relaxation states and to learn how to release the muscular tightness that so often results when you encounter stress. It is also a good way to learn how to receive the caring touch of another.

Take Time to Reflect

1. Identify a few specific areas of your life that you find most stressful (for example, trying to balance school with work, attempting to do too much in too short a time, problems with relationships, critical self-talk). What would help you to reduce your stress in these areas?

_____

_____

2. How might your telling others about all that is stressing you prevent you from really talking to others and making contact with them? Can you think of ways that you can keep yourself hidden by focusing on what stresses you?

_____

_____

3. This self-inventory is designed to assist you in pinpointing some specific ways you might better manage stress. Check all of the statements that express a goal that has meaning for you or describes a form of behavior you would like to acquire.

_____ I avoid using drugs and alcohol as a way to cope with stressful situations.
_____ I am interested in paying attention to the subtle signs of burnout, so I can take action before advanced stages of burnout set in.
_____ Learning time management skills is a priority for me.
_____ I am willing to make a schedule as a way to better organize my time.
_____ My negative self-talk often results in stressing me out. I would like to identify those thoughts that get in my way and challenge my thinking.
_____ Meditation is a practice I would be willing to experiment with for at least a month as a way to center myself and better manage stress.
_____ Mindfulness requires experiencing each moment as fully as possible. I want to acquire the kind of attention that involves focusing on here-and-now awareness.
_____ Taking short relaxation breaks appeals to me, and I am willing to do what it takes to learn relaxation methods.

4. This time management inventory can help you recognize your own time traps. Decide whether each statement is more true or more false as it applies to you and place a T for true or an F for false in the space provided.

_____ I often find myself taking on tasks because I am the only one who can do them.
_____ I often feel overwhelmed because I try to do too much in too little time.
_____ No matter how much I do, I feel that I am always behind and never quite caught up.

_____ I frequently miss deadlines.

_____ I often procrastinate.

_____ I tend to be a perfectionist, and this keeps me from enjoying my accomplishments.

_____ I am bothered by many unscheduled interruptions when doing important work.

_____ I am aware of hurrying much of the time and feeling hassled.

_____ I have a hard time getting to important tasks and sticking to them.

5. What behaviors would you most like to improve with respect to managing your time?

_____

_____

6. What beliefs or attitudes make it difficult for you to cope with stress? In other words, what do you sometimes tell yourself that increases your level of stress?

_____

_____

7. What behaviors are you willing to work on to gain better control over the stressors in your life?

_____

_____

Now that you have finished reading this chapter and completing this Take Time to Reflect, consider some of the ways you can manage the stresses you face. Reflect on some of the ways that you can take better care of yourself through practices such as meditation, relaxation exercise, paying attention to your spiritual life, maintaining good nutritional habits, getting adequate sleep and rest, and participating in a regular exercise program. Ask yourself whether your daily behavior provides evidence that you value your physical, psychological, social, and spiritual health. Once you have made this assessment, decide on a few areas you would like to improve. We suggest that you record these goals in your journal. Then begin working on a plan to change one aspect at a time. Even small changes can lead to significant improvements for you and those close to you.

SUMMARY

We cannot realistically expect to eliminate stress from our life, but we can modify our way of thinking and our behavior patterns to reduce stressful situations and manage stress more effectively. The way we process and interpret the stress of daily living has a lot to do with our mental attitude. Stress affects us physically as well as psychologically.

Conquering stress requires a willingness to accept responsibility for what we are doing to our body. We do well to listen to the messages our body gives us. If we are feeling the effects of stress in our body, this is a signal to pay attention and change what we are thinking and doing.

Remember that you are a whole being, which implies an integration of your physical, emotional, social, mental, and spiritual dimensions. If you neglect any one of these aspects of your self, you will feel the impact on the other dimensions of your being. Reflect on how well you are taking care of yourself physically, emotionally, socially, and spiritually. Ask yourself the degree to which you know your priorities and are acting on them.

In this chapter we have described a number of strategies for effectively managing stress. There is no one right way to cope with stress, which means you are challenged to devise your own personal approach to handle the stresses of daily life. Be willing to reach out to others and ask for help in more effectively dealing with stress. Although you may not be able to eliminate certain stressors in your life, there is a lot that you can do. By focusing on constructive reactions to stress and taking action, you gain personal power that enables you to manage stress instead of letting stress control you. You can apply some of the approaches that were described in this chapter to attain your goals of self-care. What is important is that you develop your own methods of self-care and consistently work at applying them to a variety of situations in everyday living.

Where Can I Go From Here?

1. How are you coping with stress? Keep an account in your journal for 1 week of the stressful situations you encounter. After each entry, note these items: To what degree was the situation stressful because of your thoughts, beliefs, and assumptions about the events? How were you affected? Do you see any ways of dealing with these stresses more effectively?

2. How are you using your time? Take an inventory of how you use your time. Be consistent in recording what you do. Keep a log of your activities for at least 1 week (2 weeks would be better) to see where your time is going. Carry a pocket notebook. Write down what you have done a couple of times each hour. After a week, add up the hours you are spending on personal, social, job, and academic activities. Then ask yourself these questions:

- Am I spending my time the way I want to?
- Am I accomplishing what I have set out to do each day? Is it what I wanted to do?
- Am I feeling rushed?

- Am I spending too much time watching television?

- Am I balancing activities that I need to do with ones that I enjoy?

- How would I like to use time differently than I did last week?

- How well am I currently managing time?

3. List three to five things you can do to feel better when you are experiencing stress (meditate, engage in deep breathing, exercise, talk to a friend, and so forth). Put this list where you can see it easily, and use it as a reminder that you have some ways to reduce stress.

4. Identify some environmental sources of stress or other stresses that are external to you. Finding a parking spot, navigating in rush hour traffic, and noise are all external factors that can put a strain on you. Once you have identified external stressors, write in your journal about how you might deal with them differently. What ways could a change in your thinking or adopting a new attitude change the impact of these external sources of stress?

5. How does stress affect your body? For at least 1 week (2 weeks would be better) record how daily stresses show up in bodily symptoms. Do you have headaches? Are you troubled with muscular aches? Do you have trouble sleeping? Does stress affect your appetite?

6. Consider the constructive ways to cope with stress presented in this chapter. Might some of these stress management strategies help you keep stress from getting the best of you? If you can select even two or three new stress management strategies and begin to practice them regularly (such as relaxation exercises, meditation, or humor), your ability to effectively curb the effects of stress are likely to be significantly improved. Write out a plan for practicing these techniques and make a commitment to a friend on what you are willing to do to better deal with your stress.

Resources for Future Study

Web Site Resources

STRESS AND YOU
http://www.chronicfatigue.org/History.html

This site is the realization of a long-held dream of Dr. Gerald E. Poesnecker. It is a part of the Chronic Fatigue Unmasked Web site and describes the biological effects of stress including the general adaptation syndrome, hypoadrenalism, and chronic fatigue. It discusses the signs of chronic fatigue and makes suggestions about getting help for it.

WESLEY SIME: STRESS MANAGEMENT
AND PEAK PERFORMANCE
http://tc.unl.edu/stress/

This site by professor and author Wesley E. Sime offers great resources on the fundamentals of stress management and an educational online tutorial.

STRESS ASSESS: NATIONAL WELLNESS INSTITUTE
**http://wellness.uwsp.edu/Health_Service/
services/stress.shtml**

This site offers an evaluation in the areas of stress sources, distress symptoms, and stress balancing strategies.

AMERICAN INSTITUTE OF STRESS
http://www.stress.org

This site provides a wealth of information and statistics on stress. American Institute of Stress addresses the following aspects of stress:

- The role of stress in health and illness

- The nature and importance of mind-body relationships

- Our inherent and immense potential for self-healing

NATIONAL INSTITUTE ON ALCOHOL ABUSE AND ALCOHOLISM (NIAAA)
http://www.niaaa.nih.gov/

The NIAAA is a part of the National Institutes of Health and provides this site, which includes resources and references about alcohol abuse and alcoholism. Included are links to publications and databases such as the National Library of Medicine Databases and Electronic Sources, press releases, conferences, and research programs.

WEB OF ADDICTIONS
http://www.well.com/user/woa/

This site by Andrew L. Homer and Dick Dillon is dedicated to providing accurate information about alcohol and other drug addictions, serving as a resource for teachers and students who "need factual information on abused drugs." It provides a collection of fact sheets arranged by drug, links to other resources, contact information for a variety of groups, meetings/conferences related to addictions, in-depth information on special topics, and places to get help with addictions.

JOB STRESS NETWORK
http://www.workhealth.org

This site offers information on job strain, projects, risk factors, and outcomes.

STRESS, TRAUMA, ANXIETY, FEARS, AND PSYCHOSOMATIC DISORDERS
http://www.mentalhelp.org/psyhelp/chap5/

This resource offers a good discussion of the nature of stress and its relationship to psychological and physical disorders. Some of the topics that are included in this chapter include: signs of stress; sources and types of stress; woundology; theories explaining stress and anxiety; ways of handling stress and anxiety; and treatment of specific anxiety-based problems.

MIND TOOLS™
http://www.mindtools.com/index.html

Mind Tools is dedicated to "helping you to think your way to an excellent life." This site provides shareware and practical suggestions for problem solving, memory improvement, increasing creativity, mastering stress, time management, goal-setting, links to stress/time management book stores, and much more.

 InfoTrac College Edition Resources

For additional readings, explore INFOTRAC COLLEGE EDITION, our online library:
http://www.infotrac.college.com/wadsworth

Hint: Enter these search terms:

stress management	yoga
time management	burnout
money management	psychosomatic illness
meditation	psychophysiological
mindfulness	

Print Resources

Benson, H. (1984). *Beyond the relaxation response.* New York: Berkeley Books.

Borysenko, J. (1988). *Minding the body, mending the mind.* New York: Bantam.

Carlson, R. (1997). *Don't sweat the small stuff . . . and it's all small stuff.* New York: Hyperion.

Easwaran, E. (1991). *Meditation.* Tomales, CA: Nilgiri Press.

Epstein, M. (1998). *Going to pieces without falling apart: A Buddhist perspective on wholeness.* New York: Broadway Books.

Feuerstein, G., & Bodian, S. (Eds.). (1993). *Living yoga: A comprehensive guide for daily life.* New York: Jeremy P. Tarcher/Putnam Books.

Fontana, D. (1999). *Learn to meditate: A practical guide to self-discovery and fulfillment.* San Francisco: Chronicle Books.

George, M. (1988). *Learn to relax: A practical guide to easing tension and conquering stress.* San Francisco: Chronicle Books.

Gunaratana, J. (1991). *Mindfulness in plain English.* Boston: Wisdom Publications.

Hales, D. (2005). *An invitation to health* (11th ed.). Belmont, CA: Wadsworth/Thomson Learning.

Nhat Hanh, T. (1992). *Touching peace: Practicing the art of mindful living.* Berkeley, CA: Parallax Press.

Nhat Hanh, T. (1997). *Peace is every step: The path of mindfulness in everyday life.* New York: Bantam Books.

Kabat-Zinn, J. (1990). *Full catastrophe living.* New York: Delacorte.

Kabat-Zinn, J. (1994). *Wherever you go, there you are: Mindfulness meditation in everyday life.* New York: Hyperion.

Rice, P. L. (1999). *Stress and health* (3rd ed.). Pacific Grove, CA: Brooks/Cole.

Rinpoche, S. (1994). *Meditation.* San Francisco: Harper.

Segal, Z. V., Williams, J. M., & Teasdale, J. D. (2002). *Mindful-based cognitive therapy for depression: A new approach to preventing relapse.* New York: Guilford.

Smith, C., & Sulsky, L. (2005). *Work stress.* Belmont, CA: Thomson Wadsworth.

6

If you want to live forever, love someone.

—Bernie Siegel

Love

Where Am I Now?

Use this scale to respond to these statements:

3 = This statement is true of me *most* of the time.

2 = This statement is true of me *some* of the time.

1 = This statement is true of me *almost none* of the time.

1. My parents showed healthy patterns of love.

2. I have a fear of losing another's love.

3. When I experience hurt or frustration in love, I find it more difficult to trust and love again.

4. I reveal myself in significant ways to those I love.

5. I am able to express loving feelings toward members of the same sex.

6. I am afraid of being accepted by those I love, and I am afraid of being rejected.

7. I realize that allowing myself to love involves both risk and joy.

8. In my loving relationships I experience trust and an absence of fear.

9. I accept those whom I love as they are, without expecting them to be different.

10. I need constant closeness and intimacy with those I love.

I n this chapter we ask you to look carefully at your style of loving by looking at the way you give and receive love. Look at the situations you create for yourself and consider how conducive these are to loving. What does love mean to you? How do you see love, intimate relationships, and sexuality as being interrelated? What makes love authentic for you? How capable are you of creating a climate in which love can flourish? Are your perceptions of love unrealistic? If so, how can you change them?

Love, as universal as it is, is not an easy subject to delve into. There are probably as many definitions of love as there are people experiencing it. In this chapter we speak about love in a way that makes it possible for you to examine your ways of loving even though you may have a very personal definition of it.

The notion of "falling in love" describes the emotion of love as it is experienced between two people typically feeling a strong physical attraction. This is a very powerful experience and oftentimes leads to a relationship. Relationships typically require a lot more than an emotion, no matter how strong the emotion may be. Relationships require loving behavior. In other words, there has to be consistency between my saying "I love you" and how I behave toward you. This kind of love is found in all loving relationships, and the behaviors of love enable the emotion of love to grow and endure. We focus on the behaviors of love because this is the area where relationships either grow or diminish. When we talk of loving oneself in this chapter, we are not talking so much about an emotional love for oneself as much as a respect, an appreciation for how we are in our world, and liking the way we behave toward others, especially those we profess to love. If we do not have this kind of love for ourselves, then in time we will be unable to accept the love, respect, and appreciation of others for us.

Love as a behavior can make living worthwhile, even during hard times. There is meaning to be found in actively caring for others and in helping them make their lives better. When we allow ourselves to love other people, we risk the possibility that they may move away, leaving us more painfully alone than we were before. Love involves commitment, which is the foundation of any genuinely loving relationship. Although commitment does not guarantee a successful relationship, it is perhaps one of the most important factors in setting the stage for nurturing and fostering a relationship.

There are many kinds of loving relationships. There is the love between parent and child, love between siblings, between friends, and romantic relationships. These various types of love have some very real differences, but all forms of genuine love embody the characteristics we have described in one way or another.

One of the purposes of this chapter is to help you clarify your views and values pertaining to love. As you read, try to apply the discussion to your own experience of love, and consider the degree to which you are now able to appreciate and love yourself. As you review your desire for love as well as your fears of loving, you are likely to recognize barriers within you that prevent you from fully experiencing love.

LOVE MAKES A DIFFERENCE

To fully develop as a person and enjoy a meaningful existence, we need to care about others and have others care about us. A loveless life is often lived in isolation and alienation. The need for love includes the need to know that our existence makes a difference to others. When we exclude physical and emotional closeness with others, we create emotional and physical deprivation.

Love in some ways never ends. Love does not have to end even with death. In *Tuesdays With Morrie,* Mitch Albom (1997) recounts a series of conversations with Morrie Schwartz, who talks about how our love for others keeps them alive in our memory. Before his death, Morrie Schwartz spoke about how "death ends a life, but not a relationship."

> AS LONG AS WE CAN LOVE EACH OTHER, and remember the feeling of love we had, we can die without ever really going away. All the love you created is still there. All the memories are still there. You live on—in the hearts of everyone you have touched and nurtured while you were here. (p. 174)

When Albom asked Morrie if he worried about being forgotten after he died, Morrie replied: "I don't think I will be. I've got so many people who have been involved with me in close, intimate ways. And love is how you stay alive, even after you are gone" (p. 133). Love can transcend death as others remember us and keep their love for us alive. Our influence in their lives may live on even after we die.

Love is expressed in many different ways. Consider the following statements:

- I need to have someone in my life I can actively care for. I need to let that person know he [she] makes a difference in my life, and I need to know I make a difference in his [her] life.

- I want to feel loved and accepted for who I am now, not for living up to others' expectations of me.

- Although I have a need for connection with people, I also enjoy my time alone.

- I am finding out that I have more of a capacity to give something to others than I had thought.

- I am beginning to realize that I need to love and appreciate myself more fully, in spite of my imperfections. If I can accept myself for who I am, then maybe I can accept love from others.

- There are special times when I want to share my joys, my dreams, my anxieties, and my uncertainties with another person. When I am listened to, I feel loved.

To enjoy a meaningful existence, we need to care about others and have others care about us.

© PhotoDisc/Getty Images

We can harden ourselves so as not to experience a need for love. We can close ourselves off from others; we can isolate ourselves by never reaching out to another; we can refuse to trust others and to make ourselves vulnerable; we can cling to an early perception that we are basically unlovable. In whatever way we do this, we pay a price.

Our love for others or their love for us may enable us to live, even in conditions of extreme hardship. In the Nazi concentration camp where he was imprisoned, Frankl (1963) noted that some of those who kept alive the images of those they loved and retained some measure of hope survived the ordeal, whereas those who gave up hope of being united with loved ones succumbed.

LEARNING TO LOVE AND APPRECIATE OURSELVES

In our counseling sessions clients are sometimes surprised when we ask them what they like about themselves. They look uncomfortable and embarrassed. They find it easier to talk about how they see themselves in positive ways if we say to them: "If your best friends were here, how would they describe you?"

© PhotoDisc/Getty Images

Active love is something we can choose to share with others.

"What characteristics would they ascribe to you?" "What reasons might they give for choosing you as a friend?"

Some have been brought up to think that it is egocentric to talk about self-love. But unless we learn how to love ourselves, we will encounter difficulties in loving others and in allowing them to love us. We cannot give to others what we do not possess ourselves. If we are able to appreciate our own worth, then we are better able to accept the love from others. This could even include loving an enemy. Nhat Hanh (1997) speaks about self-love as a prerequisite for loving others: "If you are not yet able to love yourself, you will not be able to love your enemy. But when you are able to love yourself, you can love anyone" (p. 37).

Having love for ourselves does not mean having an exaggerated picture of our own importance or placing ourselves above others or at the center of the universe. Rather, it means having respect for ourselves even though we are imperfect. It entails caring about our lives and striving to become the people we want to be.

Many writers have stressed the necessity of self-love as a condition of love for others. In *The Art of Loving*, Fromm (1956) describes self-love as respect for our own integrity and uniqueness and maintains that it cannot be separated from love and understanding of others. We often ask clients who only give to others and who have a difficult time taking for themselves: "Do you deserve what you so freely give to others?" "If your own well runs dry, how will you be able to give to others?" We cannot give what we have not learned and experienced ourselves. Moore (1994) writes that those who try very hard to be loved do not succeed because they do not realize that they have to first love themselves as others before they can receive love from others.

As we learn to treat ourselves with increasing respect and regard, we increase our ability to fully accept the love others might want to give us; at the same time, we have the foundation for genuinely loving them. Caring for ourselves and caring for others are very much connected.

AUTHENTIC AND INAUTHENTIC LOVE

Authentic love enhances us and those we love. In this section we share some of the positive meanings love has for us.

Love means that I am coming to *know* the person I love. I am aware of the many facets of the other person—not just the beautiful side but also the limitations, inconsistencies, and flaws. I have an awareness of the other's feelings and thoughts, and I experience something of the depth of that person. I can penetrate masks and roles and see the other person on a deeper level. Love also entails making myself known to the other person. Meaningful self-disclosure is essential to establishing loving relationships, especially revealing the deeper facets of ourselves.

Love means that I *care* about the welfare of the person I love and I actively *demonstrate concern* for the other. If my love is genuine, my caring is not a smothering of the person or a possessive clinging. On the contrary, my caring enhances both of us. If I care about you, I am concerned about your growth, and I hope you will become all that you can be. We do more than just talk about how much we value each other. Our actions show our care and concern more eloquently than any words. Each of us has a desire to give to the other. We have an interest in each other's welfare and a desire to see that the other person is fulfilled.

Love means having *respect* for the *dignity* of the person I love. If I love you, I can see you as a separate person, with your own values and thoughts and feelings, and I do not insist that you surrender your identity and conform to an image of what I expect you to be for me. I am not threatened by your ability to stand alone and to be who you are. I avoid treating you as an object or using you primarily to gratify my needs.

© Heidi Jo Corey

Love means making a commitment.

Love means having a *responsibility* toward the person I love. If I love you, I am responsive to what you need. This responsibility does not entail my doing for you in a way that communicates that you are incapable of doing it yourself. It does mean acknowledging that what I am and what I do affects you; I am concerned about your happiness and your sadness. I have the realization that I have the capacity to hurt or neglect you. Nhat Hanh (1992) states: "True love includes a sense of responsibility and accepting the other person as he or she is, with all strengths and weaknesses. If you like only the best things in a person, that is not love" (p. 85). He adds that authentic love implies accepting another person's weaknesses and bringing patience and understanding to help the person transform.

Love can lead to *growth* for both the person I love and me. If I love you, I am growing as a result of my love for you. You are a stimulant for me to become more fully what I might be, and my loving enhances your being as well. We each grow as a result of caring and being cared for; we each share in an enriching experience that does not detract from our being.

Love means making a *commitment* to the person I love. Commitment to another person involves risks, but commitment is the essential context of an intimate relationship. This means that the people involved have invested in their future together and that they are willing to stay with each other in times of crisis and conflict. Commitment entails a willingness to stay with each other in times of pain, uncertainty, struggle, and despair, as well as in times of calm and enjoyment. Although some people have difficulties with long-term commitments in a relationship, to what degree will they allow themselves to be loved or make themselves vulnerable if they believe the relationship is temporary? Perhaps, for some, a fear of intimacy gets in the way of developing a sense of commitment. Loving and being loved is both exciting and frightening, and we may have to struggle with the issue of how much anxiety we can tolerate.

Love means that I am *vulnerable*. Love involves allowing you to matter to me in spite of my fear of losing you. You have the capacity to hurt me as much as I am capable of hurting you. There are no guarantees that our love will endure. My love for you implies that I want to spend time with you and share meaningful aspects of my life with you.

Love means *trusting the person you love*. If I love you, I trust that you will accept my caring and my love and that you will not deliberately hurt me. I trust that you will find me lovable and that you want to be with me. I trust the reciprocal nature of our love. If we trust each other, we are willing to be open to each other and can shed masks and pretenses and reveal our true selves.

Love means *trusting yourself*. In relationships a great deal is made of trusting the person you love, yet the ability to trust yourself is equally important. Indeed, if your trust in yourself wavers, you may not be able to believe or trust in the love another wants to share with you.

Love allows for *imperfection*. Although our love relationship may be strained at times and we may feel like giving up, we have the intention of riding out challenging times. Authentic love does not imply a perfect state of happiness. We remember what we had together in the past and can envision what we will have together in our future.

Love is *freely given*. My love for you is not contingent on whether you fulfill my expectations of you. Authentic love does not mean "I'll love you when you become perfect or when you become what I expect you to become." Authentic love is not given with strings attached. There is an unconditional quality about love.

Love is *expansive*. If I love you, I encourage you to reach out and develop other relationships. Although our love for each other and our commitment to each other precludes certain actions on our parts with others, we are not totally and exclusively wedded to each other. Only a false love cements one person to another in such a way that he or she is not given room to have other meaningful relationships.

Love means that although I *want* you in my life, I am capable of functioning without you. If life is meaningless without you, it will put a lot of demands on you to be there for me. If I love you and you leave, I will experience a great loss, but I will not be destroyed. If I am overly dependent on you for my meaning and my survival, I am not free to challenge our relationship, and this is hardly a healthy sign of love.

Love means *identifying* with the person I love. If I love you, I can empathize with you, see the world through your eyes, and identify with you. This closeness does not imply a continual togetherness, for distance and separation are part of a loving relationship. Distance can intensify a loving bond, and it can help us rediscover ourselves, so that we are able to meet each other in a new way.

Love involves *seeing the potential* within the person I love. If I love you, I am able to see you as the person you can become, while still accepting who you are now. Goethe's observation is relevant here: "By taking people as they are, we make them worse, but by treating them as if they already were what they ought to be, we help make them better."

Love means *letting go* of the illusion of total control of ourselves, others, and our environment. The more I strive for complete control, the more out of control I am. Loving implies a surrender of control and being open to life's events. It implies the capacity to be surprised.

We conclude this discussion of the meanings that authentic love has for us by sharing the prayer of Saint Francis of Assisi, which to us embodies the essence of authentic love. Born in 1181, St. Francis, the founder of the Franciscan Order, is associated with the love of nature and peace among all people. Maier (1991) cites the prayer of Saint Francis of Assisi as illustrative of a heart that is filled with unconditional love. Easwaran (1991) recommends memorizing this prayer and using it as a basis for daily meditation and personal reflection. Regardless of one's possible religious affiliation or spiritual beliefs, there is an in-depth message in this prayer, which we found reproduced on a sign in the garden of the Santa Barbara Mission. Easwaran believes the words of this prayer have an almost universal appeal.

> LORD, MAKE ME AN INSTRUMENT OF YOUR PEACE.
> Where there is hatred, let me sow love;
> Where there is injury, pardon;
> Where there is doubt, faith;
> Where there is despair, hope;
> Where there is darkness, light;
> Where there is sadness, joy;
> O divine Master, grant that I may not
>   so much seek
> To be consoled as to console;
> To be understood as to understand;
> To be loved, as to love;
> For it is in giving that we receive;
> It is in pardoning that we are pardoned;
> It is in dying that we are born
>   to eternal life.

We have discussed our views on authentic love, and now we turn to an examination of the characteristics of inauthentic or false love, which has a detrimental effect on those we say we love. This list is not definitive, yet it may give you some ideas to use in thinking about the quality of your love. From our perspective, a person whose love is inauthentic:

- Needs to be in charge and make decisions for the other person.
- Has rigid and unrealistic expectations of how the other person must act to be worthy of love.
- Attaches strings to loving and loves conditionally.
- Puts little trust in the love relationship.
- Perceives personal change as a threat to the continuation of the relationship.
- Is possessive.
- Depends on the other person to fill a void in life.
- Lacks commitment.
- Is unwilling to share important thoughts and feelings about the relationship.

Most of us can find some of these manifestations of inauthentic love in our relationships, yet this does not mean that our love is necessarily inauthentic. For instance, at times you may be reluctant to let another person know about your private life, you may have excessive expectations of another person, or you may attempt to impose your own agenda. It is essential to be honest with yourself and to recognize when you are not expressing genuine love, then you can choose to change these patterns.

Take Time to Reflect

1. Examine your thoughts about opening yourself to loving another person, and complete these sentences:

   It is worth it to love because _____

   It is not worth it to love because _____

2. List some of the meanings love has for you.

   _____

   _____

3. Think of someone you love. What specifically do you love about that person? Then list some ways or times when you fail to demonstrate love for that person.

   _____

   _____

4. What are some specific steps you can take to allow others to love you more fully?

_____

_____

5. What are some steps you can take to demonstrate your love for others?

_____

_____

6. Reflect on the prayer of Saint Francis of Assisi, looking for aspects that capture what you consider to be the essence of actively loving others. What personal meaning does this prayer have for you?

_____

_____

BARRIERS TO LOVING AND BEING LOVED

Myths and Misconceptions About Love

Our culture influences our views of connection, love, intimacy, and relationships. We receive messages from our culture that can enhance our ability to give and receive love—and we also receive messages that make it difficult for us to experience love. We may have unconsciously accepted some myths about love that prevent us from forming realistic views of the nature of love. Our ability to love fully and to receive love from others is certainly influenced by such views, some of which are based on what we have heard and accepted from our culture. Our culture, especially the media, influences us on issues of loving. If we hope to challenge these myths, we must take a critical look at the messages we have received from society about the essence of love. In the following pages we present our views on some common beliefs that we think are worth examining.

The Myth of Eternal Love The notion that love will endure forever without any change is unrealistic. Although love can last over a period of time, love takes on different forms as the relationship matures. Love is complex and involves both joyful experiences and difficulties. The intensity of your love changes as you change. You may experience several stages of love with one person, deepening your love and finding new levels of richness. Conversely, you and your partner may become stagnant and the love you once shared fades.

The Myth That Love Implies Constant Closeness Betina and Luis dated throughout junior high and high school, and they went to college together because they could not tolerate any separation. They make no new friends, either with the same or opposite sex, and they show extreme signs of jealousy when the other indicates even the slightest interest in wanting to be with others. Rather than creating a better balance of time with each other and time with others, the only alternative they see is to terminate their relationship. The mistaken assumption they are operating on is that if they loved each other they would not have any need for other relationships.

Many of us can tolerate only so much closeness, and at times we are likely to need some distance from others. Another way of looking at it is that we have a dual need for both closeness with others and for solitude. Gibran's (1923) words in *The Prophet* are still timely: "And stand together yet not too near together: For the pillars of the temple stand apart, and the oak tree and the cypress grow not in each other's shadow" (p. 17).

There are times when a separation from our loved one can be beneficial. At these times we can renew our desire for the other person and also become centered again. Consider the case of Martin. He refused to spend a weekend without his wife and children, even though he said he longed for some time for himself. The myth of constant closeness and constant togetherness in love prevented Martin from taking private time. It might also have been that this covered up certain fears. What if he discovered that his wife and children could manage very well without him? What if he found that he could not stand his own company for a few days and that the reason for "togetherness" was to keep him from boring himself?

The Myth That We Fall In and Out of Love A common notion is that people "fall" in love, that they passively wait for the right person to come into their life. Buscaglia (1992) criticizes the phrase "to fall in love." He contends that it is more accurate to say that we grow in love, which implies choice and effort: "We really don't fall out of love any more than we fall into it. When love ceases, one or both partners have neglected it, and have failed to replenish and renew it. Like any other living, growing thing, love requires effort to keep it healthy" (p. 6). In *The Art of Loving*, Fromm (1956) also describes love as active: "In the most general way, the active character of love can be described by stating that love is primarily giving, not receiving" (p. 22).

Although the notion of falling in love is popular, most serious writers on the subject deny that it can be the basis for a lasting and meaningful relationship. In writing about falling in love, Nhat Hanh (1992) maintains that we construct a beautiful image that we project onto our partner. However, as reality takes hold we are apt to be shocked as our ideal picture disappears. Nhat Hanh captures the essence of genuine love: "When you first fall in love and you feel attached to the other person, that is not yet real love. Real love means loving kindness and compassion, the kind of love that does not have any conditions" (p. 59).

People often say "I love you" and at the same time are hard pressed to describe the active way in which they show this love. Words can easily be overused and become meaningless. The loved one may be more convinced by actions than by words. In our professional work with couples, we find that one person may be very verbal about being disillusioned with his or her partner's shortcomings. We often ask, "If the situation is as you describe, what do you imagine keeps you together as a couple?" A standard response is, "I love him (her)." They are often unable to identify ways in which to show this love in action.

The Myth of the Exclusiveness of Love You may believe you are capable of loving only one other person—that there is one right person for you. One of the signs of genuine love is that it is expansive rather than exclusive. By opening yourself to loving others, you also open yourself to loving one person more deeply.

Two persons may choose not to have sexual relationships with others because they realize that doing so might interfere with their capacity to freely open up and trust each other. Their sexual exclusivity does not have to preclude other genuine relationships.

Jealousy is an emotion that often accompanies feelings of exclusiveness. For example, Drew may feel insecure if he discovers that his wife, Adriana, has friendships with other men. Even if Adriana and Drew have an agreement not to have sexual relationships with others, Drew might be threatened and angry over the fact that Adriana wants to maintain these friendships with other men. He may wrongly reason: "What is the matter with me that Adriana has to seek out these friends? Her interest in other men must be a sign that something is wrong with me!" In Drew's case, his jealousy is probably rooted in his inability to truly love and accept himself. He is threatened by Adriana's desire to include others in her life. Equally, it is a mistaken notion to equate an absence of jealousy with an absence of love.

The Myth That True Love Is Selfless Lily is a mother who has always given to her children. She never lets them know that she needs anything from them, yet she complains to her friends that the children do not seem to appreciate her. She complains that if she did not initiate visits with them they would never see her. She would never say anything about her feelings to her children, nor would she ever tell them that she would like for them to contact her. If they really loved her, she thinks they would know what she needed without her having to ask for it.

People like Lily are **impaired givers;** that is, they have a high need to take care of others yet appear to have no ability to make their own needs known. They create an inequality; the receivers tend to feel guilty because they do not have a chance to reciprocate. Although these receivers may feel guilty and angry, their feelings do not seem appropriate—how could they have angry feelings toward someone who does so much for them? At the same time, impaired givers may feel resentment toward those who are always taking from them, not recognizing how difficult they are making it to receive.

It is a myth that true love means giving selflessly. For one thing, love also means receiving. If you cannot ask or do not allow others to give to you, then you are likely to become drained or resentful. In giving to others we do meet many of our own needs. There is not necessarily anything wrong in this, as long as we can admit it. For example, a mother who never sets boundaries, and rarely says no to any demands made by her children, may not be aware of the ways she has conditioned them to depend on her. They may be unaware that she has any needs of her own, for she hides them so well. In fact, she may set them up to take advantage of her out of her need to feel significant. In other words, her "giving" is actually an outgrowth of her need to feel like a good mother, not just an honest expression of love for her children. In *Care of the Soul* (1994), Thomas Moore addresses this notion of selflessness. One of his clients said, "I can't be selfish. My religious upbringing taught me never to be selfish" (p. 56). Moore observes that although she insisted on her selflessness she was quite preoccupied with herself. Selfless people often depend on others to maintain their feelings of selflessness.

Giving to others or the desire to express our love to others is not necessarily a problem. However, it is important that we recognize our own needs and consider the value of allowing others to take care of us and return the love we show them. One of us (Marianne) is finally learning the importance of letting others return favors.

MARIANNE'S STORY

*I*t has always been easy for me to show others kindness and take care of them, yet it has been a struggle for me to be on the receiving end. I am very capable of doing things myself and being self-reliant. I would rather not ask for assistance, lest I impose on people. I do see myself as a giver, and that I do not want to change. However, I do not want to create an imbalance of giving and receiving in my life. More often than not, when I do ask for help, I don't get much of a response. I have conditioned people so well that they often act helpless around me. Even capable people act helpless around me! I continue to learn that it takes a concerted effort to challenge ingrained beliefs about being a selfless giver. One way I am able to give to others is by letting others take care of me at times.

The Myth That Love and Anger Are Incompatible Many people are convinced that if they love someone they cannot get angry at them. When they do feel angry, they tend to deny these feelings or express them in indirect ways. Unfortunately, denied or unexpressed anger can do more damage to the relationship. Anger needs to be dealt with in a respectful way before it reaches explosive or implosive proportions.

© Myrleen Ferguson/PhotoEdit

There is an unconditional
quality about love.

Anger and love cannot be compartmentalized. It is difficult to feel loving toward others if we are angry at them. These unexpressed feelings tend to poison the relationship and actually destroy intimacy.

Self-Doubt and Lack of Self-Love

Despite our need for love, we often put barriers in the way of our attempts to give and receive love. One common barrier is the message we sometimes send to others concerning ourselves. If we enter relationships unsure of our lovability, we will give this message to others in subtle ways. We create a self-fulfilling prophecy; we make the very thing we fear come true by being unavailable to others in any kind of loving way.

If you are convinced that no one can love you, your conviction is probably related to experiences you had during your childhood or adolescent years. At one time perhaps you decided that you would not be loved unless you did certain expected things or lived up to another's design for your life. For example: "Unless I succeed, I won't be loved. To be loved, I must get good grades, become successful, and make the most of my life." Such an assumption can make it difficult to convince yourself later in life that you can be loved even when you are successful.

Jay tried as a child to do whatever it took to meet the expectations of others and to gain their acceptance. He gave his all to please people and to get them to like him, yet he never succeeded. Through his actions of desperately trying to win people over, he pushed them away even more. Although he thought he was doing everything right, people were uncomfortable with the way he was around them. Now he is constantly depressed and complains about how hard life is for him. He seeks sympathy and receives rejection. He needs continual reassurance, yet when he does get acceptance and reassurance, he negates it. Eventually people who know him get frustrated and rebuff him. He may never realize that he has created the cycle of his own rejection. In some important ways he continues to live by the theme that no matter what he does or how hard he tries people will still not like him, much less love him. For Jay to make changes, it is essential that he recognize those outside influences on the origins of his beliefs. Our beliefs did not originate in a vacuum. Thus to understand how our early experiences are affecting our present behavior and choices, we need to reflect on these experiences. Once we recognize the sources of the attitudes we hold about love, we are in a position to make new decisions about our thinking and acting.

Think for a moment of how many times you have completed this sentence in any of the following ways: People love me only because I am . . .

- Pretty, bright, and witty.
- Good in sports.
- A good student.
- A fine provider.
- Attractive.
- Accomplished.
- Cooperative and considerate.
- A good father [mother].
- A good wife [husband].
- A good partner.

If you have limited your ability to receive love from others by telling yourself that you are loved primarily for a single trait, it would be healthy to challenge this assumption. For example, if you say to someone, "You only love me because of my body," you might try to realize that your body is only one of your assets. You can learn to appreciate this asset without assuming that it is all there is to the person you are. If you have trouble seeing any desirable characteristics besides your physical attractiveness, you are not likely to be open to feedback about anything other than your appearance. Ideally, you will come to accept that being a physically attractive person makes it easier for others to notice you and want to initiate contact with you. However, you do not need to limit yourself by depending exclusively on how you look. When you rely exclusively on any one trait as a source of gaining love from others (or from yourself), your ability to be loved is limited to that trait and will not go very deep.

Our Fear of Love

The Fear of Isolation Despite our need for love, we often fear loving and being loved. Our fear can lead us to seal off our need for love, and it can dull our capacity to care about others. In some families relatives have not spoken to one another for years. This act of shunning is generally deliberate and aimed at controlling and isolating those who do not live within the boundaries of acceptable norms. Those who are shunned often feel invisible. Within the Amish culture, the practice of shunning is used to sanction members who violate certain norms and religious values. In its most severe form, shunning almost totally cuts off an individual from interaction within the community. Other members will not eat at the same table with those who are shunned, will not do business with them, and will not have anything to do with them socially (Good & Good, 1979).

The fear of isolation as a result of being cut off emotionally is so overwhelming that many would not even think of going against their cultural norms. The need for love and acceptance may be far stronger than giving expression to your own individual desires. Have you ever faced an emotional cut-off? If so, what was it like? Have you sometimes felt isolated because others that you cared about shunned you or treated you as though you were invisible?

The Fear of Being Discovered Some of us are afraid that if we get too close to others they will certainly discover what we are really like. We may think that at the deepest level there is nothing to us. We may question the positive reactions we receive from others and have difficulty believing that others really value us. Iyanla Vanzant (1998) realized that she wanted to be loved but was unwilling to risk being known:

> I ALSO ACKNOWLEDGED THAT I KEPT most people I professed to love at an arm's distance, never allowing them to know too much or get too close, because I was afraid of being hurt. My mouth was saying I wanted to be loved, while my mind was thinking I was unworthy. I was sending out signals indicating that I wanted to be loved, but I would only let so much love in. My fear, which I am sure is the same fear for many of us, is that too much love would kill me. I would simply melt in its presence. (p. 227)

Reflect for a moment on what she is saying. Does it resonate with your thinking and feeling?

The Uncertainty of Love   Love does not come with guarantees. We cannot be sure that another person will always love us, and we do lose loved ones. As Hodge (1967) insists, we cannot eliminate the possibility that we will be hurt if we choose to love. Our loved ones may die or be injured or become seriously ill, or they may simply leave us. "These are painful experiences, and we cannot avoid them if we choose to love. It is part of the human dilemma that love always includes the possibility of hurt" (p. 266). However, it needs to be said that avoiding the experience of love can lead to another kind of pain. A loveless existence is very painful!

Most of the common fears of risking in love are related to rejection, loss, the failure of love to be reciprocated, or uneasiness with intensity. Here are some of the ways these fears might be expressed:

- I have been so badly hurt in a love relationship, I'm not willing to take the chance of loving again.
- I fear allowing myself to love others because of the possibility that they will be seriously injured, contract a terrible illness, or in some way leave me. I don't want to care that much; that way, if I lose them, it won't hurt as much.
- I'm afraid of loving others because they might want more from me than I'm willing to give, and I might feel suffocated.
- I'm afraid that I'm basically unlovable and that when you really get to know me you'll want little to do with me.
- If people tell me they care about me, I feel I've taken on a burden, and I'm afraid of letting them down.
- I've never really allowed myself to look at whether I'm lovable. My fear is that I will search deep within myself and find little for another to love.

Maribel has struggled in overcoming early childhood messages in her quest for loving and being loved. At her present age of 26 she is still learning to deal with the fear of love. Here she describes the experience of "wearing protective armor" around her heart.

MARIBEL'S STORY

*I*ntimacy and trust do not come easy for me. Physical contact and close intimate relationships were not present during my childhood. Yet there is nothing more incredible than sharing your life with someone you love and trust completely. Even after being together almost 4 years, my boyfriend, Al, and I are still often engaged in what I sometimes call an emotional tug-of-war. He gives a little, and I feel secure. I give a little and then feel like I'm the one giving it all. We are always struggling to find a balance.

I have become aware that I wear protective armor around my heart. In my own personal therapy, I have been exploring the ways in which this wall was helpful in my childhood but may keep people at a distance now. I put my boyfriend through a test every day. If he can take the time to look beneath the tough exterior, he passes the test, and the wall comes down. I sometimes wonder if the game will ever end.

I have come to realize the vicious cycle of ebb and flow in my relationship. At times things have gotten so difficult we've actually decided to end it.

No matter what your own fears may be, you can learn, as Maribel has, to choose to open yourself to the potential for love that awaits you. In what ways can you identify with Maribel's struggle?

Take Time to Reflect

1. What did you learn about love in your family of origin?

_____

_____

2. How do you express your love to others?

_____

_____

3. How do you let another person know your own need to receive love, affection, and caring?

_____

_____

4. List some specific fears you have concerning loving others.

_____

_____

5. What barriers within you prevent others from loving you or prevent you from fully receiving their love?

_____

_____

6. List some qualities you have that you deem lovable.

_____

_____

7. What are some specific ways in which you might become a more lovable person?

_____

_____

8. What are some ways that love has played a positive role in your life?

_____

_____

IS IT WORTH IT TO LOVE?

Often we hear people say, "Sure, I need to love and to be loved, but is it *really* worth it?" Underlying this question is a series of other questions: "Is the risk of rejection and loss worth taking?" "Are the rewards of opening myself up as great as the risks?"

It would be comforting to have an absolute answer to these questions, but each of us must struggle to decide for ourselves whether it is worth it to love. Our first task is to decide whether we prefer isolation to intimacy. Of course, our choice is not between extreme isolation and constant intimacy; surely there are degrees of both. But we do need to decide whether to experiment with extending our narrow world to include significant others. We can increasingly open ourselves to others and discover for ourselves what that is like for us; alternatively, we can decide that people are basically unreliable and that it is better to be safe and go hungry emotionally.

Perhaps you know very little about love but would like to learn how to become more intimate. You might begin by acknowledging this reality to yourself, as well as to those in your life with whom you would like to become more intimate. In this way you can take a significant beginning step.

In answering the question of whether it is worth it to you to love, you can challenge some of your attitudes and beliefs concerning acceptance and rejection. You can ask yourself: "Is being rejected any worse that living a life without experiencing love?" Being rejected is not a pleasant experience, yet we hope this possibility will not deter you from allowing yourself to love someone. If a love relationship ends for you, it would be worth it to honestly search for your part in contributing to this situation without being overly self-critical. Identify some ways in which you would like to change and learn from this experience. Elana had to learn to trust again after being deeply hurt in a relationship.

ELANA'S STORY

I had a mutual loving bond with Monte, yet most of my friends had a hard time understanding why I continued in this relationship. I guess I had an idealized picture of Monte and made excuses for his insensitive behavior. I became extremely dependent on Monte and preoccupied with trying to please him at all costs, even if it meant sacrificing my own happiness to keep peace with him. My friends let me know of their concern and tried to convince me that I deserved better treatment. My response was to cut myself off from my friends so I would not have to deal with their feedback. Eventually, Monte betrayed me, which led to a crisis. I ended my relationship with Monte, but I was quite fearful of loving again, and old wounds were reopened each time I met a new man. I approached new relationships with fear and distrust, which made it difficult to open myself to love again.

With concerted work on her part, Elana became aware of how clinging to her past hampered her ability to receive love and develop friendships. Elana's immediate impulses were to flee from getting close, yet she challenged her fears with the realization that the risk of rejection did not have to keep her helpless and guarded.

As adults we are not helpless; we can do something about rejection and hurt. We can choose to challenge relationships or even leave them. We can learn to survive pain, and we can realize that being rejected does not mean we are beyond hope. Consider how the last line in Hodge's (1967) book, *Your Fear of Love,* may apply to you: "We can discover for ourselves that it is worth the risk to love, even though we tremble and even though we know we will sometimes experience the hurt we fear" (p. 270).

SUMMARY

We have a need to love and to be loved, but there are many barriers to meeting these needs. Being convinced of our unworthiness can be a major roadblock to loving others and receiving their love. Learning to give love to others and to receive love from them is contingent upon loving and appreciating ourselves. It is good to reflect on Nhat Hanh's (1992) words: "You cannot love someone else unless you love and take care of yourself" (p. 95). How can we give to others something we do not possess ourselves? Our fear of love is another major impediment to loving. Although most of us would like guarantees that our love for special people will last as long as they live, the reality is that there are no guarantees. It helps to realize that loving and the anxiety surrounding uncertainty go together and to accept that we are faced with learning to love despite our fears.

Myths and misconceptions about love make it difficult to be open to giving and receiving love. A few of these are the myth of eternal love, the myth that love implies constant closeness, the myth of the exclusiveness of love, the myth that true love is selfless, and the myth of falling into eternal love. Although genuine love results in the growth of both persons, some "love" is stifling. Not all that poses as real love is authentic, and one of the major challenges is to decide for ourselves what authentic love means to us. By recognizing our attitudes about loving, we can increase our ability to choose the ways in which we behave in our love relationships.

Where Can I Go From Here?

1. Give your personal definition of love. Do you have the love you deserve? If not, why not? Describe an incident that you experienced that would be a definition of love.

2. What have you either observed around you or experienced personally that made you say, "This is love!"

3. Think about some early decisions you made regarding your own ability to love or to be loved. Have you ever had any of these thoughts?

- I'm not lovable unless I meet others' expectations.
- I am worth loving because of the person that I am.
- I won't love another because of my fears of rejection.
- Love is what makes life worth living.

Write down some of the messages you have received and perhaps accepted uncritically. What message have you received from your family of origin? How has your ability to feel loved or to give love been restricted by these messages and decisions?

4. For a period of at least a week, pay close attention to the messages conveyed by the media concerning love. What picture of love do you get from television? What do popular songs and movies portray about love? Make a list of some common myths or misconceptions regarding love that you see promoted by the media.

5. Do you agree with the proposition that you cannot fully love others unless you first love yourself? What does this mean to you? In your journal write some notes to yourself concerning situations in which you do not appreciate yourself. Also record the times and events when you do value and respect yourself.

6. How present is love in your life right now? Do you feel that you love others in the ways you would like to? Do you feel that you are loved by others in the ways you want to be?

7. Are you an active or a passive lover? Write down the ways in which you demonstrate your caring for

those you love and then ask them to read your list and discuss with you how they see your style of loving.

8. In your journal, write about your personal story regarding love.

Resources for Future Study

Web Site Resource

LOVE PAGE
http://www.tc.umn.edu/nlhome/g296/parkx032/ LVindex.html

The Love Page was created by James Park, an existential philosopher and advocate of freedom and authenticity in relationships. This site offers many articles that challenge more traditional notions of romantic love and includes a 60-page preview of his book, *New Ways of Loving*. There are also bibliographies on a wide variety of topics dealing with love and relationships.

InfoTrac College Edition Resources

For additional readings, explore INFOTRAC COLLEGE EDITION, our online library:
http://www.infotrac.college.com/wadsworth

Hint: Enter these search terms:

love

self-acceptance

humanitarian love

self-love

brotherly love

jealousy

Print Resources

Albom, M. (1997). *Tuesdays with Morrie.* New York: Doubleday.

Buscaglia, L. (1972). *Love.* Thorofare, NJ: Charles B. Slack.

Buscaglia, L. (1992). *Born for love: Reflections on loving.* New York: Fawcett Columbine.

Easwaran, E. (1991). *Meditation.* Tomales, CA: Nilgiri Press.

Fromm, E. (1956). *The art of loving.* New York: Harper & Row (Colophon). (Paperback edition published 1974)

Nhat Hanh, T. (1997). *Teachings on love.* Berkeley, CA: Parallax Press.

Hendrix, H. (2001). *Getting the love you want: A guide for couples.* New York: Henry Holt (An Owl Book).

Jampolsky, G. G. (1981). *Love is letting go of fear.* New York: Bantam Books.

Moore, T. (1994). *Care of the soul: A guide for cultivating depth and sacredness in everyday life.* New York: Harper Perennial.

Schnarch, D. (1997). *Passionate marriage.* New York: Henry Holt.

Vanzant, I. (1998). *One day my soul just opened up.* New York: Fireside Books (Simon & Schuster).

7

It takes both imagination and effort to think of ways to revise our relationships so that they will remain alive.

Relationships

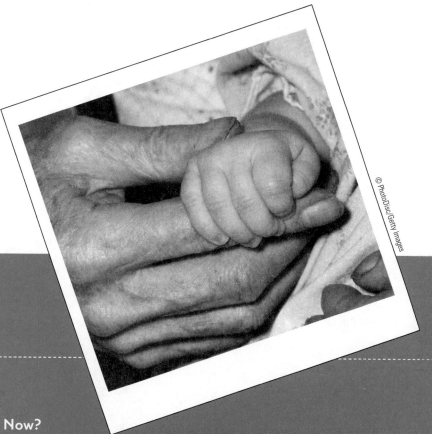

© PhotoDisc/Getty Images

Where Am I Now?

Use this scale to respond to these statements:

3 = This statement is true of me *most* of the time.

2 = This statement is true of me *some* of the time.

1 = This statement is true of me *almost none* of the time.

1. I consider the absence of conflict and crisis to be a sign of a good relationship.

2. It is difficult for me to have several close relationships at the same time.

3. In a satisfactory relationship there is no expression of anger.

4. I believe the mark of a successful relationship is that I enjoy being both with and without the other person.

5. I would like to find intimacy with one other person.

6. At times, wanting too much from another person causes me difficulties in the relationship.

7. I feel confident in what I have to offer in a relationship.

8. I am comfortable with the amount of energy I spend in my relationships.

9. I feel satisfied with my connection with others.

10. I can be emotionally intimate with another person without being physically intimate with that person.

elationships play a significant role in our lives. In this chapter we deal with friendships, marital relationships, intimacy between people who are not married, dating relationships, relationships between parents and children, and a variety of other meaningful personal relationships.

Whether you choose to marry or not, whether your primary relationship is with someone of the same or the opposite gender, you will face many similar relationship challenges. What is true for marriage is largely true for these other intimate relationships as well. The signs of growth and meaningfulness are much the same, and so are the problems.

In this chapter we invite you to reflect on what you need from your relationships, and we hope this discussion assists you in examining the quality of these relationships. The ideas in this chapter are useful tools in rethinking what kind of relationships you want, as well as in clarifying some new choices you may want to make. Take a fresh look at your relationships and decide whether you might want to improve some parts of them.

TYPES OF INTIMACY

The challenge of forming intimate relationships is the major task of early adulthood (Erikson, 1963). Being able to share significant aspects of yourself with others, understanding the barriers to intimacy, and learning ways of enhancing intimacy can help you better understand the many different types of relationships in your life.

The intimacy we share with another person can be emotional, intellectual, physical, spiritual, or any combination of these. It can be exclusive or nonexclusive, long term or brief. For example, many of the participants in the personal-growth groups we conduct develop genuine closeness with one another, even though they may not keep in touch after the termination of the group. This closeness does not come about automatically. They earn it by being different in how they relate. Instead of keeping their thoughts, feelings, and reactions to themselves, they share them in ways that they typically do not allow outside of the group setting. The cohesion comes about when people discover that they have very similar feelings and when they are willing to share their pain, anger, frustration—and their joys. Many people are reluctant to open themselves up emotionally in such short-term situations because they want to avoid the sadness of parting. Bonds of intimacy and friendship can be formed in a short period, however, and subsequent distance in space and time need not diminish the quality of the friendships formed.

When we avoid intimacy, we diminish ourselves. We may pass up the chance to get to know neighbors and new acquaintances because we fear that someone will move and that the friendship will come to an end. Sometimes we avoid intimacy with sick or dying persons because we fear the pain of losing

The challenge of forming intimate relationships is the major task of early adulthood.

them. Although such fears may be well founded, too often we deprive ourselves of the uniquely rich experience of being truly close to someone. We can enhance our lives greatly by caring about others and fully savoring the time we spend with them.

We can choose the kinds of relationships we want. By spending time reflecting on how we might want to revise some of our interactions with others, we can bring new life to our relationships. Donald's story illustrates how difficult it can be to begin to make such changes in an established relationship.

DONALD'S STORY

*M*y father seems uncaring, aloof, and preoccupied with his own concerns. I deeply wish to be physically and emotionally closer to my father, but I have no idea how to bring this about. I decided to talk to my father and tell him how I feel and what I want. My father appeared to listen, and his eyes moistened, but then without saying much he quickly left the room. I am pretty hurt and disappointed that my father wasn't more responsive when I talked to him. I just don't know what else I can do.

Donald was missing the subtle yet significant signs that his father had been touched and was not as uncaring as he had imagined. His father may be every bit as afraid of his son's rejection as Donald is of his father's rebuffs. The experience

Donald had with his father could have occurred in any intimate relationship. We can experience feelings of awkwardness, unexpressed desires, and fears of rejection with our friends, lovers, spouses, parents, or children. Donald will need to show patience with his father if he is really interested in changing the way they relate to each other.

To bring about change, we ourselves must change rather than insisting that the other person change. We have the opportunity to teach others specific ways of becoming more personal. It does little good to lament on all the ways in which the other person is not changing, nor is it helpful to focus on remaking others. Time and again in this chapter we will ask you to focus on your own wants, to look at what you are doing, and to make some decisions about how you can assume increased control of your relationships by being vulnerable rather than critical. When you take a passive stance and simply hope the other person will change in the ways that you would like, you are waiting for the other person to change rather than being different yourself.

As you read the remainder of this chapter, spend some time thinking about ways you experience intimacy in your life. Are you involved in the kinds of relationships that satisfy you? What are you willing to do to improve your relationships? What is your view of a meaningful relationship? The Take Time to Reflect exercises presented here give you an opportunity to address these questions and clarify what you are doing in your relationships.

Take Time to Reflect

1. What attracts you to a person you would like to form an intimate relationship with? Score each item using the following scale:

1 = This quality is *very important* to me.
2 = This quality is *somewhat important* to me.
3 = This quality is *not very important* to me.

_____ intelligence
_____ character (a strong sense of values)
_____ physical appearance and attractiveness
_____ financial success
_____ prestige and status
_____ a strong sense of identity
_____ a sense of humor
_____ caring and sensitivity
_____ independence
_____ a quiet person
_____ an outgoing person
_____ someone who will make decisions for me
_____ someone who is willing to make decisions cooperatively

———— someone I can depend on
———— someone I can't live without
———— someone who works hard and is disciplined
———— someone who likes to play and have fun
———— someone who has values similar to mine
———— someone I'd like to grow old with

Now list the three qualities that you value most in a person when you are considering an intimate relationship.

_____

_____

2. What do you sense you have that attracts people to you? List the qualities you see in yourself.

_____

_____

3. Identify the kinds of intimate relationships you have chosen so far in your life. What have you learned from them? If you are not now involved in an intimate relationship, what stops you?

_____

_____

4. What are the challenges and difficulties you face in being in a significant relationship? What do you get from being involved in a significant relationship?

_____

_____

MEANINGFUL RELATIONSHIPS: A PERSONAL VIEW

In this section we share some of our ideas about the characteristics of a meaningful relationship. Although these guidelines pertain to couples, they are also relevant to other personal relationships. Take, for example, the guideline, "The persons involved are willing to work at keeping their relationship healthy." Parents and children often take each other for granted, rarely spending time together. Either parent or child may expect the other to assume the major responsibility for the relationship. The same principle applies to friends or to partners in a primary relationship. As you look over our list, adapt it to the different relationships in your life, keeping in mind your particular cultural values. Your cultural background plays an influential role in your relationships, and you may need to adapt our ideas to better fit your core values. As you review our list, ask yourself what qualities you think are most important in your relationships.

We see relationships as most meaningful when they are dynamic and evolving rather than fixed. Thus any relationship may have periods of joy and excitement followed by times of struggle, pain, and distance. As long as the individuals in a relationship are willing to accept this, their relationship has a chance to change as well. The following qualities of a relationship seem most important to us.

• *Each person in the relationship has a separate identity.* Kahlil Gibran (1923) expresses this thought well: "But let there be spaces in your togetherness, and let the winds of the heavens dance between you" (p. 16). Making long-term relationships work is difficult because it is necessary to create and maintain a balance between separateness and togetherness (Lerner, 1985). If there is not enough togetherness in a relationship, people typically feel isolated and do not share feelings and experiences. If there is not enough separateness, they are apt to give up a sense of their own identity and control, devoting much effort to becoming what the other person expects.

• *Each is able to talk openly with the other about matters of significance to the relationship.* Both people openly express grievances and let each other know the changes they desire. They ask for what they want rather than expecting the other to intuitively know what they want and give it to them. For example, assume that you are not satisfied with how you and your mother spend time together. You can take the first step by letting her know, in a nonjudgmental way, that you would like to talk more personally. Rather than telling her how she is, you can focus more on telling her how you are in your relationship with her. Instead of focusing on what you don't want with your mother, you can tell her what you would like with her.

• *Each person assumes responsibility for his or her own level of happiness and refrains from blaming the other if he or she is unhappy.* Of course, in a close relationship or friendship, the unhappiness of the other person is bound to affect you, but you should not expect another person to make you happy, fulfilled, or excited. Although the way others feel will influence your life, they do not create the way you react to them. When you solely rely on others for your personal fulfillment and confirmation as a person, there are going to be problems. The best way to build solid relationships with others is to work on developing your own self. Ultimately, you are responsible for defining your goals and your life, and you have a great deal of choice in what ways you can take steps to enhance your life. Certainly you have a great deal of control when it comes to changing your attitudes about situations in which you find yourself unhappy.

In a meaningful relationship the persons involved are willing to work at keeping their relationship alive.

© Tim Kiusalaas/Corbis

● *Both people are willing to work at keeping their relationship healthy.* If we hope to keep a relationship vital, we must reevaluate and revise our way of being with each other from time to time. Consider how this guideline fits your friendships. If you take a good friend for granted and show little interest in doing what is necessary to maintain that friendship, that person may soon grow disenchanted and wonder what kind of friend you are. Lerner (1995) makes a good point when she writes about ways that we sometimes re-create old patterns and keep them alive in our current relationships. Our present relationships suffer through the process of our bringing old business into these relationships.

● *They are able to have fun and to play together; they enjoy doing things with each other.* Sometimes we do not take time to enjoy those we profess to love. One way of changing relationships in a rut is to become aware of the infrequency of joyous moments and then determine what gets in the way and what prevents us from having a more enjoyable life together. Again, think of this guideline as it applies to your close friends.

● *If the relationship contains a sexual component, each person makes some attempt to keep the romance alive.* Although sexual partners rarely experience the intensity and novelty of the early period of their relationship, they can create a climate of romance and closeness. In their lovemaking they are sensitive to each other's needs and desires; at the same time, they are able to ask each other for what they want and need. Their sex life is most often a barometer of their relationship.

● *The two people are equal in the relationship.* People who feel that they are typically the "givers" and that their partners are usually unavailable when they need them might question this imbalance. In some relationships one person may feel compelled to assume a superior position relative to the other—for example, to be very willing to listen and give advice yet unwilling to go to the other person and show any vulnerability at all. Both parties need to be willing to look at aspects of inequality and demonstrate a willingness to negotiate changes.

● *Each person finds meaning and sources of nourishment outside the relationship.* Sometimes people become very possessive in their friendships. A sign of a healthy relationship is that each avoids assuming an attitude of ownership toward the other. Although they may experience jealousy at times, they do not demand that the other person deny his or her feelings for others.

● *Each person is moving in a direction in life that is personally meaningful.* They are both excited about the quality of their lives and their projects. Applied to couples, this guideline implies that both individuals feel that their needs are being met within the relationship, but they also feel a sense of engagement in their work, play, and relationships with other friends and family members.

● *If they are in a committed relationship, they maintain this relationship by choice, not out of duty, or because of convenience.* They choose to keep their ties with each other even if things get rough or if they sometimes experience pain in the relationship. Because they share common purposes and values, they are willing to look at what is lacking in their relationship and to work on changing undesirable situations.

● *They are able to deal with conflict in their relationship.* Couples often seek relationship counseling with the expectation that they will learn to eliminate conflict, which is an unrealistic goal. More important than the absence of conflict is learning how to disagree constructively, which may entail an ongoing process of expressing anger and frustration in respectful ways.

● *They do not expect the other to do for them what they are capable of doing for themselves.* They do not expect the other person to make them feel happy, take away their boredom, assume their risks, or make them feel valued and important. Each is working toward creating his or her own identity. Consequently, neither person depends on the other for confirmation of his or her personal worth; nor does one walk in the shadow of the other. By being willing to work on making their own life meaningful, they are contributing to each other's happiness.

● *They encourage each other to become all that they are capable of becoming.* Unfortunately, people often have an investment in keeping those with whom they are intimately involved from changing. Because of their fears, they try to control their partner and thus make it difficult for their partner to be his or her authentic self. If they recognize their fears, however, they can challenge their need to block their partner's progress.

Creating and maintaining friendships, especially intimate relationships, is a major interest for many college students. There is no single or easy prescription for success; developing meaningful relationships entails the willingness to make commitments. Many students say that they do not have enough time to maintain their friendships and other relationships. If this fits for you, realize that your relationships and friendships are likely to suffer if you neglect them. You can make choices that will increase your chances of developing lasting friendships:

- Be accepting of differences between your friends and yourself.
- Learn to become aware of conflicts and deal with them constructively.
- Be willing to let the other person know how you are affected in the relationship.
- Stay in the relationship and talk even though you may experience a fear of rejection.
- Check out your assumptions about others instead of deciding for them what they are thinking and feeling.
- Be willing to make yourself vulnerable and to take risks.
- Avoid the temptation to live up to others' expectations instead of being true to yourself.

John Gottman, cofounder and codirector of the Seattle Marital and Family Institute, has conducted extensive research to determine what factors are associated with successful marital relationships. In *The Seven Principles for Making Marriage Work,* Gottman and Nan Silver (1999) describe some key characteristics of a successful relationship.

Intimate familiarity: Couples know each other's goals, concerns, and hopes.

Fondness and admiration: When couples no longer feel honor and respect for one another, it is extremely difficult to revitalize the relationship.

Connectedness: When individuals honor each other, they are generally able to appreciate each other's perspective.

Shared sense of power: When couples disagree, they look for common ground rather than insisting their way has to be supreme.

Shared goals: Partners incorporate each other's goals into their concept of what their intimate relationship is about.

Open communication: Each person in the relationship can talk fully and honestly about his or her convictions and core beliefs.

Are there gender differences regarding what people look for in an intimate relationship? According to Carroll (2005), women often report that a promising career is very important; men often report that physical attractiveness is important. People look for different personal characteristics in their partners. Carroll (2005) sums this up: "Overall, good lovers are sensitive to their partners' needs and desires, can communicate their own desires, and are patient, caring, and confident" (p. 173).

Developing meaningful intimate relationships requires time, work, and the willingness to ride out hard times. Further, to be a good friend to another, you must first be a good friend to yourself, which implies knowing yourself and caring about yourself. In this Take Time to Reflect, we ask you to focus on some of the ways you see yourself as an alive and authentic person, which is the foundation for a meaningful relationship.

Take Time to Reflect

1. What are some ways in which you see yourself as evolving in your relationships?

_____

_____

2. Are you resisting change by sticking with some old and comfortable patterns, even if they don't work? What are these patterns?

_____

_____

3. How is the person with whom you are most intimate changing or resisting change?

_____

_____

4. If you are involved in a committed relationship, in what ways do you think you and your partner are growing closer? In what ways are you going in different directions?

_____

_____

5. Are you satisfied with the relationship you have just described? If not, what would you most like to change? Would you be willing to talk to your partner about it?

_____

_____

6. Would you be happy if you had a marriage very similar to that of your parents? Explain.

_____

_____

7. To what extent do you have an identity apart from the relationship? How much do you need (and depend on) the other person? Imagine that he or she is no longer in your life, and write down the ways your life might be different.

_____

_____

A suggestion: If you are involved in a relationship, have the other person respond to the questions on a separate sheet of paper. Then compare your answers and discuss areas of agreement and disagreement.

ANGER AND CONFLICT IN RELATIONSHIPS

"We have never had a fight!" some people proudly say of their long-term relationships. Perhaps this is true, but the reasons couples do not fight can be complex. Buscaglia (1992) claims that many people try to disguise anger, sublimate it, suppress it, or project it where it does not belong. He adds that expressing anger often takes care of the situation, whereas repressed anger festers until it explodes. Iyanla Vanzant (1998) identifies anger as one of the most powerful emotions we can experience. She views passion as the driving force for life and also as the impetus for anger. Take a moment to think about how you view anger. How did you see anger expressed when you were a child? How do you deal with anger today? Do you deny your anger? What do your friends tell you about your anger? How does the way you deal with anger affect the quality of your relationships?

Expressing Anger Constructively

Expressing anger or dealing with situations involving conflict may be difficult for you because of what you have experienced and the messages you have heard about anger, conflict, and confrontation. Some of you have been told outright not to be angry. You may have observed harmful and destructive anger and made an early decision never to express these emotions (see the discussion of injunctions and early decisions in Chapter 3). You may have had mostly negative and frightening outcomes in situations involving conflict. If so, it may be necessary for you to challenge some of the messages you received from your family of origin about feeling and expressing anger.

- How was anger expressed in your home?
- Who got angry and what typically occurred?
- Did dealing with conflict and anger bring people closer together or move them farther apart?
- Is what you learned as a child about expressing anger and dealing with conflict helping or hindering you at this time in your life?

It is generally helpful to express persistent annoyances rather than to pretend they do not exist. Ideally, sources of anger are best recognized and expressed in a direct and honest way. To be able to express your anger, however, there must be safety in the relationship that will enable you to share and deal with your feelings. If you cannot trust how your reactions will be received, chances are that you will not be willing to open yourself to the other person. To us, a sign of a healthy relationship is that people are able to express feelings and thoughts that may be difficult for the other to hear, yet the message is delivered in such a way that it does not assault the other person's character.

Clearly, recognizing and expressing anger can be valuable in relationships, but anger can also be destructive or dangerous. On a daily basis we see evidence that misdirected anger is harmful and destructive. Expressing anger in relationships is not always safe, nor does it always bring about closeness.

For many people the expression of anger becomes a reflex behavior that is easily escalated. It happens without thinking, and it takes considerable effort to change this pattern. Some of you may have learned that anger leads to withdrawal of a person's love. One of our colleagues talks about the violence of silence, which is another form of destructive anger. Dealing with anger by growing silent generally does not help the situation; rather, both parties tend to pay a price for withholding their feelings. Sweeping conflict under the rug may appear to work in the short term, but over time it typically pulls the rug out from under the relationship.

Some people may be incapable of handling even the slightest confrontation, and no matter how sensitively you deliver your message, the outcome could be detrimental. If you find yourself in an abusive relationship where the outcome of anger is most often destructive, you will need to exercise great caution in how you confront that person. In such situations it may never be safe for you to express your feelings. If you recognize that anger is a problem in your relationship, we hope you will be willing to seek professional help. Many college counseling centers offer anger management workshops to assist individuals and couples in this area.

Without doubt, one of the major stumbling blocks people involved in close relationships must face is learning how to deal with anger in realistic and appropriate ways. If we avoid being judgmental and avoid being emotionally or physically abusive, anger does not have to rupture the relationship. Once conflict is recognized and dealt with appropriately, healing is possible, and we can let go of lingering resentments. This opens communication pathways that can deepen the relationship.

Ask yourself if you or your partner has a problem dealing with anger and conflict. Recognizing signs of trouble may be the first step in bringing about change. Do you recognize yourself or your partner in any of these statements?

- What you say and what you feel are not congruent. For instance, you tell the other person that you are fine, yet you are feeling angry.
- You overreact to what is said to you when it is difficult to hear.
- You typically walk away from conflict situations.
- You respond without thinking and often have regrets later about what you said.
- You often have physical symptoms such as headaches and stomachaches.
- You know you hurt the other person, yet you are unwilling to acknowledge that.
- You rarely resolve a conflict, assuming that time will take care of everything.
- You focus on the other person's flaws and rarely on your own shortcomings.
- During altercations, you bring up a litany of old grievances.
- You hold grudges and are unwilling to forgive.

Addressing Conflict and Confrontation Effectively

It is difficult to change that which you are not aware of. However, with awareness you can catch yourself in reflex behavior and begin to modify what you say and do. If some of these strategies are no longer working for you, try implementing these guidelines.

- *Recognize that conflict can be a healthy sign of individual differences and an integral part of a good relationship.* Both people in a relationship can be strong. When this leads to differences of opinion, it is not necessarily true that one is right and the other is wrong. Two people can agree that they see an issue differently.

- *See confrontation as a caring act, not an attack on the other person.* Confront a person if you care and if you are interested in bettering your relationship. Rather than being delivered as an attack, confrontation can be a conversation about some aspect of the relationship. Even though the tendency is to get defensive and attempt to fault the other person, strive to really listen and understand what the other person is saying. Deliver your message in a way that you would want it delivered to you. Respectful delivery makes for good listening.

- *Resist the temptation to plan your next response while the other person is speaking to you.* Learning to manage conflict situations is not about one person winning and another person losing. Successfully working through conflicts allows all the parties involved to retain their dignity.

- *If you do confront a person, identify your motivation.* Are you doing so out of concern? Are you expecting change in the way you deal with each other? Is your motivation to get even? Are you hoping to enhance your relationship?

- *Accept responsibility for your own feelings.* Be aware of wanting to blame others for how you feel. At times it is easy to lash out at someone close to you simply because he or she is there. Be willing to examine the source of your feelings. Even though others may elicit your feelings in a situation, this is very different from making them responsible for how you feel.

- *In confronting another, try not to make dogmatic statements about the other person.* Instead of telling others how they are, say how their behavior affects you. It is easy for us to judge others and focus on all that they are doing. It is more difficult to focus on ourselves and what we are doing.

- *Tell others how you are struggling with them.* Too often we leave out all the information that leads to a particular reaction. Instead, we give only the bottom line. We might say, "You are insensitive and uncaring." Let others know all that you have been thinking and feeling that led up to that statement. When you say all that led up to your bottom line, you are more likely to be heard.

- *Don't walk away from conflict.* Walking away from conflict does not solve the problem. However, when emotions are very highly charged and you are unable to resolve a conflict, it may be best to ask for a time-out and agree to resume discussing this issue at a later time. Do not pretend that the situation is resolved. Make a commitment to continue talking about the differences that may be separating you at a later time when both of you are able to listen to each other.

- *Recognize the importance of forgiving others who have hurt you.* If you desire intimacy with an individual, nursing grudges and pain will inhibit intimacy. Letting go of old grievances and forgiving others is essential in maintaining intimacy. Forgiveness does not imply that you have forgotten what was done to you. However, you no longer harbor feelings of resentment, nor do you seek to get even.

- *Recognize that it is essential to forgive yourself.* Sometimes others are willing to forgive us for causing them hurt, yet we may refuse to forgive ourselves for our wrongs. Morrie Schwartz (1996) offers this sage advice: "Learn to forgive yourself and to forgive others. Ask for forgiveness from others. Forgiveness can soften the heart, drain the bitterness, and dissolve your guilt" (p. 55). It is not just other people that we need to forgive—we need to forgive ourselves. As Gerald Jampolsky (1999) states, "I believe with all my heart that peace will come to the world when each of us takes the responsibility of forgiving everyone, including ourselves, completely" (p. 123).

In her commentary on forgiveness, Vanzant (1998) speaks of forgiveness as a release and a letting go. She writes: "Most people believe that when you forgive someone, you are doing something for them. The truth is, when you forgive, you are doing it for yourself. As it relates to forgiveness you must give up what you do not want in order to make room for what you do want" (p. 168). Jampolsky (1999) believes forgiving others is the first step to forgiving ourselves. For Jampolsky, the purpose of forgiveness is to release us from the past. Forgiveness can free us from the grievances we hold toward others. He writes: "We can look upon forgiveness as a journey across an imaginary bridge from a world where we are always recycling our anger to a place of peace" (p. 18). He adds that through forgiveness we can let go of fear and anger. The process of forgiving heals the wounds associated with past grievances.

In *The Art of Dying,* Weenolsen (1996) lists a number of reasons it makes sense to forgive. Here are a few of those reasons:

- An unforgiven injury is a ballast that holds you down from a destined flight. When you let go, you will soar.
- People forgive at the end of life because it is their last chance to do so.
- Forgiveness can lead to a resurrection of love.
- Forgiveness is somewhat like "spiritual pruning" on the soul. It cuts away the rotten parts so that there is room for healthy growth.

Take Time to Reflect

1. How did your family of origin deal with conflict? What did this teach you?

_____

_____

2. How do you deal with anger directed toward you?

_____

_____

3. How do you express your own anger in your current relationships?

_____

_____

4. What changes would you like to make, if any, in the manner in which you deal with conflicts in your relationships?

_____

_____

5. What importance do you place on forgiveness as a way to enhance significant relationships?

_____

_____

6. To what degree are you able to forgive yourself for any of your past transgressions or regrets? How does this influence your ability to establish meaningful connections with others?

_____

_____

DEALING WITH COMMUNICATION BLOCKS

Relationships between two people will almost certainly be challenged by difficulties. What is more important than the absence of relationship problems is recognizing them and dealing effectively with them. Basic communication skills are an important part of establishing healthy relationships. Many relationship problems stem from misunderstandings and inadequate communication. Couples who know how to communicate are happier and more satisfied with their relationship (Carroll, 2005).

A number of barriers to effective communication can inhibit developing and maintaining intimate relationships. Here are some common communication barriers:

- Failing to really listen to another person
- Selective listening—that is, hearing only what you want to hear
- Being overly concerned with getting your point across without considering the other's point of view
- Silently rehearsing what you will say next as you are listening
- Becoming defensive, with self-protection your primary concern
- Attempting to change others rather than first attempting to understand them
- Stereotyping people instead of trying to understand them
- Telling others how they are rather than telling them how they affect you
- Being blinded by prejudice
- Hanging onto old patterns and not allowing the other person to change

Many relationship problems stem from misunderstandings and inadequate communication.

- Overreacting to a person
- Failing to state what your needs are and expecting others to know them
- Making assumptions about another person without checking them out
- Using sarcasm and hostility instead of saying directly what you mean
- Avoiding responsibility by using phrases such as "You manipulate me!"

These barriers make it difficult to have authentic encounters in which both people are open with themselves and each other, expressing what they think and feel and making genuine contact. When barriers exist between people who are attempting to communicate, they typically feel distant from each other.

In *That's Not What I Meant*, Deborah Tannen (1987) focuses on how conversational styles can make or break a relationship. She maintains that male–female communication can be considered cross-cultural. The language we use as we are growing up is influenced by our gender, ethnicity, class and cultural background, and location. Boys and girls grow up in different worlds, even if they are part of the same family. Furthermore, they carry many of the patterns they established in childhood into their transactions as adults. For Tannen, these cultural differences include different expectations about the role of communication in relationships, and the subtle gender differences in communication style can lead to overwhelming misunderstandings and disappointments. Although conversational style differences do not explain all the conflicts in relationships between women and men, many problems result because partners are expressing their thoughts and feelings in different ways (Tannen, 1991). If we can sort out these differences based on conversational style, Tannen believes we will be better able to confront real conflicts and find a form of communication that will enable us to negotiate these differences.

Carl Rogers (1961), a pioneer in the humanistic approach to counseling, has written extensively on ways to improve personal relationships. For him, the main block to effective communication is our tendency to evaluate and judge the statements of others. He believes that what gets in the way of understanding another is the tendency to approve or disapprove, the unwillingness to put ourselves in the other's frame of reference, and the fear of being changed ourselves if we really listen to and understand a person with a viewpoint different from our own. Rogers suggests that the next time you get into an argument with your partner, your friend, or a small group of friends, stop the discussion for a moment and institute this rule: "Each person can speak up for himself only after he has restated the ideas and feelings of the previous speaker accurately, and to that speaker's satisfaction" (p. 332).

Carrying out this experiment requires that you strive to genuinely understand another person and achieve his or her perspective. Although this may sound simple, it can be extremely difficult to put into practice. It involves challenging yourself to go beyond what you find convenient to hear, examining your assumptions and prejudices, not attributing to statements meanings that were not intended, and not coming to quick conclusions based on superficial listening. If you are successful in challenging yourself in these ways, you can enter the subjective world of the significant person in your life; that is, you can acquire empathy, which is the necessary foundation for all intimate relationships. Rogers (1980) contends that the sensitive companionship offered by an empathic person is healing and that such a deep understanding is a precious gift to another.

Effective Personal Communication

Your culture influences both the content and the process of your communication. Some cultures prize direct communication; other cultures see this behavior as insensitive at best. In certain cultures direct eye contact is as insulting as the avoidance of eye contact is in other cultures. Harmony within the family is a cardinal value in certain cultures, and it may be inappropriate for even adult children to ever confront their parents. To do so could have detrimental consequences such as being physically and emotionally cut off. As you read the following discussion, recognize that variations do exist among cultures. Our discussion has a Euro-American slant, which makes it essential that you adapt the principles we present to your own cultural framework. Examine the ways your communication style has been influenced by your culture. You might well be satisfied with most of the communication patterns that you have acquired, in which case you will probably not see a need to change them.

From our perspective, when two people are communicating meaningfully, they are involved in many of the following processes:

- One is listening while the other speaks.
- They do not rehearse their response while the other is speaking. The listener is able to summarize accurately what the speaker has said. ("So you're hurt when I don't call to tell you that I'll be late.")
- The language is specific and concrete. (A vague statement is "I feel manipulated." A concrete statement is "I don't like it when you bring me flowers and then expect me to do something for you that I already told you I didn't want to do.")
- The speaker makes personal statements instead of bombarding the other with questions. (A questioning statement is "Where were you last night, and why did you come home so late?" A personal statement is "I was worried and scared because I didn't know where you were last night.")
- The listener takes a moment before responding to reflect on what was said and on how he or she is affected. There is a sincere effort to walk in the shoes of the other person. ("I'm sorry. It didn't even cross my mind to call you. I will be more sensitive next time.")
- Although each has reactions to what the other is saying, there is an absence of critical judgment. (A critical judgment is "You never think about anybody but yourself, and you're totally irresponsible." A more appropriate reaction would be "I appreciate it when you think to call me, knowing that I may be worried.")
- Each of the parties can be honest and direct without insensitively damaging the other's dignity. Each makes "I" statements rather than second-guessing and speaking for the other. ("Sometimes I worry that you don't care about me, and I want you to know that, rather than assuming that it's true.")
- There is respect for each other's differences and an avoidance of pressuring each other to accept a point of view. ("I look at this matter very differently than you do, but I understand that you have your own thoughts on it.")
- There is congruence (or matching) between the verbal and nonverbal messages. (If she is expressing anger, she is not smiling.)
- Each person is open about how he or she is affected by the other. (An ineffective response is "You have no right to criticize me." An effective response is "I'm disappointed that you don't like the work I've done.")
- Neither person is being mysterious, expecting the other to decode his or her messages.

These processes are essential for fostering any meaningful relationship. You might pay attention to yourself while you are communicating and take note of the degree to which you practice these principles. Decide if the quality of your relationships is satisfying to you. If you determine that you want to improve certain relationships, it will be helpful to begin by working on these skills.

Communicating With Your Parents

Our experience with our therapeutic groups has taught us how central our relationship with our parents is and how it affects all of our other interpersonal relationships. We learn from our parents how to deal with the rest of the world. We are often unaware of both the positive and negative impact our parents had, and perhaps continue to have, on us. Our groups consist of people of various ages, sociocultural backgrounds, life experiences, and vocations, yet many of the members have present struggles with their parents. It is not uncommon to have a 60-year-old man and a 20-year-old woman both expressing their frustration over not being supported by their parents. They both desire the parental approval that they have yet to experience. We find that there are also people who did get parental approval and support, yet who failed to recognize or accept it. Rather than being able to recognize what their parents *did* give them, they discount any positive aspects of the relationship. In our practice, we encounter much parent blaming, and it seems to be a challenge for many to come to terms with the fact that their parents are human. By accepting the fallibility of their parents, they make it possible to get beyond their grievances and open the channels of communication with their parents.

It is important to recognize the present effect that your parents are having on you and to decide the degree to which you like this effect, as well as any changes you may want to make. Rather than expecting your parents to make the first move, it may be more realistic for you to take the first step in bringing about the changes you desire. For example, if you hope for more physical signs of affection between you and your parents, you might initiate it. If you want more time with your mother and are disappointed with the quality of your time with her, ask yourself what is stopping you from asking for it. Too often people withdraw quickly when their expectations of others are not immediately met. If you desire intimacy with your parents, put aside your need to remake them.

GAY AND LESBIAN RELATIONSHIPS

Same-gender primary relationships are preferred by many people, yet gay, lesbian, and bisexual relationships continue to draw strong opposition. At the time of this writing, a few cities and states have granted the right to marry to same-sex couples. This has generated strong opposition with some opponents urging passage of a constitutional amendment to specify that "marriage is between a man and a woman." Recently, the U.S. Senate rejected the idea of creating such a constitutional amendment.

It is a myth that gay, lesbian, and bisexual relationships are basically different from heterosexual relationships. Common factors underlie all forms of intimate relationships; the guidelines for meaningful relationships presented earlier can be applied to friendships, parent–child relationships, and relationships between couples who are married or unmarried, gay or straight.

We cannot provide a comprehensive discussion of such a complex issue here, but we can dispel some of the myths and challenge some of the prejudices toward people based on their sexual orientation. Matlin (2004) defines some key terms pertaining to sexual identity:

- **Heterosexism** is a bias against gay males, lesbians, and bisexuals; it is a belief system that values heterosexuality as superior to homosexuality.
- A **lesbian** is a woman who is psychologically, emotionally, and sexually attracted to other women.
- **Gay men** are psychologically, emotionally, and sexually attracted to other men.
- **Bisexual** individuals are psychologically, emotionally, and sexually attracted to both women and men.

Some of you may be struggling over making a decision to identify yourself as gay (or to acknowledge and accept that in yourself). You may be affected by the prejudices of others, and you may be trying to clarify your values and decide how you want to be. The following discussion is designed to assist you in thinking about your views, assumptions, values, and possible biases and prejudices.

Psychological Views of Homosexuality

How sexual orientation is established is still not understood. Some experts argue that sexual orientation is at least partly a function of genetic or physiological factors, and others contend that homosexuality is entirely a learned behavior. Some maintain that both an internal predisposition and an environmental dimension come together to shape one's sexual orientation. And there are those who assert that sexual identity is strictly a matter of personal choice. Many gay men, lesbians, and bisexuals report that they did not actively choose their sexual orientation anymore than they did their sex. Where they see choice entering the picture is in deciding how they will act on their inclinations. Some will see that they have a choice of keeping their sexual orientation a secret or of "coming out" and claiming their affectional preference.

The American Psychiatric Association in 1973 and the American Psychological Association in 1975 stopped labeling homosexuality as a mental disorder, ending a long and bitter dispute. Along with these changes came the challenge to mental health professionals to modify their thinking and practice to reflect a view of homosexuality as being normal and healthy, rather than a manifestation of arrested psychosexual development and unresolved conflicts. Although three decades have passed since the decision to no longer consider homosexuality a form of psychopathology nor evidence of developmental

Same-gender sexual orientation can be regarded as another style of self-expression.

arrest, there is still a good deal of social prejudice, social stigmatization, and discrimination here and in many countries around the world (Pardess, 2005). Same-gender sexual orientation can be regarded as another style of self-expression.

Some heterosexual counselors see their role as actively trying to change gay couples or gay individuals to a heterosexual orientation, even if these clients do not present their sexual orientation as a problem. Some counselors will automatically attribute an individual's problems to his or her sexual orientation (Pardess, 2005). Mary Sykes Wylie (2000) writes that the current position of many evangelicals is that homosexuals cannot help being what they are and that their desire for same-gender partners is an "orientation," not a "choice." However, they believe *acting* on that unchosen orientation is both a choice and a sin. Wylie reports that "reparation therapy" is the goal of some Christian counselors who have the goal of loving gay people right out of their lifestyle and back into the straight Christian community.

Gay individuals and couples are not interested in changing their sexual orientation but seek counseling for many of the same reasons straight people do. In our consulting with counselors, we make our views quite clear. We see the counselor's responsibility as helping clients clarify their values and deciding for themselves what course of action to take. We strongly oppose the notion that counselors have the right to impose their values on their clients, to tell others how to live, or to make decisions for them. In many respects, personal issues that bring gay people to counseling are much the same as those that lead straight people to counseling, and include identity issues, relationship difficulties, and coping with crisis situations. In addition to these concerns, gay, lesbian, and bisexual individuals are often faced with dealing with the effects of prejudice, oppression, and discrimination. The task of the counselor is to help these individuals explore the problems that most concern them.

Prejudice and Discrimination Against Lesbians and Gay Men

In the past many people felt ashamed and abnormal because they had homosexual feelings. Heterosexuals frequently categorized gay and lesbian people as deviants and as sick or immoral. Pardess (2005) points out that negative views of homosexuals and opposition to homosexuality have been part of the culture of many religious traditions (Christianity, Judaism, and Islam), and in most religious settings homosexuality is considered to be morally wrong and a sin. According to Pardess, antigay prejudices are not limited to any specific cultural, social, or educational group. These prejudices exist across religions, professions, institutions, and cultures. For these and other reasons, many gay, lesbian, and bisexual individuals conceal their sexual identity, perhaps even from themselves. Furthermore, they are frequently confronted with heterosexism, interpersonal discrimination, verbal harassment, physical assault, and institutional discrimination (Matlin, 2004).

Today, the gay liberation movement is actively challenging the social stigma attached to sexual orientation, and those with same-sex partners are increasingly asserting their rights to live as they choose, without discrimination. However, just as gay men, lesbians, and bisexuals had won some rights and were more willing to disclose their sexual orientation, the AIDS crisis arose, once again creating more animosity, fear, and antipathy toward the gay population. Much of the public continues to cling to stereotypes, prejudices, and misconceptions regarding behavior between same-sex couples.

In writing about being a gay adolescent male, Pollack (1998) maintains that the tough problems they face are caused not by homosexuality but rather by society's misunderstanding of homosexuality. According to Pollack, the stereotypes and stigma that burden gay people are very much like those faced by other minorities. Like any minority group, lesbians, gay men, and bisexual individuals are subjected to discrimination, which manifests itself when gay people seek employment or a place of residence. For instance, the Department of Defense does not allow openly homosexual individuals in the military. The "Don't ask, don't tell" policy does not allow military personnel to be open about their sexual orientation. A special issue that lesbians, gay men, and bisexuals often bring to counseling is the struggle of concealing their identity versus "coming out." Dealing with other family members is of special importance to gay couples. They may want to be honest with their parents, yet they may fear alienating them.

Ann and Berit, friends of ours from Norway, wrote this personal account of the development of their relationship.

ANN AND BERIT'S STORY

We met when we were in our early 20s while attending a teacher education program in Norway. Over the years we became close friends and spent more and more time together. Even though neither of us ever married, both of us had various relationships with men, which for the most part, were not very satisfying.

Our families and friends often expressed concern and disapproval about the closeness of our relationship, which didn't appear "natural" or "normal" to them and which, they thought, might interfere with our "settling down with a good man" and starting a family. We kept our feelings for each other a secret for fear of rejection.

At one point, our relationship became a sexual one, a fact that brought out many of our self-doubts and vulnerabilities and the concern that, should we become separated, being sexually involved would make the parting even more difficult. The burden of pretending to be other than we were became increasingly heavy for us. We felt insincere and dishonest both toward each other and toward our families and friends, and we found the need to invent pat answers when others asked us why we were still single. Had we been honest, we would have said, "I'm not interested at all in a traditional marriage. I have a significant other, and I wish I didn't have to hide this very important part of my life."

BERIT'S STORY

Ann and my relationship was very anxiety producing, and I developed severe panic attacks. I saw a therapist, and my symptoms decreased. I never felt a need to explore my preference for women, but I did spend a good deal of time on the conflict between my need to do what I thought was right for me and my need to give in to external pressure to be "normal."

At the age of 40, we made the decision that we could no longer live with the duplicity. Either we would go separate ways, or we would share a life and acknowledge our relationship. After years of struggling, we were finally able to face ourselves, each other, and then the other significant people in our lives. Much to our surprise, when we did disclose the truth about our relationship, most of our relatives and friends were supportive and understanding, and some even told us that they knew of our "special" relationship. We felt a great burden had been lifted from us and began to experience a new sense of peace and happiness.

Just last year we got married. Ann's mother's first reaction to this was somewhat negative, probably because of her concern over what the neighbors and other relatives would think. However, when Ann's mother experienced nothing but positive reactions from her friends and family, her attitude changed and she accepted our marriage. My parents acted as if the marriage never took place. No remarks were ever made about the event, but they continued to treat both of us with respect, friendliness, and hospitality.

We got married first and foremost to protect each other financially. However, we are convinced that marriage overall has been an important aspect in our lives. It has made us feel more confident being the "number one" in each other's lives. It also makes a difference as to how others view us as a couple. We are both happy to live in Norway, a country that allows people of the same sex to marry.

Ann and Berit's story illustrates the struggle that many couples go through as they decide how they will live. Many of the issues that concerned Ann and Berit are the same interpersonal conflicts that any couple will eventually face and need to resolve. However, they must also deal with the pressure of being part of a segment of society that many consider unacceptable. Thus, being involved in a gay or lesbian relationship is not simply a matter of sexual preference; it involves a whole spectrum of interpersonal and practical issues. All the concerns about friendships, heterosexual relationships, and traditional marriage that we explore in this chapter apply to gay and lesbian relationships as well. Indeed, barriers to effective communication are found in every kind of intimate relationship. The challenge is to find ways of removing the blocks to honest communication and intimacy.

In categorizing relationships as heterosexual or homosexual, we sometimes forget that sex is not the only aspect of a relationship. Whatever way we choose to live, we need to examine whether it is the best choice for us. It is important that you define yourself, that you assume responsibility and accept the consequences for your own choices, and that you live out your choices with peace and inner integrity.

Take Time to Reflect

1. Are you aware of any prejudice toward people who have same-gender sexual orientations?

_____

_____

2. What are your views concerning the gay liberation movement? Should people who openly admit they are gay have rights equal to those of heterosexuals?

_____

_____

3. Do you think anyone should be denied any specific job because of his or her sexual orientation alone?

_____

_____

4. How do you react when you hear others making disparaging remarks about gay, lesbian, or bisexual individuals?

_____

_____

5. What are your thoughts about the many religions that view homosexuality as a sin?

_____

_____

SEPARATION AND DIVORCE

The principles we discuss here can be applied to separations between people who are friends, to unmarried people involved in an intimate relationship, or to married couples who are contemplating a divorce. The fear of being alone often keeps people from dissolving a relationship, even when they agree that there is little left in that relationship. People may say something like this: "I know what I have, and at least I have somebody. So maybe it's better to have that than nothing at all." Because of fear, many people remain in stagnant relationships.

Finding New Ways of Being in Relationships

An alternative to separating or stagnating is to remain in the relationship but challenge both yourself and your partner to create a different way of relating to each other. Many people have a capacity to be creative in redesigning their relationships and can avoid falling into unfulfilling routines.

At its best, marriage is a relationship that generates change through dialogue. Instead of being threatened by change, we can welcome it as necessary for keeping the relationship alive. In this way an impasse can become a turning point that enables two people to create a new way of life together. If both partners care enough about their investment in each other, and if they are committed to doing the work necessary to change old patterns and establish more productive ones, a crisis can actually enhance their relationship. People often terminate their relationships without really giving themselves or others a chance to face a particular crisis and work it through. For example, a man begins to see how unexciting his marriage is for him and to realize how he has contributed to his own unhappiness in it. As a result of changes in his perceptions and attitudes, he decides that he no longer wants to live with a woman in this fashion. However, rather than deciding to simply end the marriage, he might allow his partner to really see and experience him as the different person he is becoming. Moreover, he might encourage her to change as well instead of giving up on her too quickly. His progress toward becoming a more integrated person might well inspire her to work actively toward her own internal changes. This kind of work on the part of both people takes understanding and courage, but they may find that they can meet each other as new and changing persons and form a very different kind of relationship.

Sometimes, of course, ending a relationship seems to be the wisest course. Ending a relationship can be an act of courage that makes a new beginning possible. Our concern is that too many people may not be committed enough to each other to work together in times of crisis and struggle. As a result, they may separate at the very time when they could be making a new and different start together.

When to Separate or Terminate a Significant Relationship

How do two people know when a separation is the best solution? No categorical answer can be given to this question. However, before two people decide to terminate their relationship, they might consider these questions:

• *Has each of you sought personal therapy or counseling?* Self-exploration would lead to changes that would allow you and your partner to renew or strengthen your relationship.

• *Have you considered seeking relationship counseling?* Perhaps relationship counseling could lead to changes that would allow you and your partner to renew or strengthen your relationship. If you do get involved in relationship counseling of any type, it is important that both of you be committed to it.

• *Are you both interested in maintaining your relationship?* Perhaps one or both of you are no longer interested in keeping the old relationship, but you both at least want time together. We routinely ask both partners in a significant relationship who are experiencing difficulties to decide whether they even want to preserve their relationship. Here are some of the responses people give: "I don't really know. I've lost hope for any real change, and at this point I find it difficult to see a future together." "I'm sure that I don't want to live with this person anymore; I just don't care enough to work on improving things between us. I'm here so that we can finish the business between us and do what is best for the children." Another might say, "Even though we're going through some turmoil right now, I would very much like to care enough to make things better. Frankly, I'm not too hopeful, but I'm willing to give it a try." Whatever your response, it is imperative that you both know how the other feels about the possibility of renewing the relationship or terminating it.

• *Have you each taken the time to be alone, to get in focus, and to decide what kind of life you want for yourself and with others?* Few couples in troubled relationships arrange for time alone with each other. It is almost as if couples fear discovering that they really have little to say to each other. This discovery in itself might be very useful, for at least you might be able to do something about the situation if you confronted it; but many couples seem to arrange their lives in such a way as to prevent any possibility for intimacy.

• *What do you each expect from the divorce?* Sometimes, problems in a marriage are reflections of inner conflicts within the individuals in that marriage. In general, unless there are some changes within the individuals, the problems they experience may not end by divorce. In fact, many who divorce with the expectation of finding increased joy and freedom discover instead that they are still lonely, depressed, and anxious. Lacking insight into themselves, they may soon find a new partner very much like the one they divorced and repeat the same dynamics. Thus, a woman who finally decides to leave a man she thinks of as weak and passive may find a similar man to live with again, unless she comes to understand why she aligns herself with this type of person. Or a man who contends that he has "put up with" his wife for more than 20 years may find a similar person unless he understands what motivated him to stay with his first wife for so long. It is essential, therefore, that you come to know as clearly as possible why you are divorcing and that you look at the changes you may need to make in yourself as well as in your circumstances.

Sometimes one or both members of a couple identify strong reasons for separating but say that, for one reason or another, they are not free to do so. This kind of reasoning is always worth examining; an attitude of "I couldn't possibly leave" will not help either partner make a free and sound choice. Here are some of the reasons people give for refusing to call an end to their relationship:

• "I have an investment of 15 years with this person, and to end our relationship now would mean that these 15 years have been wasted." A person who feels this way might ask: "If I really don't see much potential for change, and if my partner has consistently and over a long period of time rebuffed any moves that might lead to improving our relationship, should I stay another 15 years?"

• "I can't leave because of the kids, but I do plan to leave as soon as they get into high school." This kind of thinking could burden children with unnecessary guilt. In a sense, it could make them responsible for the unhappiness of their parents. Why place the burden on the children if you stay in a place where you say you do not want to be? And will you find another reason to cement yourself to your partner once your children grow up? "Since the children need both a mother and a father, I cannot consider breaking up our marriage." True, children do need both a father and a mother, but it is worth asking whether they will get much of value from either parent if they see them unloving with each other. How useful is the model that parents present when they stay together and the children see how little joy they experience? Parents can set a better and more honest example if they openly admitted that they no longer choose to remain together.

● One man in a gay relationship may say, "I'm afraid to break off the relationship because I might be even more lonely than I am now." Certainly, loneliness is a real possibility. There are no guarantees that a new relationship will be established after one relationship is terminated. He might be reluctant to leave the relationship because his parents warned him of the problems he was getting into when he decided on an arrangement of living together. However, he might be more lonely living with someone he does not like, much less love, than he would be if he were living alone. Living alone might bring far more serenity and inner strength than remaining in a relationship that is no longer right for him. If he refuses to get out of a relationship because of what his parents might say about his original choice, he is almost certain to experience more alienation than he already does.

● "One thing that holds me back from separating is that I might discover that I left too soon and that I didn't give us a fair chance." To avoid this regret, partners should explore all the possibilities for creating a new relationship before making the decision to dissolve their relationship.

Leaving Abusive Relationships

At times, people find themselves in relationships that are emotionally or physically abusive, yet they are hesitant to leave these relationships. Abusive relationships have been getting a great deal of media attention, and people who have left abusive relationships often report that they did not recognize the full extent to which the relationship was toxic. Although they may have had opportunities to terminate the relationship, they rationalized that their situation was not really so bad. They often excuse the partner's behavior and find fault with themselves for bringing about the abuse. The individual doing the abuse might well demonstrate regret for hurting the partner and give promises to reform. However, soon afterward the same cycle repeats itself, and one person in the relationship feels trapped. Many times people stay in this kind of relationship because they do not know where to go, nor do they know who can help them. Here are some signs that could indicate an abusive relationship:

● Verbal put downs

● Withholding love and affection

● Striking, hitting, pushing, shoving

● Using physical or psychological threats

● Making promises, yet never keeping them

● Unpredictable behavior

- Extreme jealousy and possessiveness
- Chronic hostility and sarcasm

Not all abusive relationships involve physical violence. Subtle emotional abuse over a period of time can also erode a relationship. Remaining in such a relationship generally makes it difficult for an individual to want to reach out and form new friendships. He or she often becomes numb and is cautious about trusting anyone.

People sometimes remain in unhealthy relationships in the hopes that their situation will improve. Perhaps one of the partners believes he or she can change the other person. Frequently, this attempt ends in frustration. It is important that individuals recognize what they are not getting with their partner, and that they not deny reality. For example, abused spouses may tell themselves that they cannot possibly take a certain course of action. They may need special help. They can take a real step toward freedom when they accept the reality of their situation and find a haven in the community that will give them assistance.

Coping With Ending a Long-Term Relationship

When a long-term relationship comes to an end, a mixture of feelings, ranging from a sense of loss and regret to relief, may be present. Betty, an unmarried college student in her mid-20s, is going through some typical reactions to the breakup of a 3-year relationship with her boyfriend Isaac.

BETTY'S STORY

*A*t first I felt abandoned and was afraid of never finding a suitable replacement. I kept wondering who was at fault. I switched back and forth between blaming myself and blaming Isaac. I was depressed, and I wasn't eating or sleeping well. Then I began to withdraw from other relationships too. I felt worthless and inadequate. Because my relationship with Isaac didn't work out, it proves that I'm a failure and unlovable and that I won't be able to establish and keep any other relationships. It is a sure sign that I'll never get along with any man. Isaac found me undesirable, and I don't think I can stand the pain of this rejection.

Internal dialogue such as this kept Betty from taking any action that could change her situation. It was not the breakup itself that was causing Betty's reactions; rather, her beliefs about and her interpretations of the breakup were giving her trouble.

There are no easy ways to ending a long-standing relationship. A breakup or loss of a friend or significant other can lead to feelings of pain, anger, and grief. If you find yourself in such a situation, there are some attitudes you can assume and some behaviors you can choose that are likely to help you work through these feelings. Here are some suggestions for dealing effectively with the termination of a meaningful relationship:

- *Allow yourself to grieve.* Although grieving can be both overwhelming and painful, the alternative of denying your feelings will keep you from being able to move on and could cause you to have intimacy problems later.

- *Give yourself time.* As the saying goes, "Time heals all wounds." However long or short it takes, it is important to permit yourself to grieve based on being true to your own self and not because others feel you should be over it by now.

- *Express your anger.* Sometimes breakups leave us feeling angry and bitter. Remember that anger is a normal reaction, yet if unexpressed or overindulged in, it can cause serious problems later.

- *Depersonalize your partner's actions.* Often, when one person ends a relationship, the other is left feeling rejected as though the failure was of his or her making. A person's decision to end a relationship with you may say more about that person than it does about you.

- *Take responsibility for your own part in the relationship.* It may be easier to find fault in the other person, but exploring your own behaviors can be helpful to your healing process. The point is not to find blame but to gain insight into how you relate to people in both negative and positive ways.

- *Find a support network.* Whether you are shy or social, having people to support you can provide you with some level of stability in a time of loss and change. Seek counseling or professional help if you feel that you cannot cope with the loss on your own. Many universities offer free student counseling.

- *Keep busy.* Setting aside time to grieve is important, yet after a certain amount of time, other parts of you need to be attended to. Engaging in some form of activity can help you stay connected to the aspects of your life that continue outside the relationship.

- *Write in your journal.* Writing can help you release emotions even if you are not able to talk to others about how you are feeling. Later, it can be useful to read what you wrote to see how things have changed.

- *Make amends.* Making amends and forgiving both yourself and your partner can free you from carrying the pain and anger into future relationships. Remember, your anger hurts and burdens you more than anyone else.

- *Get closure.* Coming to some type of closure is essential to moving forward. To one person it may mean forgiveness, and for another it may include some type of a ritual or final letter. Closure does not mean it never happened. It means you have decided to live.

- *Love and learn.* At some point you will find that it can be freeing to reflect on what you have learned from the experience. Even the most abusive or unhealthy relationship can teach you something about yourself and the types of relationships you want to have.

Take Time to Reflect Complete the following sentences by writing down the first response that comes to mind. Suggestion: Ask your partner or a close friend to do the exercise on a separate sheet of paper; then compare and discuss your responses.

1. To me, intimacy means _____

2. The most important thing in making an intimate relationship successful is

_____

3. The thing I most fear about an intimate relationship is _____

4. What I like most about an intimate relationship is _____

5. One of the reasons I need another person is _____

6. One conflict that I have concerning intimate relationships is _____

7. In an intimate relationship, it is unrealistic to expect that _____

8. To me, commitment means _____

9. I have encouraged my partner to grow by _____

10. My partner has encouraged me to grow by _____

SUMMARY

In this chapter we have encouraged you to think about what characterizes a growing, meaningful relationship and to ask yourself these questions: "Do I have what I want in my various relationships?" "Do I desire more (or less) intimacy?" "What changes would I most like to make in my intimate relationships?" "In each of my relationships, can the other person and I maintain separate identities and clear boundaries?" The themes explored in this chapter can be applied to all intimate relationships, regardless of one's sexual orientation. Although same-gender relationships are not well accepted by some people in our society, it is important to realize that all couples share some common challenges.

A major barrier to developing and maintaining relationships is our tendency to evaluate and judge others. By attempting to change others, we typically increase their defensiveness. A key characteristic of a meaningful relationship is the ability of the people involved to listen and to respond to each other. They are able to communicate effectively, and they are committed to staying in the relationship even when communication is difficult. It is important to pay attention to both cultural and gender differences that make up our conversational style. Many misunderstandings are due to the different ways women and men express their thoughts and feelings.

Maintaining a relationship entails dedication and a commitment to make it work. Although there are many sources of conflict in intimate relationships, a potential problem is a sense of predictability that comes with assuming to know another person well. It takes both imagination and effort to think of ways to keep our relationships vital. At times people decide that a relationship has reached a dead end, and they give serious consideration to separating. Although this may be a solution for some situations, a relationship that has become dysfunctional can also be examined and possibly rejuvenated. Again, commitment is essential, because time will be required to resolve issues that are divisive and cause conflict.

The picture we have drawn of a growing relationship is not a dogmatic or necessarily complete one; nor will your relationships, however good they are, always approximate it. Our hope is that these reflections will stimulate your own independent thinking. You can begin by honestly assessing the present state of your intimate relationships. Then consider the choices that can lead to positive change in those areas over which you are dissatisfied.

Throughout this chapter we have emphasized that we must actively work to recognize problems in ourselves and in our relationships if we are to make intimacy as rewarding as it can be. You can choose the quality of the relationships you want in your life.

Where Can I Go From Here?

Some of these activities can be done on your own; others are designed for two persons in an intimate relationship. Select the ones that mean the most to you and consider sharing the results with the other members of your class.

1. In your journal write down some reflections on your parents' relationship. Consider these questions:

- Would you like the same kind of relationship your parents have had?
- What are some of the things you like best about their relationship?
- What are some features of their relationship that you would not want in your own relationships?
- How have your own views, attitudes, and practices regarding intimacy been affected by your parents' relationship? Would you marry a woman like your mother? A man like your father? Why or why not?

2. How much self-disclosure and honesty do you want in your intimate relationships? Reflect in your journal on how much you would share your feelings concerning each of the following with your partner.

- Your need for support from your partner
- Your angry feelings
- Your dreams
- Your friendships with other persons
- Your ideas on religion and your philosophy of life
- The times when you feel inadequate as a person
- The times when you feel extremely close and loving toward your partner
- The times in your relationship when you feel boredom, anger, or detachment

Now think about how open you want your partner to be with you. If your partner were doing this exercise, what answers do you wish he or she would give for each of the items?

3. Over a period of about a week, do some writing about the evolution of your relationship and ask your partner to do the same. Consider why you were initially attracted to each other and how you have changed since then. Do you like these changes? What would you most like to change about your life together now? List the best things about your relationship and also some problem areas you need to explore. If you could do it over again, would you select the same person? After you have each written about these and any other questions that are significant for you, read each other's writing and discuss it. This activity can stimulate you to talk more honestly with each other and can also give each of you the chance to see how the other perceives the relationship.

4. As you look at various television shows, keep a record for a couple of weeks of the messages you get regarding marriage, family life, and intimacy. What are some common stereotypes? What gender roles are portrayed? What myths do you think are being presented? Write down some of the attitudes you have incorporated from television and other media about marriage, family life, and intimacy. Do you want to rethink any of them?

Resources for Future Study

Web Site Resources

WHOLEFAMILY
http://www.wholefamily.com/

This site offers extensive information and resources on family life including the Marriage Center, the Parent Center, the Teen Center, the WholeFamily Room (where the family meets to get each other's points of view), the Senior Center, weekly dilemmas, publications, and articles on mothering.

DIVORCE CENTRAL
http://www.divorcecentral.com/

Divorce Central provides information and advice on legal, emotional, and financial issues for individuals who are considering or going through a divorce. You can use all of their services and can become a member of their online community for free. Links to other divorce-related sites are also available here.

PARTNERS TASK FORCE FOR GAY
AND LESBIAN COUPLES
http://www.buddybuddy.com/toc-cont.html

Partners Task Force for Gay and Lesbian Couples is a national resource for same-sex couples, supporting the diverse community of committed gay and lesbian partners through a variety of media. This frequently updated Web site contains more than 200 essays, surveys, legal articles, and resources on legal marriage, ceremonies, domestic partner benefits, relationship tips, parenting, and immigration.

SEXUAL ORIENTATION: SCIENCE, EDUCATION,
AND POLICY
http://www.psychology.ucdavis.edu/rainbow/

This site builds on the work of Dr. Gregory Herek's research focusing on sexual orientation, antigay violence, homophobia, and other concerns of gay, lesbian, and bisexual individuals.

YOUTH ASSISTANCE ORGANIZATION FOR GAY, LESBIAN,
AND BISEXUAL YOUTH
http://www.youth.org

Youth.Org is a service run by volunteers that was created to help self-identifying gay, lesbian, bisexual, and questioning youth. This organization provides young people with a safe space online to be themselves.

Human Rights Campaign
http://www.hrcusa.org

The Human Rights Campaign is an organization for securing equal rights for lesbians and gay men. This site provides news updates on legislation related to gay rights and descriptions of public education programs.

InfoTrac College Edition Resources

For additional readings, explore INFOTRAC COLLEGE EDITION, our online library:
http://www.infotrac.college.com/wadsworth

Hint: Enter the search terms:

intimate relationships

interpersonal relationships

intimacy

anger

anger management

conflict resolution

interpersonal communication

forgiveness

gay relationship

lesbian relationship

bisexuality

homophobia

homosexuality

heterosexuality

hetereosexism

divorce

Print Resources

Anderson, S. K., & Middleton, V. A. (2005). *Explorations in privilege, oppression, and diversity.* Belmont, CA: Thomson Brooks/Cole.

Carroll, J. L. (2005). *Sexuality now: Embracing diversity.* Belmont, CA: Thomson Wadsworth.

Crooks, R., & Baur, K. (2002). *Our sexuality* (8th ed.). Belmont, CA: Thomson Wadsworth.

Gottman, J. M., & Silver, N. (1999). *The seven principles for making marriage work.* New York: Three Rivers Press.

Jampolsky, G. G. (1999). *Forgiveness: The greatest healer of all.* Hillsboro, OR: Beyond Words.

Matlin, M. W. (2004). *The psychology of women* (5th ed.). Belmont, CA: Wadsworth/Thomson Learning.

Schwartz, M. (1996). *Morrie: In his own words.* New York: Dell (Delta Books).

Vanzant, I. (1998). *One day my soul just opened up.* New York: Simon & Schuster (Fireside Books).

Webb, D. (1996). *Divorce and separation recovery.* Portsmouth, NH: Randall.

Webb, D. (2000). *50 ways to love your leaver: Getting on with your life after the breakup.* Atascadero, CA: Impact.

Weiner-Davis, M. (1995). *Change your life and everyone in it.* New York: Simon & Schuster (Fireside Books).

When gender transcendence occurs, people can be just people.

—Basow

Becoming the Woman or Man You Want to Be

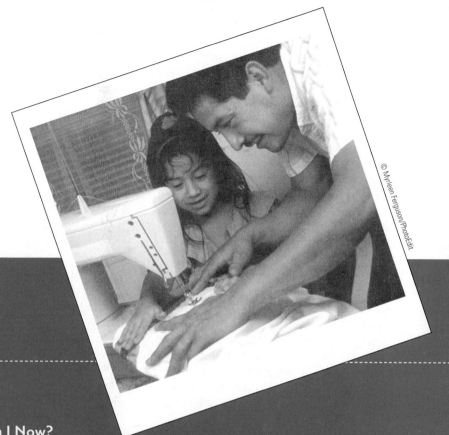

© Myrleen Ferguson/PhotoEdit

Where Am I Now?

Use this scale to respond to these statements:

> 3 = This statement is true of me *most* of the time.
>
> 2 = This statement is true of me *some* of the time.
>
> 1 = This statement is true of me *almost none* of the time.

1. It is important to me to be perceived as feminine [masculine].

2. I have a clear sense of what it means to be a man [woman].

3. It is relatively easy for me to be both logical and emotional, tough and tender, objective and subjective.

4. I have trouble accepting both women who show masculine qualities and men who show feminine qualities.

5. It is difficult for me to accept in myself traits that are often associated with the other gender.

6. I welcome the change toward more flexibility in gender roles.

7. I think I am becoming the kind of woman [man] I want to become, regardless of anyone else's ideas about what is expected of my gender.

8. I am glad that I am the gender that I am.

9. I feel discriminated against because of my gender.

10. My parents provided good models of what it means to be a woman [man].

ll of us are the products of our cultural conditioning to some extent. Behavior depends not on gender but on prior experience, learned attitudes, cultural expectations, sanctions, opportunities for practice, and situational demands. We learn behavior that is appropriate for our gender by interacting in society. **Gender-role socialization** is a process of learning those behaviors (norms and roles) that are expected of people in a particular society. Learning about gender differences does not cease with childhood; rather, it is a lifelong process.

In this chapter we invite you to examine the experiences that have directly and indirectly influenced your gender-role identity. We describe some of the detrimental effects and costs for women and men who feel they must live in accordance with rigid gender roles. **Sexism** is a bias against people on the basis of their gender. People tend to make clear distinctions between women and men, and they divide the world into two categories, male and female. Because women are viewed as being psychologically different from men, people react differently to men and women (Matlin, 2004).

Ask yourself these questions: "What did I learn about gender roles from my parents?" "From my culture?" "What attitudes prevailed in my home about gender roles, and how does this influence the woman or man I am today?" "What biases do I hold toward individuals based on gender?" "Has the way I've been socialized enhanced or hindered the manner in which I live?" With increased awareness, you will be able to assess both the positive and negative effects your gender-role socialization is having on all aspects of your life. Then you can decide what changes, if any, you want to make. We encourage you to think critically about gender-role stereotypes and to form your own standards of the woman or man you could be and want to be. This assessment requires patience and an appreciation of the difficulties involved in overcoming ingrained attitudes, but the real challenge is to translate the new attitudes that you may acquire into your actual behavior.

As you read this chapter, reflect on the models that have influenced your views of what it means to be a woman or a man and on the choices that are available to you. Societal norms provide one set of standards, but you can decide for yourself what kind of person you want to be based on what you truly value.

MALE ROLES

An increasing number of men are giving expression to both masculine and feminine dimensions of their personalities. However, many men in our society still live according to a traditional masculine model of what it is to be a man. The pressures on men to behave in ways that conflict with traditional masculine models have never been greater. Many men have put all their energy into maintaining an acceptable male image and have lost themselves. Andronico and Horne (2004) contend that "while many traditional roles have changed, most men still feel the pressure of fulfilling the three P's: Provider, Protector, and Procreator" (p. 457). According to Ronald Levant (1996), men now face pressures to make commitments in relationships, to share housework, to view sexuality in the context of loving relationships, and to curb aggression. These pressures "have shaken traditional masculinity ideology to such an extent there is now a masculinity crisis in which many feel bewildered and confused, and pride associated with being a man is lower than at any time in the recent past" (p. 259). Traditional male roles certainly pose problems for those men who take issue with what is considered to be "masculine" in our society.

Gender-role socialization begins early in life. Throughout childhood, boys are socialized to reject anything that makes them appear feminine. During adolescence, boys learn that manhood is not automatically conferred upon them; rather, it is something that is achieved through dangerous rites of passage. Boys are encouraged to compare themselves with one another, and they often worry whether they measure up (Philpot, Brooks, Lusterman, & Nutt, 1997).

In his discussion of society's messages to boys, Terrance Real (1998) states that boys learn early on that they should have fewer emotional needs than girls. While girls are encouraged to fully develop connection and relationship, boys are discouraged from developing their relational, emotional selves. Boys are encouraged to develop their assertive selves, while girls are discouraged from developing assertive action and independence.

As toddlers, boys are pressured to leave their close relationship with their mother so they can begin to become independent and self-reliant little men. William Pollack (1998) suggests that the sadness and disconnection men often experience stems from the loss of this relationship. Men sometimes have fears about commitment in long-term relationships. The fear of getting too close in adult relationships may be grounded in their reaction to this earlier loss of the maternal relationship. The move from the female world of nurturance and love to the male world of independence and competition can be drastic for boys. The pain of this loss is often repressed, yet it may surface in an intimate relationship. Men crave a return of the nurturance, but they also fear the pain of loss (see Cochran & Rabinowitz, 1996).

Real (1998) asserts that boys and men need social connection to the same degree as girls and women. Boys and men will not heal from their wounds of disconnection until they learn to place themselves inside relationships rather than above them. Real states:

> UNTIL A MAN HAS HALTED THE ACTING OUT OF HIS DISTRESS, dealt with his relationship to himself, and brought his mature self to acknowledge and deal with early wounds that remain very much alive within him, he will be inescapably impaired in his capacity to sustain a fully satisfying relationship. (p. 290)

During adolescence, boys are often subjected to shaming, and these messages are powerfully reinforced by "locker-room" experiences wherein boys are teased or isolated when they express vulnerable feelings. For example, passivity, artistic interests, celibacy, caution, and abstinence from alcohol are commonly viewed as shameful (Philpot et al., 1997). Pollack (1998) asserts that when boys feel ashamed of their vulnerability they often mask their emotions and ultimately their true selves. Because society's prevailing myths about boys do not allow for emotions such as feeling alone, helpless, and fearful, it is common for boys to feel that they do not measure up. Eventually, their sensitivity is submerged until they lose touch with themselves and become "tough" in the way society expects them to be. The result of this socialization process is a gender straightjacket.

Pollack (1998) argues that boys should be encouraged to show *all* of their emotions. Boys need to know that both their strengths and their vulnerabilities will be celebrated. In short, boys need to hear the message that all of their feelings, not just anger, are normal and "masculine."

In our work with men, we see signs that many men are struggling to live up to culturally defined standards for male behavior. In the safe environment that a therapy group can provide, we also see a strong desire in these men to modify some of the ways in which they feel they must live. For instance, they are willing to let other group members know that they do not always feel strong and that they are scared at times. As trust builds within the therapeutic group, these men become increasingly willing to share their personal pain and longings, and they struggle to accept this dimension of themselves. As these men become more honest with women, they typically discover that women are more able to accept, respect, and love the real them. The very traits that men fear to reveal to women are the characteristics that draw others closer to them. This often results in removing some of the barriers that prevent intimacy between the sexes.

Rabinowitz (2001) maintains that "a well-functioning men's group nurtures interpersonal trust, facilitates psychological awareness, encourages risk, and provides safe containment of strong emotions for its members" (p. 618). All-male groups provide men with the support they need to become aware of the restrictive roles they may have lived by and provide them with the strength to challenge the mandate of the masculine role. The group helps men to confront their disappointments and losses. Rather than denying past hurt and wounding, men are invited to openly explore these feelings, which allows for healing by the supportive action of the group. Men are able to learn that it is safe to express anger, grief, and frustration. In a supportive and challenging climate, men are able to face their fears of the unknown and to take risks. Although each man must decide what, when, and how to risk, he knows that the group will accept him regardless of the choices he makes (Rabinowitz & Cochran, 2002).

It is a commonly held belief that women and men differ substantially on a number of characteristics. Men are considered to be higher in **agency** (concern with one's own self-interests, such as competition and independence), and women are considered to be higher in **communion** (concern for one's relationship with other people). These general stereotypes have remained fairly consistent throughout recent decades (Matlin, 2004). Many men and women live restricted lives because they have accepted these cultural judgments about what it means to be male or female. Unfortunately, too many people are caught in rigid roles and expect, and sometimes receive, sanctions when they deviate from those roles or display characteristics that are not associated with their gender. People often become so involved in their roles that they become alienated from themselves. They no longer know what they are like inside because they put so much energy into maintaining an acceptable image. This was certainly the case for Abraham, who learned traditional male attitudes and behaviors from his father.

ABRAHAM'S STORY

*M*y father was hard-working, distant with us children, stoic, and prized himself for being a self-reliant individual. I learned from my father what a man is supposed to be and what behaviors are acceptable, and these attitudes were reinforced in school and by society. For a long time I did not even realize I was being restricted psychologically by these expectations, but then I faced a crisis in midlife. My father had a heart attack, and I was shocked to realize the toll that living by traditional roles had taken on him.

I began to look at the impact my definition of maleness was having on all aspects of my life, and I decided to make some changes. I realized that I had never questioned my attitudes about gender-role behavior and that I was behaving unconsciously and automatically rather than by choice. I wanted to become more expressive, but I had to struggle against years of conditioning that restricted the range of my emotional responses. I did increase my level of consciousness intellectually through reading and personal counseling, but I seem to be having trouble catching up emotionally and behaviorally. It is more difficult than I thought it would be to turn these insights into new behaviors.

Both Abraham and his father suffer from **gender-role strain** (Pleck, 1995). Societal norms for gender ideals are often contradictory, inconsistent, and unattainable. When men are unable to live up to these unrealistic societal expectations, they are subject to many psychological problems. Men who experience gender-role conflict and stress are more likely to be depressed, anxious, express hostility in interpersonal behaviors, have poor self-esteem, harbor anger, misuse substances, and engage in high-risk behavior (Mahalik, 1999a).

The next section considers some of the aspects of the traditional masculine ideology, examining stereotypes of males and identifying messages that men are given about appropriate role behavior.

Stereotypical View of Males

In general, the stereotypical male is cool, detached, objective, rational, worldly, competitive, and strong. A man who attempts to fit the stereotype will suppress most of his feelings, for he sees the subjective world of feelings as being essentially feminine. A number of writers have identified the characteristics of a man living by the stereotype and the feelings he may attempt to suppress or deny: Basow (1992), Farrell (2000), Goldberg (1983, 1987), Harris (1995), Jourard (1971), Keen (1991), Kimmel (1996), Lerner (1985, 1989), Levant (1996), Lott (1994), Mahalik (1999a, 1999b), Mornell (1979), Philpot et al. (1997), Pleck (1995), Pollack (1998), Rabinowitz and Cochran (1994, 2002), Real (1998), Rosen (2005), and Witkin (1994). Keep in mind that the following discussion is about the *stereotypical* view of males, and certainly many men do not fit this narrow characterization. It would be a mistake to conclude that this picture is an accurate portrayal of the way *most* men are or should be. However, many men in our society hear messages that dictate ways they should think, feel, and act. The limited view of the traditional male role that many men have accepted, to a greater or lesser degree, is characterized by these traits.

• *Emotional unavailability.* A man tends to show his affection by being a "good provider." Frequently, he is not emotionally available to his female partner or to his family. Because of this, she may complain that she feels shut out by him. He also has a difficult time dealing with her feelings. If she cries, he becomes uncomfortable and quickly wants to "fix her" so she will stop crying.

• *Independence.* A man is expected to be fully self-reliant. Rather than admitting that he needs anything from anyone, he may lead a life of exaggerated independence. He feels that he should be able to do by himself whatever needs to be done, and he finds it hard to reach out to others by asking for emotional support or nurturing.

• *Power and aggressiveness.* A man hears the message that he must be powerful physically, sexually, intellectually, and financially. A man receives the message that he must always be tough and fight for what he thinks is right. He is told that he must take risks, be adventurous, and resort to violence if necessary. He feels that he must be continually active, aggressive, assertive, and striving. He views the opposites of these traits as signs of weakness, and he fears being seen as soft.

- *Denial of fears.* A man hears the message that it is important to hide his fears, even in situations where he is frightened. He has the distorted notion that to be afraid means that he lacks courage, so he tries to hide his fears from himself and especially from others. He does not see that being frightened is a necessary part of courage. He fears being ashamed or humiliated in front of other men or being dominated by stronger men (Kimmel, 1996).

- *Protection of his inner self.* With other men he keeps himself hidden because they are competitors and in this sense potential enemies. He does not disclose himself to women because he is afraid they will think him unmanly and weak if they see his inner core. A woman may complain that a man hides his feelings from her, yet it is probably more accurate to say that he is hiding his feelings from himself. A man's tendency to protect his inner self begins when he is a boy and learns to hide his inner core with an image of toughness, stoicism, and strength (Pollack, 1998).

- *Invulnerability.* He cannot make himself vulnerable, as is evidenced by his general unwillingness to disclose much of his inner experience. He will not let himself feel and express sadness, nor will he cry. He interprets any expression of emotional vulnerability as a sign of weakness. To protect himself, he becomes emotionally insulated and puts on a mask of toughness, competence, and decisiveness.

- *Lack of bodily self-awareness.* Common physical stress signals include headaches, nausea, heartburn, muscle aches, backaches, and high blood pressure, but a man often ignores these stress symptoms, denying their potential consequences and failing to address their causes. He doesn't recognize bodily cues that may signal danger. For example, it is well known that heart disease and cardiovascular disease death rates are significantly higher in men than women. According to Real (1998), men die early because they do not take care of themselves. They are slow to recognize when they are sick, take longer to get help, and even after getting treatment tend not to cooperate with it as well as women do. Too often a man will drive himself unmercifully and treat his body as some kind of machine that will not break down or wear out. He may not pay attention to his exhaustion until he collapses from it.

- *Remoteness with other men.* Although he may have plenty of acquaintances, he does not confide in many male friends. Men have difficulty creating and sustaining same-gender friendships or communicating their emotional problems or vulnerability (Rosen, 2005). It is not uncommon for men to state that they do not have a single male friend with whom they can be intimate. He can talk to other men about things but finds it hard to be personal. When men talk to each other, it is often about planning what they are going to do. For a description of the process two men experience in a men's group, see Rabinowitz and Cochran (2002).

- *Driven to succeed.* A man is told that it is important to win and be competitive to get recognition, respect, and status. He has been socialized to believe success at work is the measure of his value as a man. He feels he is expected to succeed and produce, to be "the best," and to get ahead and stay ahead. He measures his worth by the money he makes or by his job title. Real (1998) contends men measure themselves with unrealistically narrow and perfectionistic standards of masculinity that leave them feeling that they rarely sufficiently measure up. One of the heaviest burdens a man carries is his need to continually prove his masculinity to himself and to others. This drive to prove himself can be a mask for deeper feelings of low self-esteem and insecurity (Rosen, 2005).

- *Denial of "feminine" qualities.* Men are frequently shut off from their emotional selves. From infancy through adulthood men are socialized to give short shrift to their emotions (Rabinowitz & Cochran, 1994). Some psychologists who have studied the traditional male role (Levant, 1996; Pleck, 1995) consider antifemininity to be the key theme associated with the male gender role. Men fear acting in any way that could be viewed as being feminine. A man hears the message that he should always be in full control of his emotions. He cannot be a man and at the same time possess (or reveal) traits usually attributed to women. Therefore, he is highly controlled, cool, detached, and shuts out much of what he could experience, which results in an impoverished emotional life. He does not give himself much latitude to deviate from a narrow band of expression. Because of his aversion to being labeled as feminine, a man finds it difficult to express warmth and tenderness or to publicly display tenderness or compassion.

- *Avoidance of physical contact.* A man has a difficult time touching freely or expressing affection and caring for other men. He thinks he should touch a woman only if it will lead to sex, and he fears touching other men because he does not want to be perceived as effeminate or homosexual.

- *Rigid perceptions.* A man tends to view gender roles as rigid categories. Women should be dependent, emotional, passive, and submissive; men are expected to be independent, logical, active, and aggressive.

- *Devotion to work.* A man is socialized with the message that work is the most important part of his identity. He puts much of his energy into external signs of success through his achievements at work. Thus, little is left over for his wife and children, or even for leisure pursuits. A man's obsession with defining himself mainly through work provides an acceptable outlet for pent-up energy. The result of getting lost in his work is forgetting to make contact with his inner spiritual self and intimate contact with others (Rabinowitz & Cochran, 1994).

- *Loss of the male spirit and experience of depression.* Because he is cut off from his inner self, he has lost a way to make intuitive sense of the world. Relying on society's definitions and rules about masculinity rather than his own leaves him feeling empty, and he experiences guilt, shame, anxiety, and depression (Keen, 1991). The secret legacy of male depression is a silent epidemic in men, a condition they hide from their family, friends, and themselves to avoid the stigma of "unmanliness" (Real, 1998). Recovery from depression entails the willingness of a man to face his pain and learn to cherish and take care of himself. Not until a man captures his own spirit will he be able to value and care for others.

African American Masculinity

Men often hide their feelings of vulnerability and are ever watchful of others' reactions, looking for indications that they might be exposed to ridicule. Hiding their true nature is characteristic of many men, regardless of their racial, ethnic, and cultural background, but the dilemma of masculine identity is especially challenging for African American men who must reclaim the manhood stolen from them by slavery and oppression (Rosen, 2005). Literary images of freed Black slaves at the turn of the century address the familiar idea of the self-made man who would reclaim his manhood (Kimmel, 1996).

Audrey Chapman (1993), a therapist with a good deal of experience working with African American men, sees their desire to connect with someone after years of frustration at not "getting it right." These men are skilled at hiding their feelings, and they see crying as the ultimate affront to manhood. Underneath their surface bravado is likely to be a scared and lonely person. Chapman emphasizes how important it is to learn to listen and be patient when these men do express what they are feeling or thinking: "If I could stress only one issue with black women, it would be the necessity of understanding and accepting the fragility of our men's psyche. They desire and need bonding as much as we do, but they need a road map to get where they long to be" (p. 225).

In teaching courses on the psychology of African American males, Caldwell and White (2001) ask students to identify images of Black males in the media and popular culture. Stereotypes such as absent father, drug dealer, pimp, gangster, and academic underachiever are often identified, and these negative and distorted images are internalized by many Black males. One way to correct such negative internalized self-images is through masculinity training and rites of passage programs for African American boys and young men, which are becoming increasingly popular. Although there are different formats for Black manhood training programs, most emphasize African American values and principles of living. These programs emphasize responsibility for self and others, wellness and self-care, respect for others, teamwork, problem solving, coping skills, responsibility for family and community, respect for women, self-discipline, and drug use prevention. Boys and young men learn how to apply principles of spirituality, connectedness with others, harmony with nature, and collective work responsibility to their daily life as essential dimensions of masculinity. Black males are taught a range of options for redefining a masculine identity and lifestyle that is psychologically healthy (Caldwell & White, 2001).

Masculinity and Latino Cultures

Like other cultural groups, Hispanic populations differ across numerous variables, making it impossible to discuss Latino masculinity as a unified entity. The typical representation of this group in the United States is largely based on stereotyped images, including little ambition, lower class, chauvinistic, uneducated, poorly groomed, and alcohol abusers (Casas, Turner, & Ruiz de Esparza, 2001). Most of these stereotypes are negative and pathological. In contrast to these stereotypes, Casas and his colleagues report that researchers have documented these value orientations associated with Latino cultures: maintaining distinct male and female gender roles, a strong sense of community, interest in the family, concept of *respeto* and dignity, present time orientation, respect for elders and children, and respect for religious and spiritual beliefs. The gender-role socialization of Hispanic American men is likely to differ in many respects from that of Euro-American males.

Asian American Masculinity

David Sue (2001) writes about the concept of masculinity in Asian American males. Sue contends that Asian men are stereotyped as being poor at sports, good in mathematics, and villains in the mass media. They are typically not viewed as possessing the traditional masculine characteristics valued in American society. Sue states that among traditional Asian American men, masculinity is determined by adherence to traditional values and successfully teaching these values to their children. Some of these traditional values include a collectivistic spirit, hierarchical relationships in which males are given higher status than females, directive and authoritarian parenting styles, emotional restraint as a sign of maturity, respect for authority, and modesty. Sue concludes that Asian males tend to experience gender-role changes differently from Euro-American males. According to Sue and Sue (2003), masculinity is not defined individually for Asian men but is a function of how they relate to others. Because of the conflict between an individualistic versus collectivistic orientation, Asian men often have the sense that they do not meet the standard of masculinity in American society. There is great pressure on Asian men to succeed academically and to have successful careers as both of these reflect on a good family upbringing. Emphasis is on not shaming or disgracing the family by failing to achieve. Asian American men often manifest these pressures by developing psychological problems that they express through bodily complaints; these somatic complaints are a common and culturally accepted means of expressing emotional stress.

It is clear that masculine identity and gender-role socialization of males in the United States cannot be accurately understood without considering the cultural context. This brief discussion reveals that African American, Hispanic American, and Asian American men experience different cultural values from

Euro-American males when it comes to gender-role socialization. Stereotypes of male roles, regardless of one's cultural background, need to be understood and challenged if men are to make choices about how they want to change certain aspects of their masculine identity.

The Price Men Pay for Remaining in Traditional Roles

What price must a man pay for denying aspects of himself and living up to an image that is not true of himself? First, he loses a sense of himself because of his concern with being the way he thinks he *should* be as a male. Many men find it difficult to love and be loved. As we have seen, they hide their loneliness, anxiety, and hunger for affection, making it difficult for anyone to love them as they really are. Part of the price these guarded males pay for remaining hidden is that they must always be alert for fear that someone might discover their inner feelings and what lies beneath the image.

Second, adhering to a rigid model of what it means to be a man keeps men looking for the perfect job, house, and partner to make them happy (Rabinowitz & Cochran, 1994). In this process men avoid knowing themselves and appreciating the richness of life. According to Weiten and Lloyd (2003), the principal costs to men of remaining tied to traditional gender roles are excessive pressures to succeed, becoming strangers to their emotional lives, and sexual difficulties. Other costs include early death, illnesses, alcoholism, a tendency to take excessive risks, depression, and workaholism.

If you are a man, ask yourself to what degree you are tied into your socialization regarding expected male patterns. What costs do you experience in striving to live up to what is expected of you as a man? Now might be a good time to reevaluate the costs associated with your gender-role identity and to consider in what ways, if any, you may want to alter your picture of what it means to be a man.

Challenging Traditional Male Roles

Are the traditional notions of what a man is supposed to be really changing in our society? Recent trends support the idea of an evolution of male consciousness, but change is a slow process. Some men are recognizing how lethal some of the messages they received are—not only for themselves but also for their relationships—and many others are challenging their childhood conditioning to overcome stereotypes and to redefine what it takes to be a man. Rabinowitiz and Cochran (2002) note that a therapy group for men provides modeling for ways to be intimate and how to trust oneself and others. The group can counteract the negative side of male gender-role socialization, with its emphasis on competition, control, and stoicism in the face of pain. In our personal-growth groups, we continue to encounter men who are willing to question the rigid patterns of masculine behavior they had adopted to conform to society's view. Leroy is one of those men.

Men are challenging traditional male roles.

© PhotoDisc/Getty Images

LEROY'S STORY

*T*o me, life was a constant struggle, and I could never let down. I was a driving and driven man, and my single goal in life was to prove myself and become a financial and business success. Life was a series of performances that involved me pleasing others and then waiting for the applause to come. But the applause was never enough, and I felt empty when the applause would die down. So I continued to push myself to give more performances, and I worked 70 to 90 hours a week. I was on my way to becoming the president of a corporation, and I was thinking that I had it made. When I got my W-2 form, I became aware that I had made more money than was in my plan for success, yet I had had a miserable year.

Then one day I became ill, landed in the hospital, and almost died. I began to look at my life and slow down, and I realized there is a world out there that does not solely involve my work. I decided that I wanted to experience life, to smell more flowers, and to not kill myself with a program I had never consciously chosen for myself. I decided to work no more than 50 hours a week. With that extra time, I decided to smell life—there are a lot of roses in life, and the scent is enticing and exciting to me. I'll thrive on it as long as I can breathe.

At age 54 Leroy showed the courage to reverse some of the self-destructive patterns that were killing him. He began deciding for himself what kind of man he wanted to be rather than living by an image of the man others thought he should be.

Like Leroy, many men are showing a clear interest in men's consciousness-raising workshops. There is a great increase in the number of conferences, workshops, retreats, and gatherings for men. Some key books have provided impetus for the men's movement. One is the poet Robert Bly's (1990) best-selling book, *Iron John*. According to Bly, men suffer from "father hunger," which results in unhappiness, emotional immaturity, and a search for substitute father figures. Bly writes and talks about the ways that having an absent, abusive, or alcoholic father results in the wounding of the children. Bly says that many mothers look to their sons to meet their own emotional needs, which are often denied to them by their husbands, and that boys feel ashamed when they are not able to psychologically fill their mothers' longing.

Some men expect the women in their lives to heal their boyhood wounds caused by their fathers, but the wounded must be the ones who do the healing. One of the bases of men's gatherings is to share common struggles, reveal their stories, and find healing in the men's collective. Sam Keen (1991) focuses on men who lacked adequate male models who demonstrated healthy male behavior and talks about the importance of men writing their autobiographies in ways that can help them become aware of their family scripts and move away from the myths that formed their socialization. The fact that men from all walks of life are becoming interested in talking about their socialization from boyhood to manhood indicates that many men are rebelling against the steep price they have paid for subscribing to traditional role behavior.

Traditional gender roles are not completely unhealthy for everyone, but we want to promote the notion of individual choice in determining what aspects of these roles you may want to retain and what aspects you may choose to modify. To make this choice, you need first to be aware of how you have been influenced by your gender-role socialization.

Traditional males should not be told that they *must* change if they hope to be healthy and happy; indeed, many aspects of traditional roles may be very satisfying to some men. However, other men are reinventing themselves without discarding many of the traits traditionally attributed to them. We suggest that you look at the potential costs associated with your gender-role identity, and then decide if you like being the way you are. The Take Time to Reflect exercises may help you discover some areas in your life that are ripe for change.

Take Time to Reflect

1. The following characteristics have been identified as gender stereotypes, some associated with women and others with men. Describe the degree to which you see each trait as a part of yourself. If you do not have this trait, explain why you would or would not like to incorporate this trait into your personality.

Emotional unavailability _____

Independence _____

Dependence _____

Aggressiveness _____

Denial of fears _____

Emotional expressiveness _____

Passive and submissive _____

Lack of bodily awareness _____

Drive to succeed _____

Avoidance of physical contact _____

Rigid perceptions _____

Devotion to work _____

2. What are your thoughts about the price you pay for accepting traditional roles?

_____

_____

3. What are some specific qualities associated with each gender that you would most like in yourself?

_____

_____

4. What did your father teach you about being a man? A woman?

_____

_____

5. What did your mother teach you about being a man? A woman?

_____

_____

6. How do you think that your culture has influenced your view of your gender-role identity?

_____

_____

FEMALE ROLES

Women today are questioning many of the attitudes they have incorporated and are resisting the pressures to conform to traditional gender-role behaviors. They are pursuing careers that in earlier times were closed to them, and more women are working. They are demanding equal pay for equal work. Women are increasingly considering their career priorities and are challenging the traditional feminine working roles. Although women now have greater opportunities to expand their career choices, there are still barriers to the changing role of women in the working world (Zunker, 2002).

Many women are making the choice to postpone marriage and child rearing until they have established themselves in careers, and some are deciding not to have children. Many are balancing both child rearing and a career, and more. Although in the past single women were perceived to be less sociable, less attractive, and less reliable than married women, choosing a single life is now an acceptable option. Single women are generally well adjusted, and they frequently report being quite satisfied with their single life (Matlin, 2004). Women are increasingly assuming positions of leadership in government and business. Women are refusing to stay in stifling or abusive relationships. In dual-career marriages, responsibilities previously allocated to one gender or the other are now often shared.

Despite these changes, women have not achieved equality with men in this society. For example, the woman's role in family life still places a great share of the responsibility on her. Women tend to be blamed for the breakdown of family solidarity, for abandoning their children, and for destroying their family by their selfishness in considering their own needs first. Even when both the woman and man work full time outside the home, the majority of household labor generally falls on the woman (Matlin, 2004). Other family members still tend to believe that when they do participate in house work they are helping the woman with a responsibility that should primarily be hers (McGoldrick, 2005). Women's lives have always required great improvisation, but never more than today.

Like men, women in our society have suffered from gender stereotypes. Gender roles and stereotypes lead to a variety of negative outcomes with respect to self-concept, psychological well-being, and physical health (Basow, 1992). People tend to adapt their behavior to fit gender-role expectations, and women have been encouraged to lower their aspirations for achievement in the competitive world. Many women are concerned that they will be perceived as unfeminine if they strive for success with too much zeal. Women pay a price for living by narrowly defined rules of what women should be. Typically, women who achieve career success continue to carry the major responsibilities of parent and spouse, and an increasing number of women are expected to become caretakers of their own and their spouse's aging parents as well (Weiten & Lloyd, 2003).

Traditional Roles for Women

Traditional gender stereotypes categorize women as passive, dependent, and unaccomplished. But women are increasingly beginning to risk operating outside these narrow limits. As is the case for traditional roles for men, the following discussion about stereotypic views of females certainly does not fit for many women. As you examine these stereotypic characteristics of the traditional portrait of femininity, think about your own assumptions about appropriate gender roles.

• *Women are warm, expressive, and nurturing.* In their relationships with other women and with men, women are expected to be kind, thoughtful, and caring. Women are so attuned to giving that they often do not allow themselves to receive nurturance or consider their own needs. Until recently, women's development was defined by the men in their lives. Their role was defined by their position in another's life, such as mother, daughter, sister, or grandmother. Rarely has there been acceptance of the notion of a woman having a right to a life for herself (McGoldrick, 2005).

- *Women are not aggressive or independent.* If women act in an assertive manner, they may be viewed as being hard, aggressive, and masculine. If women display independence, men may accuse them of trying to "prove themselves" by taking on masculine roles. Those women who are independent often struggle within themselves over being too powerful or not needing others.

- *Women are emotional and intuitive.* Women who defy their socialization may have trouble getting their emotional needs recognized. But women can be emotional and rational at the same time. Having an intuitive nature does not rule out being able to think and reason logically.

- *Women must not deviate from their female role.* A home orientation, being prone to tears and excitability in minor crises, indecisiveness, religiosity, and tactfulness are expected of the female role. If women deviate from these behavior patterns, they run the risk of being "unfeminine."

- *Women are more interested in relationships than in professional accomplishments.* Rather than competing or striving to get ahead, women are expected to maintain relationships. Many women are concerned about the quality of their relationships, but at the same time they are also interested in accomplishing goals they set for themselves.

Some of the problems associated with the traditional female role include diminished aspiration, juggling multiple roles, ambivalence about sexuality, and facing sexism and discrimination in the world of work (Weiten & Lloyd, 2003). Just as subscribing to traditional male roles stifles creativity in men, unthinkingly accepting traditional roles can result in greatly restricting women. Indeed, women can be both dependent and independent, give to others and be open to receiving, think and feel, and be tender and firm. Women who are rejecting traditional roles are embracing this complex range of characteristics.

If you are a woman, ask yourself to what degree you are tied to your socialization regarding expected female patterns. What potential conflicts might this create in your life? Now might be a good time to reevaluate the costs associated with your gender-role identity and to consider whether you want to alter your picture of what it means to be a woman.

If you are a man, reflect on how you have been affected by female roles and ways you may want to change in relation to women. Consider the flexibility you might gain if women had a wider range of traits and behaviors available to them.

Challenging Traditional Female Roles

Basow (1992) cites considerable research evidence supporting the existence of gender stereotypes, but there are signs that women are increasingly recognizing the price they have been paying for staying within the limited boundaries set for them by their culture. We are realizing that gender stereotypes influence societal practices, discrimination, individual beliefs, and sexual behavior itself.

© PhotoDisc/Getty Images

Women are challenging
gender-role stereotypes.

Basow emphasizes that gender stereotypes are powerful forces of social control but that women can choose either to be socially acceptable and conform or to rebel and deal with the consequences of being socially unacceptable. Sensitizing ourselves to the process of gender-role development can help us make choices about modifying the results of our socialization. Women are beginning to take actions that grow out of their awareness.

The changing structure of gender relations has altered what women expect of men and the role men play in women's lives. In *Composing a Life*, Mary Catherine Bateson (1990) claims that the guidelines for composing a life are no longer clear for either sex. Especially for women, previous generations can no longer be used as a model. For women, some of the basic concepts used to design a life—work, home, love, commitment—have different meanings today. Becoming a fulfilled woman entails challenging both societal and internal barriers. Lin's story reveals a woman who fought traditional socialization.

I grew up in a family where my parents' gender roles were at times reversed, and at other times mixed and ambiguous, but never traditional. This affected me in several ways. I developed into a girl whose behavior and dress was nontraditional. I experienced conflict within myself relating to the nontraditional roles my parents played. There was anger at times at both my mother and my father for not being like "other" parents.

I ended up being a tomboy—wearing a baseball cap and pants under my dresses. I climbed trees and played for hours in my self-made mud pools. It seemed that the way I was acting out my gender role was not an issue for my parents. I don't ever remember being told to "act like a young lady" or "girls shouldn't do that," although one time my mother reprimanded me for taking such wide strides when I walk. I remember it being a bit of a shock to me because I had never noticed my stride before. To this day, I'm conscious at times of my stride.

It wasn't until around the age of 12 that I began to feel the discomfort of not behaving like all the other girls. The discomfort was internal. I don't remember it ever being noticed or brought up by other kids. I felt different because the other girls seemed different. I just didn't ever feel "girly."

I didn't experience any external pressures until I had my first boyfriend. These pressures were limited to my sister's macho boyfriend who would state that I "was the one who wore the pants" and I was "the boss." These comments would feed into my own insecurities and conflicts about not being the type of girl I was "supposed" to be—and about having a boyfriend who was not being the type of man he was "supposed" to be. I often feel too strong, and my boyfriends seem too weak.

I feel like I'm supposed to be wearing skirts, dresses, and heels. But I don't wear these things, and at times I feel like I'm somehow less of a woman. I sometimes feel bad that I'm not as chatty as most of the women I work with. I've heard that people think I'm arrogant—and I assume it's because I don't stop and talk to everyone who walks across my path. I think that a good percentage of men would not like me because I'm not feminine enough. I'm too strong and too opinionated. I'm not passive. And I doubt that I'd ever be described as a "sweet girl/woman."

I have bouts of hating that I am all of these things. Society seems to be whispering that I am a bitch if I am not sweet and selfless. My bouts of disliking that I am who I am are closely matched by my strength, which says: "Who cares! I am who I am." I'm proud that I am strong and able and smart and opinionated. As I surround myself with more and more women who are like me, I am calmed. I'm proud of these women and continually try to remind myself that I should be proud of myself too.

Women and Work Choices

The number and proportion of women employed in the workplace is increasing, and more women are now looking to an occupation outside the home as a major source of their identity (Lock, 2005a). By 2020 women are expected to make up half of the U.S. labor force (Judy & D'Amico, 1997). Many women work not only out of choice but also out of necessity. Some feel the pressure of taking care of the home and holding down an outside job to help support the family. Women who are employed in satisfying occupations are as healthy and psychologically well-adjusted as women who do not work outside the home. Several studies have demonstrated that women's lives are enhanced by employment (Matlin, 2004), and women who work outside the home tend to show fewer symptoms of psychological and physical distress (McGoldrick, 2005). In writing about women and work, McGoldrick makes it clear that there are many social pressures against women feeling good about working outside the home. She notes that it is not merely the number of activities that is burdensome to a woman's well-being but also her inability to choose her roles in meeting the demands she faces.

Single parents often face tremendous pressures in providing for their families and have no viable option other than working. Consider the case of Deborah, who after her divorce said, "I know I can survive, but it's scary for me to face the world alone. Before, my job was an additional source of income and something I did strictly out of choice. Now a job is my livelihood and the means to support my children."

Today women are working in virtually all areas of the economy, but their numbers are still small in jobs traditionally performed by men. Most employed women have clerical or service jobs (Matlin, 2004). The Bureau of Labor Statistics (2001a) provides the following percentage of workers who are women in selected traditionally male occupations: engineers (10%), dentists (19%), architects (24%), physicians (28%), and lawyers (30%). Women who are in occupations traditionally filled by men are generally similar to the men in these professions in terms of personal characteristics and cognitive skills, yet the women have less self-confidence (Matlin, 2004).

In *Backlash*, Susan Faludi (1991) points out that about a third of the new jobs for women are at or below the poverty level—jobs that men turned down. In addition, the average woman earns considerably less than the average man in the same occupational category, receives fewer benefits, and works under poorer conditions. In her discussion of salary discrimination, Matlin (2004) states that women and men should receive equal pay for equal work, yet this is still not the case. Salary discrimination is a reality for women, who earn less than men do in comparable jobs. As of 2000, women in the United States who were employed full time earned only 76% of the median annual salary of men (Bureau of Labor Statistics, 2001b).

According to Carney and Wells (1999), surveys indicate that social change is accelerating as different options are becoming available to women who want to combine a career with marriage and a family. The challenge for these women is learning how to balance the difficult demands of a two-career family. Changes in women's choices do influence the attitudes of both women and men with respect to work, marriage, and children. Increasing numbers of women are postponing marriage and having children so they can pursue an education and a career. It appears that homemakers and workers of both genders are returning to school or to work after their 20s to launch new careers.

Other women are making the choice to find their fulfillment primarily through the roles of wife, mother, and homemaker. These women are not assuming these roles because they feel that they must or because they feel that they cannot enter the world of work; they want to devote most of their time to their family. These women often struggle with feeling that they should want a career outside the home because they have heard so much about finding satisfaction in that way. But they do not feel incomplete without an outside career, and they need to learn how to feel comfortable with their choice.

One woman we know, Valerie, talks about the importance of accepting her choice, despite reactions from others that she should not settle for being "merely" a mother. Valerie and her husband, Phil, had agreed that after they had children both would continue working.

VALERIE'S STORY

When our first child was born, I continued to work as planned. What I had not foreseen was the amount of energy and time it took to care for our son, Dustin. Most important, I hadn't realized how emotionally attached I would become to him. My work schedule was extremely demanding, and I was only able to see Dustin awake for one hour a day.

Phil was being Mr. Mom in the evening until I returned home, which eventually strained our marriage. I felt torn. When I was working, I felt I should be at home. I began to feel jealous of the babysitter, who had more time with Dustin than I did.

When our second son, Vernon, was born, I quit my job. Because we primarily depended on Phil's income, we thought it best that I stay home with our children. Some of my friends are pursuing a career while they take care of a family. For me, it was too difficult to manage both to my satisfaction. It means a lot to me to be involved in my sons' activities and have an influence on their lives. I have been active as a volunteer in their school, which I find very rewarding. Some of my friends cannot understand why I stay home, but I know I'm in the place where I need to be—for them and for me.

I do intend to return to my career once Vernon and Dustin begin high school, and at times I miss the stimulation my job provided. But overall I have no regrets about our decision.

Women in Dual-Career Families

One of the realities of our time is that women are increasingly assuming the dual roles of homemaker and worker. Managing both of these roles has created conflicts for women (Zunker, 2002). Although a career meets the needs of many women who want something more than taking care of their families, it dramatically

Women in dual career families often face high self-expectations.

© Jon Feingersh/The Image Bank/Getty Images

increases their responsibilities. Unless their husbands are willing to share in the day-to-day tasks of maintaining a home and rearing children, these women often experience overload, fragmentation, and chronic fatigue. The work of homemakers is often relatively invisible, frustrating, and time consuming (Matlin, 2004). Some women burden themselves with the expectation that they should perform perfectly as workers, mothers, and wives, and in short, they expect themselves to be superwomen. Living by perfectionistic standards is done at a great cost to women. Those women who feel the pressures of doing too much would do well to reevaluate their priorities and decide how they want to live. Eventually, many women realize that they simply cannot continue to balance career and home responsibilities, and they finally exclaim that enough is enough! For women who are trying to do it all, Betty Friedan's advice is worth considering: Yes, women can have it all—just not all at once.

Maureen, a physician, is another woman facing the challenge of a dual career. She holds a teaching position at a hospital. In addition to practicing medicine, she must teach interns, keep current in her field, and publish.

MAUREEN'S STORY

I enjoy pretty much everything I'm doing, but I do feel a lot of pressure in doing all that needs to be done. Much of the pressure I feel is over my conviction that I have to be an outstanding practitioner, teacher, and researcher and must also be fully available as a mother and a wife. There is also pressure from my husband, Daniel, to assume the bulk of the responsibility for taking care of our son and for maintaining the household. With some difficulty Daniel could arrange his schedule to take an increased share of the responsibility, but he expects me to consider his professional career above my own. I need to leave my job early each day to pick up our son from the day-care center. I fight traffic and get myself worked up as I try to get to the center before it closes. I put myself under a great deal of stress holding up all my roles. I feel the toll balancing family and work responsibilities is taking on my physical and emotional well-being.

Some women experience a lack of support and an actual resistance from the men in their lives when they do step outside traditional roles and exercise their options. Although Maureen did not get much resistance from her husband about maintaining her career, she received very little active support to make balancing her double life possible. The power resided with her husband, and she was expected to make decisions that would not inconvenience him greatly. Basow (1992) notes that men typically have been the dominant sex, with most of the power, and it is difficult for them to share this power with women. Those husbands who see themselves as liberated are put to the test when they are expected to assume increased responsibilities at home. They may say that they want their wives to "emerge and become fulfilled persons" but also send messages such as "Don't go too far! If you want, have a life outside of the home, but don't give up any of what you are doing at home." A woman who has to fight her husband's resistance may have an even more difficult fight with herself. Both husband and wife may need to reevaluate how realistic it is to expect that she can have a career and also assume the primary responsibility for the children, along with doing all the tasks to keep a home going. Both parties need to redefine and renegotiate what each is willing to do and what each considers essential. Ideally, women and men should be free to choose which, if either, spouse stays at home. But we have yet to reach this ideal state.

Dual-career couples are often challenged to renegotiate the rules they grew up with and that governed the early phase of their relationship. Such is the case with Deloras and Carlos. Deloras, a reentry college student who also works, reports that she generally likes most aspects of her life, yet her relationship with her husband is strained because of the direction in which she is moving.

DELORAS'S STORY

Where I struggle is with my husband, who would prefer a traditional stay-at-home wife and mother. Now that I am older, I want to discover who I am. What is sad and painful for me is that Carlos doesn't seem to appreciate the woman I am becoming. He prefers the old "doer" that I was. But I won't go back to the compliant person I was, and I will not sacrifice my true feelings and thoughts to please others.

I appreciate the importance of negotiation and listening to my husband. I love and care for him, but I am grieving because I don't have the relationship I long for. I desire a good and honest relationship where both of us are willing to be challenged and are open to change. I will be disappointed if we never get to that place.

In both of the cases just described, the husbands are resisting the growth of their wives. They do not see their wives as equal partners.

In dual-career families, both partners must be willing to renegotiate their relationship. Belinda and Burt have tried to establish a more equal partnership. Belinda is a professional woman with a husband and three young children. Her husband, Burt, shows a great deal of interest in Belinda's personal and professional advancement. She often tells her colleagues at work how much support she gets from him. When Bert was offered a higher paying job that entailed a move to another state, he declined the offer after a full discussion with his wife and children. They decided that the move would be too disruptive for all concerned. During the times when Belinda is experiencing the most pressure at work, Bert is especially sensitive and takes on more responsibility for household chores and for taking care of their children. This is an example of a dual-career couple who have created a more equitable division of responsibilities.

Just as a woman can question the traditional female stereotype, she can also question the myth that a successful and independent woman doesn't need anyone and can make it entirely on her own. This trap is very much like the trap that many males fall into and may even represent an assimilation of traditional male values. Ideally, a woman will learn that she can achieve independence, exhibit strength, and succeed while at times being dependent and in need of nurturing. Real strength allows either a woman or a man to be needy and to ask for help without feeling personally inadequate.

Relationships are often challenged as one person in the relationship moves beyond restrictive role conformity. Guiza is one of the many women struggling to break out of rigid traditional roles and move toward greater choice and self-expression.

She describes the nature of her struggle.

GUIZA'S STORY

*I*n high school I was an exceptional student and had aspirations to go to college, but I was discouraged by my family. Instead, they encouraged me to marry the "nice guy" I had been dating through high school, letting me know that I would risk losing David if I went off to college. My parents told me that David could provide a good future for me and that it was not necessary for me to pursue college or a career. Without much questioning of what I was told, I got married and had two children. Others thought I had a good life, that I was well provided for and that my husband David and I were getting along well. For me, I remember first feeling restless and dissatisfied with my life when my children went to school. David was advancing in his career and was getting most of his satisfaction from his work. Around him, I felt rather dull and had a vague feeling that something was missing from my life. I had never forgotten my aspiration to attend college, and I eventually enrolled. Although David was not supportive initially, he later encouraged me to complete my education. But he made it perfectly clear that he expected me not to neglect my primary responsibilities to the family.

As I was pursuing my college education, I often had to make difficult choices among multiple and sometimes conflicting roles. Sometimes I felt guilty about how much I enjoyed being away from my family. For the first time in my life I was being known as Guiza and not as someone's daughter or wife. Although at times David felt threatened by my increasing independence from him, he did like and respect the person I was becoming.

Guiza's situation illustrates that women can successfully shed traditional roles they have followed for many years and define new roles for themselves. Some of the themes that she and many women like her struggle with are dependence versus independence, fear of success, looking outside of herself for support and direction, expecting to be taken care of, and questioning the expectations of others.

Take Time to Reflect

1. Examine your stance on topics pertaining to roles of women. In the blank, write "A" if you agree and "D" if you disagree with the statement.

   _____ Women's socialization discourages achievement in a competitive world.

   _____ Like men, women pay a price for living by narrowly defined rules of what women should be.

   _____ Many women are labeled unfeminine if they strive for success, especially by men.

   _____ Women traditionally are encouraged to be passive and dependent.

   _____ Women are naturally more nurturing than men.

   _____ Women tend to respond emotionally to a situation, and because of that they are often considered to be irrational.

   _____ Women are still subject to discrimination in our society.

   _____ Women have more opportunity today to attain equality with men in the workplace.

   _____ Most women tend to feel more fulfilled if they work in and out of the home.

   _____ Many women today reject rigid gender roles.

2. What challenges must women face in dual-career families? What are the challenges men face in dual-career families?

   _____

   _____

3. What challenges do marriages face in dual-career families?

   _____

   _____

4. What are your thoughts about the price women must pay for accepting traditional roles?

   _____

   _____

5. What specific qualities do you most respect in women?

   _____

   _____

ALTERNATIVES TO RIGID GENDER-ROLE EXPECTATIONS

The prevalence of certain male and female stereotypes in our culture does not mean that all men and women live within these narrow confines. Tavris (1992) rejects the idea that men and women have a set of fixed personality characteristics (masculine or feminine traits) that define them. It is freeing to recognize that the qualities and behaviors expected of women and men may vary, depending on situations. Tavris suggests that the challenge is for women and men to work together in rethinking how they want to be so that they will be able to have the kind of relationships they want.

We can actively define our own standards of what we want to be like as women or as men. We do not have to uncritically accept roles and expectations that have been imposed on us or remain bound to the effect of our early conditioning—or of our own self-socialization. It is possible for us to begin achieving autonomy in our gender identity by looking at how we have formed our ideals and standards and who our models have been. We can then decide whether these are the standards we want to use in defining our gender-role identity now.

We are in a transitional period in which men and women are redefining themselves and ridding themselves of old stereotypes; yet too often we needlessly fight with each other when we could be helping each other be patient as we learn new patterns of thought and behavior. We are challenged to develop gender empathy for each other. Women and men need to remain open to each other and be willing to change their attitudes if they are interested in releasing themselves from stereotyped and rigid roles. As women and men alike pay closer attention to deeply ingrained attitudes, they may find that they have not caught up emotionally with their intellectual level of awareness.

Monica McGoldrick (2005) maintains that traditional gender roles will not change until we have worked out a new structure in relationships that is not based on the patriarchal family hierarchy. She hopes that "both men and women will be able to develop their potential without regard for the constraints of gender stereotyping that have been so constricting of human experience until now" (p. 121).

Androgyny as an Alternative

One alternative to rigid gender stereotypes is the concept of **androgyny**, the blending of typical male and female personality traits and behaviors in the same person. Androgyny refers to the flexible integration of strong "masculine" and "feminine" traits in unique ways; androgynous people are able to recognize and express both "feminine" and "masculine" dimensions. To understand androgyny, it is essential to remember that both biological characteristics and learned behavior play a part in how gender roles are actualized. We all secrete both male and female hormones, and we all have both feminine and masculine psychological characteristics, which Carl Jung labeled the *animus* and the *anima*. Taken together, the animus and the anima reflect Jung's conception of humans as androgynous (see Harris, 1996, for a more complete discussion of Jung's theory of personality).

Because women share some of the psychological characteristics of men (through their animus) and men possess some feminine aspects (through their anima), both can better understand the other. Jung was very insistent that women and men must express both dimensions of their personality. Failure to do so means that part of our nature is denied, which results in one-sided development. Becoming fully human requires that we accept the full range of our personality characteristics.

Androgynous individuals are able to adjust their behavior to what the situation requires in integrated and flexible ways. They are not bound by rigid, stereotyped behavior. Androgynous people have a wider range of capacities and can give expression to a richer range of behaviors than those who are entrapped by gender-typed expectations. Thus, they may perceive themselves as being both understanding, affectionate, and considerate and self-reliant, independent, and firm. The same person has the capacity to be an empathic listener to a friend with a problem, a forceful leader when a project needs to be moved into action, and an assertive supervisor. This fluid ability to access many qualities has been shown to correlate with good psychological health and appears to be good for both women and men (Real, 1998). Crooks and Baur (2002) suggest that androgynous people tend to be flexible and comfortable with their sexuality. Such women and men have the capacity to enjoy both the physical and emotional dimensions of sexual intimacy. Crooks and Baur state that androgynous lovers tend to be comfortable in both initiating and receiving invitations for sexual sharing, and they are probably not restricted by preconceived gender-role notions pertaining to sexuality.

According to Matlin (2004), contemporary psychologists are disenchanted with androgeny and argue that the concept of androgeny has several problems. Matlin believes that androgeny leads us to believe that the solution to gender bias is centered within the individual, whereas a proper focus should be on reducing institutional sexism and discrimination against women. Many people tend to incorporate gender stereotypes into their own concepts about themselves.

Masculinity and femininity continue to be regarded as distinctive and separate ways of behaving, yet such a dualistic view of human personality is not supported by evidence. Julia (2000) points out that the concept of gender is rooted in the premise that the sexes are diametrically defined as "female" and male." Gender-role socialization reinforces distinct and often unequal sets of behaviors for each gender. But there are wide individual differences within genders as well as across genders. In reality we are multidimensional beings, and polarities of behavioral traits are rare. People do have both feminine and masculine aspects within them. To become fully human, we need to realize the rich and complex dimensions of our being.

Gender-Role Transcendence

Gender-role transcendence involves going beyond the rigid categories of "masculine" and "feminine" to achieve a personal synthesis that allows for flexible behaviors in various situations. According to Basow (1992), androgyny may be one step on the path to transcending gender roles, but it is not the only nor necessarily the best way for personal change to occur. Basow suggests that we need to define healthy human functioning independently of gender-related characteristics. As Basow puts it: "When gender transcendence occurs, people can be just people—individuals in their own right, accepted and evaluated on their own terms" (p. 327).

When individuals go beyond the restrictions imposed by gender roles and stereotypes, they experience a sense of uniqueness because each person has different capabilities and interests. The transcendence model separates personality traits from biological sex. Those who advocate gender-role transcendence claim that this practice will enable individuals to free themselves from linking specific behavior patterns with a gender. If there were less emphasis on gender as a means of categorizing traits, they argue that each individual's capabilities and interests would assume more prominence, and individuals would be freer to develop their own unique potentials (Weiten & Lloyd, 2003).

Take Time to Reflect

1. The following statements may help you assess how you see yourself in relation to gender roles. Place a "T" before each statement that generally applies to you and an "F" before each one that generally does not apply to you. Be sure to respond as you are now rather than as how you would like to be.

   _____ Under pressure I tend to withdraw rather than express myself.
   _____ I'm more an active person than a passive person.
   _____ I'm more cooperative than I am competitive.
   _____ I have clear gender expectations.
   _____ Under pressure I tend to be competitive.
   _____ I see myself as possessing both masculine and feminine characteristics.
   _____ I'm adventurous in most situations.
   _____ I feel OK about expressing difficult feelings.
   _____ I'm very success-oriented.
   _____ I fear making mistakes.

Now look over your responses. Which characteristics, if any, would you like to change in yourself?

_____

_____

2. What are your reactions to the changes in women's views of their gender role? What impact do you think the feminist movement has had on women? On men?

_____

_____

3. Would you like to possess more of the qualities you associate with the other sex? If so, what are they? Are there any ways in which you feel limited or restricted by rigid gender-role definitions and expectations?

_____

_____

SUMMARY

The gender-role standard of our culture has encouraged a static notion of clear roles into which all biological males and females must fit. Masculinity has become associated with power, authority, and mastery; femininity has become associated with passivity, subordination, and nurturance. These concepts of masculinity and femininity are historically and socially conditioned. They are not part of a woman's or a man's basic nature.

Many men have become prisoners of a stereotypical role that they feel they must live by. Writers who address the problems of traditional male roles have focused on characteristics such as independence, aggressiveness, worldliness, directness, objectivity, activity, logic, denial of fears, self-protection, lack of emotional expressiveness, lack of bodily awareness, denial of "feminine" qualities, rigidity, obsession with work, and fear of intimacy. An increasing number of men are challenging the restrictions of these traditional roles. Books on men's issues describe the challenges men face in breaking out of rigid roles and defining themselves in new ways.

Women, too, have been restricted by their cultural conditioning and by accepting gender-role stereotypes that keep them in an inferior position.

Adjectives often associated with women include gentle, tactful, neat, sensitive, talkative, emotional, unassertive, indirect, and caring. Too often women have defined their own preferences as being the same as those of their partners, and they have had to gain their identity by protecting, helping, nurturing, and comforting. Despite the staying power of these traditional female role expectations, more and more women are rejecting the limited vision of what a woman is "expected" to be. Like men, they are gaining increased intellectual awareness of alternative roles, yet they often struggle emotionally to feel and act in ways that differ from their upbringing. The challenge for most of us is to keep pace on an emotional level with what we know intellectually about living more freely.

We described androgyny as one path toward uprooting gender-role stereotypes. However, it is not the only way, or even the best way, to bring about this change. One important way to change gender-role expectations is by focusing on systemic change aimed at reducing institutional sexism. Ideally, you will be able to transcend rigid categories of "femininity" and "masculinity" and achieve a personal synthesis whereby you can behave responsively as a function of the situation. The real challenge is for you to choose the kind of woman or man you want to be rather than to passively accept a cultural stereotype or blindly identify with some form of rebellion. When you examine the basis of your gender-role identity and your concept of what constitutes a woman or a man, you can decide for yourself what kind of person you want to be instead of conforming to the expectations of others.

In this chapter we have encouraged you to think about your attitudes and values concerning gender roles and to take a close look at how you developed them. Even though cultural pressures are strong toward adopting given roles as a woman or a man, we are not cemented into a rigid way of being. With awareness, we can challenge role expectations that restrict us and determine whether the costs of having adopted certain roles are worth the potential gains.

Where Can I Go From Here?

1. Write down the characteristics you associate with being a woman (or feminine) and being a man (or masculine). Then think about how you acquired these views and to what degree you are satisfied with them.

2. Men and women are challenging traditional roles. Based on your own observations, to what extent do you find this to be true? Do your friends typically accept traditional roles, or do they tend to challenge society's expectations?

3. Interview some people from a cultural group different from your own. Describe some of the common gender stereotypes mentioned in this chapter and determine if such stereotypes are true of the other cultural group.

4. Make a list of gender-role stereotypes that apply to men and a list of those that apply to women. Then select people of various ages and ask them to say how much they agree or disagree with each of these stereotypes. If several people bring their results to class, you might have the basis of an interesting panel discussion.

5. For a week or two, pay close attention to the messages you see on television, both in programs and in commercials, regarding gender roles and expectations of women and men. Record your impressions in your journal.

Resources for Future Study

Web Site Resources

SPSMM (Society for the Psychological Study of Men and Masculinity)
www.apa.org/divisions/div51/

A division of the American Psychological Association, SPSMM promotes the "critical study of how gender shapes and constricts men's lives" and is "committed to the enhancement of men's capacity to experience their full human potential." This site presents contemporary psychological approaches to masculinity and includes extensive links to other related Web resources.

Deborah Tannen's Homepage
http://www.georgetown.edu/tannen/

Professor Deborah Tannen is noted for her work on communication differences between women and men. Tannen has published 19 books, including *You Just Don't Understand, That's Not What I Meant!, Talking Voices, I Only Say This Because I Love You,* and *Talking from 9 to 5.* This site provides information on her books, videotapes, and a complete bibliography of professional and general interest publications.

The Wellesley Centers for Women
http://www.wellesley.edu/WCW/

The Wellesley Centers for Women works with the Center for Research on Women and the Stone Center for Developmental Services and Studies by "facilitating the development of new research, increasing efficiency, and expanding the Centers'

outreach." It shares with them "a joint mission to educate, inform and expand the ways we think about women in the world." Resources for research and publications for purchase are offered.

Women's Studies Database
http://www.inform.umd.edu/EdRes/Topic/WomensStudies/

The Women's Studies Database by the University of Maryland is a resource with links to many different areas of interest such as conferences, computing, employment, government and history, film reviews, program support, publications, and other Web sites.

Feminist Majority Foundation Online
http://www.feminist.org/

This site offers many links to a variety of feminist issues including news and events, the National Center for Women and Policing, global feminism, and a feminist online store.

Gender Talk
http://www.gendertalk.com

This site provides explanations and challenges to conventional attitudes about gender issues and gender identity.

 **InfoTrac College Edition Resources**

For additional readings, explore INFOTRAC COLLEGE EDITION, our online library:
http://www.infotrac.college.com/wadsworth

Hint: Enter these search terms:

gender-role socialization	traditional female role
gender stereotypes	dual-career family
gender-role identity	androgyny
traditional male role	gender-role transcendence

Print Resources

Basow, S. A. (1992). *Gender: Stereotypes and roles* (3rd ed.). Pacific Grove, CA: Brooks/Cole.

Bly, R. (1990). *Iron John: A book about men.* New York: Random House (Vintage).

Carter, B., & McGoldrick, M. (Eds.). (2005). *The expanded family life cycle: Individual, family, and social perspectives* (3rd ed.). Boston: Allyn & Bacon.

Faludi, S. (1991). *Backlash: The undeclared war against American women.* New York: Crown.

Farrell, W. (2000). *Women can't hear what men don't say.* New York: Penguin Putnam.

Goldberg, H. (1976). *The hazards of being male.* New York: New American Library.

Goldberg, H. (1979). *The new male: From self-destruction to self-care.* New York: New American Library (Signet).

Goldberg, H. (1983). *The new male–female relationship.* New York: New American Library.

Goldberg, H. (1987). *The inner male: Overcoming roadblocks to intimacy.* New York: New American Library (Signet).

Julia, M. (2000). *Constructing gender: Multicultural perspectives in working women.* Pacific Grove, CA: Brooks/Cole.

Keen, S. (1991). *Fire in the belly: On being a man.* New York: Bantam.

Lott, B. (1994). *Women's lives: Themes and variations in gender learning* (2nd ed.). Pacific Grove, CA: Brooks/Cole.

Matlin, M. W. (2004). *The psychology of women* (5th ed.). Belmont, CA: Wadsworth/Thomson Learning.

Miller, J. B., & Stiver, I. P. (1997). *The healing connection: How women form relationships in therapy and in life.* Boston: Beacon Press.

Mornell, P. (1979). *Passive men, wild women.* New York: Ballantine.

Pleck, J. (1995). The gender role paradigm: An update. In R. Levant & W. Pollack (Eds.), *A new psychology of men.* New York: Basic Books.

Pollack, W. (1998). *Real boys.* New York: Henry Holt.

Rabinowitz, F. E., & Cochran, S. V. (2002). *Deepening psychotherapy with men.* Washington, DC: American Psychological Association.

Real, T. (1998). *I don't want to talk about it: Overcoming the secret legacy of male depression.* New York: Simon & Schuster (Fireside).

Rosen, E. J. (2005). Men in transition: The "new man." In B. Carter & M. McGoldrick (Eds.) *The expanded family life cycle: Individual, family, and social perspectives* (3rd ed., pp. 124–140). Boston: Allyn & Bacon.

Tavris, C. (1992). *The mismeasure of women.* New York: Simon & Schuster (Touchstone).

9

It is no easier to achieve
sexual autonomy than it is to
achieve autonomy in other
areas of your life.
—C. Moore/Corbis

Sexuality

Where Am I Now?

Use this scale to respond to these statements:

3 = This statement is true of me *most* of the time.

2 = This statement is true of me *some* of the time.

1 = This statement is true of me *almost none* of the time.

1. The quality of a sexual relationship usually relates to the general quality of the relationship.

2. I find it easy to talk openly and honestly about sexuality with my friends.

3. For me, sex without love is unsatisfying.

4. I experience guilt or shame over sexuality.

5. Gender-role definitions and stereotypes affect sexual relationships.

6. Sensual experiences differ from sexual experiences.

7. Performance expectations get in the way of my enjoying sensual and sexual experiences.

8. I am clear about my own values and how they affect my sexual behavior.

9. I acquired healthy attitudes about sexuality from my parents.

10. I am concerned and knowledgeable about HIV/AIDS and other sexually transmitted infections.

People of all ages can experience difficulty talking openly about sexual matters. This lack of communication contributes to the perpetuation of myths and misinformation about sexuality despite the fact that the media give increased attention to all aspects of sexual behavior, literally bombarding us with new information and trends. Almost nothing is unmentionable in the popular media, epitomized by the number of reality television shows. Yet this increased knowledge regarding sexuality does not appear to have resulted in encouraging people to talk more freely about their own sexual concerns, nor has it always reduced their anxiety about sexuality. For many people sex remains a delicate topic, and they find it difficult to communicate their sexual wants, especially to a person close to them.

One of our goals for this chapter is to help you to recognize and appropriately express your sexual concerns. Many people experience needless guilt, shame, worries, and inhibition merely because they keep their concerns about sexuality secret. Moreover, keeping your concerns to yourself can hinder your efforts to determine your own values regarding sex. In this chapter we ask you to examine your values and attitudes toward sexuality and to determine what you want to do in this area of your life.

The reality of the HIV/AIDS crisis challenges sexually active individuals to rethink their sexual behavior. Thus, we address information necessary to prevent HIV infection (and other sexually transmitted infections as well), and we look at some misconceptions surrounding HIV and AIDS. We also take up the subjects of sexual abuse, sexual harassment, and date and acquaintance rape.

LEARNING TO TALK OPENLY ABOUT SEXUAL ISSUES

As in other areas of your life, you may want to reflect on your beliefs pertaining to sexuality. Open discussions with those you are intimate with, and with others whom you trust, can do a lot to help you challenge the unexamined attitudes and values you may have about this significant area in your life. In the past there was clearly a taboo against openly discussing sexual topics. Today, bookstores are filled with literature devoted to enhancing sexuality. Sometimes reading about sexuality results in increased concerns about performing up to what is perceived as "normal standards." Although people may have a greater awareness of sexuality, this knowledge does not always translate into a more satisfying sex life. Couples are often very uncomfortable communicating their sexual likes and dislikes, as well as their personal concerns about sex. Some people think that if their partner really loves them he or she should know intuitively what to do. To ask for what they want sexually is sometimes viewed as diminishing the value of what is received. Carroll (2005) stresses the role of good communication skills in developing healthy, satisfying relationships, including sexual relationships. Carroll adds that by talking in an honest and open way with your partner, you are able to share your sexual needs and desires, and you can learn what your partner's emotional and sexual needs are in turn. She acknowledges how difficult it is to talk about sexuality, yet says that talking about sex is a good way to move a relationship to a new level of intimacy and connection.

Although you might expect that people today would be able to discuss openly and frankly the concerns they have about sex, this is not the case. Students will discuss attitudes about sexual behavior in a general way, but they show considerable resistance to speaking of their own sexual concerns, fears, and conflicts. However, if the topic of sexuality is discussed in the classroom, it is of the utmost importance that appropriate boundaries be established and respected. Although many students want to find out how others think about sexual issues, some have reservations about sharing such deeply personal matters. Students should not be pressured to disclose their personal experiences regarding their sexual behavior. Many cultural differences exist about the norms pertaining to talking about sex in public. Within the same culture and between different cultures, variation exists in how free people are to talk about sexual topics. The religious, cultural, and moral values of students need to be taken into consideration when facilitating discussions about sexuality in the classroom.

In the therapeutic groups that we lead, we take great care to create a safe and trusting climate that will be conducive for members to discuss whatever personal concerns (including sexuality) they bring to the group. We have found it useful to give women and men an opportunity to discuss sexual issues in separate groups and then come together to share the concerns they have discovered. Typically, both men and women appreciate the chance to explore their sexual fears, expectations, and wishes, as well as their concerns about their bodies and feelings. When the male and female groups come together, the participants usually find much common ground, and the experience of making this discovery can be very therapeutic. For instance, men may fear not performing up to some expected standard or of being adequate lovers. When the men and women meet as one group, the men may be surprised to discover that women too have fears about their sexual desirability. When people talk about these concerns in a direct way, they often experience a sense of relief through hearing from others. Here are some of the concerns expressed by both men and women in our therapeutic groups:

- I often wonder what excites my partner and what she [he] would like, yet I seldom ask. Am I responsible if my partner is dissatisfied? I suppose it is important for me to learn how to initiate by asking and also how to tell the other person what I enjoy.

- I am concerned about sexually transmitted infections.

- Sex can be fun, I suppose, but it is really difficult for me to be playful and spontaneous.

- I would really like to know how other women feel after a sexual experience.

- As a man, I frequently worry about performance expectations, and that gets in the way of my making love.

- There are times when I become involved in a sexual relationship because I feel lonely.

- There are times when I really do not want intercourse but would still like to be held and touched and caressed. I wish my partner could understand this about me and not take it as a personal rejection.

These are a few of the common concerns people express about sexuality. Knowing that others have similar concerns can help people to feel less alone with their anxieties about sexuality. Look over the list and identify the statements that seem to fit for you. Ask yourself if you are ready to reexamine your beliefs about some of these issues.

DEVELOPING YOUR OWN SEXUAL VALUES

You can and should decide what sexual practices are acceptable for you, and this decision making is enhanced when you are able to explore sexual issues without needless guilt or shame. It is important that your sexual behavior be consistent with your value system. Take a few minutes to reflect on your attitudes about sexual behavior and consider these questions in exploring the pros and cons of being sexually active:

- How do I feel about my decision to be sexual or nonsexual?

- Does my choice to be sexually active conflict with my religious beliefs or cultural values?

- Do I feel pressured into having sex?

- What are my reasons for choosing to have sex at this time?

- Am I willing to talk openly with my partner about sex prior to initiating a sexual relationship?

- Am I prepared for the emotional dimensions of a sexual relationship?

- If birth control is an issue, have my partner and I considered options and chosen a safe and effective method?

- Have my partner and I discussed our sexual histories?

- Am I prepared to discuss and effectively use protection against sexually transmitted infections?

Sexual Abstinence as an Option

You may have decided that abstaining from sexual intercourse until marriage is congruent with your value system. An increasing number of adolescents and young adults are choosing **sexual abstinence** until they enter a committed, long-term, monogamous relationship. A television news special reported that between 50% and 75% of adolescents engage in sexual intercourse before they graduate from high school, but there is also a growing group of young people committed to sexual abstinence until marriage. About 2.5 million adolescents have taken pledges to abstain from premarital sex (Hales, 2005).

But what does abstinence really mean? Does it merely mean to abstain from sexual intercourse? Carroll (2005) indicates that abstinence means different things to different people. Some who decide to be abstinent refrain from all sexual activity. Others may engage in a range of sexual behaviors, but they choose not to engage in sexual intercourse. It appears that oral sex has increased among adolescents and that some do not consider this sex. As you can see, there are many meanings of the concept of abstinence.

Choosing celibacy or sexual abstinence is a viable option. Some choose it out of moral or cultural convictions, others as a way to prevent pregnancy and sexually transmitted infections, and some because of various fears. Fear is not necessarily a bad reason. For example, the fear of driving under the influence of drugs and alcohol makes good sense. So does the fear of an unwanted pregnancy. According to Hales (2005), many people who were sexually active in the past are also choosing abstinence because the risks of medical complications associated with sexually transmitted infections increases with the number of sexual partners one has. Hales adds that one of the safest, healthiest options for many is abstinence. For many people, abstinence is a deliberate choice regarding their body, mind, spirit, and sexuality.

If you are choosing to be sexually abstinent, you should know that you are not alone. Answering these questions will help you understand the values that support your decision: "What meaning do I attach to celibacy?" "Is my choice to be celibate based on a full acceptance of my body?" "Do I believe I am a sexually desirable person?" "Do I fear that being celibate stands in the way of the level of intimacy I desire?"

Even in marriage or other committed relationships, celibacy is sometimes necessary due to illness or other physical conditions. In these situations, it is important to cultivate emotional intimacy even though there is no physical intimacy.

Formulating Your Sexual Ethics

Designing a personal and meaningful set of sexual ethics is not an easy task. It can be accomplished only through a process of honest questioning. Examine the role of your family of origin and your culture as the background of your sexual ethics. Are the values you received from your family and your culture congruent with your views of yourself in other areas of your life? Which of them are important in enabling you to live responsibly and with enjoyment? Which values might you want to modify?

Developing our own values means assuming responsibility for ourselves, which includes taking into consideration how others may be affected by our choices. For instance, some people struggle with wanting to act out sexually with many partners, even though this behavior goes against their personal value system. Their struggle is between giving behavioral expression to their sexual desires and feeling guilty because they are not living by their values. In an adult relationship, the parties involved are capable of taking personal responsibility for their own actions. For example, in the case of premarital or extramarital sex, each person must weigh these questions: "Do I really want to pursue a sexual relationship with this person at this time?" "What consequences are there if I do or don't?" "What are my commitments?" "Who else is involved, and who might be affected?" "How does my decision fit in with my values generally?"

It is no easier to achieve sexual autonomy than it is to achieve autonomy in other areas of your life. While challenging your values, you need to take a careful look at how you could easily engage in self-deception by adjusting your behavior to whatever you might desire at the moment. Pay attention to how you feel about yourself in regard to any past sexual experiences. You might ask: "Do I feel enhanced or embarrassed by my past experiences?"

Sex can be a positive or a negative force, depending on how it is used. At its best, our sexuality provides a deep source of enjoyment, brings pleasure, enhances overall well-being, and demonstrates love, caring, and affection. At its worst, sex can be used to hurt others. Sex is abused when it is manipulative, used as a punishing force, used to get favors, used as a tool of aggression and control, is aimed at dominating another, or when it evokes guilt.

Learning to establish your boundaries is of major importance in being true to your own values. We encourage you to stand by your convictions and not be shamed by having clear boundaries. What is important is that you respect the boundaries of others as you would want them to respect your boundaries. Hales (2005) offers some useful guidelines in establishing boundaries.

- Be aware of your own values. If you believe that sex is to be shared only by people who are close in other ways, be true to your beliefs. Do not feel that you have to apologize for a "no."

- If you are feeling pressured to go against your values, let the person know that you are uncomfortable. Be simple, clear, and direct.

- Establish your boundaries sooner rather than later. For example, it is easier to say, "I don't want to go to your apartment" than to deal with unwelcome advances once you are there.

- If saying no to sex ends a relationship, this is a sign that it was not much of a relationship in the first place.

Take Time to Reflect

1. What influences have shaped your attitudes and values concerning sexuality? In the following list, indicate the importance of each factor using this scoring system:

   1 = This is a *very important* influence.
   2 = This is a *somewhat important* influence.
   3 = This is *unimportant* as an influence.

   For each item you mark with a 1 or a 2, briefly indicate the nature of that influence.

   _____ Parents _____

   _____ Church _____

   _____ Friends _____

   _____ Siblings _____

   _____ Movies _____

   _____ School _____

   _____ Books _____

   _____ Television _____

   _____ Spouse _____

   _____ Grandparents _____

   _____ Your own experiences _____

   _____ Other influential factors _____

2. Try making a list of specific values that guide you in dealing with sexual issues. As a beginning, respond to the following questions:

   a. How do you feel about sex with multiple partners versus monogamous sex? Give your reasons.

   _____

   _____

b. What is your view of sex outside of marriage or a committed relationship?

_____

_____

c. How would it affect you if you separated love from sex?

_____

_____

MISCONCEPTIONS ABOUT SEXUALITY

We consider the following statements to be misconceptions about sex. As you read over this list, ask yourself what your attitudes are and where you developed these beliefs. Could any of these statements apply to you? How might some of these statements affect your ability to make choices concerning sexuality?

- If I allow myself to become sexual, I will get into trouble.
- Women are not as sexually desirable when they initiate sex.
- Men need to prove themselves through sexual prowess.
- As I get older, I am bound to lose interest in sex.
- If my partner really loved me, I would not have to tell him or her what I liked or wanted. My partner should know what I need intuitively without my asking.
- I cannot hope to overcome any negative conditioning I received about sex as I was growing up.
- Acting without any guilt or restrictions is what is meant by being sexually free.
- Being sexually attracted to a person other than my partner implies that I don't really find my partner sexually exciting.
- Being attracted to someone of the same gender is abnormal.
- The more physically attractive a person is, the more sexually exciting he or she is.
- With the passage of time, any sexual relationship is bound to lose its excitement.

SEX AND GUILT

Guilt Over Sexual Feelings

As in the case of shame over our bodies, we need to look at our guilt and determine whether we are unnecessarily burdening ourselves. Not all guilt is unhealthy, but there is a real value in learning to challenge guilt feelings and let go of those that are unfounded.

Many people express fears as they begin to recognize and accept their sexuality. It is important to learn that we can accept the full range of our sexual feelings yet decide for ourselves what we will do behaviorally. For instance, we remember a man who said that he felt satisfied with his marriage and found his wife exciting but was troubled because he found other women appealing and sometimes desired them. Even though he had made a decision not to have extramarital affairs, he still experienced a high level of anxiety over having sexual feelings toward other women. At some level he believed he might be more likely to act on his feelings if he fully accepted that he had them. It was important for him to learn to discriminate between having sexual feelings and deciding to take certain actions.

In making responsible, inner-directed choices about whether to act on your sexual feelings, consider these questions:

- Will my actions negatively affect another person or myself?
- Will my actions exploit another's rights?
- Are my actions consistent with my values and commitments?

Each of us must decide on our own moral guidelines, but it is unrealistic to expect that we can or should control our feelings in the same way we control our actions. By controlling our actions, we define who we are; by denying our feelings, we become alienated from ourselves.

Guilt Over Sexual Experiences

Although some people are convinced that college students do not suffer guilt feelings over their sexual behaviors, our observations show us that this is not the case. Some college students, whether single or married, young or middle-aged, report a variety of experiences over which they feel guilt. Guilt may be related to masturbation, extramarital (or "extrapartner") affairs, sexual promiscuity, same-sex behavior, or sexual practices that are sometimes considered abnormal.

Our early sexual learning is a crucial factor in later sexual adjustment because current guilt feelings often stem from both unconscious and conscious decisions made in response to verbal and nonverbal messages about sexuality. Peers often fill the void left by parents. However, reliance on the same-sex peer group usually results in learning inaccurate sexual information, which can later lead to fears and guilt over sexual feelings and activities. Most sex information from the peer group is imparted during the early teen years, and because of that we carry into adulthood many distorted and inaccurate notions about sex.

Movies, television, magazines, and newspapers provide information that is often a source of negative learning about sexuality. Material dealing with rape, violent sex, and venereal disease is blatantly presented to children. This slanted information often produces unrealistic and unbalanced attitudes about sexuality and can foster fears and guilt that can have a powerful impact on the ability to enjoy sex as an adult.

We acquire a sense of guilt over sexual feelings and experiences as a result of a wide diversity of sources of information and misinformation. Not all guilt is neurotic, nor should it necessarily be eliminated. When we violate our value system, guilt is a consequence. This guilt can serve a useful purpose, motivating us to change the behavior that is not congruent with our ethical standards. In freeing ourselves of undeserved guilt, the first step is to become aware of early verbal and nonverbal messages about sexuality and gender-role behavior. Once we become aware of these messages, we can explore them to determine in what ways we might want to modify them.

Take Time to Reflect

1. Complete the following statements pertaining to sexuality:

   a. I first learned about sex through _____

   b. My earliest memory about sex is _____

   c. The way this memory affects me now is _____

   d. One verbal sexual message I received from my parents was _____

   e. One nonverbal sexual message I received from my parents was _____

   f. An expectation I have about sex is _____

   g. When the topic of sexuality comes up, I usually _____

   h. While I was growing up, a sexual taboo I internalized was _____

2. Are there any steps you would like to take toward learning to accept your body and your sexuality more than you do now? If so, what are they?

   _____

   _____

3. Do you experience guilt over sexual feelings? If so, what specific feelings lead to guilt?

_____

_____

4. How openly are you able to discuss sexuality in a personal way? Would you like to be more open in discussing your sexuality or sexual issues? If so, what is preventing this openness?

_____

_____

5. How have your cultural, spiritual, and religious background and values affected your view of sex?

_____

_____

LEARNING TO ENJOY SENSUALITY AND SEXUALITY

Sensual experiences involve all of our senses and can be enjoyed separately from sexual experiences. Although sexuality involves sensual experiences, **sensuality** does not have to lead to sexual activity.

Performance standards and expectations often get in the way of sensual and sexual pleasure, particularly for men. Some men measure themselves by unrealistic standards and may fear losing their sexual adequacy. In spite of the appearance of drugs such as Viagra and Cialis, men continue to be concerned about their ability to respond sexually. Instead of enjoying sexual and sensual experiences, many men become oriented toward **orgasm,** an explosive physical release at the height of sexual activity. For some men, the fact that they or their partner experiences an orgasm signifies that they have performed adequately. They may expect their partner always to have an orgasm during intercourse, primarily out of their need to see themselves as good lovers. For example, Roland stated in his human sexuality class that he would not continue to date a woman who did not have an orgasm with him. Several of the other male students were in full agreement with Roland's attitude. With this type of orientation toward sex, it is not surprising that these men have problems with intimacy.

© W. Hill, Jr./The Image Works

Intimacy can be conceived of as a close emotional relationship characterized by a deep level of caring for another person and is a basic component of all loving relationships.

Listening to Our Bodies

Television and e-mail commercials promoting Viagra have given men another way to ensure sexual responsiveness. **Erectile dysfunction (ED),** sometimes referred to as impotence, is the consistent inability to achieve and maintain a penile erection required for adequate sexual relations. Most men are unable to achieve or maintain an erection on occasion for any number of reasons: fatigue, stress, or alcohol or drug abuse (Hales, 2005). Sometimes there is a physical reason, and sometimes this is due to the side effects of certain prescription drugs. In addition, ED is frequently due to psychological factors such as feelings of guilt, prolonged depression, hostility or resentment, anxiety about personal adequacy, fear of pregnancy, or a generally low level of self-esteem. Men who experience erectile dysfunction might ask themselves, "What is my body telling me?"

When we are unable to be sexually responsive, our bodies are often sending us an important message about our emotional health or possibly about our relationship. Although ED is an anxiety-provoking situation for men, it can paradoxically create and promote the potential for making significant changes. Goldberg (1987) contends that ED is a lifesaving and life-giving response. If the context is properly understood, and if the man's fragile masculine self-image is able to tolerate the anxiety over not performing adequately, he has the opportunity to become aware of his flawed emotional interaction. His inability to function sexually can thus be the only authentic response he has left to measure the defects in the interchange. Although he is telling himself that he should be close, his body is telling the real truth, for it knows that he does not want to be close for some reason. ED can be a pathway to a man's deeper feelings because it represents a central threat to his ego, makes him vulnerable, and motivates him to seek help. If men are able to pay attention to their body signals, they can see that the penis serves as a monitoring device in the relationship. Goldberg likens erectile dysfunction to a psychological heart attack, which can either result in psychological death or be a catalyst for the man to restructure his patterns of living. A behavioral approach aimed at reducing anxiety has proven quite successful in treating erectile dysfunctions due to psychological factors. The treatment has several phases: sensate focus, followed by genital stimulation, and then penetration (Crooks & Baur, 2002).

Some women have difficulty responding sexually, especially experiencing orgasm. This is often due to unrealistic expectations, which affect sexual behavior and intimacy. Stress is also a major factor that can easily interfere with being in a frame of mind that will allow a woman's body to respond. Although her partner may climax and feel some degree of satisfaction, she might be left frustrated. This is particularly true if the couple engages in sex late at night when they are both tired or if they have been under considerable stress. If her body is not responding, it could well be a sign that stress and fatigue are making it difficult for her to relax and give in to a full psychological and physical release. Rather than interpreting her lack of responsiveness as a sign of sexual inadequacy, she would be wise to pay attention to what her body is expressing. Her body is probably saying, "I'm too tired to enjoy this." For an in-depth discussion of this subject, we recommend the book, *For Women Only: A Revolutionary Guide to Overcoming Sexual Dysfunction and Reclaiming Your Sex Life*, by Jennifer Berman and Laura Berman (2001), which addresses female sexual arousal and treatments for sexual problems.

Asking for What We Want

Paying attention to the messages of our body is only a first step. We still need to learn how to express to our partner specifically what we like and enjoy sexually. Women and men both tend to keep their sexual wishes to themselves instead of sharing them with their partner. They have accepted the misconception that their partner should know intuitively what they like, and they resist telling their partner what feels good to them out of fear that their lovemaking will become mechanical or that their partner will only be trying to please them.

Often a woman will complain that she does not derive as much enjoyment from sex as she might because the man is too concerned with his own pleasure or is orgasm-oriented. Although she may require touching and considerable foreplay and afterplay, he may not recognize her needs. Therefore, it may be helpful for her to express to him what it feels like to be left unsatisfied, but in a way that minimizes defensiveness on his part. It needs to be mentioned that in some cultures there is an injunction against women asking for what they want in a sexual relationship. Thus it is essential to consider the cultural context here.

It is not uncommon for a woman to ask a question such as, "Does touching always have to lead to sex?" She is probably implying that there is a significant dimension missing for her in lovemaking—namely, the sensual aspect. The case of Tiffani and Ron illustrates this common conflict in lovemaking.

TIFFANI'S STORY

*A*nytime I want to be affectionate with Ron, he wants to have sexual intercourse. I really resent Ron's inability to respond to my need for affection without making a sexual demand. When I sense that Ron wants to be sexual with me, I start a fight to create distance.

In turn, he feels rejected, humiliated, and angry. I want to feel close to Ron both physically and emotionally, but his all-or-nothing response makes me afraid to be affectionate with him.

It is important to learn how to negotiate for what you want. Being sensual is an important part of a sexual experience. Sensuality pertains to fully experiencing all of our senses, not just sensations in our genitals. Many parts of the body are sensual and can contribute to our enjoyment of sex. Although there is great enjoyment in the orgasmic experience, many people are missing out on other sources of enjoyment by not giving pleasure to themselves and their partners with other stimulation. A range of sexual behavior is open to couples if they make their expectations clear and if they talk about sexuality as part of their relationship.

SEX AND INTIMACY

Intimacy is a close emotional relationship characterized by a deep level of caring for another person and is a basic component of all loving relationships. Positive sexual experiences contribute to our deepest need to connect to another person. In our discussions with college students, we often hear that they are seeking to be loved by a special person, and they want to trust giving their love in return. Although intimacy is part of all loving relationships, it is a mistake to assume that sexuality is part of all loving and intimate relationships. In Chapter 7 we explored many forms of intimate relationships that do not involve sex. Here we address the links between sex and intimacy.

Take a moment to reflect on what sex means to you and how sex can be used to either enhance or diminish you and your partner as persons. Is sex a form of stress release? Does it make you feel secure? Loved? Accepted? Nurtured? Is it fun? Does it signify commitment? Is it abusive? Pleasurable? Is it shameful or positive? Ask yourself: "Are my intimate relationships based on a genuine desire to become intimate, to share, to experience joy and pleasure, to both give and receive?" Asking yourself what you want in your relationships and what uses sex serves for you may also help you avoid the overemphasis on technique and performance that frequently detracts from sexual experiences. Although technique and knowledge are important, they are not ends in themselves, and overemphasizing them can cause us to become oblivious to the needs of our partner. An abundance of anxiety over performance and technique can only impede sexual enjoyment and rob us of the experience of genuine intimacy and caring. It may be helpful for you to examine where your views about sex come from and the meaning you attach to sexuality. Knowing where you stand can make it easier to make choices about what you do and do not want sexually.

Take Time to Reflect

1. Complete the following sentences:

   a. To me, being sensual means _____

   b. To me, being sexual means _____

   c. Sex without intimacy is _____

   d. Sex can be an empty experience when _____

   e. Sex can be most fulfilling when _____

2. Look over the following list, quickly checking the words that you associate with sex:

_____ fun	_____ dirty	_____ routine
_____ ecstasy	_____ shameful	_____ closeness
_____ procreation	_____ joy	_____ release
_____ beautiful	_____ pressure	_____ sinful
_____ duty	_____ performance	_____ guilty
_____ trust	_____ experimentation	_____ vulnerability

Now look over the words you have checked and see whether there are any significant patterns in your responses. How would you summarize your attitudes toward sex?

_____

_____

AIDS: A CONTEMPORARY CRISIS

If you have not already done so, you will inevitably come in contact with people who have tested positive for HIV, people who have AIDS, people who have had sexual contact with someone who has tested HIV-positive, and people who are close to individuals with HIV or AIDS.

AIDS already affects a wide population and will continue to be a major health problem. You simply cannot afford to be unaware of the personal and societal implications of this epidemic. Unless you are educated about the problem, you are more likely to engage in risky behaviors or live needlessly in fear. Accurate information is vital if you are to deal with the personal and societal implications of the AIDS epidemic.

You need to be able to differentiate between fact and fiction about the virus and about this disease. Because this is a relatively new disease, we continue to discover new information. Thus, the material we provide here is continually being updated and expanded. You can contact the Centers for Disease Control and Prevention (CDC) National AIDS Hotline (1-800-342-AIDS) for free written material, for updated information, and for answers to your questions.

Ignorance and fear of AIDS is fueled by conflicting reports and misinformation about the ways in which the disease is spread. But there is no reason to remain ignorant today because the basic information you need about this disease is available from the CDC and through AIDS workshops or by contacting your local public health department or one of the many HIV clinics that are being started all over the country.

As well as finding out about HIV and AIDS, we suggest you explore your own sexual practices, drug behaviors, and your attitudes, values, and fears pertaining to HIV/AIDS. Better understanding on all fronts will better equip you to make informed, wise choices.

Basic Facts About AIDS

What Is AIDS? **Acquired immunodeficiency syndrome (AIDS)** is the last stage of a disease caused by the **human immunodeficiency virus (HIV),** which attacks

do you have time?
five people worldwide die of **AIDS** every minute

take a minute: visit www.worldAIDSday.org
1st December is World AIDS Day. For confidential information and advice on safer sex, HIV and AIDS call **0800 567 123** anytime

© AWARE Limited 2003 and The National AIDS Trust

and weakens the body's natural immune system. Without a working immune system, the body gets infections and cancers that it would normally be able to fight off. By the time an individual develops AIDS, the virus has damaged the body's defenses (immune system). HIV was first isolated by French and American scientists in late 1983 and early 1984. People who have AIDS are vulnerable to serious illnesses that would not be a threat to anyone whose immune system was functioning normally. These illnesses are referred to as "opportunistic" infections or diseases. AIDS weakens the body's immune system against invasive agents so that other diseases can prey on the body. The course of HIV infection is unpredictable. Some individuals progress to full-blown AIDS and die within several months. Others have no symptoms as long as 10 years or more after being infected with HIV (Edlin, Golanty, & Brown, 2000).

What Do We Know About HIV/AIDS? At this time, much is known about how HIV is transmitted and how it can be avoided. What is not known is how to destroy the virus. Although there is not yet a vaccine, treatment is improving with early detection and intervention. The vast majority of people with HIV infection will eventually develop AIDS. However, with early treatment, the HIV infection can generally be retarded and the onset of AIDS can be delayed. HIV-positive individuals can live relatively symptom-free lives for many years, and new medications are now available to treat the opportunistic infections that often kill people with AIDS. Without treatment, half of HIV-infected people will develop an AIDS-related illness within 10 years (CDC, 1994c). Once the HIV virus infects a person's body, the immune system attempts to fight the virus, but it is unable to destroy it. Because of the way the HIV virus attacks the immune system, it becomes less effective in fighting off other infections that the body is exposed to or is carrying. Gradually, the immune system becomes weaker and weaker. Many people who were infected with HIV in the 1980s have yet to be diagnosed with AIDS. There is still a great deal we do not know about the virus and whether everyone infected will eventually develop AIDS. But most people who become infected become ill to some degree within 5 to 15 years after infection.

Recent research from the Centers for Disease Control and Prevention has determined that many factors play a role in the progression of HIV infection to other illness (including AIDS). Health behaviors known to be cofactors for facilitating the progression of HIV include these:

- Restricted breathing pattern
- Low levels of fluid or water intake
- Poor appetite or inadequate nutrition
- Inadequate or disrupted sleep
- Excessive use of alcohol and other drugs
- Lack of physical exercise
- High levels of stress

By changing their behavior to reduce the number of cofactors, people with HIV can slow and possibly stop the progression of their infection.

How Is HIV Transmitted?   HIV can be transmitted by unprotected sexual intercourse (vaginal, oral, or anal) with a person infected with the virus or by sharing needles with an infected person during intravenous drug use. Babies born to HIV-infected women may become infected before or during birth or through breast-feeding after birth. Although some cases have developed through blood transfusions, this risk has been practically eliminated since 1985 when careful and widespread screening and testing of the blood supply for evidence of HIV became standard practice (CDC, 1994c). "High concentration" agents of transmission of HIV include blood, semen, vaginal secretions, and breast milk. The virus can be spread by women or men through heterosexual or homosexual contact. It may also be possible to become infected with HIV through oral intercourse because the act often involves semen and vaginal secretions that may contain HIV. The virus can enter the body through the vagina, penis, rectum, or mouth or through breaks in the skin. The risk of infection with the virus is increased by having multiple sexual partners and by sharing needles among those using drugs. People are most liable to infect someone in the first few months of being infected themselves. This is a major problem because individuals may test HIV-negative during this time. It is possible for people carrying the virus to infect others even if they do not know they are infected. They may feel fine and be without symptoms of the illness yet still be HIV-positive and be able to transmit HIV infection.

The virus has been found in "low concentration" in a number of body fluids and secretions, such as saliva, urine, and tears. However, you do not "catch" AIDS in the same way you catch a cold or the flu. It cannot be passed through a glass or eating utensils. The AIDS virus is not transmitted through everyday contact with people around you in the workplace, at school, or at social functions. You cannot get AIDS by being near someone who carries the virus. The virus is hard to get and easily avoided. It is a misconception that it is spread through casual contact or from a mosquito bite, a casual kiss, swimming pools, eating food prepared by someone who is HIV infected, or a toilet seat. HIV infection is best prevented by abstinence, fidelity between noninfected partners, avoiding sharing needles, and consistently using latex condoms.

Who Gets AIDS? Some people who are infected with HIV have not developed AIDS. Most of the AIDS public health effort has been focused on persons with high-risk behaviors such as bisexual and gay men, intravenous drug users, and blood transfusion recipients. College students are at risk for contracting HIV because of high rates of sexual activity, multiple sex partners, inadequate protection during sexual activity, and sexual activity following drinking (Carroll, 2005). Some people have been lulled into feeling safe because they believe they are not associated with a high-risk group. But this epidemic is shifting and is spreading to women, youth, and minorities. Indeed, most cases of HIV infection worldwide are due to unprotected heterosexual intercourse. Here are the statistics provided by the World Health Organization:

- 80% transmitted through heterosexual intercourse
- 10% transmitted through homosexual intercourse
- 5% to 10% transmitted through injection drug use
- 3% transmitted through breast-feeding and blood transfusions

AIDS has been called an "equal opportunity disease" because it is found among people of all ages, genders, races, and sexual orientations. Unlike people, AIDS does not discriminate. It is behavior that puts people at risk—not the group to which they belong. The largest growth in HIV infection is occurring among women. According to the Joint United Nations Programme on HIV/AIDS and the World Health Organization (2002), from a worldwide perspective, in 2002 there were 42 million people living with HIV/AIDS, and 5 million people were newly infected in that year. The total deaths due to AIDS in 2002 were 3.1 million, and in the United States 43,950 new cases of AIDS were reported (CDC, 2003).

What Symptoms Are Associated With HIV Infection? HIV may live in the human body for years before symptoms appear. These people are asymptomatic. Although many individuals infected with the virus have no symptoms, some people develop severe and prolonged fatigue, night sweats, fever, loss of appetite and weight, diarrhea, and enlarged lymph glands in the neck. Anyone having one or more of these symptoms for more than 2 weeks should see a health care provider. Of course, other diseases besides HIV can cause similar symptoms.

What Kind of Test Is There for HIV Infection? An HIV antibody test looks for antibodies, not the virus. People can test negative but be positive during a 6-month window period. This is why it is important to get a second test about 6 months after a person thinks he or she might have been exposed to the virus. Many people who test positive either remain symptom free or develop less serious illnesses. Two separate tests for HIV (called ELISA and Western blot), when used together, are accurate more than 99% of the time (CDC, 1994b, 1994c). The ELISA test, which is widely used in the United States and around the world, can be performed relatively quickly and easily. This test requires two visits: one to receive pretest counseling and to have blood drawn for HIV testing, and another visit to receive test results and additional counseling and possibly referrals. If the results are positive, the test is repeated to check it. Edlin and colleagues (2000) report that the most accurate test for HIV infection is the Western blot, which provides an indirect measure of HIV infection. It does not measure whether a person has AIDS or will get AIDS, and the test cannot tell whether the individual will eventually develop signs of illness related to the viral infection or, if so, how serious the illness might be. Testing is completely anonymous and confidential, but it is important to inquire if the test site provides these safeguards.

In addition to the ELISA and the Western blot tests, another approach to HIV testing is the "rapid HIV test." The rapid test produces results in 20 to 30 minutes and allows testing, counseling, and referrals to be done in one visit, which has these advantages:

- It is more cost effective for agencies due to fewer outreach visits to give results.
- More people will get their results because return visits are not necessary.
- People who test positive can get medical attention sooner.
- It can lead to a reduction of potential exposures because people learn about their condition earlier.
- Posttest counseling can be done with the results.

As is true of the current ELISA antibody procedure, an initial positive HIV test result based on the rapid test should be confirmed by the Western blot.

Along with the rapid test, posttest counseling is offered that addresses the following:

- Information about the importance of HIV testing
- Ways to reduce the risk of becoming infected with HIV
- Next steps for persons who have a reactive test result
- Need for additional testing of persons whose rapid test results are negative but who have had a recent exposure to HIV

Early intervention is the key. One of the problems with AIDS antibody tests is that false-positive results can create unnecessary anxiety. Any positive HIV test result should be rechecked (Edlin et al., 2000). A positive result does not mean that you have AIDS. It means that you have been infected with the HIV virus, that your body has developed a reaction to it, and that you can transmit it to others. If you suspect that you have been exposed to the virus, it is crucial that you get tested as soon as possible because there are clear benefits to early medical attention for HIV infection. If you are infected with HIV, the virus slowly weakens your ability to fight illness, but early medical care and medicines can help your body resist the virus. Medicines do this by slowing the growth of HIV and delaying or preventing certain life-threatening conditions (CDC, 1994c).

What Are Common Reactions to Testing HIV-Positive? Upon learning that they are HIV-positive, it is not uncommon for people to experience a gamut of emotional reactions from shock, to anger, to fear and anxiety, to grieving for the loss of sexual freedom, to alarm over the uncertain future. Some feel that they have been given a death sentence. They will need to find a support system to help them cope with the troubled times that lie ahead.

HIV-positive individuals can live long and relatively symptom-free lives. Many new medications are now available to treat the opportunistic infections that often killed people with AIDS in years gone by. Today much more is known about the disease than was the case when AIDS was first discovered, and research toward a cure is continuing.

Why Is a Stigma Attached to AIDS? Both those who have AIDS and those who discover that they have the HIV virus within them struggle with the stigma attached to this disease. People who are HIV-positive live with the anxiety of wondering whether they will come down with this incurable disease. Most of them also struggle with the stigma attached to AIDS. They live in fear not only of developing a life-threatening disease but also of being discovered and thus being rejected by society in general and by significant persons in their lives.

Of course, people with AIDS must also deal with this stigma. Many of the social fears felt by people with HIV or AIDS are realistic. Some family members actually disown the person with AIDS out of fear. This type of treatment naturally inspires anger, depression, and feelings of hopelessness in the person who has been rejected. He or she may express this anger by asking, over and over: "What did I do to deserve this? Why me?" This anger is sometimes directed at God for letting this happen, and then the person may feel guilty for having reacted this way. Anger is also directed toward others, especially those who are likely to have transmitted the virus.

How Is HIV/AIDS Treated? At this point, those who carry the virus are likely to have it for the rest of their lives. No drugs currently available will completely destroy HIV, but new drugs and vaccines are being tested. The availability of an increasing number of antiretroviral agents and the rapid evolution of new information has introduced substantial complexity into treatment regimens for people with HIV infections.

Although optimism for treating HIV infections has increased, a cure for AIDS is still a remote hope (Edlin et al., 2000). Although not a cure, antiviral agents including azidothymidine (AZT), dideoxyinosine, and others appear to retard the progress of the disease in some patients. Several experimental drugs have also shown efficacy in delaying the onset of AIDS. According to Edlin and colleagues, the majority of HIV-infected patients require powerful drugs to keep HIV in check and to prevent progression to AIDS. They list three classes of drugs that block HIV multiplication in infected individuals: reverse transcriptase inhibitors (AZT and 3TC), nonnucleoside reverse transcriptase inhibitors (Nevirapine, Delavirdine, and Loviride), and newly developed protease inhibitors (Saquinavir, Rotonavir, and Indinavir). These and other drugs must be taken daily to prevent HIV from infecting additional cells. Although no treatment has yet been successful in restoring the immune system, doctors have been able to treat the various acute illnesses affecting those with AIDS.

How Can the Spread of HIV Be Prevented? Pollack (1998) reports that AIDS is now the second leading cause of death in the United States among people ages 25 to 44. He adds that 1 in 5 of all reported AIDS cases are diagnosed in the 20- to 29-year-old age group. Most people who are diagnosed with AIDS in their 20s were probably teenagers when they first became infected. An increasing number of teenagers are being infected with HIV each year, and by the time they reach their 20s many of them may develop the symptoms of AIDS. Because the impact of AIDS has been devastating, Pollack urges parents and schools to teach children and adolescents about sex and sexuality, including the reality of AIDS and ways to prevent this disease. Because this reality unravels and even ends human life, Pollack feels it is absolutely critical that young people receive objective information and are exposed to an honest discussion that may enable them to make better choices regarding their sexual behavior.

Designing prevention programs that really work is a real challenge. Conflicting reports and evidence about AIDS and misinformation about the ways in which the disease is spread can block programs aimed at prevention. But the HIV/AIDS crisis shows no signs of decreasing, and education to stop the spread of the disease is the key to prevention. Individuals can do a lot to avoid contracting the disease. These specific steps aimed at prevention have been taken from a number of sources:

- All sexually active individuals need to know the basic facts about this disease and how to avoid the risk of infection.

- Engaging in sex with multiple partners is high-risk behavior. The more partners you have, the more you increase your risk. Restricting intercourse to only one uninfected partner is low-risk or no-risk behavior.

- Having sex with persons with AIDS, with those at risk for AIDS, or with those who have tested positive on the HIV antibody test is high-risk behavior.

- Effective and consistent use of latex condoms and spermicidal barriers will reduce the possibility of transmitting the virus, but they are not 100% effective in preventing HIV or other sexually transmitted illnesses. It is essential that latex condoms be used correctly from start to finish with each act of intercourse. When condoms are used reliably, they not only prevent pregnancy up to 98% of the time but also provide a high degree of protection against a variety of sexually transmitted illnesses, including HIV infection. For more detailed information about condoms, see the CDC (1999a) publication *Condoms and Their Use in Preventing HIV Infection and Other STDs.*

- Making responsible choices is of the utmost importance in avoiding sexually transmitted illnesses, including HIV infection. Sexual abstinence is certainly a safe course to follow. If you choose to practice abstinence as a way to prevent infection, this strategy will be effective only if you always abstain.

- If you intend to have unprotected sexual intercourse, you are engaging in unsafe behavior and subjecting yourself to the risks of infection. Any form of unprotected sex is risky, including oral sex. Rather than thinking in terms of "safe sex," it is helpful to consider practices that are "unsafe," "relatively safe," and "safer." In *What You Can Do to Avoid AIDS*, Earvin "Magic" Johnson (1992) emphasizes that "the most responsible thing you can do is to act as though you yourself and anybody you want to have sex with could have HIV and to practice safer sex every time" (p. 67).

- It is wise to talk with your partner about his or her past and present sexual practices, sexually transmitted infection (STI) history, and sex history. It is important to negotiate safer sex with your partner.

- Safer sex behavior includes choosing not to be sexually active; restricting sex to one mutually faithful, uninfected partner; and not injecting drugs. Safer sex practices are especially critical if you sense that your partner may not be totally honest about his or her past or present sexual practices.

- If you use intravenous drugs, do not share needles.

- Avoid using drugs and alcohol, which cloud your judgment. Many college students attend parties in which there is a great deal of peer pressure to "drink and have fun." Intoxication lessens inhibitions, which often leads to unprotected sex.

It takes a good bit of courage to take a stand and not engage in the irresponsible use of drugs and alcohol, especially when many of your friends may be drinking excessively. Furthermore, if you are drunk and have unprotected sex, the chances are increased that you will be infected if your partner is carrying the virus because your immune system is lowered.

• People who carry the HIV virus often are not sick and may be unaware that they are infected. You can be HIV-positive and still look fine and feel well. If you have engaged in a high-risk behavior, get an HIV test to determine your health status.

Educate Yourself

Educational programs aimed at prevention have helped considerably in reducing the spread of AIDS (Carroll, 2005). It is easier today to increase your knowledge about HIV/AIDS. Simply having information will not prevent you from getting AIDS (or from contracting other STIs), but it will help you make sound behavioral choices. In the early days of the AIDS epidemic, the emphasis was on providing information and education. But information is changing rapidly today, and it is difficult for some people who are at risk to trust what they hear from the medical profession. Some individuals do not believe the information they are given and become defensive. Others may remain in a state of denial because they do not want to change their sexual behavior. Education is only one step in the change process; information alone is not sufficient to create the environment for individuals to change. Behavior change is tough, especially when dealing with very personal behaviors such as sexuality. Assess your own knowledge about HIV/AIDS and determine whether you are practicing safer sex. What can you do to protect yourself and your sexual partners from contact with this virus?

More information about AIDS and HIV-related illnesses can be obtained from your doctor, your state or local health department, your local chapter of the American Red Cross, and the Public Health Service's toll-free HIV and AIDS hotline (1-800-342-AIDS). This national hotline is for anyone with questions about HIV and AIDS, and it functions 24 hours a day in every state. These information specialists are well trained, respect privacy, and can provide information and referrals to appropriate sources. The National AIDS Clearinghouse (1-800-458-5231) also provides information on HIV/AIDS. Updated pamphlets (some of which are listed at the end of this chapter) can also be requested by contacting either of these hotlines. Additional sources of information on HIV/AIDS and other STIs include these agencies:

• HIV/AIDS Treatment Information Service, 1-800-HIV-0440

• National Gay and Lesbian Task Force AIDS Information Line, 1-800-221-7044

• AIDS National Interfaith Network, 202-546-0807

- Public Health Service AIDS Hotline, 1-800-342-AIDS
- National Institute on Drug Abuse Hotline, 1-800-662-HELP
- National Sexually Transmitted Diseases Hotline, 1-800-227-8922
- Centers for Disease Control and Prevention, 404-639-3534
- American Red Cross, 1-800-375-2040
- World Health Organization, 202-861-4354

Magic Johnson (1992) sums up the message we have attempted to convey in this section on HIV and AIDS. His message deserves reflection.

> TAKE RESPONSIBILITY. It's your life. Remember: The safest sex is no sex, but if you choose to have sex, have safer sex each and every time. HIV happened to me, so I know it could happen to you. I want you to stay safe. Your life is worth it. (p. 156)

OTHER SEXUALLY TRANSMITTED INFECTIONS

It is a reality that unprotected sexual practices frequently result in contracting some form of **sexually transmitted infection (STI).** Some of the more common STIs include herpes, genital warts, chlamydial infection, gonorrhea, and syphilis. Some STIs can be transmitted without direct genital-to-genital contact. Effective and consistent protection is necessary to protect yourself and your partner. All STIs are treatable, yet all are not curable. If you or someone you know discovers symptoms associated with STIs, seek medical treatment as soon as possible. If STIs go untreated, they can cause sterility, organ damage, and life-threatening complications.

The safest way to prevent the transmission of STIs is abstinence and other activities that do not include the exchange of body fluids. One alternative to abstinence is to consider long-term monogamy, where both partners have been laboratory tested for STIs. As a way to reduce the risk, it is a good practice to avoid using drugs and alcohol, which can interfere with your judgment and may cause you to make unsafe choices about sex. Another approach to reducing the risk is to use preventive measures (such as condoms) consistently and effectively. The National Sexually Transmitted Diseases Hotline (1-800-227-8922) can provide you with additional information on STIs.

What it boils down to is this: If you choose to be sexually active, in addition to getting information and educating yourself about a safer sex plan, it is essential that you develop the skills to negotiate your safer sex plan with your partner. Magic Johnson (1992) has some outstanding advice for those who are considering becoming sexually active. He suggests asking yourself these questions:

- Am I prepared to practice safer sex each time I have sex?
- Am I prepared to consistently and effectively use contraception each time I have heterosexual sex?
- Am I prepared to deal with the consequences if I or my partner becomes infected with HIV or another STI or becomes pregnant?
- Am I prepared to say "no" when I think it is not right for me?

If you cannot answer "yes" to each of these questions, you are ill prepared to take on the responsibilities that are basic to this level of intimacy.

Young adults often feel that they are immune to any harm, and thus they tend to disregard good advice. Others may remain in a state of denial because they do not want to change their sexual lifestyle. In his keynote address at the Evolution of Psychotherapy conference, Elliot Aronson (2000) spoke about the value of self-persuasion as opposed to direct persuasion by others as a way to reduce risky sexual behavior in young adults. Only a small percentage of young people who are sexually active use condoms with regularity, and fear-arousing campaigns are not effective in changing these patterns of sexual behavior. Aronson encourages young adults to persuade themselves to change dysfunctional attitudes and behavior, and his work in schools teaching self-persuasion has had results far superior to traditional external approaches. If people learn to challenge their own beliefs and make new decisions based on internal motivation, they have gained personal power over their lives. By persuading yourself to act in accordance with what you know, you can lessen your chances of contracting a sexually transmitted infection.

Take Time to Reflect

1. What are your attitudes, values, and fears pertaining to HIV/AIDS and other STIs?

_____

_____

2. What steps are you willing to take to avoid contracting HIV and other STIs?

_____

_____

3. Have you known anyone who is HIV-positive or who has AIDS? How did you react when you first heard this news? Has your relationship with this person changed because of this?

_____

_____

4. What kind of education about HIV/AIDS have you been exposed to? What kind of education do you think is most needed?

_____

_____

5. Simply having information will not prevent you from contracting HIV or other STIs. What other factors, besides education, will help you make sound behavioral choices?

_____

_____

SEXUAL ABUSE AND HARASSMENT

In this section we discuss three topics that involve some form of abuse of sexuality: incest, rape, and sexual harassment. In each of these cases, power is misused or a trusting relationship is betrayed for the purpose of gaining control over the individual, for degrading, oppressing, or exploiting a person. Individuals are robbed of choice—except for the choice of how to react to being violated. Incest, date and acquaintance rape, and sexual harassment all entail abusive power, control, destructiveness, and violence. As such, these practices are never justifiable. In all of these forms of sexual abuse, a common denominator is the reluctance of victims to disclose that they have been wronged. In fact, many victims suffer from undue guilt and believe they were responsible for what occurred. This guilt is exacerbated by segments of society that contribute to the "blaming the victim" syndrome. The victims should not be given further insult by being blamed for cooperating or contributing to the violence that was forced upon them. Survivors of sexual abuse often carry psychological scars from these experiences that stifle their ability to accept and express the full range of their sexuality, as well as many other aspects of their lives.

Incest: A Betrayal of Trust

Incest involves any form of inappropriate sexual behavior that is brought about by coercion or deception. Vanderbilt (1992) defines incest as "any sexual abuse of a child by a relative or other person in a position of trust and authority over the child. It is the violation of the child where he or she lives—literally and metaphorically" (p. 51). Today the subject of incest is being given much-deserved attention by both helping professionals and the general public, and it appears that incest is far more widespread than ever before thought. Incest occurs on all social, economic, educational, and professional levels, and at least 1 out of 10 children is molested by a trusted family member (Forward & Buck, 1988). Incest is a betrayal of trust and a misuse of power and control. It can never be rationalized away. The responsibility of the perpetrator can never be diminished.

In our personal-growth groups for relatively well-functioning people, we find a startling number of women who report incidents of incest and sexual experimentation with fathers, uncles, stepfathers, grandfathers, and brothers. To a lesser extent, we come across men who have been subjected to incest. Vanderbilt (1992) indicates that incest is a felony offense in all 50 states, although its definition varies from state to state, as does the punishment. Although females are more often incest victims, males also suffer the effects of incestual experiences.

In our therapy groups many women bring up the matter of incest because they feel burdened with guilt, anger, hurt, and confusion over having been taken advantage of sexually and emotionally. They feel like they are victims, but some of them also see themselves as conspirators. They may believe they were to blame—a belief that is often reinforced by others. They may have liked the affection and love they received even though they were probably repulsed by the sexual component. Because children realize that adults have power over them, they tend to be compliant, even in situations that seem strange. Typically, these experiences happen in childhood or early adolescence; the women remember feeling helpless at the time, not knowing how to stop the man, and also being afraid to tell anyone. Some of the reasons children give for not telling others about the abuse include not knowing that it was wrong, feeling ashamed, being frightened of the consequences of telling, fearing that others might not believe that such abuse occurred, fearing the loss of affection from their family and friends, and hoping to protect other siblings from incest. However, once they bring out these past experiences, intense, pent-up emotions surface, including hatred and rage for having been treated in such a way and feelings of having been raped and used.

In *Betrayal of Innocence,* Forward and Buck (1988) describe recurring themes that emerge from the incest experiences of almost every victim. From the victim's perspective, these themes include a desire to be loved by the perpetrator; a tendency to put up little resistance; an atmosphere of secrecy surrounding the incest; feelings of repulsion, fear, and guilt; the experience of pain and confusion; fears of being punished or removed from the home; and feelings of tremendous isolation and of having no one to turn to in a time of need. Most often the victim feels responsible for what occurred.

Children who have been sexually abused by someone in their family feel betrayed and typically develop a mistrust of others who are in a position to take advantage of them. Oftentimes the sexual abuse is only one facet of a dysfunctional family. There may also be physical abuse, neglect, alcoholism, and other problems. These children are often unaware of how psychologically abusive their family atmosphere really is for all members of the family.

The effects of these early childhood experiences can carry over into adulthood, for both women and men. Men often have many of the same patterns that are carried over because of the trauma of sexual abuse. For now we address the impact of childhood sexual abuse on the woman. The woman's ability to form sexually satisfying relationships may be impaired by events she has suppressed for many years. She may resent men, associating them with the father or other man who initially took advantage of her. If she could not trust her own father, then what man can she trust? She may have a hard time trusting men who express affection for her, thinking that they, too, will exploit her. She may keep control of relationships by not letting herself be open or sexually playful and free with men. She may rarely or never allow herself to fully give in to sexual pleasure during intercourse. Her fear is that if she gives up her control, she will be hurt again. Her guilt over sexual feelings and her negative conditioning prevent her from being open to enjoying a satisfying sexual relationship. She may blame men for her feelings of guilt and her betrayal and victimization. She may develop severe problems with establishing and maintaining intimate relationships, not only with her partner but also with her own children. In adulthood she may marry a man who will later victimize his own children, which perpetuates the pattern of her experiences in growing up. In this way the dynamics from childhood are repeated in adulthood.

Veronika Tracy (1993) conducted a research study to determine the impact of childhood sexual abuse on women's sexuality. Her study compared a group of women who were sexually abused with a group of women who had not experienced sexual abuse. She found that the women with a reported history of sexual abuse in childhood tended to have lower self-esteem, a greater number of sexual problems, less sexual satisfaction with a partner, less interest in engaging in sex, a higher propensity for sexual fantasies that involved force, and more guilt feelings about their sexual fantasies. Many of the women who were sexually abused reported that they were not able to achieve orgasm with a partner, but only by themselves. Her research revealed that women who were sexual abuse survivors often blocked out their negative experiences, only to remember the sexual abuse as they became sexually active. Paradoxically, as the women began to feel safer with a partner, their sexual activity often triggered memories of the abuse, which tended to interfere with their ability to maintain satisfying intimate relationships.

We have found that it is therapeutic for most women and men who have a history of sexual abuse to share the burden associated with their abuse that they have been carrying alone for so many years. In a climate of support, trust, care, and respect, these individuals can begin a healing process that will eventually enable them to move beyond the abuse. Before this healing can occur, they generally need to fully express suppressed feelings, usually of anger and hatred. A major part of their therapy consists of accepting the reality that they were indeed victims and learning to direct their anger outward, rather than directing their anger toward themselves. We stress that it is important for this catharsis to occur in the group in symbolic ways. With the assistance of their therapist, they may be able to confront the perpetrator and those who did not protect them. Sometimes the perpetrator in question will no longer be alive, or the individual may decide that he or she does not want to confront the aggressor.

As we mentioned, it is not uncommon for people to assume the guilt and responsibility for these inappropriate sexual activities. Even though they may have been only 7 years old or younger, they firmly believe they should have prevented the abuse from happening. They fail to realize that the adults in their lives were violating them and did not provide the safe environment in which they could have developed and matured as sexual beings.

The process of recovery from the psychological wounds of incest varies from individual to individual, depending on a number of complex factors. Many incest victims cut off their feelings as a survival tactic. Part of the recovery process involves regaining the ability to feel, getting in touch with buried memories, and speaking truths. They will likely have to deal with these questions: "What is wrong with me?" "Why did this happen in my life?" "Why didn't I stop it?" "What will my future be like?" Victims may vacillate between denying the incestuous experiences and accepting what occurred. As they work through their memories surrounding the events, they eventually accept the fact that they were involved in incest. They typically feel sadness, grief, and then rage. It is hoped that eventually they are able to shift the responsibility to the perpetrator and to release themselves from this responsibility and guilt.

According to Forward and Buck (1988), one of the greatest gifts that therapy can bestow is a full and realistic reversal of blame and responsibility from the victim to the victimizers. In her therapeutic practice with victims of incest, Susan Forward attempts to achieve three major goals:

- Assist the client in externalizing the guilt, rage, shame, hurt, fear, and confusion that are stored up within her.
- Help the survivor place the responsibility for the events primarily with the aggressor and secondarily with the silent partner.
- Help the client realize that although incest has damaged her dignity and self-esteem she does not have to remain psychologically victimized for the rest of her life.

Through role playing, release of feelings, and sharing her conflicts with others in the group, the survivor often finds that she is not alone in her plight, and she begins to put these experiences into a new perspective. Although she will never forget these experiences, she can begin the process of letting go of feelings of self-blame and eventually arrive at a place where she is not controlled by these past experiences. In doing so, she is also freeing herself of the control that these sexual experiences (and the feelings associated with them) have had over her ability to form an intimate relationship with her partner.

We have worked with some adult men who were incest victims during childhood and adolescence. Regardless of gender or cultural background, the dynamics of incest are similar, and thus the therapeutic work is much the same for both women and men. If you have been sexually abused in any way, we suggest that you seek professional help. It is not uncommon for people to block out experiences such as sexual abuse, only to have memories and feelings surface at a later time. Counseling can provide you with an opportunity to deal with feelings and unresolved problems that may linger because of earlier experiences. Support groups for incest survivors also can be most beneficial. These self-help resources may also be useful for victims of child sexual abuse (Vanderbilt, 1992):

- Self-Help Clearinghouse, St. Clare's-Riverside Medical Center, Denville, NJ 07834 (201-625-9565) publishes *The Self-Help Directory*, a guide to mutual-aid self-help groups and how to form them.
- Incest Survivors Anonymous, P.O. Box 5613, Long Beach, CA 90805-0613 (213-428-5599) assists in forming 12-step groups.
- SARA (Sexual Assault Recovery Anonymous) Society, P.O. Box 16, Surrey, British Columbia V3T 4W4 Canada (604-584-2626) provides self-help information for adults and teens who were sexually abused as children.
- The National Council on Child Abuse and Family Violence, 1155 Connecticut Avenue NW, Suite 400, Washington, DC 20036 (202-429-6695) may also be helpful.

In addition to counseling or support groups, many fine books deal with sexual abuse, which can be of value. For an excellent book that helps survivors and their partners understand and recover from the effects of sexual abuse, we recommend *The Sexual Healing Journey*, by Wendy Maltz (2001).

Date and Acquaintance Rape

In our contacts with college students it has become clear to us that date rape is prevalent on the campus. **Rape** involves physically or psychologically forcing sexual relations on another person. **Acquaintance rape** takes place when a woman is forced to have unwanted sex with someone she knows. This might involve friends, coworkers, neighbors, or relatives. **Date rape** occurs in those situations where a woman is forced to have unwanted intercourse with a person in the context of dating. Rape is an act of aggressive sexuality, or a form of sexual assault where power is misused to dominate another person.

Earlier in this chapter we identified some misconceptions about sexuality. One of these misconceptions is that men are by nature sexually aggressive. Thus men may feel that they are expected to be this way. As a consequence, they may misinterpret a woman's "no" as a "maybe" or a sign of initial resistance that can be broken down. Dating partners may not say what they really mean, or they may not mean what they say. This phenomenon is reinforced by the linkage of sex with domination and submission. In our society masculinity is equated with power, dominance, and sexual aggressiveness, and femininity is associated with pleasing men, sexual passivity, and lack of assertiveness (Basow, 1992).

Weiten and Lloyd (2003) offer a number of suggestions to people in dating relationships as a way of reducing date rape:

- Recognize that date rape is an act of sexual aggression.
- Familiarize yourself with the characteristics of men who are likely to engage in date rape, and avoid dating such men.
- Beware of using excessive alcohol or drugs, which can lower your resistance and distort your judgment.
- Exercise control over your environment—agree to go only to public places until you know someone well.
- Communicate your feelings, thoughts, and expectations about sex in a clear and open manner.
- Be prepared to act aggressively if assertive refusals do not stop unwanted sexual advances.

Both date rape and acquaintance rape can be considered as a betrayal of trust. Much like in incest, when a woman is forced to have sex against her will, her dignity as a person is violated. Not believing that she is in danger, she may make herself vulnerable to a man, and then experience hurt. She might have explicit trust in a man she knows, only to discover that he cannot be trusted to respect her boundaries. The emotional scars that are a part of date rape are similar to the wounds inflicted by incest. As is the case with incest victims, women who are raped by people they know often take responsibility and blame themselves for what occurred, and they are often embarrassed about or afraid of reporting the incident. According to Carroll (2005), forcible rape is one of the most underreported crimes in the United States. Carroll states that some of the reasons that women do not report rape include that they do not think they were really raped, they fear that others won't believe them, they are not sure anything will be done legally, and they feel shame and humiliation about the incident.

Currently, many college campuses offer education directed at the prevention of date rape. The focus of this education is on the importance of being consistent and clear about what you want or do not want with your dating partner, as well as

Sexual harassment diminishes choice and surely is not flattering.

© Royalty-free/Digital Vision/Getty Images

providing information about factors contributing to date rape. Rape prevention programs are increasing, and these programs are designed for women, men, and both women and men. Programs for women are designed for women to increase their awareness of high-risk situations and behaviors and to teach them how to protect themselves. Those targeted for men emphasize responsibility and respect for women. It is the man's responsibility to avoid forcing a woman to have sex with him, and he must learn that her "no" really does mean "no." It is clear that campus preventive programs need to be designed for both women and men. Both women and men can benefit from discussion groups or workshops on rape prevention. In such programs the focus is generally on topics such as interpersonal communication and predicting potential problem areas.

Sexual Harassment

Sexual harassment is repeated and unwanted sexually oriented behavior in the form of comments, gestures, or physical contacts. This phenomenon is of concern on the college campus, in the workplace, and in the military. Women experience sexual harassment more frequently than do men. Sexual harassment is abuse of the power differential between two people. Those who have more power tend to engage in sexual harassment more frequently than those with less power (Basow, 1992). Title VII of the 1964 Civil Rights Act prohibits sexual harassment. A company can be held liable for the coercive actions by its employees.

You may have witnessed, or been the victim of, some of these forms of sexual harassment:

- Comments about one's body or clothes
- Physical or verbal conduct of a sexual nature
- Jokes about sex or gender-specific traits
- Repeated and unwanted staring, comments, or propositions of a sexual nature
- Demeaning references to one's gender
- Unwanted touching or attention of a sexual nature
- Conversations tinted with sexually suggestive innuendoes or double meanings
- Questions about one's sexual behavior

Men sometimes make the assumption that women like sexual attention, when in fact they may resent being related to in strictly sexual terms. Sexual harassment diminishes choice, and surely it is not flattering. Harassment reduces people to objects to be demeaned. The person doing the harassing may not see this behavior as being problematic and may even joke about it. Yet it is never a laughing matter. Those on the receiving end of harassment often report feeling responsible. However, as in the cases of incest and date rape, the victim should never be blamed.

Many incidences of sexual harassment go unreported because the individuals involved fear the consequences, such as getting fired, being denied a promotion, risking a low grade in a course, or encountering barriers to pursuing their careers. Fear of reprisals is a foremost barrier to reporting.

If you are on the receiving end of unwanted behavior, you are not powerless. Because sexual harassment is never appropriate, you have every right to break the pattern. The initial step is to recognize there is a problem pertaining to sexual harassment. The next step is to make it clear to the person doing the harassing that his or her behavior is unacceptable to you and that you want it stopped. If this does not work, or if you feel it would be too much of a risk to confront this individual, you can talk to someone else. If the offensive behavior does not stop, keep a detailed record of what is taking place. This will be useful in showing a pattern of unwanted behavior when you issue a complaint.

Most work settings and colleges have policies and procedures for dealing with sexual harassment complaints. You do not have to deal with this matter alone if your rights are violated. Realize that the college community does not take abusing power lightly and that procedures are designed to correct abuses.

When you report a problematic situation, know that your college most likely has staff members who will assist you in bringing resolution to this situation. As is true for preserving the secret of incest, it will not help if you keep the harassment a secret. By telling someone else, you are breaking the pattern of silence that burdens sexual harassment victims.

Take Time to Reflect

1. Recent legislation requires that information identifying registered (convicted) sex offenders be made available to the public. What is your reaction to this ruling? How do you think you would react if you knew one of your neighbors had been convicted of molesting children?

_____

_____

2. Of the suggestions discussed in this chapter for reducing date or acquaintance rape, which strategies make the most sense to you? Are you using any of these strategies currently?

_____

_____

3. Sexual harassment is common on both college campuses and in the workplace. What specific behaviors that you would deem sexual harassment have you witnessed or experienced yourself?

_____

_____

SUMMARY

Sexuality is part of our personhood and should not be thought of as an activity divorced from our feelings, values, and relationships. Although childhood and adolescent experiences do have an impact on shaping our present attitudes toward sex and our sexual behavior, we are in a position to modify our attitudes and behavior if we are not satisfied with ourselves as sexual beings.

If we are successful in dealing with barriers that prevent us from acknowledging, experiencing, and expressing our sexuality, we increase our chances of learning how to enjoy both sensuality and sexuality. Sensuality can be a significant path toward creating satisfying sexual relationships, and we can learn to become sensual beings even if we decide not to have sexual relationships with others. Sensuality implies a full awareness of and a sensitivity to the pleasures of sight, sound, smell, taste, and touch. We can enjoy sensuality without being sexual, and it is a mistake to conclude that sensuality necessarily leads to sexual behavior. Nevertheless, sensuality is very important in enhancing sexual relationships. Intimacy, or the emotional sharing with a person we care for, is another ingredient of joyful sex.

One significant step toward evaluating your sexual attitudes is to become aware of the myths and misconceptions you may harbor. Review where and how you acquired your views about sexuality. Have the sources of your sexual knowledge and values been healthy models? Have you questioned how your attitudes affect the way you feel about yourself sexually? Is your sexuality an expression of yourself as a complete person? The place that sex occupies in your life and the attitudes you have toward it are very much a matter of your choice. It is no easier to achieve sexual autonomy than it is to achieve autonomy in other areas of your life.

A significant step toward developing your own sexual views is to learn to be open in talking about sexual concerns, including your fears and desires, with at least one other person you trust. Guilt feelings may be based on unfounded premises, and you may be burdening yourself needlessly by feeling guilty about normal feelings and behavior. You may feel very alone when it comes to your sexual feelings, fantasies, fears, and actions. By sharing some of these concerns with others, you are likely to find out that you are not the only one with such concerns.

The AIDS crisis has had a significant impact on sexual behavior. Although ignorance and fear of AIDS are rampant, education can be the key to dispelling them. There are many misconceptions pertaining to who gets AIDS, how it is transmitted, and the stigma attached to it. Along with a better understanding of this disease and of other STIs, education can put you in a good position to make informed choices in expressing your sexuality.

Incest and date rape are examples of betrayals of trust, sexual aggression, and violence. Those involved do not have much choice in a situation that is foisted upon them. The consequences are potentially dire both physically and psychologically, for the victims often have difficulty forming trusting relationships and enjoying sexuality.

The themes explored in the chapters on love and relationships are really impossible to separate from the themes of this chapter. Think about love, sex, and relationships as an integrated dimension of a rich and full life.

Where Can I Go From Here?

I. Write down some of your major questions or concerns regarding sexuality. Consider discussing these issues with a friend, your partner (if you are involved in an intimate relationship), or your class group.

2. In your journal trace the evolution of your sexual history. What were some important experiences for you, and what did you learn from these experiences?

3. What sexual modeling did you see in your parents? What attitudes and values about sex did they convey to you, both implicitly and explicitly? What would you most want to communicate to your children about sex?

4. List as many common slang words as you are able to think of pertaining to (a) the male genitals, (b) the female genitals, and (c) sexual intercourse. Review this list and ask yourself what sexual attitudes seem to be expressed. What do you think this list implies about your culture's attitude toward sexuality? Reflect for a moment on the particular slang words regarding sex that are used in your culture. What attitudes about sex are conveyed by these words?

5. Go to a community family-planning agency or the campus health center. Pick up pamphlets on HIV, AIDS, STIs, and safer sex practices. Recruit a health educator as a guest speaker for some group you belong to or for your class.

6. Incest is a universal taboo. Explore some of the reasons for this taboo. You might investigate cross-cultural attitudes pertaining to incest. Do you view sexual experimentation between siblings during childhood as incest? Discuss.

7. The media are giving increasing attention to the topics of incest and sexual abuse of children. What do you think this current interest in these subjects implies?

Resources for Future Study

Web Site Resources

SEXUAL HEALTH NETWORK
http://www.sexualhealth.com/

This site is "dedicated to providing easy access to sexuality information, education, counseling, therapy, medical attention, and other sexuality resources," especially for people with disabilities, illness, or other health-related problems.

SEXUALITY INFORMATION AND EDUCATION COUNCIL OF THE UNITED STATES (SIECUS)
http://www.siecus.org

This organization is devoted to providing information on a range of topics pertaining to sexuality. SIECUS promotes comprehensive education about sexuality and advocates the rights of all individuals to make responsible sexual choices.

QUEER RESOURCES DIRECTORY (QRD)
http://www.qrd.org/QRD/

The QRD focuses on issues relating to sexual minorities: "groups which have traditionally been labeled as 'queer' and systematically discriminated against." This site is "an electronic library with news clippings, political contact information, newsletters, essays, images, hyperlinks, and every other kind of information resource of interest to the gay, lesbian, and bisexual community."

HIV/AIDS AEGIS
http://www.aegis.com/

This is the largest and one of the most important Internet resources dealing with HIV and AIDS.

This site provides an extensive collection of related links, documents, and news articles.

NATIONAL CENTER FOR HIV, STD,
AND TB PREVENTION
http://www.cdc.gov/hiv/dhap.htm

The Centers for Disease Control and Prevention (CDC) offers current information, fact sheets, conferences, publications, and information on the prevention and treatment of HIV/AIDS.

NATIONAL CENTER FOR ASSAULT PREVENTION
http://www.ncap.org/aboutncap.htm

This center provides services to children, adolescents, mentally retarded adults, and elderly.

ADVOCATES FOR YOUTH
http://www.advocatesforyouth.org

This organization develops programs and materials to educate youth on sex and sexual responsibility.

NATIONAL COMMITTEE FOR THE PREVENTION
OF CHILD ABUSE
http://www.preventchildabuse.org

This is a resource that provides literature on child abuse prevention programs.

RAPE ABUSE AND INCEST NATIONAL
NETWORK
http://www.rainn.org

This site offers news, hotlines, a list of local crisis centers, and statistics on the incidence of rape and incest.

InfoTrac College Edition Resources

For additional readings, explore INFOTRAC COLLEGE EDITION, our online library:
http://www.infotrac.college.com/wadsworth

Hint: Enter these search terms:

sexuality

sensuality

celibacy

sexual abstinence

acquired immunodeficiency syndrome

human immunodeficiency virus

erectile dysfunction

sexually transmitted illness

sexually transmitted infection

safe sex

sexual abuse

sexual harassment

incest

date rape

acquaintance rape

Print Resources

Bass, E., & Davis, L. (1994). *The courage to heal: A guide for women survivors of child sexual abuse* (3rd ed.). New York: Harper Perennial.

Berman, J., & Berman, L. (2001). *For women only: A revolutionary guide to overcoming sexual dysfunction and reclaiming your sex life.* New York: Henry Holt.

Black, C. (1987). *It will never happen to me.* New York: Ballantine.

Carroll, J. L. (2005). *Sexuality now: Embracing diversity.* Belmont, CA: Thomson Brooks/Cole.

Centers for Disease Control and Prevention. (1994). *Voluntary HIV counseling and testing: Facts, issues, and answers.* Rockville, MD: Author.

Centers for Disease Control and Prevention. (1999). *Condoms and their use in preventing HIV infection and other STDs.* Rockville, MD: Author.

Centers for Disease Control and Prevention. (1999). *HIV and its transmission.* Rockville, MD: Author.

Crooks, R., & Baur, K. (2002). *Our sexuality* (8th ed.). Belmont, CA: Wadsworth/Thomson Learning.

Finklehorn, D. (1984). *Child sexual abuse: New theory and research.* New York: Free Press.

Forward, S., & Buck, C. S. (1988). *Betrayal of innocence: Incest and its devastation.* New York: Penguin.

Johnson, E. M. (1992). *What you can do to avoid AIDS.* New York: Times Books.

Jones, L. (1996). *HIV/AIDS: What to do about it.* Pacific Grove, CA: Brooks/Cole.

King, B. M. (1999). *Human sexuality today* (3rd ed.). Upper Saddle River, NJ: Prentice-Hall.

Maltz, W. (2001). *The sexual healing journey: A guide for survivors of sexual abuse.* New York: HarperCollins.

Meiselman, K. C. (1990). *Resolving the trauma of incest: Reintegration therapy with survivors.* San Francisco: Jossey-Bass.

10

Working to live—living
to work.

Work and
Recreation

Where Am I Now?

Use this scale to respond to these statements:

   3 = This statement is true of me *most* of the time.

   2 = This statement is true of me *some* of the time.

   1 = This statement is true of me *almost none* of the time.

   1. I am in college because it is necessary for the career I want.

   2. My primary reasons for being in college are to grow as a person and to fulfill my potential.

   3. I am in college to give me time to decide what to do with my life.

   4. I would not work if I did not need the money.

   5. Work is a very important means of expressing myself.

   6. I expect to change jobs several times during my life.

   7. A secure job is more important to me than an exciting one.

   8. If I am unhappy in my job, it is probably my fault, not the job's.

   9. I expect my work to fulfill many of my needs and to be an important source of meaning in my life.

   10. I have a good balance between my work and my recreation.

D eriving satisfaction from work and recreation are of paramount importance. As you will see, work has an impact in many areas of our lives, and the balance we find between work and recreation can contribute to our personal vitality or be a stressful experience that ultimately results in burnout. **Recreation** is derived from "re-create," which means to restore, to refresh, to put new life into, and to create anew. Recreation involves leisure time and what we do away from work.

Work is a good deal more than an activity that takes up a certain number of hours each week. If you feel good about your work, the quality of your life will improve. If you hate your job and dread the hours you spend at it, your relationships and your feelings about yourself are bound to be affected. It is important to reflect on the attitudes we have toward work and recreation and to be aware of the impact of these attitudes on our lives. It is certainly worth the effort to think about ways to improve the quality of the many hours we devote to work and to recreation in our daily life.

If you are a reentry student, you may already have a career. You may be working at a job, carrying out responsibilities in the home, and also being either a part- or full-time college student. Your college work may be preparing you for a career change or a job promotion. If you have not yet begun a career, you can use this chapter to examine your expectations about work. Make an assessment of your personal interests, needs, values, and abilities, and begin the process of matching these personal characteristics with occupational information and trends in the world of work. In *Taking Charge of Your Career Direction*, Robert Lock (2005b) acknowledges that choosing an occupation is not easy. Externally, the working world is constantly changing; internally, your expectations, needs, motivations, values, and interests may change. Deciding on a career involves integrating the realities of these two worlds. Lock emphasizes the importance of *actively choosing* a career.

> Accept the responsibility of choosing an occupation and then be willing to live with the consequences of that decision. Of course, these words are easy to say but difficult to practice. (p. 6)

One way to assume an active role in deciding on a career is to talk to other people about their job satisfaction. However, it is essential that you explore your thoughts about a career. Zunker (2002) contends that it is most important to "use personal agency," which involves taking responsibility for your career development. One of the major factors that might prevent you from becoming active in planning for a career is the temptation to put off doing what needs to be done to choose your work. Rather than actively choosing a career, some people allow themselves to merely "fall into" a job.

Career development researchers have found that most people go through a series of stages when choosing an occupation or, more typically, several occupations to pursue. As with life-span stages, different factors emerge or become influential at different times throughout this process. Therefore, it could well be a mistake to think about selecting *one* occupation that will last a lifetime. It may be more fruitful to choose a general type of work or a broad field of endeavor that appeals to you. You can consider your present job or field of study as a means of gaining experience and opening doors to new possibilities, and you can focus on what you want to learn from this experience. It can be liberating to realize that your decisions about work can be part of a developmental process and that your jobs can change as you change or can lead to related occupations within your chosen field.

The fast pace of social and technological change in today's world is forcing people to adapt to a changing world of work. The changing workforce and changing workplace have implications for career decision making. In writing about these changes, Zunker (2002) emphasizes that the workplace will become more diverse in the 21st century. Increasing numbers of women will enter the workplace, and the workforce will become more culturally diverse. The average American entering the workforce today will change occupations, not just jobs, three times (Bolles, 2000; Naisbitt & Aburdene, 1991). This means that people entering the workforce need to have more than specific knowledge and skills; they need to be able to adapt to change. One career may pave the way to another.

Before continuing with this chapter, let's clarify the terms "career," "occupation," "job," and "work." A **career** can be thought of as your life's work. A career spans a period of time and may involve one or several occupations; it is the sequence of a person's work experience over time. An **occupation** is your vocation, profession, business, or trade, and you may change your occupation several times during your lifetime. A **job** is your position of employment within an occupation. Over a period of time you may have several jobs within the same occupation. A job is what you do to earn money to survive and to do the things you would like to do. **Work** is a broad concept that refers to something you do because you want to, and we hope, because you enjoy it. Ideally, your job and your work involve similar activities. Work is fulfilling when you feel you are being compensated adequately and when you like what you are doing.

YOUR COLLEGE EDUCATION AS YOUR WORK

You may already have made several vocational decisions and held a number of different jobs, you may be changing careers, or you may be in the process of exploring career options and preparing yourself for a career. If you are in the midst of considering what occupations might best suit you, it would be helpful to review the meaning that going to college has for you now. There is certainly some relationship between how you approach your college experience and how you will someday approach your career.

School may be your primary line of work for the present, but for those of you who are engaged in a career and have families, school is not likely to be your main source of work. Regardless of your commitments outside of college, it is a good idea to reflect on why you are in college. Ask yourself these questions: "Why am I in college?" "Is it my choice or someone else's choice for me?" "Do I enjoy most of my time as a student?" "Is my work as a student satisfying and meaningful?" "Would I rather be somewhere else or doing something other than being a student? If so, why am I staying in college?"

Some people are motivated to go to college because it offers opportunities for personal development and the pursuit of knowledge. Others are in college primarily to attain their career objectives, and some go because they are avoiding making other choices in their lives. Clarifying your own reasons for being in college can be useful in the process of long-range career planning.

In Chapter 1 we asked you to review your experiences as a learner and your learning style. You were encouraged to take steps to become an active and involved student. This would be a good time to review the goals you set and determine how well you are progressing toward them. If you established a contract to take increased responsibility for your own learning and to get personally involved in this book and the course, reevaluate how you are doing. Consider setting new goals, modifying your original goals, or trying new behavior in reaching your goals.

If you like the meaning your college experience has for you as well as your part in creating this meaning, you are likely to assume responsibility for making your job satisfying. If you typically do more than is required as a student, you are likely to be willing to go beyond doing what is expected of you in your job. If you are the kind of student who fears making mistakes and will not risk saying what you think in class, you may carry this behavior into a job. You may be afraid of jeopardizing your grades by being assertive, and someday you may be unassertive in the work world out of fear of losing your job or not advancing. If you have taken on too many courses and other projects, planned poorly, procrastinated, and fallen behind, you may feel utter frustration and exhaustion by semester's end. Reflect for a moment on the degree to which this same pattern might show up in your work.

Make an honest inventory of your role as a student. If you are not satisfied with yourself as a student, consider how you can change this situation. If you decide that your present major is not what really interests you, you are no more wedded to your course of study than you are to one particular job in the future. Determine for yourself why you are in college and what you are getting from and giving to this project.

CHOOSING AN OCCUPATION OR CAREER

What do you expect from work? What factors do you stress in selecting a career or an occupation? In working with college students, we find that many of you have not thought seriously about why you are choosing a given vocation.

For some, parental pressure or encouragement is the major reason for being in college. Others have idealized views of what it would be like to be a lawyer, an engineer, or a doctor. Many college students have not looked at what they value the most and whether these values can be attained in their chosen vocation. John Holland's (1997) theory of career decision making is based on the assumption that career choices are an expression of personality. Holland believes the choice of an occupation should reflect the person's motivation, knowledge, personality, and ability. Occupations represent a way of life. Dave's personal story illustrates this search for a satisfying career. Dave chose college without knowing what he wanted. Eventually he found a direction by pursuing what interested him.

DAVE'S STORY

I went to college right out of high school even though I wasn't sure that college was for me. I went because I thought I needed a college degree to get a good job and to succeed.

My first year was a bit rough because of the new surroundings. In my classes I felt like a number, and it didn't seem to matter if I attended classes or not. College provided a wide range of freedom. I was the one who was responsible to show up for class. It was hard for me to handle this freedom. Needless to say, my grades took a nosedive. I was placed on academic probation. As a result, I decided to go to a community college. But my pattern of not taking school seriously remained the same.

Although I wanted to eventually finish college, I knew that university life was not right for me at this time. I decided to move out of my parents' home and worked full time. Although I was working, I managed to take a few night classes at a community college. I knew that if I left college completely it would be harder to ever return.

Eventually I accepted a job with a promotional marketing firm. I was given more responsible assignments, and I really enjoyed what I was doing. I asked myself: "How could I apply what I enjoyed doing and make it a career?" This question led me to doing research on the sports entertainment field to discover a career path.

Knowing what I wanted as a career made selecting a major relatively easy. I majored in business with a marketing emphasis and did extremely well. My journey took me from academic disqualification to graduating with honors.

Following my interests has led to an exciting career. I look forward to getting up and going to work, which is both fun and challenging. I am able to combine my sports hobbies with my profession. This work is personally rewarding, and I feel energized and motivated on the job. My work doesn't seem like "work." To me, this is one of the keys to a meaningful life.

The Disadvantages of Choosing an Occupation Too Soon

So much emphasis is placed on what you will do "for a living" that you may feel compelled to choose an occupation or a career before you are really ready to do so. In our society we are pressured from an early age to grow up, and we are encouraged to identify with some occupation. Children are often asked: "What are you going to be when you grow up?" Embedded in this question is the implication that we are not grown up until we have decided to be something. By late adolescence or young adulthood, the pressure is on to make decisions and commitments. Young adults are expected to make choices that will affect the rest of their lives, even though they may not feel ready to make these commitments. Our society expects young people to identify their values, choose a vocation and a lifestyle, and then settle down (Carney & Wells, 1999). The implication is that once young people make the "right decision" they should be set for life. Yet deciding on a career is not that simple.

One of the disadvantages of focusing on a particular occupation too soon is that students' interest patterns are often not sufficiently reliable or stable in high school or sometimes even in the college years to predict job success and satisfaction. Furthermore, the typical student does not have enough self-knowledge or knowledge of educational offerings and vocational opportunities to make realistic decisions. The pressure to make premature vocational decisions often results in choosing an occupation in which one does not have the interests and abilities required for success. At the other extreme are those who engage in delay, defensive avoidance, and procrastination. An individual on this end of the scale drifts endlessly and aimlessly, and life may be pretty well over when he or she asks, "Where am I going?" It is clear that either extreme is problematic. We need to be cautious in resisting pressures from the outside to decide too quickly on a life's vocation, yet we also need to be alert to the tendencies within ourselves to expect that what we want will come to us easily. You may remember from Chapter 2 that Erikson calls for a psychological moratorium during adolescence to enable young people to get some distance from the pressure of choosing a career too soon. A moratorium can reduce the pressure of having to make key life choices without sufficient data. As young people gain experience, they are likely to develop a new perspective about what they want from a career and from life.

Factors in Career Decision Making

Factors that have been shown to be important in the occupational decision-making process include motivation and achievement; attitudes about occupations; abilities and aptitudes; interests; values; self-concept; temperament and personality styles; socioeconomic level; parental influence; ethnic identity; gender; and physical, mental, emotional, and social handicaps. In choosing your

The fast pace of social and technological change in today's world is forcing people to adapt to a changing world of work.

© Yang Liu/Corbis

vocation (or in evaluating the choices you have made previously), consider which factors really mean the most to you. Let's take a closer look at how some of these factors may influence your vocational choice, keeping in mind that a career choice is a process, not an event.

Motivation and Achievement Setting goals is at the core of the process of deciding on a vocation. If you have goals but do not have the energy and persistence to pursue them, your goals will not be met. Your need to achieve along with your achievements to date are related to your motivation to translate goals into action plans. In thinking about your career choices, identify those areas where your drive is the greatest. Also, reflect on specific achievements. What have you accomplished that you feel particularly proud of? What are you doing now that moves you in the direction of achieving what is important to you? What are some of the things you dream about doing in the future? Did you ever have a dream of what you wanted to be when you grew up? What happened to that dream? Were others encouraging or discouraging of this dream? Thinking about your goals, needs, motivations, and achievements is a good way to get a clearer focus on your career direction.

Attitudes About Occupations We develop our attitudes toward the status of occupations by learning from the people in our environment. Typical first graders are not aware of the differential status of occupations, yet in a few years these children begin to rank occupations in a manner similar to that of adults. As students advance to higher grades, they reject more and more occupations as unacceptable. Unfortunately, they rule out some of the very jobs from which they may have to choose if they are to find employment as adults. It is difficult for people to feel positive about themselves if they have to accept an occupation they perceive as low in status. At this point ask yourself: "What did I learn about work from my parents?" "What did I learn about work from my culture?"

Abilities Ability or aptitude has received a great deal of attention in the career decision-making process, and it is probably used more often than any other factor to evaluate potential for success. **Ability** refers to your competence in an activity. **Aptitude tests** are designed to measure specific skills or the ability to acquire certain proficiencies. Assessment of aptitudes provides a useful frame of reference for evaluating potential careers (Zunker, 2002). Both general and specific abilities should be considered in making career choices. (See Chapter 1 for a discussion of how multiple intelligences influence our abilities.) You can measure and compare your abilities with the skills required for various professions and academic areas of interest to you. Ask yourself: "How did I determine what abilities I have?" "What influence did my family of origin have on my perception of my abilities?" "How did others, such as teachers and friends, influence my perception?"

Interests Your interests reflect your experiences or ideas pertaining to work-related activities that you like or dislike. In career planning, primary consideration is given to interest measurements, which can be done in a three-step process: (1) discover your areas of interest, (2) identify occupations in your interest areas, and (3) determine which occupations correspond to your abilities.

Interest inventories are useful tools because the results can be used to compare your interests with those of others who have found job satisfaction in a given area (Zunker, 2002). Interest alone does not necessarily mean that you have the ability to succeed in a particular occupation. Both abilities and interests are integral components of career decision making.

Several interest inventories are available to help you assess your vocational interests. If you were going to select just one instrument, we recommend Holland's Self-Directed Search (SDS) interest inventory, which is probably the most widely used interest inventory. Other interest and personality inventories you may want to consider taking are the Vocational Preference Inventory, the Strong Interest Inventory, the Kuder Occupational Interest Inventory, and the Myers-Briggs Type Indicator. This last instrument assesses types of human personality. For further information about such inventories, contact the counseling center at your college.

Values Your values indicate what is important to you and what you want from life. It is important to assess, identify, and clarify your values so you will be able to choose a career that enables you to achieve what you value. An inventory of your values can help you discern patterns in your life and see how your values have emerged, taken shape, and changed over time. Work value inventories measure values associated with job success and satisfaction (Zunker, 2002).

Your **work values** pertain to what you hope to accomplish through your role in an occupation. Both general values and work values need to be considered in making career decisions because values tend to remain fairly stable over the life span (Zunker & Osborn, 2002). Work values are an important aspect of your total value system, and knowing those things that bring meaning to your life is crucial if you hope to find a career that has personal value for you. A few examples of work values include helping others, influencing people, finding meaning, achievement, prestige, status, competition, security, friendships, creativity, stability, recognition, adventure, physical challenge, change and variety, opportunity for travel, moral fulfillment, and independence. Because specific work values are often related to particular occupations, they can be the basis of a good match between you and a position.

Self-Concept People with a poor self-concept are not likely to envision themselves in a meaningful or important job. They are likely to keep their aspirations low, and thus their achievements will probably be low. They may select and remain in a job they do not enjoy or derive satisfaction from because they are convinced this is all they are worthy of. Choosing a vocation can be thought of as a public declaration of the kind of person we see ourselves as being.

Personality Types and Choosing a Career

According to John Holland (1997), people are attracted to a particular career by their unique personalities. People who exhibit certain values and particular personality traits are a good match with certain career areas. Holland has identified six worker personality types, and his typology is widely used as the basis for books on career development, vocational tests used in career counseling centers, and self-help approaches for making career decisions.* Because his work has been so influential in vocational theory, it is worth going into some detail about it here.

As you read the descriptions of Holland's six personality types, take the time to think about the patterns that fit you best. Remember that most people do not fall neatly into one category but have characteristics from several types. When you come across a phrase that describes you, put a check mark in the

---

*Holland's (1997) six personality types are realistic, investigative, artistic, social, enterprising, and conventional. Our discussion of these six types is based on Holland's work as refined by Jim Morrow (retired professor of counseling, Western Carolina University, North Carolina). For more information about Holland's personality types and implications for selecting a career, we highly recommend John Holland's (1994) *Self-Directed Search (Form R)*. For further information contact Psychological Assessment Resources, Inc., P.O. Box 998, Odessa, FL 33556 or telephone (1-800-331-TEST).

space provided. Then look again at the six personality types and select the three types (in rank order) that best describe the way you see yourself. As you become more aware of the type of person you are, you can apply these insights in your own career decision-making process.

Realistic Types

_____ are attracted to outdoor, mechanical, and physical activities, hobbies, and occupations

_____ like to work with things, objects, and animals rather than with ideas, data, and people

_____ tend to have mechanical and athletic abilities

_____ like to construct, shape, and restructure and repair things around them

_____ like to use equipment and machinery and to see tangible results

_____ are persistent and industrious builders but seldom creative and original, preferring familiar methods and established patterns

_____ tend to think in terms of absolutes, dislike ambiguity, and prefer not to deal with abstract, theoretical, and philosophical issues

_____ are materialistic, traditional, and conservative

_____ do not have strong interpersonal and verbal skills and are often uncomfortable in situations in which attention is centered on them

_____ tend to find it difficult to express their feelings and may be regarded as shy

Investigative Types

_____ are naturally curious and inquisitive

_____ need to understand, explain, and predict what goes on around them

_____ are scholarly and scientific and tend to be pessimistic and critical about nonscientific, simplistic, or supernatural explanations

_____ tend to become engrossed in whatever they are doing and may appear to be oblivious to everything else

_____ are independent and like to work alone

_____ prefer neither to supervise others nor to be supervised

_____ are theoretical and analytic in outlook and find abstract and ambiguous problems and situations challenging

_____ are original and creative and often find it difficult to accept traditional attitudes and values

_____ avoid highly structured situations with externally imposed rules but are themselves internally well-disciplined, precise, and systematic

_____ have confidence in their intellectual abilities but often feel inadequate in social situations

_____ tend to lack leadership and persuasive skills

_____ tend to be reserved and formal in interpersonal relationships

_____ are not typically expressive emotionally and may not be considered friendly

Artistic Types

_____ are creative, expressive, original, intuitive, and individualistic

_____ like to be different and strive to stand out from the crowd

_____ like to express their personalities by creating new and different things with words, music, materials, and physical expression like acting and dancing

_____ want attention and praise but are sensitive to criticism

_____ tend to be uninhibited and nonconforming in dress, speech, and action

_____ prefer to work without supervision

_____ are impulsive in outlook

_____ place great value on beauty and esthetic qualities

_____ tend to be emotional and complicated

_____ prefer abstract tasks and unstructured situations

_____ find it difficult to function well in highly ordered and systematic situations

_____ seek acceptance and approval from others but often find close interpersonal relationships so stressful that they avoid them

_____ compensate for their resulting feelings of estrangement or alienation by relating to others primarily indirectly through art

_____ tend to be introspective

Social Types

_____ are friendly, enthusiastic, outgoing, and cooperative

_____ enjoy the company of other people

_____ are understanding and insightful about others' feelings and problems

_____ like helping and facilitating roles like teacher, mediator, adviser, or counselor

_____ express themselves well and are persuasive in interpersonal relationships

_____ like attention and enjoy being at or near the center of the group

_____ are idealistic, sensitive, and conscientious about life and in dealings with others

_____ like to deal with philosophical issues such as the nature and purpose of life, religion, and morality

_____ dislike working with machines or data and at highly organized, routine, and repetitive tasks

_____ get along well with others and find it natural to express their emotions

_____ are tactful in relating to others and are considered to be kind, supportive, and caring

Enterprising Types

_____ are outgoing, self-confident, persuasive, and optimistic

_____ like to organize, direct, manage, and control the activities of groups toward personal or organizational goals

_____ are ambitious and like to be in charge

_____ place a high value on status, power, money, and material possessions

_____ like to feel in control and responsible for making things happen

_____ are energetic and enthusiastic in initiating and supervising activities

_____ like to influence others

_____ are adventurous, impulsive, assertive, and verbally persuasive

_____ enjoy social gatherings and like to associate with well-known and influential people

_____ like to travel and explore and often have exciting and expensive hobbies

_____ see themselves as popular

_____ tend to dislike activities requiring scientific abilities and systematic and theoretical thinking

_____ avoid activities that require attention to detail and a set routine

Conventional Types

_____ are well-organized, persistent, and practical

_____ enjoy clerical and computational activities that follow set procedures

_____ are dependable, efficient, and conscientious

_____ enjoy the security of belonging to groups and organizations and make good team members

_____ are status-conscious but usually do not aspire to high positions of leadership

_____ are most comfortable when they know what is expected of them

_____ tend to be conservative and traditional

_____ usually conform to expected standards and follow the lead of those in positions of authority, with whom they identify

_____ like to work indoors in pleasant surroundings and place value on material comforts and possessions

_____ are self-controlled and low-key in expressing their feelings

_____ avoid intense personal relationships in favor of more casual ones

_____ are most comfortable among people they know well

_____ like for things to go as planned and prefer not to change routines

Relationships Among the Personality Types As you were reading the descriptions of the six personality types, you probably noticed that each type shares some characteristics with some other types and also is quite different from some of the others. To help you compare and contrast the six types, Holland's "hexagon" illustrates the order of the relationships among the types (see Figure 10.1).

Each type shares some characteristics with those types adjacent to it on the hexagon. Each type has only a little in common with those types two positions removed from it, and it is quite unlike the type opposite it on the hexagon. For example, the investigative type shares some characteristics with the realistic and artistic types, has little in common with the conventional and social types, and is quite different from the enterprising type. If you read the descriptions of the six types once more with the hexagon in mind, the relationships among the types will become clearer.

People who feel that they resemble two or three types that are not adjacent on the hexagon may find it difficult to reconcile the conflicting elements in those type descriptions. It is important to remember that the descriptions provided are for "pure" types and that very few people resemble a single type to the

Figure 10.1
Holland's Hexagon

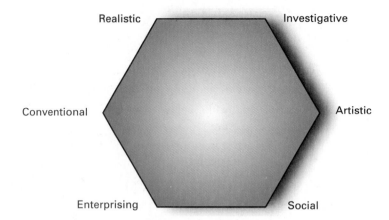

exclusion of all others. This is why we ask you to select the three types that you think best describe you.

Once you have compared your personal traits with the characteristics of each of the six types, it is possible to find a general area of work that most matches your personal qualities, interests, and values. This topic is addressed in the next section. The Take Time to Reflect exercise will assist you in assessing your personality type. It is important to have someone you know assess you as well as doing so yourself.

Take Time to Reflect   This exercise will help you become familiar with Holland's personality types.

1. Read the descriptions and other information furnished about Holland's six personality types at least two or three times.

2. Which of the six personality types best describes you? No one type will be completely "right" for you, but one of them will probably sound more like you than the others. Consider the overall descriptions of the types; do not concentrate on just one or two characteristics of a type. As soon as you are satisfied that one type describes you better than the others, write that type down on the space for number 1 at the end of this exercise.

3. Which of the six types next best describes you? Write that type down in the space for number 2. Write down the type that next best describes you in the space for number 3.

4. Next, give the descriptions of the six types to someone who knows you very well. Ask them to read the descriptions carefully and order them in terms of their resemblance to you, just as you have done. Do not show or tell them how you rated yourself.

5. After the other person finishes rating you, compare your own rating with theirs. If there is not close agreement among the three types on both lists, ask the other person to give examples of your behaviors that prompted his or her ratings. The other person may not have rated you very accurately, or your behavior may not portray you to others as you see yourself. The purpose of this exercise is to familiarize you with Holland's personality types. It may have a "bonus" effect of better familiarizing you with yourself.

Your rating of yourself:

1. _____

2. _____

3. _____

Rating by someone who knows you well:

1. _____

2. _____

3. _____

THE PROCESS OF DECIDING ON A CAREER

Holland (1997) originally developed his system as a way of helping people make occupational choices. After you have identified the three personality types that most closely describe you, this information can be used in your career decision-making process.

Personality Types and Careers

It is more likely that you will be successful in your career if your own personality types match those of people who have already proven themselves in the career that you hope to pursue. Central to Holland's theory is the concept that we choose a career to satisfy our preferred person orientation. However, you will need to have at least basic skills in all areas. For example, if you are a strong investigative type, you might need to brush up on your enterprising skills in order to do well in the interview situation. Holland has developed elaborate materials that can help you assess your personality type and compare it with the dominant types in various occupations or fields of study. Here is a list of possible occupations or fields of interest associated with each personality type.

Realistic Type: carpenter, electronics engineer, emergency medical technology, mechanical engineering, industrial design, sculpture, law enforcement, photography, wildlife conservation management, orthodontics assistant, culinary arts, locomotive engineer, camera repair, cement masonry, jewelry repair, diesel mechanics, optician, floral design, marine surveying, automotive technology.

Investigative Type: economics, marketing, linguistics, biology, dentistry, food technology, optometry, medicine, physician's assistant, pollution control and technology, surveying, quality control management, meteorology, public health administration, highway engineering, veterinary medicine, biochemistry, cardiology, chemistry.

Artistic Type: acting/theater, creative writing, dance, journalism, commercial art, music, technical writing, fashion illustration, art education, graphic arts and design, cosmetology, fashion design, audiovisual technology, furniture design, interior decorating and design, photography, architecture, landscape architecture, stage design.

Social Type: education, motion pictures/cinema, probation and parole, recreation education/leadership, social work, hospital administration, rehabilitation counseling, nursing, psychology, school administration, labor relations, religious education, television production, library assistant, air traffic control, real estate, physical therapy, home economics, beautician, dental assistant.

Enterprising Type: accounting, travel agency management, park administration, dietetics, laboratory science, banking and finance, industrial engineering, international engineering, fire science management, records management, fashion merchandising, business administration, travel administration, marketing, law, international relations, outdoor recreation.

Conventional Type: computer and data processing, office machine technology, bookkeeping, building inspection, computer operator, court reporter, library assistant, medical records technology, personnel clerk, secretarial science, quality control technology, orthodontics assistant, electrical technology, medical secretary.

A Suggestion After you have looked at the lists above, underline any fields of interest that appeal to you and then make notes on why certain occupations or fields of study are attractive to you. Reflect on occupations that both appeal to you as well as areas you would want to avoid. What are your reasons for picking certain fields of study or occupations and for rejecting others?

Another Suggestion It might be helpful to make use of various standardized assessment devices. There are several things you can do to assist you in self-assessment. For one, consider visiting the career counseling center at your college or university and inquire about standardized assessments that are available. Consider also using Computer-Assisted Career Guidance (CACG) assessment. The use of CACG assessment has steadily increased because results are immediately available. Computer-based assessment programs interpret results by occupational fit with lists of career options (Zunker, 2002).

Steps You Can Take

The process of selecting a career is more than a simple matter of matching information about the world of work with your personality type. You will find it useful to go through some of these steps several times. For example, gathering and assessing information is a continual process rather than a step to be completed.

- **Begin by focusing on yourself.** Continue to identify your interests, abilities, aptitudes, values, beliefs, wants, and preferences. Keep these questions in mind: "Who am I?" "How do I want to live?" "Where do I want to live?" "What kind of work environment do I want?" "What do I want to do for a living?" This self-assessment includes taking into consideration your personality style. Ask yourself: "Do I function well in a system that is structured or unstructured?" "How much and what type of supervision do I need?" "Do I prefer to work alone or with others?"

- **Generate alternative solutions.** This stage is closely related to the next two. Rather than first narrowing your options, consider a number of alternatives or different potential occupations that you are drawn to. In this step it is wise to consider your work values and interests, especially as they apply to Holland's six personality types.

- **Gather and assess information about the alternatives generated.** In the process of expanding your list of career possibilities, recognize that you will likely devote a great deal of time to your occupation. Be willing to research the occupations that attract you. Doing so will increase your chances of being able to live the way you want. Ask yourself, "Where do I best fit?" "Will the occupation I am considering be psychologically and financially satisfying to me?" "Do I have the resources to meet the challenges and responsibilities of the occupation?" "What are the typical characteristics of people who enter into this occupation?" Find an occupation that matches your interests, values, and talents, and read about the educational requirements of the occupation. Talk to as many people as you can who are involved in the occupations you are considering. Ask them how their occupation may be changing in the years to come. Examine the social, political, economic, and geographic environment as a basis for assessing factors that influence your career choice.

- **Weigh and prioritize your alternatives.** After you arrive at a list of alternatives, spend adequate time prioritizing them. Consider the practical aspects of your decisions. Integrate occupational information and the wishes and views of others with your knowledge of yourself.

- **Make the decision and formulate a plan.** It is best to think of a series of many decisions at various turning points. In formulating a plan, read about the preparation required for your chosen alternative. Ask, "How can I best get to where I want to go?"

Choosing a career is best
thought of as a process,
not a one-time event.

- **Carry out the decision.** After deciding, take practical steps to make your vision become a reality. Realize that committing yourself to implementing your decision does not mean that you will have no fears. The important thing is not to allow these fears to keep you frozen. You will never know if you are ready to meet a challenge unless you put your plan into action. This action plan includes knowing how to market your skills to employers. You need to learn how to identify employment sources, prepare résumés, and meet the challenges of job interviews.

- **Get feedback.** After taking practical steps to carry out your decision, you will need to determine whether your choices are viable for you. Both the world of work and you will change over time, and what may look appealing to you now may not seem appropriate at some future time. Remember that career development is an ongoing process, and it will be important to commit yourself to repeating at least part of the process as your needs change or as occupational opportunities open up or decline.

For a more detailed discussion of the steps we have outlined, see *Taking Charge of Your Career Direction* (Lock, 2005b). Lock emphasizes these key components of the career-planning process: being aware and committed, studying the environment, studying yourself, generating occupational alternatives, gathering information about occupational prospects, making decisions, implementing a plan of action, and obtaining feedback or reevaluating this career decision-making process.

Take Time to Reflect This survey is aimed at getting you to reflect on your basic attitudes, values, abilities, and interests in regard to occupational choice.

1. Rate each item, using the following code:

1 = This is a *most important* consideration.
2 = This is *important* to me, but not a top priority.
3 = This is *slightly important*.
4 = This is of *little* or *no importance* to me.

_____ Financial rewards
_____ Security
_____ Challenge
_____ Prestige and status
_____ Opportunity to express my creativity
_____ Autonomy—freedom to direct my project
_____ Opportunity for advancement
_____ Variety within the job
_____ Recognition
_____ Friendship and relations with coworkers
_____ Serving people
_____ Source of meaning
_____ Chance to continue learning
_____ Structure and routine

Once you have finished the assessment, review the list and write down the three most important values you associate with selecting a career or occupation.

_____

_____

2. In what area(s) do you see your strongest abilities?

_____

_____

3. What are a few of your major interests?

_____

_____

4. Which one value of yours do you see as having some bearing on your choice of an occupation?

_____

_____

5. At this point, what kind of work do you see as most suitable to your interests, abilities, and values?

_____

_____

CHOICES AT WORK

Just as choosing a career is a process, so is creating meaning in our work. If we experience a dead end in our job or do not find avenues of self-expression through the work we do, we eventually lose our vitality. In this section we look at ways to find meaning in work and at approaches to keeping our options open.

The Dynamics of Discontent in Work

If you are dissatisfied with your job, one recourse is to look for a new one. Change alone, however, might not produce different results. In general it is a mistake to assume that change necessarily cures dissatisfactions, and this certainly applies to changing jobs. To know whether a new job would be helpful, you need to understand as clearly as you can why your present job is not satisfactory to you. Consider some of the external factors that can devitalize you in your job and the pressures your job often creates. It is also critical to deal with those factors within yourself that lead to discontent at work. The emphasis of our discussion will be on what you can do to change some of these factors in the job and in yourself.

You may like your work and derive satisfaction from it yet at the same time feel drained because of irritations produced by factors that are not intrinsic to the work itself. Such factors may include low morale or actual conflict and disharmony among fellow workers, authoritarian supervisors who make it difficult for you to feel any sense of freedom on the job, or organizational blocks to your creativity. Countless pressures and demands can sap your energy and lead you to feel dissatisfied with your job. These include having to meet deadlines and quotas, having to compete with others instead of simply doing your best, facing the threat of losing your job, feeling stuck in a job that offers little opportunity for growth, dealing with difficult customers or clients, or having to work long hours or perform exhausting or tedious work. Another source of dissatisfaction might be encountering other people at your work who are younger and less experienced than you who are making close to your current salary or perhaps even more.

A stress that is particularly insidious—because it can compound all the other dissatisfactions you might feel—is the threat of cutbacks or layoffs, an anxiety that becomes more acute when you think of your commitments and responsibilities. In addition to the strains you may experience on the job, you may also have the daily stress of commuting to and from work. You may be tense before you even get to work, and the trip home may only increase the level of tension or anxiety you bring home with you. One real problem for many is that relationships with others are negatively affected by this kind of pressure. If your work is deenergizing, you may have little to give your children, partner, and friends, and you may not be receptive to their efforts to give to you. You may not be able to avoid working in a less than desirable job, but you cannot afford to ignore the effects this may have on your overall life. If you are in an unsatisfying work situation, look for other ways of nourishing yourself.

All these factors can contribute to a general discontent that robs your work of whatever positive benefits it might otherwise have. Experiencing this kind of discontentment in your work can spoil much of the rest of your life as well. The alternative is to look at the specific things that contribute to your unhappiness or tension and to ask yourself what you can do about them. You can also ask what you can do about your own attitudes toward those pressures and sources of tension.

Self-Esteem and Work

With downsizing and layoffs, people sometimes find themselves out of work due to circumstances beyond their control. Unemployment is a reality that can erode self-esteem. Maria's story illustrates how self-esteem and identity are often anchored to your ability to engage in meaningful work, and how losing your job can be devastating.

MARIA'S STORY

*T*wo years ago I had an accident at work that forever changed who I was and required that I modify my future goals and plans. After hurting my back, I was told that I was no longer able to continue in the job that I had been engaged in for 16 years. I didn't want to believe this, and for a time I was in denial. When this harsh reality eventually hit me, I became depressed.

I didn't know who I was anymore. Working had been my life. It was my identity. I felt lost and very empty inside, and my self-esteem plummeted. I found myself making very little money, and at my age this was a failure. Being on worker's compensation, I was required to get training in a different line of work. Changing careers at this point in my life was a most difficult task. I was both angry and scared.

I realized the hardest part for me was that I had little control over what I was going through. I had to rely on the decisions of my doctors and the insurance company. To make matters even worse, I had to live at home with my parents. This felt like another loss of identity, because I ceased to be the head of my own household.

Coping with these circumstances was difficult, yet not impossible. The first thing I did was pray that God would help me through this crisis, making me stronger and restoring my self-esteem. I also relied on my friends, who gave me support and encouragement. I told myself that I was a good person, no matter what the circumstances. It took hard work, help from others, and positive thinking to keep my self-esteem afloat.

Maria's story demonstrates how losing a job had a negative impact on her life. But she learned a crucial lesson. Maria learned to separate her worth as a person from her job performance. She realized that she was a good person even though her options had been limited by losing her job.

Creating Meaning in Work

Work can be a major part of your quest for meaning, but it can also be a source of meaninglessness. Work can be an expression of yourself; it can be "love made visible" (Gibran, 1923, p. 27). It can be a way for you to be productive and to find enjoyment in daily life. Through your work you may be making a significant difference in the quality of your life or the lives of others, and this may give you real satisfaction. But work can also be devoid of any self-expressive value. It can be merely a means to survival and a drain on your energy. Instead of giving life meaning, your work can be contributing to burnout and even an early death. Ask yourself: "Is my work life-giving?" "Does it bring meaning to my life? If not, what can I do about it?"

If your job is depleting you physically and emotionally instead of energizing you, what course of action might you consider? What are your options if you feel stuck in a dead-end job? Are there some ways that you can constructively deal with the sources of dissatisfaction within your job? When might it be time for you to change jobs as a way of finding meaning? A helpful strategy could be exploring what you most want from your work, such as variety, a flexible schedule, and direct contact with people. If what you want is lacking in your work environment, you could always discuss alternatives with your employer. Many employers are likely to renegotiate rather than lose a quality person.

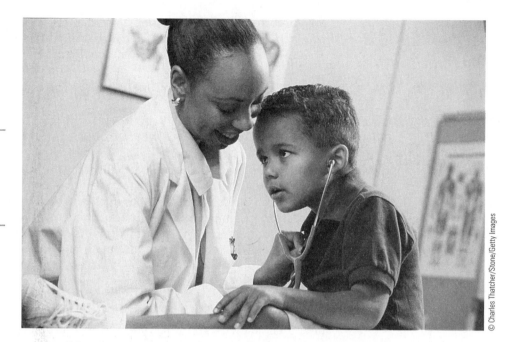

© Charles Thatcher/Stone/Getty Images

Through your work you may be making a significant difference in the quality of your life or the lives of others.

One way to examine the issue of meaninglessness and dissatisfaction in work is to look at how you really spend your time. It would be useful to keep a running account for a week to a month of what you do and how you relate to each of your activities. Which of them are taxing your vitality, and which are energizing you? Although you may not be able to change everything about your job that you do not like, you might be surprised by the significant changes you can make to increase your satisfaction. Some people adopt a passive stance in which they complain about the way things are and dwell on those aspects that they cannot change. Instead, a more constructive approach is to focus on those factors within your job that you *can* change. Even in cases where it is impractical to change jobs, you can still change your attitude and how you respond to a less than ideal situation.

Perhaps you can redefine the hopes you have for the job. Of course, you may also be able to think of the satisfactions you would most like to aim for in a job and then consider whether another job more clearly meets your needs and what steps you must take to obtain it. You might be able to find ways of advancing within your present job, making new contacts, or acquiring the skills that eventually will enable you to move on.

Although making changes in your present job might increase your satisfaction in the short term, the time may come when these resources no longer work and you find yourself stuck in a dead-end job that leads toward frustration. Changing jobs as a way to create meaning is possible, but you have to be prepared to deal with potential consequences. Changing jobs might increase your satisfaction with work, but changing jobs after a period of years can entail even more risk and uncertainty than making your first job selection.

Shifting Your Attitudes About Work

What attitudes do you hold about work that may either help or hinder you in achieving success in the world of work in the future? Zunker (2002) believes certain attitudes and beliefs are crucial to finding success as a future worker. The worker of the future will need to develop new and different attitudes about work itself and about career development through **personal agency**—certain attitudinal and behavioral characteristics such as a belief that one's career develops through effort, initiative, and self-development. Examples of basic shifts in attitudes include assuming responsibility for the future, being committed to lifelong learning, viewing the future with vision and creativity, being able to tolerate uncertainty, and viewing change as both positive and necessary. Some behaviors associated with personal agency are exhibiting a high level of resourcefulness and imagination, striving to use one's abilities to the fullest, cooperating with coworkers and supervisors, using effective interpersonal skills, planning for unknown changes, and assuming full responsibility for one's career development. Reflect for a moment on attitudes and behaviors that you think you now have that will help you achieve success as a future worker. What would help you the most to best deal with the demands of the future world of work? What attitude shifts could you make to find increased meaning in your work?

You may be enthusiastic about some type of work for years and yet eventually become dissatisfied because of the changes that occur within you. With these changes comes the possibility that a once-fulfilling job will become less than satisfying. If you outgrow your job, you can learn new skills and in other ways increase your options. Because your own attitudes are crucial, when a feeling of dissatisfaction sets in, it is wise to spend time rethinking what you want from a job and how you can most productively use your talents. Look carefully at how much the initiative rests with you—your expectations, your attitudes, your behaviors, and your sense of purpose and perspective.

CHANGING CAREERS IN MIDLIFE

Being aware of options can be an important asset at midlife. Most of the people we know have changed their jobs several times, and they may also have experienced a career change. Does this pattern fit any people you know? Whether or not you have reached middle age, ask yourself about your own beliefs and attitudes toward changing careers. Although making large changes in our lives is rarely easy, it can be a good deal harder if our own attitudes and fears are left unquestioned and unexamined.

A common example of midlife change is the woman who decides to return to college or the job market after her children reach high school age. Many community colleges and state universities are enrolling women who realize that they would like to develop new facets of themselves. This phenomenon is not unique to women. Many middle-aged men are reentry students pursuing an advanced degree or a new degree. Some men quit a job they have had for years, even if they are successful, because they want new challenges. Men often define themselves by the work they do, and work thus becomes a major source of the purpose in their lives. If they feel successful in their work, they may feel successful as persons. If they become stagnant in work, they may feel that they are ineffectual in other areas. People sometimes decide on a career change even as they approach late adulthood.

Thomas Bonacum was drafted into the army at age 21 and became a drill instructor. After leaving the army, Tom completed his degree in engineering, which led to a job as an industrial engineer. A few years later he was laid off and then joined the police department. During the time he was a police officer, he returned to college to get another degree in criminal justice. He became a police sergeant and eventually taught criminal justice for 4 years in the police academy during his 22 years in police work.

After the death of his wife of 35 years, "Father Tom" made a significant change of careers. With the support and encouragement of his four grown children, he entered the seminary in his late 50s and was ordained as a Catholic priest at age 60. Even after Father Tom retired, at the age of 77, he still kept active in the church and conducted services on weekends as long as his health allowed him to do so. He died at the age of 81.

Father Tom is an example of a person who was able to translate a dream into reality. When he graduated from high school, he tried to become a priest but discovered that he was not ready for some of the people in church, and they were not ready for him. He exemplifies a man who was willing to make career changes throughout his life and who dared to pursue what might have seemed like an impossible career choice. Many of us would not even conceive of such a drastic career change, yet Father Tom not only entertained this vision but also realized his dream.

For many it may be extremely risky and seemingly unrealistic to give up our job, even if we hate it, because it provides us with a measure of financial security. This is especially true during economically difficult times. The costs involved in achieving optimal job satisfaction may be too high. We might choose to stay with a less-than-desirable career yet at the same time discover other avenues for satisfaction. If you feel stuck in your job, ask yourself these questions: "Does my personal dissatisfaction outweigh the financial rewards?" "Is the price of my mental anguish, which may have resulted in physical symptoms, worth the price of keeping this job?"

RETIREMENT

Many people look forward to retirement as a time for them to take up new projects. Others fear this prospect and wonder how they will spend their time if they are not working. The real challenge of this period, especially for those who retire early, is to find a way to remain active in a meaningful way. Some people consciously choose early retirement because they have found more significant and valuable pursuits. For other people, however, retirement does not turn out as expected, and it can be traumatic. Can people who have relied largely on their job for meaning or structure in their lives deal with having much time and little to do? How can people retain their sense of purpose and value apart from their life's work?

Options at Retirement

It is a mistake to think of retired people as sitting around doing nothing. Many retired individuals keep themselves actively involved in community affairs, volunteer work, pursuit of new careers, engaging in recreation more fully and with more enjoyment, and having a fuller life than when they were employed full time. At the age of 76 Angela finally retired. Soon after her retirement, she became deeply involved in managing a retirement community. Doing this as a volunteer did not lessen the meaning of this kind of work for Angela.

For people who were in positions of power, the adjustment to retirement is sometimes difficult. They need to come to terms with the reality that once they retire they may no longer have the respect and admiration that they received in their professional roles. If most of the meaning of their lives was derived from their work position, they may be at a loss when they are without the work that filled so many of their needs. It is important to prepare for retirement and to find other sources of meaning so that you remain engaged with life.

Adjustments at Retirement

Some individuals are at a loss when they retire, and they really did not want to quit working as soon as they did. Ray worked for 32 years as a salesman for a large dairy company. Here is Ray's description of his experience with work and retirement.

RAY'S STORY

I loved my work. My job was my life. I looked forward to going to work, I liked helping people, and I thrived on the challenges of my career. I worked for 50 hours a week, and at age 57 I stopped very abruptly. While I had made some plans for my financial retirement, I was not prepared for the emotional toll that not working would take on me. My work was my identity, and it helped me to feel worthwhile. For at least 2 years, I did not know what to do with myself. I sat around and began feeling depressed. It took me some time to adjust to this new phase in my life, but eventually I began to feel that I mattered. With the help of some friends I began to take on small jobs outside the home. I managed rentals, did repair work, and did some volunteer work at my church. Simply getting out of the house every day gave me another opportunity to contribute, which changed my attitude.

Today, at 83, I can honestly say that I like my life. Leisure is something I value now, rather than fearing it, which was the case in my younger years. There are plenty of work projects to keep me busy. Fortunately, I love fishing and golfing. Each year I go on several fishing trips, and my wife and I do a lot of traveling. By being active in the church, I've learned the value of fellowship and sharing with friends. I've found that I don't have to work 50 hours a week to be a productive human being. Just because I'm retired doesn't mean that I want to sit in a rocking chair most of the day. While I retired from my career, I have not retired from life.

Although many people take early retirement in their 50s, retirement generally comes later in life than was the case a couple of decades ago. Most people who are over 65 will continue to find some form of work, even if they decide to retire from a full-time job. They may work part time, serve as community volunteers, become consultants, or become self-employed. People in their 60s and 70s may seek work not only because they want to feel a sense of purpose but because they want to support themselves for greatly elongated later lives (Sheehy, 1995).

In their study of retired people, Moen and Fields (2002) note several trends: Approximately 39% of retired men and about 20% of retired women are engaged in part-time work; 45% of the men and 62% of the women are doing volunteer work for more than 10 hours a week; and 61% of the men and 51% of the women are involved in community organizations. Although these retired persons have left behind them their full-time work, it is clear that they are finding meaningful ways to structure their lives in new ways.

Retirement can usher in new opportunities to redesign your life and tap unused potentials, or it can be a coasting period where people simply mark time until their end. A couple who did not deal well with retirement are Leona and Marvin. Both had very active careers and retired relatively early. They began to spend most of their time with each other. After about 2 years they grew to dislike each other's company. They both began to have physical symptoms and became overly preoccupied with their health. Leona chronically complained that Marvin did not talk to her, to which he usually retorted, "I have nothing to say, and you should leave me alone." They were referred by their physician for marital counseling. One of the outcomes of this counseling was that they both secured part-time work. They found that by spending time apart they had a greater interest in talking to each other about their experiences at work. They also began to increase their social activities and started to develop some friendships, both separately and together. Marvin and Leona recognized that they had retired too early from life as well as from work.

Just because people no longer work at a job does not mean that they have to cease being active. Many options are open to retired people who would like to stay active in meaningful ways. This is the time for them to get involved with the projects they have so often put on the back burner due to their busy schedules. A high school teacher who retired at 55 is now making wooden toys for underprivileged children with a group of men, and he is devoting a great deal of his time to making bookshelves for his church. This offers both companionship and doing something productive for those in need. It is essential for retirees to keep themselves vital as physical, psychological, spiritual, and social beings.

Retirees do have choices and can create meaning in their lives. They may discover that retirement is not an end but rather a new beginning. As Schlossberg (2004) points out, retirement is not simply an event in a person's life: retirement is best viewed as an evolving process that changes over time. Retirement is a major transition in a person's life that brings a unique set of choices and challenges. Transitions change our lives by altering our relationships, routines, roles, and assumptions. These shifts are characterized by leaving old patterns and moving onto new paths. Once people retire, says Schlossberg, they have different relationships with their colleagues, different daily routines, different roles, and different assumptions that affect both the structure of their lives and their interactions. The process of replacing these relationships, routines, roles, and assumptions is an evolutionary process that often gives rise to considerable uncertainty and anxiety.

There are many choices open to us as we embark on the path toward retirement. Indeed, a major challenge we face as we retire is deciding which path we will take to continue to find meaning in life. Schlossberg (2004) identified the following five paths: continuers, adventurers, searchers, easy gliders, and retreaters.

> *Continuers* do more of the same, but they package their main activities in new ways. They use their skills and maintain their interests and values associated with their previous work, but they modify them to fit retirement.

> *Adventurers* are characterized by seeking something new. They view retirement as an opportunity to create a new path, and they look for new ways of organizing their time and space.

> *Searchers* spend much of their time engaged in trial-and-error activities. Although they are separating from their past, they have not yet found their niche. They may pursue a path and discover that it is not rewarding, and then continue looking for a more satisfying path.

Recreation implies flowing with the river rather than pushing against it and making something happen.

© PhotoDisc/Getty Images

Easy gliders are content to go with the flow. They thrive on unscheduled time and select activities that appeal to them. In short, they value the newfound freedom that retirement provides for them to embrace life.

Retreaters are those who have given up on forging a new and rewarding life. They often feel disengaged from life.

Schlossberg reminds us that the word *retirement* is often used to imply giving up work. However, there are now many different models of retirement, and most people choose from a combination of paths. We are not locked into one path but instead may be traveling on several paths.

THE PLACE OF WORK AND RECREATION IN YOUR LIFE

One way to look at the place that work and recreation occupy in your life is to consider how you divide up your time. In an average day, most people spend about 8 hours sleeping, another 8 hours working, and the other 8 hours in routines such as eating, traveling to work, and leisure. If your work is something that you enjoy, then at least half of your waking existence is spent in meaningful activities. Yet if you dread getting up and hate going to work, those 8 hours can easily have a negative impact on the other 8 hours you are awake.

Work and the Meaning of Your Life

If you expect your work to be a primary source of meaning but feel that your life is not as rich with meaning as you would like, you may be saying, "If only I had a job that I liked, then I'd be fulfilled." This type of thinking can lead you to believe that somehow the secret of finding purpose in your life depends on something outside yourself.

If you decide that you must remain in a job that allows little scope for personal effort and satisfaction, you may need to accept the fact that you will not find much meaning in the hours you spend on the job. It is important, then, to be aware of the effects that your time spent on the job have on the rest of your life and to minimize them. More positively, it is crucial to find something outside your job that fulfills your need for recognition, significance, productivity, and excitement. By doing so, you may develop a sense of your true work as something different from what you are paid to do.

Your job may provide you with the means for the productive activities that you engage in away from the job, whether they take the form of hobbies, creative pursuits, volunteer work, or spending time with friends and family. One high school teacher we know finds himself discouraged over how little his students are interested in learning. Rather than expecting to get all his rewards from teaching, he finds meaning in making things and remodeling his house. He loves to travel, work on antiques, and read. Although he enjoys aspects of his teaching profession, he finds many of his rewards outside the classroom. If this person did not find his own rewards—many of them beyond his job—he would soon feel trapped in an unfulfilling job. The point is to turn things around so that you are the master rather than the victim of your job. Too many people are so negatively affected by their job that their frustration and sense of emptiness spoil their eating, leisure time, family life, sex life, and relationships with friends. For some, job dissatisfaction can be so great that it results in physical or psychological illness.

If you can regain control of your own attitudes toward your job and find dignity and pride elsewhere in your life, you may be able to lessen these negative effects. Seeking counseling is one means to achieve greater control of your life. It can be an excellent way for you to deal with the frustrating and negative effects that work has on you and those around you. Counseling often helps people recognize the stagnant roles they are caught up in both at work and in their personal relationships—and then assists them in creating more satisfying ways of being.

Recreation and the Meaning of Your Life

Work alone does not generally result in fulfillment. Even rewarding work takes energy, and most people need some break from it. Recreation involves creating

If we do plan for creative ways to use leisure, we can experience both joy and continued personal growth.

© Gerald Corey

ourselves anew and is a vital path to vitality. **Leisure** is "free time," the time that we control and can use for ourselves. Whereas work requires a certain degree of perseverance and drive, recreation requires the ability to let go, to be spontaneous, and to avoid being obsessed with what we "should" be doing. Recreation implies flowing with the river rather than pushing against it and making something happen. Compulsiveness dampens the enjoyment of leisure time, and planned spontaneity is a contradiction in terms.

The balance between work and recreation depends on the needs of the individual. Some people schedule recreational activities in such a manner that they actually miss the point of recreation. They "work hard at having a good time." Others become quickly bored when they are not doing something. For Bob and Jill, leisure is more of a burden than a joy. He is a laborer, she is a hairstylist, and both of them work hard all week. They say they like a weekend trip to the river, but their "vacation" includes driving in a car with two whiny children who constantly ask when they will get there. After coping with traffic, they often feel more stressed once they return home from the river. They need to assess whether their leisure is meeting their needs.

As a couple, we (Marianne and Jerry) attribute different meanings to our leisure time. I (Jerry) tend to plan most of the things in my life, including my leisure time. I often combine work and leisure. Until recently, I seemed to require less leisure than some people, because most of my satisfactions in life came from my work. Although at one point in my life I was doing everything I wanted to professionally, I continued to feel challenged in learning limits and in finding a balance in nonwork areas of my life. A hard lesson for me to learn was to pause before too readily accepting yet another invitation for doing another workshop, another keynote speaker engagement, or another book project. Because I lived with an overcrowded schedule and accepted too many invitations, I was challenged to learn the value of carefully reflecting on the pros and cons of accepting any invitation, no matter how tempting it appeared. Although I enjoyed most of what I was doing, I eventually recognized that it took time and energy. I had the difficult task of learning to say "no" to some delightful offers.

Many of my "hobbies" are still work-related, and although my scope tends to be somewhat narrow, this has been largely by choice. I am aware that I have had trouble with unstructured time. I am quite certain that leisure has represented a personal threat; as if any time unaccounted for is not being put to the best and most productive use. However, I am learning how to appreciate the reality that time is not simply to be used in doing, producing, accomplishing, and moving mountains.

Although it is a lesson that I am learning relatively late in life, I am increasingly appreciating times of being and experiencing, as well as time spent on accomplishing tasks. Experiencing sunsets, watching the beauty in nature, and being open to what moments can teach me are ways of using time that I am coming to cherish. Although work is still a very important part of my life, I am realizing that this is only a part of my life, not the totality of it.

Marianne, in contrast, wants and needs unstructured and spontaneous time for unwinding. I (Marianne) am uncomfortable when schedules are imposed on me. I do not particularly like to make detailed life plans, for this gets in the way of my relaxing. Although I plan for trips and times of recreation, I do not like to have everything I am going to do on the trip planned in advance. I like the element of surprise. It feels good to flow with moments and let things happen rather than working hard at making things happen. Also, I do not particularly like to combine work and leisure. For me, work involves considerable responsibility, and it is hard for me to enjoy leisure if it is tainted with the demands of work, or if I know that I will soon have to function in a professional role.

The objectives of planning for a career and planning for creative use of leisure time are basically the same: to help us develop feelings of self-esteem, reach our potential, and improve the quality of our lives. If we do not learn how to pursue interests apart from work, we may well face a crisis when we retire. In fact, many people die soon after their retirement. If we do plan for creative ways to use leisure, we can experience both joy and continued personal growth.

A Couple Who Are Able to Balance Work and Recreation

Judy and Frank have found a good balance between work and recreation. Although they both enjoy their work, they have also arranged their lives to make time for leisure.

Judy and Frank were married when she was 16 and he was 20. They now have two grown sons and a couple of grandchildren. At 59 Frank works for an electrical company as a lineman, a job he has held for close to 35 years. Judy, who is now 55, delivers meals to schools.

Judy went to work when her two sons were in elementary school. She was interested in doing something away from home. Judy continues her work primarily because she likes the contact with both her coworkers and the children whom she meets daily.

Frank is satisfied with his work, and he looks forward to going to the job. Considering that he stopped his education at high school, he feels he has a good job that both pays well and offers many fringe benefits. Although he is a bright person, he expresses no ambition to increase his formal education. A few of the things Frank likes about his work are the companionship with his coworkers, the physical aspects of his job, the security it affords, and the routine.

Judy and Frank have separate interests and hobbies, yet they also spend time together. Both of them are hardworking, and they have achieved success financially and personally. They feel pleased about their success and can see the fruits of their labor. Together they enjoy their grandchildren, their friends, and themselves.

Judy and Frank enjoy their work life and their leisure life, both as individuals and as a couple. A challenge that many of us will face is finding ways of using our leisure as well as they do. Just as our work can have either a positive or a negative influence on our life, so, too, can leisure. These Take Time to Reflect exercises will help you consolidate your thoughts on how work and leisure are integrated in your life.

Take Time to Reflect

1. List a few of the most important benefits that you get (or expect to get) from work or college.

   _____

   _____

2. To what extent do you allow for leisure time? What was modeled by way of leisure time and recreation in your family of origin?

   _____

   _____

3. Are there any ways that you would like to spend your leisure time differently?

_____

_____

4. What leisure activities make you feel creative and energetic?

_____

_____

5. Could you obtain a job that would incorporate some of the activities you have just listed? Or does your job already account for them?

_____

_____

6. What do you think would happen to you if you could not work? Write what first comes to mind.

_____

_____

SUMMARY

Choosing a career is best thought of as a process, not a one-time event. The term _career decision_ is misleading because it implies that we make one choice that we stay with permanently. Most of us will probably have several occupations over our lifetimes, which is a good argument for a general education. If we prepare too narrowly for a specialization, that job may become obsolete, as will our training. In selecting a career or an occupation, it is important to first assess our attitudes, abilities, interests, and values. The next step is to explore a wide range of occupational options to see what jobs would best fit our personality. Becoming familiar with Holland's six personality types is an excellent way to consider the match between your personality style and the work alternatives you are considering. Choosing an occupation too soon can be risky because our interests change as we move into adulthood. Passively falling into a job rather than carefully considering where we might best find meaning and satisfaction can lead to dissatisfaction and frustration.

Retirement can be a time with new opportunities to redesign ones life, or it can be a time when one is coasting and feeling lost. Especially for those who retire early, the real challenge of retirement is to find a way to keep active in a meaningful way. Many retired people become involved in community affairs, volunteer work, pursuit of new careers, and new recreational activities, and may therefore lead fuller lives than they did when they worked full time. Some people consciously choose early retirement because they have found more significant and valuable pursuits. Yet for others, retirement can be a period of disillusionment. People who are retired do have choices and they can create meaningful lives without employment. Many retired people have found that retirement is not an end to life but rather a new beginning.

Because we devote about half of our waking hours to our work, it behooves us to actively choose a form of work that can express who we are as a person. Much of the other half of our waking time can be used for leisure. With the trend toward increased leisure time, cultivating interests apart from work becomes a real challenge. Just as our work can profoundly affect all aspects of our lives, so, too, can leisure have a positive or negative influence on our existence. Our leisure time can be a source of boredom that drains us, or it can be a source of replenishment that energizes us and enriches our lives.

Although work is seen as an important source of meaning in our lives, it is not the job itself that provides this meaning. The satisfaction we derive depends to a great extent on the way we relate to our job, the manner in which we do it, and the meaning that we attribute to it. Perhaps the most important idea in this chapter is that we must look to ourselves if we are dissatisfied with our work. We can increase our power to change unfavorable circumstances by recognizing that we are mainly responsible for making our lives and our work meaningful.

Where Can I Go From Here?

1. Interview a person you know who dislikes his or her career or occupation. Here are some questions you might ask to get started:

- If you don't find your job satisfying, why do you stay in it?

- Do you feel that you have much of a choice about whether you'll stay with the job or take a new one?

- What aspects of your job bother you the most?

- How does your attitude toward your job affect the other areas of your life?

2. Interview a person you know who feels fulfilled and excited by his or her work. Begin with these questions:

- What does your work do for you? What meaning does your work have for the other aspects of your life?

- What are the main satisfactions for you in your work?

- What challenges or barriers did you have to deal with in getting established in your work?

- How do you think you would be affected if you could no longer pursue your career?

3. Interview your parents and determine what meaning their work has for them. How satisfied are they with the work aspects of their lives? How much choice do they feel they have in selecting their work? In what ways do they think the other aspects of their lives are affected by their attitudes toward work? After you have talked with them, determine how your attitudes and beliefs about work have been influenced by your parents. Are you pursuing a career that your parents can understand and respect? Is their reaction to your career choice important to you? Are your attitudes and values concerning work like or unlike those of your parents?

4. If your college has a career counseling program available to you, consider talking with a counselor about your plans. You might want to explore taking career interest and aptitude tests. If you are deciding on a career, consider discussing how realistic your career plans are. For example:

- What are your interests?

- Do your interests match the careers you are thinking about pursuing?

- Do you have the knowledge you need to make a career choice?

- Do you have the aptitude and skills for the careers you have in mind?

- What are the future possibilities in the careers you are considering?

5. If you are leaning toward a particular occupation or career, seek out a person who is actively engaged in that type of work and arrange for a time to talk with him or her. You might even see if job shadowing is a possibility. Ask questions concerning the chances of gaining employment, the experience necessary, the satisfactions and drawbacks of the position, and so on. In this way, you can make the process of deciding on a type of work more realistic and perhaps avoid disappointment if your expectations do not match reality.

6. Most career counseling centers in colleges and universities now offer one or more computer-based programs to help students decide on a career. One of the main reasons for the steady increase in the use of computer-assisted career guidance assessments is that results can be readily available. These computer-based programs interpret results to clients in terms of occupational fit with lists of career options (Zunker & Osborn, 2002). One popular computer-based program is known as the System of Interactive Guidance and Information, more commonly referred to as SIGI PLUS (SP) (Educational Testing Service, 1996). SP is a comprehensive, interactive program aimed at helping people in the process of making a career decision. This program consists of eight sections, from which users can select those most appropriate to their decision: Self-Assessment, Search, Information, Skills, Preparing, Coping, Deciding, and Next Steps. Taking the SP will aid you in identifying specific occupations you might want to explore.

Schedule an appointment in the career counseling center at your college to participate in a computer-based occupational guidance program. In addition to SIGI PLUS, other programs are the Career Information System (CIS), the Guidance Information System (GIS), Choices, and Discover. Each of these programs develops lists of occupations to explore. Other instruments assess values. One is Super's Work Values Inventory. Consider taking the Myers-Briggs Type Indicator, which is an inventory that indicates your temperament style. You can take the Keirsey Temperament Sorter online (www.Keirsey.com). Meet with a career counselor to discuss these value assessment instruments.

7. The abbreviated description of Holland's six personality types and the exercise in this chapter should not be thought of as a complete and accurate way to assess your personality. If you are interested in a more complete self-assessment method that also describes the relationship between your type and possible occupations or fields of study, we strongly recommend that you take Form R of the *Self-Directed Search* (Holland, 1994). The *Self-Directed Search* (SDS) consists of a test as well as these booklets designed to accompany this test: (1) You and Your Career, (2) The Occupations Finder, (3) The Educational Opportunities Finder, (4) The Leisure Activities Finder, and (5) Assessment Booklet: A Guide to Educational and Career Planning. All of these resources are available from Psychological Assessment Resources, P.O. Box 998, Odessa, FL 33556 or by telephone (1-800-331-8378). In addition to the SDS, other inventories that are useful in constructing a list of occupational alternatives from which to choose a career include the *Career Decision-Making System* (CDM) and the *Career Occupational Preference System* (COPS). The online reference for SDS is http://www.self-directed-search.com.

8. Here are some steps you can take when exploring the choice of a major and a career. Place a check before each item you are willing to seriously consider. I am willing to

_____ Talk to an adviser about my intended major.

_____ Interview at least one instructor regarding selecting a major.

_____ Interview at least one person I know in a career that I am interested in

_____ Make a trip to the career development center and just look around.

_____ Make use of computer-assisted career guidance assessments.

_____ Inquire about taking a series of interest and work values tests in the career development center.

_____ Take the SIGI or some similar computer-based instrument.

_____ Take an interest inventory.

_____ Talk to my parents about the meaning work has for them.

_____ Write in my journal about my values as they pertain to work.

_____ Browse through books that deal with careers.

_____ Read a book on careers.

9. Apply the seven steps of the career-planning process to your own career planning. Set realistic goals to do one or more of the following or some other appropriate activity:

- Choose a major that most fully taps my interests and abilities.
- Take time to investigate a career by gathering further information.
- Develop contacts with people who can help me meet my goals.
- Take steps that will enable me to increase my exposure to a field of interest.

In your journal, write down at least a tentative plan for action. Begin by identifying some of the key factors associated with selecting a career. Write down the steps you are willing to take at this time. (Your plan will be most useful if you identify specific steps you are willing to take. Include seeking the help of others somewhere in your plan.)

Resources for Future Study

Web Site Resources

THE OCCUPATIONAL OUTLOOK HANDBOOK
http://www.bls.gov/oco/

The *Occupational Outlook Handbook* is a "nationally recognized source of career information, designed to provide valuable assistance to individuals making decisions about their future work lives" and it "describes what workers do on the job, working conditions, the training and education needed, earnings, and expected job prospects in a wide range of occupations." Users can download pages on the careers of their choice.

THE CATAPULT ON JOB WEB
http://www.jobweb.com/search/sitemap.htm

The National Association of Colleges and Employers has created a comprehensive set of resources for job seekers and job offerings. The site includes searching employment listings, resources for career practitioners, career library resources, and professional development resources.

U.S. DEPARTMENT OF LABOR
http://www.dol.gov/

This online site serves as a way to explore topics such as wages, worker productivity, unsafe working conditions, and the legal rights of workers, including protection from sexual harassment.

CAREERS.WSJ.COM
http://www.careerjournal.com/

This site contains daily updates of employment issues and more than 1,000 job-seeking articles.

JOBWEB
http://www.jobweb.com/

This site includes information on job searches, employment listings, and college-based resources.

THE RILEY GUIDE: EMPLOYMENT OPPORTUNITIES AND JOB RESOURCES ON THE INTERNET
http://www.rileyguide.com/

This site contains hundreds of annotated links regarding a wide variety of topics related to employment and careers.

ELDERHOSTEL
http://www/elderhostel.org

This site provides "adventures in lifelong learning" for adults ages 55 and older. It is a not-for-profit organization with a catalog of high-quality, affordable, educational programs lasting 1 to 4 weeks year round and throughout the world.

 InfoTrac College Edition Resources

For additional readings, explore INFOTRAC COLLEGE EDITION, our online library:
http://www.infotrac.college.com/wadsworth

Hint: Enter these search terms:

career development

career decision making

career decision

occupational interest

occupational ability

personality type

leisure time

Print Resources

Bolles, R. N. (2000). *What color is your parachute?* Berkeley, CA: Ten Speed Press.

Carney, C. G., & Wells, C. F. (1999). *Working well, living well: Discover the career within you* (5th ed.). Pacific Grove, CA: Brooks/Cole.

Holland, J. L. (1997). *Making vocational choices: A theory of vocational personalities and work environments* (3rd ed.). Odessa, FL: Psychological Assessment Resources, Inc.

Lock, R. D. (2005a). *Job search: Career planning guide, Book 2* (5th ed.). Pacific Grove, CA: Brooks/Cole.

Lock, R. D. (2005b). *Taking charge of your career direction: Career planning guide, Book 1* (5th ed.). Pacific Grove, CA: Brooks/Cole.

Schlossberg, N. K. (2004). *Retire smart, retire happy.* Washington, DC: American Psychological Association.

Sharf, R. S. (2002). *Applying career development theory to counseling* (3rd ed.). Belmont, CA: Brooks/Cole.

Smith, C., & Sulsky, L. (2005). *Work stress.* Belmont, CA: Thomson Wadsworth.

Terkel, S. (1975). *Working.* New York: Avon.

U.S. Department of Labor. (1998). *Occupational outlook handbook, 1998–1999.* Washington, DC: U.S. Government Printing Office.

Zunker, V. G. (2002). *Career counseling: Applied concepts of life planning.* Belmont, CA: Brooks/Cole.

Zunker, V. G., & Osborn, D. S. (2002). *Using assessment results for career counseling.* Belmont, CA: Brooks/Cole.

11

In solitude we make the time
to be with ourselves, to
discover who we are, and to
renew ourselves.

Loneliness
and Solitude

© PhotoDisc/Getty Images

Where Am I Now?

Use this scale to respond to these statements:

    3 = This statement is true of me *most* of the time.

    2 = This statement is true of me *some* of the time.

    1 = This statement is true of me *almost none* of the time.

1. I stay in unsatisfactory relationships to avoid being lonely.

2. I like being alone.

3. I don't know what to do with my time when I am alone.

4. Even when I'm with people I sometimes feel lonely and shut out.

5. At this time in my life I like the balance between my solitude and my time with others.

6. I know the difference between being lonely and being alone.

7. My childhood was a lonely period of my life.

8. My adolescent years were lonely ones for me.

9. Currently I am satisfied with the way in which I cope with my loneliness.

10. I sometimes arrange for time alone so that I can reflect on my life.

Being with others and being with ourselves are best understood as two sides of the same coin. If we do not like our own company, why should others want to be with us? If we are not able to enjoy time alone, it will be difficult to truly enjoy time with others. If we have a good relationship with ourselves and enjoy our solitude, we have a better chance of creating solid, give-and-take relationships with others. Although the presence of others can surely enhance our lives, no one else can completely share our unique world of feelings, thoughts, hopes, and memories. In some respects we are alone, even though we may have meaningful connections with others.

We invite you to think of being alone not as something to be avoided at all costs but as a part of the human condition and a valuable part of human experience. Each of us is ultimately alone in the world. Appreciating that aloneness can enrich our experience of life.

THE VALUE OF LONELINESS AND SOLITUDE

It is important to distinguish between being alone and being lonely. Loneliness and solitude are different experiences, and each has its own potential value. **Loneliness** is generally triggered by certain life events—the death of someone we love, the decision of another person to leave us (or we them), a move to a new city, a long stay in a hospital, or a major life decision. Loneliness can occur when we feel set apart in some way from everyone around us, which can have its roots in the lack of attachment in early childhood. We also experience loneliness when our network of social relationships is lacking or when there are strains on these relationships. People who are particularly vulnerable to loneliness include those who are divorced, separated, or widowed and those who live alone (Hales, 2005). Sometimes feelings of loneliness are simply an indication of the extent to which we have failed to listen to ourselves. However it occurs, loneliness is generally something that happens to us rather than something we choose to experience. We do choose the attitude we take toward loneliness, however, and we can choose how we will deal with it. If we allow ourselves to experience our loneliness, even if it is painful, we may be surprised to find sources of strength and creativity within ourselves.

Unlike loneliness, solitude is something that we choose for ourselves. In **solitude,** we make time to be with ourselves, to discover who we are, and to renew ourselves. In her beautiful and poetic book *Gift From the Sea,* Anne Morrow Lindbergh (1955/1975) describes her own need to get away by herself to find her center, to simplify her life, and to nourish herself so that she could give to others again. She relates how her busy life, with its many and conflicting demands, fragmented her, so that she felt "the spring is dry, and the well is empty" (p. 47).*

Through solitude, she found replenishment and became reacquainted with herself:

> WHEN ONE IS A STRANGER TO ONESELF, then one is estranged from others too. If one is out of touch with oneself, then one cannot touch others. . . . Only when one is connected to one's own core is one connected to others. . . . For me, the core, the inner spring, can best be refound through solitude. (pp. 43–44)

If we do not take time for ourselves but instead fill our lives with activities and projects, we run the risk of losing a sense of centeredness. As Lindbergh puts it, "Instead of stilling the center, the axis of the wheel, we add more centrifugal activities to our lives—which tend to throw us off balance" (p. 51). Her own solitude taught her that she must remind herself to be alone each day, even for a few minutes, to keep a sense of herself that would then enable her to give of herself to others.

Solitude provides us with the opportunity to examine our life and gain a sense of perspective. It gives us time to ask significant questions such as, "Have I become a stranger to myself?" and "Have I been listening to myself, or have I been distracted and overstimulated by my busyness?" We can use times of solitude to look within ourselves, to renew our sense of ourselves as the center of choice and direction in our lives, and to learn to trust our inner resources instead of allowing circumstances or the expectations of others to determine the path we travel. Some people believe that when they are alone they are lonely. However, if we accept our aloneness, we can give ourselves to our projects and our relationships out of our freedom instead of running to them out of our fear. In writing about solitude, Father William McNamara (cited in Shield & Carlson, 1999) says that it is a misunderstanding to equate solitude with isolation. In his view, the opposite is true. When we enter into genuine solitude, we then have the ability to enter into the center of our being and connect in a meaningful way with others. Silence and solitude provide avenues for coming to know ourselves better, for becoming centered, and for forming meaningful relationships. The Dalai Lama (2001) stresses that to make changes in our lives we need solitude, by which he means "a mental state free of distractions, not simply time alone in a quiet place" (p. 78).

We may miss the valuable experience of solitude if we allow our life to become too frantic and complicated. We may fear that others will think we are odd if we express a desire for solitude. Indeed, others may sometimes fail to understand our desire to be alone and may try to persuade us to be with them.

---

*This and all other quotations from this source are from *Gift From the Sea*, by A. M. Lindbergh. Copyright 1955 by Pantheon Books, a division of Random House, Inc.

Some people who are close to you may feel vaguely threatened, as if your need for time alone means that you have less affection for them. Indeed, their own fears of being left alone may lead them to try to keep you from taking time away from them.

We need to remind ourselves that we can tolerate only so much intensity with others and that ignoring our need for distance can breed resentment. For instance, a mother and father who are constantly with each other and with their children may not be doing a service either to their children or to themselves. Eventually they are likely to resent their "obligations." When they take time out, they may be able to be more fully present to each other and to their children.

Many of us fail to experience solitude because we allow our lives to become more and more frantic and complicated. We may fear that we will alienate others if we ask for private time, so we alienate ourselves instead. Society provides us with many distractions that are often hard to resist. It seems that solitude is neither valued nor encouraged. The message that it is better to be constantly busy rather than inactive often begins during early childhood. An abundance of activities are planned for children, which allows for little quiet time. Counselors see children who suffer from stress and an already overstuffed life. These children learn early on to become impatient with lack of stimulation, and they are quick to point out that they are bored with the absence of activity.

We may feel uneasy about wanting and taking time alone for ourselves. We might even make up excuses if we want to have some time alone. Claiming what we need and want for ourselves can involve a certain risk; failing to do so also involves a risk—a loss of a sense of self-direction and being centered, which does involve a certain amount of solitude.

LEARNING TO CONFRONT THE FEAR OF LONELINESS

There is probably good reason to have some fear of loneliness because there is some evidence that loneliness influences both our physical health and our psychological well-being. Loneliness is most likely to cause emotional problems when it is chronic rather than when it is an occasional concern (Hales, 2005). People who report being lonely tend to report more depression, use of drugs as an escape, and higher blood pressure (Rice, 1999). Some evidence points to loneliness as being associated with higher risks for heart disease, lessened longevity, and increased risk for recurrent illness (Hafen, Karren, Frandsen, & Smith, 1996). This is probably more true for those who are chronically lonely and who have few people with whom they share their lives.

We may think of loneliness in a negative light if we associate the lonely periods in our lives with pain and struggle. Furthermore, we may identify

We can sometimes cope with the fear of loneliness by surrounding ourselves with people and social functions.

© Corbis

being alone with being lonely and either actively avoid having time by ourselves or fill such time with distractions and diversions. We may associate being alone with rejection of self and being cut off from others. Paradoxically, out of fear of rejection and loneliness, we may even make ourselves needlessly lonely by refusing to reach out to others or by holding back in our intimate relationships. At other times, because of our fear of loneliness, we may deceive ourselves by thinking that we can overcome loneliness only by anchoring our life to another's life. The search for relationships, especially ones in which we think we will be taken care of, is often motivated by the fear of being isolated.

Silence can be threatening for those of us who want to escape from loneliness because it forces us to reflect and touch deep parts of ourselves. We may attempt to escape from facing ourselves by keeping so busy that we leave little or no time to reflect. Here are some ways we do this:

- We schedule every moment and overstructure our lives, so we have no opportunity to think about ourselves and what we are doing with our lives.
- We strive for perfect control of our environment, so we will not have to cope with the unexpected.
- We surround ourselves with people and become absorbed in social functions in the hope that we will not have to feel alone.
- We numb ourselves with alcohol or drugs.

- We immerse ourselves in our responsibilities.
- We eat compulsively, hoping that doing so will fill our inner emptiness and protect us from the pain of being lonely.
- We spend many hours with the computer, video games, and television.
- We go to centers of activity, trying to lose ourselves in a crowd. By escaping into crowds, we avoid coming to terms with deeper layers of our inner world.

The world we live in surrounds us with entertainment and escapes, which makes it difficult to hear the voice within us. Paradoxically, in the midst of our congested cities and with all the activities available to us, we are often lonely because we are alienated from ourselves. To better understand this paradox, listen to Stella talk about her life and her fears. Stella is a young woman who often fears separateness from others, even though she immerses herself in many relationships and activities. Outsiders tend to envy her "fun-filled" life and wish they were in her place. In a moment of candor, however, she will admit that she feels her life to be empty and that she is in a desperate search for substance.

STELLA'S STORY

I am petrified when I have to spend any time alone in my apartment. I schedule my life so that I spend as little time by myself as possible. I have a long list of phone numbers to call, just in case my panic overwhelms me. My stereo or television is typically blaring so that I am unable to pay attention to what is going on with me. I want so much to fill my inner emptiness. I have a hard time liking myself or thinking I have much value. I look to others for my security, yet I never really find it. In my therapy I am learning to stay with being uncomfortable with myself long enough to face some of my fears.

In some ways Stella illustrates the quiet desperation that is captured in Edward Arlington Robinson's poem "Richard Cory" (1897/1943):

Whenever Richard Cory went down town,
We people on the pavement looked at him:
He was a gentleman from sole to crown,
Clean favored, and imperially slim.
And he was always quietly arrayed,
And he was always human when he talked;
But still he fluttered pulses when he said,
"Good morning," and he glittered when he walked.

And he was rich—yes, richer than a king—
And admirably schooled in every grace:
In fine, we thought that he was everything
To make us wish that we were in his place.
So on we worked and waited for the light,
And went without the meat, and cursed the bread;
And Richard Cory, one calm summer night,
Went home and put a bullet through his head.

The way we present ourselves to the world oftentimes belies the loneliness we feel, as the cases of Stella and Richard Cory demonstrate. Pretending to others to be what we are not, as well as anchoring our lives to others as a way of avoiding facing ourselves, results in our losing our sense of self and leads to alienation.

In our therapy groups, we meet people who hide dimensions of themselves. Out of fear of being rejected, they deprive others of getting to know them. During the group sessions, they reveal themselves in ways that are totally unknown to even the most intimate people in their lives. As they reveal themselves in the context of the group, and generally receive support and reinforcement, they are more willing to show that hidden self to the significant people in their lives. Through this self-disclosure, individuals learn to appreciate facets of themselves that they were estranged from.

We often surround ourselves with people, trying to convince ourselves that we are not lonely. From our perspective, if we want to get back into contact with ourselves, we must begin by looking at the ways we have learned to escape from our loneliness. We can examine our relationships to see if we at times use others to fill that void. We can ask whether the activities that fill our time actually satisfy us or whether they leave us empty and discontented. For some of us, being alone may be less lonely than being in a relationship. To truly confront loneliness, we need to spend more time alone, strengthening our awareness of self as the true center of meaning and direction in our lives.

CREATING OUR OWN LONELINESS THROUGH SHYNESS

Do you believe you are shy? **Shyness** refers to anxiety and excessive caution in interpersonal relationships. Some specific characteristics that identify shy individuals are timidity in expressing themselves; being overly sensitive to how they are perceived and reacted to; being embarrassed easily; and experiencing bodily symptoms such as blushing, upset stomach, anxiety, and racing pulse (Weiten & Lloyd, 2003). Shy people are almost always uncomfortable in social situations, especially if they become the center of attention or if they are expected to speak up. Shyness does not necessarily have to be a problem for you. In fact, you might decide you like this quality in yourself—and so might many others who know you. Shyness becomes a problem only when you hold back from expressing yourself in ways you would like. You can learn to say and do what you would like when you are with others and still retain your shy nature.

According to Phil Zimbardo (1987), founder of the shyness clinic at Stanford University, shyness is an almost universal experience. In one study 80% of those questioned reported that they had been shy at some point in their lives. Of those, more than 40% considered themselves shy at that time. This means that 4 out of every 10 people you meet, or 84 million Americans, are shy. Shyness exists on a continuum. That is, some people see themselves as chronically shy, whereas others are shy with certain people or in certain situations. It is important to realize that shyness might be influenced by your culture. This is why it helps to define "shyness" for yourself. You may be shy in some situations, yet in many situations shyness may not be a part of your personality.

Shyness can lead directly to feelings of loneliness. Zimbardo (1987) believes shyness can be a social and psychological handicap as crippling as many physical handicaps, and he lists these consequences of shyness:

- Shyness prevents people from expressing their views and speaking up for their rights.
- Shyness may make it difficult to think clearly and to communicate effectively.
- Shyness holds people back from meeting new people, making friends, and getting involved in many social activities.
- Shyness often results in feelings such as depression, anxiety, and loneliness.

You may be aware that shyness is a problem for you and that you are creating your own loneliness, at least in part. You may ask, "What can I do about it?" You can begin by challenging those personal fears that keep you from expressing the way you truly think and feel. It is likely that one reason for your shyness is not having the interpersonal skills that make it possible to express your feelings and thoughts. Put yourself in situations where you will be forced to make contact with people and engage in social activities, even if you find doing this is scary and uncomfortable.

It helps to understand the context of your shyness, especially to identify those social situations that stimulate your shy behavior. Also, it is useful to pinpoint the reasons or combination of factors underlying your shyness. According to Zimbardo (1987, 1994), a constellation of factors explain shyness: being overly sensitive to negative feedback from others, fearing rejection, lacking self-confidence and specific social skills, being frightened of intimacy, and personal handicaps.

A good way to identify those factors that contribute to your shyness is to keep track in your journal of those situations that elicit your shy behavior. It helps to write down what you are truly experiencing and then what you actually do in such situations. Pay attention to your self-talk in these difficult situations. For example, your self-talk may be negative, actually setting you up to fail. You may say silently to yourself: "I'm unattractive, so who would want anything to do with me?" "I'd better not try something new because I might look ridiculous." "I'm afraid of being rejected, so I won't even approach a person I'd like to get to know." "People are not really interested in what I am thinking and feeling." "Others are evaluating and judging me, and I'm sure I won't measure up to what they expect." These are the kinds of statements that are likely to keep you a prisoner of your shyness and prevent you from making real contact with others. You can do a lot yourself to control how your shyness affects you by learning to challenge your self-defeating beliefs and by substituting constructive statements. Coping with shyness involves becoming aware of, examining, and changing your thinking about shyness and yourself (Zimbardo, 1994). Learning new ways of thinking about yourself involves pushing yourself to test out your new beliefs by acting in new ways.

People who have difficulty dealing with shyness often withdraw socially. However, social withdrawal generally exacerbates matters and can lead to loneliness. Tracy's experience in coping with shyness illustrates how you can overcome inhibitions and can come out of your shell.

TRACY'S STORY

When I first began my college education, I was really shy. I would not raise my hand to ask questions in class, I studied by myself, and I did not pursue friendships with my peers. My shyness developed out of a belief that I would look stupid if I asked questions and that my peers would think I was not really smart if they studied with me. If I pursued friendships, I was convinced that people would eventually realize I was not fun or outgoing. I believe my shyness in these early years contributed to my failure at my first college.

When I decided to leave my first college, I made a commitment to myself that I would do what it took to succeed in earning my education at my new school. Part of this commitment was to speak up in class, ask questions, form study groups, and make friends. This was really scary for me, but I knew that not reaching out kept me lonely.

I did not want to live that way anymore. I made contact with my teachers and actually became involved in my learning process. As I became involved with my studies and my peers, my self-confidence increased. Along with this came higher grades. I began to believe that I was smart, that I did ask good questions, that others were not judging me, and that others liked who I was, and most important, I liked who I was.

If you are shy, the best first step to take is to accept this as part of who you are. Then challenge yourself to get involved in activities and to make contact with others. Even though you are shy, monitor your thoughts, feelings, and actions to become more aware of the process you are going through. Like Tracy, you can take steps to make contact with others and challenge negative self-talk that is keeping you in your shell.

Take Time to Reflect

I. In what ways do you try to escape from your loneliness?

_____

_____

2. Does this avoidance work for you? If not, what might you do to change?

_____

_____

3. If shyness is a problem for you, how might you be creating your own loneliness with the ways you deal with your shyness?

_____

_____

4. In what ways do you value time spent alone?

_____

_____

5. List a few of the major decisions you have made in your life. Did you make these decisions when you were alone or when you were with others?

_____

_____

A journal suggestion: If you find it difficult to be alone, try being alone for a little longer than you are generally comfortable with. You might simply let your thoughts wander freely, without hanging on to one line of thinking. In your journal describe what this experience is like for you.

LONELINESS AND OUR LIFE STAGES

How we deal with feelings of loneliness can depend to a great extent on our experiences of loneliness in childhood and adolescence. Later in life we may feel that loneliness has no place or that we can and should be able to avoid it. It is important to reflect on our past experiences, because they are often the basis of our present feelings about loneliness. In addition, we may fear loneliness less if we recognize that it is an inevitable part of living in every stage of life. There are many areas in which we may experience loneliness. Our differences, such as gender, race, sexual orientation, and language, or being a foreigner in a foreign land can result in feelings of loneliness. Once we get beyond viewing loneliness as something that must be overcome at any cost, we may be less concerned about periods when we face loneliness. It helps to recognize that some loneliness is a natural dimension of the human condition and we need to avoid pathologizing the experience of loneliness.

Loneliness and Childhood

Reliving childhood experiences of loneliness can help you come to grips with present fears about being alone or lonely. Here are some typical memories of lonely periods that people we have worked with in therapy have relived:

- A woman recalls the time her parents were fighting in the bedroom and she heard them screaming and yelling. She was sure that they would divorce, and in many ways she felt responsible. She remembers living in continual fear that she would be deserted.

- A man recalls attempting to give a speech in the sixth grade. He stuttered over certain words, and children in the class began to laugh at him. Afterward he developed extreme self-consciousness in regard to his speech, and he long remembered the hurt and loneliness he had experienced.

- An African American man recalls how excluded he felt in his all-White elementary school and how the other children would talk to him in derogatory ways. As an adult, he can still, at times, experience the pain associated with these memories.

- A woman recalls the fright she felt as a small child when her uncle made sexual advances toward her. Although she did not really understand what was happening, she remembers the terrible loneliness of feeling that she could not tell her parents for fear of what they would do.

- A man recalls the boyhood loneliness of feeling that he was continually failing at everything he tried. To this day, he resists undertaking a task unless he is sure he can handle it, for fear of rekindling those old feelings of loneliness.

- A woman vividly remembers being in the hospital as a small child for an operation. She remembers the loneliness of not knowing what was going on or whether she would be able to leave the hospital. No one talked with her, and she was all alone with her fears.

As we try to relive these experiences, remember that children do not live in a logical, well-ordered world. Our childhood fears may have been greatly exaggerated, and the feeling of fright may remain with us even though we may now think of it as irrational. Unfortunately, being told by adults that we were foolish for having such fears may only have increased our loneliness while doing nothing to lessen the fears themselves.

At this point you may wonder, "Why go back and recall childhood pain and loneliness? Why not just let it be a thing of the past?" It is important that we re-experience some of the pain we felt as children to understand how we may still be affected by this pain now. We can also look at some of the decisions we made during these times of extreme loneliness and ask whether these decisions are still appropriate. Frequently, strategies we adopted as children remain with us into adulthood, when they are no longer appropriate. For instance, suppose that your family moved to a strange city when you were 7 years old and that you had to go to a new school. Kids at the new school laughed at you, and you lived through several months of anguish. You felt desperately alone in the world. During this time you decided to keep your feelings to yourself and build a wall around yourself so others could not hurt you. Although this experience is now long past, you will still defend yourself in the same way because it is now a reflex response. In this way old fears of loneliness might contribute to a real loneliness in the present. If you allow yourself to experience your grief and work it through, emotionally as well as intellectually, you can overcome past pain and create new choices for yourself.

Take Time to Reflect Take some time to decide whether you are willing to recall and relive a childhood experience of loneliness. If so, try to recapture the experience in as much detail as you can, reliving it in fantasy. Then reflect on the experience, using the following questions as a starting point.

1. Describe in a few words the most intense experience of loneliness you recall having as a child or an adolescent.

_____

_____

2. How do you think the experience affected you then?

_____

_____

3. How do you think the experience may still be affecting you now?

_____

_____

Journal suggestions: Consider elaborating on this exercise in your journal. How did you cope with loneliness as a child? How has this influenced the way you deal with loneliness in your life now? If you could go back and put a new ending on your most intense childhood experience of loneliness, what would it be? You might also think about times in your childhood when you enjoyed being alone. Write some notes to yourself about what these experiences were like for you. Where did you like to spend time alone? What did you enjoy doing by yourself? What positive aspects of these times do you recall?

Loneliness and Adolescence

Adolescents and young adults are more likely to experience loneliness than people from older age groups (Weiten & Lloyd, 2003). For many people loneliness and adolescence are practically synonymous. Adolescents often feel that they are all alone in their world, that they are the only ones to have had the feelings they do, and that they are separated from others by some abnormality. Bodily changes and impulses alone are sufficient to bring about a sense of perplexity and loneliness, but there are other stresses to be undergone as well. Adolescents are developing a sense of identity. They strive to be successful yet fear failure. They want to be accepted and liked, but they fear rejection, ridicule, or exclusion by their peers. Most adolescents know the feeling of being lonely in a crowd or among friends. They often have fears of being ostracized. Conformity can bring acceptance, and the price of nonconformity can be steep.

As you recall your adolescent years—and, in particular, the areas of your life that were marked by loneliness—reflect on these questions:

- Did you feel included in a social group? Or did you sit on the sidelines, afraid of being included and wishing for it at the same time?

- Was there at least one person you felt you could talk to—one who really heard and understood you, so that you didn't feel alone?

- What experience stands out as one of the loneliest times during these years? How did you cope with your loneliness?

- Did you experience a sense of confusion concerning who you were and what you wanted to be as a person? How did you deal with your confusion? Who or what helped you during this time?

Adolescents often feel that they are all alone in the world.

© Corbis

- How did you feel about your own worth and value? Did you believe you had anything of value to offer anyone or that anyone would find you worth being with?
- How did your culture affect the way you viewed loneliness?
- Did you hear the message that loneliness is something to be avoided?

Ethnic minority adolescents often face cultural isolation. Tatum (1999) believes adolescents from the same ethnic background congregate with their own group as a way to avoid social isolation and loneliness. Black youths in particular face unique challenges in terms of feeling connected to others, knowing who they are, and believing in their abilities. They may buy into the stereotypes of racism that contribute to feeling alone and different. Natalie's story shows how a person can find an identity and begin to trust herself. At the time of this writing, Natalie is enrolled in a doctoral program.

NATALIE'S STORY

*I*n high school I was told that I was not college material and that "Mexicans are good with their hands." A block that I've had to deal with is the stereotype of Mexican women as being submissive and unable to stand up for themselves—which I've heard all my life from many teachers.

During my senior year in high school, I met Sal, who invited me to a Chicano Youth Leadership Conference. This conference made my outlook about myself change. Up to that point I was a stranger in my own land. I had no cultural identity and no strength to speak up. People there believed in me and told me that I could go to college and be successful. It was the first time that others had more faith in my abilities than I did. Sal became my mentor and challenged me to never underestimate the power I have. He made me feel so proud as a young Chicana and proud of my people. This was my spark to stand up and help the Chicano community.

Can you identify in any way with Natalie's story? Have you ever had difficulty believing in yourself? If so, did this affect your ability to feel connected to others? As you reflect on your adolescence, try to discover some of the ways in which the person you are now is a result of your experiences of loneliness as an adolescent. Do you shrink from competition for fear of failure? In social situations are you afraid of being left out? Do you feel some of the isolation you did then? If so, how do you deal with it? How might you have changed the way you deal with loneliness?

Loneliness and Young Adulthood

In our young adult years we experiment with ways of being, and we establish lifestyles that may remain with us for many years. You may be struggling with the question of what to do with your life, what intimate relationships you want to establish, and how you will chart your future. Dealing with all the choices that face us at this time of life can be a lonely process. Loneliness can be a result of not having any validation from others.

How you come to terms with your own aloneness can have significant effects on the choices you make—choices that, in turn, may determine the course of your life for years to come. For instance, if you have not learned to listen to yourself and to depend on your own inner resources, you might succumb to the pressure to choose a relationship or a career before you are really prepared to do so, or you might look to your projects or partners for the sense of identity that you ultimately can find only in yourself. Alternatively, you may feel lonely and establish patterns that only increase your loneliness. This last possibility is well illustrated by the case of Saul.

Saul was in his early twenties when he attended college. He claimed that his chief problem was his isolation, yet he rarely reached out to others. His general manner seemed to say "Keep away." It is likely that Saul's negative self-talk made it difficult for him to make contact with others, which increased the chances that others would want to stay away from him. His social withdrawal resulted in him feeling lonely.

One day, as I (Jerry) was walking across the campus, I saw Saul sitting alone in a secluded spot, while many students were congregated on the lawn, enjoying the beautiful spring weather. Here was a chance for him to do something about his separation from others; instead, he chose to seclude himself. He continually told himself that others didn't like him and, sadly, made his prophecy self-fulfilling by his own behavior. He made himself unapproachable and, in many ways, the kind of person people would avoid.

In this time of life we have the chance to decide on ways of being toward ourselves and others as well as on our vocation and future plans. We can work on our responsibility for our own loneliness and create new choices for ourselves. If you feel lonely on the campus, ask yourself what you are doing and can do about your own loneliness. Do you decide in advance that the others want to keep to themselves? Do you assume that there already are well-established cliques to which you cannot belong? Do you expect others to reach out to you, even though you do not initiate contacts yourself? What fears might be holding you back? Where do they seem to come from? Are past experiences of loneliness or rejection determining the choices you now make?

Life circumstances and cultural factors also pave the way to a lonely existence. Many young adults make the journey from their country to the United States, and for some this new life can be a very frightening and lonely experience. The loneliness immigrants feel may have a lot to do with not knowing how to be a part of a new culture. They may want to hold onto ways that are familiar to them, yet they are generally expected to give up many of their customs. They may find it difficult to connect with people in the mainstream culture and often feel isolated. Language barriers or accents may make it difficult for them to understand others or to make themselves understood to others. Depending on the country immigrants come from, they may experience discrimination. Even if they want to take on the ways of their new culture, they often miss their country of origin and struggle with retaining their original values and adopting new values.

We know of some young people who came from Africa to the United States to get a college education. Some of these immigrants experience guilt over leaving significant people behind, especially if their new life is better than the one at home where people are often struggling to meet their most basic needs. In one case, a young man lost his financial aid targeted for his education when it was discovered that he was sending some of this money to family members at home. He experienced a major dilemma when he was expected to help those at home who were in desperate living situations, especially when he was using money to better himself by getting an education. Although he wanted to take advantage of getting a college education, he also felt a loyalty to his family and his community at home. Not only did he experience guilt over having so much personally, but he felt the loneliness of making decisions that affected so many besides himself.

I (Marianne) came to the United States from Germany as a young adult. Although there were many exciting and challenging aspects of moving here, I did experience the loneliness of missing my family and my country. There were times when I did not know how to fit into the mainstream of society and felt that I was not truly understood. I learned to balance embracing the American way of life while retaining my identity as a German. At times I felt disloyal and was conflicted when I was expected to make changes that were unacceptable because of the way I was brought up. I remember the loneliness I felt over conflicts of being expected to fully accept all American values, and at the same time to reject some of the values of my childhood. In speaking with other immigrants I have found a shared struggle over retaining our continued appreciation to our original culture without being seen as being disloyal to the country that many of us have chosen to live in.

Loneliness and Middle Age

Many changes occur during middle age that can result in new feelings of loneliness. Although we may not be free to choose some of the things that occur at this time in our lives, we are free to choose how we relate to these events. Here are some possible changes and crises of middle age:

- Our significant other may decide to permanently separate from us, which is likely to result in an overwhelming sense of rejection and loneliness. Will we decide never to trust anyone again? Will we mourn our loss and, after a period of grieving, go on with our life?

- Our life may not turn out the way we had planned, which can pave the way to a lonely existence. We may not enjoy the success we had hoped for, we may feel disenchanted with our work, or we may feel that we passed up many fine opportunities earlier. The key point is what choices will we make in light of this reality? Will we remain stuck in loneliness and hopelessness and berate ourselves endlessly about what we could have done and should have done? Will we allow ourselves to stay trapped in meaningless work and empty relationships, or will we look for positive options for change?

- Our children may leave home, and with this change we may experience emptiness and a sense of loss. If so, what will we do about this transition? Will we attempt to hang on? Can we let go and create a new life with new meaning? When our children leave, will we lose our purpose in life? Will we look back with regret at all that we could have done differently, or will we choose to look ahead to the kind of life we want to create for ourselves now that we do not have the responsibilities of parenthood?

These are just a few of the changes that many of us confront during midlife. Although we may feel that events are not in our control, we can still choose how we respond to these life situations. For example, Amy and Gary made different decisions about how to deal with their loneliness after divorce, and their attitudes have been central to how they experience their loneliness.

Amy and Gary had been married for more than 20 years before their recent divorce, and they have three children in their teens. Amy is 43; Gary is 41. Here is Gary's story.

GARY'S STORY

I felt resentful at first and believed that somehow we could have stayed together if only Amy had changed her attitude. I live alone in a small apartment and get to see my kids only on weekends. I see my divorce as a personal failure, and I still feel a mixture of guilt and resentment. I hate to come home to an empty apartment with no one to talk to and no one to share my life with. I wonder whether women would find me interesting once they got to know me, and I fear that it's too late to begin a new life with someone else.

For her part, Amy also had many ambivalent feelings about divorcing.

AMY'S STORY

*A*fter the divorce I experienced panic and aloneness as I faced the prospect of rearing my children and managing the home on my own. I wonder whether I can meet my responsibilities and still have time for any social life. I am concerned that men may not be interested in me, especially with my three teenagers.

Even though I'm unsure of myself, I have dated some. At first I felt pressured by my parents to get married again. Yet I'm doing my best to resist this pressure. I'm choosing to remain single for the time being. Although I feel lonely at times, I don't feel trapped.

The loneliness of later years can be accentuated by the losses that come with age.

© Joel Gordon

Experiences like those of Gary and Amy are very common among middle-aged people who find themselves having to cope with feelings of isolation and abandonment after a divorce. Some, like Gary, may feel panic and either retreat from people or quickly run into a new relationship to avoid the pain of separation. If they do not confront their fears and their pain, they may be controlled by their fear of being left alone for the rest of their lives. Others, like Amy, may go through a similar period of loneliness after a divorce yet refuse to be controlled by a fear of living alone. Although they might want a long-term relationship again some day, they avoid rushing impulsively into a new relationship to avoid feelings of pain or loneliness.

Loneliness and the Later Years

Our society emphasizes productivity, youth, beauty, power, and vitality. As we age, we may lose some of our vitality and sense of power or attractiveness. Many people face a real crisis when they reach retirement, for they feel that they are being put out to pasture—that they are not needed anymore and that their lives are really over. Loneliness and hopelessness are experienced by anyone who feels that there is little to look forward to or that he or she has no vital place in society, and such feelings are particularly common among older adults.

The loneliness of the later years can be accentuated by the losses that come with age—loss of sight, hearing, memory, and strength. Older people may lose their jobs, hobbies, friends, and loved ones. A particularly difficult loss is the death of a spouse with whom they have been close for many years. In the face of such losses, a person may ultimately ask what reason remains for living. It may be no coincidence that many old people die soon after their spouses have died or shortly after their retirement.

Charles, 65, lost his wife, Betsy, to cancer after a year's battle. During the last few months of Betsy's life, members of the local hospice organization helped Charles care for her at home. Here is an account of Charles's attempt to deal with her death.

CHARLES'S STORY

Before Betsy's death she expressed a desire to talk to me about her impending death. I could not tolerate the reality of her illness and her dying, so I never talked with her. Even though Betsy has been dead for some time, I still feel guilty for not listening to her and talking. When I look at her chair where she sat, I feel an overwhelming sense of loneliness. At times I feel as though my heart is going to explode. I rarely sleep through the night, and I get up early in the morning and look for tasks to keep me busy. I feel lost and lonely, and it is difficult for me to be in the house where she and I lived together for more than 45 years. Her memories are everywhere. My friends continue to encourage me to talk about my feelings. Although my friends and neighbors are supportive, I'm worried that I'll be a burden for them. I wish that I had died instead of Betsy, for she would have been better able to deal with my being gone than I'm able to cope with her passing.

C. S. Lewis, in *A Grief Observed* (1961), poetically compares grief to a long and winding valley where any bend may reveal a totally new landscape. He writes about his own grief over observing the death of his wife from cancer:

> AND GRIEF STILL FEELS LIKE FEAR. Perhaps, more strictly, like suspense. Or like waiting; just hanging about waiting for something to happen. It gives life a permanently provisional feeling. It doesn't seem worth starting anything. I can't settle down. I yawn, I fidget, I smoke too much. Up until this I always had too little time. Now there is nothing but time. Almost pure time, empty successiveness. (p. 29)

The pangs of aloneness or the feeling that life is futile reflect a drastic loss of meaning rather than an essential part of growing old. Viktor Frankl (1969) has written about the "will to meaning" as a key determinant of a person's desire to live. He notes that many of the inmates in the Nazi concentration camp where he was imprisoned kept themselves alive by looking forward to the prospect of being released and reunited with their families. Many of those who lost hope simply gave up and died, regardless of their age.

At least until recently our society has compounded the elderly person's loss of meaning by grossly neglecting the aged population. Although many elderly are well-taken care of in a convalescent home and are visited by their family members, many others are left alone in an institution with only minimal human contact.

Sometimes, however, older people choose a lonely existence rather than participating in the activities and human relationships that could be open to them. Rudy is an example of an older man who feels basically lost and does not seem able to find a direction that brings him satisfaction. Rudy is 85 years old. His wife died 15 years ago, and he remained in his large house. He reports that he has real difficulty being at home for any length of time. He leaves the house early in the morning in his pickup truck and spends most of his day doing crossword puzzles, except for the time he spends walking a few miles. When he finally returns home late at night, he faces the loneliness he attempted to escape from early in the morning. Although he has occasional contact with extended family at holiday gatherings, he rarely initiates contact with them during the rest of the year. He shies away from people out of his fear of burdening them. What he fails to realize is how much he still has to offer and how much others could benefit from their association with him. His inability to recognize and appreciate what he could offer to others keeps him a prisoner of his loneliness.

TIME ALONE AS A SOURCE OF STRENGTH

We hope you will welcome your time alone. Once you fully accept it, your aloneness can become the source of your strength and the foundation of your relatedness to others. Maya Angelou is a person who schedules time for herself so she can retain her center. She lives a very full life, and she finds ways to retain her vitality. She schedules one day a month for herself; nothing is scheduled and her friends know not to call her. Reflecting on Maya Angelou's practice, can you see yourself as actively creating alone time? Sometimes we get so busy attending to day-to-day routines that we forget to reflect and provide ourselves with spiritual and emotional nourishment. Taking time to be alone gives you the opportunity to think, plan, imagine, and dream. It allows you to listen to yourself and to become sensitive to what you are experiencing. In solitude you can come to appreciate anew both your separateness from and your relatedness to the important people and projects in your life. Remember, if you are not a good friend to yourself, it will be difficult to find true friendship in the company of others.

SUMMARY

We have a need to be with others that is best satisfied through many forms of intimate relationships. Yet another essential dimension of the human experience is to be able to creatively function alone. Unless we can enjoy our own company, we will have difficulty finding real joy in being with others. Being with others and being with ourselves are two sides of the same coin.

Some people fail to reach out to others and make significant contact because they are timid in social situations and are relatively unassertive. Many people report that they are troubled by shyness or have had problems with being shy in the past. Shyness can lead to feelings of loneliness, yet shy people can challenge the fears that keep them unassertive. Shyness is not a disorder that needs to be "cured," nor are all aspects of being shy negative. It is important to recognize that certain attitudes and behaviors can create much of the loneliness we sometimes experience.

Each period of life presents unique tasks to be mastered, and loneliness can be best understood from a developmental perspective. Particular circumstances often result in loneliness as we pass through childhood, adolescence, young adulthood, middle age, and the later years. Most of us have experienced loneliness during our childhood and adolescent years, and these experiences can have a significant influence on our present attitudes, behavior, and relationships. It helps to be able to recognize our feelings about events that are associated with each of these turning points.

Experiencing loneliness is part of being human, for ultimately we are alone. We can grow from such experiences if we understand them and use them to renew our sense of ourselves. Moreover, we do not have to remain victimized by early decisions that we made as a result of past loneliness. We do have choices. We can choose to face loneliness and deal with it creatively, or we can choose to try to escape from it. We have some choice concerning whether we will feel lonely or whether we will make connections with others. We can design our activities so that we reject others before they reject us, or we can risk making contact with them.

Where Can I Go From Here?

I. Allocate some time each day to be alone and reflect on anything you wish. In your journal note the thoughts and feelings that occur to you during your time alone.

2. If you have feelings of loneliness when you think about a certain person who has been or is now significant to you, write a letter to that person expressing all the things you are feeling (you do not have to mail the letter). For instance, tell that person how you miss him or her or write about your sadness, your resentment, or your desire for more closeness.

3. Imagine that you are the person you have written your letter to, and write a reply to yourself. What do you imagine that person would say to you if he or she received your letter? What do you fear (and what do you wish) he or she would say?

4. If you sometimes feel lonely and left out, try some specific experiments for a week or so. For example, if you feel isolated in most of your classes, make it a point to get to class early and initiate contact with a fellow student. If you feel anxious about taking such a step, try doing it in fantasy. What are your fears? What is the worst thing you can imagine might happen? Record your impressions in your journal. If you decide to try reaching out to other people, record in your journal what the experience is like for you.

5. Recall some periods of loneliness in your life. Select important situations in which you experienced loneliness, and spend some time recalling the details of each situation and reflecting on the meaning each of these experiences has had for you. Now you might do two things:

- Write down your reflections in your journal. How do you think your past experiences of loneliness affect you now?

- Select a friend or a person you would like to trust more and share this experience of loneliness.

6. Many people rarely make time exclusively for themselves. If you would like to have time to yourself but just have not gotten around to arranging it, consider going to a place you have never been or to the beach, the desert, or the mountains. Reserve a weekend just for yourself; if this seems too much, then spend a day completely alone. The important thing is to remove yourself from your everyday routine and just be with yourself without external distractions.

7. Spend a day or part of a day in a place where you can observe and experience lonely people. You might spend time near a busy downtown intersection, in a park where old people congregate, or in a large shopping center. Pay attention to expressions of loneliness, alienation, and isolation. How do people seem to be dealing with their loneliness? Later, you might discuss your observations in class.

8. Imagine yourself living in a typical rest home—without any of your possessions, cut off from your family and friends, and unable to do the things you now do. Reflect on what this experience would be like for you; then write down some of your reactions in your journal.

Resources for Future Study

Web Site Resource

THE SHYNESS HOME PAGE
http://www.shyness.com/

The Shyness Institute offers this Web site as "a gathering of network resources for people seeking information and services for shyness." It is an index of links to articles, associations, and agencies that work with shyness.

 ### InfoTrac College Edition Resources

For additional readings, explore INFOTRAC COLLEGE EDITION, our online library:
http://www.infotrac.college.com/wadsworth

Hint: Enter these search terms:

loneliness	social isolation
solitude	aloneness
shyness	

Print Resources

Block, D. (1991). *Listening to your inner voice: Discover the truth within you and let it guide your way.* Center City, MN: Hazelden.

Lindbergh, A. (1975). *Gift from the sea.* New York: Pantheon. (Original work published in 1955)

Moustakas, C. (1961). *Loneliness.* Englewood Cliffs, NJ: Prentice-Hall (Spectrum).

Zimbardo, P. G. (1994). *Shyness.* Reading, MA: Addison-Wesley.

12

Contemplate death if you would learn how to live.

Death and Loss

© PhotoDisc/Getty Images

Where Am I Now?

Use this scale to respond to these statements:

> 3 = This statement is true of me *most* of the time.
>
> 2 = This statement is true of me *some* of the time.
>
> 1 = This statement is true of me *almost none* of the time.

1. The fact that I will die makes me take life seriously.

2. I find funerals depressing.

3. If I had a terminal illness, I would want to know how much time I had left to live so I could decide how to spend it.

4. Because of the possibility of losing those I love, I do not allow very many people to get close to me.

5. If I live with integrity, I am unlikely to have regrets at the end of my life.

6. My greatest fear of death is the fear of the unknown.

7. I have had losses in my life that seemed in some ways like the experience of dying.

8. There are ways in which I am not really alive emotionally.

9. I am not especially afraid of dying.

10. I fear the deaths of those I love more than I do my own.

I n this chapter we invite you to look at your attitudes and beliefs about your own death, the deaths of those you love, and other forms of significant loss. An honest understanding and acceptance of death and loss can lay the groundwork for a meaningful life. If we accept that we have only a limited time in which to live, we can make choices that will make the most of the time we do have.

Related to accepting the reality of death is the notion that suffering is a natural part of human existence. The Dalai Lama (Dalai Lama & Cutler, 1998) speaks of the importance of learning to face the realities of old age, illness, and death. According to the Dalai Lama, many of us have an intense aversion to facing our pain and suffering. If we accept that suffering is a part of life, then we are in a better position for dealing with the problems that we will inevitably experience. The attitude we assume toward suffering is extremely important because it influences our ability to cope with suffering when it arises. The Dalai Lama writes, "If we can transform our attitude towards suffering, adopt an attitude that allows us greater tolerance of it, then this can do much to help counteract feelings of mental unhappiness, dissatisfaction, and discontent" (p. 140).

In this chapter we ask you to consider the notion of death in a metaphorical way and to think about these questions: "In what ways am I not as alive as I might be?" and "What will I do with my awareness of the ways in which I'm not fully alive?" Finally, we address the importance of fully experiencing grief when we suffer significant losses.

This discussion of death and loss has an important connection with the themes of the previous chapter, loneliness and solitude. When we accept the reality of our eventual death, we get in touch with our ultimate aloneness. This awareness of our mortality and aloneness helps us realize that our actions do count, that we do have choices concerning how we live, and that we must accept the final responsibility for the way we live life.

An awareness of death can enable us to give meaning to life. It can stimulate us to look at our priorities and to ask what we value most. In this way our willingness to come to terms with death can teach us how to live. Running from death is running from life, for as Gibran (1923) writes, "Life and death are one, even as the river and the sea are one" (p. 71).

This chapter is also a bridge to the next chapter, which deals with meaning and values. Our knowledge that we will die can encourage us to ask ourselves whether we are living by values that create a meaningful existence; if not, we have the time and opportunity to change. On this topic, Morrie Schwartz observes: "Everyone knows they're going to die, but nobody believes it. If we did, we would do things differently" (Albom, 1997, p. 81). This notion of doing things differently is illustrated by Norma's response to the question of how she would feel if she found that she had only a short time to live.

NORMA'S STORY

I'm 53 years old, and I have accomplished more in my life than I ever thought possible. So far, my life has been rich and gratifying. I have a husband and four children with whom I generally have a good relationship. Although I know they have a need for me in their lives, they could function well without me. I am not afraid of death, but I would consider death at this time in my life as terribly unfair. There is so much more I want to do. Within me are many untapped talents that I haven't had time to express. Many of my present projects take an enormous amount of time, and although they are mostly satisfying, I've put on hold many other personal and professional aspirations.

At times I feel an overwhelming sense of sadness and disappointment over the possibility of running out of time to do those things I was meant to do. Time seems to go by so fast, and I often wish I could stop the clock. It is my hope to live to an old age, yet I do confront myself with the reality that I may not be that fortunate, which provides me with the impetus to want to make changes in my life. The reality of mortality challenges me to reflect on what I would regret not having done if I were to die soon. This reality helps me not to postpone my plans to later, because there may not be a later. The greatest tragedy for me would be, if, on my dying day, I would say that I didn't live my life, rather I lived someone else's life.

Can you relate to Norma's account? Are you living the kind of life you want? What do you most want to be able to say that you have experienced or accomplished before you die?

OUR FEARS OF DEATH

There are many aspects of death, including leaving behind those we love, losing ourselves, encountering the unknown, and coping with the humiliation and indignity of a painful or long dying. For many people it is not so much death itself they fear as the process of dying. They may ask, "What will my process of dying be like?"

Morrie Schwartz was an elderly professor who was dying. Each Tuesday he met with one of his former students, Mitch, to share his insights about living and dying. Morrie said: "The truth is, once you learn how to die, you learn how to live" (Albom, 1997, p. 82). For Morrie, wasting life is even sadder than dying. Morrie talked about his fears of dying, which included losing more and more of his faculties and becoming increasingly dependent. However, he chose to face his fears and deal with them rather than letting his fears consume him. Even though he knew he was dying, Morrie realized that he had a choice regarding how he would deal with the end of this life: "Am I going to withdraw from the world, like most people do, or am I going to live? I decided I'm going to live— or at least try to live—the way I want, with dignity, with courage, with humor, with composure" (p. 21). One of the lessons we can learn from reading *Tuesdays With Morrie* is that we do not have to stay away from someone who is dying. There is much that we can learn by sharing in the last days of someone we love.

When they are dying, some people want to discuss what they are going through, yet their loved ones may not be able to handle such conversations. Although Morrie was quite ready to talk about his death and the meaning of dying and living, Mitch was not ready to hear about death and was uncomfortable discussing this subject for some time. Certainly the life of Mitch Albom was enriched by his encounters with Morrie in his death process. Albom found new meaning in life, but only by eventually being willing to really listen to Morrie and to talk about what Morrie needed to talk about.

Some people are reluctant to talk about dying with those close to them. For example, our daughter Heidi wrote to a friend's mother who was diagnosed with cancer. The mother did not want those close to her to talk about her condition. It was Heidi's hope that her friend's mother would recognize that she could give those who love her a gift by letting them share her struggle and allowing them to take care of her. Heidi had this kind of open relationship with her grandmother, as can be seen in Heidi's letter.

HEIDI'S LETTER

*O*ne of my greatest memories with my Gram is sitting at the foot of her big queen chair and me on the little wooden stool. My face lay in her lap and her rose soft hand stroked my cheek. We both cried over the news of her being diagnosed with bladder cancer. We cried and cried and cried, then we laughed and then cried some more. As she would say, we bared our souls and left nothing unsaid. I value that experience and others like it and see its true power. The tears washed over us, and it bathed a fear and helped us both let go and embrace. In the beginning, Gram wanted to hide her diagnosis from others. She didn't want them to worry. But I encouraged her to tell all, which she finally did. What I saw happening was those who were always taken care of by her were given the gift to nurture and take care of such a strong and powerful woman. It is a gift I personally treasure. I still carry the glow of that power.

At this point pause to reflect on what you fear about dying. Have you had the experience of being with a dying person? If so, what was this like for you?

Do you tend to avoid talking with people who are dying? What seems to arouse the greatest fears in you? How might these fears influence the way you are choosing to live now?

DEATH AND THE MEANING OF LIFE

Life and death are two facets of the same reality. Learning about death, dying, and bereavement is a pathway to learning about life and living, and the reverse is also true (Corr, Nabe, & Corr, 2003). When we avoid facing the reality of death or our reflecting on death, our capacity for life can be diminished. Acceptance of death does not have to be a morbid topic, for it can revitalize our goals and assist us in finding a deeper purpose for living.

Existentialists view the acceptance of death as vital to the discovery of meaning and purpose in life. One of our distinguishing characteristics as human beings is our ability to grasp the concept of the future and, thus, the inevitability of death. Our ability to do so gives meaning to our existence, for it makes our every act and moment count. Rather than living in the fear of death, we can view it as a challenge and as an opportunity.

From the Stoics of ancient Greece—who proclaimed "Contemplate death if you would learn how to live"—until modern times, we have been challenged to face our future. Seneca commented that "no man enjoys the true taste of life but he who is willing and ready to quit it." And Saint Augustine said, "It is only in the face of death that man's self is born." Those who are terminally ill provide a sharply defined example of facing the reality of death and of giving meaning to life. Their confrontation with death causes them to do much living in a relatively brief period of time. The pressure of time forces them to choose how they will spend their remaining days. Irvin Yalom (1980) found that cancer patients in group therapy had the capacity to view their crisis as an opportunity to instigate change in their lives. Once they discovered that they had cancer, many experienced these inner changes that enabled them to find a powerful focus on life:

- A rearrangement of life's priorities, paying little attention to trivial matters
- A sense of liberation; the ability to choose to do those things they really wanted to do
- An increased sense of living in the moment; no postponement of living until some future time
- A vivid appreciation of the basic facts of life; for example, noticing changes in the seasons and other aspects of nature
- A deeper communication with loved ones than before the crisis
- Fewer interpersonal fears, less concern over security, and more willingness to take risks (p. 35)

Cultural and religious beliefs affect the way people view death.

We are finite beings, and what we do with our lives counts. We can make a conscious decision to fully affirm life, or we can passively let life slip by us. We can settle for letting events happen to us, or we can actively create the kind of life we want. Our time is invaluable precisely because it is limited.

Cultural and religious beliefs affect the way people view death. Some belief systems emphasize making the most of this life, for it is viewed as the only existence. Other belief systems focus on the natural continuity and progression of this temporal life into an afterlife. Just as our beliefs and values affect our fear of death, so do they affect the meaning we attribute to death. Regardless of our philosophical or spiritual views on the meaning of life and death, a wide range of choices is still open to us to maximize the quality of our present life.

Both of our daughters, Heidi and Cindy, were very much a part of their grandmother's final few weeks. Although this was a difficult time for them, they both learned many invaluable lessons about living from their grandmother, not only at this time when she was dying but also during the many years of her life. Cindy wrote down some of these "lessons my Gram taught me."

- Look the ones you love deeply in the eyes and without words let them know you love them and that they mean the world to you. Look at them so intensely and with such mindfulness that they feel as if you are the only person in the room with them.

- Say thank you and be grateful. Recognize your blessings, even in the face of despair.
- Say you are sorry when you have hurt or offended someone.
- Touch the ones you love and invite them to touch you. Touch heals and touch penetrates the soul and fills you up with joy.
- Laugh, smile, and be playful. Let laughter enter every relationship you have with every person you know.
- Tell people how much you care about them. If you have a compliment or a kind thought about someone, speak it in the moment.
- Do not judge others without trying to understand them. Even if they have done you harm or wronged you, find a way to let it go and to forgive.
- If you live a life of compassion and love and concern for others, you too will receive these gifts at the end of your days.
- Be open and share your fears and pain with each other.
- Sit patiently with other people's pain. If you share your sorrows, they become less heavy and can easily be transformed into love and peacefulness.
- Take an interest in what other people do. Be genuine and curious in who they are. Ask about the welfare of others.
- Share your wisdom and life lessons without giving advice. Tell stories about your own struggles and accomplishments without being arrogant or self-centered.
- Pray and put faith in God. Always know that you are not alone and that you are connected to something beyond yourself. Trust this, ask for strength when you need to, and remember to give thanks as well.

Take Time to Reflect

1. What do you experience when you think about your own death?

_____

_____

2. Do you like the way you are living your life? List some specific things you are not doing now that you would like to be doing.

_____

_____

3. If you had only 6 months left to live, what would you do differently?

_____

_____

4. Does the fact that you will die give meaning to your life? If so, how?

_____

_____

5. In what ways do you think your fears about death and dying might be affecting the choices you make now?

_____

_____

SUICIDE: ULTIMATE CHOICE, ULTIMATE SURRENDER, OR ULTIMATE TRAGEDY?

Suicide, the taking of one's own life, is one of the leading causes of death in the United States, and it is on the increase. Yet in spite of how common suicide is, we avoid talking about it and rely on these common but untrue myths (Marcus, 1996):

- There are no warning signs.
- People who talk about committing suicide will not do it.
- Young people are more likely than old people to kill themselves.
- Once a suicidal crisis has passed, the person is out of danger.
- Suicide is genetic.
- People who are suicidal want to die.

Although it is true that some people do not give any signs that they intend on taking their lives, generally there are warning signs that give some indication that a person is suicidal (Marcus, 1996). Here are some signs that an individual may be a suicidal risk:

- Suicidal thoughts and threats
- Previous suicidal threats or comments

- Preoccupation with death, including talk of feeling hopeless and helpless
- Giving away prized possessions
- Discussing specific methods and a time for killing oneself
- Depression
- Isolation and withdrawal from friends and family
- Extreme changes of behavior and sudden personality changes
- A sudden need to get one's life in order
- A sudden appearance of calm or peace after a period during which some of these above-listed characteristics were evident

These signs should be taken seriously, and interventions should be made to help bring about a change in the suicidal person.

Those considering suicide often feel that they are trapped in a dead-end existence and that life is unbearable. They simply do not want to go on in such deadening patterns, and they may feel that the chances of change are slim. Although there are undoubtedly options for living differently, they are unable to see any. Suicidal thoughts can be overwhelming during this time of emotional blindness.

Is suicide an ultimate choice, an ultimate surrender, or an ultimate tragedy? This question is complex, with no easy answer. We each make conscious choices about how we live or die. Some people believe suicide to be the ultimate surrender, the result of not being willing to struggle or of being too quick to give up without exploring other possibilities. At times you may have felt a deep sense of hopelessness, and you may have questioned whether it was worth it to continue living. Have you ever felt really suicidal? If so, what was going on in your life that contributed to your desire to end it? What factor or factors kept you from following through with taking your life? What hidden meanings does suicide have for you?

Taking one's life is a powerful act, and the underlying emotional messages and symbolic meanings can be equally powerful:

- A cry for help: "I cried out, but nobody cared!"
- A form of self-punishment: "I don't deserve to live."
- An act of hostility: "I'll get even with you; see what you made me do."
- An attempt to control and exert power over people: "I will make others suffer for the rest of their lives for what they did to me."
- An attempt to be noticed: "Maybe now people will talk about me and feel sorry for the way they treated me."
- A relief from a terrible state of mind: "Life is too stressful, and I see no hope at all."
- An escape from a difficult or impossible situation: "I am a burden to everybody. It will be a relief to them when I am gone."

- A relief from hopelessness: "I see no way out of the despair I feel. Ending my life will be better than hating to wake up each morning."
- An end to pain: "I suffer extreme physical pain, and there is no end to it. My suicide will end it."

Reactions to Suicide

Often death is associated with the ending of pain. Those who commit suicide may resort to this final and deliberate act as a way to put an end to either physical or emotional suffering. Yet for survivors, the death of someone they were close to often marks the beginning of suffering (Pehrsson & Boylan, 2004). Suicide leaves surviving family members with emotional turmoil, unanswered questions, and an emptiness that is difficult to deal with (Kaslow & Aronson, 2004). The sudden death of a loved one, especially due to suicide, sets the survivors on a grief-stricken journey (Marcus, 1996). When a family member commits suicide, the immediate reaction is generally shock and distress. Soon afterward those left behind experience a range of feelings such as denial, shock, anger, shame, guilt, grief, depression, fear, blame, rejection, and abandonment. When family members are in denial, they may invent reasons that will contribute to their refusal to accept the death as a suicide. Anger is quite common and is often directed toward the deceased. Anger may also be aimed at oneself, friends, family members, health care providers, insurance companies, and others in the community (Kaslow & Aronson, 2004). There may be a sense of shame because of religious teachings about suicide. Survivors often experience guilt over what they could and should have done to prevent the tragedy. "Maybe if I had been more sensitive and caring," they might feel, "this terrible thing wouldn't have happened." Survivors also may experience fear over the possibility that this act will be repeated by another family member or, perhaps, even by themselves.

Survivors generally need considerable time and opportunity to process feelings such as anger, self-blame, and guilt before they can begin to accept the loss. Survivors frequently cannot understand or even feel their own numbed pain. It is extremely important that they find a person they can talk to about their loss, or their emptiness may never be filled. Eventually they face the task of reconstructing their lives without the person they lost, but this is unlikely to happen until they have dealt with their reactions to the suicide (Pehrsson & Boylan, 2004).

Counseling can be useful in helping survivors deal with their reactions to the suicide of a friend or family member. The nature of the unfinished business, how it is handled, and how the survivor is affected by it all have an impact on the grief process. Typically, those who are left behind experience a deep sense of abandonment, rejection, loneliness, and isolation. For those who are mourning a suicide, a good support system and communication with a nonjudgmental person can be most useful (Corr et al., 2003). If family members are willing to seek counseling (either individually or as a family), they can be taught how to express feelings that they might otherwise keep to themselves. Counseling encourages the survivors to talk about the things they may be rehearsing over and over in their heads, and it can help them to talk about their thoughts and feelings with one another. Counseling can help correct distortions that survivors may hold, prepare for their future, let go of regrets and blame, and give expression to their anger. Because of their deep sadness, without professional help it may be difficult for family members to become aware of, much less express to one another, the anger that they feel.

Ending Life as an Act of Mercy

Can suicide be an act of mercy? Can suicide be rational? Some victims of painful and terminal illnesses have decided when and how to end their lives. **Rational suicide** means that a person has decided—after going through a decision-making process and without coercion from others—to end his or her life because of extreme suffering involved with a terminal illness. Many people are opposed to active measures to end life, yet they also oppose interventions that unnecessarily prolong life by artificial and unusual means. Certainly there is a difference between suicide and allowing nature to take its course in cases of extreme illness. **Assisted suicide** involves providing lethal means to cause a person's death, with the individual performing the act that ends his or her own life. **Hastened death** involves speeding up the dying process, which can entail withholding or withdrawing life support. To date only one state (Oregon) has enacted legislation allowing physician-assisted suicide for terminally ill patients. This form of rational suicide is sometimes argued to be morally and ethically appropriate in circumstances involving terminal illness and unendurable suffering (Corr et al., 2003).

In his book, *Life and Death Decisions: Psychological and Ethical Considerations in End-of-Life Care*, Kleespies (2004) writes about the importance of advance care planning. **Advance directives** are designed to protect the self-determination of people who have reached a point in their illness when they are not able to make decisions on their own about their care. The fear of being kept alive when they are in a vegetative state has resulted in directives for people at any age. Through the use of advance directives, people can go on record with their preferences for medical treatment while they are mentally capable of making decisions, with the anticipation that the time may come when they will no longer have the capacity to make these choices. Generally, there are two forms of advance directives. One form involves completing a **living will** by which the person specifies his or her preferences for end-of-life care. Another form involves identifying a person to make decisions on one's behalf when one can no longer do so. According to Kleespies, advance directives have been viewed as a means of exercising mercy and protecting the autonomy of individuals by giving them the right to make their wishes clear to both family members and treatment staff pertaining to their own end-of-life care.

Take a few minutes to think about how you might respond if you were critically ill and chances were just about nonexistent that you would improve. Might there come a time in your life when there was nothing for you to live for? Imagine yourself in a skilled nursing facility, having lost control of all your bodily functions. You are unable to read, to carry on meaningful conversation, or to go places, and you are partially paralyzed by a series of strokes. Would you want to be kept alive at all costs, or might you want to end your life? Would you feel justified in doing so? What might stop you?

Now apply this line of thought to other situations in life. Is your life yours to do with as you choose? Do you believe it is permissible to commit suicide at *any* period in your life? Suppose you tried various ways of making your life meaningful, but nothing worked and nothing changed. Would you continue to live until natural causes took over? Would you feel justified in ending your own life if your active search had failed to bring you peace?

FREEDOM IN DYING

The process of dying involves a gradual diminishing of the range of choices available to us. But even in dying, we can choose how we handle what is happening to us. The following account deals with the dying of Jim Morelock, a student and close friend of mine (Jerry's).*

Jim is 25 years old. He is full of life—witty, bright, honest, and actively questioning. He had just graduated from college as a human services major and seemed to have a bright future when his illness was discovered.

About a year and a half ago, Jim developed a growth on his forehead and underwent surgery to have it removed. At that time, his doctors believed the growth was a rare disorder that was not malignant. Later, more tumors erupted, and more surgery followed. Several months ago, Jim found out that the tumors had spread throughout his body and that, even with cobalt treatment, he would have a short life. Since that time he has steadily grown weaker and has been able to do less and less; yet he has shown remarkable courage in the way he has faced this loss and his dying.

Some time ago Jim came to Idyllwild, California, and took part in the weekend seminar that we had with the reviewers of this book. On this chapter, he commented that although we may not have a choice concerning the losses we

---

*This account is being repeated as it appeared in this book's first edition. Many readers have commented to us about how touched they were as they read about Jim's life and his death, and in this way he seems to have lived on in one important respect.

Jim Morelock

Courtesy of Betty Jane Morelock

suffer in dying, we do retain the ability to choose our attitude toward our death and the way we relate to it.

Jim has taught me (Jerry) many things during these past few months about this enduring capacity for choice, even in extreme circumstances. Jim has made many critical choices since being told of his illness. He chose to continue taking a course at the university, because he liked the contact with the people there. He worked hard at a boat dock to support himself, until he could no longer manage the physical exertion. He decided to undergo chemotherapy, even though he knew that it most likely would not result in his cure, because he hoped that it would reduce his pain. It did not, and Jim has suffered much agony during the past few months. He decided not to undergo any further chemotherapy, primarily because he did not want to prolong his life if he could not really live fully. He made a choice to accept God in his life, which gave him a sense of peace and serenity. Before he became bedridden, he decided to go to Hawaii and enjoy his time in first-class style.

Jim has always had an aversion to hospitals—to most institutions, for that matter—so he chose to remain at home, in more personal surroundings. As long as he was able, he read widely and continued to write in his journal about his thoughts and feelings on living and dying. With his friends, he played his guitar and sang songs that he had written. He maintained an active interest in life and in the things around him, without denying the fact that he was dying.

More than anyone I (Jerry) have known or heard about, Jim has taken care of unfinished business. He made it a point to gather his family and tell them his wishes, he made contact with all his friends and said everything he wanted to say to them, and he asked Marianne to deliver the eulogy at his funeral services. He clearly stated his desire for cremation; he wants to burn those tumors and then have his ashes scattered over the sea—a wish that reflects his love of freedom and movement.

Jim has very little freedom and movement now, for he can do little except lie in his bed and wait for his death to come. To this day he is choosing to die with dignity, and although his body is deteriorating, his spirit is still very much alive. He retains his mental sharpness, his ability to say a lot in a very few words, and his sense of humor. He has allowed himself to grieve over his losses. As he puts it, "I'd sure like to hang around to enjoy all those people that love me!" Realizing that this isn't possible, Jim is saying good-bye to all those who are close to him.

Throughout this ordeal, Jim's mother has been truly exceptional. When she told me (Jerry) how remarkable Jim has been in complaining so rarely despite his constant pain, I reminded her that I'd never heard her complain during her months on duty. I have been continually amazed by her strength and courage, and I have admired her willingness to honor Jim's wishes and accept his beliefs, even though at times they have differed from her own. She has demonstrated her care without smothering him or depriving him of his free spirit and independence. Her acceptance of Jim's dying and her willingness to be fully present to him have given him the opportunity to express openly whatever he feels. Jim has been able to grieve and mourn because she has not cut off this process.

This experience has taught me (Jerry) much about dying and about living. Through him, I have learned that I do not have to do that much for a person who is dying other than to be with him or her by being myself. So often I have felt a sense of helplessness, of not knowing what to say or how much to say, of not knowing what to ask or not to ask, of feeling stuck for words. Jim's imminent death seems such a loss, and it is very difficult for me to accept it. Gradually, however, I have learned not to be so concerned about what to say or to refrain from saying. In fact, in my last visit I said very little, but I feel that we made significant contact with each other. I have also learned to share with him the sadness I feel, but there is simply no easy way to say good-bye to a friend.

Jim is showing me (Jerry) that his style of dying will be no different from his style of living. By his example and by his words, Jim has been a catalyst for me to think about the things I say and do and to evaluate my own life.

Take Time to Reflect

1. If you were close to someone during his or her dying, how did the experience affect your feelings about your life and about your own dying?

_____

_____

2. How would you like to be able to respond if a person who is close to you were dying?

_____

_____

3. If you were dying, what would you most want from the people who are closest to you?

_____

_____

THE STAGES OF DEATH AND LOSS

Death and dying have become topics of widespread discussion among psychologists, psychiatrists, nurses, physicians, sociologists, clergy, and researchers. Whereas these topics were once taboo for many people, they are now the focus of seminars, courses, and workshops, and a number of books give evidence of this growing interest.

Dr. Elisabeth Kübler-Ross is a pioneer in the contemporary study of death and dying. In her widely read books *On Death and Dying* (1969) and *Death: The Final Stage of Growth* (1975), she discusses the psychosocial aspects of death and the experience of dying. Thanks to her efforts, many people have become aware of the almost universal need dying persons have to talk about their impending death and to complete their business with the important people in their lives. She has shown how ignorance of the dying process and of the needs of dying people—as well as the fears of those around them—can rob those who are dying of the opportunity to fully experience their feelings and arrive at a resolution of them.

A greater understanding of dying can help us come to an acceptance of death, as well as be more helpful and present to those who are dying. For this reason, we describe the **five stages of dying** that Kübler-Ross has delineated, based on her clinical work with terminally ill adult cancer patients. She emphasizes that these are not neat and compartmentalized stages that every person passes through in an orderly fashion. At times a person may experience a combination of these stages, perhaps skip one or more stages, or go back to an earlier stage he or she has already experienced. In general, however, Kübler-Ross found this sequence: denial, anger, bargaining, depression, and acceptance.

Denial

After the initial shock of learning that death will happen soon, denial is a normal first reaction. Most people move on and deal with their impending death in other ways after some time, but denial may recur at a later time. During the stage of denial, the attitudes of a dying person's family and friends are critical. If these people cannot face the fact that their loved one is dying, they cannot help him or her move toward an acceptance of death. Their own fear will blind them to signs that the dying person wants to talk about his or her death and needs support.

Anger

It is important that people recognize the need of those who are dying to express their anger, whether they direct it toward their doctors, the hospital staff, their friends, their children, or God. If this displaced anger is taken personally, any meaningful dialogue with the dying will be cut off. Moreover, people have reason to be enraged over having to suffer in this way when they have so much to live for. Rather than withdrawing support or taking offense, the people who surround a dying person can help most by allowing the person to fully express whatever he or she is feeling. In this way they help the person to ultimately come to terms with his or her death.

Bargaining

Kübler-Ross (1969) sums up the essence of the bargaining stage as follows: "If God has decided to take us from this earth and he did not respond to any angry pleas, he may be more favorable if I ask nicely" (p. 72). Bargaining typically involves a change in behavior or a specific promise in exchange for more time to live. Such bargains are generally made in secret, often with God. Basically, the stage of bargaining is an attempt to postpone the inevitable end.

Depression

Depression occurs when a dying person faces the losses that dying brings and begins to mourn what is already lost and what is still to be lost. In *Tuesdays With*

Morrie (Albom, 1997), Morrie was asked if he felt sorry for himself. He replied that in the mornings he often cries as he watches his body wilt away to nothing. "I feel around my body, I move my finger and my hands—whatever I can still move—and I mourn what I've lost. I mourn the slow, insidious way in which I'm dying" (pp. 56–57). He added that he then stops mourning and concentrates on all the good things still in his life. What Morrie describes is more like sadness and mourning of his losses than it is depression.

Just as it had been important to allow dying people to fully vent their anger, it is important to let them express their sadness and to make their final plans. Dying people are about to lose everyone they love, and only the freedom to grieve over these losses will enable them to find some peace and accept the reality of their death.

Acceptance

Kübler-Ross (1969) found that if patients have had enough time and support to work through the previous stages, most of them reach a stage at which they are neither depressed nor angry. Acceptance of death can be reached if they work through the many conflicts and feelings that dying brings:

> ACCEPTANCE SHOULD NOT BE MISTAKEN for a happy stage. It is almost devoid of feelings. It is as if the pain has gone, the struggle is over, and there comes a time for "the final rest before the long journey," as one patient phrased it. (p. 100)

At this stage, the dying person is often tired and weak. Acceptance does not imply submission, defeat, or doing nothing. Instead, acceptance is a form of dealing with reality. It involves a gradual separation from people, life, ties, and roles. Of course, some people never achieve an acceptance of their death, and some have no desire to. Brenner (2002) captures this notion when he writes: "Not all people who are dying have a beautiful, blissful, insightful, forgiving, loving experience. Many are downright angry and resentful" (p. 90).

The Significance of the Stages of Dying

The value of Kübler-Ross's description of the dying process is that the stages describe and summarize in a general way what patients may experience and therefore add to our understanding of dying. But these stages should not be interpreted as a natural progression that is expected in most cases, and it is a mistake to use these stages as the standard by which to judge whether a dying person's behavior is normal or right. Just as people are unique in the way they live, they are unique in the way they die. Sometimes people who work with the terminally ill forget that the stages of dying do not progress neatly, even though they cognitively know this reality. One practitioner told us: "Although I had read Kübler-Ross's book and knew the stages that a dying person was supposed to go through, many of my terminal patients had not read the same book!"

Patients who do not make it to the acceptance stage are sometimes viewed as failures. For example, some nurses get angry at patients who take "backward" steps by going from depression to anger, or they question patients about why they have "stayed so long in the anger stage." People have a range of feelings during this process: hope, anger, depression, fear, envy, relief, and anticipation. Those who are dying have great fluctuations in their moods. Therefore, these stages should not be used as a method of categorizing, and thus dehumanizing, the dying; they are best used as a frame of reference for helping them.

People facing death cope with this reality in a variety of ways. Some persons cope by becoming angry, others by withdrawing, and others by examining some meaning in their lives that would make death more acceptable. The key point is that different people cope with their death in different ways. Corr and colleagues (2003) identify three significant lessons from Kübler-Ross's stage-based approach:

- Those who are coping with dying often have unfinished business that they want to deal with before they die.
- Those who are caretakers for the dying need to actively listen and understand the needs of the dying person.
- Those who are close to those who are dying can learn a great deal about both living and dying from them.

In our view, Kübler-Ross made many people aware of the needs of the dying. She also shed light on the notion that bereavement involves some predictable stages of grief over a period of time. Some of her contributions may have been misunderstood and misinterpreted because too many people have viewed her stages as a linear process, which is not what she intended.

A Task-Based Model for Coping with Dying

Kübler-Ross's stage-based model is one approach to understanding ways of coping with dying. Other researchers have proposed alternative approaches to understanding death and dying. One of these is Corr's (1992) **task-based model** for coping with dying. Corr believes that any useful account of coping must address the whole human being, take into account the differences among individuals, and consider all who are involved. His model identifies four main areas of task work in dealing with dying: the physical, psychological, social, and spiritual.

- **Physical tasks** pertain to bodily needs and physical conditions such as coping with pain and nausea and other physical conditions. These basic bodily needs must be attended to in order to meet other needs (psychological, social, and spiritual). The aim is often to minimize physical distress.

- **Psychological tasks** are associated with autonomy, security, and richness in living. Personal dignity is especially important for those who are dying.
- **Social tasks** have to do with sustaining and enhancing the interpersonal attachments valued by the dying person. For many who are dying, their social interests narrow and their priorities shift.
- **Spiritual tasks** pertain to common themes such as meaningfulness, connectedness, transcendence, and fostering hope. People who are coping with dying often are concerned with the meaning of their lives, the meaning of suffering, and the impact of the reality of death on their remaining time.

These four tasks correspond to the four dimensions of human life, and they are approached differently by different individuals. Some of these tasks may not be undertaken, and some may be more or less important for different individuals. The task-based model is aimed at fostering empowerment and participation in coping with dying by focusing on choices. People have choices in the ways in which they will cope with life-threatening illness and dying. Certain tasks may be dealt with for a time and then set aside as the person works on other tasks. People can choose to work on one, all, or none of these series of tasks. According to Corr, it is never possible to finish all of the tasks facing an individual, even if one particular task is completed. Generally, work on these tasks ends with death. For those who live on, certain tasks may be addressed in coping with bereavement.

The Hospice Movement

There is a trend toward more direct involvement of family members in caring for a dying person. An example of this is the **hospice program.** The term *hospice* was originally used to describe a resting place for weary travelers during the Middle Ages. Later, hospices were established for children without parents, for the incurably ill, and for the elderly. In recent years hospice programs have spread rapidly through Europe, North America, and many other parts of the world. They offer care for those who are in the final stages of the journey of life. Generally, hospice services are provided in the dying person's home. Much hospice home care takes the place of more expensive and impersonal multiple hospitalizations. The hospice movement also gives permission to those who are losing a significant person to feel the full range of emotions during the bereavement process.

Both volunteers and a trained staff provide health care aid, including helping the patient and the family members deal with psychological and social stresses. Hospice workers provide useful information to the patient and to family members of what to expect. Hospices aim to provide services that help dying persons experience a sense of self-worth and dignity and to provide support for the family members so that they can prepare for the eventual separation.

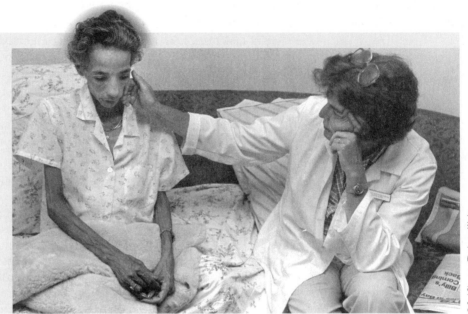

The hospice movement came in response to what many people perceived as the inadequate care for the dying in hospitals.

© Carl Glassman/The Image Works

The hospice philosophy and its key principles are summarized by Corr and colleagues (2003) thusly:

- Hospice is a philosophy with the main focus on end-of-life care.
- The hospice philosophy affirms life, not death.
- Hospice is a form of palliative or symptom-oriented care with the goal of maximizing the present quality of living and minimizing discomfort. Hospice care is aimed at making people as comfortable as possible who are terminally ill or who have no reasonable hope of benefit from cure-oriented intervention.
- Hospice offers care to the patient-and-family unit.
- Hospice seeks to re-create caring communities to help dying persons and their families.
- Hospice programs offer both formal and informal programs of support for volunteers and staff members.
- Hospice is holistic care.
- The hospice approach combines professional skills and human presence through interdisciplinary teamwork.
- Hospices typically offer continuing care and a variety of counseling services for those who survive the death of someone they love.
- Hospice philosophy can be applied to a variety of individuals and the members of the family who are coping with an illness, dying, death, and bereavement.

Sometimes the purpose of hospice is misunderstood, especially in light of the controversy surrounding physician-assisted suicide. As a family, we were recently confronted with one of the misconceptions regarding the aims of hospice. During the last few weeks of Josephine Corey's (Jerry's mother) life, several family members had decided to request the services of hospice. However, one family member was extremely opposed to this decision because of his mistaken belief that hospice would withhold treatment and by doing so would accelerate her death. He was willing to go to a hospice agency to talk about his concerns, which resulted in a different way of thinking about what hospice could offer. As an entire family, we felt a tremendous amount of support from the hospice staff and also came to realize how much more difficult this situation would have been had we not asked for their help. The various hospice workers were a genuine source of comfort to each of the family members. They also provided the opportunity for Josephine Corey to live out her last few weeks in her own home, which was one of her wishes.

GRIEVING OVER DEATH, SEPARATION, AND OTHER LOSSES

In a way that is similar to the stages of dying, people go through stages of grief in working through death and various other losses. **Grief work** refers to the exploration of feelings of sorrow, anger, and guilt over the experience of a significant loss. This process is often not an easy or simple one. Some people refuse to accept the death of a child or a spouse. They may get stuck in denial of their feelings and be unable to face and work through their pain over the loss. At some point in the grief process, people may feel numb or that they are functioning on automatic pilot. Once this numbness wears off, the pain seems to intensify. This is when professional assistance could be most useful.

To put to rest unresolved issues, we need to express our anger, guilt, regrets, and frustrations. When we deny pain, we inevitably suffer more in the long run and are unable to express a range of feelings. This unexpressed pain tends to eat away at people both physically and psychologically and prevents them from accepting the reality of the death of a loved one. We are reminded of a woman who reported that she was overcome with emotions and could not stop crying at the funeral of an acquaintance. What surprised her was the way her reaction contrasted with her "strength and composure" over the death of her husband. What she did not realize was that she had not allowed herself to grieve over the loss of her husband and that years later she was having a delayed grief reaction.

Allowing Yourself to Grieve

Grief is a psychologically necessary and natural process after a significant loss. However, the norms in many cultures make it very difficult for people to experience a complete grief process after they have suffered a loss. For example, in our society there appears to be a cultural norm that fosters an expectation of a "quick cure," closure, and a focus on how long it is taking some people to "get back to normal." As is the case with any unexpressed emotion, unresolved grief lingers in the background and prevents people from letting go of losses and from forming new relationships. Also, unresolved grief is considered a key factor in the onset of a variety of somatic complaints and physical illnesses. They may experience psychological and behavioral difficulties, yet seldom recognize that these symptoms are related to a loss (Freeman, 2005).

Most writers on the psychological aspects of death and loss agree that grieving is necessary. Only by working through grief, by dealing with a loss both emotionally and intellectually, can bereaved individuals make their way back to the living world of hope and love (Hales, 2005). Although people may successfully work through their feelings pertaining to loss, it can be expected that the loss may always be with them. In successful grieving, however, people are not immobilized by the loss, nor do they close themselves off from other involvements. Another commonality in all these theories is that they recognize that not all people go through the grieving process at the same rate, nor do all people move neatly and predictably from one stage to another. Some writers emphasize that there is no correct way to grieve, implying that the grief process assumes many forms and faces (Freeman, 2005).

Earlier we described the task model of coping with dying, and in a like manner, a task model can be applied to working through intense grieving. Many researchers have begun to pay more attention to the various *tasks* associated with bereavement, some of which include being able to verbalize what happened to their loved one, visiting the grave site, and being able to reminisce about past memories (Abeles, Victor, & Delano-Wood, 2004). Worden (2002) proposes thinking of mourning in terms of four tasks to be accomplished:

1. *Accept the reality of the loss.* Before mourning can begin, the death of a person needs to be faced. Accepting this loss needs to be done both intellectually and emotionally. For many there will be a time lag before they are able to experience the emotional impact of the reality of a loss.

2. *Work through the pain of grief.* When the bereaved accept the reality of their loss, pain usually follows. Those in mourning need to experience and express the emotional pain of a loss and at the same time learn to nurture themselves both physically and emotionally.

3. *Adjust to an environment in which the deceased is missing.* Learning to develop a new relationship with the deceased is a gradual and unfolding process.

Although the bereaved do not have to let go of all ties to the person who has died, it is important to say good-bye and to grieve the loss.

4. *Emotionally relocate the deceased and move on with life.* Mourners eventually need to develop a new sense of identity based on a life without the deceased. This task involves restructuring the relationship with the deceased in a way that is satisfying but that also reflects the changed circumstances of life and death.

In writing about bereavement associated with the death of one's spouse, Kaslow (2004) identifies these tasks associated with the healing process: relinquishing roles, forming a new identity, assuming control and responsibility for one's life, forgiving the loved one for dying, finding new meaning in life, and renewing hope. Worden (2002) maintains that those who are mourning must accomplish these tasks before their mourning can be completed. These tasks in mourning reflect a proactive stance in managing one's loss and grief. Although these tasks require effort, this effort on the part of the grieving person can be instrumental in gaining increased control over his or her life.

A chronic state of depression and a restricted range of feelings suffered by some people are often attributed to some unresolved reaction to a significant loss. Such individuals seem to fear that the pain will consume them and that it is better to shut off feelings. What they fail to realize is that there is a consequence for this denial in the long run. This consequence can lead to the inability to feel closeness and joy. These people can go on for years without ever expressing emotions over their loss, being convinced that they have adequately dealt with it. Yet they might find themselves being flooded with emotions for which they have no explanation. They may discover that another's loss opens up old wounds for them, wounds they thought they had successfully healed.

My (Marianne's) father died 17 years ago. Although I grieved his death and found support from my friends and family, I find that even years later there are times when I am flooded with emotions of sadness over his loss. Sometimes these emotions take me by surprise, and I do not always know what triggered them. On several occasions when I felt the sadness, I realized afterward that it was a particular anniversary date that had to do with his life and death. My unconscious was more in tune than was my conscious mind. Sometimes people who have lost a loved one expect to complete their grieving in a set time, such as 1 year. It is important to realize that there is no predictable schedule. Instead, people who are grieving need to experience their sadness and not tell themselves that they should be over this by now. Freeman (2005) puts this matter well when he writes:

> GRIEF AND MOURNING ARE UNIQUELY INDIVIDUAL PROCESSES, and no one has the correct timetable for their completion. The process of healing might take a year, or it might take a lifetime. Whatever the time, the bereaved should not travel alone. (p. 74)

Cultural Differences on Grieving

Most cultures have rituals designed to help people with the grieving process. Examples are the funeral practices of the Irish, the Jewish, the Russians, and others, whereby painful feelings are actually triggered and released. Many cultures have a formal mourning period (usually a year), and in these cultures the mourners are directly involved in the funeral process. In the United States those who suffer from a loss are typically "protected" from any direct involvement in the burial, and people are often praised for not displaying overt signs of grief. Many of our rituals make it easy for us to deny our feelings of loss and therefore keep us from coming to terms with the reality of that loss. It has become clear that practices that include denial are not genuinely helpful. Today, increasing emphasis is being placed on providing ways for people to participate more directly in the dying process of their loved ones (such as the hospice movement) and in the funeral process as well.

If you are experiencing bereavement and are able to express the full range of your thoughts and feelings, you stand a better chance of adjusting to a new environment. Indeed, part of the grief process involves making basic life changes and experiencing new growth. If you have gone through the necessary cycle of bereavement, you will be better equipped to become reinvested with a new purpose and a new reason for living. What major losses have you had, and how have you coped with them? Have you lost a family member, a close friendship, a job that you valued, a spouse through divorce, a material object that had special meaning, a place where you once lived, a pet, or your faith in some person or group? Are there any similarities in how you responded to these different types of loss? Did you successfully work through your feelings about the losses? Or did you allow yourself to express your feelings to someone close to you? In recalling a particular loss, are the feelings still as intense as they were then?

In learning to resolve grief, regardless of its source, people need to be able to talk about what they are telling themselves internally and what they are feeling. They may eventually face up to the fact that there is no rational reason that will explain their loss.

Stages of Grief Over a Divorce or a Significant Loss

The five stages of dying described by Kübler-Ross can also be applied in understanding other significant losses. To illustrate, we describe a divorce in terms of the five stages. Of course, you can broaden this concept to see whether it applies to separation from your parents, the experience of breaking up with a girlfriend or boyfriend, or the process of seeing your children mature and leave home. The stages can also provide understanding of the process you go through after losing a job and face the anxieties of unemployment. Although not all people who experience divorce, the breakup of a long-term relationship, or some other loss necessarily go through the stages in the same way, we have found that many people do experience a similar questioning and struggling.

Denial Many people who are divorcing go through a process of denial and self-deception. They may try to convince themselves that their marriage is not all that bad, that nobody is perfect, and that things would be worse if they did separate. Even after the decision is made to divorce, they may feel a sense of disbelief. If it was the other person who initiated the divorce, the remaining partner might ask: "Where did things go wrong? Why is she [he] doing this to me? How can this be happening to me?"

Anger Once people accept the reality that they are divorcing, they frequently experience anger and rage. They may say: "I gave a lot, and now I'm being deserted. I feel as if I've been used and then thrown away." Many people feel cheated and angry over the apparent injustice of what is happening to them. Just as it is very important for dying people to express any anger they feel, it is also important for people who are going through the grief associated with a divorce or other loss to express their anger. If they keep it bottled up inside, it is likely to be turned against them and may take the form of depression, a kind of self-punishment.

Bargaining Sometimes people hope that a separation will give them the distance they need to reevaluate things and that they will soon get back together again. Although separations sometimes work this way, it is often futile to wish that matters can be worked out. Nevertheless, during the bargaining stage one or both partners may try to make concessions and compromises that they hope will lead to reconciliation.

Depression In the aftermath of a decision to divorce, a sense of hopelessness may set in. As the partners realize that reconciliation is not possible, they may begin to dwell on the emptiness and loss they feel. They may find it very difficult to let go of the future they had envisioned together. They may spend much time ruminating over what their lives might have been like if they had made their relationship work. It is not uncommon for people who divorce to turn their anger away from their spouse and toward themselves. Thus they may experience much self-blame and self-doubt. They may say to themselves: "Maybe I didn't give our relationship a fair chance. What could I have done differently? I wonder where I went wrong? Why couldn't I do something different to make our relationship work?" Depression can also be the result of the recognition that a real loss has been sustained. It is vitally important that people fully experience and express the grief (and anger) they feel over their loss. Too often people deceive themselves into believing that they are finished with their sadness (or anger) long before they have given vent to their intense feelings. Unresolved grief (and anger) tends to be carried around with a person, blocking the expression of many other feelings. For instance, if grief isn't worked through, it may be extremely difficult for a person to form new relationships, because in some ways he or she is still holding on to the past relationship. It is important to note that grief work is not limited to expressing and working through feelings. Grief entails exploring the cognitive dimension; many people experience problems because they do not challenge some of their beliefs about a loss. Dealing with grief needs to be done on both a cognitive and an emotional level.

Acceptance   If people allow themselves to mourn their losses, the process of grief work usually leads to a stage of acceptance. In the case of divorce, once the two persons have finished their grieving, new possibilities begin to open up. They can begin to accept that they must make a life for themselves without the other person and that they cannot cling to resentments that will keep them from beginning to establish that life. They can learn from their experience and apply that knowledge to future events.

In summary, these stages are experienced in different ways by each person who faces a significant loss. Some people, for example, express very little anger; others may not go through a bargaining stage. Nevertheless, the value of a model such as this one is that it provides some understanding of how we can learn to cope with the various losses in our lives. Whatever the loss may be and whatever stage of grieving we may be experiencing, it seems to be crucial that we freely express our feelings. Otherwise, we may not be able to achieve acceptance.

BEING "DEAD" PSYCHOLOGICALLY AND SOCIALLY

We find it valuable to use the metaphor of death in dealing with the notion of being "dead" in a variety of psychological and social ways. What is dead or dying in us may be something we want to take a look at.

Sometimes being alive requires letting go of old and familiar ways of being that we may need to mourn before we can really move on. An example might be when you let go of the security of living with your parents in exchange for testing your independence by living alone and supporting yourself. In the process you may have lost something that was valuable to you, even if it was incompatible with your further development and growth. The following questions may help you understand some of the potentially dead areas of your life.

Are You Caught Up in Deadening Roles?

Our roles and rituals can eventually trap us. Instead of fulfilling certain roles while maintaining a separate sense of identity, we may get lost in our roles and in the patterns of thought, feeling, and behavior that go with them. As a result, we may neglect important aspects of ourselves, limiting our options of feeling and experiencing. We may feel lost when we are unable to play a certain role: a supervisor may not know how to behave when he or she is not in a superior position to others, an instructor may be at loose ends when there are no students to teach, or a parent may find life empty when the children have grown.

Do you see yourself living by certain routines and roles? Is today a copy of yesterday? Do you depend on being able to identify with those roles to feel alive and valuable? Have you made the mistake of believing that who you are is expressed by a single role, no matter how much you value that role? What if your roles were taken away one by one? Could you find other ways of being and thinking? At this time in your life you might find that you are so caught up in the student role that you have little time or energy left for other dimensions of your life. When roles begin to deaden us, we can ask whether we have taken on a function or identity that others have defined instead of listening to our own inner promptings.

Are You Alive to Your Senses and Your Body?

Your body expresses to a large degree how alive you are. It shows signs of your vitality or reveals your tiredness with life. Use your body as an indication of the degree to which you are affirming life. As you look at your body, ask yourself these questions: "Do I like what I see? Am I taking good care of myself physically? What am I expressing by my posture? What does my facial expression communicate?"

Ask yourself if you are alive to your senses. Perhaps you rarely stop to notice the details of your surroundings. If you take time to be alive to your senses, you will feel renewed and interested in life. Ask yourself, "What sensations have particularly struck me today? What have I experienced and observed? What sensory surprises have enlivened me?"

Nhat Hanh (1992) reminds us that a simple truth that we know intellectually is that our final destination is the cemetery. So, why are we in a hurry to get there? He suggests that learning the art of mindful living involves moving in the direction of life by fully savoring the present moment. Most of Nhat Hanh's books contain simple but profound thoughts on how to be alive to our senses and how to take in and fully appreciate the beauty in nature. Ask yourself: "Am I willing to slow down and embrace life by being in tune with my senses?"

Can You Be Spontaneous and Playful?

Can you be playful, fun, curious, explorative, and spontaneous? Even as adults we can continue to be playful. Humor shakes us out of our patterned ways and promotes new perspectives. If you find that you are typically realistic and objective to the point that it is difficult for you to be playful or light, you might ask what inner messages are blocking your ability to let go. Are you inhibited by a fear of

Are you alive to your senses
and your body?

© Corbis

being wrong? Are you afraid of being called silly or of meeting with others' disapproval? If you want to, you can begin to challenge the messages that say: "Don't!" "You should!" "You shouldn't!" You can experiment with new behavior and run the risk of seeming silly or of "not acting your age."

Are You Alive to Your Feelings?

We can numb ourselves to most of our feelings, joyful or painful. We can decide that feeling involves the risk of pain. In choosing to cut off one feeling, we might be cutting off other feelings. Closing ourselves to our lows usually means closing ourselves to our highs as well.

Because of the ways we sometimes insulate ourselves, we may find it difficult to recognize our flat emotional state. To begin assessing how alive you are emotionally, ask yourself these questions:

- Do I let myself feel my sadness and grieve over a loss?
- Do I try hard to cheer people up when they are sad instead of allowing them to experience their feelings?
- Do I let myself cry if I feel like crying?
- Am I ever ecstatic?
- How many people have I let myself get close to in my life?
- Do I suppress certain emotions—insecurity, fear, dependence, tenderness, and anger?

Are Your Relationships Alive?

Our relationships with the significant people in our lives can lose a sense of vitality. It is easy to become set in routine ways of being with another person and to lose any sense of surprise and spontaneity. Long-term relationships are vulnerable to this kind of predictability. Breaking out of routine patterns in relationships takes conscious effort and can be anxiety provoking. Look at the significant relationships in your life and think about how alive both you and the other person is in each relationship. Does the relationship energize you, or does it drain you? Are you settling into a comfortable relationship at the expense of a dynamic relationship? If you recognize that you are not getting what you want in your friendships or intimate relationships, ask what you are willing to do to revitalize them. Focus on how you can change yourself rather than how you can change another. Consider what specific things you would like to ask from the other person. Simply talking about relationships can do a lot to bring new life into them.

Are You Alive Intellectually?

Children typically display much curiosity about life, but this is often time lost as they grow older. By the time we reach adulthood, we can easily become caught up in our activities, devoting little time to considering why we are doing them and whether we even want to be doing them.

Assess the degree to which you keep yourself intellectually active in your classes. In the initial chapter we focused on ways to integrate mental and emotional dimensions of learning. One way of keeping mentally alert is by reflecting on how you can apply whatever you are learning in your classes to your personal development. How might you apply the notion of staying intellectually alive as a student? Have you given up on asking any real and substantive questions that you would like to explore? Have you settled for merely going to classes and collecting the units you need to obtain a degree? Are you open to learning new things? Are you changing as a learner?

Are You Alive Spiritually?

There is growing empirical evidence that people's spiritual values and behaviors can promote physical and psychological coping, healing, and well-being (Miller, 1999). This finding has led many health practitioners and those in the counseling profession to conclude that an individual's spiritual values should be viewed as a potential resource in the healing process rather than as something to be ignored (Richards, Rector, & Tjeltveit, 1999). Religious beliefs and practices affect many dimensions of human experience, including how to handle guilt feelings, authority, and moral questions, to name a few. To what degree do your spiritual beliefs enhance your life?

As a healer, Bernie Siegel (1988) views spirituality as encompassing the belief in some meaning or order in the universe. From his perspective, there is a loving and intelligent force behind creation. Regardless of what label is used for this force, contact with it allows us the possibility of finding peace and resolving seeming contradictions between the inner world and the outer. How do you define spirituality for yourself? What moral, ethical, or spiritual values guide your life? Whether you belong to an organized religious group or simply contemplate the beauty of the natural world, you are on a spiritual quest. Take time to reflect on this aspect of your life.

Take Time to Reflect

1. How alive do you feel psychologically and socially? When do you feel the most alive?

_____

_____

2. When do you feel the least energy and vitality?

_____

_____

3. What specific things would you most like to change about your life? What can you do to make these changes?

_____

_____

HOW WELL ARE YOU LIVING LIFE?

Some people may never really take the time to evaluate how they live. Are you one of those who has gotten lost in the routine of daily existence to the extent that you do not take time to assess the quality of your living? Imagine that you are told that you have only a limited time to live. You begin to look at what you have missed and how you wish things had been different; you begin to experience regrets over the opportunities that you let slip by; you review the significant turning points in your life. You may wish now that you had paused to take stock at many points in your life, instead of waiting until it was too late.

One way to take stock of your life is to imagine your own death, including the details of the funeral and the things people might say about you. Try actually writing down your own eulogy or obituary. This can be a powerful way of summing up how you see your life and how you would like it to be different. In fact, we suggest that you try writing three eulogies for yourself. First, write your actual eulogy—the one you would give at your own funeral, if that were possible. Second, write the eulogy that you fear—one that expresses some of the negative things someone could say of you. Third, write the eulogy that you would hope for—one that expresses the most positive aspects of your life so far. After you have written your three eulogies, write down in your journal what the experience was like for you and what you learned from it. Are there any specific steps you would like to take now to begin living more fully? Reflect on how you might live your life today to bring about your hoped-for eulogy. As an additional step, consider sealing your eulogies in an envelope and putting them away for a year or so. Then, at this later date, do the exercise again and compare the two sets of eulogies to see what changes have occurred in your view of your life.

Before he died 30 years ago, Jim Morelock gave me (Jerry) a poster showing a man walking in the forest with two small girls. At the top of the poster were the words "TAKE TIME." Jim knew me well enough to know how I tend to get caught up in so many activities that I sometimes forget to simply take time to really experience and enjoy the simple things in life. You have been challenged to complete the Take Time to Reflect exercises throughout this book. If you have taken the time for yourself, you should have a good idea of what your life is like now. What can you do today to ensure that you will live the life you want?

SUMMARY

In this chapter we have encouraged you to devote some time to reflecting on your eventual death. Doing so can help you examine the quality and direction of your life and help you find your own meaning in life. The acceptance of death is closely related to the acceptance of life. Recognizing and accepting the fact of death gives us the impetus to search for our own answers to questions like these: "What is the meaning of my life?" "What do I most want from life?" "How can I create the life I want to live?"

Although terminally ill people show great variability in how they deal with their dying, a general pattern of stages has been identified: denial, anger, bargaining, depression, and acceptance. These same stages can apply to other types of loss, such as separation and divorce. Alternative models explaining how people cope with dying place emphasis on tasks to be accomplished. Both the stage model and the task model of coping with dying can also be applied to people who are working through grief over a significant loss. In dealing with losses, grieving is necessary. Unless we express and explore feelings of sorrow, anger, and guilt over our losses, we are not likely to move on with life.

If we can honestly confront the reality of death, we can change the quality of our lives and make real changes in our relationships with others and with ourselves. We often live as though we had forever to accomplish what we want. Few of us ever contemplate that this may be the last day we have. The realization that there is an end to life can motivate us to get the most from the time we have. The fact of our finality can also be an impetus toward fulfilling our unmet goals. Thus it is crucial that we live in a manner that will lead to few regrets. The more we fail to deal with immediate realities, the greater the likelihood that we will fear death.

Where Can I Go From Here?

1. For at least a week take a few minutes each day to reflect on when you feel most alive and when you feel most "dead." Do you notice any trends in your observations?

2. If you knew you were going to die soon, in what ways would you live your life differently? What might you give up?

3. Imagine you are on your deathbed. Who would you want to be there? What would you want them to say to you, and what would you want to say to them?

4. For about a week write down specific things you see, read, or hear relating to practices of dealing with death in our culture.

5. Let yourself reflect on how the death of those you love might affect you. Consider each person separately, and try to imagine how your life today would be different if that person were not in it. Write these impressions in your journal.

6. Investigate what type of hospice program, if any, your community has. Who is on the staff? What services does it offer? If you are interested in learning more about hospice services, or to identify a local hospice program, call the Hospice Helpline at (800) 658-8898, or contact the National Hospice Organization, 1901 N. Moore Street, Suite 901, Arlington, VA 22209 (telephone: 703-243-5900).

Resources for Future Study

Web Site Resource

SUICIDE . . . READ THIS FIRST
http://www.metanoia.org/suicide/

This site is for those who are dealing with suicidal issues in themselves or others. This site speaks straight to the issue and guides readers through a thoughtful series of steps to resolve their issues. Suicide and suicidal feelings are dealt with including helpful resources and links for more information.

This resource provides guidelines for online help and raises questions such as: How serious is our condition? Why is it so hard for us to recover from being suicidal? Also provided are practical suggestions in helping someone who may be suicidal, online sources of help, and some useful suggested reading.

InfoTrac College Edition Resources

For additional readings, explore INFOTRAC COLLEGE EDITION, our online library:
http://www.infotrac.college.com/wadsworth

Hint: Enter these search terms:

dying

death AND dying

stages of dying

hospice

bereavement

grief work

suicide

suicide prevention

rational suicide

physician-assisted suicide

advance directive

Print Resources

Albom, M. (1997). *Tuesdays with Morrie.* New York: Doubleday.

Capuzzi, D. (Ed.). (2004). *Suicide across the life span: Implications for counselors.* Alexandria, VA: American Counseling Association.

Corr, C. A., Nabe, C. M., & Corr, D. M. (2003). *Death and dying, life and living* (4th ed.). Belmont, CA: Wadsworth.

Freeman. S. J. (2005). *Grief and loss: Understanding the journey.* Belmont, CA: Brooks/Cole.

Kübler-Ross, E. (1969). *On death and dying.* New York: Macmillan.

Marcus, E. (1996). *Why suicide? Answers to 200 of the most frequently asked questions about suicide, attempted suicide, and assisted suicide.* San Francisco: HarperCollins.

Siegel, B. (1988). *Love, medicine, and miracles.* New York: Harper & Row (Perennial Library).

Siegel, B. (1989). *Peace, love, and healing. Bodymind communication and the path to self-healing: An exploration.* New York: Harper & Row.

13

We need to develop the ability to listen to our inner selves and trust what we hear.

Meaning and Values

© PhotoDisc/Getty Images

Where Am I Now?

Use this scale to respond to these statements:

3 = This statement is true of me *most* of the time.

2 = This statement is true of me *some* of the time.

1 = This statement is true of me *almost none* of the time.

___ 1. At this time in my life I have a sense of meaning and purpose.

___ 2. Most of my values are similar to those of my parents.

___ 3. I have challenged and questioned most of the values I now hold.

___ 4. Religion/spirituality is an important source of meaning for me.

___ 5. I'm generally faithful to my values.

___ 6. My values and my views about life's meaning have undergone much change over the years.

___ 7. The meaning of my life is based in large part on my ability to have a significant impact on others.

___ 8. I let others influence my values more than I would like to admit.

___ 9. I am willing to reflect on my own biases and prejudices and to challenge them.

___ 10. I welcome diversity more than being threatened by it.

I n this chapter we encourage you to look critically at the why of your existence, to clarify the sources of your values, and to reflect on questions such as these: "Where have I been, where am I now, and where do I want to go?" "What steps can I take to make the changes I have decided on?" Our quest for meaning involves asking three key existential questions, none of which have easy or absolute answers: "Who am I?" "Where am I going?" "Why?"

"Who am I?" is a question that will be answered differently at different times in our lives. When our values no longer seem to supply meaning or give us direction, we are faced with the choice of a deadening existence or creating a new of way of life. You must decide whether you are going to allow others to define you or whether you will redefine yourself based on the values of your choosing.

"Where am I going?" questions our plans for a lifetime. What process do we expect to use to attain our goals? Like the previous question, this one demands periodic review as life goals are rarely set once and for all.

Asking "Why?" and searching for understanding is a human characteristic. We face a rapidly changing world in which earlier values give way to new ones or to none at all. Part of the quest for meaning requires an active search to make sense of the world in which we find ourselves.

Many who achieve power, fame, success, and material comfort nevertheless experience a sense of emptiness. Although they may not be able to articulate what is lacking in their lives, they know that something is amiss. The astronomical number of pills and drugs humans consume to allay the symptoms of this "existential vacuum"—depression and anxiety—is evidence of our failure to find values that enable us to make sense of our place in the world.

The need for a sense of meaning is manifested by an increased interest in spirituality and religion, especially among young people in college. A student told us that in her English class of 20 students 4 of them had selected religion as a topic for a composition dealing with a conflict in their lives. Other signs of the search for meaning include the widespread interest in Eastern and other philosophies, the use of meditation, the number of self-help and inspirational books published each year, experimentation with different lifestyles, and even the college courses in personal growth.

OUR QUEST FOR IDENTITY

Achieving personal identity does not necessarily mean stubbornly clinging to a certain way of thinking or behaving. Instead, it may involve trusting ourselves enough to become open to new possibilities. We are challenged to reexamine our patterns and our priorities, our habits and our relationships. Above all, we need to develop the ability to listen to our inner selves and trust what we hear. In this way we can come to define the core values that shape us.

Values are core beliefs that influence how we act. To make true choices, we must examine the sources of our values and the extent to which they are enhancing our life. If we have questioned our values, and they fit for who we are, there is a greater chance that we will live in harmony with these values.

Sometimes we may decide to go against our cultural upbringing to create an identity that is congruent with our own values. This was true for Jenny, a Vietnamese woman who developed a different set of values from her mother.

JENNY'S STORY

*T*here were many instances when I wanted to be alone or to take time off from work to relax. There would be an attack of accusatory statements indicating that I was selfish, that I was wasting too much time on myself, and that I wasn't devoting enough time to my family obligations. Even the way I spent my money was met with criticism, because I did not save it for a better cause like my family. I spent many hours explaining to my mother about how much it meant to me to buy myself nice things and to spend some of my time enjoying life. In the eyes of my mother and her culture, I was the selfish one. I had to understand this perspective and edit it to my own values.

Pause now and assess how you experience your identity at this time in your life. This Take Time to Reflect exercise may help you do so.

Take Time to Reflect

I. What are some of your key values? To identify some of your values, rate the importance of each of these items using this scale:

3 = This is *extremely important* to me.
2 = This is *somewhat important* to me.
1 = This is *not important* to me.

_____ A relationship with God
_____ Loving others and being loved
_____ Enjoying an intimate relationship
_____ Engaging in recreation
_____ Family life

_____ Security
_____ Courage
_____ Work and career
_____ Laughter and a sense of humor
_____ Intelligence and curiosity
_____ Being open to different cultures and experiences
_____ Taking risks in order to change
_____ Being of service to others
_____ Making a difference in the lives of others
_____ Appreciating nature
_____ Independence and self-determination
_____ Interdependence and cooperation
_____ Having control of my life
_____ Being financially successful
_____ Having solitude and time to reflect
_____ Being productive and achieving
_____ Being approved of by others
_____ Facing challenges
_____ Compassion and caring
_____ Engaging in competition

Look over the items you rated as "3" (extremely important). If you had to select the top three values in your life, which would they be?

_____

_____

2. How are these three values a part of your everyday life?

_____

_____

3. How often do you experience each of the things you have just listed? What prevents you from doing the things you value as frequently as you would like?

_____

_____

4. What are some specific actions you can take to add meaning to your life?

_____

_____

5. Who are you? Try completing the sentence "I am . . ." six different ways by quickly writing down the words or phrases that immediately occur to you.

I am _____

I am _____

I am _____

I am _____

I am _____

I am _____

OUR SEARCH FOR MEANING AND PURPOSE

We are the only creatures we know of who can reflect on our existence and, based on this capacity for self-awareness, exercise individual choice in defining our lives. With this freedom, however, comes responsibility and a degree of anxiety. If we truly accept that the meaning of our lives is largely the product of our own choosing—and that the emptiness of our lives is the result of our failure to choose—our anxiety is increased. To avoid this anxiety, we may refuse to examine the values that govern our daily behavior or to accept that we are, to a large degree, what we have chosen to become. Instead, we may make other people or outside institutions primarily responsible for our direction in life.

In *Tuesdays With Morrie* (Albom, 1997) the dying Morrie shared a gem worth reflecting upon: "Learn how to die, and you learn how to live" (p. 83). Morrie makes some perceptive comments that go to the heart of finding purpose and meaning in life:

> SO MANY PEOPLE WALK AROUND with a meaningless life. They seem half asleep, even when they're busy doing things they think are important. This is because they're chasing the wrong things. The way you get meaning into your life is to devote yourself to loving others, devote yourself to community around you, and devote yourself to creating something that gives you purpose and meaning." (p. 43)

Morrie is not talking about making money or stockpiling material items. He is speaking to the necessity of finding a cause outside of yourself, giving to others, and striving to make the world a better place.

One obstacle in the way of finding meaning is that the world itself may appear meaningless. When we look at the absurdity of the world in which we live, it is easy to give up the struggle or to seek some authoritative source of meaning. Yet creating our own meaning is precisely our challenge as human beings.

Many clients who enter psychotherapy do so because they lack a clear sense of meaning and purpose in life. Yalom (1980) states the **crisis of meaninglessness** in its most basic form: "How does a being who needs meaning find meaning in a universe that has no meaning?" (p. 423). Along with Frankl (1963), Yalom concludes that humans require meaning to survive. To live without meaning and values provokes considerable distress, and in its most severe form may lead to the decision for suicide. We need clear ideals to which we can aspire and guidelines by which we can direct our actions.

Viktor Frankl, a European psychiatrist, dedicated his professional life to the study of meaning in life. The approach to therapy that he developed is known as **logotherapy,** which means "therapy through meaning" or "healing through meaning." According to Frankl (1963, 1965, 1969, 1978), what distinguishes us as humans is our search for purpose. The striving to find meaning in our lives is a primary motivational force. Humans choose to live and even to die for the sake of their ideals and values. Frankl (1963) notes that "everything can be taken from a man but one thing: the last of the human freedoms—to choose one's attitude in any given set of circumstances, to choose one's own way" (p. 104). Frankl points out the wisdom of Nietzsche's words: "He who has a why to live for can bear with almost any how" (as cited in Frankl, 1963, p. 164). Drawing on his experiences in the death camp at Auschwitz, Frankl asserts that inmates who had a vision of some goal, purpose, or task in life had a much greater chance of surviving than those who had no sense of mission. We are constantly confronted with choices, and the decisions we make or fail to make influence the meaning of our lives.

This relationship between choice and meaning is dramatically illustrated by Holocaust survivors who report that although they did not choose their circumstances they could at least choose their attitude toward their plight. Consider the example of Dr. Edith Eva Eger, a clinical psychologist, who was interviewed about her experiences as a survivor of a Nazi concentration camp (see Glionna, 1992). At one point, Eger weighed only 40 pounds, yet she refused to engage in the cannibalism that was taking place. She said, "I chose to eat grass. And I sat on the ground, selecting one blade over the other, telling myself that even under those conditions I still had a choice—which blade of grass I would eat." Although Eger lost her family to the camps and had her back broken by one of the guards, she eventually chose to let go of her hatred. She finally came to the realization that it was her captors who were the imprisoned ones. As she put it: "If I still hated today, I would still be in prison. I would be giving

Hitler and Mengele their posthumous victories. If I hated, they would still be in charge, not me." Her example supports the notion that even in the most dire situations it is possible to give a new meaning to such circumstances by our choice of attitudes.

Sometimes our choices are stripped from us, as in the extreme cases illustrated by Viktor Frankl and Edith Eger. In a like manner, Francis Bok (2003), in his very moving book, *Escape From Slavery*, tells his story of his village in the Sudan being pillaged and his being taken as a slave for many years. He reports his childhood horrifying experiences with near death and his attempts to escape, only to be captured. His father told Bok that he was special and that he would always do something important in life. His father's faith in him inspired him to never give up hope and to continue to struggle even in extreme circumstances. Bok found ways to avoid totally surrendering, even though almost all of his freedoms were taken from him. With his attitude and constant thoughts of escaping from slavery, Bok was able to retain some degree of control over his life. Although a couple of his attempts at escaping almost resulted in his death, he finally did escape his bondage because of his hope and the risks he took. Since that time he has devoted his life to doing whatever he could to inform people in the United States about the trials of the Sudanese people. At 23 years old, Bok is an associate at the Boston-based American Antislavery group. In 2000 he became the first escaped slave to testify before the Senate Committee on Foreign Relations in hearings on Sudan. He speaks throughout the United States, has been featured in magazines and television, and met with President George W. Bush at the White House. Francis Bok's story illustrates how he was able to find meaning at a very desperate time in his life and how his work today is motivated by giving meaning to his earlier experiences. He is an example of a person who is making a significant difference by what he is choosing to do with his life.

Many of us find meaning by striving to make a difference in the world. We want to know that we have touched the lives of others and that somehow we have contributed to helping others live more fully. Although self-acceptance is a prerequisite for meaningful interpersonal relationships, there is a quest to go beyond self-centered interests. Ultimately, we want to establish connections with others in society, and we want to make a contribution. This notion is captured by Alfred Adler's concept of social interest, which was addressed in Chapter 1.

Bellah and his colleagues (1985) conclude that meaning in life is found through intense relationships with others rather than through an exclusive and narrow pursuit of self-realization. In their interviews, many people expressed a desire to move beyond the isolated self. Healthy relationships are two-sided transactions characterized by reciprocal giving and taking. Sacrificing yourself, without getting anything in return, is not the way to achieve a meaningful life. We must find a balance in our concern for ourselves and our desire to further the interests of the community.

Meaning in life is found in relationships with others.

© PhotoDisc/Getty Images

THE FOUNDATIONS OF MEANING

What Is the Meaning of Life?

In 1988 the editors of *Life* magazine asked a wide spectrum of people from all walks of life the question "What is the meaning of life?" David Friend's (1991) *The Meaning of Life* is the product of 300 thoughtful people. This mosaic of responses offers a variety of approaches to understanding life. As you read, think about the responses that resonate most closely with your own values.

• "We believe that we are in fact the image of our Creator. Our response must be to live up to that amazing potential—to give God glory by reflecting His beauty and His love. That is why we are here and that is the purpose of our lives" (South African civil rights leader, Archbishop Desmond Tutu, p. 13).

• "The meaning of life is to live in balance and harmony with every other living thing in creation. We must all strive to understand the interconnectedness of all living things and accept our individual role in the protection and support of other life forms on earth. We must also understand our own insignificance in the totality of things" (Wilma Mankiller, Chief of the Cherokee Nation, p. 13).

- "It's my belief that the meaning of life changes from day to day, second to second. We're here to learn that we can create a world and that we have a choice in what we create, and that our world, if we choose, can be a heaven or hell" (Thomas E. O'Connor, AIDS activist and lecturer, p. 20).

- "Since age two I've been waltzing up and down with the question of life's meaning. And I am obliged to report that the answer changes from week to week. When I know the answer, I know it absolutely; as soon as I know that I know it, I know that I know nothing. About seventy percent of the time my conclusion is that there is a grand design" (Maya Angelou, writer and actress, p. 20).

- "I believe we as humans have the great challenge of living in harmony with the planet and all its parts. If we achieve that harmony we will have lived up to our fullest potential" (Molly Yard, feminist activist, p. 27).

- "I believe we are here to do good. It is the responsibility of every human being to aspire to do something worthwhile, to make this world a better place than the one he found. Life is a gift, and if we accept it, we must contribute in return. When we fail to contribute, we fail to adequately answer why we are here" (Armand Hammer, industrialist, physician, and self-made diplomat, p. 29).

- "While we exist as human beings, we are like tourists on holiday. If we play havoc and cause disturbance, our visit is meaningless. If during our short stay—100 years at most—we live peacefully, help others and, at the very least, refrain from harming or upsetting them, our visit is worthwhile" (Dalai Lama, spiritual leader of Tibetan Buddhism, p. 49).

- "The purpose of human life is to achieve our own spiritual evolution, to get rid of negativity, to establish harmony among our physical, emotional, intellectual and spiritual quadrants, to learn to live in harmony within the family, community, nation, the whole world and all living things, treating all of mankind as brothers and sisters—thus making it finally possible to have peace on earth" (Elisabeth Kübler-Ross, psychiatrist and author, p. 65).

What is the meaning of your life? How would you answer this complex question in a few brief sentences? To help you refine your answer, let's look at some of the dimensions of a philosophy of life.

Developing a Philosophy of Life

A **philosophy of life** is made up of the fundamental beliefs, attitudes, and values that govern a person's behavior. You may not have thought much about your philosophy of life, but the fact that you have never explicitly defined the components of your philosophy does not mean you are completely without one. All of us operate on the basis of general assumptions about ourselves, others, and the world. The first step in actively developing a philosophy of life is to formulate a clearer picture of your present attitudes and beliefs.

We have all been developing an implicit philosophy of life since we first began to wonder about life and death, love and hate, joy and fear, and the nature of the universe. If we were fortunate, adults took time to engage in dialogue with us rather than discouraging us from asking questions and fostered our innate curiosity.

During the adolescent years, the process of questioning usually assumes new dimensions. Adolescents who have been encouraged to question and to think for themselves as children begin to get involved in a more advanced set of issues. Many adolescents struggle with these questions:

- Are the values I've believed in all these years the values I want to continue to live by?

- Where did I get my values? Are they still valid for me? Are there additional sources from which I can derive new values?

- Is there a God? What is the nature of the hereafter? What is my conception of a God? What does religion mean in my life? What kind of religion do I choose for myself? Does religion have any value for me?

- What do I base my ethical and moral decisions on? Peer group standards? Parental standards? The normative values of my society?

- What explains the inhumanity I see in the world?

- What kind of future do I want? What can I do to help create this kind of future?

A philosophy of life is not something we arrive at once and for all during our adolescent years. Developing our own philosophy of life continues as long as we live. As long as we remain curious and open to new learning, we can revise and rebuild our conceptions of the world. Life may have a particular meaning for us during adolescence, a new meaning during adulthood, and still another meaning as we reach old age. Indeed, if we do not remain open to basic changes in our views of life, we may find it difficult to adjust to changed circumstances. You may find the following suggestions helpful as you go about formulating and reforming your own philosophy:

- Create time to be alone in reflective thought.

- Consider what meaning the fact of your eventual death has for the present moment.

- Make use of significant contacts with others who are willing to challenge your beliefs and the degree to which you live by them.

- Adopt an accepting attitude toward those whose belief systems differ from yours and develop a willingness to test your own beliefs.

All of these suggestions require that you are willing to challenge yourself and the beliefs you hold. Keeping track of yourself can provide unexpected rewards.

Take Time to Reflect

Complete the following sentences by writing down the first responses that come to mind:

1. My parents have influenced my values by _____

2. Life is worth living because of _____

3. One thing that I most want to say about my life at this point is _____

4. If I could change one thing about my life at this point, it would be _____

5. If I had to answer the question "Who am I?" in a sentence, I'd say _____

6. What I like best about me is _____

7. I keep myself vital by _____

8. I am unique in that _____

9. When I think of my future, I _____

10. I feel discouraged about life when _____

11. My beliefs and values have been influenced by _____

12. I feel most powerful when _____

13. If I don't change, _____

14. I feel good about myself when _____

15. To me, the essence of a meaningful life is _____

16. I suffer from a sense of meaninglessness when _____

RELIGION/SPIRITUALITY AND MEANING

Religious faith, or some form of personal spirituality, can be a powerful source of meaning and purpose. For some, religion does not occupy a key place, yet a personal spirituality may be a central force. Spiritual values help many people make sense out of the universe and the purpose of our lives on this earth. Like any other potential source of meaning, religious faith or spirituality seems most authentic and valuable when it enables us to become as fully human as possible. It can help us get in touch with our own powers of thinking, feeling, deciding, willing, and acting.

In *The Art of Happiness: A Handbook for Living*, the Dalai Lama and Howard Cutler (1998) offer some thought-provoking ideas about basic spiritual values and the subject of religion:

- Religions are aimed at nourishing the human spirit.
- Diversity in religions can be celebrated, and it is important to respect and appreciate the value of the different major world religions.
- Religion can be used to help reduce conflict and suffering in the world, not as a source to divide people.
- Involvement in any religion can create a feeling of belonging and a caring connection with others.
- Religious beliefs can provide a deep sense of purpose and meaning in life. These beliefs can offer hope in the face of adversity and suffering and can offer a perspective when we are overwhelmed by life's problems.

However, the Dalai Lama acknowledges that the majority of people on this earth are nonbelievers in religion, and it is essential to help them become good and moral human beings without any religion. The ultimate goal of all religions is to produce better human beings who will demonstrate caring and acceptance of others.

The Dalai Lama (2001) teaches that religious beliefs are but one level of spirituality, and he talks about **basic spiritual values,** which include qualities of goodness, kindness, love, compassion, tolerance, forgiveness, human warmth, and caring. All religions have the same basic message in that they all advocate these basic human values. Love, compassion, and forgiveness are not luxuries, but are essential values for our survival. **Compassion,** an essential part of one's spiritual development, involves caring about another's suffering and doing something about it. Whether we are believers or nonbelievers, this kind of spirituality is essential. True spirituality results in making people calmer, happier, and more peaceful, and it is a mental attitude that can be practiced at any time. The Dalai Lama has consistently emphasized that inner discipline offers the foundation of a spiritual life, which is also the fundamental pathway to achieving happiness.

Mother Teresa, who became known to the world for her selfless work with the poor people in Calcutta, India, talks about compassion in action. She believes that God and compassion are one and the same. Much like the Dalai Lama, Mother Teresa views compassion as attempting to share and understand the suffering of people. Mother Teresa states: "Religion has nothing to do with compassion; it is our love for God that is the main thing because we have all

Religious beliefs can provide a deep sense of purpose and meaning in life.

been created for the sole purpose to love and be loved" (cited in Shield & Carlson, 1999, p. 181).

Rabbi Harold Kushner (cited in Shield & Carlson, 1999) believes that encountering God consists in doing the right thing. For Rabbi Kushner, we make room in our lives for God when we do things that make us truly human, such as helping the poor, working for social justice, and keeping in check our exaggerated sense of self-importance. The Dalai Lama, Mother Teresa, and Rabbi Kushner seem to agree that leading a religious life is characterized by action. Acting on our beliefs is what matters.

Andrew Harvey (cited in Shield & Carlson, 1999) writes that there are three ways in which we can have a relationship with the divine: through prayer, meditation, and service. It is essential to combine prayer (talking to God) with a simple daily practice of meditation (listening to God). But Harvey says that prayer and meditation are not enough. We need to put what we learn about divine love into practice through service to others. Harvey points to a common message from all the great figures—from Lao Tzu to Buddha to Confucius to Jesus—we must give our love to those around us. Harvey writes: "Prayer, meditation, and service, lived together, can engender the divine life if they are pursued with humility, reverence, and simplicity of heart" (p. 76).

At this point, what do you think is the heart of your spirituality or religion? Reflect on the following questions about your religion or your spirituality to determine whether it is a constructive force in your life:

- Is the way that I live my life congruent with my religion or spirituality?
- Does my religion or spirituality assist me in better understanding the meaning of life and death?
- Does my religion or spirituality allow acceptance for others who see the world differently from me?
- Does my religion or spirituality encourage me to put my beliefs into action?
- Does my religion or spirituality provide me with a sense of peace and serenity?
- Is my religious faith or value system something I actively chose or passively accepted?
- Do my core religious and spiritual values help me live life fully and treat others with respect and concern?
- Does my religion or spirituality help me integrate my experiences and make sense of the world?
- Does my religion or spirituality encourage me to exercise my freedom and to assume responsibility for the direction of my own life?
- Are my religious beliefs or spirituality helping me become more the person I would like to become?
- Does my religion or spirituality encourage me to question life and keep myself open to new learning?

As you take time for self-examination, how able are you to answer these questions in a way that is meaningful and satisfying to you? If you are honest with yourself, perhaps you will find that you have not critically evaluated the sources of your spiritual and religious beliefs. Although you may hesitate to question your belief system out of a fear of weakening or undermining your faith, the opposite might well be true; demonstrating the courage to question your beliefs and values might strengthen them. Increasing numbers of people seem to be deciding that a religious faith or a spiritual orientation is necessary if they are to find order and purpose in life.

For further reading on spirituality and religion, we recommend two books. In *For the Love of God: Handbook for the Spirit*, Benjamin Shield and Richard Carlson (1999) present an extraordinary group of teachers and thinkers sharing their thoughts and personal experiences of the divine. In Mother Teresa's (1997) little book, *In the Heart of the World*, a variety of thoughts, stories, and prayers provide useful sources of reflection.

OUR VALUES IN ACTION

Values for Our Daughters

When our daughters Heidi and Cindy were growing up, we hoped they would come to share these important values with us:

- Have a positive and significant impact on the people in their lives
- Be willing to take risks and make mistakes
- Form their own values rather than unquestioningly adopting ours
- Like and respect themselves and feel good about their abilities and talents
- Be open and trusting rather than fearful or suspicious
- Respect and care for others
- Continue to have fun as they grew older
- Be able to express their feelings and always feel free to come to us and share meaningful aspects of their lives
- Remain in touch with their power and refuse to surrender it
- Be independent and have the courage to be different from others if they want to be
- Have an interest in a religion that they freely chose
- Be proud of themselves, yet humble
- Respect the differences in others
- Not compromise their values and principles for material possessions
- Develop a flexible view of the world and be willing to modify their perspective based on new experiences
- Give back to the world by contributing to make it a better place to live in

Our daughters are now independent adults, yet they continue to value time with us and to invite us to be involved in their lives. Although their lives are not problem-free, they typically show a willingness to face and deal with their struggles and are succeeding in making significant choices for themselves. If you have children or expect to have children someday, you might pause to think about the values you would like them to develop, as well as the part you will need to play in offering them guidance.

Becoming Aware of How Your Values Operate

Your values influence what you do; your daily behavior is an expression of your basic values. We ask you to take time to examine the source of your values to determine if they are appropriate for you at this time in your life. Furthermore, it

© Heidi Jo Corey

We want to know that we have touched the lives of others and that somehow we have contributed to helping others live more fully.

is essential that you be aware of the significant impact your value system has on your relationships with others. In our view, it is not appropriate for you to push your values on others, to assume a judgmental stance toward those who have a different view, or to strive to convert others to adopt your perspective on life. Indeed, if you are secure in your values and basic beliefs, you will not be threatened by those who have a different set of beliefs and values.

In *God's Love Song*, Maier (1991) wonders how anyone can claim to have found the only way, not only for him- or herself but also for everyone else. As a minister, Sam Maier teaches that diversity shared is not only beautiful but also fosters understanding, caring, and the creation of community. He puts this message in a powerful and poetic way:

> IT IS HEARTENING TO FIND COMMUNITIES where the emphasis is placed upon each person having the opportunity to:
>
> - share what is vital and meaningful out of one's own experience;
> - listen to what is vital and meaningful to others;
> - not expect or demand that anyone else do it exactly the same way as oneself. (p. 3)

Reverend Maier's message is well worth contemplating. Although you might clarify a set of values that seem to work for you, we hope that you will respect the values of others that may be quite different from yours. One set of values is not right and the other wrong. The diversity of cultures, religions, and worldviews provides a tapestry of life that allows us the opportunity to embrace diverse paths toward meaning in life. Whatever your own values are, they can be further clarified and strengthened if you entertain open discussion of various viewpoints and cultivate a nonjudgmental attitude toward diversity. Ask yourself these questions:

- Where did I develop my values?
- Have I questioned my values?
- Do I have a need that everything remain the same and nothing changes?
- Are my values open to modification?
- Do I find a consistency between what I say I believe in and what I do?
- Do I feel so deeply committed to any of my values that I am likely to push my friends and family members to accept them?
- How would I communicate my values to others without imposing those values?
- Am I willing to accept people who hold different values?
- Do I avoid judging others even if they think, feel, or act in different ways from me?

Take Time to Reflect

1. At this time, what are some of the principal sources of meaning and purpose in your life?

_____

_____

2. Have there been occasions in your life when you have allowed other people or institutions to make key choices for you? If so, give a couple of examples.

_____

_____

3. What role, if any, does religion or spirituality play in your life?

_____

_____

4. If you were to create a new religion, what virtues and values would you include? What would be the vices and sins?

_____

_____

5. What are some of the values you would most like to see your children adopt?

_____

_____

EMBRACING DIVERSITY

Living in a multicultural society, we are a people with many diverse backgrounds. It is a challenge to learn to embrace and appreciate diversity rather than be threatened by it. Unless we are able to accept this challenge, we remain isolated and separate from one another.

One barrier to forming meaningful connections with others is the existence of negative attitudes toward those who are different from us. We sometimes choose to live in an **encapsulated world,** ignoring consideration of the diversity of worldviews different from our own and seeking support from those who think and value as we do. This narrowness prevents us from learning from those who may have a different worldview than our own, and it results in fewer options to participate fully in the human community. It also allows us to remain unchallenged in our own world.

Meaning in life can be found by paying attention to the common ground we all share and by becoming aware of universal themes that unite us in spite of our differences. In the early chapters of this book, we emphasized that a meaningful life is not lived alone but is the result of connectedness to others in love, work, and community. In accepting and understanding others, we discover deeper meanings in life. If we live in isolation, we are placing a barrier between ourselves and those who are different from us.

In this section we invite you to explore the costs of prejudice and discrimination—which grow out of fear and ignorance. We ask you to reflect on a philosophy of life that embraces understanding and acceptance of diverse worldviews. At times the phrase "tolerance for diversity" is used, which we think could carry a negative connotation of "putting up with diversity." This section deals more with understanding, accepting, embracing, respecting, and celebrating diversity. Too often people judge those who are different from them, rather than appreciating differences and recognizing that there is no one right way. Consider those attitudes and behaviors you are willing to change that will allow you to increasingly accept and respect others, whether they are like or different from you.

Stereotypes as Barriers to Understanding Others

A **stereotype** is a judgmental generalization applied to an individual without regard to his or her own uniqueness. Stereotypes create boundaries that prevent us from seeing our interconnectedness as members of the human race. This social isolation limits our capacity to experience the richness that can be part of diverse human relationships. Here are a few examples of stereotypes: "Men are unemotional and uncaring." "Lesbians hate men." "Asians are talented in mathematics." "Italians are emotional." "Most Irish are alcoholics." "Most old people are sad and lonely." "Women are passive." Stereotypes are very common in our society, partly because they make complex problems seem simple. But putting people in boxes is hardly treating them as individuals, and most of us would resist being categorized this way.

Prevailing assumptions are generally held onto tenaciously. Once people have made an assumption, they are mainly interested in whatever proves it. People are likely to call someone an "exception" rather than change a stereotype. For example, if you believe all men are "macho," you are likely to look for and find macho men. However, if you take on the challenge of examining this generalization, you will likely find many exceptions to a generalized view. If you become aware of making any unexamined assumptions or generalizations, look for evidence that will disconfirm the expectations you have about a particular group of people. Unless challenged, your stereotypes can keep you separate and prevent you from getting to know people who could enhance your life.

Vontress, Johnson, and Epp (1999) reject the tendency to stereotype people according to the ethnic, racial, or cultural groups into which they were born. Instead, they recognize that each of us is unique and that we share important concerns about life. The challenge is to move beyond the stereotypes and prejudices that set people apart and strive to understand each individual in his or her subjective world.

Think about stereotypes you may hold and reflect on ways that they serve as barriers in getting to know another person. Ask yourself how stereotypes get in your way of understanding people on an individual basis. How are you affected by having certain characteristics assigned to you based on your gender, sexual orientation, ethnicity, culture, religion, age, or ability? How does the act of placing a label on you or on others affect your relationships?

Once you become aware of stereotypes, explore where you acquired those beliefs. Did you get messages from your parents? From people in your community? From your friends? From your teachers? From your church? The chances

If we live in isolation, we are walling ourselves off from the possibilities of engaging in social interest.

© Joel Gordon

are that you have acquired stereotypes on a less than conscious level. Once you become aware of their existence, you can modify them and begin to act differently based on your new awareness and your revised perceptions.

What Can You Do to Better the World?

Some claim that the world is getting worse and that humanity is doomed. Even if you do not accept this premise, you might find some evidence for the need for bettering humanity. But where can we start? Bettering humanity may seem like an overwhelming task, but it is less staggering if we start with ourselves. It is easier to blame others for the ills of the world than to accept that we might be contributing to this malady. We might ask ourselves, "What am I doing, even in the smallest way, that contributes to the problems in our society? And what can I do to become part of the solution to these problems?"

Prejudice, discrimination, hatred, and intolerance, especially toward those who are different from us, are all paths toward an empty existence. **Prejudice,** a preconceived notion or opinion about someone, can be overt or covert. Prejudice refers to negative attitudes; **discrimination** refers to biased behavior (Matlin, 2004). People can be obvious and blatant about their particular prejudices, or they can hide them. Prejudice can be a very subtle thing, and it may occur outside of conscious awareness. **Unintentional racism,** such as believing that we are free of any traces of prejudice, can be as harmful as intentional racism (Ridley, 1995).

Becoming aware of our own subtle prejudice and unintentional racism is the first step toward change. Laughing at or being impatient with someone who has an accent, telling or laughing at racial jokes, speaking in generalities about a whole group of people as though they are all the same, and assuming that our culture is superior to any other are all signs of prejudice founded on racist attitudes. If you want to become more accepting of others, reflect on some of the ways you have acquired your beliefs about particular groups of people and begin to question the source of those beliefs.

Prejudice has negative consequences. For the victims, it results in acts of discrimination and oppression that keep them from participating fully in the mainstream of society. People often feel intimidated by differences, whether these are differences in skin color, lifestyle, or values embraced. At the root of prejudice is fear, low self-esteem, ignorance, and feelings of inferiority. Prejudice is a defense mechanism that protects individuals from facing undesirable aspects of themselves by projecting them onto others. Treating others in a demeaning way may give these people an illusion of superiority.

White Privilege

In discussing prejudice, discrimination, and oppression, we are often made aware of the negative impact on both its targets and those doing the discriminating and oppressing. Less often do we talk about the privileges that come with being a part of a group that does the discriminating. If racism in America puts people of color at a disadvantage, it is essential to recognize that **White privilege** puts Whites at an advantage. Although not all White people consciously discriminate against people of color, it is clear that Whites in general, especially White males, enjoy certain privileges. We are including this discussion here because we find this concept worthy of reflection. White people may feel guilty or react with defensiveness when their unearned privileges are pointed out. If you are White, we hope you will not quickly close your mind to what is implied by White privilege but consider carefully the degree of truth in this concept.

According to Peggy McIntosh (1998), a professor at Wellesley College, North American culture is based on the hidden assumption that being White is normative. This White-as-normative concept implies that White people have certain privileges that they generally take for granted. In *Overcoming Our Racism*, Derald Wing Sue (2003) defines White privilege as the unearned advantages and benefits that accrue to White people by virtue of a system normed on the values and perceptions of their group. Sue states: "White privilege automatically confers dominance, control, and power to White Americans, and on the other side, it automatically disempowers and oppresses people of color"

(p. 138). McIntosh (1988) describes White privilege as an invisible knapsack of unearned assets that White people enjoy that are not extended to people of color. White privilege is a phenomenon that is both denied and protected. Although she was taught about racism as something that puts others at a disadvantage, she was not taught the corollary: that White privilege gives White people distinct advantages. She lists 46 conditions in which being White is an unearned advantage, and McIntosh has experienced some of the following examples of unearned privileges that are not extended to people of color:

1. I can be in the company of people of my race most of the time.
2. I can go shopping alone and be assured that I will not be followed or harassed by store detectives.
3. If a traffic cop pulls me over or if the IRS audits my tax return, I can be sure I haven't been singled out because of my race.
4. I can criticize our government and talk about how much I fear its policies without being viewed as a cultural outsider.
5. I can do well in a challenging situation without being called a credit to my race.
6. I can be sure that my children will be given curricular materials that testify to the existence of their race.
7. I can be late to a meeting without having the lateness reflect on my race.
8. I can easily find academic courses and institutions that give attention only to people of my race.
9. I can be sure that if I need legal or medical help, my race will not work against me.
10. I can be concerned about racism without being seen as self-interested or self-seeking.

In unpacking the invisible knapsack of White privilege, McIntosh (1988, 1998) lists conditions of daily experience that she had once taken for granted as neutral, normal, and universally applicable to everybody. Once we realize that we benefit from this privileged and unearned race advantage, what might we be willing to do to lessen its effects? McIntosh indicates that one of our choices is to use our unearned advantage to reduce these invisible privilege systems and to use our conferred power to try to reconstruct power systems on a broader base. Do not judge or harshly criticize yourself if you realize that you do indeed have certain privileges based on skin color or gender. Give yourself credit for being open enough to recognize the limitations of your socialization, for this is the beginning of the change process.

In *Explorations in Privilege, Oppression, and Diversity*, Sharon Anderson and Valerie Middleton (2005) challenge readers to dismantle privilege by acknowledging that it does exist, that oppression is a result of privilege, and that privilege is reinforced at institutional and societal levels. These authors contend that knowledge alone will not lead to change; rather, people need to act on what they know:

> THE DIFFICULTY IN UPROOTING SYSTEMS OF PRIVILEGE is privilege's invisibility and the power it has to provide advantages to its beholders—advantages many do not want to lose. However, the consequence of maintaining this system of advantage is that it serves to disadvantage and oppress others. The uprooting process comes with recognizing our own points of privilege, which is the forerunner of true cultural sensitivity and cultural competence. (p. xiii)

Breaking Down the Barriers That Separate Us

There are always barriers to understanding, regardless of how similar or different we are. Language difficulties and value differences can make intercultural communication challenging. Awareness of these obstacles is the first step toward increasing communication and breaking down the walls that separate people. Here are some ideas about how you can break down the barriers that keep you separate from other people:

- Acknowledge and understand your own biases and prejudices.
- Challenge your prejudices by looking for data that do not support your preconceived biases.
- Challenge your fears and anxieties about talking about racial or cultural differences.
- Do volunteer work in an agency that provides services to people who are culturally different from you.
- Look for similarities and universal themes that unite you with others who differ from you in certain ways.
- Avoid judging differences; view diversity as a strength.
- Be respectful of those who differ from you.
- Attempt to learn about cultures that differ from your own.
- Talk about yourself and your experience with people who differ from you. Try to keep it simple and not global.
- Be willing to test, adapt, and change your perceptions.

In relating to people who differ from us culturally, we will undoubtedly make mistakes. We can learn from our cultural blunders if we recognize them and admit them. In the process of working through a problem, we can recover from such blunders. It is crucial that we avoid becoming defensive, remain open and flexible, and focus on ways to resolve a conflict or a misunderstanding.

Unity and diversity are related concepts, not polar opposites. It is not that diversity is good and right and homogeneity is bad and wrong. Both sameness and difference are part of the rainbow. Vontress and his colleagues (1999) take the position that it is important to recognize that people are more alike than they are different. As humans we share some common ground that enables us to understand one another despite our differences. Concerns about loving, living, relating, and dying are human problems that transcend culture.

Recently I (Jerry) had an opportunity to do some lecturing in Korea, an experience that revealed to me that regardless of our differences we do share common ground that makes it possible to understand people from diverse cultures. I gave lectures on group counseling to graduate students in counseling, mental health practitioners, and university professors who taught counseling and social work.

In reflecting on this experience, what surprised me greatly was the apparent fit of Western ideas with the Korean culture. Before I accepted the invitation to give these lectures, I considered carefully if many of the basic concepts and assumptions underlying the practice of group work in the United States would be appropriate for the Korean culture. Many of the ideas that Marianne and I have written about in our book, *Groups: Process and Practice* (Corey & Corey, 2006), seemed to work well in a variety of settings in Korea. Although our ideas and approach to group counseling were developed in the United States, this basic philosophy was well received by the students and professionals who made up the audience.

As a counselor educator in the United States, I felt that it was an honor and a privilege to be able to teach about group counseling in Korea. Rather than simply convey factual material, my main hope was to share an attitude toward counseling that might be useful to both students and professionals alike. During my interactions with people, I was struck by the many common life themes we share, even though we have our differences. This trip confirmed my belief that although it is essential to be aware of and respect cultural differences, it can be a mistake to make assumptions about any particular cultural group without making room for individual variances.

Embracing Versus Denying Our Cultural Heritage

I (Jerry) am a first-generation Italian American. Both of my parents were from Italy, yet neither of them seemed to think it was important that I learn to speak Italian, nor did they teach me much about my cultural heritage. When I was a child, we spent almost every Sunday at a family gathering at my maternal grandparents' house. Most of the conversation was in Italian, and I felt lost and separate from my extended family because I could not understand what was being said. Not passing on family history or Italian customs was a common practice among recent immigrants at that time. They believed it was best for their offspring to blend into the dominant society and not stand out by being different.

My father, Guiseppi Cordileone, came to the United States from Italy when he was 7 years old, not knowing a word of English. He had an extremely hard life, growing up in an orphanage without contact with his parents. In spite of many odds against him, he eventually managed to become a dentist. Once he began his dental practice, he was concerned that people might not want to come to an Italian dentist. He changed his name from *Cordileone* (meaning "heart of the lion") to *Corey*. It was likely that my father had some shame about his roots, and he also wanted to prevent his children from experiencing the prejudice and discrimination that he experienced.

Being around a nuclear and extended immigrant Italian family, I learned at an early age that people see the world through different eyes and express themselves in different ways. I came to appreciate differences rather than judge them. Because of my father's experiences, I became aware that people were discriminated against because of their ethnicity. Today, immigrants might still be encouraged to blend into the mainstream, but they are not as likely to do so to the degree I experienced as a child.

Not all immigrants actively deny their cultural roots. Many take pride in passing on their language, customs, and values to their children. I (Marianne) earlier mentioned that I emigrated from Germany to the United States as a young adult. I was surprised that many first-generation offspring did not speak their parents' language and knew very little about their ancestors. I made a decision that I wanted our daughters to learn as much as possible about their German heritage and language. So that Heidi and Cindy would not be teased by their friends for speaking German, I taught some of the neighborhood children German lessons. This proved to be a fun experience and was positive for all concerned. Living in a typical middle-class neighborhood, I had observed that people oftentimes did not know how to react when they were in the presence of others who spoke a foreign language.

Most Americans speak English only, and people speaking another language are sometimes viewed as being secretive, impolite, exclusionary, and cliquish—even when English speakers are not part of the interaction. I (Marianne) will sometimes speak to fellow Germans in my own language, even among Germans who also understand English. Doing so is not aimed at excluding others who do not understand German; rather, it is a way of being more intimate and forming a more meaningful connection. During such encounters, speaking English may lose the meaning and feeling of what I want to convey. The book (not the movie) *Lost in Translation* (Hoffman, 1990) addresses this issue of losing the emotional quality and connection when translating from one's primary language.

Building Connections by Reaching Out to Others

The more you know about your own culture, the more you will be able to understand the cultures of others. If you have a sense of your own cultural background and values, you have a framework for appreciating the values of people in another culture. And the more you know about diverse cultures, the better able you will be to connect with them in a positive way.

Many people incorrectly assume that cultural diversity relates only to one's race or ethnicity. Broadly conceived, **culture** pertains to the knowledge, language, values, and customs that are passed from person to person and from one generation to the next generation. We possess both an individual cultural identity and a group identity with a variety of cultures. Culture is one aspect of our experience that makes us similar to some people and different from others. It is clear that in the United States we are affected by the ever-changing and increasing diversity of our culture. The global community will continue to become more interdependent, and we will need to understand and build connections with diverse cultures. One threat to building these connections is a form of ethnic bias, a kind of nationalism that includes the view that the United States has a higher status than other countries have (Matlin, 2004).

It is relatively easy to get caught in the trap of an **ethnocentric bias,** using our own culture or country as a standard of what is right and good and judging other cultures or countries by our own frame of reference. Our central challenge is to learn to welcome diversity. One living example of this can be found in Glide Memorial Church in San Francisco. The pastor of this church, the Reverend Cecil Williams, along with the executive director of the church, Janet Mirikitani, are committed to welcoming diverse people into their spiritual community, a community that truly embraces love and acceptance. Reverend Williams (1992) works to empower individuals who are recovering and provides assistance to troubled communities. The pastor does not see his congregation as a melting pot where all people are blended together. Instead, Glide Memorial Church is more akin to a salad bowl filled with different leaves. Reverend Williams does far more than preach about love to a packed congregation on Sunday; he is actively engaged in spreading the meaning of love. He demonstrates ways to find meaning and purpose in life through acts of love. Through the efforts of Glide, hundreds of homeless are fed each day, substance abusers are given hope of a new kind of life, and society's outcasts are welcomed into a loving community. By giving people unconditional love and acceptance, Reverend Williams and his people bring out the best in those they encounter.

We challenge you to reflect on ways you can augment the meaning of your life by making connections with others and striving to make a significant difference. You can change the world in small ways by touching the lives of others through your acts of kindness and generosity. The purpose of your life can take on expanded dimensions if you are interested in making the world a better place for all of us. This process of making a difference in the human community begins with seeing ways that diversity can enhance life.

The *Quick Discrimination Index* can help you assess your attitudes toward cultural diversity. Even if you think you are free of prejudice toward others, you may discover some subtle biases. Once you are aware of them, you can begin working toward tolerance and acceptance.

The Quick Discrimination Index*

We hope you will take and score this social-attitude survey, which is designed to assess sensitivity, awareness, and receptivity to cultural diversity and gender equity. This is a self-assessment inventory, and it is essential that you strive to respond to each item as honestly as possible. This inventory is not designed to assess how you should think about cultural diversity and gender equity issues; rather, its aim is to assess subtle racial and gender bias. You can use this inventory to become more aware of your attitudes and beliefs pertaining to these issues.

DIRECTIONS: Remember there are no right or wrong answers. Please circle the appropriate number to the right.

	Strongly Disagree	Disagree	Not Sure	Agree	Strongly Agree
1. I do think it is more appropriate for the mother of a newborn baby, rather than the father, to stay home with the baby (not work) during the first year.	1	2	3	4	5
2. It is as easy for women to succeed in business as it is for men.	1	2	3	4	5
3. I really think affirmative-action programs on college campuses constitute reverse discrimination.	1	2	3	4	5
4. I feel I could develop an intimate relationship with someone from a different race.	1	2	3	4	5
5. All Americans should learn to speak two languages.	1	2	3	4	5
6. It upsets (or angers) me that a woman has never been president of the United States.	1	2	3	4	5
7. Generally speaking, men work harder than women.	1	2	3	4	5
8. My friendship network is very racially mixed.	1	2	3	4	5
9. I am against affirmative-action programs in business.	1	2	3	4	5
10. Generally, men seem less concerned with building relationships than women.	1	2	3	4	5
11. I would feel OK about my son or daughter dating someone from a different race.	1	2	3	4	5
12. It upsets (or angers) me that a racial minority person has never been president of the United States.	1	2	3	4	5
13. In the past few years, too much attention has been directed toward multicultural or minority issues in education.	1	2	3	4	5
14. I think feminist perspectives should be an integral part of the higher education curriculum.	1	2	3	4	5
15. Most of my close friends are from my own racial group.	1	2	3	4	5
16. I feel somewhat more secure that a man rather than a woman is currently president of the United States.	1	2	3	4	5

The Quick Discrimination Index (continued)

	Strongly Disagree	Disagree	Not Sure	Agree	Strongly Agree
17. I think that it is (or would be) important for my children to attend schools that are racially mixed.	1	2	3	4	5
18. In the past few years too much attention has been directed toward multicultural or minority issues in business.	1	2	3	4	5
19. Overall, I think racial minorities in America complain too much about racial discrimination.	1	2	3	4	5
20. I feel (or would feel) very comfortable having a woman as my primary physician.	1	2	3	4	5
21. I think the president of the United States should make a concerted effort to appoint more women and racial minorities to the country's Supreme Court.	1	2	3	4	5
22. I think white people's racism toward racial-minority groups still constitutes a major problem in America.	1	2	3	4	5
23. I think the school system, from elementary school through college, should encourage minority and immigrant children to learn and fully adopt traditional American values.	1	2	3	4	5
24. If I were to adopt a child, I would be happy to adopt a child of any race.	1	2	3	4	5
25. I think there is as much female physical violence toward men as there is male physical violence toward women.	1	2	3	4	5
26. I think the school system, from elementary school through college, should promote values representative of diverse cultures.	1	2	3	4	5
27. I believe that reading the autobiography of Malcolm X would be of value.	1	2	3	4	5
28. I would enjoy living in a neighborhood consisting of a racially diverse population (Asians, blacks, Latinos, whites).	1	2	3	4	5
29. I think it is better if people marry within their own race.	1	2	3	4	5
30. Women make too big a deal out of sexual-harassment issues in the workplace.	1	2	3	4	5

The total score measures overall sensitivity, awareness, and receptivity to cultural diversity and gender equality. Of the 30 items on the QDI, 15 are worded and scored in a positive direction (high scores indicate high sensitivity to multicultural/gender issues), and 15 are worded and scored in a negative direction (where low scores are indicative of high sensitivity). Naturally, when tallying the total score response, these latter 15 items need to be *reverse-scored*. Reverse scoring simply means that if a respondent circles a "1" they should get five points; a "2" four points, a "3" three points, a "4" two points, and a "5" one point.

The following QDI items need to be *reverse-scored*: 1, 2, 3, 7, 9, 10, 13, 15, 16, 18, 19, 23, 25, 29, 30.

Score range = 30 to 150, with high scores indicating more awareness, sensitivity, and receptivity to racial diversity and gender equality.

Take Time to Reflect

1. To what extent do you feel threatened by people who think and believe differently from you? Do you tend to be drawn to human diversity, or do you tend to shy away from those with a different worldview?

_____

_____

2. What value do you place on diversity as part of your philosophy of life?

_____

_____

3. How many, if any, of the important people in your life are culturally different from you?

_____

_____

4. What steps are you willing to take to move in the direction of challenging your prejudices or restricted ways of thinking?

_____

_____

5. What one action can you take to make a significant, even though small, difference in society? To what extent do you believe you are able to influence others?

_____

_____

SUMMARY

Seeking meaning and purpose in life is an important part of being human. Meaning is not automatically bestowed on you; it is the result of your active thinking and choosing. We have encouraged you to recognize your own values and to ask both how you acquired them and whether you can affirm them for yourself out of your own experience and reflection. This task of examining your values and purposes continues throughout your lifetime.

If you are secure about your value system, you will also be flexible and open to new life experiences. At various times in your life you may look at the world somewhat differently, which may lead to modifying some of your values. This is not to say that you will change your values without giving the matter considerable thought. Being secure about your values also implies that you do not need to impose them on other people. We hope you will be able to respect the values of others that may differ from your own. You can learn to accept people who have a different worldview from your own without necessarily approving of all of their behavior. If you are clear about the meaning in your own life, and if you have developed a philosophy of life that provides you with purpose and direction, you will be more able to interact with others who might embrace different value systems. Being able to talk openly with these people can be a useful avenue for your own personal development.

In this chapter we have focused on the central role of values as a basis for meaning in life. In addition to finding meaning through projects that afford opportunities for personal growth, we have seen that meaning and purpose extend to the broader framework of forming linkages with others in the human community. Accepting others by respecting their right to hold values that may differ from yours is a fundamental dimension of a philosophy of life that embraces diversity. Prejudice, based on fear and ignorance, is often a barrier that separates us from others instead of uniting us. We hope you will welcome diversity as a bridge to link yourself with others who differ from you. It may be overwhelming to think of solving the global problems of prejudice and discrimination, but you can begin in smaller but still significant ways by changing yourself. Once you recognize the barriers within yourself that prevent you from understanding and accepting others, you can take steps to challenge these barriers.

Where Can I Go From Here?

1. Ask a few close friends what gives their lives meaning. How do they think their lives would be different without this source of meaning?

2. Make a list of what you consider to be the major accomplishments in your life. What did you actually do to bring about these accomplishments?

What kinds of future accomplishments would enhance the meaning of your life?

3. Writing a paper that describes your philosophy of life can help you integrate your thoughts and reflections about yourself. Ideally, this paper will represent a critical analysis of who you are now and the factors that have been most influential in contributing to the person that you are.

The following outline for your paper is very comprehensive, and writing such a paper can be a major project in a course. As you review the outline, select one or two major topics and use them as a focus for your paper. Feel free to use or omit any part of the outline, and modify it in any way that will help you to write a paper that is personally significant. You might also consider adding poetry, excerpts from other writers, and pictures or works of art. If you take this project seriously, it will help you clarify your goals for the future and suggest the means to obtain them.

a. Who are you now? What influences have contributed to the person you are now? In addressing this question consider factors such as influences during childhood and adolescence.

b. How are love and intimacy factors in your life? Consider some of the following elements as you develop your answer:

- Your need for love
- Your fear of love
- The meaning of love for you
- Dating experiences and their effect on you
- Your view of gender roles
- Expectations of others and their influence on your gender role
- Attitudes toward the opposite sex
- Meaning of sexuality in your life
- Your values concerning love and sex

c. What place do intimate relationships and family life occupy in your life?

- The value you place on marriage
- How children fit in your life
- The meaning of intimacy for you
- The kind of intimate relationships you want

- Areas of struggle for you in relating to others
- Your views of marriage
- Your values concerning family life
- How social expectations have influenced your views
- Gender roles in intimate relationships

d. What are your thoughts about death and meaning?

- Your view of an afterlife
- Religious views and your view of death
- The way death affects you
- Sources of meaning in your life
- The things you most value in your life
- Your struggles in finding meaning and purpose
- Religion and the meaning of life
- Critical turning points in finding meaning
- Influential people in your life

e. Whom do you want to become? In addressing this question consider some of the following:

- How you see yourself now (strengths and weaknesses)
- How others perceive you now
- What makes you unique
- Your relationships with others
- Present struggles

f. How would you describe your future with others? (Consider the kind of relationships you want and what you need to do to achieve them.)

g. What are your future plans for yourself?

- How you would like to be 10 years from now

- What you need to do to achieve your goals
- What you can do now
- Your values for the future
- Choices you see as being open to you now

Resources for Future Study

Web Site Resource

WEB OF CULTURE
http://www.webofculture.com/

Although this site is intended for businesses, it includes a wide range of issues and approaches to increase cross-cultural understanding. It features extensive worldwide information on subjects such as capitals, currency, gestures, headlines, and languages.

InfoTrac College Edition Resources

For additional readings, explore INFOTRAC COLLEGE EDITION, our online library:
http://www.infotrac.college.com/wadsworth

Hint: Enter these search terms:

meaning in life

personal meaning

philosophy of life

religious faith

value systems

human diversity

prejudice

racism

Print Resources

Albom, M. (1997). *Tuesdays with Morrie.* New York: Doubleday.

Anderson, S. K., & Middleton, V. A. (2005). *Explorations in privilege, oppression, and diversity.* Belmont, CA: Thomson Brooks/Cole.

Bellah, R. N., Madsen, R., Sullivan, W. M., Swidler, A., & Tipton, S. M. (1985). *Habits of the heart: Individualism and commitment in American life.* New York: Harper & Row (Perennial Library).

Bok, F. (with Tivnan, E.). (2003). *Escape from slavery.* New York: St. Martin's Press.

Dalai Lama. (1999). *Ethics for a new millennium.* New York: Riverhead Books.

Dalai Lama. (2001). *An open heart: Practicing compassion in everyday life.* Boston: Little Brown.

Dalai Lama, & Cutler, H. C. (1998). *The art of happiness: A handbook for living.* New York: Riverhead Books.

Frankl, V. (1963). *Man's search for meaning.* New York: Washington Square Press.

Frankl, V. (1969). *The will to meaning: Foundation and applications of logotherapy.* New York: New American Library.

Joy, W. B. (1979). *Joy's way: A map for the transformational journey.* Los Angeles, CA: Jeremy P. Tarcher.

Katz, J. (1999). *Running to the mountain: A journey of faith and change.* New York: Villard.

Mother Teresa. (1999). *In the heart of the world.* New York: MJF Books.

Ridley, C. R. (1995). *Overcoming unintentional racism in counseling and psychotherapy.* Thousand Oaks, CA: Sage.

Seligman, M. E. P. (1993). *What you can change and what you can't.* New York: Fawcett (Columbine).

Shield, B., & Carlson, R. (Eds.). (1999). *For the love of God: Handbook for the spirit.* New York: MJF Books.

Sue, D. W. (2003). *Overcoming our racism: The journey to liberation.* San Francisco, CA: Jossey-Bass.

Tatum, B. D. (1999). *"Why are all the Black kids sitting together in the cafeteria?"* New York: Basic Books.

Vontress, C. E., Johnson, J. A., & Epp, L. R. (1999). *Cross-cultural counseling: A casebook.* Alexandria, VA: American Counseling Association.

Williams, C. (1992). *No hiding place: Empowerment and recovery for our troubled communities.* San Francisco: Harper.

14

Avenues to personal growth
are as varied as the people
who choose them.

Pathways to Personal Growth

Where Am I Now?

Use this scale to respond to these statements:

   3 = This statement is true of me *most* of the time.

   2 = This statement is true of me *some* of the time.

   1 = This statement is true of me *almost none* of the time.

☐ 1. I am motivated to keep up with regular journal writing.

☐ 2. I would like to begin meditation practices.

☐ 3. I intend to incorporate relaxation methods into my daily life.

☐ 4. Now that I have read this book, I see that I have more choices available to me than I realized.

☐ 5. Personal growth is a journey rather than a fixed destination.

☐ 6. I really intend to do what it takes to continue the self-exploration I have begun through this course and book.

☐ 7. If I had a personal problem I could not resolve by myself, I would seek professional assistance.

☐ 8. I dream a lot and am able to remember many of my dreams.

☐ 9. I see dreaming as a way to understand myself and to remain psychologically healthy.

☐ 10. I intend to develop an action plan as a way to begin the changes I most want to make in my life.

T hroughout this book you have been invited to discover new choices you might like to make. In this relatively brief chapter, we invite you to review what you have learned and determine where you will go from here. If you have invested yourself in the process of questioning your life, now is a good time to make a commitment to yourself (and maybe to someone else) to actively put to use what you have been learning about yourself. Will you stop here, or will this be a commencement—a new beginning in the best sense?

You can deliberately choose experiences that will help you become the person you want to be. As you consider what experiences for continued personal growth you are likely to choose at this time, be aware that as you change you can expect that what brings meaning to your life will also change. The projects you were deeply absorbed in at an earlier time in your life may hold little meaning for you today. And where and how you discover meaning today may not be the pattern for some future period.

Often, we make resolutions about what we would like to be doing in our lives or about experiences we want to share with others, and then we fail to carry them out. Are there activities you value yet rarely get around to doing? When you stop to think about it, how would you really like to be spending your time? What changes are you willing to make today, this week, this month, this year? What kind of plan can you devise that will help you attain these changes? How will you deal with difficulties you encounter in making the changes you desire? We encourage you to reflect on the previous chapters and identify some of the areas that stand out most for you.

Growth has no small steps. Every step is significant because it is a step in a new direction. You can choose to do many things on your own (or with friends or family) to continue your personal development. A few of the resources available to you for continued personal growth are outlined in the pages that follow. Different resources may fit your needs at different stages of your personal growth. We invite you to investigate any of these avenues that you feel are appropriate for you at this time.

PATHWAYS FOR CONTINUED SELF-EXPLORATION

Develop a Reading Program

One excellent way to motivate yourself to explore life is through reading, including selected self-help books. The References and Suggested Readings section at the end of this book includes a variety of books that can give you a start on developing a personal reading program. Many students and clients tell us how meaningful selected books have been for them in putting into perspective

You can choose experiences that will help you become the person you want to be.

© PhotoDisc/Getty Images

some of the themes they have struggled with, and we encourage you to take advantage of this resource. What are some areas that you are most interested in reading about? What are a few books that you might select? Would it be helpful to create a schedule to make reading a priority?

Continue Your Writing Program

Along with setting up a reading and reflection program for yourself, another way to build on the gains you have made up to this point is to continue the practice of journal writing. If you have begun a process of personal writing in this book or in a separate notebook, maintain this practice. Even devoting a short period a few times each week to reflecting on how your life is going and then recording some of your thoughts and feelings is useful in providing you with an awareness of patterns in your behavior. You can learn to observe what you are feeling, thinking, and doing; then you have a basis for determining the degree to which you are successfully changing old patterns that are not working for you. Have you been regularly making use of journal writing as a part of this course? Have you gotten any insights as a result of journal writing?

Practice Ongoing Self-Assessment

Throughout this book you have been challenged to assess the ways that you think, feel, and act on a variety of topics. Review your responses to the Where

© Todd Gipstein/Corbis

Growth can occur in small ways, and there are many things you can do on your own to continue your personal development.

Am I Now? statements at the beginning of each chapter and assess your written responses to the Take Time to Reflect exercises. Taking time to consolidate your thoughts will enhance your learning and provide you with some signposts for future changes. Did you find any persistent themes in your review of these chapter exercises? In Chapter 1 you were introduced to choice theory, which emphasizes the role of self-evaluation as a first step toward change. What are some of the areas of your life that are working for you? Are there any aspects of your life that are not presently working for you?

Contemplate Self-Directed Behavior Change

Now that you have finished this book, you have probably identified a few specific areas where you could do further work. If you decide that you are frequently tense and that you do not generally react well to stress, for example, you might construct a self-change program that includes practicing relaxation methods and breathing exercises. Identify some target areas for personal change and set realistic goals. Then develop some specific techniques for carrying out your goals, and practice the behaviors that will help you make those changes. What kind of self-change program are you most interested in launching? What might help you to begin and to maintain your program? Design an action plan (see Chapter 1) and commit yourself to its implementation.

Take Advantage of Support Groups

Most colleges and community mental health centers offer a variety of self-help groups that are facilitated by a person who has coped or is coping with a particular life issue. A good support group will help you see that you are not alone in your struggle. The experience can also provide you with alternatives that you may not be considering. Other examples of support groups include those that deal with rape or incest, consciousness-raising groups for women and for men, groups for reentry students, groups for people concerned about gay and lesbian issues, and medical self-help groups. We suggest that you proceed with some caution in selecting a support group, asking yourself if this is the right kind of group for you at this time in your life.

COUNSELING AS A PATH TO SELF-UNDERSTANDING

We hope you will remain open to the idea of seeking counseling for yourself at critical transition periods in your life or times when you feel particularly challenged with life events or choices to be made. Reading this book and participating in this kind of class may have raised personal issues that you were unaware of before. To wrestle with choices about life is human, and taking this course has probably shown you that you are not alone with your struggles. We encourage you to trust yourself to make your own choices, but even a few counseling sessions at the right time can assist you in clarifying your options and can provide you with the impetus to formulate action plans leading to change.

In our view, it is essential to attend to your physical, psychological, social, and spiritual well-being. When you find that you cannot give yourself the help you need or get needed assistance from your friends and family, you may want to seek out a professional counselor. When people are physically ill, they generally seek a physician's help. Yet when people are "psychologically ill," they often hesitate to ask for help. Counseling does not necessarily involve a major revamping of your personality. Instead of getting a major overhaul, you might need only a minor tune-up! Many people refuse to take their car to a mechanic unless it breaks down because they do not want to take the time for preventive maintenance. Some will avoid a trip to the dentist until they are in excruciating pain with a toothache. Likewise, many people wait until they are unable to function at home, at work, or at school before they reach out for professional counseling. Your road to personal growth will be smoother if you opt for a few tune-ups along the way.

You do not have to be in a crisis to benefit from either individual or group counseling. Counselors can help their clients move ahead when they feel stuck in some aspect of living. If you can identify with any of these statements, you might consider seeking counseling:

- I feel out of control in my life.
- I am unhappy with where I am heading.
- I think that I make a lot of bad choices.
- I am the victim of a crime or a survivor of some form of abuse.
- I have no sense of what to do with my life.
- I am often depressed.
- I am in a very unhappy relationship.
- I have several addictions.
- I don't like myself.
- I am experiencing a spiritual crisis.
- I am experiencing a significant loss.
- I am having problems related to work or school.
- I am under chronic stress and have stress-related ailments.
- I have been discriminated against and experienced oppression.
- I am ending a significant relationship.
- I feel that I am using only a fraction of my potential.

In a study of student problems in college counseling centers, Benton, Robertson, Tseng, Newton, and Benton (2003) found that college students who seek counseling today frequently have problems associated with normal developmental issues and relationship concerns, along with more severe problems such as anxiety, depression, suicidal ideation, and personality disorders. From 1996 to 2001, these researchers identified the following problem areas (by percentage) experienced by students seeking help in college counseling centers:

- Stress and anxiety = 63%
- Situational problems = 58%
- Relationship concerns = 56%
- Family issues = 45%
- Developmental issues = 41%
- Depression = 41%
- Academic skills = 34%
- Medication used = 22%
- Educational/vocational concerns = 22%
- Physical problems = 14%
- Abusive relationships = 12%

- Grief reactions = 10%
- Suicidal ideation = 9%

Counselors are mentors who guide you in making use of your inner resources. Good counselors do not attempt to solve your problems for you. Instead, they teach you how to cope with your problems more effectively. In many respects counselors are psychological educators, teaching you how to get the most from living, how to create more joy in your life, how to use your own strengths, and how to become the person you want to be.

A counselor's function is to teach you how to eventually become your own therapist. Counselors do not change your beliefs through brainwashing; rather, they assist you in examining how your thinking affects the way you feel and act. A counselor will help you identify specific beliefs that may be getting in the way of your living effectively. You will learn how to critically evaluate your values, beliefs, thoughts, and assumptions. Counseling can teach you how to substitute constructive thinking for self-destructive thinking. If you find it hard to identify and express feelings such as joy, anger, fear, or guilt, counseling can help you learn to do so. If your present behavior prevents you from getting where you want to go, counselors can help you explore alternative ways of acting.

Therapeutic work can be difficult for you *and* for the counselor. Self-honesty is not easy. Confronting and dealing with your problems takes courage. By simply going in for counseling, you have taken the first step in the healing process. Recognizing the need for help is itself significant in moving forward. Self-exploration requires discipline, patience, and persistence. There may be times when progress seems slow, for counseling does not work wonders. Indeed, at times you may feel worse before you get better because old wounds are brought to the surface and explored.

Selecting the counselor who is right for you is of the utmost importance. Just as it is important to go to a physician you trust, it is critical that you find a counselor whom you can trust. Ask questions about the counselor's training and background before you make a commitment to work with that person. In fact, ethical therapists feel a responsibility to inform their clients about the way counseling works. Another good way to find an effective therapist is to ask others who have been in counseling. A personal referral to a specific person can be useful. However you select a counselor, do some research and make a thoughtful decision. Counseling is a highly personal matter, and you stand a greater chance of doing the hard work self-learning demands if you trust your counselor.

Remember, counseling is a process of self-discovery aimed at empowerment. Counseling is not an end in itself. You will eventually stop seeing a counselor, but the process you have begun does not end; you are responsible for the quality of your life. If your counseling is successful, you will learn far more than merely how to solve a specific problem. You will acquire skills of self-examination and assessment that you can use to confront new problems and challenges as they arise. Ultimately, you will be better equipped to make your own choices about how you want to live.

DREAMS AS A PATH TO SELF-UNDERSTANDING

Dreams can reveal significant clues to events that have meaning for us. If we train ourselves to recall our dreams—and this can indeed be learned—and discipline ourselves to explore their meanings, we can get a good sense of our struggles, wants, goals, purposes, conflicts, and interests. Dreams can shed a powerful light on our past, present, and future dynamics and on our attempt to construct meaning. Dreaming helps us deal with stress, work through loss and grief, resolve anger, and bring closure to painful life situations. Our dreams can provide us with a path toward greater understanding of ourselves and our relationships with others.

In *Teach Yourself to Dream,* Fontana (1997) tells us that "dreams are our chance to eavesdrop on a conversation between our unconscious and conscious minds, offering us opportunities to understand ourselves better and achieve greater inner harmony" (p. 8). We can learn how to reveal the special meaning of our dreams, how to make our dreams more vivid, and how to use our dreams for guidance in times of personal difficulty. Many of the messages we receive in dreams are associated with concerns, anxieties, and hopes of daily life:

> IN A BROAD SENSE, dreams often relate to what might be, rather than what actually is. A dream could thus suggest that you might wish to enlarge your horizons, or to explore new avenues and opportunities. Sometimes dreams seem to warn us of dangers, or to caution us to think more carefully about a particular course of action. The one clear message is that dreams are far too important to be ignored. (p. 23)

If you learn to recall your dreams and to pay attention to the wisdom of your unconscious, dreams can be healing. Many people forget their dreams because they do not value them as being important enough to remember (Fontana, 1997). In Western culture most of us are brought up to believe dreams serve no real purpose and that they should not be taken seriously. Fontana suggests that we would do well to reassess our negative attitudes about dreaming and change them. He advises that we tell ourselves that our dreams are helpful, that we remember them, and that we welcome what our dreams can teach us about becoming more fulfilled and effective human beings.

As much as we believe in the healing capacity of dreams, we have some concerns in writing about this topic. Indeed, a little knowledge can be a dangerous thing. Sometimes people attempt to analyze their dreams (and the dreams of their friends and family members) without a full understanding of the complexity of dream interpretation. We caution you to avoid analyzing and interpreting dreams of others unless you have the necessary education and training in dream work.

One of the best ways to keep track of your dreams is to record them in your journal. Sharing a dream with someone you trust can be self-revealing and helpful. If you journal around themes in your dreams, you may begin to see more parallels between your sleeping and waking life.

Until recently, I (Jerry) rarely had dreams that I could remember. But a few years ago I attended a conference focused on exploring dreams. I began to record whatever fragments of dreams I could recall, and interestingly, during this conference I started to recall some vivid and rich dreams. I have made it a practice to record in my journal any dreams upon awakening, along with my impressions and reactions to the dreams. It helps me to share my dreams with Marianne or other friends; especially useful is comparing impressions others have of my dreams.

All the images in my dreams are manifestations of some dimension within me. In Gestalt fashion, I typically allow myself to reflect on the ways the people in my dreams represent parts of myself. "Becoming the various images" in the dream is one way for me to bring unconscious themes forward. I am finding that my dreams have a pattern and that they are shorthand ways of understanding conflicts in my life, decisions to be made at crossroads, and themes that recur from time to time. Even a short segment of a dream often contains layers of messages that make sense when I look at what is going on in my waking state.

Exploring the Meaning of Dreams

People have been fascinated with dreams and have regarded them as significant since ancient times. But dreams have been the subject of scientific investigation only since the mid-19th century. Dreams are not mysterious; they are avenues to self-understanding.

Fritz Perls, a founder of Gestalt therapy, discovered some useful methods to assist people in better understanding themselves. He suggested that we become friends with our dreams. According to Perls (1969, 1970), the dream is the most spontaneous expression of the existence of the human being; it is a piece of art that individuals chisel out of their lives. It represents an unfinished situation, but it is more than an incomplete situation, an unfulfilled wish, or a prophecy. Every dream contains an existential message about oneself and one's current struggle. Gestalt therapy aims at bringing a dream to life by having the dreamer relive it as though it were happening now. This includes making a list of all the details of the dream, remembering each person, event, and mood in it, and then becoming each of these parts by acting and inventing dialogue. Perls saw dreams as "the royal road to integration." By avoiding analysis and interpretation and focusing instead on becoming and experiencing the dream in all its aspects, the dreamer gets closer to the existential message of the dream.

Rainwater (1979) offers some useful guidelines for dreamers to follow in exploring their dreams:

- Be the landscape or the environment.

- Become all the people in the dream. Are any of them significant people?

- Be any object that links and joins, such as telephone lines and highways.
- Identify with any mysterious objects, such as an unopened letter or an unread book.
- Assume the identity of any powerful force, such as a tidal wave.
- Become any two contrasting objects, such as a younger person and an older person.
- Be anything that is missing in the dream. If you do not remember your dreams, then speak to your missing dreams.
- Be alert for any numbers that appear in the dream; become these numbers and explore associations with them.

When you wake from a dream, is your feeling state one of fear, joy, sadness, frustration, surprise, or anger? Identifying the feeling tone may be the key to finding the meaning of the dream (Rainwater, 1979). As you play out the various parts of your dream, pay attention to what you say and look for patterns. By identifying your feeling tone and the themes that emerge, you will get a clearer sense of what your dreams are telling you.

Dreams are full of symbols. Gestalt therapists contribute to dream work by emphasizing the individual meaning of symbols. The person assigns meaning to his or her own dream. For example, an unopened letter could represent a person who is clinging to secrets. An unread book might symbolize an individual's fear of not being noticed or of being insignificant. A Gestalt therapist might ask the person, "What is the first thing that comes to you when you think about an unopened letter?" One person replies, "I want to hide. I don't want anyone to know me." Another individual says, "I wish somebody would open me up." To understand the personal meaning of a dream, a therapist often asks, "What might be going on in your life now where what you just said would make sense?" In Gestalt therapy no established meaning fits everyone; rather, meaning is deciphered by each individual.

Dreams are a rich source of meaning. Dreams are the link between our inner and outer lives, and they give us a unique opportunity to listen to and learn from our inner wisdom. Your dreams can provide you with a direction in making better choices and living more fully. If you are interested in doing further reading about dreams, we highly recommend Fontana's (1997) book, *Teach Yourself to Dream.*

Dare to Dream

Dreams can reveal significant aspects of our past and present struggles. As a gateway to the unconscious, dreaming can also inform us of our future strivings. To better design a personal vision for your future, we encourage you to dream when you are awake as well as when you are asleep. Don Quixote dared "to dream the impossible dream." We encourage you to follow a similar path. The greatest hindrance to your growth may be a failure to allow yourself to imagine all the possibilities open to you. You may have restricted your vision of what you might become by not allowing yourself to formulate a vision or pursue your dreams. If you reflect thoughtfully on the messages in your dreams, a range of choices will unfold for you. We have met many people who continue to surprise themselves with what they have in their lives. At one time they would not have imagined such possibilities—even in their wildest dreams—but their dreams became reality for them. Too many of us restrict our vision of the possible by not allowing ourselves the luxury of reflecting on an impossible dream. Dare to dream, and then have the courage to follow your passions.

CONCLUDING COMMENTS

If you have become more aware of personal issues than you were when you began the course, and if you have an eagerness to continue on the path of self-examination and reflection, you have already taken the first steps down the path of self-actualization. Sometimes people expect dramatic transformations and feel disappointed if they do not make major changes in their lives. Remember that it is not the big changes that are necessarily significant; rather, it is your willingness to take small steps that will lead to continued growth. Only you can change your own ways of thinking, feeling, and doing. Look for subtle ways of increasing your personal freedom.

The knowledge and skills that you have gained from both the course and the book can be applied to virtually all of your future experiences. Recognize that there is no one path for you to follow. You will encounter many paths and make critical decisions at various transition points in your life. Remain open to considering new paths.

At this point you probably have a clearer vision of the personal goals that you most want to pursue. Make plans to accomplish these new goals, but avoid overwhelming yourself with too many things to do lest you become discouraged. Personal change is an ongoing process that really does not come to an end until you do. We sincerely wish you well in your commitment to take the steps necessary, no matter how small, in your journey to becoming the person you were meant to be. Remember that even a journey of a thousand miles begins with the first step—so start walking!

Where Can I Go From Here?

1. If you have trouble remembering your dreams, before you go to sleep (for about a month) tell yourself "I will have a dream tonight, and I will remember it." Keep a paper and a pen near your bed, and jot down even brief dream fragments you may recall when you wake up. If you do not recall dreaming, at least write that down. This practice may increase your ability to remember your dreams.

2. If you are aware of dreaming fairly regularly, develop the practice of writing your dreams in your journal as soon as possible upon awakening.

Look at the pattern of your dreams; become aware of the kinds of dreams you are having and what they might mean to you. Simply reading your descriptions of your dreams can be of value to you.

3. Make a list of all the reasons you would not want to seek out a counselor when you are in psychological pain or coping with a problem that hampers your personal effectiveness. Apply this same list to whether you would seek out a physician when you are in physical pain. Compare your answers to determine your attitudes regarding psychological health and physical health.

4. What have been the highlights of this course and book? What changes in yourself have you noticed? What have you learned that you can take with you wherever you go?

5. If you have invested yourself in this book and in this course, you have acquired a set of skills that you can continue to use, one being the art of self-assessment. Respond to each of the following questions in your journal. Do not check off the question until you feel you have responded as fully as you can.

    a. Have you felt good about the kind of student you have been this term? If the rest of your college career will be much like this term, what will that be like for you?

    b. Go back to the discussion of becoming an active learner in Chapter 1. To what degree have you become more involved and active as a student and as a learner?

    c. What kind of student are you? How far have you progressed since you began this book? What are some of the most significant steps you have taken?

    d. You were invited to become a coauthor of this book by writing in it and personalizing the material. Take time to reread some of what you wrote in the Take Time to Reflect sections and in your journal. What patterns do you see in your thoughts?

    e. Describe the student and person you would like to be one year from today. Consider these questions as you imagine different directions:

- If you had right now what you wanted in your life, what would that be?
- If you were the kind of student today that you would like to be, how would you be?
- What might be getting in your way of being the kind of person and student that you would like to be?
- What are a few specific actions you need to take if you want to accomplish new goals?
- What will help you to stick with a plan aimed at becoming more of the person and student you want to become?

Resources for Future Study

Web Site Resources

AMERICAN ASSOCIATION OF MARRIAGE AND FAMILY THERAPY
http://www.aamft.org/

This site explains how professional therapy can help couples and families experiencing difficulty. The site also offers links to important family and marriage-related resources including their "Find a Therapist" service.

MENTAL HEALTH NET
http://www.mentalhelp.net/

This is an excellent site that explores all aspects of mental health. Many psychological disorders and treatments are discussed along with professional issues. There are links to more than 8,000 mental health resources.

THE ALBERT ELLIS INSTITUTE
http://www.rebt.org/

This site describes rational emotive behavior therapy (REBT). The site also offers facts about the

Institute, questions and answers about REBT, a forum for asking Dr. Ellis questions directly, resources for self-help, therapist referrals, workshop schedules, professional services and products, and a complete selection of all of the Institute's publications and products.

THE EFFECTIVENESS OF PSYCHOTHERAPY: THE *CONSUMER REPORTS* STUDY
http://www.apa.org/journals/seligman.html

This article by Martin E. P. Seligman discusses the *Consumer Reports* (November 1995) study on the effectiveness of psychotherapy.

DR. IVAN'S DEPRESSION CENTRAL
http://www.psycom.net/depression.central.html

This site by psychiatrist Ivan K. Goldberg, M.D., provides very extensive coverage of mood disorders and treatments and has links to other sites on mood and other disorders.

 **InfoTrac College Edition Resources**

For additional readings, explore INFOTRAC COLLEGE EDITION, our online library:
http://www.infotrac.college.com/wadsworth

Hint: Enter these search terms:

support group	dream AND therapy
dreams	dream AND couns
dream work	dream AND psych

Print Resources

Fontana, D. (1997). *Teach yourself to dream: A practical guide.* San Francisco: Chronicle Books.

Hwang, P. O. (2000). *Other-esteem: Meaningful life in a multicultural society.* Philadelphia, PA: Accelerated Development (Taylor & Francis).

Kottler, J. A. (2001). *Making changes last.* Philadelphia, PA: Brunner-Routledge (Taylor & Francis Group).

Miller, T. (1995). *How to want what you have: Discovering the magic and grandeur of ordinary existence.* New York: Avon.

Moulton, P., & Harper, L. (1999). *Outside looking in: When someone you love is in therapy.* Brandon, VT: Safer Society Press.

Seligman, M. E. P. (1990). *Learned optimism: How to change your mind and your life.* New York: Pocket Books.

Seligman, M. E. P. (1993). *What you can change and what you can't.* New York: Fawcett (Columbine).

Stone, H., & Stone, S. (1993). *Embracing your inner critic: Turning self-criticism into a creative asset.* San Francisco: Harper.

Vanzant, I. (1998). *One day my soul just opened up.* New York: Simon & Schuster (Fireside).

References and Suggested Readings*

ABELES, N., VICTOR, T. L., & DELANO-WOOD, L. (2004). The impact of an older adult's death on the family. *Professional Psychology: Research and Practice, 35*(3), 234–239.

ADLER, A. (1958). *What life should mean to you.* New York: Capricorn.

ADLER, A. (1964). *Social interest: A challenge to mankind.* New York: Capricorn.

ADLER, A. (1969). *The practice and theory of individual psychology.* Paterson, NJ: Littlefield.

AINSWORTH, M. D. S., BLEHAR, M. C., WATERS, E., & WALL, S. (1978). *Patterns of attachment: A psychological study of the strange situation.* Hillsdale, NJ: Erlbaum.

ALBOM, M. (1997). *Tuesdays with Morrie.* New York: Doubleday.

AMERICAN ASSOCIATION FOR WORLD HEALTH. (1994). *AIDS and families* [Booklet]. Washington, DC: Author.

AMERICAN PSYCHOLOGICAL ASSOCIATION. (2004). Guidelines for psychological practice with older adults. *American Psychologist, 59*(4), 236–260.

ANDERSON, S. K., & MIDDLETON, V. A. (2005). *Explorations in privilege, oppression, and diversity.* Belmont, CA: Thomson Brooks/Cole.

ANDRONICO, M. P., & HORNE, A. M. (2004). Counseling men in groups: The role of myths, therapeutic factors, leadership, and rituals. In J. L. DeLucia-Waack, D. Gerrity, C. R. Kalodner, & M. T. Riva (Eds.), *Handbook of group counseling and psychotherapy* (pp. 456–468). Thousand Oaks, CA: Sage.

ARNETT, J. J. (2000). Emerging adulthood: A theory of development from the late teens through the twenties. *American Psychologist, 55*(5), 469–480.

ARONSON, E. (2000, May 28). *The social psychology of self-persuasion.* Keynote address at the Evolution of Psychotherapy Conference, Anaheim, CA.

*BASOW, S. A. (1992). *Gender: Stereotypes and roles* (3rd ed.). Pacific Grove, CA: Brooks/Cole.

BATESON, M. C. (1990). *Composing a life.* New York: Plume.

BEISSER, A. R. (1970). The paradoxical theory of change. In J. Fagan & I. L. Shepherd (Eds.), *Gestalt therapy now* (pp. 77–80). New York: Harper & Row (Colophon).

*BELLAH, R. N., MADSEN, R., SULLIVAN, W. M., SWIDLER, A., & TIPTON, S. M. (1985). *Habits of the heart: Individualism and commitment in American life.* New York: Harper & Row (Perennial).

*BENSON, H. (1976). *The relaxation response.* New York: Avon.

BENSON, H. (1984). *Beyond the relaxation response.* New York: Berkeley Books.

BENSON, H. (2000, May 25). *Timeless healing: The power and biology of belief.* Keynote address at the Evolution of Psychotherapy Conference, Anaheim, CA.

BENTON, S. A., ROBERTSON, J. M., TSENG, W., NEWTON, F. B., & BENTON, S. L. (2003). Changes in counseling center client problems across 13 years. *Professional Psychology: Research and Practice, 34*(1), 66–72.

BERMAN, J., & BERMAN, L. (2001). *For women only: A revolutionary guide to overcoming sexual dysfunction and reclaiming your sex life.* New York: Henry Holt.

BERNE, E. (1975). *What do you say after you say hello?* New York: Bantam.

*BLOOMFIELD, H. H. (WITH FELDER, L.). (1983). *Making peace with your parents.* New York: Ballantine.

*BLOOMFIELD, H. H. (WITH FELDER, L.). (1985). *Making peace with yourself: Transforming your weaknesses into strengths.* New York: Ballantine.

*BLY, R. (1990). *Iron John: A book about men.* New York: Random House (Vintage).

*BOK, F. (WITH TIVNAN, E.). (2003). *Escape from slavery.* New York: St. Martin's Press.

---

* An asterisk before an entry indicates a source that we highly recommend as supplementary reading.

*BOLLES, R. N. (2000). *What color is your parachute?* Berkeley, CA: Ten Speed Press.

BORYSENKO, J. (WITH ROTHSTEIN, L.). (1988). *Minding the body, mending the mind.* New York: Bantam.

BORYSENKO, J. (1996). *A woman's book of life: The biology, psychology and spirituality of the feminine life cycle.* New York: Riverhead.

BOWLBY, J. (1969). *Attachment and loss: Vol. 1. Attachment.* London: Hogarth Press.

BOWLBY, J. (1973). *Attachment and loss: Vol. 2. Separation.* New York: Basic Books.

BOWLBY, J. (1980). *Attachment and loss: Vol. 3. Loss, sadness, and depression.* New York: Basic Books.

BOWLBY, J. (1988). *A secure base.* New York: Basic Books.

BRANNON, L., & FEIST, J. (2004). *Health psychology: An introduction to behavior and health* (5th ed.). Belmont, CA: Wadsworth/Thomson Learning.

BRENNER, P. (2002). *Buddha in the waiting room: Simple truths about health, illness, and healing.* Hillsboro, OR: Beyond Words.

BUREAU OF LABOR STATISTICS. (2001a). *Current population survey data for 2000 by detailed occupation and sex.* Retrieved December 27, 2001, from ftp://ftp.bls.gov/pub/special.requests/If.aat11.txt

BUREAU OF LABOR STATISTICS. (2001b). *Employment characteristics of families summary.* Retrieved December 27, 2001, from http://www.bls.gov/news.release/famee.txt

*BURNS, D. D. (1981). *Feeling good: The new mood therapy.* New York: New American Library (Signet).

*BUSCAGLIA, L. (1972). *Love.* Thorofare, NJ: Charles B. Slack.

BUSCAGLIA, L. (1992). *Born for love: Reflections on loving.* New York: Fawcett (Columbine).

CALDWELL, L. D., & WHITE, J. L. (2001). African-centered therapeutic and counseling interventions for African American males. In G. R. Brooks & G. E. Good (Eds.), *The new handbook of psychotherapy and counseling with men, Volume 2* (pp. 737–753). San Francisco: Jossey-Bass.

CAPUZZI, D. (ED.). (2004). *Suicide across the life span: Implications for counselors.* Alexandria, VA: American Counseling Association.

CARDUCCI, B. J. (1999). *Shyness: A bold new approach: The latest scientific findings, plus practical steps for finding your comfort zone.* New York: HarperCollins.

CARLSON, R. (1997). *Don't sweat the small stuff . . . and it's all small stuff.* New York: Hyperion.

CARLSON, R., & SHIELD, B. (EDS.). (1996). *Handbook for the heart: Original writings on love.* Boston: Little, Brown.

*CARNEY, C. G., & WELLS, C. F. (1999). *Working well, living well: Discover the career within you* (5th ed.). Pacific Grove, CA: Brooks/Cole.

*CARR, J. B. (1988). *Crisis in intimacy: When expectations don't meet reality.* Pacific Grove, CA: Brooks/Cole.

CARROLL, J. L. (2005). *Sexuality now: Embracing diversity.* Belmont, CA: Thomson Wadsworth.

CARTER, B., & MCGOLDRICK, M. (EDS.). (2005). *The expanded family life cycle: Individual, family, and social perspectives* (3rd ed.). Boston: Allyn & Bacon.

CASAS, J. M., TURNER, J. A., & RUIZ DE ESPARZA, C. A. (2001). Machismo revisited in a time of crisis. In G. R. Brooks & G. E. Good (Eds.), *The new handbook of psychotherapy and counseling with men, Volume 2* (pp. 754–779). San Francisco: Jossey-Bass.

CENTERS FOR DISEASE CONTROL AND PREVENTION. (1994a). *HIV/AIDS surveillance report, 6*(1), 1.

CENTERS FOR DISEASE CONTROL AND PREVENTION. (1994b). *Surgeon general's report to the American public on HIV infection and AIDS.* Rockville, MD: Author.

CENTERS FOR DISEASE CONTROL AND PREVENTION. (1994c). *Voluntary HIV counseling and testing: Facts, issues, and answers.* Rockville, MD: Author.

CENTERS FOR DISEASE CONTROL AND PREVENTION. (1999a). *Condoms and their use in preventing HIV infection and other STDs.* Rockville, MD: Author.

CENTERS FOR DISEASE CONTROL AND PREVENTION. (1999b). *HIV and its transmission.* Rockville, MD: Author.

CENTERS FOR DISEASE CONTROL AND PREVENTION. (2003). *HIV/AIDS Surveillance Report: Cases of HIV Infection and AIDS in the United States, 2002, Volume 14.* Washington, DC: National Center for HIV, STD and TB Prevention, Department of Health and Human Services. Retrieved from http://www.cdc.gov/hiv/stats/hasr1402.htm

CHAPMAN, A. B. (1993). Black men do feel about love. In M. Golden (Ed.), *Wild women don't wear no blues: Black women writers on love, men and sex.* New York: Doubleday.

CHOUDHURY, B. (1978). *Bikram's beginning yoga class.* New York: Jeremy P. Tarcher (Putnam).

COCHRAN, S. V., & RABINOWITZ, F. E. (1996). Men, loss, and psychotherapy. *Psychotherapy, 33*(4), 593–600.

COREY, G., COREY, C., & COREY, H. (1997). *Living and learning.* Belmont, CA: Wadsworth.

COREY, M. S., & COREY, G. (2006). *Groups: Process and practice* (7th ed.). Belmont, CA: Thomson Brooks/Cole.

CORR, C. A. (1992). A task-based approach to coping with dying. *Omega, 24,* 81–94.

*CORR, C. A., NABE, C. M., & CORR, D. M. (2003). *Death and dying, life and living* (5th ed.). Belmont, CA: Wadsworth.

COURTNEY-CLARKE, M. (1999). *Maya Angelou: The poetry of living.* New York: Clarkson Potter.

*COVEY, S. R. (1990). *The seven habits of highly effective people.* New York: Simon & Schuster (Fireside).

CROOKS, R., & BAUR, K. (2002). *Our sexuality* (8th ed.). Belmont, CA: Thomson Wadsworth.

*DALAI LAMA. (1999). *Ethics for the new millennium.* New York: Riverhead.

DALAI LAMA. (2001). *An open heart: Practicing compassion in everyday life.* Boston: Little Brown.

*DALAI LAMA, & CUTLER, H. C. (1998). *The art of happiness: A handbook for living.* New York: Riverhead.

DAWSON, G. (2000). *Life is so good.* New York: Random House Value.

DEETS, H. B. (2000, January/February). The graying of the world: Crisis or opportunity? *Modern Maturity,* p. 82.

DELANY, S. L., & DELANY, A. E. (WITH HEARTH, A. H.). (1993). *Having our say: The Delany sisters' first 100 years.* New York: Dell (Delta).

DONATELLE, R., SNOW-HARTER, C., & WILCOX, A. (1995). *Wellness: Choices for health and fitness.* Redwood City, CA: Benjamin/Cummings.

*EASWARAN, E. (1991). *Meditation.* Tomales, CA: Nilgiri Press.

EDLIN, G., GOLANTY, E., & BROWN, K. (2000). *Essentials for health and wellness* (2nd ed.). Sudbury, MA: Jones & Bartlett.

EDUCATIONAL TESTING SERVICE. (1996). *SIGI PLUS.* [Computer program]. Princeton, NJ: Author.

*ELKIND, D. (1984). *All grown up and no place to go.* Reading, MA: Addison-Wesley.

*ELLIS, A. (2001). *Overcoming destructive beliefs, feelings, and behaviors.* Amherst, NY: Prometheus Books.

*ELLIS, A., & HARPER, R. A. (1997). *A guide to rational living* (3rd ed.). North Hollywood, CA: Wilshire.

EPSTEIN, M. (1998). *Going to pieces without falling apart: A Buddhist perspective on wholeness.* New York: Broadway Books.

ERIKSON, E. (1963). *Childhood and society* (2nd ed.). New York: Norton.

ERIKSON, E. (1968). *Identity: Youth and crisis.* New York: Norton.

ERIKSON, E. (1982). *The life cycle completed.* New York: Norton.

FADIMAN, A. (1997). *The spirit catches you and you fall down.* New York: Farrar, Straus & Giroux.

FALUDI, S. (1991). *Backlash: The undeclared war against American women.* New York: Crown.

FARRELL, W. (2000). *Women can't hear what men don't say.* New York: Penguin Putnam.

FEUERSTEIN, G., & BODIAN, S. (EDS.). (1993). *Living yoga: A comprehensive guide for daily life.* New York: Jeremy P. Tarcher (Putnam).

FIELD, F. M. (1998). Massage therapy effects. *American Psychologist, 53*(12), 1270–1281.

*FONTANA, D. (1997). *Teach yourself to dream: A practical guide.* San Francisco: Chronicle Books.

*FONTANA, D. (1999). *Learn to meditate: A practical guide to self-discovery and fulfillment.* San Francisco: Chronicle Books.

*FORWARD, S., & BUCK, C. S. (1988). *Betrayal of innocence: Incest and its devastation.* New York: Penguin.

*FRANKL, V. (1963). *Man's search for meaning.* New York: Washington Square Press.

*FRANKL, V. (1965). *The doctor and the soul.* New York: Bantam.

*FRANKL, V. (1969). *The will to meaning: Foundation and applications of logotherapy.* New York: New American Library.

*FRANKL, V. (1978). *The unheard cry for meaning.* New York: Bantam.

*FREEMAN, S. J. (2005). *Grief and loss: Understanding the journey.* Belmont, CA: Thomson Brooks/Cole.

FRIEND, D. (1991). *The meaning of life.* Boston: Little, Brown.

*FROMM, E. (1956). *The art of loving.* New York: Harper & Row (Colophon). (Paperback edition 1974)

GARDNER, H. (1983). *Frames of mind: The theory of multiple intelligences.* New York: Basic Books.

*GEORGE, M. (1998). *Learn to relax: A practical guide to easing tension and conquering stress.* San Francisco: Chronicle Books.

*GIBRAN, K. (1923). *The prophet.* New York: Knopf.

*GLASSER, W. (1998). *Choice theory: A new psychology of personal freedom.* New York: Harper & Row.

*GLASSER, W. (2000). *Counseling with choice theory: The new reality therapy.* New York: Harper & Row.

GLIONNA, J. M. (1992, January 12). Dance of life. *Los Angeles Times.*

GOLDBERG, H. (1976). *The hazards of being male.* New York: New American Library.

GOLDBERG, H. (1979). *The new male: From self-destruction to self-care.* New York: New American Library (Signet).

GOLDBERG, H. (1983). *The new male–female relationship.* New York: New American Library.

*GOLDBERG, H. (1987). *The inner male: Overcoming roadblocks to intimacy.* New York: New American Library (Signet).

*GOLEMAN, D. (1995). *Emotional intelligence.* New York: Bantam.

GOOD, M., & GOOD, P. (1979). *20 most asked questions about the Amish and Mennonites.* Lancaster, PA: Good Books.

*GOTTMAN, J. M., & SILVER, N. (1999). *The seven principles for making marriage work.* New York: Three Rivers Press.

GOULD, R. L. (1978). *Transformations: Growth and change in adult life.* New York: Simon & Schuster (Touchstone).

GOULDING, M., & GOULDING, R. (1979). *Changing lives through redecision therapy.* New York: Brunner/Mazel.

GOULDING, R., & GOULDING, M. (1978). *The power is in the patient.* San Francisco: TA Press.

HAFEN, B. Q., KARREN, K. J., FRANDSEN, K. J., & SMITH, N. L. (1996). *Mind/body health.* Boston: Allyn & Bacon.

HALDEMAN, D. C. (2001). Psychotherapy with gay and bisexual men. In G. R. Brooks & G. E. Good (Eds.), *The new handbook of psychotherapy and counseling with men, Volume 2* (pp. 796–815). San Francisco: Jossey-Bass.

HALES, D. (1987). *How to sleep like a baby.* New York: Ballantine.

HALES, D. (2005). *An invitation to health* (11th ed.). Belmont, CA: Wadsworth/Thomson Learning.

HARLOW, H. F., & HARLOW, M. K. (1966). Learning to love. *American Scientist, 54,* 244–272.

HARRIS, A. S. (1996). *Living with paradox: An introduction to Jungian psychology.* Pacific Grove, CA: Brooks/Cole.

HARRIS, I. M. (1995). *Messages men hear: Constructing masculinities.* Bristol, PA: Taylor & Francis.

*HIRSCHMANN, J. R., & MUNTER, C. H. (1995). *When women stop hating their bodies: Freeing yourself from food and weight obsession.* New York: Fawcett (Columbine).

HODGE, M. (1967). *Your fear of love.* Garden City, NY: Doubleday.

HOFFMAN, E. (1990). *Lost in translation: A life in a new language.* New York: Penguin Books.

HOLLAND, J. L. (1994). *Self-directed search (form R).* Odessa, FL: Psychological Assessment Resources, Inc.

HOLLAND, J. L. (1997). *Making vocational choices: A theory of vocational personalities and work environments* (3rd ed.). Odessa, FL: Psychological Assessment Resources, Inc.

HOLMES, T. H., & RAHE, R. H. (1967). The social readjustment rating scale. *Journal of Psychosomatic Research, 11,* 213–218.

*HWANG, P. O. (2000). *Other-esteem: Meaningful life in a multicultural society.* Philadelphia, PA: Accelerated Development (Taylor & Francis).

*JAMPOLSKY, G. G. (1981). *Love is letting go of fear.* New York: Bantam.

*JAMPOLSKY, G. G. (1999). *Forgiveness: The greatest healer of all.* Hillsboro, OR: Beyond Words.

JOHNSON, E. M. (1992). *What you can do to avoid AIDS.* New York: Times Books.

JOINT UNITED NATIONS PROGRAMME ON HIV/AIDS AND THE WORLD HEALTH ORGANIZATION. (2002). *AIDS epidemic update.* Geneva, Switzerland: UNAIDS.

JONES, C., & SHORTER-GOODEN, K. (2003). *Shifting: The double lives of black women in America.* New York: HarperCollins.

JORDAN, J. V., KAPLAN, A. G., MILLER, J. B., STIVER, I. P., & SURREY, J. L. (1991). *Women's growth through connection: Writings from the Stone Center.* New York: Guilford.

JOURARD, S. (1971). *The transparent self: Self-disclosure and well-being* (rev. ed.). New York: Van Nostrand Reinhold.

*JOY, W. B. (1979). *Joy's way: A map for the transformational journey.* Los Angeles, CA: Jeremy P. Tarcher.

JUDY, R., & D'AMICO, C. (1997). *Workforce 2020: Work and workers in the 21st century.* Indianapolis, IN: Hudson Institute.

*JULIA, M. (2000). *Constructing gender: Multicultural perspectives in working with women.* Pacific Grove, CA: Brooks/Cole.

JUNG, C. G. (1961). *Memories, dreams, reflections.* New York: Vintage Books.

KABAT-ZINN, J. (1990). *Full catastrophe living.* New York: Delacorte.

KABAT-ZINN, J. (1994). *Wherever you go, there you are: Mindfulness meditation in everyday life.* New York: Hyperion.

KASLOW, N. J., & ARONSON, S. G. (2004). Recommendations for family interventions following suicide. *Professional Psychology: Research and Practice, 35*(3), 240–247.

*KATZ, J. (1999). *Running to the mountain: A journey of faith and change.* New York: Villard.

*KEEN, S. (1991). *Fire in the belly: On being a man.* New York: Bantam.

KIMMEL, M. (1996). *Manhood in America: A cultural history.* New York: Free Press.

KINOSIAN, J. (2000, May–June). Right place, write time. *Modern Maturity.*

KLEESPIES, P. M. (2004). *Life and death decisions: Psychological and ethical consideration in end-of-life care.* Washington, DC: American Psychological Association.

KOBASA, S. C. (1979a). Personality and resistance to illness. *American Journal of Community Psychology, 7,* 413–423.

KOBASA, S. C. (1979b). Stressful life events, personality and health: An inquiry into hardiness. *Journal of Personality and Social Psychology, 37,* 1–11.

KOBASA, S. C. (1984, September). How much stress can you survive? *American Health,* 64–67.

KOTTLER, J. A. (2001). *Making changes last.* Philadelphia, PA: Brunner-Routledge (Taylor & Francis).

*KÜBLER-ROSS, E. (1969). *On death and dying.* New York: Macmillan.

KÜBLER-ROSS, E. (1975). *Death: The final stage of growth.* Englewood Cliffs, NJ: Prentice-Hall (Spectrum).

*LERNER, H. G. (1985). *The dance of anger: A woman's guide to changing the patterns of intimate relationships.* New York: Harper & Row (Perennial).

LERNER, H. G. (1989). *The dance of intimacy: A woman's guide to courageous acts of change in key relationships.* New York: Harper & Row (Perennial).

LEVANT, R. F. (1996). The new psychology of men. *Professional Psychology: Research and Practice, 27*(3), 259–265.

*LEVINSON, D. J. (1978). *The seasons of man's life.* New York: Knopf.

LEVINSON, D. J. (WITH LEVINSON, J. D.). (1996). *The seasons of woman's life.* New York: Ballantine.

LEWIS, C. S. (1961). *A grief observed.* New York: Seabury.

*LINDBERGH, A. (1975). *Gift from the sea.* New York: Pantheon. (Original work published in 1955)

*LOCK, R. D. (2005a). *Job search: Career planning guide* (5th ed.). Belmont, CA: Thomson Brooks/Cole.

*LOCK, R. D. (2005b). *Taking charge of your career direction: Career planning guide* (5th ed.). Belmont, CA: Thomson Brooks/Cole.

*LOTT, B. (1994). *Women's lives: Themes and variations in gender learning* (2nd ed.). Pacific Grove, CA: Brooks/Cole.

MAHALIK, J. R. (1999a). Incorporating a gender role strain perspective in assessing and treating men's cognitive distortions. *Professional Psychology: Research and Practice, 30*(4), 333–340.

MAHALIK, J. R. (1999b). Interpersonal psychotherapy with men who experience gender role conflict. *Professional Psychology: Research and Practice, 30*(1), 5–13.

*MAIER, S. (1991). *God's love song.* Corvallis, OR: Postal Instant Press.

MALTZ, W. (2001). *The sexual healing journey: A guide for survivors of sexual abuse.* New York: HarperCollins.

*MARCUS, E. (1996). *Why suicide? Answers to 200 of the most frequently asked questions about suicide, attempted suicide, and assisted suicide.* San Francisco: HarperCollins.

MASLACH, C. (1982). *Burnout: The cost of caring.* Englewood Cliffs, NJ: Prentice-Hall (Spectrum).

MASLOW, A. (1968). *Toward a psychology of being.* New York: Van Nostrand Reinhold.

MASLOW, A. (1970). *Motivation and personality* (2nd ed.). New York: Harper & Row.

MASLOW, A. (1971). *The farther reaches of human nature.* New York: Viking.

MATLIN, M. W. (2004). *The psychology of women* (5th ed.). Belmont, CA: Wadsworth/Thomson Learning.

*McGOLDRICK, M. (2005). Women and the family life cycle. In B. Carter & M. McGoldrick (Eds.), *The expanded family life cycle: Individual, family, and social perspectives* (3rd ed., pp. 106–123). Boston: Allyn & Bacon.

*McGOLDRICK, M., & CARTER, B. (2005). Self in context: The individual life cycle in systemic perspective. In B. Carter & M. McGoldrick (Eds.), *The expanded family life cycle: Individual, family, and social perspectives* (3rd ed., pp. 27–46). Boston: Allyn & Bacon.

McINTOSH, P. (1988). *White privilege and male privilege: A personal account of coming to see correspondences through work in women's studies.* [Working paper #189]. Wellesley, MA: Wellesley College Center for Research on Women.

McINTOSH, P. (1998). White privilege: Unpacking the invisible knapsack. In P. S. Rothenberg (Ed.), *Race, class, and gender in the United States: An integrated study* (4th ed., pp. 165–169). New York: St. Martin's Press.

*MILLER, J. B., & STIVER, I. P. (1997). *The healing connection: How women form relationships in therapy and in life.* Boston: Beacon Press.

MILLER, T. (1995). *How to want what you have: Discovering the magic and grandeur of ordinary existence.* New York: Avon.

MILLER, W. R. (ED.). (1999). *Integrating spirituality into treatment: Resources for practitioners.* Washington, DC: American Psychological Association.

MOEN, P., & FIELDS, V. (2002). Midcourse in the United States: Does unpaid community participation replace paid work? *Aging International, 27*(3), 21–48.

*MOORE, T. (1994). *Care of the soul: A guide for cultivating depth and sacredness in everyday life.* New York: Harper (Perennial).

MORNELL, P. (1979). *Passive men, wild women.* New York: Ballantine.

MOTHER TERESA. (1999). *In the heart of the world.* New York: MJF Books.

MOULTON, P., & HARPER, L. (1999). *Outside looking in: When someone you love is in therapy.* Brandon, VT: Safer Society Press.

*MOUSTAKAS, C. (1961). *Loneliness.* Englewood Cliffs, NJ: Prentice-Hall (Spectrum).

NAISBITT, J., & ABURDENE, P. (1991). *Megatrends 2000.* New York: Avon.

*NHAT HANH, T. (1991). *Peace is every step: The path of mindfulness in everyday life.* New York: Bantam.

NHAT HANH, T. (1992). *Touching peace: Practicing the art of mindful living.* Berkeley, CA: Parallax Press.

*NHAT HANH, T. (1997). *Teachings on love.* Berkeley, CA: Parallax Press.

OUELLETTE, S. C. (1993). Inquiries into hardiness. In L. Goldberger & S. Breznitz (Eds.), *Handbook of stress: Theoretical and clinical aspects* (2nd ed.). New York: Free Press.

PARDESS, E. (2005). Pride and prejudice with gay and lesbian individuals: Combining narrative and expressive practices. In C. L. Rabin (Ed.), *Understanding gender and culture in the helping process: Practitioners' narratives from global perspectives.* (pp. 109–128). Belmont, CA: Thomson Wadsworth.

PARHAM, T. A. (1989). Cycles of psychological nigrescence. *The Counseling Psychologist, 17*(2), 187–226.

PEHRSSON, D. E., & BOYLAN, M. (2004). Counseling suicide survivors. In D. Capuzzi, (Ed.), *Suicide across the life span: Implications for counselors* (pp. 305–324). Alexandria, VA: American Counseling Association.

PELUSO, P. R., PELUSO, J. P., WHITE, J. F., & KERN, R. M. (2004). A comparison of attachment theory and individual psychology: A review of the literature. *Journal of Counseling and Development, 82*(2), 139–145.

*PERLS, F. S. (1969). *Gestalt therapy verbatim.* New York: Bantam.

PERLS, F. S. (1970). Four lectures. In J. Fagan & I. L. Shepherd (Eds.), *Gestalt therapy now* (pp. 14–38). New York: Harper & Row (Colophon).

PHILPOT, C. L., BROOKS, G. R., LUSTERMAN, D. D., & NUTT, R. L. (1997). *Bridging separate gender worlds: Why men and women clash and how therapists can bring them together.* Washington, DC: American Psychological Association.

PISTOLE, C., & ARRICALE, F. (2003). Understanding attachment: Beliefs about conflict. *Journal of Counseling and Development, 81*(3), 318–328.

PLECK, J. (1995). The gender role paradigm: An update. In R. Levant & W. Pollack (Eds.), *A new psychology of men.* New York: Basic Books.

*POLLACK, W. (1998). *Real boys.* New York: Henry Holt.

RABIN, C. L. (ED.). (2005). *Understanding gender and culture in the helping process: Practitioners' narratives from global perspectives.* Belmont, CA: Thomson Wadsworth.

RABINOWITZ, F. E. (2001). Group therapy for men. In G. R. Brooks & G. E. Good (Eds.), *The new handbook of psychotherapy and counseling with men, Volume 2* (pp. 603–621). San Francisco: Jossey-Bass.

*RABINOWITZ, F. E., & COCHRAN, S. V. (1994). *Man alive: A primer of men's issues.* Pacific Grove, CA: Brooks/Cole.

*RABINOWITZ, F. E., & COCHRAN, S. V. (2002). *Deepening psychotherapy with men.* Washington, DC: American Psychological Association.

*RAINWATER, J. (1979). *You're in charge! A guide to becoming your own therapist.* Los Angeles: Guild of Tutors Press.

*REAL, T. (1998). *I don't want to talk about it: Overcoming the secret legacy of male depression.* New York: Simon & Schuster (Fireside).

*RICE, P. L. (1999). *Stress and health* (3rd ed.). Pacific Grove, CA: Brooks/Cole.

RICHARDS, P. S., RECTOR, J. M., & TJELTVEIT, A. C. (1999). Values, spirituality, and psychotherapy. In W. R. Miller (Ed.), *Integrating spirituality into treatment: Resources for practitioners* (pp. 133–160). Washington, DC: American Psychological Association.

RIDLEY, C. R. (1995). *Overcoming unintentional racism in counseling and psychotherapy.* Thousand Oaks, CA: Sage.

*RINPOCHE, S. (1994). *Meditation.* San Francisco: Harper.

ROBINSON, E. A. (1943). *The children of the night.* New York: Scribner's.

ROGERS, C. R. (1961). *On becoming a person: A therapist's view of psychotherapy.* Boston: Houghton Mifflin.

ROGERS, C. R. (1980). *A way of being.* Boston: Houghton Mifflin.

ROSEN, E. J. (2005). Men in transition: The "new man." In B. Carter & M. McGoldrick (Eds.), *The expanded family life cycle: Individual, family, and social perspectives* (3rd ed., pp. 124–140). Boston: Allyn & Bacon.

SCHAFER, W. (2000). *Stress management for wellness* (4th ed.). Belmont, CA: Wadsworth.

*SCHLOSSBERG, N. K. (2004). *Retire smart, retire happy: Finding your true path in life.* Washington, DC: American Psychological Association.

*SCHNARCH, D. (1997). *Passionate marriage.* New York: Henry Holt.

SCHULTZ, D., & SCHULTZ, S. E. (2005). *Theories of personality* (8th ed.). Pacific Grove, CA: Brooks/Cole.

*SCHWARTZ, M. (1996). *Morrie: In his own words.* New York: Dell (Delta Book).

SELIGMAN, M. E. P. (1990). *Learned optimism: How to change your mind and your life.* New York: Pocket Books.

*SELIGMAN, M. E. P. (1993). *What you can change and what you can't.* New York: Fawcett (Columbine).

SHARF, R. S. (2002). *Applying career development theory to counseling.* Pacific Grove, CA: Brooks/Cole.

SHEEHY, G. (1976). *Passages: Predictable crises of adult life.* New York: Dutton.

SHEEHY, G. (1981). *Pathfinders.* New York: Morrow.

SHEEHY, G. (1992). *The silent passage.* New York: Random House.

*SHEEHY, G. (1995). *New passages: Mapping your life across time.* New York: Random House.

SHIELD, B., & CARLSON, R. (EDS.). (1999). *For the love of God: Handbook for the spirit.* New York: MJF Books.

*SIEGEL, B. (1988). *Love, medicine, and miracles.* New York: Harper & Row (Perennial).

*SIEGEL, B. (1989). *Peace, love, and healing. Bodymind communication and the path to self-healing: An exploration.* New York: Harper & Row.

SIEGEL, B. (1993). *How to live between office visits: A guide to life, love, and health.* New York: HarperCollins.

*SIZER, F., & WHITNEY, E. (2000). *Nutrition: Concepts and controversies* (8th ed.). Belmont, CA: Wadsworth.

SMITH, C., & SULSKY, L. (2005). *Work stress.* Belmont, CA: Thomson Wadsworth.

STEINER, C. (1975). *Scripts people live: Transactional analysis of life scripts.* New York: Bantam.

*STONE, H., & STONE, S. (1993). *Embracing your inner critic: Turning self-criticism into a creative asset.* San Francisco: Harper.

SUE, D. (2001). Asian American masculinity and therapy. In G. R. Brooks & G. E. Good (Eds.), *The new handbook of psychotherapy and counseling with men, Volume 2* (pp. 780–795). San Francisco: Jossey-Bass.

SUE, D. W. (2003). *Overcoming our racism: The journey to liberation.* San Francisco, CA: Jossey-Bass.

SUE, D. W., & SUE, D. (2003). *Counseling the culturally diverse: Theory and practice* (4th ed.). New York: Wiley.

*TANNEN, D. (1987). *That's not what I meant: How conversational style makes or breaks relationships.* New York: Ballantine.

*TANNEN, D. (1991). *You just don't understand: Women and men in conversation.* New York: Ballantine.

TATUM, B. D. (1999). *"Why are all the black kids sitting together in the cafeteria?"* New York: Basic Books.

*TAVRIS, C. (1992). *The mismeasure of women.* New York: Simon & Schuster (Touchstone).

*TERKEL, S. (1975). *Working.* New York: Avon.

TRACY, V. M. (1993). *The impact of childhood sexual abuse on women's sexuality.* Unpublished doctoral dissertation. La Jolla University: San Diego, CA.

*TRAVIS, J. W., & RYAN, R. S. (1994). *Wellness workbook* (3rd ed.). Berkeley, CA: Ten Speed Press.

VANDERBILT, H. (1992, February). Incest: A four-part chilling report. *Lear's, 4*(12), 49–77.

*VANZANT, I. (1998). *One day my soul just opened up.* New York: Simon & Schuster (Fireside).

VERGEER, G. E. (1995). Therapeutic applications of humor. *Directions in Mental Health Counseling, 5*(3), 4–11.

*VONTRESS, C. E., JOHNSON, J. A., & EPP, L. R. (1999). *Cross-cultural counseling: A casebook.* Alexandria, VA: American Counseling Association.

*WEBB, D. (1996). *Divorce and separation recovery.* Portsmouth, NH: Randall.

*WEBB, D. (2000). *50 ways to love your leaver: Getting on with your life after the breakup.* Atascadero, CA: Impact.

*WEENOLSEN, P. (1996). *The art of dying: How to leave this world with dignity and grace, at peace with yourself and your loved ones.* New York: St. Martin's Press.

*WEIL, A. (2000). *Eating well for optimum health: The essential guide to food, diet, and nutrition.* New York: Knopf.

WEINER-DAVIS, M. (1995). *Change your life and everyone in it.* New York: Simon & Schuster (Fireside).

*WEITEN, W., & LLOYD, M. A. (2003). *Psychology applied to modern life: Adjustment at the turn of the 21st century* (7th ed.). Belmont, CA: Wadsworth.

*WILLIAMS, B., & KNIGHT, S. M. (1994). *Healthy for life: Wellness and the art of living.* Pacific Grove, CA: Brooks/Cole.

*WILLIAMS, C. (1992). *No hiding place: Empowerment and recovery for our troubled communities.* San Francisco: Harper.

WITKIN, G. (1994). *The male stress syndrome: How to survive stress in the '90s* (2nd ed.). New York: Newmarket.

WORDEN, J. W. (2002). *Grief counseling and grief therapy: A handbook for the mental health practitioner* (3rd ed.). New York: Springer.

*WUBBOLDING, R. E. (2000). *Reality therapy for the 21st century.* Muncie, IN: Accelerated Development (Taylor & Francis).

WYLIE, M. S. (2000). Soul therapy. *Family Therapy Networker, 24*(1), 26–37, 60–61.

*YALOM, I. D. (1980). *Existential psychotherapy.* New York: Basic Books.

ZIMBARDO, P. G. (1987). *Shyness.* New York: Jove.

*ZIMBARDO, P. G. (1994). *Shyness.* Reading, MA: Addison-Wesley.

ZUNKER, V. G. (2002). *Career counseling: Applied concepts of life planning.* Belmont, CA: Brooks/Cole.

ZUNKER, V. G., & OSBORN, D. S. (2002). *Using assessment results for career counseling.* Belmont, CA: Brooks/Cole.

Photo Credits

Index

TO THE OWNER OF THIS BOOK:

We hope that you have found *I Never Knew I Had a Choice: Explorations in Personal Growth,* 8th edition, useful. So that this book can be improved in a future edition, would you take the time to complete this sheet and return it? Thank you.

School and address: _____

Department: _____

Instructor's name: _____

1. What I like most about this book is: _____

_____

_____

2. What I like least about this book is:

_____

_____

3. My general reaction to this book is:

_____

_____

4. The name of the course in which I used this book is:

_____

5. Were all of the chapters of the book assigned for you to read? _____

   If not, which ones weren't? _____

6. In the space below, or on a separate sheet of paper, please write specific suggestions for improving this book and anything else you'd care to share about your experience in using this book.

_____

_____

_____

BUSINESS REPLY MAIL

FIRST-CLASS MAIL   PERMIT NO. 34   BELMONT CA

POSTAGE WILL BE PAID BY ADDRESSEE

Attn: Christine Northup
BrooksCole/Thomson Learning
10 Davis Drive
Belmont, CA   94002-9801

OPTIONAL:

Your name: _____ Date: _____

May we quote you, either in promotion for *I Never Knew I Had a Choice: Explorations in Personal Growth,* 8th edition, or in future publishing ventures?

Yes: _____ No: _____

Sincerely yours,

Gerald Corey

Marianne Schneider Corey

More Praise for *The Bingo Palace*

"Grounded in harsh reality, Erdrich's prose attains a full-throated mystery and magic akin to that of Gabriel Gárcia Márquez or Toni Morrison. . . . Erdrich's brilliance lies in transforming the American Indian fascination with games of chance into a compelling metaphor for the intricacies of fortune.

"In *The Bingo Palace*, Louise Erdrich has taken a chance of her own and scored big. It's another triumph for one of our best writers of fiction."

—*New York Newsday*

"*The Bingo Palace* is a masterpiece. . . . Writing in prose both dense and colloquial, with characters and subject matter that continue to be engrossing, Erdrich has again created a world that is at once familiar, foreign and magical."

—*Glamour*

"Louise Erdrich's books all have stoic wisdom, an unwillingness to judge, a commitment to objective observation that records each emotional event entirely, without ever sacrificing complexity of meaning. *The Bingo Palace* is full of that wisdom."

—*Los Angeles Times Book Review*

"*The Bingo Palace* is the story of two men in love with the same woman, surely the oldest plot around, but one that Louise Erdrich reinvents with delicacy humor and boldness . . . so vivid are the images and carefully constructed scenes, that both place and passion become immediate and memorable."

—*New York Daily News*

"In the hands of the sort of accomplished novelist that Erdrich has become, we can know a place as even its own residents only dimly do. In these novels of Erdrich's we come to see not only the history and myths that form the narrative a community tells about itself, but the patterning in the generations of a family and . . . insights into the most private matters of the individual heart and psyche."

—*USA Today*

"Erdrich's rich, pleasurable mix of family histories, tribal gambling and humanist vision is homebred magic realism played by an expert."

—*Elle*

THE BINGO PALACE

by Louise Erdrich

THE BINGO PALACE

LOUISE ERDRICH

HarperPerennial
A Division of HarperCollinsPublishers

Parts of this book have been previously published in the following: Chapter Seven as "The Bingo Van" in *The New Yorker,* Chapter Twelve as "Fleur's Luck" in the *Georgia Review,* Chapter Twenty-four as "I'm a Mad Dog Biting Myself for Sympathy" in *Granta.*

A hardcover edition of this book was published in 1994 by HarperCollins Publishers.

HarperCollins books may be purchased for educational, business, or sales promotional use. For information please write: Special Markets Department, HarperCollins Publishers, Inc., 10 East 53rd Street, New York, NY 10022.

First HarperPerennial edition published 1995.

Designed by C. Linda Dingler

The Library of Congress has catalogued the hardcover edition as follows:

Erdrich, Louise.
  The bingo palace / Louise Erdrich. — 1st ed.
   p. cm.
  ISBN 0-06-017080-8 (cloth)
  1. Indians of North America—North Dakota—Fiction. 2. Man–woman relationships—North Dakota—Fiction. 3. Bingo—North Dakota—Fiction. I. Title.
PS3555.R42B5 1994
813'.54—dc20   93–37684

ISBN 0-06-092585-X (pbk.)
95 96 97 98 99 ❖/RRD 10 9 8 7 6 5 4 3 2 1

To Michael,
U R lucky 4 me

ACKNOWLEDGMENTS

Megwitch, Merci, B-4 and after 4 bingo guidance, Susan Moldow, Lise, Angela and Heid Ellen Erdrich, Sandi Campbell, Delia Bebonang, Thelma Stiffarm and Duane Bird Bear family, Pat Stuen, Peter Brandvold, Alan Quint, Gail Hand, Pauline Russette, Laurie SunChild, Marlin Gourneau, Chris Gourneau, Bob and Peggy Treuer and family, Two Martin, Trent Duffy, Tom MacDonald, Michael Dorris, as ever, for his generous devotion to this book. Thanks go to my father, Ralph Erdrich, for keeping track of bingo life, and again, my grandfather, Pat Gourneau, who played so many cards at once.

CONTENTS

Contents

CHAPTER ONE

THE MESSAGE

ON MOST WINTER DAYS, LULU LAMARTINE DID NOT STIR UNTIL the sun cast a patch of warmth for her to bask in and purr. She then rose, brewed fresh coffee, heated a pan of cream, and drank the mix from a china cup at her apartment table. Sipping, brooding, she entered the snowy world. A pale sweet roll, a doughnut gem, occasionally a bowl of cereal, followed that coffee, then more coffee, and on and on, until finally Lulu pronounced herself awake and took on the day's business of running the tribe. We know her routine—many of us even shared it—so when she was sighted before her normal get-up time approaching her car door in the unsheltered cold of the parking lot, we called on others to look. Sure enough, she was dressed for action. She got into her brown Citation wearing hosiery, spike-heeled boots, and, beneath her puffy purple winter coat, a flowered dress cut evening low. She adjusted her rearview mirror, settled her eyeglasses on her nose. She started the engine, pulled away onto the downslope winding road. From the hill, we saw her pass into the heart of the reservation.

She rolled along in quiet purpose, stopping at the signs, even yielding, traveling toward one of two places open at that early hour. The gas pumps—she could be starting out on a longer trip—or the post office. These were the two choices that we figured out among ourselves. When she passed the first, we knew it must be the second, and from there, we relied on Day Twin Horse to tell us how Lulu entered the post office beneath the flags of the United States, the Great Seal of North Dakota, and the emblem of our Chippewa Nation, and then lingered, looking all around, warming herself like a cat at the heat register and tapping at her lips with a painted fingernail.

Day Twin Horse watched her, that is, until she turned, saw him looking, and set confusion into motion. First she glared a witch gaze that caused him to tape a finger to the postal scale. The tape seemed to have a surprising life all of its own so that, as he leaned over, extracting the finger, balling up the tape, Day Twin Horse became more and more agitated. For while he struggled with the sticky underside, Mrs. Josette Bizhieu entered, impatient as always, carrying three packages. Tending to her needs, Postmaster Twin Horse was unable to keep an eye on Lulu as she wandered, flicking at the dials of the tiny boxes that held other people's bills. He did not see her pause to read the directions on the Xerox machine, or lean over the glass display case showing pen sets, stamp mugs, albums that could be purchased by collectors. He did not see her stop before the wanted posters, flick through quickly, silently, riffling the heavy roll until she came to the picture of her son.

It was Josette herself, sharp and wary as her namesake bobcat, who tipped her chin down, turned her face just a fraction to watch Lulu Lamartine as she reached into the fall of criminals and with one quick tug, evenly, as if she were removing a paper towel from a toothed dispenser, tear away government property. Holding the paper, Lulu walked over to the copier. She carefully slid the picture onto the machine's face, inserted two coins into the coin box. Satisfaction lit her face as the machine's drum flashed and whirred. She removed the original, then the copy of the picture as it emerged. She folded it into an envelope and carried it quickly to the Out of Town slot, where Josette now held her packages as if deciding which to mail first. Seeing the drop of Josette's gaze, Lulu quickly posted the letter, but not before Josette caught the city part of the address, already written onto the outside of the stamped envelope.

Fargo, North Dakota. There it was—the well-known whereabouts of that stray grandson whom Lulu Lamartine and Marie Kashpaw shared uneasily between themselves. So Lulu Lamartine was sending the picture of the father to the son. Perhaps it was a summons home. A warning. Surely, it meant something. There was always a reason behind the things Lulu did, although it took a while to find them, to work her ciphers out for meaning. Now Lulu walked directly through the glass front doors, leaving Josette and Day Twin Horse in the post office.

The two gazed after her, frowning and pensive. Around them, suddenly, they felt the drift of chance and possibility, for the post office is a place of near misses, lit by numbers. Their gazes fixed upon the metal postal box doors—so strictly aligned and easily mistaken for one another. And then the racks constructed for the necessary array of identical-looking rubber stamps that nevertheless could send a letter halfway around the world. Of course, there were the stamps themselves, either booklets or sheets sold in waxed cellophane envelopes. Eagles. Flowers. Hot air balloons. Love dogs. Wild Bill Hickok. The ordinary world suddenly seemed tenuous, odd. Josette reared back in suspicion, narrowing her clever eyes. Day Twin Horse regarded his olive-colored tape. The roll again was docile and orderly in his hands. He ran his fingernail across the surface searching for the ridge to pull, the cut, but the plastic was seamless, frustrating, perfect, like the small incident with Lulu. He couldn't find where to pull and yet he knew that in her small act there was complicated motive and a larger story.

As it turned out, however, there was not much more to know about the things Lulu did on that particular day. It was later on that we should have worried about, the long-term consequences. All the same, we tried to keep a close eye upon her doings, so we know that soon after she left the post office Lulu Lamartine purchased, from the fanciest gift shop in Hoopdance, a brass and crystal picture frame. She brought it back to her apartment, laid it down upon her kitchen table. Josette, who sat right there with a glass of water, winding down from all her errands, told how Lulu used her nail file to press aside the tiny clamps that held in the backing. She removed the fuzz-coated cardboard, then the inner corrugated square, and lastly, the flimsy reproduction of a happy wedding couple. She tossed the sentimental photograph aside, positioned the wanted poster against the glass. She smoothed down the cheap paper, replaced the backing, then turned the portrait around front to gaze upon the latest picture of her famous criminal boy.

Even in the mug-shot photographer's flash, the Nanapush eyes showed, Pillager bones, the gleam of one earring at his cheek. Gerry Nanapush had a shy rage, serious wonder, a lot of hair. She looked for traces of herself—the nose surely— and of his father—the grin, the smile held in and hidden, wolf-white, gleaming. Looking down the length of her rounded arms, her face was thoughtful, Josette said, too shrewd, bent on calculation. In fact, we never thought Lulu Lamartine wore the proper expression anyway—that of a mother resigned. Her undevout eyes were always dangerously bright, her grin was always trying to get loose and work a spell. Her face was supple, her arms strong, and even touched with arthritis, she had the hands of a safecracker. Still, we thought the business would end with the picture sitting on the shelf. After all, he was recently caught and locked up again for good. We never thought she'd go so far as she finally managed. We believed Lulu Lamartine would content herself with changing the picture's resting spot, carrying it back and forth until she finally centered it upon her knickknack shelf, a place where you couldn't help noticing it upon first entering her apartment.

Lulu's totaling glance followed Josette that day, not the picture's rigid stare, but the two pairs of eyes were so alike that it always took a decision of avoidance to enter the place. Some of us tried to resist, yet were pulled in just the same. We were curious to know more, even though we'd never grasp the whole of it. The story comes around, pushing at our brains, and soon we are trying to ravel back to the beginning, trying to put families into order and make sense of things. But we start with one person, and soon another and another follows, and still another, until we are lost in the connections.

We could pull any string from Lulu, anyway, it wouldn't matter, it would all come out the same degree of tangle. Start with her wanted-poster boy, Gerry Nanapush, for example. Go down the line of her sons, the brothers and half brothers, until you get to the youngest, Lyman Lamartine. Here was a man everybody knew and yet did not know, a dark-minded schemer, a bitter and yet shaman-pleasant entrepreneur who skipped money from behind the ears of Uncle Sam, who joked to pull the wool down, who carved up this reservation the way his blood father Nector Kashpaw did, who had his own interest so mingled with his people's that he couldn't tell his personal ambition from the pride of the Kashpaws. Lyman went so far as to court a much younger woman. He loved and failed, but that has never kept down Kashpaws, or a Lamartine either, for very long.

Keep a hand on the frail rope. There's a storm coming up, a blizzard. June Morrissey still walks through that sudden Easter snow. She was a beautiful woman, much loved and very troubled. She left her son to die and left his father to the mercy of another woman and left her suitcase packed in her room to which the doorknob was missing. Her memory never was recovered except within the thoughts of her niece, Albertine—a Kashpaw, a Johnson, a little of everything, but free of nothing.

We see Albertine dancing at the powwow, long braid down her back and shawl a blue swirl. We see her hunched over the medical library books resisting a cigarette ever since anatomy class. We see her doing what the *mookamon* call *her level best,* which is going at it, going at it until she thinks her head will fall off into her hands. It seems her task to rise and sink, to rush at things fast and from all directions like the wind, to bowl down every adversary with her drama. We see her hurt when the strong rush fails. We see her spring back, collecting power.

We shake our heads, try to go at it one way, then another. The red rope between the mother and her baby is the hope of our nation. It pulls, it sings, it snags, it feeds and holds. How it holds. The shock of throwing yourself to the end of that rope has brought many a wild young woman up short, slammed her down, left her dusting herself off, outraged and tender. Shawnee Ray, Shawnee Ray Toose and her little boy, for instance. The old men shut their eyes and try not to look directly at this young woman's beauty because a hot flame still leaps to life, focused and blue, and what can they do about it? Better to let the tongue clack. We've heard Shawnee Ray talks to spirits in the sweat lodge in such a sweet way, in such an old-time way, respectful, that they can't help but answer. We don't know how she's going to get by that boss *ikwe* Zelda Kashpaw, who put up a stockade around her own heart since the days when she herself was a girl. We don't know how it will work out, come to pass, which is why we watch so hard, all of us alike, one arguing voice.

We do know that no one gets wise enough to really understand the heart of another, though it is the task of our life to try. We chew the tough skins, we wonder. We think about the Pillager woman, Fleur, who was always half spirit anyway. A foot on the death road, a quick shuffle backwards, her dance wearies us. Yet some of us wish she'd come out of the woods. We don't fear her anymore—like death, she is an old friend who has been waiting quietly, a patient companion. We know she's dawdling, hanging back as long as she can, waiting for another to take her place, but in a different way from when she put her death song into other people's mouths. This time she's waiting for a young one, a successor, someone to carry on her knowledge, and since we know who that person must be, our knowledge makes us pity her. We think she's wrong. We think Fleur Pillager should settle her bones in the sun with us and take a rest, instead of wasting her last words on that medicine boy.

Lipsha Morrissey.

We're all disgusted with the son of that wanted poster. We give up on that Morrissey boy Marie Kashpaw rescued from the slough. Spirits pulled his fingers when he was a baby, yet he doesn't appreciate his powers. His touch was strong, but he shorted it out. Going back and forth to the city weakened and confused him and now he flails in a circle with his own tail in his teeth. He shoots across the road like a coyote, dodging between the wheels, and then you see him on the playground, swinging in a swing, and again he has made himself stupid with his dope pipe. He tires us. We try to stand by him, to bring him back, give him advice. We tell him that he should ground himself, sit on the earth and bury his hands in the dirt and beg the Manitous. We have done so much for him and even so, the truth is, he has done nothing yet of wide importance.

We wish that we could report back different since he last told his story, but here's the fact: that boy crossed the line back to the reservation, proud in his mother's blue Firebird car, and then he let his chances slip. For a while it looked like he'd amount to something. He stuck with high school, scored high in the state of North Dakota in the college tests. He gave us all a shock, for we thought he was just a waste, a load, one of those sad reservation statistics. Offers came into his Grandma

Marie's mailbox—everything from diesel mechanics to piloting aircraft. But then he proved us right. For nothing captured his interest. Nothing held him. Nothing sparked.

He got onto a crew that was turning an old abandoned rail-road depot into a first-class restaurant, which was the fad in renovation. It came out picture-perfect, except that when the trains came through plates fell, glasses shook, and water spilled. Next, he worked in a factory that made tomahawks. He helped to bring that enterprise down around his own ears, and didn't stay to clean up the mess, either, but skipped off down to Fargo. There, he found work in a sugar beet plant, shoveling sugar. He shoveled mountains of it, all day, moving it from here to there. He called back on the party line, always collect, to his Grandma Marie, and always he was complaining.

Well, we could imagine. What kind of job was that anyway, for a Chippewa? We weren't very pleased with the picture. When he got back to his room, he held a dustpan underneath his shoes and socks and emptied the sugar in a little pile. He shook his pants in the bathtub and brushed his hair and washed the sugar down the drain. Still, the grains crackled underfoot and the carpet thickened. The shag strands stuck together, the sweetness drew roaches and silverfish, which he sprayed dead. Nothing was ever clean, he told Marie, us listen-ing. The sugar settled into syrup and the spray acted like a seal, so that layers of sticky glaze collected and hardened.

Just like him. He was building up a seal of corrosion, hard-ening himself, packing himself under. We heard from sources we don't like to talk about that he was seen down in the bars, the tougher spots, the dealer hangouts and areas beneath the bridges where so much beyond the law gets passed hand to mouth. Like father, we thought, only moving our eyes to say it, like father, there he goes. And then one day Lulu's mailed pic-ture of Gerry Nanapush arrived in Fargo, a wanted-poster mes-sage regarding his father that evidently made the boy stop and look around himself. This was his life—a fact we could have told him from the first phone call. There he was, sitting at the fake wood-grain table, listening to cars go by in the street below. He was covered with a sugary chip-proof mist of chemicals, preserved, suspended, trapped like a bug in a plastic weight. He was caught in a foreign skin, drowned in drugs and sugar and money, baked hard in a concrete pie.

We didn't know him, we didn't want to, and to tell the truth we didn't care. *Who he is is just the habit of who he always was,* we warned Marie. *If he's not careful, who he'll be is the result.*

Perhaps a drumming teased in the bones of his fingers, or maybe his whole face smarted as if he'd slapped himself out of a long daze. Anyway, he stood up and found himself out the door taking what he could carry—jackets, money, boom box, clothes, books, and tapes. He walked down the hall and stairs, out into the street. He stuffed his car full and then, once he got behind the wheel, all that mattered was the drive.

We saw him immediately as he entered the gym during the winter powwow. He slid through the crowd during the middle of an Intertribal song. We saw him edge against the wall to watch the whirling bright dancers, and immediately we had to notice that there was no place the boy could fit. He was not a tribal council honcho, not a powwow organizer, not a medic in the cop's car in the parking lot, no one we would trust with our life. He was not a member of a drum group, not a singer, not a candy-bar seller. Not a little old Cree lady with a scarf tied under her chin, a thin pocketbook in her lap, and a wax cup of Coke, not one of us. He was not a fancy dancer with a mirror on his head and bobbing porcupine-hair roach, not a traditional, not a shawl girl whose parents beaded her from head to foot. He was not our grandfather, either, with the face like clean old-time chewed leather, who prayed over the microphone, head bowed. He was not even one of those gathered at the soda machines outside the doors, the ones who wouldn't go into the warm and grassy air because of being drunk or too much in love or just bashful. He was not the Chippewa with rings pierced in her nose or the old aunt with water dripping through her fingers or the announcer with a ragged face and a drift of plumes on his indoor hat.

He was none of these, only Lipsha, come home.

LIPSHA MORRISSEY

WALKING INTO THE LIGHTS OF THE HIGH SCHOOL GYM THAT evening, I stop as if to ask directions to a place I've always known. The drums pound, lighting my blood. My heart jumps. I am all at once confused and shy-faced and back where I belong without a place to fit, a person to turn to, a friend to greet. Of course, it doesn't take long before I glimpse satin, the trademark of my cousin Albertine Johnson. Her patience with that slippery fabric is well known, and sure enough, as if I'd even imagined the sky blue color, the darker shadows she would pick, my eyes latch right onto her the first time she circles past and catches me with the corner of her gaze.

I watch her. A dusky blue eagle spreads its beaded wings across her back, and she carries a blue shawl with all shades from navy to turquoise fringe swinging from the borders. Her leggings are beaded blue and her moccasins are that same color. She's put her red-brown hair in one simple braid right down her back, a tapering rope held on each side with a matching rosette and a white plume that lifts softly with each of her steps. Right about here, I ordinarily would begin to tell you all about Albertine: how she went away to school, how her life got so complicated and advanced. However, because she's dancing along with a friend, my story doesn't turn out to be a record of Albertine at all. She comes later. No, the hero of my tale, the mad light, the hope, is the second woman I see dancing at the winter powwow.

Our own Miss Little Shell.

I follow the soft light of Albertine's expression to where it catches the harder radiance of Shawnee Ray Toose, who takes that glow of my cousin's and somehow beams it at me, in a complex ricochet that leaves me, as they sway by, with the dazzling impression of lights glinting off Shawnee's teeth. I step forward, to catch a better glimpse of them both, but my eyes somehow stay hooked to Shawnee Ray. The back view of her jingle dress, which is made of something snaky and gleaming dark red, grabs me hard and won't let go. The material fits so close, and her belt, labeled Miss Little Shell in blazing beads, so tight around her waist.

I blink and shake my head. My eyes want to see more, more, closer, but my hands save me, as I fold my arms and press myself back into the crowd. Still, every time those two women sweep by me I am fixed. I can't ignore the display of Shawnee Ray's sewn-in breasts, carried in a circle, around and around, like prizes in a basket, and those jingles sewn all over her in Vs, so that each wet-looking red curve goes by ringing with her body music. I catch her profile, tough and bold. Her hair is twisted into some kind of braid that looks stitched onto her head, and a crown is pinned there, made of winking stones. Once, when I look too long at her, I think she feels the touch of my attention, because all of a sudden she tips onto her toes, high, higher. She rises into the popcorn air, and she begins to step free and unearthly as a spirit panther, so weightless that I think of clouds, of sun, of air above the snow light.

Then she lands, bounds lower, and puts a hand to her hip. She raises her other arm, proud, and poises her fan high.

Shawnee carries the entire wing and shoulder of a big mother eagle. I picture her lifting off, snagging that bird midflight, and then neatly lopping it in half. You can see Shawnee

Ray deep in the past, running down a buffalo on a little paint war-horse, or maybe on her own limber legs. You can see her felling the animal with one punch to the brain. Or standing bent-elbowed with a lance. You can see her throwing that spear without hesitation right through a cavalry man or a mastodon. Shawnee Ray, she is the best of our past, our present, our hope of a future.

There are her parents, I see now. Elward Strong Ribs, second husband to big Irene Toose. They are back to the reservation for a visit. Shawnee's real dad died a while ago in a bad accident, and after Irene married again the new couple went to work in Minot. Shawnee Ray was left here on the reservation to finish high school and, oh yes, to have her baby, which everyone now takes for granted.

Tonight, Elward and Irene are sitting as far apart as they can place themselves on side-by-side folding chairs, trying not to look at their girl too often, or to seem too pleased with her or not pleased enough with one another. They try not to notice that Irene's other daughters, the Toose girls, are not in the gym but most likely out in the parking lot or farther off, drinking in the dark hills beyond. They try not to notice their own position, the best one, right in front but not too near the Rising Wind drum, and try not to talk too long to any one person or show their favor although they nod in agreement with the medium-stout woman in the heavy black-velvet beaded dress who stands next to them with a child in her arms.

Zelda Kashpaw.

When women age into their power, no wind can upset them, no hand turn aside their knowledge; no fact can deflect their point of view. It is like that with the woman I was raised to think of as a sister and call aunt in respect, the velvet beaded lady holding Shawnee Ray's little boy. Upon seeing Zelda Kashpaw, I remember to dread her goodness. I remember to fear her pity, her helping ways. She is, in fact the main reason coming home is never simple: with Zelda, I am always in for something I cannot see but that is already built, in its final stages, erected all around. It is invisible, a house of pulled strings, a net of unforced will, a perfect cat's cradle that will spring to life as soon as Zelda is aware of me. I step back. Her head whips around. What am I thinking? My aunt knows all there is to know. She has a deep instinct for running things. She should have more children or at least a small nation to control. Instead, forced narrow, her talents run to getting people to do things they don't want to do for other people they don't like. Zelda is the author of grit-jawed charity on the reservation, the instigator of good works that always get chalked up to her credit.

Zelda stands firm, a woman to whom much is obliged. She moves within an aura of repayment schedules, and, as always, it is clear I owe her big even though I don't yet know what for. This happens in many different and mysterious ways. How amazed I am so often in my life to find myself acting, as I believe, from true and deep motivations, only to discover later that Zelda has planned what I am doing.

For instance, she knows all about my return. My summons by Grandma Lulu. No words needed. Zelda has now left the Strong Ribs and Toose family and moved over next to me. She carries Shawnee Ray's little boy, Redford, carefully in her arms, but he is only bait for calculations. I know that much by this time. It is no matter that I have driven the back roads. No matter that I haven't talked to or in any way informed my aunt of my traveling decisions. It turns out that all along, without knowing it, I am just following her mental directions.

"I told them you'd make it," she says, putting down the boy, who runs directly into the circle and manages somehow to evade the trampling moccasins of the big-bellied war dancers who lurch past, too proud and heavy with bone plate and paint to lift their knees. Redford zips straight to his mother's side and she scoops him immediately close. His round-cheeked face sweetens, his eyes go big and tender, light with dark fascination. Nobody talks too much about Redford's father, for it often seems that his presence is everywhere—he has a foot through every basket, a nose for scams and schemes. If I say it out, it is only to introduce what is known and whispered. The boy is the son of my half uncle and former boss, Lyman Lamartine.

I often brag on Lyman, for even though I think of him as a big, bland Velveeta, I am proud I am related to this reservation's biggest cheese. The fact is, a tribal go-getter has to pasteurize himself. He has to please every tribal faction. He has to be slick, offend nobody, keep his opinions hid. By way of doing this, Lyman has run so many businesses that nobody can keep track—cafés, gas pumps, a factory that made tomahawks, a flower shop, an Indian Taco concession, a bar which he has added to and parlayed from a penny-card bingo hall and kitchen-table blackjack parlor into something bigger, something we don't know the name of yet, something with dollar signs that crowd the meaning from our brain. My uncle took an interest in me after my A.C.T. scores turned out so high, though I don't think he ever personally liked me. It is well known that he and Shawnee Ray are long-term engaged, that dates for a wedding keep getting set, wrangled over, broken. What isn't clear to anyone is just who does the breaking or the setting, whose feet are hot, whose cold.

"Redford's big," I remark to Zelda. She is fanning herself with a paper plate she has stored in her beaded bag, and waits for me to say more. Zelda was once called raven-haired and never forgot, so on special occasions her hair, which truly is an amazing natural feature, still sweeps its fierce wing down the middle of her back. She wears her grandmother Rushes Bear's skinning knife at her strong hip, and she touches the beaded sheath now, as if to invoke her ancestor.

My aunt recently launched herself into the local public eye when Shawnee let it be known she would keep her baby. With her parents moving off, and her sisters' drinking habits a bad legend, Shawnee needed a place to stay. Zelda took her in for the price of free-rein interference. She stepped to the front and erected a structure for the whole situation. She swept, tidied, and maneuvered an explanation and a future that would fit expectations and satisfy all hearts.

Through furious gossip, Zelda has got Shawnee and her man semi-engaged, and is doing her best to make arrangements for them both to marry. A pang shoots through me, now, when I think of marriage between Shawnee Ray and Lyman. I am surprised to find that I experience the disappointment of a hope I never knew I harbored.

Most people are jealous of Lyman, and maybe I am no better. He is an island of *have* in a sea of *have-nots*. And even more than that, he's always been a little special, picked out. Though short, he is a guy with naturally football-padded shoulders, a dentist grin, a shrewd and power-cleaned presence in a room. Lyman owns a beautiful Italian-cut three-piece suit. His shirts are sparkling white, his collars ringless, his bolo-tie stones not glass but semiprecious rocks. Some think that he is following in the footsteps of his old man, Nector Kashpaw, and will eventually go off to Washington to rise into the Indian stratosphere. Some green envy talk has him quitting the local bingo, running for an elected office, making politician's hay. As if business and popularity are athletic events, he keeps himself in tip-top shape, especially for a guy his age. His vested middle is made for a woman to throw herself at, clawing the buttons, which are sewn on double-tight. A girl could do an entire load of laundry on his washboard stomach. I know, because I've seen him bench press, that his biceps are smooth, rounded, and hard as the stones in lakes.

I could go on and on about Lyman. The truth is, our relationship is complicated by some factors over which we have no control. His real father was my stepfather. His mother is my grandmother. His half brother is my father. I have an instant crush upon his girl.

Reading is my number-one hobby, and I have browsed a few of the plays of the old-time Greeks. If you read about a thing like Lyman and me happening in those days, one or both of us would surely have to die. But us Indians, we're so used to inner plot twists that we just laugh. We're born heavier, but scales don't weigh us. From day one, we're loaded down. History, personal politics, tangled bloodlines. We're too preoccupied with setting things right around us to get rich.

Except for Lyman, who does a whole lot of both.

As an under-the-table half sister, Zelda Kashpaw is in his corner, and she tries to help him out in the community. She blesses his and Redford's future in a hundred conversations via phone and tribal mall, asks positive input from the priests, from her friends the Sisters. She leads novenas for unwed mothers. She helps Shawnee in every way—would have had the baby for her if she could, and nursed it too, with the rich, self-satisfying milk of her own famous kindness. It's gotten so, by this time, no one can mention the current situation of Redford and Shawnee Ray without acknowledging Zelda's goodness in the same breath.

"Isn't that a fine thing Zelda's doing?" people repeat to each other. "Shawnee Ray is lucky to have her take such an interest."

Yes, Zelda racks points up sky high with her tireless energy. She fixes it for Redford to get a naming ceremony and she arranges files and blood quantums in the tribal office where she works, so that he is enrolled as a full-blood. She gathers WIC food to feed him, and is always at the Sisters' door when they open it to sell or give away donated clothing. People let her snatch what she wants, knowing it is for the child, who is always, at every moment, dressed like an ad in a magazine. Even if Shawnee Ray sews his outfit, as she has the one he wears right now—old-time leggings, a ribbon shirt of dotted calico—the word soon leaks that Zelda bought the "special" fabric.

Just to check, I point at Redford.

"Nice fabric," I observe.

Zelda draws herself up with a penetrating air.

"*You* might think so," she answers. "But it was not what I wanted. They never have exactly what you're looking for! I had to go to three shops, then finally I gave up and drove all the way to Hoopdance." She frowns, shakes her head remembering the gasoline expended and the many unworthy bolts that passed between her critical thumb and first finger.

"And Shawnee Ray, she looks like she's doing pretty good." I am casual, unable to help myself from mentioning her name.

"Pretty good." Zelda's hand goes into that beaded bag. She draws out a foil-wrapped brick and presses it toward me. The thing is heavy as a doorstop. I don't need to ask—it is Zelda's old-time holiday fruitcake, made with traditional hand-gathered ingredients, chokecherries pounded with the pits still in them, dried buffalo meat, molasses, raisins, prunes, and anything else that carries weight. Winter traction, I think as I heft it. I thank her, and then, when that is not enough, thank her again for saving it for me through the new year and its aftermath.

Accepting my gratitude, Zelda turns her attention full onto me. I can feel her scan my brain with the sudden zero-gaze of medical machines. A map of my feelings springs up in blue light, a map that Zelda focuses to read.

Miss Little Shell.

Suddenly I am watching so hard for the flash and wave of red that I miss Zelda's reaction, which is too bad, because if I could only have seen what she was rerouting and recasting to fit her intentions and visions, I could perhaps have headed off all that came to pass. But too late. I have this impression that my regard of Shawnee Ray, my watching of her, is natural. So I stand there and continue looking, as in me there begins to form some vague swell of feeling. I believe at the time it is fate at work, but of course, it turns out to be Zelda.

* * *

You may undergo your own incarceration. You may witness your demise piece by piece. You may be one kind of fool who never gets enough or another who gets too much. Lipsha, I tell myself, you didn't have to come back. You got your father's poster in the mail, courtesy of Grandma Lulu. Staring at this haunted face, you had the impulse to change your life. But to put that moment into operation is more complicated than you thought. You are looking for a quick solution, as usual, but once you get into Zelda's range that won't matter. Something else is at work. I have to ask myself if there is more—am I drawn back specifically to watch the circle where that pretty Toose now appears? And Shawnee Ray herself, our hope of a future, is she aware, too, and has she rolled me into each one of her snuff-can-top jingles? Sewed me into her dress with a fine needle? In/out. In/out. Lipsha Morrissey. My man. Can it be possible?

Once I allow myself to consider anything, it is almost sure those thoughts don't quit, so I sink down holding Zelda's gift. I find myself in a bland steel chair and I wait, watching the floor, dazzled with new prospects. I am out of shape for being told what to do by everything around me. I've been out in a world where nobody cares to manipulate me, and maybe I take this unseen plotting as a sign of concern, even comfort, and fall back under its spell. That might be it, because even when another part of the design comes clear, soon after, I don't register its meaning.

Lyman Lamartine attacks the polished wood floor with his pounding feet. He whips by me and I hardly glance up except to register that he is now good at yet another thing. Lyman has inherited, and wears now, the outfit of his champion grass-dancing brother Henry. It is old-timey looking compared to the other yarn-draped and ribboned ones, but there is something classical about it, too. His antique roach has white fluffies bobbing on the wrapped springs of two car chokes, long silky fringes from an upholstery outlet, a beautifully beaded necktie and a pointed collar, matching armbands, and over his forehead, shading his shifty eyes, a heart-shaped mirror.

Lyman gets bigger when people stare at him, his chest goes out, his nostrils flare. He grows visibly as he swings into motion. Which is maybe why he is so good at dancing. The more people who watch him the faster and huger he spins, as if he feeds off their stares. He takes the title of his dance literally and plays out a drama in his head. He believes in himself like nobody else. Now I watch close, closer, and get lost in things I see: a guy on the lookout, quick footed, nervous, sneaking up on someone unsuspecting. Crouching. Snaking down in long grass. The grass, it closes over him. You only see its movement as he creeps along, as he knits himself into the scene. Wind riffles through, bending, charming the stems and stalks and plumes. The sneaking what . . . warrior? No, *lover,* pokes his head up. Puts it down. Now he's getting close. More grass blows, waves. His victim sleeps on. Suddenly Lyman springs. Four times, right on the drumbeat, he jumps in a circle, his feet landing in a powerful stance, his heart mirror shining like a headlight, glancing sharp, piercing, pointing, straight into the deep brown eyes of Shawnee Ray, who winces, blinks, then opens her eyes wide and skeptical to take in his crazed and sudden dancing.

Aunt Zelda, of course, stands right next to Shawnee, focusing that love light to a narrow laser. She leans over, accomplishing through small remarks great articles of destiny. As she talks, she jiggles Redford, whose dark brown hair and beaming eyes are fixed upon his father. Shawnee Ray turns away from Lyman. Zelda pops a piece of candy into Redford's mouth so as not to distract the two. Shameless, playing on resistless baby greed, Zelda keeps the boy occupied and totally set on the hand that contains the rest of the packaged sweets.

Hold on now, the tangle, the plot, the music of homecoming thickens. Lyman has one great advantage. Zelda shoots her webs right at him from a distance, and he allows them to stick. They are in on this together, although he doesn't know it yet. Sensing that invisible-string guide ropes have been erected to assist his approach, Lyman simply walks over, smiling at his own son. He is friendly, unconcerned over looks and whispers. He says hello to Shawnee Ray, reaches into Zelda's embrace and takes Redford, who strains toward him with thrilled arms and an open face. Zelda's lips press together, sealed on her own directions like an envelope. Having insisted everything should be up front and normal, these are the fruits, her reward.

I have to admire Lyman right then, for he clearly has kept a firm connection with his little boy. Perhaps I should take lessons from him, but I don't. I don't have the broad vision, or I am otherwise unprepared. Maybe the net that whirls clean around him falls by accident, with firm links, over me. I hardly know what happens next, although I hear it coming, the sounds of her approach. Then those steak-rare, ringing hips are suddenly before me, eye level, and I look up, over what the basket carries, into Shawnee's downcast and commanding eyes.

"You're back," she states. "For good?"

"For bad," I joke.

She doesn't laugh.

I glance away from her, anywhere but at her, and try to compose myself. I have the sense of weight descending, and then of some powerful movement from below. I have this sudden knowledge that no matter what I do with my life, no matter how far away I go, or change, or grow and gain, I will never get away from here. I will always be the subject of a plan greater than myself, an order that works mechanically, so that no matter what I do it will come down to this. Me and Shawnee Ray, impossible, unlikely. I don't know if I give in then, or if I respond to the sight of her slender, silver-ringed, strong, and pointed fingers resting for a moment on my own bare hands. I only know that I close my ears to the drum music, my heart to the blowing wind, and stare at the random swirls of plastic within plastic, the stained linoleum on the gym floor that spreads so calm and thick beneath my feet, and changes each time I blink my eyes so that a leaping bull becomes a howitzer and then an apple tree tipped with small candles, or a hill into which a pleasant little door opens, into more doors than I can count, darker ones that lead farther back, intricately, toward spaces I have never seen and no place I can name.

CHAPTER THREE

SOLITARY

EVEN IN DIRECT AND SKILLED COMPETITION WITH DEATH itself, Albertine did not escape the iron shadow of her mother's repressed history. Her name was the feminine of the middle name of her mother's first boyfriend, Xavier Albert Toose. When, as a little girl, she had complained about it to her mother, Zelda had looked sternly at her and asked if she would rather have been named after Swede, her father, morose and handsome in a fading photograph.

Recently, in a ceremony that Xavier Toose himself had run, and in the presence of Fleur Pillager, she had received a traditional name, one belonging originally to a woman she had heard of spoken in her grandmother's low voice as a healer. Since then, whenever she had a moment, Albertine worked her way through notebooks and trapper's diaries and fitful church records to try to find some reference to Four Soul.

She'd sunk deep in the scattered records of the Pillagers, into the slim and strange substance of the times and names. The words soaked into her, the names almost hurt with the intimations of unknown personality. Ogimaakwe, Boss Woman; Chokecherry Girl; Bineshii, Small Bird, also known as Josette. There was Unknown Cloud. Red Cradle. Comes from Above. Strikes the Water.

And there was Four Soul, only a scratch on the record of

Chippewa taken down by Father Damien in that first decade when people, squeezed westward, starving, came to the reservation to receive rations and then allotted land.

Everywhere she looked, once she got up from the desk, reminders of her mother's notorious benefactions—books, hair clips, many sets of earrings, food by the item and box, lacy note cards, pictures. Her suitcase for home was always halfway packed, her heart dutifully filling, a holy-water font for guilt. Albertine was one of those who took on too much in order to remain perpetually dissatisfied with herself. It worked—a plume of spent fuel trailed her days, headlong in concentration, and her nights were black. Exhaustion was her pleasure, usually, but tonight she was too keyed up to settle into sleep and she switched on the television.

A vibrant, low-pitched, and authoritative male voice described a microwaved meal. Albertine dropped her head back, sank into the knitted pillow on her couch, wrapped one of Zelda's patchworked afghans around herself, and tucked it under her chin. Next the voice described the careful recording of all personal and phone conversation and showed a long and shining corridor of white paint, linoleum tile, blue and brown lines. An hour of gym a day, metal rings. SORT team. A description of headgear, helmets, pads. Albertine leaned forward, turned up the volume, stared intently into the screen. A different voice began to speak on the subject of penitentiary life.

I spend my time dwelling on revenge and try to deal with the monsters crawling out of the ashes.

And still another voice.

Chained and spread-eagled in the isolation four days.

And then his face, impossibly smiling, but different, a soft wilderness, a temple of unconfused purpose, much different from the man she had known, in person. That Gerry Nanapush had absorbed and cushioned insults with a lopsided jolt of humor. He had been a man whose eyes lighted, who shed sparks, who had once leaped out a hospital window and popped a wheelie at the hospital entrance to mark his daughter's birth. Gerry's look now was so hungry and his gaze so razor desperate that there seemed no depth or end to the moment that the two confronted one another across blank space.

At his trial, as the verdict was handed over, when the voice dropped the words into the paneled courtroom the spectators in the back of the room had risen, startled from the benches to their feet shouting *no* at once, in one thrilled and throttled voice, breaking it across the air. *No. No.*

Albertine said it out loud now, again, at the sight of Gerry. *No.* But he was frozen air now, caught in the shadows of the beamed videotape just as he was in the Xeroxed posters and Insty-Printed newsletters and movies and stories of appeal. The television image dissolved, but as if the ink blackened and spread, her mind continued to leak apprehension until the air dimmed, until the constant and underlying level of fatigue hooked her under.

Chapter Four

LIPSHA'S LUCK

Marie Kashpaw sat at the round wooden table in her Senior Citizens apartment, touching her wracked hands together lightly. Through sheer nylon drapes, the winter sun cast a buttery light on the table, warming her knobbed fingers. She knew that her youngest would come by to visit soon, and she was gathering peace. She prayed to no saints, but she believed in steadiness and luck. This one worried her. He was different from the others, wilder, anxious. She had taken him in as abandoned, but he had felt like her own from the beginning. Though he was grown, she still babied him, kept his school pictures taped to her refrigerator, still bought his clothes on sale, still saved money for him in a jar.

Maybe she had put her fierceness into guarding children for so long that she didn't know how to quit. Maybe she petted him too much, gave in too easy, spoiled him with her mercy. Lulu Lamartine said so, but Marie did not agree. Long ago, she had decided to grant Lipsha extra. Because of the way he was found in the slough, half drowned, he needed more than other children. She had tried to mother his mother, June, but it had been too late to really save her. June had worn out the world with her hurt, headlong chase. June was damaged goods, found once freezing in an outhouse, in a ditch, on the steps of the Sisters, and at last starving in the woods. Some children, you could not repair.

As a baby, Lipsha knew how to make his hands into burrs that would not unstick from Marie's clothing. He gripped her so strongly that he left small marks on her skin. And even older, he hugged her, desperate, when the others weren't look-ing. Sometimes she caught him holding to his face a piece of soft leather that she had given him as a doll. She had caught him weeping for no reason. She had caught him playing dead in a pile of leaves and dirt.

Now Marie heard his footsteps in the hall, his knock on the door, and she stroked the doeskin bag that held Nector's pipe. The quilled parcel was laid out before her, carefully, on a cro-cheted place mat.

Peendigaen.

Lipsha came in looking ragged, his hair a chopped off mass that touched his shoulders, his mustache thin hairs curving down beside his lips. His skin was clear and mild, a pale brown like his mother's, and his eyes were hers too, beautiful and slightly upturned at the corners. He gave her a serene and foolishly sweet look, shrugged, sat down at the table.

"What's this?"

"Nector's pipe."

He was wearing a black baseball jacket, black jeans, a white shirt full of slogans. She said nothing more and he swal-lowed his carelessness into a quiet and attentive frown. For a few moments, they listened to snow drip from the eaves over the window, and gathered in the brilliance of sun, strained through the net of curtains. The pipe in its bag rested between them and their thoughts were small fractions, shards of sight. Lipsha remembered and saw the calm way that Nector's supple hands tamped down kinnikinnick in the bowl. Marie heard his voice speaking the old language in chunky phrases, his prayers that went on too long and always included everyone. Nector's eyes had always slightly crossed into the distance, his arms made a light swaying motion with the pipe as he asked for favors.

"You know how to use it," Marie said. "He taught you."

Lipsha raised his face to hers and let the warmth of her intentions fill him until a shy smile rippled nervously over his features and he blinked, looked down at the bag, and made his face serious again. He still seemed unbelieving when she put the pipe into his hands. As he held it in his open palms he seemed about to speak. Once or twice he cleared his throat, shook his head, but he didn't find words.

An hour or two of asking around for jobs made Lipsha restless, and he decided to take a break and play a few video games at the newly built tribal mall, a complex erected to keep cash revenues in local hands. His initials soon lighted the bottoms of two screens, his scores were highest. When he got bored he wandered out of the dim hole-in-the-wall and sat on a scarred wooden bench bolted to the floor. One wish led to another and he soon persuaded himself that it wouldn't hurt to call up Shawnee Ray, just to talk. He walked to the pay phone, hopeful, and took it as a sign when it was not taped up and broken, but in working order. He knew the number because he was raised at the old Kashpaw place where Shawnee now lived with Zelda. He dialed and forgot to breathe. He didn't expect her to say anything important right off, but she answered his sudden offhand question whether she wanted to go out with him the way she danced, put her foot right down on the beat.

"Sure."

A raw hot space bloomed in Lipsha's chest.

"Hey. Are you there?"

Shawnee sounded worried, and the small note of concern in her voice charmed and exalted Lipsha. He stammered and an eager grin formed on his face. Ideas galloped at him right and left and he couldn't stop them, tame them. He tried to make small talk for a few more minutes, set a time to pick up Shawnee, said good-bye, and then stood in the entryway of the mall building with the phone clutched in his fingers. He looked down at the tiny black holes of the mouthpiece and it suddenly occurred to him that it had been brushed by many, many lips, maybe even Shawnee's. Tenderly, he placed the receiver on its cradle. With his sleeve, he smoothed the shining chrome rectangle beside it. Passing public phones, he usually slipped his hand into the dark apertures of their coin boxes in the hope of a stray quarter. A wholly different impulse gripped him now. He took an extra coin from his pocket and fed it into the slot in the machine's forehead. He pushed his arms into the air, pulled them down tight, in fear and pleasure, whispered, "Yes!"

That night, he drove to Zelda's and waited outside the front door of the little house. Although the night was cold, Shawnee Ray was sitting on the steps and now she rose, walked quickly to Lipsha's car, hands shoved in her jacket pockets. The door opened and Zelda posed in the kitchen light, waving slowly, once, twice, solemn but with an unreadable expression of satisfaction on her face. Lipsha put down his car window, waved back, and Zelda disappeared. Shawnee slid into the front bucket seat and latched herself securely.

"Is this a date?" Shawnee's voice was worried.

There was a long still space in which the car bounced slowly over the winding access road.

"I always hated dates, where you plan out fun." Lipsha talked quickly, nervous. "It always seems like no matter what you do you're not having enough of it, or having it only for the other person's benefit, or not having the kind of fun you are supposed to be having. It seems like your fun is suspect, or that your fun is really no fun, you know?"

"Because I'd rather this wasn't a date," continued Shawnee Ray.

"How about we go to Canada?" Lipsha suggested. "Ho Wun's."

"Why not?"

Lipsha could almost feel Shawnee's smile open in the dark. The nearest Chinese restaurant was located in a tiny town across the border and it was a romantic place, the walls covered in red paper patterned with flocked lanterns, signs for happiness, benevolence, and luck. Black bean sauce shrimp. Dumplings. Flower petal soup. All of these were on the menu. Rich foods, exotically chopped vegetables that they could exclaim over. They headed into the black north along a new stretch of highway.

"So, how's Lyman?" asked Lipsha, then bit his lip, surprised he'd spoken Lyman's name right out like that. He didn't know why he'd said it so abruptly, it was just that he wondered so hard about Shawnee and Lyman, whether or how they were involved, and his tongue had slipped.

"He's okay, I guess." Shawnee Ray's tone was careful, stiff.

"How's your uncle Xavier?"

"Okay."

"How's your mom?"

"Fine."

"How's Zelda?"

"Good."

"How, how, how," said Lipsha. "I feel like a Hollywood Sioux."

Shawnee laughed once, abruptly, and then immediately the atmosphere inside the car thickened and grew rubbery. Everything Lipsha said from then on bounced back at him unchanged, so he turned on the radio and twisted the dial to find something besides the Christian preaching that jammed the airwaves. *Sometimes His ego raps to me,* a male voice said. Quickly he switched the station and the miles zoomed by until they reached the lighted building next to the highway, the checkpoint people from the reservation always breezed through when they went up to Canada.

Lipsha rolled down his window to answer the usual questions, but here's where it started, that little wrinkle in destiny which he somehow came to believe that Zelda might have arranged. The incident grew out of nothing more than a border guard's dark mood, or maybe an unfilled quota, or just a fit of thoroughness. The guard, an elderly clean-cut type with a deep crisp voice, asked Lipsha to step out of the car. Lipsha turned off the ignition and did so. The officer reached to the dashboard and gently removed the ashtray and brought it beneath the floodlit awning to examine. Lipsha got back into the driver's seat, tried to smile confidently at Shawnee, but she wasn't looking at him. The guard took a long time poking through the ashes with a ballpoint pen before he came up with something. He walked back, leaned down to the car window.

"I have bad news," he said, holding between his thumb and forefinger what looked like a tiny seed. His voice was formal and neutral. "I am compelled to search this vehicle."

Carefully, hands folded before them, heads bowed, Lipsha and Shawnee stepped out of the car, into the linoleum-floored and fluorescent-lighted room, and sat down across from one another on hard benches.

Shawnee Ray was wearing a big fluffy parka that made her shoulders huge. She tapered like a bodybuilder to her hips. Her hair had been sprayed-curled and it punched out all over her head, as if frozen stiff in fear or rage. Her eyes were irritated, not at all afraid. Lipsha sat down next to her, breathed her sharp perfume in deep breaths, narrowed his eyes against the harsh overhead glare. Shawnee Ray stared at her hands, calm in her lap. She found the patterned stitching on the back of her green knit gloves of exquisite interest and seemed so fascinated that Lipsha didn't dare drag her away from her involvement. Meanwhile, in the parking lot outside, he could hear the cheerful sound of boxes and bags thumping the asphalt.

"Sorry. I almost feel like this trouble's my fault."

"It is your fault," said Shawnee. "Where'd that seed come from?"

"I don't know."

"And another thing. Zelda told me you'd call, right after the powwow. How'd she know?"

"I guess she saw me looking at you."

Shawnee glanced up and then froze, caught in the lock of Lipsha's stare, so direct he scared himself at first, until he found he was looking hopefully and peacefully into Shawnee's eyes as into a beautiful and complicated new computer game whose pleasures and secrets he could not yet and might never measure. Shawnee's face transformed as she returned his frank stare, her outer features melting with her inner warmth. If the electricity went off, Lipsha felt sure, thinking of this moment later, she would have glowed with her own blossoming light. Her hair softened into a cloud, ready to be touched by welcome hands.

Lipsha's heart pumped hard, thinking for itself. He could hear things put back into his car now—from outside there was the sound of jamming, squeezing, slamming. What did he care? It was time to change this false configuration. The *not yet* of his potential life was the perfect match for Shawnee's *I am,* her *is,* he reasoned, while Lyman's *always was* fit precisely with the *no doubt* of some other unnamed and successful woman. The structure of this date had been strictly arranged, he now understood. Zelda was behind it, as with everything in which she had an interest. Lyman was along, too—not in the backseat, but certainly stuck between them in spirit. In the all-revealing light and silence of that waiting room, Lipsha believed he saw that whatever love there was between Shawnee and Lyman was canned love, love they ate from Zelda's shelf, love they couldn't even admit to not having because of the *should be* of the whole situation. That is, Lyman should be in love with Shawnee because he had fathered her child, and Shawnee should welcome him back into her arms for the same reason.

As for Lipsha, he remembered Zelda's mysterious parting

look, and a word from his high school chemistry class sprang into his head. She intended him to be that third element introduced so that two neutral substances would strongly react. He was a drop of jealousy—strong, clear, and bitter: a catalyst. He pondered this with all of his powers, but the understanding that he almost reached flew from his hands and was of no consequence anyway, for just as he was about to try to rearrange Zelda's plans by driving all other men but himself from Shawnee's mind—he was concentrating all these thoughts into what he hoped would be a shattering kiss—it was as if Zelda knew. It was as if she sensed this danger and with swift magic counteracted Lipsha from a distance.

The guard stepped back into the door with the small, foil-wrapped brick of Zelda's old-time pemmican fruitcake resting in the open palm of one hand. In the other, he carried the elaborate bag that contained the sacred pipe that had once belonged to Nector Kashpaw.

"You'll be staying here until I can get you picked up," the guard said, jingling Lipsha's car keys. "You're in federal protective custody until I can get a lab analysis on this."

"But," Lipsha began, "that's—"

"Don't bother," said the guard, not unkind. He almost smiled, grim with satisfaction. "I've heard it all and I've seen it all. But this is a pipe and I know hash."

And then, staring calmly at the two, the guard put down the fruit bread, opened the quilled bag, and took out the bowl of the pipe and the long, carved stem. He held out his hands and there, as they watched, under the strong lights, he looked from one piece to the other and decided to connect the pipe as one. So many things would happen in the next months, soon after, that Lipsha wouldn't have time to take in or understand. But always, he would think back to that action, which seemed to happen slowly and to last for timeless moments. It seemed, on thinking back, that there, in the little border station, in the hands of the first non-Indian who ever attached that pipe together, sky would crash to earth.

"Please, don't," Lipsha whispered.

But the frowning man carefully and methodically pressed the carved stem to the bowl and began to turn it and jam it until the two sections locked into place. The eagle feather hung down, the old trade beads clicked against each other three times. Then there was silence, except for the buzzing lights. The guard turned to make his phone call, walked counterclockwise, around the room and desk. The pipe hung from his hand, backwards, casual as a bat. The eagle feather dragged lower, lower, until it finally touched the floor.

TRANSPORTATION

WHEN I THINK OF ALL OF THE UNCERTAINTIES TO FOLLOW, the collisions with truth and disaster, I want to dive, to touch and lift that broad feather. I want to go back in time and spin the Firebird around, screeching with a movie flourish, to zoom back into the story, separate the pipe, swallow that one lone seed. And yet, as there is no retreating from the moment, the only art left to me is understanding how I can accept the consequence. For the backwardness, the wrongness, the brush of heaven to the ground in dust, is a part of our human nature. Especially mine, it appears.

As I sit with Shawnee Ray in that blinding room, waiting for the police to drive up wailing their sirens, I talk fast. I am trying to edge out the one idea I do not want Shawnee Ray to pursue.

"Just picture the lab analysis when it comes back," I try to joke. "Raisins, dried buffalo meat, *pukkons,* suet, prunes, tire rubber . . ."

She doesn't answer. Her head stays bowed.

"You're thinking," I venture.

She just sighs, gets up, and walks over to the phone.

It only takes Lyman Lamartine a half hour to respond to the call that ricochets from Shawnee to Zelda and probably on all through the tribal party-line wire. He drives into the border station yard with a powerful crackle of his studded snow tires. I can't help but hope he might slide through to Canada, but Lyman never slips off course. Each tiny silver nail bites ice. Standing at the window, both Shawnee Ray and I watch as he confers with the guard, using soothing hand gestures, shaking his head, smiling briefly, and then examining with zealous eyes the pipe offered to him, holding forth then, explaining tradition with a simple courtesy I wish that I could imitate. He wears a tie and silver-bowed eyeglasses. His hair is long, but cut in a careful shag that brushes the collar of his overcoat. After a while, the conversation seems to take on a friendlier overtone, for the guard nods his head once, and then straightens with an air of discovery.

"Zelda must have called him," says Shawnee Ray. Her face, in its frame of harsh feathers, is flushed and anxious. I am going to ask her just how I should conduct myself in this unusual situation, what to say, whether she can give me any clues, when Lyman and the guard come inside.

Shawnee doesn't turn to greet Lyman, her stare just widens as she continues to gaze out the window, seemingly struck by the view of parking lot asphalt and dark-night snowy earth. I am at such a loss that I act completely normal, and walk over to Lyman to talk to him, far enough away so she will not hear our conversation. There aren't enough words on the reservation for our line of kin anymore. It's less confusing to decide on one thing to call them and leave out the tangles.

"Hello, my uncle," I say, once the guard has busied himself with a phone call and paperwork. "It's decent of you to show up and get this straightened out, so I just want to say thanks, and to assure you that Shawnee Ray had nothing to do with the mess."

"I never dreamed she did."

"And, see, you were right."

Lyman still holds the pipe carefully in his two hands.

Weighing it, he slowly disconnects the bowl and stem. I reach to take them, but he keeps turning the pieces around and around in his hands as though they were magnetized. The stem is long as my arm, double barreled, one of a kind. It is quilled the old way, and the bowl is carved by some expert long forgot, the red stone traded from South Dakota.

"I'll give you three hundred," he says.

I don't register his meaning at first. I stand still, waiting for him to finish his inspection. Passed to Nector from his old man, Resounding Sky, that pipe is that very same one smoked when the treaty was drawn with the U.S. government. So there are some who say that it was badly used and has to be re-blessed, and it is, I don't argue, a pipe that capped off the making of a big fat mistake. This is the same pipe refused by Pillagers who would not give away our land, the same one that solemnized the naming ceremony of a visiting United States president's wife, but it is also the pipe that started the ten-summer sundance. It is a kind of public relations pipe, yet with historical weight. Personal too. This pipe is my inheritance from Nector. I feel his love dishonored by the rude treatment it received from the guard, on my account. Standing there regarding it, guilty, I wait for the sky to drop. I wait for the earth to split, for something to go terribly wrong, but the only thing that happens is I take a job.

"I suppose," says Lyman, putting the pipe reluctantly back into my hands, "you don't have a place to keep this museum piece."

"I'm kind of between places," I acknowledge. "I had the pipe stowed in a little suitcase in my car trunk."

Lyman drops his chin low and looks up at me from under his brows.

"You working?"

"I'm between jobs, too."

"Maybe," says Lyman, his teeth showing a little, "you could work for me again. Close by. Where I could keep an eye on you."

Neither of us glances at Shawnee Ray, but we both automatically lower our voices.

"Could be," I put the pipe in its bag, tuck it back into my jacket, against my heart, "I'll take you up on that. Stay close. Where I can keep an eye on you, too."

So that's how I am hired to rise early and clean out the bingo hall. Once in a while, I substitute bartend too. My place of employment is an all-purpose warehouse containing an area for gambling that Lyman hopes to enlarge, a bingo floor that converts to a dance area, and a bar, and there are even a few older makes of video games blinking dimly against one wall. At five each morning I roll from bed in a room behind the bar, fill a bucket with hot water, add a splash of pink soap, wring out my mop, and set to work. After I swab the linoleum, I sling my rag across the seats and counters. I wash down the walls where people stagger, reach their hands out to break their fall, hands they've used to fix cars, calm horses, tie steel in the new interstate highway, hands that have slipped low with the oil of popcorn. Hands that are blood-related to my own hands, knuckle and bone.

It is my duty to retrieve what people drop when their nerves go numb in the lounge. Every morning, I pick up all that has fallen from their pockets, wedged beneath the plastic seats of booths. All the evidence of the night before comes to me, and as I accumulate what was lost, I feel lighter, as if the keys and the pens and the pennies and the dimes have no gravity, as if they drop off a weightless planet. As I clean, I see and hear all of the dramas replayed. Scenes resurrect from their own peaceful wreckage and surround me with the echoes of crashing noise.

In those still blue hours, the drunks and the nuns who pray for them are the only other people with their eyes open. I sometimes imagine those Sisters up the hill with clouds floating above their brains. Pure white clouds full of milk. As their lips move, the clouds pass over us, raining drops of mercy on the undeserving and the good.

Wisps of vapor, on the other hand, pour from the ears of my brothers and sisters in the deeps of their binges and write, in vague ballooned letters over their heads at this hour, *Where the fuck can I get the next one?*

The answer: *Here. Just hang tough till seven.*

From outside, my place of work is a factorylike Quonset hut—aqua and black—one big half-cylinder of false hope that sits off the highway between here and Hoopdance. By day, the place looks shabby and raw—a rutted dirt parking lot bounds the rippled tin walls. Bare and glittering with broken glass, the wide expanse is pocked by deep holes. The Pabst sign hangs crooked and the flat wooden door sags as if it was shoved shut in too many faces, against hard fists. But you can't see dents in the walls or rips or litter once darkness falls. Then, because the palace is decked with bands of Christmas tree lights and traveling neon disks that wink and flicker, it comes at you across the flat dim land like a Disney setup, like a circus show, a spaceship, a constellation that's collapsed.

Inside it's always sour twilight. The atmosphere is dense and low, as if a storm is on the wind. You don't walk through the door, it's more like you're swallowed, like God's servant who the fish gulped down. Steel ribs arch overhead and the floor is damp. I can't get it dry even with a fan. The booths are covered in a thick plastic torn and carved in old patterns, glued back together in raised scars where I've fixed them with Vinyl-repair. But nobody notices how it looks after nine o'clock.

On one side, the bar is fixed so all the bottles are backed by mirrors and the bartender can see the customers even when his hands are busy with the pumps. The popcorn machine is at the end of the counter, and it's the best lighted spot in the house. The bulbs in the hood flood golden radiance down on four or five barstools where women gravitate. They know how the light makes their eyes soft and dark, how the salt and butter clings to them, gets into their clothes, and mixes with sweat, cologne, and Salem smoke to produce a smell that is almost a substance, a kind of magic food that leaves a man emptier and hungrier after one whiff.

The bingo palace drives itself through wet nights according to these hungers. Except for the bright glow of the glass case of yellow popcorn, and the stage, bathed in purple, the great low room is a murk that hazes over and warms. Lovers in the booths or the unmatched dinette sets wrap their arms and legs together and send charged looks through rings of smoke. Smoke hangs low like a heavy cloud, collects at one level, shifts and bobs above the heads of the players and dancers. Smoke deepens, poised calm as a lake, over the tables.

People come and go underneath the cloud. Some to the bar, some to the bingo. There are the road workers, in construction, slab muscled and riding temporary money, new pickups with expensive options and airbrushed curlicues on the doors. Local businessmen with French names and Cree blood, guys with green eyes and black hair, talk in the quieter corners, making deals with flat hand gestures. Farmers visit—a Scandinavian family group or two—always quiet and half asleep and worked raw. When the men take off their Grain Belt or John Deere hats, the upper halves of their pale foreheads float and bob in the dark as they nod and talk.

Indian men, old ones with slicked-back gray hair, black-framed Indian Health Service glasses, and spotless white shirts of western cut and pearl snaps, sit straight up at the tables. Although they speak in low, soft voices, you can hear everything they say through the din. Within their company, there's sometimes a woman in a flowered pantsuit, hair swept into a bead rosette. She sips her beer, nods, adds a word at the right moment, and through the force of her quiet, runs the entire show.

Near the radiant circle at the popcorn machine, against the Lally poles, around the back entrance, lounge the younger Indian guys. Without seeming to notice the eyes that turn on them, or don't—and I know because I'm usually attempting to be one of them—these guys strut like prairie grouse. Some wear straw Stetsons with side or front medallions of pheasant feathers, and some wear mesh CAT hats, black and gold, with beaded brims. A few have long ponytails that flood to their waist, or thick loose hair they toss back over their shoulders. Some leave on their dark glasses, even inside. Some wear rude-colored western shirts, or fancy ones with roses and briars and embroideries of rising suns. Heavy-metal leather, surfer shirts, glow-in-the-dark rings around a few necks. Anything to make a girl look. There are tall men already with hard, belligerent paunches and slender boys with mysterious, clear faces and sly ways with their hands. But all of us, every one, wear boots and jeans within which our hips move, proud, with lazy joy, smooth as if oiled with warm crankcase or the same butter that the women at the bar lick off their fingers and smear on the men's hands when they dance—or go elsewhere. For the large unlit parking lot behind the palace is full of empty-looking cars that shudder, rock on their springs, or moan and sigh as the night wears on.

Now, you say, what about that truth and disaster I mentioned? It starts here at the bingo palace, with one of those ladies I just told you about who runs things by sitting quiet in the middle of the room. Aunt Zelda, of course.

Every time Aunt Zelda got annoyed with life in general she came to sit in Lyman's bar—not to drink, but to disapprove of her surroundings. On the night I get my luck fixed, I feel my aunt's presence the moment she steps through the doors. Her eyes flick and probe the dark booths as she sails forward, and her mouth twitches in righteous shock. I don't even have to turn around or look in the mirror to know it is her. She clicks across the floor loud as a calculator, then scrubs the end stool clean with a hankie fished from her sleeve.

"A tonic water, please," she requests in a controlled voice. I reach over and splash the stuff into a glass with ice. Then I squeeze a rag carefully to wipe the counter, and I set her glass on a little white square napkin from a special pile, unsoiled by liquor slogans or printed bathroom jokes. Cautiously, I put forth the question. "Lime?" She gives a short nod, a little yank of her cuffs. Her shoulders shrug slightly down. I spear not one, but two lime chunks on a little plastic sword and dunk them into her glass.

Only then does she take possession of her stool.

"On the house." I wave away the open metal jaws of her tiny purse. She snaps it shut, thanks me, cranks up her posture one more notch.

"You give this place just what it needs," I tell her, "an air of class."

When she doesn't respond, I repeat the compliment again, with more conviction, and she smiles, curving the corners of the pointed lips she has carefully painted upon her mouth.

"Salute," she toasts with light sophistication. Her sip prints the glass with her sharp lip-print, blurring her determined mouth further yet.

It will take glass after glass of formal prepared tonic waters very gradually laced with gin to bring the human shape back to her face. My motive is good—to make Shawnee Ray's life a little easier, for once the slight amounts of alcohol start having their effect, Zelda's basic niceness is free to shine forth. Right and left, she always forgives the multitude. Her smile relaxes—gleaming, melted pearls. From her corner she sheds a more benign opinion like a balm. No matter how bad things get, on those nights when Zelda stays long enough, there is eventually the flooding appeasement of her smile. It is like having a household saint.

But you have to light a candle, make a sacrifice.

Zelda is aware that her chemistry experiment has had unexpected results—here I am mixing drinks for my boss, the intended husband of the girl she fostered, while that girl herself, Shawnee Ray, is not out with Lyman Lamartine but at home intensively mothering her little boy. Zelda shouldn't play so hard and loose with the unexpected, that is my opinion. People's hearts are constructed of unknowable elements and even now, I feel sure, there is some unexplainable interest in me on the part of Shawnee Ray. I have to admit that our first date wasn't much. Still, she has consented to talk to me on the phone once or twice since that night.

I don't push my luck, but just go along for a while tending to my job, allowing the others to run interference with Zelda. As usual, she has a lot of people to maneuver, and so she hasn't had the time to concentrate full force on me. I am satisfied, want to stay that way. I like my aunt, even though I find it difficult to keep from getting run over by her unseen intentions.

Eighteen-wheeler trucks. Semis, fully loaded, with a belly dump. You never know what is coming at you when Zelda takes the road. Maybe it is the wariness, maybe I just want to head her off. Maybe I am stepping out in front of her with a red flag, or maybe I forget to put on my orange Day-Glo vest. Whatever happens, the fact is I get careless with Zelda's drinks. The trade is slow. I suppose I am tired and forget to measure. I add just that little bit too much to Zelda's tonics that sends her barreling at me full throttle. Too bad I am standing on the center line.

Starting out, she explains to me how my great grandmother, that dangerous Fleur Pillager, tried to kill herself by loading her pockets with stones and marching into Matchimanito Lake. Only, here's what stones she picked: the very ones that rested by her bedside, the very ones that she had always talked to. The perfect ones. The round ones. They knew her and so they helped her. They wouldn't let her sink. Spirit stones, they floated her up.

Aunt Zelda next confides to me the identity of her first boyfriend, the only man she ever loved. That is Shawnee Ray's uncle, Xavier Toose. Zelda says right out, strangely, that he lost his fingers for touching her. Then she falls silent, stares long at the mirror behind me, just moving her lips. I try to change the subject of her brooding thoughts by asking her how Redford is doing, but as though I have prodded a tape back into the reel she begins to speak again of Xavier, well-known traditional singer whom I last saw at the powwow, hand cupped at his ear like an animal paw. As he drummed, his voice shivered all the high notes with the Rising Wind singers.

Again she stops. "So, do you want me to tell it?" she asks.

"Tell what?"

"Do you want me to tell you this here story?"

I want to say no, to gently tap the faucet of her words shut, but her eyes are too brilliant, her need too harsh.

"It's what you might call," she says, her face both dreamy and sharp of sight, "a tale of burning love."

It's a concept with which I'm very recently familiar, so I lean closer, and I open my ears.

"Xavier Toose was the lookingest man around here, and a smart one too, but he wasn't the man I was saving myself to marry. That special man had to be white, so he would take me away from the reservation to the Cities, where I'd planned my life all out from catalogs and magazines. I resisted Xavier Toose, and yet my heart annoyed me when he sat down in our kitchen. Beating so loud, beating out the rabbit dance, beating hard enough to choke my throat, my heart pounded when I watched him stretch his slim legs from the wooden chair. He knew that when he spoke, my ears caught the lower registers, the love line underscoring all he said, the real and hidden meanings.

"There were other things. I lighted candles to the saints to stop my thoughts, but they did no good. I dreamed of him every single night. I think he knew it. I think he doctored my tea. Yet, he was wrong for me, didn't fit into my futures, where I saw myself holding a pan over a little white stove. In those wish dreams, I was dressed in pink, dressed in pale blue. I was someone with an upstairs to her downstairs, a two-story woman.

"Not Xavier. He was a man who would live in an old-time cabin. He was heading for a life of happy-time powwowing, if he didn't get caught up in drink. Oh yes, those days he drank some. I saw him doing the circuits, singing and drumming. He would hold down a low-pay job to support the bigger task it was to be an Indian. Now he's a ceremony man, Xavier, religious and quiet, but then he had a little of the devil in him.

"Time went on, and I refused him once a season. Spring. Summer. Fall. Then came winter. The question would be asked for the last time. The fourth time, in the old ways, you accept or refuse forever. So it seemed like we were down to a pitched battle. He visited every night and people assumed I'd said yes. But I hadn't said that word to Xavier because he hadn't asked outright although he kept looking at me, staring at me, with patient determination.

"Then came Saint Lucy's, the longest night of the year. He came over to our house and as the light ran soft and dusky he whispered, smiled, flashed the new ring on the tip of his finger. Unwilling, I followed him out to the barn, placing no in my mouth like a pebble to throw. Once inside, we stood by the dark stalls and he showed me the golden French band he'd bought with haying money.

"'Want it?' he asked.

"I couldn't find the courage to talk so I shook my head *no*.

"'Sure?'

"My heart was giving out on me, going fast. My face curved to meet his. Staring into his eyes, my gaze lost focus.

"'Go away,' I said.

"'I'm not going to leave tonight until you tell me the truth.

You love me but you want a white man, I know the way you are. You wouldn't be happy, though. You need a guy like me.'

"Xavier had stashed a bottle of whiskey in the manger, underneath some hay, and now he brought it out, offered me a drink. I took a sip and the burn almost choked me, I took another and my head cleared.

"'I won't leave. I'll sit outside your window lighting matches all night.' He laughed. 'I'll get drunk on your doorstep. Say yes!'

"I turned away from him and slammed back into the house, mad, yet my heart was dancing to return to the stalls, the warmth of his hands, already seamed with so much work. But I was strong, this just goes to show you. I did not go back. From the wide bed I shared with my little sisters, I pulled a blanket around my shoulders and I watched. After the lights were out I saw his matches, one after the other, flare in the windless night. One small light, then another. I dozed off and still saw those small flickers in the depth of blue, against the blue snow.

"The next morning, my brothers brought him in. They found Xavier hunched and frozen, still sitting in a curl of drifted snow. One hand was on his heart, they said, the other clutched the bottle. It was the hand on his heart that froze, though, and from that hand he lost his fingers."

Zelda stops, drinks long, and then looks me steady in the eye to see how I react.

"Go home now, Auntie, please go home," I beg.

But she will not, in fact, she's just getting started, one story hinging into the next. She tells me how my grandma Lulu found a dead man in the woods, and how she herself stood by to watch her own father burning down the Lamartine's house. She tells me that is why she's glad that she refused Xavier Toose. "Love wrecks things, love is a burning letter in the sky, a nuisance," she growls. She says things that she should keep to herself, keep quiet about, never speak. She goes and tells me why I owe her everything.

"You're sweet," Zelda sways forward, her hair semifrowzled.

"I got it from the time I worked the sugar beet plant," I explain.

"You got it from yourself." Her black eyes wander. "Not from your mother."

"My mother?"

I can't help it, my ears flare for more. So I ball up my rag, lean on the counter, and ask the thing I shouldn't ask.

"What about her?"

And then Zelda tells me the raw specifics of how my mother left me with Grandma. She tells me facts that make me miserable. She does the worst thing of all: she tells me the truth.

"I don't know how she could have done it." Zelda shakes her head, her mouth rolled tight.

"What?"

"I hate to talk about it in front of you." She hedges to draw out the intensity. "But then, you already heard about the gunnysack."

My aunt is enjoying herself. She pretends not to, but actually loves giving out the facts and the painful details. I could stop her, but the mention of my mother makes me helpless. No matter what June Morrissey has done to me, no matter that she's gone, I still love her so. I can't hear enough, or so I believe.

"That gunnysack was a joke." I speak confident. "Grandma kidded me once that my real mom was about to throw me in the slough. But no mother—"

Zelda interrupts me, nods agreement. "No mother, she was sure no true mother. June Morrissey, Kashpaw, whatever she was, she threw you in."

"*N'missae*," I say now, real slow, calling her my oldest sister. "You had a little extra to drink tonight. I spiked your tonic. Don't get mad at me. It's on the house."

But she is shaking her head at my version of the subject that has risen in her memory.

"She chucked you," Aunt Zelda continues. "I should know. It was me who dragged you out."

"You never said that before." I check the gin bottle. I cannot tell exactly how much I've poured.

"I was always a watcher, the one who saw. I was sitting on the back steps when I looked down the hill. There was June, slinging a little bundle into the slough."

"That's gin talking," I say. I tell her right out like that, and even throw down my rag on the counter. But I cannot turn away or stop listening as she continues in a voice that grows more hoarse, fascinated and too believable.

"I'll never forget that moment, Lipsha. Cloudy summer's day. I was all sly and I waited until June left. Then I went to see for myself what she had tossed into the water." Zelda stops here, bites her lower lip, and twists the glass in her hands. "I don't know how long I waited. If I'd known it was you, I would have ran down right away."

"Wasn't me." I make my voice firm, loud. "Wasn't Lipsha. No mother . . ."

No use. Zelda hardly notices me. She's talking about the moment she lived through at the edge of that pothole of water brown as coffee and sprouting cattails and lilies and harboring at its edges ducks and mudhens and flashy mallards.

"I waded in." Her voice grows strong, definite and sure. "I went in mud up to my knees and then into water over my head, so I had to swim around and try to remember where June had aimed the gunnysack. I started diving and must have made three, four tries before I touched the bag's edge. It took me two more dives to haul it up because"—now Zelda pauses for emphasis, glaring through me like I'm not there—"June had added *rocks*. I lugged that heavy sack to dry land, pulled it out. Then I packed it with the rocks banging, through the woods and into the field." Zelda bites her straw as she remembers me once more. "I would have opened it as soon as I got it out, Lipsha, if I'd known it was you."

I am getting this feeling now, this sick wrench that comes upon a person when they don't want to witness what is happening right in front of them.

"It wasn't me!" My voice is loud and one or two bleary loungers look over, curious. My mind is buzzing. My arms are weakening, deadening with the feeling that they want something big to hold on to, a tree, a rooted sapling, a hunkered crowd of earth, another person. But Zelda isn't someone to tolerate surprises. I can't grab her, and anyway she is the source of my confusion, so I stand my ground, even though I feel a tremble starting down low in my feet. I don't move as her voice continues.

"I opened that sack once I was out of the woods. I cried when I saw it was a baby! When you saw me you blinked your eyes wide and then you smiled. You were in that sack for twenty minutes, though, maybe half an hour."

"I was not."

"Maybe longer." She takes no argument. "Something else has always bothered me though." She scratches at the counter with a swizzle. "Lipsha, you were in that slough a long time."

"No, I wasn't."

She stops completely and stares at me, and then she whispers.

"So why weren't you drowned?"

And because I am mad at her for making up that stupid fucking story and all, I stare right back.

"Watch out," I snap my eyes at her. *"You'll take my place!"*

I hiss these words into Zelda's face, using the same dangerous threat that my great grandmother, Fleur Pillager, is supposed to have said to her long-ago rescuer, who died soon and took her place on death's road. I employ the family warning, and Zelda does draw back. A tiny light of fear strikes itself in and out of her eyes as quick as a motel match. But she isn't one to accept into herself a curse. She is too strong a boss woman, and veers off my Pillager words with a quick sign of the cross.

I would like to do the same with hers, but odd thing is, I can't. I tell myself that in her cups she became inventive, that she embroidered my case history in her memory, beadworked it with a colorful stitch. She's wrong, I keep promising myself. Wrong as wrong.

Wrong, I repeat, turning in that night. Wrong, I keep insisting in my mind as I turn out the lights. Wrong, wrong, wrong, I fall into my dreams. I tell myself that Zelda scared the story up, she made it happen. She never found me in a gunnysack. I remind myself that I believe what Grandma Kashpaw told me—that I was given to her in a sad but understandable way by a mother who was beautiful but too wild to have raised a boy on her own. I had come to terms with that story, forgave how June was so far out on the edge of life that she couldn't properly care for me.

I want to keep that firm ground, that knowledge, but my dreams are frightening water.

That night, deeper places draw me down. I sink into black softness, my heart beating fast, straining in the trap of my chest. I wake with a thump, as though I've hit the bottom of my waterbed. I jump onto the floor and pull on my jeans, switch on the lights, decide to make a round, a kind of house check, and maybe, although I rarely do indulge, drink down a free drink.

I walk quietly into the shadowy echoes of emptiness. I pass the bar, then steer around to the other side. I am just in the process of selecting a bottle, when I look into the mirror.

And see June.

Her face is a paler blur than the dark, her eyes are lake quartz, and she gazes with sad assurance at me out of the empty silence. She wears a pink top that glows faintly, as does the Bailey's Irish Cream filling her small glass. Her hair is black, sweeps down along her chin in two smooth feathers. There is no age to her—ancient, brand-new, slim as a girl. Take your pick. She is anyone, everyone. She is my mother.

She looks the way she did when I was little, those times I glimpsed her walking back from her trips to town. She looks the way she should have if she stayed and kept the good ways and became old and graceful. She watches me across the long, low room. There is no smoke to part, to make way for her gaze. There is no noise to hear over. I can't claim that she is obscured. I can't claim her voice is covered.

June carefully opens her purse and taps out a cigarette. Darkness moves in front of her and by the time I turn around and shuffle to the other side of the room, her chair is empty. She has moved. My hair freezes on my neck to see her on the other side of the bar. I get a prickle down my back and I go fainting and weak all over. Stumbling, I almost turn tail.

"You have to face her," I tell myself, trying to calm my heart. "She's visiting for a reason."

In places, the concrete base of the bar has humped beneath the flooring and buckled. On cold nights, from my little den, I hear it shift. I catch that low sound now, a thump and crack. Then there is a still moment when nothing moves. Outside, there is no wind, not a faraway motor. No voice raised. No sound in the open fields. No dog barks, nothing.

Suddenly the furnace breathes out and complains. Ice tumbles in the freezer slot of the refrigerator.

I shake.

Now I always told myself before that there was a good side to ghosts. My reasoning goes along on the base of the following uncertainties: Beyond this world, is there another? Dimensions, how many? Which afterlife? Whose God will I face if there is one, whose court? A ghost could answer the basic question, at least, as to whether there is anything besides the world I know, the things I touch. If I see a ghost, possibilities will open. I have told myself all this, and yet, finally in the presence of one, I shake.

I keep telling myself that my mother means me no harm and besides, it can't have been easy for her to appear. She has surely walked through fire, crossed water, passed through the great homely divide of fenced pasture and fields scoured flat by the snow. She has walked the three-day road back, the road of the dead. She has put herself out royally to get here, is what I'm saying. I tell myself I should at least have the guts to find out why.

I take a deep breath and enter the vast, still plain of the bingo palace. I flick on the lights, but they are low-watt anyway, so dim they hardly make a difference. Each step I take, I stop and listen for the echo, the trail. Each time I stop, I hear the silence, loud as a rush of heat. My heart pushes the blood to my head in pulses that glow behind my eyelids, and my fingers burn at the tips as if they were dipped in ice. I reach the stool, the one where I've seen her sitting, and then I touch it with my palm and it seems to me the back is warm.

"Where's my car?" she asks right beside me, then, as if we are continuing a conversation in time. "I came back because I was just wondering where you put it. Where the hell is my car?"

"It's outside," I answer, but my voice sounds like I'm talking from a hollow well.

"What did you do with it?" Her tone is pointed. "Crack it up?"

"No."

"Well, what?"

"It's kind of stalled," I tell her.

"'Kind of'? What do you mean 'kind of'?"

"All it needs is a little jump-start."

"I'll give you jump-start. Shit!"

She throws herself down at a table, angry, and nods at the chair. I am now in a weakened state, my legs wobble, soft rags.

If I'd known that accepting the blue Firebird paid for with the insurance money from her death would piss her off this bad—even from beyond the grave—well, forget it. Even after what Zelda said, I guess I still imagined my mother as gentle toward me, hopefully guilt-struck, but either that was wishful thinking or she is in a mood that night. Her voice is hard and she has no time for small talk. I figure that there is maybe some trouble, something disagreeable going on wherever she has come from, a situation from which she needs relief, or at least transportation.

After sitting there and stewing in our own silence for what seems a long time to me, I get the nerve to speak.

"June . . . Mom," I gently begin, surprised to hear how the last word sounds in my voice, "what do you want from me?"

Lukewarm puffs of smoke quiver in the air between us, and she frowns.

"I'm in a rush. I gotta go, but listen here. Do you play bingo?"

"I never did yet," I inform her. "Well, hardly ever."

"Now you do."

She dangles the lighted cigarette from her lips and again opens her purse, searches with both hands, carefully draws out a flimsy booklet, and pushes it across the table between us. I see that the papers are bingo tickets, marked with little squares containing letters and numbers. I begin to flip through the book politely, the way you look at photos of someone's vacation to Sturgis, wondering what her intention could be, but there is nothing in the tickets that looks out of the ordinary. When I lift my head to thank her, no one is there. She has evaporated into the spent daze of smoke that wreathes her chair.

I run outside, coatless in the freezing black air, and I call my mother's name but there is no answer. Above me, in the heaven where she came from, cold stars ring down and stabs of ancient light glitter, delicate and lonely. Grand forms twist out of unearthly dust. As I watch, then, sure enough, one star breaks from its rank and plunges.

It is happening. I know it. My luck is finally shifting. I go back inside and crawl into my sleeping bag bed, and eventually I begin to lose the sense of fear and of excitement, to float down through the connections. I wake slightly, once, imagining that from beyond the thickly insulated walls of the bar, I hear the muffled rev of an engine. I worry vaguely about my car, but sleep is a deep wave's trough. I turn over, roll down the watery slope.

CHAPTER SIX

JUNE'S LUCK

AT FIRST IT WAS JUST THAT JUNE'S MOTHER WENT CLUMSY, knocking the tin cups from their nails, the bucket hollow against the stove. In the middle of the night, she sang an old round-dance song and laughter screamed out from her place behind the curtain. Dawn came and June rose by herself, found a little cold bannock in the unfired oven. She scraped ashes off and put it into her mouth, chewed the sweet, burnt crumbles. June left for the school bus but then, halfway down the path, a cloud spun into her face. She ran back, touched her sleeping mother on the cheek, jumped away, and was gone once she stirred.

Lucille Lazarre was thin through the hips and arms, but her stomach was thick and solid as a tree trunk. She looked huge standing at the door when June came home from the Sisters' school. June had made good marks that day and had won a scapular of bronze felt. Her older brother, Geezhig, who had stayed in town the night before, elbowed roughly past his mother but Lucille grabbed him and hugged him against her. He looked down at his feet and held his neck stiff while she rubbed at his hair with her warm palms. She didn't stop, kept rubbing harder.

"Let me go."

She pushed him away, turned to June. Her eyes were red

around the edges, burning, her lips were dry and purple. Her long hair fell almost to her waist. When, on good days, she sat in a chair making baskets and let June braid and brush, June imagined that she wore her mother's hair, that she sat inside its safe tent.

June reached out now, tried to catch a strand, a mistake she realized even before her mother's hand slapped. Still, it happened so quickly that June did not react at first. She squinted across the sting of the blow at Lucille's blouse, at the blue patterns of teapots, turned upside down. Lucille's tan skirt was long and stained as though she had been standing near fire and the smoke had drifted up her body. Now, because of the slap, the clothing seemed covered with a strange glaze, a shining, beaded substance that winked fiercely. June rubbed her eyes, turned away, then ran outside, pushing off the sand of her mother's voice. For the next few hours she sat high in her tree.

When June went into the house again, her mother's face looked chalked in, coated with white dust. She was sitting on the chair, alone and still. There was no bottle in her hand, none to see anywhere, and June crept past her to the corner of heaped blankets where she slept with Geezhig. It was soon completely dark, and she rolled against Geezhig's bony back, slept until he tapped on her face, lightly, calling her awake.

"Run off in the bush," he said. "Go on, little sister."

Lucille's boyfriend was there, a man named Leonard whom they both made fun of for his big red lips. His body was a powerful lump, short and thick, and he thrust out his head before him as he moved, like a wedge. He wore his hair short, bristling, so they called him porcupine. His nose was darker than the rest of his face, but he didn't smell sour like a porcupine, he smelled wonderful. He wore some kind of *mookamon* juice that sweetened him for Lucille.

The air around June's face seemed cold. She sank lower, under the scratchy old army blankets, where her body had hollowed a nest. Usually, her mother had to hit Geezhig anyway, and got to her only when she wasn't so angry, when her arm had gone slack and lazy. June curled up and shut away Geezhig's voice. It was too cold outside to sleep covered over with leaves. She stayed. The voices boomed around her with great and muffled drumming sounds and filled her body with a loose warmth. In sleep, she didn't have to hear them, and so she relaxed into their cries and curled against a wall of noise.

Light blared. June's head, thick, rang. Then she flew and hit. Sprawled flat, she gagged for breath. Her chest was pressed flat as pages. She saw the center of a yellow wheel, churning, throwing off sparks that filled big sails.

Across golden water, her mother screamed. *"Where is he?"* June's air bubbled in and out and fear shot her toward the doorway. She nearly slipped by, twisting like a cat, but Leonard's hands were loaded springs and he caught her and scuffled her down. June's mother cuffed her once, not too hard. But then, different than ever before, she kneeled with her knees pinching in June's waist and with a string of cotton clothesline fastened complicated tangles around her arms and tied her daughter to the leg of the cast-iron stove.

"No more running away!"

Lucille's breath rushed in and out, ragged, sick. She got the bottle and went off, tilting it over her with every other step. June twisted against the knots, tried to scramble or bite herself free, but the ropes were put on every which way and tightened the harder she fought. Leonard's feet clumped down once, but he never came near. Then she heard him walk over to the lean-to door, near where her mother kept her bed, and although the floor was rough dirt, the dust choking, cold, she went dreamy. Finally, sleep sifted into her brain.

She felt his hand across her mouth, big and heavy with tough pads. She smelled the sweetness, spice, the incense of his perfumes and under it the sour yeast and heavy flowers of his armpits. He touched her, his hands like hot bells. He took off her ropes but kept her bound up with his fingers. They were steel clamps. They found her, found her, until she galloped against him. No matter where she went, his tongue came down. Then the wheel sang again, flew off its spokes and banged into a brilliant wall. There was a way a man could get into her body and she never knew. Pain rang everywhere. June tried to climb out of it, but his chin held her shoulder. She tried to roll from underneath, but he was on every side. Skeins of sparks buzzed down, covered her eyes and face. Then she was so small she was just a burning dot, a flung star moving, speeding through the blackness, the air, faster and faster and with no letup until she finally escaped into a part of her mind, where she made one promise before she went out.

Nobody ever hold me again.

THE BINGO VAN

WHEN I WALK INTO BINGO THAT NIGHT IN LATE WINTER I AM a player like any regular person, drenched in casual wishes, in hopes. Upon first entering, I look for any friends I might have from the past or the present, or any relations, and right off, I see Grandma Lulu. She has five tickets spread in front of her. Her neighbors each have only one. When the numbers roll, she picks up a bingo dauber in each hand. It is the Early Birds' game, one-hundred-dollar prize, and nobody has got too wound up yet or serious.

"Lipsha, go get me a Coke," commands Lulu when someone else bingos. "Yourself too."

I hit the concession, snag our soft drinks and come back, set them down, pull up to the table, and lay out my ticket. Like I say, my grandmother, she plays five, which is how you get the big money. In the long run, much more than even, she is one of those rare Chippewas who actually profit by bingo. But then again, these days it is her preferred way of gambling. No pull-tabs. No blackjack. No slot machines for her. She never goes into the back room, never drinks. She banks all of her cash. I think I can learn from Lulu Lamartine, so I watch her close.

Concentration. Before the numbers even start, she sits down in her lucky place, a chair that nobody else dares take, fourth row and fourth to the right by the eastern wall. She composes her face to calm, snaps her purse shut. She shakes her daubers upside down so that the foam-rubber tips are thoroughly inked. She looks at the time on her watch. The Coke, she takes a drink of that, but no more than a sip. She is a narrow-eyed woman with a round jaw, curled hair. Her eyeglasses, blue plastic, hang from her neck by two chains. She raises the ovals to her eyes as the caller takes the stand. She holds her daubers poised while he plucks the ball from the chute. He reads it out. B-7. Then she is absorbed, scanning, dabbing, into the game. She doesn't mutter. She has no lucky piece to touch in front of her. And afterward, even if she loses a blackout by one square she never sighs or complains.

All business, that's Lulu. And all business pays.

I believe I could be all business too, like her, if not for the van that sits behind the curtain. I don't know it right away, but that is the prize that will change the order of my life. Because of the van, I'll have to get stupid first, then wise. I'll have to keep floundering, trying to catch my bearings in the world. It all sits ahead of me, spread out in the sun like a naming giveaway. More than anything, I want to be the man who can impress Shawnee Ray.

"Lipsha Morrissey, you got to go for a vocation," says Grandma Lulu, during break.

"Maybe I'll win at bingo," I say to her, in hope.

Her smile is still and curved as a cat's, her cheeks round and soft, her fingernails perfect claws of blazing tropic pink.

"'Win at bingo,'" she repeats my words thoughtfully. "Everybody wins once. It's the next time and the next time you got to worry about."

But she doesn't know that I am playing bingo on the advice of a ghost, and I haven't mentioned my position as night watchman at the bar. I suppose I want her to think of me as more successful than I really am, so I keep my mouth shut although, after all, I shouldn't be so shy. The job earns me a place to sleep, twenty dollars per week, and as much beef jerky, beer nuts, and spicy sausage sticks as I can eat.

I am now composed of these three false substances. No food in a bar has a shelf life of less than forty months. If you are what you eat, I will live forever, I decide.

And then they pull aside the curtain, and I forget my prediction. I see that I wouldn't want to live as long as I have coming, unless I own *the van*. It has every option you can believe—blue plush on the steering wheel, diamond side windows, and complete carpeting interior. The seats are easy chairs, with little built-in headphones, and it is wired all through the walls. You can walk up close during intermission and touch the sides. The paint is cream, except for the design picked out in blue, which is a Sioux Drum border. In the back there is a small refrigerator and a padded platform for sleeping. It is a starter home, a portable den with front-wheel drive, a place where I can shack with Shawnee Ray and her little boy, if she will consent. If she won't live there, though, at least she will be impressed.

Now, I know that what I feel is a symptom of the national decline. You'll scoff at me, scorn me, say what right does that waste Lipsha Morrissey, who makes his living guarding beer, have to comment outside of his own tribal boundary? But I am able to investigate the larger picture, thanks to my mother's directions and thanks to Lulu, from whom I soon learn to be one-minded in my pursuit of a material object.

After that first sighting, I go play the bingo whenever I can get off from bar duty or cleanup. Lyman never stops me, for I think it seems economical for his workers to return their profits to the palace by spending off-hours at the long tables or drinking beers. Every bit of time that I spend listening for bingo numbers, I grow more certain I am close. There is only one game per night at which the van is offered, a blackout game, in which you have to fill every slot. The more cards you buy, the more your chance increases. I try to play five numbers like Grandma Lulu, but they cost five bucks each.

To get my van, I have to shake hands with greed.

I get unprincipled. As I might have already said, my one talent in this life is a healing power I get passed down through the Pillager branch of my background. It's in my hands. I snap my fingers together so hard they almost spark. Then I blank out my mind, and I put on the touch. I have a reputation up to now for curing sore joints and veins. I can relieve ailments caused in an old person by one half century of grinding stoop-over work. I have a power in myself that flows out, resistless. I have a richness in my dreams and waking thoughts. But I do not realize I will have to give up my healing source once I start charging for my service.

You know how it is about charging. People suddenly think you are worth something. Used to be, I'd go anyplace I was called, take any price offered or take nothing. Once I let it go around that I expect a twenty for my basic work, however, the phone at the bar rings off the hook.

"Where's that medicine boy?" they want to know. "Where's Lipsha?"

I take their money. And it's not like beneath the pressure of a twenty I don't try, for I do try even harder than before. I skip my palms together, snap my fingers, position them where the touch inhabiting them should flow. But when it comes to blanking out my mind, I consistently fail. For each time, in the center of the cloud that comes down into my brain, in perfect focus, the van is now parked.

One afternoon, Grandma Lulu leaves word that I should come over to her apartment to work on a patient, and though she doesn't name money, I know from her voice it is an important customer. Maybe he's her latest boyfriend. For sure, he has a job or some SSI. So I go over there. Entering her place, as usual, I exchange salutes with my own father from his picture on her shelf of little china mementos.

"I'd like you to meet Russell Kashpaw," Grandma says, and with that, I shake the hand of our state's most decorated war hero, who is recovering from multiple strokes and antique shrapnel wounds. Russell sits in a wheelchair. His job, at which he does the most business after the bars close, is tattooing people with pictures of roses, skulls, Harleys, and kung fu dragons. He lives down a curved road, off in the bush, and you can see his work displayed on almost any night.

Russell looks like a statue, not the type you see in history books, I don't mean those, but the kind you see for sale as you drive along the highway. He is a native Paul Bunyan, carved with a chain saw. He is rough-looking, finished in big strokes. I shake Russell Kashpaw's hand, hoping to feel some pulse surge, some information. I shake it longer, waiting for electrical input, but there is nothing.

"Sometimes there's a lot of static in these old war wounds," I say out loud. "Where do you feel the knot?"

In a low and commanding voice, heavy on the details, he begins to describe his aches, his pains, his spasms, his creaks and cricks. My two grandmas and their neighbor, that gossiper Mrs. Josette Bizhieu, are in the room with me. The three of them nod and tut at every one of Russell Kashpaw's symptoms and in glowing words assure him that he's come to the right place for a cure. So I rub my hands together hard and fast, inspired, then I press my burning palms to the sides of his shoulders, for it is the back of his neck and spine that are giving him the worst aggravations today. But though I knead him like I see Grandma making her buns and rolls, and though I heat my hands up again like a lightning strike, and though I twist my fingers into wire pretzels, I cannot set the touch upon him proper.

He was so shot up there's metal in him, shorting out my energy. He is so full of scars and holes and I can't smooth him straight. I don't give up, though. I try and I try until I even seem to hurt him worse, gripping desperate, with all my might.

"Holy buckets," he yells.

"Damn, Mr. Kashpaw. I'm sorry!"

I'm all balled up like some kind of tangled yarn of impulse. I'm a mess of conflicting feedback, a miserable lump of burnt string. And worst of all, the eyes of my Grandmas are on me with increasing letdown and disappointment, as I fail, and fail my patient once again. Russell pays me but he isn't happy, and neither am I, for I know, as soon as right now, the talk will gather and flash from lip to lip starting at the Senior Citizens and fanning through the houses, down the roads. My touch has deserted me. My hands are shocked out, useless. I am again no more than the simple nothing that I always was before.

I suppose after that I begin to place my desperations in the bingo. I long for the van like I've started to wish for Shawnee. And then, there comes an incident that sets me back in my quest.

Instead of going for the van with everything, saving up to buy as many cards as I can play when they get to the special game, I go short-term for variety with U-Pick-em cards, the kind where you have to choose the numbers for yourself.

First off, I write down my shoe and pants size. So much for me. I take my birth date and a double of it after that. Still no go. I write down the numbers of my Grandma's address and her anniversary dates. Nothing. Then I realize if my U-Pick-em is going to win, it will be more like revealed, rather than a forced kind of thing. So I shut my eyes right there in the middle of the long bingo table and I let my mind white out, fizzing like the screen of a television, until something forms. The van, as always. But on its tail this time a license plate is officially fixed and bolted. I use that number, write it down in the boxes.

And then I bingo.

I get two hundred dollars from that imaginary license. It is in my pocket when I leave that night. The next morning, I have fifty cents. But it's not like you think it is with Shawnee Ray, and I'll explain that. She doesn't want something from me, she never cares if I have money and never asks for it. Her idea is to go into business. To pay for college, she wants to sell her original clothing designs, of which she has six books.

I have gotten to know Shawnee a little better with each phone call, but the time has come that I can't think up another excuse to dial her number. She is so decided in her future that she intimidates me—it is her A+ attitude, her gallons of talents and hobbies. Though I want to ask her out again, the embarrassing memory of our first date keeps intruding on my mind. Finally I tell myself, "Lipsha, you're a nice-looking guy. You're a winner. You know the washer's always broken at Zelda's house. Pretend to run into Shawnee at the laundry."

So I scout the place for days until she finally shows, then I go right up to her at the Coin-Op and I make a face of surprise, which against my better judgment gets taken over by immediate joy. Just seeing her makes my head spin and my hands clench my chest. For the hundredth time, I apologize for how I've gotten her in trouble. Then I say, "Care to dance?" which is a joke. There isn't anyplace to dance at a laundromat. Yet, I can tell she likes me at least as much as the week before. We eat a sandwich and a cookie from the machine and then while her clean clothing dries Shawnee says she wants to take a drive, so we tag along with some others in the back of their car. They go straight south, toward Hoopdance, where action is taking place.

"Shawnee Ray," I whisper as we drive along, "I can't stop thinking of you."

"Lipsha." She smiles. "I can't stop thinking of you too."

I don't say anything about Lyman Lamartine and neither does she, but I have this sudden sense of him right then as perched behind us in the back window, head bobbing side to side like a toy car dog. Even so, Shawnee Ray and I move close together on the car seat. My hand is on my knee, and I think of a couple different ways I could gesture, casually pretend to let it fall on hers, how maybe if I talk fast she won't notice, in the heat of the moment, her hand in mine, us holding hands, our lips drawn to one another. But then I decide to give it all up, to boldly take courage, to cradle her hand as at the same time I look into her eyes. I do this. In the front, the others talk between themselves. We just sit there. Her mouth turns raw and hot underneath the weight of my eyes and I bend forward. She leans backward. "You want to kiss me?" she asks. But I answer, not planning how the words will come out, "Not here. Our first kiss has to be a magic moment only we can share."

Her eyes flare softer than I'd ever imagined, then widen like a deer's, and her big smile blooms. Her skin is dark, her long hair a burnt brown-black color. She wears no jewelry, no rings, that night, just the clothing she has sewed from her own designs—a suit jacket and a pair of pants the tan of eggshells, with symbols picked out in blue thread on the borders, the cuffs, and the hem. I take her in, admiring, for some time on that drive before I realize that the reason Shawnee Ray's cute outfit nags me so is on account of she is dressed up to match my bingo van. I can hardly tell her this surprising coincidence, but it does convince me that the time is perfect, the time is right.

They let us off at a certain place and we get out, hardly breaking our gaze from each other. You want to know what this place is. I'll tell you. Okay. So it is a motel, a long low double row of rooms painted white on the outside with brown wooden doors. There is a beautiful sign set up featuring a lake with some fish jumping out of it. We stand beside the painted water.

"I haven't done this since Redford," she says in a nervous voice. "I have to call Zelda and tell her I'll be late."

There is a phone outside the office, inside a plastic shell. She walks over there. I know without even listening that when Shawnee Ray asks whether it is okay with Zelda to stay out later than usual no names will be mentioned but Lyman's will probably be implied.

"He's sleeping," she says when she returns.

I go into the office, stand before the metal counter. There is a number floating in my mind.

"Is room twenty-two available?" I ask for no reason.

I suppose, looking at me, I look too much like an Indian. The owner, a big woman in a shiny black blouse, notices that. You get so you see it cross their face the way wind blows a disturbance on water. There is a period of contemplation, a struggle in this woman's thinking. Behind her the television whispers. Her mouth opens but I take the words from it.

"This here is Andrew Jackson," I say, offering the bill. "Known for booting our southern relatives onto the trail of tears. And to keep him company, we got two Mr. Hamiltons."

The woman turns shrewd, and takes the bills.

"No parties." She holds out a key attached to a square of orange plastic.

"Just sex." I cannot help but reassure her. But that is talk, big talk from a person with hardly any experience and nothing that resembles a birth control device. I am not one of those so-called studs who can't open up their wallets without dropping out a foil-wrapped square. No, Lipsha Morrissey is deep at heart a romantic, a wild-minded kind of guy, I tell myself, a fool with no letup. I go out to Shawnee Ray, and take her hand in mine. I am shaking inside but my voice is steady and my hands are cool.

"Let's go in." I show the key. "Let's not think about tomorrow."

"That's how I got Redford," says Shawnee Ray.

So we stand there.

"I'll go in," she says at last. "Down two blocks, there's an all-night gas station. They sell 'em."

Okay. Life in this day and age might be less romantic in some ways. It seems so in the hard twenty-four-hour light, trying to choose what I needed from the rack by the counter. It is quite a display, there are dazzling choices—textures, shapes, even colors. I notice I am being watched, and I suddenly grab what is near my hand, two boxes, economy size.

"Heavy date?" my watcher asks.

I suppose the guy on the late shift is bored, can't resist. His T-shirt says Big Sky Country. He is grinning in an ugly way. So I answer.

"Not really. Fixing up a bunch of my white buddies from Montana. Trying to keep down the sheep population."

His grin stays fixed. Maybe he has heard a lot of jokes about Montana blondes, or maybe he is from somewhere else. I look at the boxes in my hand, put one back.

"Let me help you out," the guy says. "What you need is a bag of these."

He takes down a plastic sack of little oblong party balloons, Day-Glo pinks and oranges and blues.

"Too bright," I say. "My girlfriend's a designer. She hates clashing colors." I am breathing hard suddenly, and so is he. Our eyes meet and take fire.

"What does she design?" he asks. "Bedsheets?"

"What does yours design?" I reply. "Wool sweaters?"

I put money between us. "For your information," I say, "my girlfriend's not only beautiful, but she and I are the same species."

He pauses, asks me which species.

"Take the money," I order him. "Hand over my change and I'll be out of here. Don't make me do something I'd regret."

"I'd be real threatened." The guy turns from me, ringing up my sale. "I'd be shaking, except I know you Indian guys are chickenshit."

As I turn away with my purchase, I hear him mutter something and I stop. I thought I heard it, but I wasn't sure I heard it. Prairie nigger.

"What?" I turn. "What'd you say?"

"Nothing."

The guy just looks at me, lifts his shoulders once, and stares me in the eyes. His are light, cold, empty. And mine, as I turn away, mine burn.

I take my package, take my change.

"Baah . . . ," I cry, and beat it out of there.

It's strange how a bashful kind of person like me gets talkative in some of our less pleasant border-town situations. I take a roundabout way back to room twenty-two and tap on the door. There is a little window right beside it. Shawnee Ray pulls the curtains aside, frowns, and lets me in.

"Well," I say in that awkward interval. "Guess we're set."

She takes the bag from my hand and doesn't say a word, just puts it on the little table next to the bed. There are two chairs. Each of us takes one. Then we sit down and turn inward to our own thoughts. The romance isn't in us now for some reason, but there is something invisible that makes me hopeful about the room.

It is a little place just over the reservation line, a modest kind of place, a clean place. You can smell the faint chemical of bug spray the moment you step inside it. You can look at the television hung on the wall, or examine the picture of golden trees and waterfall. You can take a shower for a long time in the cement shower stall, standing on your personal shower mat for safety. There is a little tin desk. You can sit down there and write a letter on a sheet of plain paper. You can read in the

Good Book someone has placed in the drawer. I take it out, New Testament, Psalms, Proverbs. It is a small green book, no bigger than my hand, with a little circle stamped in the corner, a gold ring containing a jug, a flame.

As we sit there in the strumming quiet, I open the book to the last page and read, like I always do, just to see how it ends. I have barely absorbed the last two pages when Shawnee Ray gets curious, touches my hand, asks what I am doing. Her voice is usually bold but at that moment I think of doves on wires. Whatever happens, I think, looking at her, I want to remember. I want a souvenir. I might never be hopeful for the rest of my life the way I am hopeful right now. I suppose it says something about me that the first thing I think of is what I can steal. But there it is, the way I am, always will be, ever was. I think of taking the lampshade, made of reed, pressed and laced tight together. That is possible, but not so romantic. The spread on the double mattress is reddish, a rusty cotton material. Too big, too easy to trace. There is an air conditioner. That might not be noticed until winter finishes. There are ashtrays and matches, a sad, watery mirror, and a couple postcards of the motel itself with its sign of the fish. But what I finally close my hands on, what I put in my pocket, is the little Bible, the bright plastic Gideon's.

"I don't know why we're here," I say at last. "I'm sorry."

Shawnee Ray removes a small brush from her purse.

"Comb my hair?"

I take the brush and sit on the bed just behind her. I start at the ends, very careful, but there are hardly any tangles to begin with. Her hair is a quiet dark without variation. "Your lamp doesn't go out by night," I whisper, in a dream. She never hears me. My hand follows the brush, smoothing after each stroke, until the fall of her hair is a hypnotizing silk. I lift my hand away from her head and the strands follow, electric to my touch, in soft silk that hangs suspended until I return to the brushing. She never moves, except to switch off the light, and then the television. She sits down again in the total dark and asks me to please keep on and so I do. The air goes thick. Her hair gets lighter, full of blue static, charged so that I am held in place by the attraction. A golden spark jumps on the carpet. Shawnee Ray turns toward me. Her hair floats down around her at that moment like a tent of energy.

Well, the money part is not related to that. I give it all to Shawnee Ray, that's true. Her intention is to buy material and put together the creations that she draws in her notebooks. It is fashion with a Chippewa flair, as she explains it, and sure to win prizes at the state home-ec contest. She promises to pay me interest when she opens her own boutique. It is after the next day, after we have parted, after she has picked up the very-dried-out laundry and after I have checked out the bar I was supposed to night watch, that I go off to the woods to sit and think. Not about the money, which is now Shawnee's and good luck to her, not even about the Bible I have lifted and find myself reading, again, again, whenever I am lonesome. I don't want to think about these things, but about the bigger issue of Shawnee Ray and me.

She is two years younger, yet she has direction while I am aimless, lost in hyperspace, using up my talents which are already fading from my hands. I wonder what our future can hold, even if she breaks it off with Lyman Lamartine. One thing is sure, I'll get fired from my job if Shawnee and I get together. I never knew a man to support his family playing bingo, and ever since the Russell Kashpaw failure the medicine calls for Lipsha are getting fewer by the week, and fewer, as my touch fails to heal people, flees from me, and stays concealed.

I sit on ground where Pillagers once walked. The trees around me are the dense birch and oak of old woods. Matchimanito Lake drifts in, gray waves, white foam in a bobbing lace. Thin gulls line themselves on a sandbar. The sky turns dark. I close my eyes and that is when, into my mind, the little black star shoots. It comes out of the darkness, though it is darkness itself. I see it pass and diminish and remember my mother's visit.

Here's luck. June's moment, a sign to steer me where I go next.

"This is the last night I'm going to try for the van," I tell myself. After my mother's visit, the book of bingo tickets that she gave me disappeared for a while and then, one early morning, cleaning out the bar, I found them stuffed into the seam of a plastic booth. To me, they are full of her magic—ghostly, charged. I never dared use them before. I'll use them now, I decide. This or never is the time. I'll use these last-ditch tickets, and once they're gone I'll make a real decision. I'll quit working for Lyman, go full out for Shawnee Ray, open the Yellow Pages at random and where my finger points, I will take that kind of job.

Of course, I never count on actually winning the van.

I am playing for blackout on the shaded side of those otherworldly tickets. As usual, I sit with Lulu. Her vigilance helps me. She lets me use her extra dauber and she sits and smokes a filter cigarette, observing the quiet frenzy that is taking place around her. Even though that van has sat on the stage five months, even though nobody has yet won it and everyone says it is one of Lyman's scams, when it comes to playing for it most people buy a couple cards. That night, I've just got one, but it is June's.

A girl reads out the numbers from the hopper. Her voice is clear and bright on the microphone. Lulu points out one place I have missed on the winning ticket. Then I have just two squares left to make a bingo and I suddenly sweat, I break into a chill, I go cold and hot at once. After all my pursuit, after all of my plans, I am N-36 and G-52. I narrow myself, shrink into the spaces on the ticket. Each time she reads a number out and it isn't 36 or 52 I sicken, recover, forget to breathe.

I almost faint with every number she reads out before N-36. Then right after that G-52 rolls off her lips.

I scream. I am ashamed to say how loud I yell. That girl comes over, gets Lyman Lamartine from his office in the hallway behind the big room. His face goes raw with irritation when he sees it's me, and then he cross-checks my numbers slow and careful while everyone hushes. He researches the ticket over twice. Then he purses his lips together and wishes he didn't have to say it.

"It's a bingo," he finally tells the crowd.

Noise buzzes to the ceiling, talk of how close some others came, green talk. Every eye is turned and cast on me, which is uncomfortable. I never was the center of looks before, not Lipsha, who everybody takes for granted around here. Not all those looks are for the good either—some are plain envious and ready to believe the first bad thing a sour tongue can pin on me. It makes sense in a way. Of all those who stalked that bingo van over the long months, I am now the only one who has not lost money on the hope.

Okay, so what kind of man does it make Lipsha Morrissey that the keys do not burn his hands one slight degree, and he beats it out that very night, quick as possible, completing only the basic paperwork? I mean to go tell Shawnee Ray, but in my disbelief I just drive around without her, getting used to my new self. In that van, I ride high, and maybe that's the thing. Looking down on others, even if it's only from the seat of a van that a person never really earned, does something to the human mentality. It's hard to say. I change. Just one late evening of riding the reservation roads, passing cars and pick-ups with a swish of my tires, I start smiling at the homemade hot rods, at the clunkers below, at the old-lady sedans nosing carefully up and down the gravel hills.

Once, in the distance, flying through my headlights at a crossroads like a spell, I think I see the blue Firebird, mine formerly and, I presume, now rightfully my mother's. After all, she told me she was coming for it on the night she gave me the bingo tickets. After all, the next morning it was gone. I reported it stolen and I filed a complaint with the tribal police, but that was duty, for the car insurance. I know who has it now. Riding along in my van, I wish her well. I am happy with what I have, alive with satisfaction.

I start saying to myself that I shouldn't visit Shawnee because by then it's late, but I finally do go over to Zelda's anyway. I pull into the driveway with a flourish I cannot help. When the van slips into a pothole, I roar the engine. For a moment, I sit in the dark, letting my headlamps blaze alongside the door until it opens.

The man who glares out at me is Lyman Lamartine.

"Cut the goddamn lights!" he yells. "Redford's sick."

I roll down my window, ask if I can help. I wait in the dark. A dim light switches on behind Lyman and I see some shadows—Zelda, a little form in those pajamas with the feet tacked on, a larger person pacing back and forth. I see Shawnee arguing, then picking up her little boy.

"Come in if you're coming," Lyman calls.

But here's the gist of it. I just say to tell Shawnee hello for me, that I hope Redford is all right, and then I back out of there, down the drive, and leave her to fend for herself. I could have stayed. I could have drawn my touch back from wherever it had left. I could have offered my van to take Redford to the IHS. I could have sat there in silence as a dog guards its mate, its own blood, even though I was jealous. I could have done something other than what I do, which is to hit the road for Hoopdance, looking for a better time.

I cruise until I see where the party house is located that night. I drive the van over the low curb, into the yard, and I park there. I watch until I recognize a couple cars and the outlines of Indians and mixed-bloods, so I know that walking in will not involve me in what the newspapers term an episode. The door is white, stained and raked by a dog, with a tiny fan-shaped window. I go through and stand inside. There is movement, a kind of low-key swirl of bright hair and dark hair tossing alongside each other. There are about as many Indians as there aren't. This party is what we call, around here, a hairy buffalo and most people are grouped with paper cups around a big, brown plastic garbage can that serves as the punch bowl for the all-purpose stuff, which is anything that anyone brings, dumped in along with pink Hawaiian Punch. I grew up around a lot of the people, know their nicknames, and I recognize others I don't know so well but am acquainted with by sight. Among those last, there is a young redheaded guy.

It bothers me. I recognize him, but I don't know him. I haven't been to school with him or played against him in any sport. I can't think where I've seen him, until later, when the heat goes up and he takes off his bomber jacket. Then Big Sky Country shows, plain letters on a blue background.

I edge around the corner of the room into the hall and stand there to argue with myself. Will he recognize me or am I just another face, a forgotten customer? He probably isn't really from Montana, so he might not have been insulted by our little conversation or even remember it anymore. I reason that he probably picked up the shirt while vacationing. I tell myself that I should calm my nerves, go back into the room, have fun. What keeps me from doing that is the sudden thought of Shawnee, our night together, and what I bought and used.

When I remember, I am lost to the present moment. One part of me catches up with the other.

I have a hard time getting drunk. It's just the way I am. I start thinking and forget to fill the cup, or recall something I have got to do, and end up walking from a party. I have put down a full can of beer before and wandered out to weed my Grandma's rhubarb patch or to work on a cousin's car. But that night, thinking of Lyman's face, I start drinking and keep on going and never remember to quit. I drink so hard because I want to lose my feelings.

I can't stop thinking of you too.

I hear Shawnee Ray's voice say this out loud, just behind me where there is nothing but wall. I push along until I come to a door and then I go through, into a tiny bedroom full of coats, and so far with nobody either making out or unconscious on the floor. I sit on a pile of parkas and jean jackets in this alcove within the rising hum of the party outside. I see a phone and I dial Shawnee Ray's number. Of course, Zelda answers.

"Get off the phone," she says. "We're waiting for the doctor."

"What's wrong with Redford?" I ask. My head is full of ringing coins.

There is a silence, then Shawnee's voice is on the line. "Could you hang up?"

"I'm coming over there," I say.

"No, you're not."

The phone clicks dead. I hold the droning receiver in my hand, and try to refresh my mind. The only thing I see in it clear enough to focus on is the van. I decide this is a sign for me to pile in behind the wheel, drive straight to Zelda's house. So I put my drink on the windowsill, then slip out the door and fall down the steps, only to find them waiting.

I guess he recognized me and I guess he really was from Montana, after all. He has friends, too. They stand around the van and their heads are level with the roof, for they are tall.

"Let's go for a ride," says the T-shirt guy from the all-night gas pump.

He knocks on the window of my van with his knuckles. When I tell him no thanks, he leaps on the hood. He wears black cowboy boots, pointy-toed and walked-down on the heels, and they leave small depressions every time he jumps and lands.

"Thanks anyhow," I repeat. "But the party's not over." I try to get back into the house, but like in a bad dream, the door is stuck or locked. I holler, pound, kick at the very marks that a desperate dog has left, but the music rises and nobody hears. So I end up behind the wheel of the van. They act very gracious. They urge me to drive. They are so polite, I try to tell myself, they aren't all that bad. And sure enough, after we have proceeded along for a while, these Montana guys tell me they have chipped together to buy me a present.

"What is it?" I ask.

"Shut up," says the pump jockey. He is in the front seat next to me, riding shotgun.

"I don't really go for surprises," I say. "What's your name anyhow?"

"Marty."

"I got a cousin named Marty."

"Fuck him."

The guys in the back exchange a grumbling kind of laughter, a knowing set of groans. Marty grins, turns toward me.

"If you really want to know what we're going to give you, I'll tell. It's a map. A map of Montana."

Their laughter turns hyena-crazed and goes on for too long.

"I always liked the state," I allow in a serious voice.

"No shit," says Marty. "Then I hope you like sitting on it." He signals where I should turn and all of a sudden I realize that Russell Kashpaw's place is somewhere ahead. He runs his tattoo den from the basement of his house, keeps his equipment set up and ready for the weekend, and of course, I remember how in his extremity of pain I failed him.

"Whoa." I brake the van. "You can't tattoo a person against his will. It's illegal."

"Get your lawyer on it tomorrow." Marty leans in close for me to see his unwinking eyes. I put the van back in gear, but just chug along, desperately, thinking. Russell does a lot of rehabilitation in the old-time sweat lodge, and for income or art has taken up this occupation that he learned overseas and can do sitting down. I don't expect him to have much pity on me, and I graphically imagine needles whirring, dyes, getting stitched and poked, and decide that I'll ask Marty, in a polite kind of way, to beat me up instead. If that fails, I will tell him that there are many states I would not mind so much, like Minnesota with its womanly hourglass for instance, or Rhode Island which is small, or even Hawaii, a soft bunch of circles. I think of Idaho. The panhandle. That has character.

"Are any of you guys from any other state?" I ask, anxious to trade.

"Kansas."

"South Dakota."

It isn't that I really have a thing against those places, understand, it's just that the straight-edged shape is not a Chippewa preference. You look around, and everything you see is round, everything in nature. There are no perfect boundaries, no natural borders except winding rivers. Only human-made things tend toward cubes and squares—the van, for instance. That is an example. Suddenly I realize that I am driving a four-wheeled version of the state of North Dakota.

"Just beat me up, you guys. Let's get this over with."

But they laugh even harder, and then we are at Russell's.

The sign on his basement door reads Come In. I am shoved from behind and strapped together with five pairs of heavy football-toughened hands, so I am the first to see Russell, the first to notice he is not a piece of all the trash and accumulated junk that washes through the concrete-floored cellar, but a person sitting still as any statue, in a corner, on his wheelchair that creaks and sings when he pushes himself toward us with long, powerful old man's arms.

"Please!" I plead with a desperate note in my voice. "I don't want—"

Marty squeezes me around the throat and tousles up my hair.

"Cold feet. Now remember, Mr. Kashpaw, just like we talked about on the phone. Map of Montana. You know where. And put in a lot of detail."

I try to scream.

"Like I was thinking," Marty goes on, "of those maps we did in grade school showing products from each region. Cows' heads, oil wells, missile bases, those little sheaves of wheat and so on. . . ."

Russell Kashpaw looks from Marty to me and back and forth again, skeptical, patient, and then he strokes his rocklike cliff of a chin and considers the situation.

"Tie him up," says Kashpaw at last. His voice is thick, with a military crispness. "Then leave this place."

They do. They take my pants and the keys to the van. I hear the engine roar and die away, and I roll side to side in my strict bindings. I feel Russell's hand on my shoulder and suddenly, from out of nowhere, caught in a wrinkle in my brain, words jump like bread into my mouth.

I start babbling. "Please, Russell. I'm here against my will, kidnapped by Montana boys. Take pity!"

"Be still." Russell Kashpaw's voice has changed, now that the others are gone, to a low sound that matches with his appearance and does not seem at all unkind. I fix my pleading gaze upon him. A broke-down God is who he looks like from my worm's-eye view. His eyes are frozen black, his hair crewcut, half dark, half gray, his scarred cheeks shine underneath the blazing tubes of light in the ceiling. You never know where you're going to find your twin in the world, your double. I don't mean in terms of looks, I'm talking about mindset. You never know where you're going to find the same thoughts in another brain, but when it happens you know it right off, just like you were connected by a small electrical wire that suddenly glows red hot and sparks. That's what happens when I stare up at Russell Kashpaw, and he suddenly grins.

He puts a big hand to his jaw.

"I don't have a pattern for Montana," he tells me. He unties my ropes with a few quick jerks, sneering at the clumsiness of the knots. Then he sits back in his chair again, and watches me get my bearings.

"I never wanted anything tattooed on me, Mr. Kashpaw, not that I have anything against a tattoo," I say, so as not to hurt his professional feelings. "It was a kind of revenge plot though."

He sits in silence, a waiting quiet, hands folded and face composed. By now I know I am safe, but I have nowhere to go and so I sit down on a pile of magazines. He asks what revenge, and I tell him the story, the whole thing right from the beginning. I tell him how my mother came to me, and go farther back, past the bingo, from when I entered the winter powwow. I leave out the personal details about Shawnee and me but he gets the picture. I mention all about the van.

"That's an unusual piece of good fortune."

"Have you ever had any? Good fortune?"

"All the time. Those guys paid plenty. Maybe they'll want it back, but then again, why don't you just look sore—you know, kind of rub your ass the next time you see them. Keep them off my back too."

He opens a book on the table, a notebook with plastic pages that clip in and out, and hands it over to me.

"You can pick a design out," he says.

I pretend interest—I don't want to disappoint him—and leaf through the dragons and the hearts, thinking how to refuse. Then suddenly I see the star. It is the same one that scattered my luck in the sky after my mother left me alone that night, it is the sight that came into my head as I sat in the woods. Now here it is. The star falls, shedding rays, reaching for the edge of the page. My luck's uneven, but it's coming back. I have a wild, uncanny hope. I get a thought in my head, clear and vital, that this little star will bring my touch back and convince Shawnee I am serious about her.

"This one. Put it here on my hand."

Russell nods, gives me a rag to bite, and plugs in his needle.

Now my hand won't let me rest. It throbs and aches as if it came alive again after a hard frost. I know I'm going somewhere, taking this hand to Shawnee Ray. Even walking down the road in a pair of big-waisted green pants belonging to Russell Kashpaw, toward the bingo palace, where I keep everything I own in life, I'm going forward. My hand is a ball of pins, but when I look down I see the little star shooting across the sky.

I'm ready for what will come next. That's why I don't fall on the ground and I don't yell when I come across the van parked in a field. At first, I think it is the dream van, the way I always see it in my vision. Then I notice it's the real vehicle. Totaled.

My bingo van is dented on the sides, kicked and scratched, and the insides are scattered. Ripped pieces of carpet, stereo wires, glass, are spread here and there in the new sprouts of wheat. I force open a door that is bent inward. I wedge myself behind the wheel, tipped over at a crazy angle, and I look out. The windshield is shattered in a sunlight burst, a web through which the world is more complicated than I thought, and more peaceful.

I've been up all night and the day stretches long before me, so I decide to sleep where I am. Part of the seat is still wonderfully upholstered, thick and plush, and it reclines now—permanently, but so what? I relax to the softness, my body warm as an animal, my thoughts drifting. It makes no sense, but at this moment I feel rich. Sinking away, it seems like everything worth having is within my grasp. All I have to do is reach my hand into the emptiness.

CHAPTER EIGHT

LYMAN'S LUCK

THE TWO MEN SAT ACROSS FROM ONE ANOTHER AT A scratched plastic table in the palace bar. Lipsha Morrissey hunched over his arms, cradled his hand, rocked forward in his chair. Lyman leaned back slightly, palms placed neatly on the tabletop. Ever since he'd seen the pipe returned from the authorities and put back into the boy's possession, Lyman hadn't been able to get the thought of it from his head. He wanted that pipe with a simple finality that had nothing to do with its worth as a historical artifact. Although he didn't examine all of his motivations, he knew that the desire had something to do with his natural father, for when he imagined himself smoking the pipe that had once belonged to Nector Kashpaw, he saw himself drawing the sacred object solemnly from its bag and also presenting it to friends, to officials, always with the implication that it had, somehow, been passed down to him by right.

The prestige of owning that pipe had dogged Lyman's thoughts so consistently that he had tried several times to actually buy it from Lipsha. Always, he'd been shyly refused, but now he thought he might reason a little more aggressively. Lyman knotted his square, heavy hands, looked down at his blue class ring. The stone drank deep light. He cocked his head to one side and his wide-spaced eyes figured.

"I'm not trying to persuade you for myself," he said to Lipsha. "Consider it this way—you would be donating the pipe back to your people."

Lipsha licked the end of a straw and shook his head with a distracted smile.

"I'd keep it on permanent display," Lyman continued. "Put it out where the public could look at it, in a glass case maybe, right at the casino entrance. Keep it yourself and you're liable to lose it. Something might happen, just like at the border crossing."

"We got it returned though," Lipsha reminded Lyman. "They took it illegal, they admitted that."

"I'm not saying the loss was your fault." Lyman shook his head, frowning into the steeple of his fingers. "I'm just saying *things happen*."

"Things do happen," Lipsha agreed.

"To you, they happen all the time."

"I guess." Lipsha crumpled his fingers together in a tight package, and looked down at the little star that shot across the back of his hand. Titus, the bartender, placed a hamburger before him. Titus was dressed in black—black jeans, biker's boots, T-shirt, black plastic diver's watch. His long curls, dry and electric, hung about his shoulders. He gazed at Lyman, then back at Lipsha.

"You ain't got a hangover, do you?" Titus asked Lipsha. "Never deal with Lyman when you're not a hundred percent. He's after that pipe."

"Tell me about it." Lipsha kept on eating. His jaws slowed until he was merely pretending to chew, once, twice. His hair fell out of its band and he suddenly stuffed the rest of the burger into his mouth. He swallowed, staring down at the table, hair flopped across his face, then tossed his head back, hooked the loose strands behind his ears.

"I don't think I better sell."

"Why not?" Lyman's face clouded over as he attempted to control his irritation.

"You ever heard the story about the mess of porridge?"

"What?"

"One brother gives his birthright to the other for some breakfast. It's in the Bible."

Lyman's look eased slightly and he almost started to laugh.

"That hamburger's on the house." He then frowned in deepening suspicion. He began to smooth one hand over the other, back and forth, like he was petting a dog. He worked his hands together faster, faster, and then finally spoke in a quick, dry tone.

"Nector Kashpaw was *my* real father."

"What does that have to do with it?"

"Goddamn it, Lipsha! Think about it once. Everybody could be getting inspiration from this pipe, it's a work of genuine art, it's spiritual. Only you'd rather keep it in your leaky trunk, or stuffed in your footlocker. Somewhere like that. You don't deserve it!"

Lipsha stared at his uncle's face, his mouth slightly open, dazed, strangely serene in his contemplation.

Lyman's voice lowered to its most persuasive register. "It belongs to all of us, Lipsha. It especially belongs to me."

"Like Shawnee Ray?"

Lyman tucked his mouth in at the corners, reeled back a little as if at the surprising unfairness of the question. He clenched his jaw, spoke sternly, adopting a minister's logical, reasoning tones.

"Shawnee Ray doesn't 'belong' to me, Lipsha. She goes out with me because she chooses to, because she sees something in me she admires, because she has, I like to think, good taste— she values hard work, intelligence. She goes out with me because of *her,* Lipsha, not because I make her do it."

As Lipsha listened, his stare became wide-eyed, almost frantic, piercing.

"I'll trade you the pipe!" he suddenly cried out.

"For what?"

"Shawnee Ray. Here's the deal: I give you the pipe, and you lay low, step aside."

"You sonofabitch!"

Lipsha raised his hands, palms out, grinning crazily as Lyman jumped up, unable to contain his agitation. He went about the bar, straightening stools, dusting off tables, lifting the chairs and setting them down. He took a grape soda from the glass-door cooler, sat down again with a bowl of popcorn.

"You want me to go get the pipe now?" Lipsha asked, his grin stretching huger.

Lyman halted with a handful of popcorn halfway to his mouth, one eye glinting past his fist.

"I'll write the check," he said.

"It's not for *sale*." Lipsha was composed and patient now. "Trade only. You get the pipe, I get to let Shawnee make her own decision."

Lyman drew his head back, sank his chin to his chest in thought. He stared at the counter, his eyes staring blank, then shrewd.

"She's going to love hearing that you tried to do this," he said.

Lipsha turned away, at a loss. For moment after long moment neither man said anything. The only sounds in the bar were a low cloud of conversation around the pool table, the intermittent clocking of balls, Titus in the back room on the phone. The popcorn machine popped over, spilled, and a last kernel exploded, weakly, in the yellow air.

Packing his suitcase for the Indian Gaming Conference, Lyman weighed the pipe for a moment in his hands. Quickly, carefully, he set the pipe, in its pouch, within the inside pocket

of his carry-on case and pulled all of the zippers shut. He shuffled through his tickets: Bismarck to Denver, Denver to Reno.
His reservations: Sands Regency. The confirmation card was
inked in purple with tiny stars flying off the letters of the hotel.
He went through everything twice, picked up his bag, and carried it to the spare living room of his government house. He
shrugged his arms into his leather suit jacket, brown and supple, made sure all his windows were shut, then locked and
triple-locked his front door.

Lyman hadn't been to desert country before. He followed
the signs to Ground Transportation, and stood alongside the
service way, waiting for the hotel shuttle. The air passing in
and out of his lungs tasted of the color of dust, faintly tinged, a
dry and melancholy tone. All the buildings he could see were a
washed-out yellow margarine color. He strolled to stretch his
legs. The buckets of palms, set here and there, smelled of cat
piss. He was already sweating in his leather jacket, boiling. His
hair fell in limp, damp clumps. Although he had helped to
organize the conference, he felt anxious and uncertain, ready
to turn around and fly back home. Then the shuttle pulled to
the curb and he put his bag inside and tipped his head back
and was convinced, suddenly, that something was going to
happen to him. His mouth watered, tears formed at the corners of his eyes, his thoughts were eager, and his heart
pumped, hot and alert. He tried to contain it but a kick of
adrenaline surged up when he walked into the lobby of the
Sands and heard the high, manic warble of the slot machines,
the controlled shouts of pit bosses, the whine and crash of
someone's bad hand sinking, dark, out of view.

He forced himself to get his key at the front desk, and then
he made himself go to his room. The decor was jungle bronze,
the bed vast and tigerish. Foil and black leopard spots surrounded the mirror and trimmed the desk, table, the chairs of
molded plastic. Green shag carpeted the floor, long flows of

greasy yarn. He took his wallet out of his pocket, put it in his bag, set the bag down inside his room, backed out, and shut the door.

Crossing the grand floor of the casino, the biggest he'd ever been in, Lyman passed through windows—areas of noise and intensity blocked off from other shapes of smoke and voice. The ceiling was low and mirrored, the cushioned floor spread, the rug endless, the color of good barbecue. The place was dizzyingly lighted, divided by pathways and velvet-roped rotundas into dreamlike parkways. Pleasure soaked into him like resin. He entered caves of darkness where ice cream, chilled in blue polar cases, was sold in a thousand flavors. A doorway crusted in rhinestones. A great orange containing Orange Julius. An elevator dispensing trim hostesses smelling of chlorine from the upstairs swimming pool and offering to spray you with Obsession. Fascinated, awed, he watched a couple of elderly women in identical lime green pantsuits play the quarter slots. He waited, like them, for the glad sound of the payout. He navigated the banks of video poker machines and came out the other side with his hands still clenched in his pockets. A red Camaro. Vintage baby blue Mustang. Lyman ran his fingers over the hoods of the cars that people were playing for in the rear bank of the casino. He passed the five-dollar blackjack tables, passed the ten. He doubled back to show that he could do it. He passed the hundred and then the five-hundred tables. He ambled the entire circle again and as he stood, not watching, looking sideways, breathing carefully, his hands lifted from his pockets in a magical arc.

That was when he whirled, almost ran to the elevators, got on, and rode up to his floor. The attraction and detail of it all was too much, overwhelming, and his eyes fairly ached from straining to see it all. Once inside his room, he reached immediately for the phone, dialed room service, ordered a large fruit salad with cottage cheese. He called back, added a diet soda, called back again, ordered a plate of Super Grande Nachos, then sat in front of the window and willed himself to wait. There was a long blank, a space of time which he knew that he should fill in by focusing on the presentation that he had to deliver the next day. Or he could make a telephone call— surely someone he knew from other, more local tribal gaming conferences had arrived. Surely he was not the only one to book his flight so early, to arrive so soon. He looked at his watch. So slow! He would have done better going out onto the streets, getting directions to a real restaurant, or just walking around to burn away his appetite.

And why not? So what?

He jumped to his feet and searched out his wallet, patted his pockets. Outside the door, he passed the waiter with the cart, making for his room with bored determination, and nearly stopped. But then he saw the salad—large quarter of a pineapple, spiky top still attached, and watermelon, slices of honeydew, red grapes. It looked as though the plastic wrap was molded to the fruit. He kept walking, took the elevator down to the lobby. Just before he went out into the street, he veered around the shining columns, past the churning machines, to the tables where the same people were still tapping and releasing their cards.

People drifted away, the air dimmed and brightened under sizzling marquees. Five hours later, Lyman got up from the blackjack table. He stretched his arms and tipped the dealer. He was seven hundred dollars happier than he was when he sat down. "Now," he said to himself, *"now."* He was advising himself to go, to leave, to find the Italian restaurant recommended to him by the dealer, who clearly wanted to get rid of him. "La Florentine," he said definitively, and stood up. He nodded at the other players, still absorbed in the next hand, counting chips and cards in their heads. Lyman's winnings made a cool package in his hands and he walked to the cashier, but then, as there was a short line, he decided not to wait. He would walk around the slot machines again, uncramp his legs. He passed the ice cream stand and ordered a peanut butter parfait, then put the package under his arms and ate the sundae, standing there, watching people move and shuffle about, jingling their white plastic buckets of quarters.

His features were a mask. His outside expression was fixed, serene, but beneath that, on the real face that was hidden, he could feel his look of bewildered dread. A sudden jittery anxiety coursed through him along with the cold ice cream. His senses dulled. His mouth went numb, he could not taste, couldn't hear above casino clatter, couldn't feel his own hands spooning the peanut sauce between his lips. A certainty clapped down like a wet hand and his brain let go. Fixed hard on the dim comfort of his own surrender he relaxed into it, threw away the rest of his ice cream, and carried the seven hundred dollars in chips back to the high stakes table.

He would have played it, too, but for the accident. An elderly man in a neat white shirt and plaid pants bumped into him halfway across the room, and the jolt sent the chips to the ground. Lyman, ashamed after they were picked up, mumbled that he had been on his way to the cashier. Then, as if a different program had taken over in his brain, he actually did go there, cashed the chips, walked back through the crowd. It was as though he was now surrounded by a force field. He was immune. He got into the elevator and let himself back into his room. Sitting by the window, watching other windows and lights, he peeled off layers of plastic wrap from the tray of food, ate the warm fruit, the corn-chip wedges disintegrating into salsa and sour cream. He ate everything and drank the watery soda. Then he slept, dreamless, the seven hundred curled in an ashtray beside his head.

It was two A.M. when he woke, starting into clarity, his brain on and humming like a machine connected to that money. He dressed quickly and combed his hands through his hair, went downstairs knowing that he couldn't miss. And he couldn't. For the next hour he played perfect games, steadily and easily accumulating chips until he was far ahead. The wins came slower for a while, but the chips kept accumulating. A thousand, then two, then more. Right about there, when he perched just under three thousand, he felt a low wave, a green slide of nausea, and told himself to leave. But he was two people then, split, and could not unstick himself. He started losing his way in a muddy sluice of sloppy plays, and he got desperate. His luck turned unpredictable and he played on, but the momentum had died. The spell was slack. Slowly and unremittingly, things soured. It was for the nostalgia of feeling the luck, wanting it to return, as much as for the money, that he kept playing after he had nothing left.

At four A.M. he stood before the cash machine and punched in his PIN number again and again, unbelieving, but he'd gone beyond his limit.

At four fifteen he cashed the loan from the Bureau of Indian Affairs that had just come in to finance the tribal gaming project. He put half in chips and half in another cashier's check. He started hitting, then the losses dragged him down again and he went bust.

At five he cashed the other check.

At six he brought Nector's pipe to the all-night pawnshop and got a hundred dollars for it.

"I'll be back by noon," he promised the clerk.

At seven in the morning he had nothing left that he could turn to collateral, but he still felt good, drained but on top of things, alert and clean. He walked straight out the double glass doors and stood quietly, hands hanging at his sides, in the cool, dry Nevada dawn. In the Sands parking lot, he watched the sky go from silver to blue and felt the sun's light strengthen. Beyond the railroad tracks, he remembered a bridge, and as though he could smell the water, taste it now, he walked toward it. The trees, the grassy park at its edge, lay only two blocks off and he soon entered the sounds of morning, the click of aspen, a lower murmur. Mild breezes swelled against him, and he smelled the sage in dry flower and the oils of broken cedar twigs. He walked over to the rail beside the river's bank, thought hopefully of jumping in, but the Truckee River was only a foot or so in depth, wandering among gray rocks, too weak to flow, too shallow to run.

INSULATION

WHAT I COME UP WITH IN MY FISTS WHEN I REACHED MY HAND INTO the nowhere place is insulation. You might call it money, but I know different. If you are poor and you suddenly get bingo rich you'll see money the way I first do. Not so much for what it gets you, but what it keeps away—cold, heat, sore feet, nicotine fits and hungry days, even other people. I debate for a while about just what I should do. I look inside my Gideon's, and chance on a verse from Luke. *Divide the inheritance,* it instructs. I already did that, I figure, sharing Nector's pipe with Lyman Lamartine. In return for not telling Shawnee Ray about my offer to purchase her undivided attention, he borrows the pipe for an undetermined amount of time.

Insulation buys insulation, that's how it goes with me. Every time I play for money using one of June's remaining bingo tickets, I win a small amount. The first time, it's fifty dollars, just gas money, but the trend continues. A week goes by and I win six hundred altogether, the next week two, then six again, nothing for days, then drips and drabs, but always I keep acquiring the insulation. With my mother's bingo tickets, luck is magnetized. She watches over me, at last, in the form of hundreds and twenties. I stuff it all into my pocket. Some blows out into the hands of my buddies, but the greater part collects beneath my mattress.

With money, I notice as time wears on, the spring comes on milder, even those blazing weeks that drop suddenly to freezing. When it is hot, I sleep easy at night beneath the fake breeze in my room. Some would call it a nice new cooling system. I call it insulation. I keep hoping that insulation will impress Zelda Kashpaw so much that she will stop standing in my way, for after that morning when I dozed in the wrecked van and awakened to the shattered window and rattling black spines of last year's sunflowers, I have no thoughts for anyone but Shawnee Ray. Sometimes, falling asleep in the blowing dark, I remember how we tangled together. It was so natural, as if we grew into a single plant. And now I ache for her, now my arms are broken stems. I try to look at other women with serious and measuring anticipation, but it doesn't work. I can't get the feeling right.

I scold my heart for sitting turned over on the table like an empty cup. Still, I can't accept no one else but Shawnee Ray. Even though I tell myself that love is just an image, like the mental picture of your home—which when you get back is full of anxious demands and people, far from perfect—even though I tell myself to go on from where I left off, my heart is stubborn.

I am fixed in the twilight zone of Shawnee Ray's arms. My love is so strong that it busts the barriers and the morals, it whines through padding and steel targets like a bullet, it strikes. It hurts. But the only actual evidence I have of the beautiful things that went on are mental touchtones. Room twenty-two. Twin twos. Inside my mind I erect brass posts and loop thick ropes of wine-colored velvet at the flimsy door. I cordon off that scene, the love tableau, from common touch. I go there the way a person goes to a museum. I close my eyes to get refreshed. Fragrance that clings to my fingers, my skin. Raw cinnamon. Fresh salt. An animal smell that is the taste of actual sensation, of an ache, of joy stuffed into me with each touch so that I grow beyond the boundaries of my own body into one larger, sweeter, more skilled.

I can't get rid of her. My heart keeps beating out her name.

Yet, the more I jump toward love the faster it flees. The more furious I throw my mental life into its capture, the more elusive it becomes, an animal that learns avoiding a trap. Love is hard, loneliness a sure bet. All the songs I listen to and moan over bear this truth. When do you ever hear a song about the fullness and the romance, the dream come into its own? No matter how hard I try, love is just beyond the tips of my fingers, precious as a field of diamonds and elusive, receding fast. The big-bang world is love—we have sex and everything explodes and ever after the pieces are whirling free.

Thanks to the insulation cash, I get my van fixed and then I start lying in wait for Shawnee Ray. I want to talk to her, see her face, put my hand on her knee. The money buys me gas so that I can idle my van in place. I sit outside the grocery store, or on the road to the Kashpaw place, or at the junior college— anywhere that my own Miss Little Shell might pass. It isn't long before I catch her at the entrance to the post office and wave her over to me. She comes eagerly, walking light on her feet, swinging a pack full of schoolbooks. She jumps into the seat next to me and for a minute we don't breathe, just stare into each other's eyes, feasting on the surprising nearness of each other.

"I tried to call you."

"You shouldn't. Zelda, Lyman, they're both—"

"What should I do? I can't stop thinking about you."

She swings her face aside. "I thought I'd marry him—I mean, he thought so too."

"You're still seeing Lyman, then?"

"I never stopped." She looks at me almost defiantly, as if I have a right to feel jealous, a fact I file away to thrill over later.

She pauses, gathers herself, and speaks as if she's memorized the lines she has to say. "It was always understood, since Redford. You should probably leave me alone for a while, let me try and get my bearings."

"Do you love me, though?" I speak low, trying to press my voice against her.

She looks at me so long, so tenderly, with such a wistful darkness in her eyes that she really doesn't need to answer my question at all. In the days that follow, I keep that look of hers like a wallet-size photo filed behind clear plastic in my mind. Whenever I find my heart racing after her in longing, in panic at her retreat, I flip to that little picture of her overwhelmed with matching wishes and I somehow convince myself that although harsh time might pass, although we might have explosive troubles, there is no doubt that a loving future together will be ours.

It's not like that's the only pressure on my mind, either, for I've never figured out what Lyman's done with the pipe. About a week after Lyman returns from his conference trip, I ask for it back. With a face like ash, eyes wary, Lyman Lamartine tells me that he hasn't presently got possession of it but he is working on its return.

"Return?" I almost shout.

He won't say from where, and I think maybe a collector has approached from a museum, like they do. He won't talk to me, just fixes control on himself and glares. There is a tone underneath his statement, a pulled string, a fear I never heard in him, a roughness that was never part of his slippery line. I regret about lending the pipe to him, but still, because of the red eyes and outgrown shaggy haircut, he seems less groomed, more human, somebody I can almost trust.

We all got holes in our lives. Nobody dies in a perfect garment. We all got to face the nothingness before us and behind. Call it sleep. We all begin in sleep and that's where we find our end. Even in between, sleep keeps trying to claim us.

To stay awake in life as much as possible—that may be the point.

Money helps, though not as much as you think when you don't have it. Anyway, this is temporary bingo-luck money, nothing sure. No matter how I'm tempted to resign as night watchman, I think of Shawnee Ray and do not quit my job. But the fact is, things don't bother me as much at the bar as they did before. New sound system in my room so I can play my songs at any hour. New shirts in my boxes so I don't have to wash the old ones out so often at the Senior Citizens, which means I don't have to listen to so much old-people criticism of me. Insulation. People don't laugh at Lipsha, knowing they might need a loan. Instead of putting on the touch, these days I get touched up, for cash. People don't come around just to visit me and take up my time—except for Lyman Lamartine, who was always insulated, comfortable about money, cool about the changes it can make in a person's life.

Over the weeks, he seems to recover, gains back his old, easy ways, and lands back on top of the reservation heap. He tells me that he has the pipe back, but asks if I mind if he keeps it for a couple more weeks, and although I am suspicious I tell him that it is all right. He says he has to have it exorcised, has to have it reblessed, but no matter how much I prod he will not tell me what has happened. It is strange, the way I feel about him, for our history is a twisted rope and I hold on to it even as I saw against the knots. He is my rival, he is my enemy, and yet I've beat him already by sleeping with Shawnee Ray and I feel guilt even though I never went to church. It's just built into me. In his presence, I'm always mild mannered, eager to help, sorry for him, shamed because it turns out that he does love her. Only not as much as me. Nobody, I am sure, could love another human as much I am starting to love Miss Little Shell.

I do complain to Lyman, though.

"You said if you had the pipe, you wouldn't see her," I remind him.

"I know I said that," Lyman admits, giving me a long look. "But I can't stop—could you?"

The problem is, I understand just how he feels and I know just how much he must need Shawnee Ray, and although a wave of red hatred passes over me, shimmers between us, I can't deny that I approve of his feelings. He was there first, but then, is Shawnee Ray some sort of mining claim? Is she a right-of-occupancy apartment? Is she sunken treasure, found loot? Of course not. My hands itch for Lyman's neck.

"Have you opened up a bank account for all that money you're winning?" he asks me, and I'm grateful that he manages to divert our attention to hard currency.

"Got the cash hid," I tell him.

He shakes his head, lets his mouth form a little smile. "You need financial advice."

I shrug. "I scored big in the college testing, even though I don't talk so perfectly as you do, even though money doesn't make any sense to me."

"You've got the aptitude, but not the latitude," says Lyman. "I can provide the latter."

"Thanks anyway. You helped me enough by giving me this job in the first place."

He has to admit that's true. "You were a risk, Lipsha. But you'll pay off."

"In spades."

"In spades." He allows a laugh, but again his eyes stay on me too long, figuring.

Time draws us into the dead center of the afternoon. We are sitting at an empty table, again, as we often do before the rush is on. The false lights shine on us and upon our hamburger plate specials, which as usual Lyman has thoughtfully ordered. He doesn't make me pay, even though my bingo luck was good that week. He doesn't even mention the bingo, but I know my streak is on his mind. He is anxious to save my money almost as if it were his own, which it is, in a sense. I soon find, to my surprise, that as we talk about the money itself, I am eager to discuss the amounts that are passing through my hands, because I never had the chance before, see, the chance to talk about money. It's no fun to talk about the stuff with poor people—in the first place they don't know what you're talking about, and in the second they can't help but think, *hand it over, asshole.* I find it so pleasant just to discuss dollars and cents in matter-of-fact ways, as though money isn't so unusual a thing to own.

"Money is alive," Lyman tells me. "You don't just stuff it somewhere, leave it. You have to put it in a place where it grows."

"Money's dead stuff, but I like it."

I bite a big hunk from my sandwich. It has everything on it, pickles, mayo, all the works, just like my life now that I am rich.

"Have you ever heard of compound interest, Lipsha?" Now Lyman looks serious. I nod to keep the conversation going, and he continues. "Interest is growth. How can I put this?" He drums his fingers. "You let your money out to work for you, like each dollar is a horse, and you lend the herd out to people who pay you back extra for the privilege. It grows, it accumulates."

"The facts of life," I joke.

Lyman has no humor about this. "The real facts. The sex of money. How it reproduces if you pile it up high enough and put it in the right circumstances."

I put down my tasteless hamburger and all of a sudden lose my humor, too. "Tell me everything you know."

The blood beats in my ears and swirls about inside my head. I keep my mind centered as closely as possible on Lyman's words, but I'm not sure I can swallow all his wisdom. I'm not used to this level of possession, see, and every so often while the Lamartine talks I want to ditch the conversation and break into a maniac frenzy of expensive laughter.

"Success wrecks as many people as failure," he says, "especially Indians. We're not programmed for it."

"I had luck from the beginning though, always," I argue. "I'm a lucky guy."

Lyman shakes his head. "You've never had luck you can put your hands on."

"It don't matter."

"You ever hear about the crayfish pots, Lipsha? Listen. There's these three fishermen. An Irishman, a Frenchman, and an Indian. They're picking crayfish from a streambed one day, and they each have a bucket. They're all picking at the same rate, the same number of these crayfish. The Irishman fills his, but he turns his back and the crayfish all get out. The Frenchman fills his, but he turns his back and his crayfish get out too. But when the Indian turns around, though, his bucket's still full. The others can't believe it, they ask how come. The Indian says it's simple. He picked out all Indian crayfish—the minute one of them tries to climb out the others pull him back."

"What's the message?"

"Think about it."

All that comes to me is how Grandma let me take her money for a bus ticket that I needed, how Albertine lent me her own school loan from the U.S. government, how Grandma Lulu put me down for benefits, how people had helped me, how they tried to get me to make something of my life.

"Don't let anybody ever tell you money doesn't make people nicer, kinder, better," says Lyman to gag me.

Maybe he's right, yet all I can think is that the good people I have known so far in life have been cash poor. However, this conversation does make me appreciate them, for their kindness must have come twice as hard. I don't like to say this, I don't like to make a judgment, but I do think that Lyman Lamartine has an ax to grind down to dust ever since his fake tomahawk factory blew up in everybody's face. And yet, the bingo palace that he so recently maneuvered to open is doing bigger business and contributing to the overall economic profile of our reservation, as it says in his brochures. So what was his problem? He should be proud, but you see, here is the thing about Lyman Lamartine. Here's the implicating factor. There is a secret in his face that only someone who formerly possessed the touch can see. A secret.

I watch him as he talks to me and counsels me about which bank in the area is the most stable, how he'll help me open my account. I study him as he asks, point blank, for me to toss in my hand with his next project, which will be a more profitable, a more enormous bingo hall with drawing power that will attract not only surrounding residents but also people from as far away as Grand Forks and Winnipeg. There was a temporary hang-up of his plans, he allows, but he won't give up. He's going forward. He won't be stopped.

The secret is, though, that he doesn't believe what he's doing is completely as simple as making money.

"It's a mixed bag of trouble, like you," he laughs at one point. "There's lots of ways to make money, and gambling is not the nicest, not the best, not the prettiest. It's just the way available right now."

"The easiest."

"That's right, too."

I'm lighthearted and secure in my luck. From Lyman's disallowing smile and considering eyes, however, I know he thinks I'm a fool, much too simple for his complicated advice, which he gives me anyway.

"Go after something real," he says in a meaningful tone. I let the sentence gather strength between us, let each word lock onto the next like the muscles in the balanced arms of two wrestlers. It is a challenge, it is an ignorance, for he doesn't know what I'm really after.

Shawnee Ray, Shawnee Ray, my love. I think about her in the shape of clean beer glasses, in their sleek-waisted forms. I think about her in the napkins, which I am sure she uses politely at Zelda's. I think about her as I stock the little rack of pocket combs and beer nuts and I even think about her as I replenish the jars of pickled eggs that sit on the counter. She is everywhere. The band plays slow wailing country love songs each evening and my heart gives, just sinks down, all riddled with holes. I leak love. I grin like a fool when I think of her, wipe too hard on counters and tables as though I am polishing her body—smooth, washed by motel showers, warm to my touch and kiss. I have a picture of her from the newspaper, one of her high school fashion-show triumphs, and I hold the newsprint so often to my lips that the ink smears onto me, indelible, fading to silver her graven image.

A wandering procession of Shawnee Ray pictures trails constant through my brain. I write notes to send her, poems, songs that I compose into my old high school spiral-bound. I place imaginary phone calls, in which I try to hold my breath and speak in a mannerly voice while every moment I am thinking, Please, my baby heart, please, please. I try to keep my promise, let her alone to think, but one morning she answers my desperate call on the first ring. She tells me that the thinking has paid off, that she feels more together, and that I should just keep leaving her alone.

"What?"

"You've been wonderful to me, I can't thank you enough."

"Hey, wait!"

Something doesn't figure in what she's saying, it is all contradictions. At the sudden thought that maybe Lyman has managed to weasel his way back into the front of her affections, my pulse surges ahead and I feel an animal's strength.

"I'm still thinking," she says, sounding a little lame now, her voice halting.

"You've been thinking too much! Stay there, I'm coming over."

I hang the phone up on her loud refusal, and I jump into the van. But I do not entirely lose my head. It is a Sunday, so first I make sure that Zelda is at Holy Mass. Then I bring Shawnee a bundle of flowers from the grocery store in the mall. I purchase these purple daisies and hot red carnations that look like they'll last in a vase. I think of chocolates and I think of a laser stunner or a book or a head of lettuce, something to give to Redford. I don't get these things for fear that Shawnee Ray will think that I am flaunting my money in her face, but I want to buy her a new house, a pet, a car red as the fresh blood she is bleeding from my heart.

I drive over to Zelda's house, get out of the van carrying the flowers. I knock on the door. It is a warm day and a humid breeze is rattling the cottonwood leaves and the lilac brush that grow in the yard. Zelda lives in the original old log house from way back when, a place tucked together by Resounding Sky, added to over years gone by with layer on layer of Sheetrock and plaster, which is why the walls, so thick, keep in the warmed air in winter, and the cool of night all summer. The wood siding is now painted a bright turquoise, and the inside is very close, different now, partitioned off by Zelda into rooms and hallways, so the place has to me a watery slough feeling even though there is no water near except down the hill. It is dim in the house, underwater pleasant.

Shawnee Ray answers the door. I hold out the flowers, almost brushing them into her face. Her warm eyes light before she remembers to give me a suspicious look.

"What do you want?"

"Just to visit with you for a little while."

I hang my head. She knows me as Lipsha, con and fluke rich man. Maybe, like everybody else, she is waiting to see how I'll blow it, lose my money, ditch her, end up back where I belong. Still, as she stands in the door, I thank her in a humble voice for allowing me to enter. She doesn't say a word, just looks at me like what's-he-trying-to-pull and motions at me to carry my flowers through a little hall down to the back of the house.

In spite of her attitude, peace overcomes me as I stand at the entrance to her room. Hopeful thoughts tear at my heart.

"It is an honor to be here," I tell her.

She raises one eyebrow.

"What do you really want?" she asks.

Silence hangs behind her words, and my true feelings surge up through my hands. Her bedroom is bright. Yellow radiance streams through the window that looks out over a brushy little gully. Her bed is crushed against that wall and surrounded very neatly by calendars, drawings, typed sayings, and rows of dried plants. She has a drum hanging from a strap on the wall next to a leather-wrapped beater, the handle decorated with orange and blue cut-glass beads. Her window is protected with not one but three dream catchers, and I remember her saying that Redford sometimes has nightmares. Right now, he's at church with Zelda, but I imagine him sleeping next to Shawnee, curled tight in a little ball, right under that window on a small cot and mattress. I cannot help but see myself there too, my fingers laced above, protecting them both from spirits as they dream together calm as winter bears.

There are also cardboard boxes in the room, half full of folded clothes and books. The drawers are open, I see now, and there is an air of something started that I've interrupted.

"I can't visit long, I'm packing."

"You're moving out?"

"Maybe. Pretty soon, anyway. Right now, I have to go get Zelda and Redford from the Sisters' and finish this."

She puts some things away and picks up a sewing project, trying not to look at me. There is a full concentration in the set of her back, in the arched-over heel of her neck, in her tumbled hair. Then—this hits me with a hammer—she puts the sweetest pair of eyeglasses onto her face. They are just glass, with no rims, like a grandmother or a nun would wear. I can hardly stand it, I get weakened down my thighs and my arm ticks and trembles holding out the flowers. I want at that moment to take off all of her clothes and make important love to her. No, not all she wears. I would leave on those little spectacles, which I would breathe on and smudge and smear and kiss. She has pins in her mouth, and that gets to me too, I mean the danger. I would take them out of her teeth one by one and stick them into her little heart-shaped pincushion before I put my lips on hers.

But she herself removes the pins carefully. "Just about done," she promises when her mouth is empty. "Would you mind trying this on?"

She holds up a leather vest with fringes, lined with calico and piped with satin ribbon.

"It's cool," I say, almost in reverence, taking it from her hands and shrugging my arms into the armholes, which are cut generous. "It fits good, just like you already knew the size."

"Well, naturally." She eases it off me. "I measured Lyman before I cut it out."

I unflex a small aluminum lawn chair propped against the wall and sit down in it—obviously, it is there for Lyman, too.

Shawnee Ray looks at me, blank and quizzical, then picks up the flowers from my lap and takes the rubber band off and carefully saves it in a drawer. She sticks the stems into a glass of water that she's been drinking from before I came into the room. Then she arranges the stems one by one like a professional. Here's the thing, though. She smiles on them so nice, too nice. In reaction, within my heart, I feel myself rising up with jealousy of those flowers, of how they make her smile but the smile is not for me, of how she gives admiring looks at their beautiful colors.

I put my hand out, between us, and I show her my little

tattooed star. It is sinking fast below my knuckles. Although I feel bashful about this I tell her that I got it put onto my hand just for her. She doesn't seem to understand, and lifts her eyebrows at me, all confused and burdened.

"Don't you like stars?"

"Not really."

"Oh."

"I mean, it's fine if you do," she assures me in a polite way. "Tattoos really turn me off."

I bury my hand in my pocket. "Hey!" I exclaim, trying to divert her attention and make a new subject of conversation that might impress her. "Guess who I talked to? Lyman."

She looks wary, so I try to set her mind at ease.

"He gave me money advice. We're like this now." I set my two fingers hard together and hold them up before her.

She does not respond, so I speak louder. "He wants me to throw in with him on a big investment scheme. A project. We even opened a bank account with both of our names on it."

She shakes her head and puts her hands on her hips.

"Don't you even want to know the idea?"

Her eyes are brilliant beams. Of course she does, so I go right ahead and outline the deal. But as I talk, as I get farther into it, make more and more of the details apparent to her, things I should maybe not even reveal, her expression becomes both interested and troubled.

I stop. "What's wrong? What?"

"Where's this land you're talking about, this big resort area that sits on an undeveloped lake? Where is this place?"

"Just a lake," I tell her. "Left wild. The ownership got so fractionated now that the shore has reverted to tribal ownership status, or will when . . . "

Her face takes on a gathering distance as she picks up on the dot-dot-dots of my reluctance to fill her in completely on the information.

I try to divert the subject. "What about going out with me tomorrow? What about the next day and the next day after that?"

"What do you mean, Lipsha, 'tribal'? Does someone live up there now?"

I can't lie, but I can't answer. I look down at my beautiful new shitkickers, the spangled snakehide boots that bingo money bought me, and I get stubborn seeing this magnificence in which I walk. Why should I answer?

She gets pointed.

"Why won't you tell me? What are you hiding?"

"I don't want to talk about it."

"You brought it up."

"Yeah, so now I'm dropping it. Let's go out. I miss you."

"Quit dodging around. Where's this land for the bingo palace? What lake?"

"Dancing." I insist more forcibly.

"I want a straight answer."

I don't know what possesses me then or makes my tongue fly. I'm hurt, I suppose, though that's not enough of an excuse. I sling my phrase out so hard it sounds angry.

"You know I'm crazy about you."

Shawnee doesn't react, just frowns and puts her hands to each side of her face.

"Stop it," she says.

"No way."

Now it is like the words that filled me for so long spill right over. "If you're moving out of Zelda's, come live with me. Let's start over, start from nowhere, begin where we left off."

I can't calculate anymore. I know I'm sounding strange, but the words wash out of me like stormy waves.

"Where we left off, Shawnee Ray! Me underneath and your hair swinging over me. Don't be afraid. It's just Lipsha, a short visit, a couple flowers, no drugs. It's true." I pause, seeing her surprised face. I amend myself. "Maybe right now, at this moment, I'm acting unusual, but these are unusual times and things are happening throughout the world that none of us expected. Shawnee!"

I stop cold. She is staring at me in a spell of mystification.

"You listen to the news?" I continue. "Foreign crisis, the crash of stocks and rise of the Japanese. You can't fault me for my feelings for you. You can't take your loving off me like it was a blanket. It's part of me now."

I put my hands to my jeans and start unzipping. Her eyes lose that glazed look, sharpen, and grow deep as a snared doe.

"Don't stare that way, don't let me scare you."

She folds her arms and then gives herself a shake, unclenches her hands, and turns to her sewing machine.

"Sure, turn away, don't look. You might see something that you want. I'm in your power. No matter if you like it or not. I'll do anything for you. Just test me. Anything, at any time, at a minute's notice. Or how's this. You don't need to give me any notice. A bottle of orange pop, a cheap motel, and you. That's all I'm asking for my payment. Eternity was in that room. I don't believe in religions. I don't believe in any gods. I just believe . . . "

I fall silent, for my pants slide so loud to the floor they seem to crash, and I am hobbled until I reach down and kick off my boots. She glares at me and color comes over her face. I watch to see the effect of my words, my dropping clothes, hoping she'll burn and collapse in passion and be mine, but she does none of those things. Her cheeks go hot and a shine of tears comes into her eyes but she gathers control, pushes her rich hair back, and keeps looking at me steady and speculating.

"At least you wear socks."

I feel words rising in me, so many I can't keep my mouth shut.

"You know what I believe in?"

I leave that question and stare at Shawnee until that shine

of her emotions returns. I can't help myself. I know I'm making a fool of myself, that this is dangerous, stupid, but I speak softly to her now as I work the tight buttons of my shirt apart one by one.

"Shawnee, I know that you staying with me that night was an impulse move, a great disservice to Zelda, and of course to Lyman. Don't get me wrong. I like Lyman, he's two ways my relative and I understand his feelings for you. You're a perfect accessory to his future. You go with his life, his success, all those ramifications. You'd make a great Senator's wife. Just don't bother doing anything else. Do your duty. Five years time will go by and you'll look at Lyman's face and he'll smile that straight business smile and you'll want my crooked face. He'll say something good, and you'll want me bad. The feel of me will unfreeze in you. Something will grind, come to life, and you'll burn for my eyes looking in your eyes while we—"

She slams her hands down on the table of her sewing machine.

"I'm sorry. I'm going overboard and I know you don't like that kind of talk, but I heard it from you once and you meant it. I know you did. I've made mistakes, and it seems as though nothing's gone right since. But Shawnee, with him, Lyman, sure, he points out your intelligence. But the effect is this: all you do is *about him.* What a good selection *he* made. How interesting *he* was to go back and claim his son, and his son's mother, who luckily turned out smart and beautiful. With me, you'll have to be about yourself. With me, you own who you are. In fact, you'll have to be smarter, stronger, better, 'cause my life ain't gonna shine any light. My deeds won't bounce down on you and give you a halo."

"That's for sure." Shawnee starts the sewing machine up with a foot pedal, feeds a piece of material beneath the needle with a businesslike motion, but her fingers shake.

"Take your foot off that sewing pedal!"

I am losing ground, but I try to contain myself. "You've got to listen to me even though I am making no sense. In fact, because I am making no sense, you should listen harder. We'll get to the truth quicker if we don't worry about logic. You've got feelings for me, hid, and you won't let them out because the world and its big fat woes conquers and prevails on you and you feel you have to serve other people with your life. Your own feelings don't mean shit. You try to road grade and pave them over. Your love for me is just bumps on an icy road. Potholes, honey sweetheart, but they'll bust your suspension. I'll always be there when you think your life is running smooth."

She is shaking with her emotions, and so am I, plus I have no more clothes to shed and I'm feeling foolish. She stands up and throws half a flowered shirt at me.

"You'll do anything for me, anything, you say?"

Her face is wild, her lips stuck in a line.

I nod, blazing my eyes into hers, all want and willingness.

"Put that on," she whispers, intense. "Then get out of here."

I pick up what she's thrown.

"This here is half a shirt," I tell her, just as intense.

"Get out of here!" she shouts.

I don't step back though. The edge is so near. The mournful mirror in that little room beckoned me once to go through, and at this moment I try. I put out my hands, and now the words of grief break from my chest.

"Didn't I give you what you wanted? I gave it to you and I gave it to you like I never did with no one else. Don't you remember how you lay in my arms like a dreamy animal and sighed, and how I made my breath go with yours, perfect in trust, like we were sleeping all winter in a den, you and me? What do you want, what have I done? I was so proud! I got the love medicine!"

Then she speaks, looking at me steady and sad.

"You got the medicine, Lipsha. But you don't got the love."

When she says it, like that, right then, it is as though I am stunned with truth. I can't see for the dazzlement, but I know in one instant that she's right. I stumble backward, but then she sees how I feel and gently takes the shirt from my grip and puts it down on her machine.

"Let me try then," I ask her, in a voice I never heard myself use before. I pry out my words from the heart. "Please, let me have another chance."

So we sink down on the floor, right there in the doorway, and this time it is different than before. You ever seen a couple orange-black butterflies kiss and hover above the ground? This is even more delicate. It is their shadows beneath, that's who the two of us are. Two tender shadows touching in, touching out. Two hungers made out of the dim shade we cast.

But if it was only our shadows moving, loving in that room, what of the other, the heavier and solid-footed selves who stood apart passing judgment, what of us?

CHAPTER TEN

SHAWNEE'S LUCK

AFTER SHE SHUT THE DOOR BEHIND LIPSHA MORRISSEY, AFTER she heard him drive out of the yard, Shawnee whirled from the door and walked straight back into her room. She ripped off her shirt, popping a button, chose a different one, her arms jerking the material. She swore impatiently, monotonously, in surprise at herself. She pulled on a clean pair of jeans, then kicked them into a corner. She yanked a purple dress off a hook, then sat on the edge of her bed and crumpled the skirt against her stomach. Her face twisted and she unfolded her hands between her knees, drew her palms up the insides of her thighs. Breathing heavily, she rested her hands at her center, pressing herself back together. She put her arms out suddenly, pounded on the mattress, opened and closed her fists in front of her eyes, and then slapped herself so hard on the cheeks it made her laugh.

She threw herself deliberately, eagerly, down on the floor and started doing push-ups, then she rolled over, hooked her feet underneath the bed frame. Glaring, eyes fixed upon the stitching of her blue cotton star quilt, she continued with sit-ups. She did a hundred, hands across her breasts, and then she lowered herself back into the little oval rag rug and slammed her palms down over her face.

She supposed it was just pure good fortune that you ever

loved the person who was right for you. Or who loved you in the way that was most likely to bring happiness, the way that fit the world. Where was that Mister Right all of the magazines talked about? She always saw him as an illustrated profile in her high school history book, or a chapter-end picture and short biography in her English text. Backlighted, smiling, every hair in its place, date and place of birth typed in carefully underneath his studio portrait, that was her picture of the man she would marry.

Lyman fit that studied blank as if the negative had been developed. Lyman Lamartine, Bingo Chief, the subtitle read. In strict opposition to the glossy smile, however, a photograph referring to Mister Wrong now obsessed her. Visiting Marie Kashpaw at Lulu Lamartine's apartment, Shawnee had been unable to turn from the smeared, inky, unshadowed frankness of the framed wanted poster of the father of Lipsha Morrissey. Her gaze was drawn to the shelf, her mind kept scratching for resemblances.

She could see Lipsha whenever she shut her eyes. He was a mess, his shirttails out, hair flapping, mouth sweet in a grin that would change unexpectedly and for reasons that she found interesting. She never knew what he would say. There was a mystery to him, an ease, a calm way that he had with his hands and lips. Now, thinking about how they had just made love, she shivered and in her head a cicada buzz of panic whined. It was unbearable, it made her furious, all her plans were out of whack and useless. She loved him.

Shawnee stood up, went to the table, sat down. She smoothed flat the soft piece of deerskin that her uncle Xavier had given her and cut out a pair of small moccasin soles. The way her uncle would, the Chippewa way instead of the Sioux, she put the tiny gathers in the top, sewed bits of an old flannel blanket inside. Tonight, she decided, she would stitch a tiny bluebird on each toe in order to remember the ones she'd seen, so fierce around their fence-post nests.

As she sewed together two crescents of muskrat fur for each ankle, she grew more calm, but she still wished that she could swear off men altogether. Except for Redford, they were too much trouble. Who would not prefer, after all, to live in a world of women? To need men, to love men, was a great nuisance and a misery. To sit and sew with her sisters in a room was like entering a country where she had always belonged. Shawnee missed Tammy and Mary Fred and her mother so fiercely that she winced at the stab of her longing. Her breathing deepened, she put her work down and restlessly took up the beading needle.

Women made more sense, had their priorities in place, seemed to know just who they were and where they came from, unless they got mixed up with men. Most women, that is, but not Zelda Kashpaw, whose fierce grip made everyone she loved uneasy. Ever since Zelda had insisted on keeping Redford, full-time, if Shawnee Ray decided to dance at the big-money powwows, ever since Zelda had started holding on too tightly, Shawnee Ray had been slowly packing up to move, but she had to be secretive about it and not raise Zelda's suspicions or hurt her feelings. And she couldn't rely on her own mother—here was the fact that proved her point—because her new stepfather's needs and attitudes and opinions came first. Shawnee had only herself to depend on. For the past week, she had been checking on a special she had heard about, a memorial dance at a big Montana powwow. Three thousand dollars, winner take all, for women's all-around—traditional, shawl dance, and jingle dress.

Shawnee knew that she could win that prize.

Zelda was a man-woman, Shawnee had decided. Aligned with Lyman Lamartine, the two kept her soldered in their own hopes. Her sisters had no hopes, no reason to manipulate her. The trouble was, every time she made up her mind to go and stay with Tammy and Mary Fred, she would hear that one of them was deep in a binge, or arrested, or maybe worse, converted and spouting Bible verse. She would go to them anyway, she decided now, and stay back in the bush for a while, where she didn't have to worry about pleasing so many people. Where Lyman wouldn't visit her. Where Lipsha might. Where she could sort out her life and make her plans.

Shawnee put down her needle and the butterfly that she was beading onto a clip that would match the pattern on her shawl. Into her hand, she took the little moccasins and cradled her head in her folded arms, in the smoky tanned scent of home-cured hides. Tears dropped onto the edge of her sewing table fast as hard rain, but she soon stopped them, pushing her hands hard across her face.

Zelda's eyes were bright as pointed stars. She was standing in the same doorway where Lipsha Morrissey had argued, begged, pleaded, and thrown off his clothes. Stepping into Shawnee's room, Zelda walked across the rag-braided rug. Shawnee lowered her gaze and looked away as the older woman pivoted with hard assurance. Hands firm on her hips, Zelda was solid as a truck. She absolutely opposed Shawnee Ray's return to Tammy and Mary Fred.

"Who took care of you when you needed it? Who does Redford call his grandma even now?"

"You," said Shawnee.

"It's for your own good," said Zelda, softening. "I just want to stop your wild-goose chasing. That contest—I know the woman . . . she'll never come up with the money. "

"She lost her daughter."

"Because she left, went to the Cities, never really came home. Just like some."

"You're scared I'll be like Albertine?" Shawnee looked steadily at the older woman, and then spoke coaxingly. "She comes home, she's going to be a doctor. You're lucky with her, you know that."

"I don't call it coming home," said Zelda. "She never stays!"

"Why should she?" Shawnee lost patience. "You drive everyone around you crazy!"

"Oh, I do? I do?" Zelda's voice grew strange, exultant. "Do I drive them so crazy when I take them in, pay their bills, feed them, help them raise their little boys?"

Shawnee turned away, face smarting, confused with guilt.

"No." Her voice small, but then her tone strengthened. "You can't get Albertine back by holding on to me. I'm going to stay with my sisters, just for a little while."

Zelda's features hardened, she firmed her shoulders, settled her hands carefully together to disguise her anxious fears. She reminded Shawnee Ray that people would think that Zelda threw her out, that Lyman would object, that she had no way of raising money for a bus ticket to that Montana powwow, that she owed Zelda her affection, and that, although her sisters had been observed at the end of the previous summer, kneeling on the beaten grass beneath a tent awning and receiving Jesus, they had not attended a single AA or Assembly of God meeting since, and people said that they had backslid powerfully, lost their low-pay jobs.

"You can't go there," reported Zelda once again. Her hair was caught up in a beaded shield, pinned there with a sharp wooden stick; her cheekbones were dusted with magenta blush and her mouth was set firmly into a line of opposition. She stared down at Shawnee Ray, who had never given her a moment's trouble up until this conversation. Zelda expected that the young woman would shrug, gently take out her books, and after the thoughtful lecture, forget the whole idea. Instead, Shawnee met Zelda's eyes with an expression of stubbornness and puzzled fear, and for a long time, neither one of them would look away. Finally, Zelda took a breath, shrugged lightly, and walked out the door.

Shawnee heard Zelda in the kitchen soothing Redford and sifting cereal into a bowl. She heard the rubber seal of the refrigerator unsticking, the coffee sighing through the little white plastic machine on her counter. Hands calm on her knees, Shawnee considered what she would do next. She stared at the little night table, behind which she kept the envelope of money from Lipsha Morrissey. It was her freedom, her train ticket, her camping money, and Zelda didn't know she had it. Shawnee walked to her closet and carefully removed the dress she had been working on late at night. It was velvet, beaded in the old style with fiercely twisting roses and flowers, with thorns and striped leaves. That was one outfit, and she'd almost finished with the dress she was trimming and hemming to match her butterfly shawl. That was two. And three, her jingle dress, hot red, cast light in a corner. Shawnee Ray pushed herself out of her chair and walked into the kitchen.

Redford flung open his arms at the sight of his mother. She cupped his face in her hands and kissed him twice, and when he turned back to his food, she addressed Zelda.

"I'm taking Redford."

"Shawnee Ray!" Zelda spoke loudly, fearfully, too quickly. "I don't want you to go for your own good. They're a bad influence on you."

"I'll come back if things get out of hand," Shawnee said in her most adult, reassuring voice. "I'm just going to visit, and besides, they've been sober for over a year now."

"That's not true!"

"Just because you don't see them much in town these days doesn't mean they're drinking. Mary Fred started going to sweat lodge with Uncle Xavier. He's been studying with an old man up north. He knows a lot about old-time medicine, and he's helping them out, maybe curing them."

"There's no cure for what they've got," said Zelda.

Shawnee's face shaded with an increase of determination. She scooped Redford from his seat at the table and tramped quickly back into her room. He wailed in surprise and then, pleased to be alone with his mother, began to laugh and talk in small and broken words.

Zelda folded her arms across her chest and stood underneath the burning overhead light fixture, staring at the closed back of the door. As she poised that way, unmoving, her expression took on gravity and thought became solid intention. Her face was fixed in lines, rapt and determined, all goodness, from which there was no escape.

MINDEMOYA

I WALK OUT OF SHAWNEE RAY'S ROOM, AND AS I GO THROUGH the dimness of that hibernation household, as I find my way back out into the friendly fixed interior of my bingo van, her love medicine words stick with me. I know I'll never get rid of them, the shock and strangeness of their meaning. I start the van, press down the gas, slowly pull out of the driveway, and I realize I'm different now, changed. Our sex on the floor was not the medicine, not this time, but love. True love. She can't deny it, and I won't let her confuse me with the love ways of Lyman Lamartine.

It's true, I got the medicine, but not the way she thinks. I never made love so you would notice it with anyone but her. I know to touch away hurt, but not touch on pleasure. It's Lyman who learned that skill, I know for a fact from his younger days that he made it happen for women and for girls since the year he was fourteen years old. He always loved girls so he and his brother Henry wanted to be with them all the time, make them go completely open in their arms, drive them wild as dogs to bite their ankles, make their hands into combs, claws, feather mittens. Whatever. I admit I have a medicine that was given to me in my hands, but the fact is until Shawnee Ray I never really used it for sex, never fell in love. I always said I wanted staying power, like my Grandma

Kashpaw showed me she possessed. I always bragged that I wished to find the woman who would love me until one of us died or went crazy. The truth is, I've been looking.

Now I fear I have also lost my direction, got so far off the road that, at this moment when I know I have met the one, Shawnee Ray, she does not believe me.

"You really fucked this up," I say to myself. "Lipsha, you got so slick with your hands that you polished off all the rough edges. You ain't believable! And as for Lyman, he has roughed up his style just enough so it looks innocent!"

Even that does not seem right, or enough, and it bothers me that my understanding is so frail. A little portion of sweet heaven is allotted to each of us by our fate.

That was mine, I think as I bounce the gravel road. Sure as hell she'll forget me once Lyman snows her with his brilliant words.

I go back to the bar and sit down to try and get prepared for the experience of losing her even after this last occurrence. I can't. I put on spongy shoes and decide to do something unlike myself, to go out running on the new clay high school track. So I drive over there. I get out of my van in the afternoon wind, so high and brilliant, and I start to move my legs. My jeans are too tight, but I keep going anyway, thinking that the red marks they leave on my skin will remind me of the advice from myself that I hope I'll take. Around the red road I travel, first desperate and stiff jointed, then freer, looser, more myself as I sweat and burn off my anxious hope into beat exhaustion. My chest feels wracked, and very soon I slow to a slog and then walk. I remember back to the days when I tried to doctor my own grandpa with the store-bought love medicine that ended up so tragic and confused. I remember back to my original wish to visit up at the Pillager woman's place, and how my heart quailed and I was too much of a Morrissey coward to do the thing. Maybe all my love medicine was store-bought after all, maybe it was fake, maybe I relied too heavily on the commercial stuff and am only now understanding what it takes to get the real.

"Crazy courage," I shout to the empty bleachers. "Just watch!"

I tip up on my toes and heft my knees and then I take off fast as that shooting star—but about fifty yards along the track I have to throw myself down to earth. I'm half dead, my breath a seared feather in my chest, my weak and half-broke heart thumping. I smell the chemical-sprayed grass, the fertilized dirt underneath. To put my face in the dirt makes me think of lying underneath it. I don't want to die without Shawnee Ray's love, and to get it I'll have to acquire a love medicine that's better than Lyman Lamartine's.

I make my way back to my van through the bleachers. The fact is, I can't afford my own fears anymore. The sky stretches bare and wide, building clouds in the east above me, banks of sleet or rain. I will not let up in my intentions. During the first dry-off of the season, the Old Lady Pillager is always known to come to town. She is by rights my great grandmother, the one who started it all in motion. I will find her, I will follow her, I will make my love request. And I will hope not to die of her darker medicines as a result.

When I finally glimpse the old lady people fear, she is walking down the broad dirt road that leads from deep bush into town. It is a weekday spring morning. The new heat is surprising, and people are taking long and social routes to work—that is, until they see her. As the Pillager passes by, men and women rush indoors to punch their time cards, swing their cars toward parking lots. Some fade back into the bars and shadows of the post office, those who can't cross their breasts or touch the holy medal of a saint. I do none of these things. I am unnoticeable. For in waiting for the Pillager I have become a kind of a fixture, a railing, a piece of carved cement on the Agency steps. Anyway, I happen to glance up from filling out my papers and there she is.

Fleur.

They say that strange things happen when the old lady is around. A dog falls over dead and all of its hair drops out. Gossiping mouths twist to one side and stick that way. Cold winds blow out of nowhere, in places there isn't even a fan system. Yellow jackets build a nest in a loaf of baking bread. And then those drownings: three times she was cast in the lake, and men were taken by the spirits each instance when she came to life, as if she put their name on the list to the death road, replacing hers. These things happened, frightful incidents, but also there is good.

People forget the good, because the bad has more punch. The old lady cures fevers, splints bones, has brought half the old-timers in the Senior's Lounge into this world. That's right. She's older than any of them, so old no one remembers how old. She's a Pillager, the adopted daughter of Old Man Nanapush, this healing doctor witch. She must be a hundred. She's so old that people don't use her name anymore. She's just the Old Lady, Mindemoya. As far as I know, she's just got one surviving child in town, my grandma Lulu, and I watch now to see if she is going to visit the apartment.

Of course, since she walks right by and never notices Lipsha Morrissey, who never amounted to a sack of nothing until the bingo, I am able to get a close look at her. Fleur comes nowhere near the government buildings, she does not let her gaze stray to either side or notice how her path has emptied out. She is a tall woman with a hunch to her shoulders and a face honed and heavy as a sharpened tool. She taps the dust before each step with a stick that looks burnt, made out of twisted diamond willow, a type of slough tree stronger than rebar steel. Her head is knotted in a white scarf and earrings flash, two small green fires at her jawbone. Her feet are

big in a pair of old-fashioned men's-type boots. She wears a
long dress, an odd style considering her frightful reputation,
for it is a girl's dress, flounced, covered with rosy flowers, sagging in the front with ruffles. She walks quickly, covers ground
so fast that before I think to stand up and maybe talk to her,
she is halfway up the hill. In a few minutes she is just an inno-
cent-looking speck of pink and white moving farther on, and
then she vanishes between the fat green shrubs and brush
around the entrance to the church.

A cousin of mine, a Morrissey girl named Layla, who works
in the offices, comes outside and leans against the steel banisters.

"They said Mindemoya was out here."

"Where?" I ask.

I don't know why, but in that moment something closes in
me as if to protect the old lady, though she hardly needs me,
and though I like this cousin Layla all right and she doesn't
mean any harm but is only curious.

"I never saw her," I say. "And I was sitting right here."

Layla stares all around us—at the wide cottonwoods that
lean over the clinic, at the school buses pulled up in the big
yard across the hill, at the mottled brown brick and thick gray
windows of the Senior Citizens apartments, at the road where
Fleur has passed. Things look normal. Cars rush or calmly
putter back and forth.

"They say she heads there on her feast day," Layla whispers.
"Every year."

"I wouldn't know."

Layla frowns toward the hill.

"How come you don't just go and see if she's there?" I ask.

But Layla only scuffs her foot a little, disappointed, and
then walks back into the offices where she keeps the records of
each tribal member filed for her boss—that is, Zelda, who has
the record and whereabouts of everyone's ancestors and secret
relatives handy to herself. I sit down again. I am waiting for
proof-positive self-identification, a complicated thing in Indian

Country. I am waiting for a band card, trying out of boredom to prove who I am—the useless son of a criminal father and a mother who died with her hands full of snow—but in trying to prove myself to the authorities, I am having no luck, for Zelda is a solid force to reckon with. I don't have my enrollment and entitlements stabilized, not yet, nor do I have my future figured exactly out. Still, the reason I have been hanging out has just walked down the road.

I stand there on the steps. Duplicates of applications and identification papers weigh down my hands.

"Here." I shove them at Layla. She takes them.

"File it under 'L' for Love Child," I say, walking off.

The way things occur and come together is strange as music. Like I said, the old lady is actually my great grandma, though I never even spoke to her face-to-face before that time. I decide that I will follow her into the church and as I enter I will cross myself with holy water. Then I might be safe enough to go up to her and introduce myself as her descendant, Lipsha, and tell her what I need her to do for me. Of course, the blessed water might not work. She might have medicine to counteract it, she might say something like she said to Flying Nice and I will have to take her place on death's road the next time she is summoned to go. People say that's how she got to live this long. Rumor is, there's no limit to her life. She takes the future of others and makes it her own, sucks it in through a hollow reed, through a straw, a bone.

I get nervous, so instead of tagging the old lady directly into church, I go over to the Senior Citizens, where both of my grandmas keep themselves. Grandma Kashpaw is orderly and always in charge, set up in an apartment decorated with souvenir plates from far-off grandchildren, the walls lined with closets of carefully saved paper sacks and used clothes and brand-new thermal blankets. Grandma Lulu isn't neat like her, and at her place everything is strewn out: papers and Congressional records and magazines. The two live around the corner from one another, down the hall, but I stop first to see my grandma Lulu, on the Pillager side. The old lady is her mother, after all.

"Mindemoya's in town," I inform her without a preview.

Lulu rises from her chair, dusts off her hips, and walks into her kitchen nook to move around some pots and pans on the stove. The smell of browning potatoes and seared meat and onions spreads from that alcove when she lifts a cover. Lulu was once flowery and soft, smelling of perfume, but in her old age she's gotten compact and tensed down. Her arms are hard and brown, as if she does push-ups, and her smell is sharper now—of ink, office products, white erasing fluids. Except for the time she spends at the bingo palace, her pleasure time, she is full speed into politics and each of the spray perfume bottles on her dresser wears a ring of dried unused sweetness. She is out to reclaim the original reservation, no less. It was once six times bigger.

"She comes in on her feast day, gets supplies," I state, when Lulu doesn't answer.

"Not her feast day. My dad's." She speaks briefly and flips the meat, keeps on stirring something with a metal spoon. A purple smell rushes at me. She is cooking a pot of chokecherry jelly.

"Who was he?"

She turns, arches her thin black eyebrows, and gives the pan a sudden, annoyed shake.

That is my cue to quit, I know it, but this time I want more. My father's eyes, shrouded and full of Nanapush light, watch me from my grandma's knickknack shelf. My family people are full of secrets, things they hide from each other and from themselves. Beginnings are lost in time and the ends of things are unpronounceable. I was one of those dark secrets too, according to Zelda, a boy whose mother tried to drown him in a slough but who survived, and whose convict-hero father was silenced by the higher authorities of this country.

Grandma Kashpaw raised me, and Grandma Lulu started the ball rolling toward explaining it all. So I count on Lulu, now, to tell me more.

"You don't like to talk about the old lady," I say. "But she's your mother."

"You have an itchy mind." Lulu sets down before me a plate holding venison, limp brown rings of onions, potatoes mashed with a fork, buttered and peppered. She settles herself into a chair across from me. On her plate there is a slice of soft white bread glazed with cooling jelly. Her eyes shoot out tiny points of black light. She is watchful. The fashion-plate wig she wears today is teased in soft spiked waves like beaten egg whites. I pick up the knife and fork and start cutting the meat, eat it, try to think of another approach, the way a wrestler might circle, arms out to grapple. But I miss my opening. She dives in first and takes me down.

"Even if I told you what you want to know, it wouldn't do you any good."

"Why not?"

"You're too simple. You think you got things figured out. But you young Indians today are living on a different planet."

"Maybe I'm ignorant," I say, putting down my fork, both mad and reasonable. "But if I had a mother here alive, at least I wouldn't hate her."

"I don't hate the old lady," Lulu says, pausing for a moment, evening her voice. "I understand her."

Which leaves me something to think over.

Outside the Senior Citizens, the air is dry and still unnaturally hot for spring. Wheels of fine gray dirt hang lazy over the road. The new leaf buds click and the church seems to yawn before me, a big, empty, white, board building with long colored windows and a square steeple topped by a little painted roof of dark green shingles. The reservation spreads downhill, and I have a good view of the town, its gas station, its tree-shaded bar, and the small box houses built by government administration. Some sag, gray and unpainted, and others seem alert, bright pink, lime, blue, bristling with stovepipes, antennas, little windmills, for it is popular these days to make lawn ornaments out of long poles and twirling plastic milk jugs cut in various surprising shapes. Screen doors snap. Children swirl their tin trucks in the dirt. Women lean down the steps to frown at their dead plots of grass. The houses are all built helter-skelter, streets put in later. They dribble away onto flat prairie to the south and trees take them over to the north and begin to enfold them in quick-growing bush.

To that side, out of the leathery green trees, a road of coarse tan gravel floats in the morning heat. I follow it to the first of the church steps. At the top, I reach forward and open the heavy brown door, then I step inside. The air is dark and heavy with the scent of spent incense. The pews are dim furrows of empty quiet. As I enter, I can hear the wind rush up suddenly outside, in the trees, and my heart taps quickly. In the center of the church, Fleur Pillager sits straight, suspended. I kneel down beside her. She ignores me. I cough.

"*Booshoo.*" I offer a hello.

"What do you want?"

She booms this out, echoing, using the old Chippewa language that I can barely understand or much less answer. I hardly even know the French mix and so I speak English and say that I am her great grandson, right out, just like that. She only nods as an answer so that I wonder if she places me. After a while she says, "*Geget na?*", "Is that right?", like a question, pulling down her mouth. I don't know where to go from there, so we just sit side by side.

She doesn't do anything that I can see from the corner of my eye. Her hand doesn't move to toss a pinch of powder or make some sign that will hang over me. She carries no purse where she could keep, say, her medicine charm, a child's finger wrapped in a strip of doehide like people say. I already looked at the dirt to make sure she left the footprints of the big men's boots, not tracks of the bear. Just thinking about those objects freezes my voice box, and I can't answer when she finally does.

"I've got to go to the store."

She clips her words off in English perfect as a nun. We stand. She is not the type to genuflect before the altar, she just turns heel and walks toward the door. I open it and step out. She has leaned her stick against the building and I hand it back.

"Could I carry your groceries home for you?" I ask.

When she smiles at me, unblinking, showing her sharp old teeth, I gulp air, feel a flutter of black wings in my heart. It is her grin that can kill, I've heard, the slow spread of fierce pleasure on her face. But nothing happens to me.

"It's a long walk, grandson," is all that she says, and she is right.

Maybe I have smoked too much into my lungs so far in life, or maybe I have weakened myself with sugar, I don't know, except I can't keep up with her. She can't be a hundred, more like ninety years at most, she moves along so fast. I carry the bag, just a few things—flour, oatmeal, a number ten can of coffee, and some potatoes. I am glad I wore my running shoes in which I gathered strength, yet she is shaming me, this old-time, maybe *djessikid* woman.

I do tell her my name halfway there, not that she asks for it. She frowns at the Morrissey part and says that she doesn't agree that she is related to any of that clan. I hesitate to remind her that my grandmother is her daughter, Lulu, but I do sense Fleur Pillager is being polite, not saying to me that the Morrisseys are no-goods, a family that for bad give the Lazarres a run.

"I'm not a Morrissey by blood though," I say, "or not hardly." I explain how my mother left me off with Grandma Kashpaw because I was the son of a Nanapush man related through the Pillagers. It is then that she nods her head, in time to her walking. The name Kashpaw means something to her.

"If you're a Pillager then claim so. Don't say Morrissey."

"Would the Pillagers claim me back?"

She looks over at me, turns her mouth down. "Why not? There's none of us left."

We walk on in quiet, the sun traveling down lower and lower into the windless trees. I have had my imagination turned on full volume at the time, but I do think that the woods go all silent as she passes, the birds choke on their own songs, the rabbits stop skipping, trees go stiff, deer freeze in their huddled bush. Cars pass at first—none stopping to offer us a ride—then fewer, and even fewer as we go down roads and gravel turnoffs that get us closer to earth, narrow, sift to dirt, then peter out in unused and nearly grown-over ruts and go on, still after that, in trackless scrub and finally stop in sheer grass and sage surrounded by bush. She must have got up in the middle of the night to walk into town from all of this distance. I knew the reservation inside out, I thought, but it turns out I knew it by car, not foot. Now it feels like we're lost, off the radar, and at this a weakness grips my legs.

We have come around to the far end of Matchimanito Lake, which is right where Lyman Lamartine intends to erect his gambler's paradise.

I am not now, and nor have I ever been, interested in visiting here. It is a spirit place, good if you are good and bad if you have done bad things, like me. I am relieved that there is no sign of the water itself yet, no opening through the brush, no gleam of dark waves catching the sky. There is also no way further into the bush that I can see, no path, and yet the old lady points forward with her black stick and before I know it she walks straight into a clump of sumac. Vanishes.

I follow as best I can. The trunks are dense, twisting against me, and the leaves seem to wrap around me so I can't keep the springtime flash of her dress in my line of vision. I keep edging forward, easing under dead falls and squeezing through crossed tangles. The air grows dense, buzzing, and smells of ripped green wood and heavy sunlight. I try backing up once but the twigs and leaves have closed behind me in sharp knots. This is a one-way woods. She has me. She is drawing me forward on a magic string coughed up from her insides. She is an owl waiting on the other end with her claws out, with her tongue like a meat fork. I crouch down, shaking, and try to get my bearings, but then I think I feel the wood ticks crawling eagerly into my socks and I jump, lunging, and run straight through a singed burn-out filled with raspberry brush, out into a small grassy rise. Her house sits on top, bleak but normal, in the shadows of a denser olden growth beyond which the lake winks, fine and blue surfaced, all postcard perfect and false. She is there, too, bent over, her elbow sawing up and down, working the curved iron handle of a pump.

"You made it," she says without turning. She picks the bucket up and walks into her house. It is an old-time place, a low, long house of sawed beams tamped smoothly between with yellow gumbo clay, dug up from underneath the top soil. The roof has a little tin chimney and I stand there long enough to see it puff smoke. Her windows are small, polished clean, empty, not hung at the sides with curtains. I gulp down my fear to remember that Fleur Pillager has cured diseases, brought children into the world. I am her own blood. But I still wish I had some medicine to protect me.

"You're thirsty," she says when I finally step through the door.

Her house reminds me of Lulu's apartment, for it is stacked to the low ceiling with papers, with folders, with bundled envelopes and boxes of rippled cardboard that seem to hold still more files and newspapers and clippings. The place smells of paper, mildewed, dried, leaked on, but carefully saved. For there is care in the arrangement of these stacks against the old, whitewashed inside walls that are covered everywhere with hairline cracks and patterns of tangled thready lines.

"I'm making tea."

I sit, and my gaze naturally drops down on the rubbed and faded pattern of her oilcloth on the table. It is covered with pen lines, rushing on straight, sloping, doubling back.

"Somebody wrote on your tablecloth," I say, and then I shut my mouth, for it isn't probably a good idea to be so observant. But she doesn't mind.

"You're thirsty," she repeats.

"No, I'm not," I say, weakening and dizzy. "Maybe a little."

She gets up, hands me a dipper of water from her metal pail, then takes the kettle off her stove and throws a handful of dried, crushed leaves into a stew pot with the hot water. After a moment, she pours two cups and puts one in front of me. She spoons out a blob of honey that looks like it was raked from a tree. Her hand is brown and bony, long fingered and dry like it has been baked in the sun. I take a hot, sweet, fragrant gulp, and my vision clears, yet all the rest of me is fuzzy, dense, too heavy to move. I look at the strange lines on her walls, between the neat stacks of letters, and pick out familiar patterns.

"Someone wrote there, too," I point out stupidly, leaning forward and instantly realizing that I am reading a set of words, a sentence, something that loops toward the window, which makes no sense to me and which I can't understand. I open my mouth, but can't think of anything to add, so shut it and examine my folded hands while Fleur gets up again and begins to stir something in a black iron pot. She has an old woodstove maybe from the thirties, a big thing with winged nickel handles on the doors. Her bed sags beneath a bearskin that doesn't look dead but shines like live fur. A red trader's blanket is folded at the foot. The bed is held up not by legs but by more files and books. Above it there is a shelf, and on that, a shallow round drum. Beaver and ermine and otter skins hang there, a bandolier-type tobacco bag, beaded all over, braids of sweet grass, sage bundles, and other things, too, in pouches, things that I try very hard not to look at too close. There is a bowl on the floor that holds stones, completely round stones that the water from the lake has washed smooth. The sight of them makes my mouth go dry again, for I know that they are not just rocks but spirit rocks, full of existence, and that she probably talks to them at night and tells them what to do for her, who to visit, who to bother.

It's getting dark now, and before me she sets a plate of bean soup which I dig into so as not to offend her, though as I eat, the taste of smoke and grease and heavy comfort soothes me into an almost ordinary mind frame. One plate, another, and now my tongue feels thick and swollen. I drink more water from the dipper. The air is dark and full. The old lady lights a glass kerosene lamp and goes outside. I stand up, splash my face from the basin of water she's left, afraid that I have fallen under some sort of spell, drunk a sleeping powder in the hot tea, eaten herbs disguised by salt in the bean soup. But as soon as the water touches my face I feel all right. I wash myself a little better with a slab of harsh yellow lye soap, the kind I remember from my first years of life. No pink Camay here like at Lulu's, no towels either. I dry my hands and face on my shirt and then stand at the door to be ready when she comes back.

It is cool out, now, and she wears a long green sagging sweater. She eases past me and pours hot water from her kettle into a basin, starts washing the bowls and spoon. Her back is turned. Her elbows move rhythmically, her hands scour, the lamp flares golden, and I calm myself, knowing this is my chance.

"I need a love medicine."

My words drop in a well. She does not answer, but continues at her task, and then, unexpectedly, too quickly for an old lady, she whirls around and catches me in the dim light, looks steadily into my eyes until I blink, once, twice. When I open my eyes again, she broadens, blurs beyond my reach, beyond belief. Her face spreads out on the bones and goes on darkening and darkening. Her nose tilts up into a black snout and her eyes sink. I struggle to move from my place, but my legs are numb, my arms, my face, and then the lamp goes out. Blackness. I sit there motionless and my head fills with the hot rasp of her voice.

CHAPTER TWELVE

FLEUR'S LUCK

THE FOURTH AND LAST TIME SHE CAME BACK TO THE RESERVATION, Fleur Pillager was dressed in stark white. Her padded-shoulder suit, pinched at the waist, caught the spring sun. She moved in a glare, a shield of new light. She carried gloves, wore gleaming high heels. A short-brimmed hat tipped a spotted veil across her face. Those of us who dared to notice saw that her braids had grown thick as tails and hung long down her back, bound together with a red strip of cloth. The oldest people frowned when they heard that detail, remembering how in the old days the warriors arranged their hair, tied back when they prepared to meet an enemy.

Fleur's car was also white and it was large, a Pierce-Arrow with a Minnesota license plate. Inside, sulking in the passenger's seat, a boy raised and lowered hand to chewing mouth, methodically drawing one licorice whip after another from a crisp red-and-white-striped bag of candy he had insisted on buying at the trader's store.

Everyone knew and did not know her. There were no cries of greeting, no hands held admiringly to the face and smiles. No one smoothed Fleur's hair down on each side of her forehead and said *Daughter, daughter, we've missed you. Peendigaen. Sit and eat some of this good soup.* No one offered her bread and tea. Only sharp-eyed gossipers already hurried to build story

139

onto story, jumped to wonder at the white suit of foreign cut, the luxury car, the boy.

It was reported that he held his candy in his fist at the trader's store, and ate it looking straight into the faces of the Migwans girls, who watched each dark twist as it passed before them. Sugar-hypnotized, mouths watering, they swallowed and looked down as he continued to chew, staring at them with no curiosity.

Like her clothes, her hat, her purse and car, the boy, too, was white. No trace, the old ladies bent close to the problem agreed, no trace, no sign of Fleur Pillager in him. Perhaps she was just caring for the boy, son of a rich *mookamon*, perhaps she was—and there was no word to use as description but one was quickly invented—hired milk.

And yet the car and clothes were troubling. Stolen perhaps, though the Pillager acted as though she owned them. But then, she'd always acted as though she owned everything and nothing: sky, earth, those who crossed her path, road, and Pillager land. It was because she owned herself, they said, because she was a four-souled woman. Like her grandmother, Fleur Pillager possessed more souls than she had a right to. It was not proper. Even now, who knew how many she had left to use? She could not be killed, that fact was now proved once more. For here she was again, a presence that did not stand to reason. She should have been dead, but perhaps, knowing death was near, she had thrown a soul out into the world, a decoy, and lived on without harm.

And here, too, was another worrisome detail, a source of argument, for where did they go, those souls? Whom did they inhabit, haunt? Why, after she survived the sickness, did the fox bark under Two Hat's window and why, after she did not drown yet again, did that owl sit at the entrance to the church, just over the doorway on the pine branch, blinking with pale eyes at the Sunday worshipers, of whom only Josette Bizhieu

was brave enough to offer tobacco and speak these words—
"Grandfather, I see that you are watching us, but go. Do not
bother us. We were good to you. Do not be lonely for us where
you are."

And after that, why did it happen that although Josette
Bizhieu had been polite and the grandfather lifted soundlessly
into the air, it did no good. Josette's mother and her sister's
small daughter died together, same day, same hour. Sometime
later, in the road, the black dog stood guarding air. Why did
these things happen when Fleur Pillager was around? Or did
they happen all of the time, perhaps, and was her presence a
way of putting order to the random way death struck?

Whatever it was, soon darker rumors were afloat.

The boy and Fleur went to the house of Nanapush. The car
sat nightlong in the yard and all the next day and the next day
no one drove it, a nuisance, for it meant all those interested
had to find an excuse to pass by the old man's place if they
wanted to see for themselves the thing Fleur drove, or catch a
glimpse of her young boy.

He had a blue rubber ball, which he threw in the yard but
never very high, and caught in his hands. He had an orange,
which he peeled, tossing down the brilliant skin. He had a
black umbrella, which he raised and stood beneath when the
sky opened and it rained. It was a small umbrella, just right for
a child. This caused great interest. Even more than the car, it
struck the envious full on. Since when did children carry
umbrellas? And was this a fact now to be expected, that children would not get wet from rain, and if so, how were they to
become vulnerable to knowledge? For it was well known that
the rain must fall occasionally upon that soft place on the skull
of a child in order for that child to understand the language of
adults. From that source, they then learned both the ways of
animals and, these days, to please teachers in the schools of the
nuns and United States government.

If children were to stand beneath umbrellas, what next? And anyway, what child besides this white boy of Fleur's ever would consent to remain so motionless?

For he hardly moved at all, it was true. He stood in the yard as rain drove down, returning stare for glance, watching all who dared approach until they grew uneasy, lost their curiosity. Those light eyes! That pale hair! Then the sun came out, and someone noticed, as well, that he did not cast a shadow. This, at last, answered many questions.

He must be a soul Fleur had tossed out in the face of death. An argument. Bait. He was a piece of her own fate used to divert attention from her real business, which was something now thrown open for speculation.

Since old Nanapush had saved her from death, since he was her only friend on the reservation, her visiting the man stood to reason. Yet, to stay so long indoors? To talk endlessly together in the yard? To allow the mud of spring to come over their feet and ruin that white suit as, together, they went out every day to check his traplines in the woods? Or were they up to something else? Marking out certain boundaries? Old lines, old places, old grounds of the long dead Pillagers?

And still, that white car. And still, that pale boy in the yard. And soon, very soon, eventually and as expected, the Agent.

After the Pillager land around the lake was stripped bare by the lumber company and of no more use, as the logging companies moved on west, it was put up for sale and bought by the former Indian Agent, Jewett Parker Tatro, a man now wealthy in land but in little else. He still lived in government housing, clung to a place just at the edge of town. He longed for the great yellow barns and brick house of his New England childhood, a dairy farm broken up among his brothers, sold piece by piece from under them, and he wanted to return. But no one was interested in purchasing the land for which he had cheated so carefully and persistently. And he was restless. Since his retirement, he showed up anywhere two people gathered.

Now he stood carefully aside, gaunt and lean, his beard a tough gray horn jutting off his chin, his eyes as black as any full-blood's, watching.

The white Pierce-Arrow. His look glittered and intensified when Fleur stepped from Nanapush's door. His eyes became the beacons of his wishes. He walked alongside the machine, stepping with the eager reverence of a prospective owner. Once or twice he smoothed his hand across the hood, kicked the tires, jiggled the grille, and tugged the chromed bumpers. He put his hand to the window to make a shadow through which he could see inside, where, that morning, the boy sat, this time eating nothing, but dressed in a fine, fawn-colored suit, and wherefrom he emerged. Jewett Parker Tatro had in his life managed with such thorough ease to acquire anything that pleased him—beaded moccasins, tobacco bags, clothing, drums, rare baskets, property of course—that when he saw the car he made an immediate assumption. He could get it from Fleur, just like he had acquired her land, and he would. He had not yet determined the method, but there was no question that this would happen. There was only time between him and the capture of his desire.

Even the boy did not deflect his attention, though if Tatro had not been preoccupied, he would have asked questions enough to form an explanation. The automobile, the clarity of his own greed, concentrated him. He looked at the car, he looked at Fleur, and that is when we realized that the decoy was not the boy, as we previously believed, but the car. Large parcels and belongings would soon change owners. From wherever she had been Fleur had studied the situation and kept track of time, calculated justice, assessed possibilities. That was not a white woman's powder in her purse. Gamblers in the old days kept a powder of human bones—dried, crushed, pounded fine—to rub on their hands. So did she. So we were not surprised when, casually and unimportantly, with no reference to anything else or anyone, even though plenty of those who had the time to watch had gathered, Fleur and Nanapush sat down in front of the house and then, with no ceremony, took out a new deck of cards.

The two of them began to play. Jewett Parker Tatro was riveted with interest. He caught his breath. Deepened lights shown in the pits of his eyes, but even he knew better than to play cards with Fleur Pillager, and so he did not approach. However, as if in his stead, the boy joined the game, and there were those who counted the tipped balance that became the rocking vertigo that culminated in the Agent's undoing as the instant he saw the boy sit down to play, and at the same time, did not truly see him.

The boy leaned to the rough little table in the trampled yard, twisted his spoiled face at the watchers, and made himself at home with Nanapush and Fleur. Jewett Tatro approached, struck ground with his hand-carved cane. He came near enough to see everything and yet did not although he squinted his eyes. And then, according to those who were there, in paying strict attention to Fleur the Agent watched the wrong person, for those who really knew how to observe kept their eyes on the boy as he took his place between his elders. They saw the smoothness of his face, the shut innocence, the vacant look that absorbed without interest. They saw his smile gleam, once, knew that dullness was a veil. They saw the smallness of him, the childish candy fat, the tightness of his rich-boy suit. And then, unfurling from his cuffs and wrists, they saw his hands. His wrists appeared, his palms, and then the fingers—long and pale, strong, spidery, and rough. The boy shuffled with an organist's blur and the breath of the little crowd held. He dealt. There were those who found slim shade to watch, those who rolled cigarettes of pouch tobacco, those who smoothly stroked their chins or grinned with excitement, and those who turned and walked silently back down the road. Once the Agent sat down, it didn't matter who stayed or who left. For to all, the outcome was obvious.

Fleur was never one to take an uncalculated piece of revenge. She was never one to answer injustice with a fair exchange. She gave back twofold. When the Agent got up from his chair she would have what he owned, or the boy would, the two one and the same. As for the Agent, the car, you do not feed bait to a gasping fish. What does it matter? You simply extract the hook.

CHAPTER THIRTEEN

LYMAN'S DREAM

FROM THE OUTSIDE, STARING INTO THE LIGHTED FACE OF THE video slot machine, he looked like anyone. His jaw hung slightly open, his hands worked the levers, the buttons, he watched the bars reel over in a whirl and fashion themselves into regular shapes before him. He was playing Caribbean Gold, working for the treasure chest. Knives spun. Brown pirates and ladies. Skulls, flags, and golden coins. The mystery intensified. The quiet of the hushed air surrounded him. Slowly, with an endless burst, the tension vaulted over him but Lyman dipped into an automatically refilling bucket of quarters and continued, and continued, until he had pushed so many coins into the heavy slot that his hands were raw, stiff as wax.

The microprocessors inside the machine were starting to question, to hum, to whine with the weight of self-importance. Lyman was even money, then he was gaining, when all of a sudden Shawnee's face flashed in the little video square. Once. Twice. Three times. Then Redford clanked down beside her. He played a quarter, another, then a whole handful, but his own face did not appear in the magic line along with theirs. Sometimes Zelda's, sometimes Lipsha's. Sometimes the face of the old Pillager woman leapt glaring from nowhere. But never his own.

His own reflection was lodged at the bottom of the river where his brother Henry had jumped in and drowned. His face was composed of Kashpaw's face. Shawnee's wishes moved him, her religious interests sent him into the woods. Her hopes were his. Lyman's hands were strung with his mother's clever nerves. His feet were the size of his father's tracks—ambitions, chances, progress reports, and hope. He was everybody else's creature but his own. And yet, as quarter after quarter fed off his fingers, he began to receive a hint of himself, an ID picture composed of his economic tribulations and triumphs, a personal glimpse from the outside. He was drive. He was necessity. If not him, there was no one who would plan his plans, lift his voice, scheme, and bring the possibilities into existence.

The face of Fleur Pillager appeared before him and the walls melted into leaves and standing poplar, then into brush, into darkness so intense his eyes strained miserably before he shut them. He was sitting face-to-face with the old lady, listening, as Lipsha had described, to the hot rasp of her bear voice.

Land is the only thing that lasts life to life. Money burns like tinder, flows off like water, and as for the government's promises, the wind is steadier.

She spoke to him, and her tone was not the quiet blessing of other elders he knew, but a hungry voice, still fierce, disdainful and impatient.

This time, don't sell out for a barrel of weevil-shot flour and a mossy pork.

Blinking, back to himself, part of the world again, Lyman smoothed his dirty hair off his face and lay back on his blankets in the backyard of his house. The air was light and cool. Over him, in a twisting and muscular arch, the veined brawn of an old oak tree clasped at and released patches of sky. The towering air was colored such a sweet blue he could not stop looking. Perhaps he had dreamed and perhaps she had really come to him. Maybe during his sleep she had sat by him and spoken those words into his ear. *Put your winnings and earnings in a land-acquiring account. Take the quick new money. Use it to purchase the fast old ground.* He almost laughed at the certainty and possibility. Use a patch of federal trust land somewhere, anywhere near his employee base. Add to it, diversify, recycle what money came in immediately into land-based operations.

He saw wheatland accumulating, a pasta plant, then sunflowers. Acres of sunflowers turning with the day. He saw a possible big-time resort. A marina. Boats, pleasure-seekers. He saw Shawnee Ray painting and sewing and making beautiful things in a little studio with a wide glass window looking out into the stillness, the depth, the unforced beauty of the woods and lakes. He saw Redford, from time to time, accompanying him to his office and tapping out requests for information on accounts on his computer. Whatever else happened, he would be a good father, that is, he would be himself—instead of trucks, he would play store. Teach value for value, pound for pound. Already, he was sure, Redford had an investor's eye.

Lyman's secret in life was that he had never, not ever, not in any part of himself, ever given up. His boots also had filled with water on the evening he dove into the gray swell of icy water after his brother. Lyman wasn't a good swimmer, he didn't know how to stroke and kick, and he felt in one moment during the struggle exhausted. His body had loosened fearfully, another movement seemed impossible. And then from somewhere, he couldn't tell where, because it wasn't in him but outside him, the pull, one inch, the next inch, the tiny article of faith.

RELIGIOUS WARS

LOVE WON'T BE TAMPERED WITH, LOVE WON'T GO AWAY. PUSH it to one side and it creeps to the other. Throw it in the garbage and it springs up clean. Try to root it out and it only flourishes. Love is a weed, a dandelion that you poison from your heart. The taproots wait. The seeds blow off, ticklish, into a part of the yard you didn't spray. And one day, though you worked, though you prodded out each spiky leaf, you lift your eyes and dozens of fat golden faces bob in the grass.

After I get clear of the old lady's house, I never am quite sure about all the things that she told me, for it seems as though the important ones have entered my understanding from the inside. Scenes without words appeared that night. Dreams. I saw Fleur Pillager when she was young, heard her speak in low voices, telling me her bear thoughts, laughing in tongues. For although she took pity on me, accepted me as her relation, she gave me nothing I could use outright—no love teas, no dried frog hearts, no hints or special charms. *Admit your love,* I think she said, *take it in although it tears you up.* I don't have a choice about it, anyway, for I am lost. Everything that I take in about Shawnee Ray mixes me up bad, but I let it happen. She makes my heart seize like an overheated engine. I think of her and feel myself melt down to a metal sludge. From that molten mess, I still hope she'll fix my heart into the shape

151

she wants, like she does the patterns of her original designs. And then one day I hear the rumor that she's got a different plan in mind.

"That girl's got ambition," they all say, for Shawnee Ray has gone over to the All Red Road Powwow in Montana to dance the jingle dress and sell her designed clothes. College money, she tells everyone. She is going to get schooled in the arts. On the phone, she had said that she will soon pay me back the money that I gave her for fabric. Now I know where she's going to get it. Odds are she'll beat her competitors and come home in a week with big prize money. Knowing Shawnee Ray, she won't bingo that money away, either. She will put her money down on an apartment, get a baby-sitter, take classes, embark upon some kind of major, acquire two initials, three, then four behind her name, all of which will cause her to be hired by an art gallery, or maybe she'll go political, into a law firm, a lobby group, an Indian gaming agency in Washington, where she will be swallowed in the brilliance of a successful life and I will never be able to follow.

I can hardly lift the mop. I throw it across the bar like a messy javelin, and then I go back into my room and lie down on the rocking plastic waves of my bed thinking that my heart will explode with spirals of love and confusion and fear of what comes next. I believe Shawnee loves me, I trust in my vision, but in deference to Lyman's fatherhood she is deflecting her sights once again from me. I am doing what I can do, try-ing to be irresistible by being responsible. I counsel myself that I should stay away from Shawnee Ray and not try to change her decision, but over and over in my mind's sight I see her foot press the sewing pedal, I see her little round glasses fog. I see back, to before that scene, and I am caught. Again, I watch her emerge from the rushing water in the motel room.

She lies down beside me, takes my hand, moves over me, her breasts both full and pointed, her waist a band of flexible emotion, and between her legs a rough and stirring sweetness. Again, with Shawnee Ray, I enter the trailless forest. I never slept all that long-ago motel night. As dawn spilled, I watched the ice blue radiance stray over the flimsy mutton-colored curtains and my heart quailed in me. I know it wasn't long before we had to check out. That was when the mirror in that small room spoke to me, dim, calling me right through its shadowy door. All night Shawnee Ray had tossed and grumbled at me, kicking and rolling and touching my hand. I knew it was just the way people don't fit the first time they are together, and I longed to change that, to make our love habit.

Hopeless, as I've said. Breathing hard, listening to Titus open up the bar, curled around my lonely pillow, I remember her saying those fatal words.

You got the medicine, but you don't got the love.

Does she believe that even now? Did she argue me out of her heart? I get so downcast after time that I begin to open the book too much, the plastic Bible which is still my only souvenir of that long-ago night. In the beginning pages there is a section for the desperate. Big problems, all of which I personally suffer, are given neat reference points, conveniently labeled. Adultery, Adversity, Anxiety, Conceit, Confidence (False), Covetousness, Crime, Death, Deceit, Depravity, Divorce, Doubt, Drunkenness, Enemies, Excuses, Extravagance, Falsehood, Fault finding, Fear, Flesh, Greed, Hatred, Intemperance, Judging, Lip service, Lust, Pride, Revenge, Self-exultation, Sin, Submission, Swearing, Temptation, Tribulation, and Worldliness. There is also Backsliding, Bitterness, Defeat, Depression, Loneliness (Overcoming), Trouble (In), and Weariness.

Weariness gets it about right for me and so I find the chapter in Matthew about the yoke being easy, the burden light, and I fix on the words *gentle* and *lowly in heart*. Lowly in heart describes me so perfect and describes what I can't be, also— humble and contented with what I got. A job. Money. People who don't hate me. I get to wondering if the Son of Man had any mad-green love affairs. Unless He did, He could never understand us humans, I am sure.

I page through, wondering: Where does it come from, this beautiful sickness of the heart? Why would I choose the feeling it over the not feeling it? Why, although she doesn't even love me back the same, do I feel thankful to Shawnee Ray Toose? It comes to me, in time, that part of my emotion for her is all mixed up with the love that she has for her little boy. I love her the more as she resists me in favor of her son's father. Somehow, I'm proud she loves her little boy enough to stay away from bad risks like Lipsha Morrissey.

I am getting riskier with every day, too, like something in my brain has sunk out of sight. Darker thoughts inhabit me. I think of Stan Mahng, this guy I used to know who got a crush on a girl from off-reservation and ran away with her to Colorado. They were heard from once, twice, and then she returned alone and soon married a completely different person. Only thing was, she had Stan's baby one month into that sudden union, and when Stan returned from the mountains and he heard about that, he went over to their house in the hope of getting to see his child. They let Stan in the door and anyway, real polite, he visited with them, and held his little baby. Then he left without hardly saying anything, for he was a quiet kind of guy, and went off to ice-fish on Matchimanito Lake, where his cousin's house was set.

Well, they saw Stan go in the icehouse door, but they never saw him come out. He carried in his ice auger, used a pruning saw to enlarge the fishing hole big enough so that he could slide through with rocks tied on his feet. There he sat, on the bottom of the lake until spring thaw.

I get to thinking of others. Stacy Cuthbert, who killed her rival with a shovel. Of Martha May Davis, who held up a Stamart and used the money next day to buy herself a thousand-dollar white lace wedding dress. I think of my own grandmother

Lulu with all her towering love of men, of how Nector Kashpaw set her house on fire from the heat of his attraction. Naturally, I think of the frozen hand of Xavier Toose, and the long-running gossip that has followed Fleur Pillager into her old age, about how she loved men outside, against trees, in the water, between the dangerous crystal-set tables in the high society of Saint Paul, Minnesota. I think of the other Pillager named Moses whose *windigo* love howl still rings across the lake from his island of stone, where he died of desire. I wonder how it was my grandmother Marie stayed so calm in love, or why it was that Zelda lost her love-luck after Xavier and never married a Chippewa.

And after all that, I keep coming back to Stan Mahng. It is as though I see him down there all winter, on the lake bottom. At last he was in a place that ran deep as his own feelings. I almost felt glad for how he finally found that spot. The cold might have been unpleasant, but it drove out the heat of sorrow. Sometimes a light beam shot through the ice, a slash of raving silver, but most often, I think, only the resolving dark.

One early morning night, before I rise to my daily job, I decide that I have a problem that the good little book must help me deal with and I turn the beginning list of pages for a reference to the thought of Suicide. But there is nothing there. I look through twice, and then a third time, thinking maybe it will be under another heading like Contemplating, suicide, or Feeling like, suicide, or Committed, suicide, but there is no mention of this area at all. I'm just curious, it's not like I have a noose in my hands, a pistol, a garment bag, or pills. I'm just thinking that it would be nice to have a verse handy just in case scriptures come up short.

I get furious at the absence. So mad that I throw the book across the room with all my force. And it hits my stereo, it turns my stereo on, and through the speakers, through the system, through the electronic noodles, at that moment my life or death answer comes, top volume.

. . . life is but a joke . . .

Cold air flows up my spine to the roots of my hair as the man himself, Jimi Hendrix, speaks to me, breathes at me past death, drags me out of my cave to flat turquoise spaces where the wildcats announce themselves and towers crumble into sand and mountains fall against karate chops and I am not to worry. If life only is a joke then I'll get lost in it. Leave behind all the serious shit. Live like he did with a big smile of crazed pain and genius upon his face. Get religious, for want of anything more ridiculous.

For I have to admit the book knocked on the power. If life's a joke, then suicide's a bad punch line, I guess. I reach in the corner for the Bible, smooth the fluttered pages, and ease myself cautiously onto my bed again to ponder.

We never ask for all this heat and silence in the first place, it's true. This package deal. It's like a million-dollar worthless letter in the mail. You're chosen from the nothingness, but you don't know for what. You open the confusing ad and you think, Shall I send it in or should I just let the possibilities ripen? You don't know shit! You are left on your own doorstep! You are set there in a basket, and one day you hear the knock and open the door and reach down and there is your life.

I relax deeper into my bed, and as I lie there a peculiar thing happens. I feel time pass. Or more rightly, since it is always ticking by, I become aware of its passage. I sense it running through my hands, my fingers touching the hem, my mouth catching at the flavor, just a fleeting change upon my lips. The music beats onward, the guitar licks like holy fire, burning time like paper, like a match to alcohol. My thoughts enlarge. Outside, trees are sieving air and seeding and whipping through the black gates of clockwork. All around us, time. Time over us. The sky never twice, the river once. No moment the same. Time glimpsed like a mighty book, swift pages turning fast in us and slow in stone. Time gathering, a muscle of space, a rhythmical flex of darkness curving like a cat, and me, Lipsha Morrissey, one hair on its ass.

Why fight the joke, why rush the moment? Who the hell knows how it all turns out?

After this, my day proceeds in the usual manner. Nothing seems so terribly different, and yet, those big spaces that collide in my room set me on a further linkage of considerations. Thoughts of God bother me and will not quit. I wonder whether I should start reciting Bible quotes to Shawnee Ray, whether my becoming a witness of some kind, a Christian martyr, might press a button in her heart.

For the fact is, you can think big, but your real concerns are little. Schemes and hopes. I would go down-dirty, I would do anything to get Shawnee Ray. It occurs to me that she is also involved in some of our more traditional religious pursuits, and I can maybe get to her through her own uncle, Xavier Toose. I know that Lyman is involved as well, and now I wonder to myself whether getting the real old-time traditional religion wouldn't help my case.

With religion there is always that personal impossibility, a barrier which stops me, of believing in a God in the first place. Where and who? No spirit ever was revealed to me, I got no message through a burning bush. I never heard words spoken in my head unless I did a garbage lid of drugs. First of all, I think about the Catholics, maybe signing up with them somehow. I am attracted to their ritual motions, although when the nuns tell you straight-faced that you are eating the real true and precious body and the blood of Christ, you have to wonder. How come the Catholics make such a big deal out of converting cannibals? Drinking blood, eating flesh, it goes on every Mass. Also Confession is a thing I can't agree with. I say it's cheap. You kneel down in that box and say what you done. And then, basically, you get off scot-free, only cranking out a few Hail Marys or some Our Fathers. No restitution demanded, no community service.

I suppose it is natural, too, after all my thinking, and after my experience with Old Lady Pillager, that I should also take an interest in the Chippewa religion. Not that I am about to go crawling after illusions. No, my main motive in getting traditional is the hope of attracting Shawnee Ray's attention to my staying power.

So I go looking for a home to rest in Shawnee Ray's heart. I want a place where I can belong, but I end up as part of a surprising configuration. I go looking for a god I cannot resist, try to get to heaven through the ozone hole, land on any old star. I look for peace, I look for love. I end up in a religious war.

I go to Lyman in order to scope out the possibilities, to get the angle, and to check out his religious technique along with his love strategies. It is a sweet, new summer weekday at his government house, and I find him inside with the telephone in his hand, clouds of smoke around his head, the television laugh track slashing air, radio chiming in the other room. There is a worried look on his face and excitement in the intense way he mouths his words. He gestures at me, points at a chair that is set among his exercise machines, all pulleys, weights, and dials. I make myself at home and overhear his business talk. Casino talk, state compact talk, blackjack equipment talk, which goes on and on until I pour myself a coffee, sit down, and watch him so steadily that finally he catches my eye once, twice, and then hangs up.

"Your mother is my grandmother, you're my half uncle and half brother and my boss," I say, quickly, before the phone rings again. "So I am going to ask a favor of you."

"Shoot."

"My favor is religious," I go on. "I haven't ever done an official sort of spiritual quest, just the kind of grab-you-by-the-collar stumble, you know the type of thing. So I'm in the market for a more high-type vision, and I don't know where to go for it, who to ask."

At that, Lyman takes the phone off the hook, a thing I've never seen him do before. He walks into his small living room, hits the television power button. Sit-com characters are blipped into the vacuum, and Lyman sits down across from me in a stiff, low plaid chair. I see that his grass dance outfit and his accessories—strings of yarn, fluff and feathers, ankle bells and moccasins—are spread all across the room, on the coffee table and the plastic end tables. He has been chewing for his own moccasins, I see, softening some hide in the traditional and ancient way. To my mind, this is both a touching and an awful thing, Lyman repairing his brother's grass dance outfit, a thing most unusual for a big shot like him. I know he's doing it in order to impress Shawnee Ray. I am jealous to see that they have the use of a needle and thread in common. I am uneasy at the evidence of the depth of Lyman's love design.

"It so happens I'm going to go see Xavier Toose. Bring him some tobacco. You know why?"

Of course I don't.

Lyman picks up a wristband, squints at his needle in concentration, running at it with a bit of waxed thread. He tells me that he needs to debate a few things and ask advice. He is trying to think whether to include me in some plan that he has in mind. I can tell that he is going through an inside struggle. He finally bests himself.

"You gave me the pipe. I can't refuse you." He sighs. "I'll ask Toose to put you out for a fast, for a quest, the same time as me."

"With you?"

"We won't be together or anything, just be waiting for a vision at the same time."

Things are moving quicker than I hoped, maybe even than I wanted. I had in mind something a little less radical than four or maybe six days alone in the bush with no food.

"Sure you never had a vision?" asked Lyman.

I think back. I was cracked on the head by an old vet with a wine bottle. That was by accident, but I decided then and there I would not join the army. I was visited by the form of my mother in the Northern Lights. I talked to her sitting in a bar so close we could have clasped fingers. I saw dandelions, me in the grass, picking handfuls, gathering up the yellow pollen in a ditch and putting those tart flowers to my face when I thought of Shawnee Ray. I had those kind of visions. I saw blank-outs of my own past, like the time when Zelda swore how she found me in the slough or when Jimi spoke. I saw things here and there and everywhere but lost my powers of the touch nonetheless.

"Sure," I say, "I had plenty of visions, but I ain't satisfied with them."

I honestly admire Lyman's ease in the larger world, and I appreciate his taking me in his hand like this with the money, now the religion, his basic good nature. Of course, he doesn't get the whole picture, doesn't know that despite denying all rumors I am planning to slowly zero in upon Shawnee Ray. He doesn't know I am a spy, a thief scoping out his love medicines. I keep on trying to convince myself that if he has genuine love for Shawnee, it is lodged in his heart so deep the point has disappeared from view like a fine-point needle. But seeing his devoted work on that grass dance clothing makes me pause before I think of the moving strands of fringe and ribbon, at which thought I shiver and grow weak with longing at the memory of the swing of Shawnee's hair.

There it is, soft morals, but how can you argue? Lyman is trying to do his duty. Shawnee Ray is full of noble attitude. I am a creature of the same old underhanded shit. Not only that, but I am up against the heavens themself. The supernatural world. If there does happen in the scheme of the universe to be a prime creator, a God who takes our actions personal, my plan to grab some spirit power just in order to impress a woman might be construed as low, as not in keeping with the big dedications of others, like Lyman.

But that's how much I love Shawnee Ray. Heaven is a dangerous place, I already know that from lying in her arms. How much worse than to live without her could it be to live in hell? For some reason, as if God was up there, I look out Lyman's window. It is one of those wide unvariable days when the sky is like the inside of a big, white opal shell. Streaks of dim pale reflections hang windless on one side of the horizon. On the other, darker shades cast fuming shadows.

No, I don't hate Lyman the way I probably should, since he is my rival for the woman I adore down to her heels. I can't get behind inventing faults, he's just another guy. I don't even dislike him, and in fact, I actually enjoy hanging around with my uncle, beating him at pool, drinking a beer or two, talking business. That morning, I make my report on my bingo winnings and hand over my bank account, which is mounting with comfortable persistence. The numbers put Lyman into such a good mood that he makes a new pot of coffee, spoons some flavored nondairy creamer into mine, a treat he bought at his own convenience store. He all but invites me to stay. So I decide to help him out a little since he's helping me, to string beads or whatever he has in mind. He offers me a piece of leather to chew, but I politely refuse. The smoky taste helps him cut down on cigarettes, he says, and then he starts biting the leather, chomping it in a sad way, a hungry way, until I begin to feel a space yawn inside me.

We get to talking. I can't help asking, since the subject is so unavoidable, and I'm nervous, and since after all we are related, about his brother Henry, the one who died, a relative I never knew. Lyman sits back in his couch chair for a minute, relaxed as I've never seen him, and suddenly he breaks out into a smile. Not even a sad smile. He's looking at the dark cloth of the fringe-trimmed shirt that Henry once wore.

"I can see him," he says, "that time we traveled on the pow-wow trail. We brought our things along in a suitcase and sometimes we just sat underneath the arbor, in that dry heat, listening to the popple leaves curl when the drum stopped. There was that silence between the songs, when all the talk seems so far away, when the announcer starts teasing the dancers back to the arena—it's like your heart is waiting to beat. You take a breath, another breath, and then you're laughing at something, or you're hungry again, ready to go snagging, to walk by that camp full of beautiful sisters.

"We both danced sometimes, when the mood came upon us, and those times, oh well, my brother Henry, he was the best, they'd all say it. The most promising grass dancer, though he didn't always win because that wasn't the point with Henry—he danced to move within his own thoughts. We were different. I danced for prize money."

Lyman leans forward now and laughs low and hard at himself, but then he softens, sips his coffee, and after a while he starts in again, not even looking at me.

"Once we sat on the side of a hill in August when the grass had grown long, tasseled out and feathered. It was lush, a rainy summer. We watched the opposite side of an ungrazed hill where the grass was moving, going, rushing, as if a great hand was pushing it from underneath. You know how that is, how it makes you reach to understand it—that grass changing. Sometimes it was as if a different hand from above pressed down, fingers spread, showing the silver underside of fur. Coursing, streaming, that grass fled. Then changed direction. At lower currents it was rising up, green smoke.

"And Henry says to me, not drunk, just speaking from the heart, 'Little Brother, I see the earth breathing, coming at me, almost like it's playing with me.'

"In return, I was almost going to make a joke. But then I

saw he was right in what he said, so I did not speak. We were both of us in the grip of something, then. Modest power, but unrelenting power. The grass will cover him, I thought. For the grass was running in the dried sloughs and in the ditches. Wind, earth, water—all of it flowed together as the lick of green flames, as the grass.

"And I said, 'Henry, *don't go.*'

"That's all I said to him. He'd enlisted in the Marines. Still, he never heard me, I don't think. By then, he was far away in his thoughts, already gone.

"Just like you are, Little Brother," says Lyman, looking close at me, "just like you always were. Just like you'll always be."

And I have to look away, almost afraid to think, to feel the way he's just called me his little brother. Because I love his girl, I cannot meet his gaze. We could have maybe gotten more in tune somehow, right then, in the quiet of his house, but we are set up to fail by the sight of Shawnee Ray in both our minds. Shawnee Ray at the center pole, behind the eagle staff, before the loudspeakers, dancing in the arbor, all flashing light of cut beads and jingles.

I take a deep breath. I take another. It stabs, full of sorrow. We are so related I can hardly find the knot. I feel all embarrassed by these lost emotions and I can't open up my heart, except finally to make a lame comment and then suggest that we go someplace and eat.

"Eat," says Lyman.

He looks down at the dance shirt he has picked up and holds in his hands. I see, as we regard the cloth together, how the light shines through the worn-out places where the weave has thinned and pulled. The shirt is old, frail, of a Kleenex softness, faded; all through it the threads look ready to part.

Almost immediately, as we pull out onto the road, I can't help but go on to try to change the subject. I ask, in a casual voice, how Lyman and Shawnee are doing these days.

"Okay," he says, distracted.

We ride awhile longer, and I still can't hold back.

"What do you mean, okay?" I ask.

"Just okay," he says. "Well, not so good."

My heart leaps up at my throat, but he won't say anything else more specific about their troubles.

"She's so smart, that Shawnee Ray," I sigh, attempting to draw him out as we drive along.

"She's got a good head on her shoulders," he responds, almost suspiciously, as we leave the dusty gravel and enter the highway to town. "She could amount to something, but she's got two Achilles' heels named Mary Fred and Tammy."

"Her sisters."

"One's the ball and the other's the chain. It wouldn't be so bad, but she left Redford with them."

"Why not with you?" I ask.

Lyman shrugs. "She's not thinking, or I backed her into a corner. She says I'm in too thick with Zelda, trying to block her, keep her down on the farm so to speak. She says she does not intend to spend her whole life as a bingo caller, but hey, who said that was the deal? I'm grooming her."

"Oh."

Lyman's back to his business self, done with the memories and the spiritual side of life, and I try to be quick to follow.

"She's going to be my manager," he goes on. "Shawnee's good with people."

"That's true."

"Except for this thing with Redford. Talk about a lack of judgment! Of course, I've got a court order going through and by tomorrow I should have him back."

I think this is strange, all of a sudden him going to court, and I am filled with a carbonating heat.

"You can't take Redford—I mean, you're not even on the records as his dad."

"How would you know?" Lyman shakes his head. "You're unbelievable. Zelda's in that office, remember, and I do have some rights even if Shawnee Ray won't marry me."

"Lyman, she's a good mother," I now say.

"Good? Oh yes, too good a mother, up until now."

The way he says this, mouth turned down, ironical, it seems to me like he is happy that she made a mistake at last, if that's even what it is. He talks like he doesn't place particular value on her uplifting ways, or is making them into something negative, like he's tried, in fact, to take her down. I don't answer for a minute, for it occurs to me that being a smart woman and a good mother are two things I never valued quite enough in Shawnee Ray either. What I think about more than anything else is the sex—day in and day out those thoughts preoccupy my brain. But now, I put my mind onto her other qualities: I picture the way she holds Redford in her strong arms, and how she brings him walking in the woods to show him a bird, a leaf. I have watched her unbeknown, seen her hugging him so close as they walk the supermarket aisle together to pick up a jug of milk. She gets all fierce when her boy is threatened, so I know now that she must have been unhinged by our love on the floor, desperate to escape, half crazy to leave him with her sisters.

I get a piercing pain right beneath the hollow of my heart. I see her rocking Redford, kissing him, touching his face with her finger, and it presses a panic jolt. First off, there is no way I can imagine June Morrissey doing that to me, and my thoughts veer away in longing. The subject makes my throat choke up with envy. I try to swallow. Even left for a week with Tammy and Mary Fred, I wish I was that little boy, I wish that I was Redford.

I make an attempt to control myself, for I see now that Lyman sees himself as Redford's father and I see myself as Redford's competition. That is not right. I want everything about Shawnee Ray, even her motherhood. Only, I want her to mother me, to heal me. I've helped stand in the way of her future just as much as Lyman. Between the three of us, including Redford, we've all but torn her into equal pieces. I roust myself from these thoughts, new thoughts, things I cannot tell Lyman. I don't trust him and I'm angry at how he's forced her to his will. The two of us have now reached the Dairy Queen. I try to shake my shoulders free, but they're loaded with heavy chips of resentment. I don't like knowing the deeper Lyman, the side of him that loved his brother. It makes it so much harder to do him dirt. We get out of the car and stroll into the air-conditioned area where customers are spooning cold mushwax into their mouths.

"What do you want?" I ask Lyman. I take out my wallet, full of bingo money I'm determined to use.

"Hot dog. Large Diet Pepsi. I'll pay."

"No," I say. "I've got my money out. I'll pay."

Lyman, used to always footing the bill, is almost shocked.

We get our food and sit down at a little plastic table. We unwrap the hot dogs and I try to take a bite, to stuff my mouth, before I speak, but it is like I have no further resistance to my angers.

"You don't know her!" I suddenly throw down my hot dog on the table. "You don't understand her. You don't know who she is! And here you are, trying to discredit her!"

"Who?"

Lyman doesn't take my meaning at all, he just looks at me all quizzical and then, after a while of watching me, when I don't answer, just glare at him, Lyman considers. He cocks his head to the side, opens his mouth, shuts it, then sits back with his pop and puts the straw between his teeth.

"Shawnee Ray," he mumbles, making sure.

I almost knock my pop over on the table, because I lean so suddenly right into his face.

"I know her," I say. "I know her better than you do."

"Really?" He is still not even threatened. It is frustrating, because I don't want to overplay my hand. I get so upset looking at the strong arms and winning bone structure of Lyman Lamartine that my teeth clench on the plastic straw. I raise the straw up, and then I spray pop onto our reservation's biggest tamale. His face goes numb. He looks down at his shirt.

"Stupid little punk."

"Motherfucker!"

That gets him and he dives, like from the high board, right over the little tabletop where I am waiting with all the rage I have tempered in my heart. Our fight is about the biggest mess I've ever started, for that's the way you get when related friends turn to sudden enemies—you hate worse than any strangers. You have to pound out the old affection along with all the new aggravation. But unfortunately a few other folks get involved, too. Doing a flying drop kick, I knock into an entire large-size family who are carefully turning from the ice cream counter and balancing five-topping sundaes with whipped cream and cherries. The cherries explode into the air, the walnut bits zing sideways, the ice cream blobs collide at super speed.

The father sluices pineapple and chocolate down some lady's bosom front, and there begins an immediate and deadly argument about who will pay the bill for the dry cleaning. Lyman's arm, in the meantime, goes haywire as he staggers backward groping for purchase. I have delivered a near knock-out connecting punch. His hand goes down in a super nacho plate. The random eater, annoyed, throws the remains at me but I see it coming, duck, and it happens to catch a customer who has just entered from a construction site and is pulling off his hard hat. From there on, until I grab Lyman from the grip of someone big who is massaging a banana split into his growing-out-traditional hair, I can't really describe or explain. It is just one big explosion.

Then we are back in the car. We are driving. We are licking all flavors of creamy substances off of our arms and hands.

"I never fought you before," says Lyman, excited and almost joyful.

"I never fought you before, either," I admit, but I'm not happy.

"Hey," he says, holding a hand out, dripping strawberry topping.

"Hey." I clasp it. "No hard feelings."

But the truth is, lying low after that incident the next two days, I do have harder feelings to deal with than I ever thought. For then we have this conversation in which Lyman says things that complicate my simple hatred of the thing he is doing.

"Lipsha, I have this confession to make," says Lyman. "I'm probably messed up these days because of Shawnee. Something's going on with her, but I don't know what. It's not just this trip, it's something deeper."

My heart sings so hard in a sudden key I have trouble quieting it. I take my breath deep.

"You just got to know this," he blurts out, his voice a strained cry. "I'm so crazy for her I could die, real easy, and Redford's my boy. Would you leave him with those unstable sisters of hers, now would you? Think about it. Shawnee Ray, she's in my head every minute, and I know she's not the same about me. She never forgave me after the things I did. . . . Once, I broke up with her. She was pregnant, but that's history. I'm loving her so hard I think she'll crack, let her feelings well up inside, you know? I just don't know how to go much farther, and I was thinking, see, just wondering if you had any advice. I'm drinking my pride, here. You, a young guy, you might have a way with girls, Lipsha. Things you can tell me. Maybe you could let me in on your secrets."

He gets red in the face after that, bashful, like any moment he could break down and wail. I feel like some low form of life. What am I supposed to say? I cast about in my mind, come up empty of everything but guilt. Here I thought he had the love ways, the smooth ways that I could imitate, but it turns out he's just as confused and oppressed by love as me. Lyman's such a complicated guy there's something uncanny about him, scary, like it's a disease of the spirit, a kind of sainthood that's out of control.

It is tempting to confess everything. I've got to be wary though. For some reason an adage I never knew comes into my mind. *Lie down with dogs, get up with fleas. Lie down with saints, get up with holes in your hands and feet.* I mutter something hopeless about my clumsiness and fears that I hope reassures him, and then I put a hand on his hard shoulder just a moment to let him know that I understand the depth.

As it happens, mixing it up with Lyman doesn't unwedge either my friendship feelings for him or my love for Shawnee Ray, and that last gets worse than ever, so bad that I wake up in the morning and moan and whine before I can slosh out of bed. I know I should quit thinking about her, but I don't exactly have a choice for she's just *there* wherever I turn, *there* when I let my guard down, *there* when I want her and *there* when I don't. Each day, I try to put her out of my mind. For an hour or two I'm in the struggle, I'm talking and arguing, for a while I'm in the fight, resisting all thoughts of Shawnee Ray Toose. And then I weary of it. I get bored of my own resistance. I think of her hand where I want it or her smile flashing, sweet, over her left shoulder. I cannot win out against myself. I just poop out and say, "I'm bad, I have evil tendencies." I accept it, accept myself, and taste her nipple in my mouth. Of course, it's not that I see my love for Shawnee Ray as evil. It's the part where I want to steal her away from my uncle Lyman that is hard to defend against my conscience.

I work late and turn in later, pretend that I have a reason to sleep. I try to step aside, knowing of the reality of Lyman's feelings. But Shawnee gets in the way of my resolution so easily, my heart is all sprung doors and busted windows when it comes to her. I keep recalling our first shocking kiss. I eat, but only strange things, the snacks that Shawnee Ray and I shared at our one meal at the Coin-Op—a Polish sausage sandwich and a chocolate chip cookie. I begin to wish that we'd included a fruit or two, something fresh at least. I drink tea, which she likes, instead of my thick black coffee, and I imagine her soft and slippery touch at any hour when my mind is temporarily unoccupied. It is as though my out-of-the-body sex with Shawnee those two times has increased my longing to an unbearable degree. I can't turn it off. I can't live with it. This uncooked and useless desire with no hope that lives inside me seems like some sort of curse. A net of burning threads. A snare trap that hangs loose around my neck waiting for her hands to jerk me dead.

So it is a relief when Lyman comes into the bar a few nights later. He orders the usual diet pop and suggests tomorrow is a good time to visit Xavier Toose. He says that Redford and Shawnee are now back with Zelda, where they belong. He says he's fixed things, that all is under control. I should take off a week. I am more than ready. I clasp my arms so brotherly around him that he startles in surprise. My face is wide and pure, a shining sun, and I am prepared to see a vision that will fix my mind higher, above the belt.

CHAPTER FIFTEEN

REDFORD'S LUCK

REDFORD WAS AWAKE, WATCHING OUT FOR HIS MOTHER. SHE would come back for him soon with the money she'd win at the big powwow dancing jingle dress. First place and nothing less, she had said. He knew he had to wait for her, and he had to be as good as possible, but Mary Fred was hard to sleep with. Her feet, limp and brown as two trout, hung over the edge of the cot in the shed. Her round arms reached out and slapped at things she saw in her dreams. Redford had been knocked awake out of his own dream where he was hiding in a washing machine.

"*Tss*," his aunt mumbled, half awake, "wasn't nothing." But Redford sat up after her breathing went deep again, and he watched.

There was something coming and he knew it.

It was coming from far off but he had a picture of it in his mind. It was a large thing made of metal with many barbed hooks, points, and drag chains on it, something like Grandma Zelda's potato peeler, only a giant one that rolled out of the sky, scraping clouds down with it and jabbing or crushing everything that lay in its path on the ground.

Redford watched Mary Fred carefully, trying to figure. If he woke her up, maybe she would know what to do about the thing, but he thought he'd wait until he saw it for sure before he shook her. He liked that he could look at a grown-up woman for as long and close up as he wanted, but something about Mary Fred's face scared him. He took a strand of her crackly, curled hair and held it in his hands as if it was the rein to a horse. She had a salty, half-sour, almost puppy smell that wasn't a comfort. He wanted to touch the satin roses sewed on her pink sweater, but he knew he shouldn't do that even in her sleep. If she woke up and found him touching the roses, she would tell him to quit.

He felt drowsy, slumped down, and put his legs beneath the blanket. He closed his eyes and dreamed that the cot was lifting up beneath him, that it was arching its canvas back and then traveling very fast and in the wrong direction, for when he looked up he saw they were advancing to meet the great metal thing with hooks and barbs and all sorts of sharp equipment to catch their bodies and draw their blood. He heard its insides as it rushed toward them, purring softly like a powerful motor, and then they were right in its shadow. He pulled the reins as hard as he could and the horse reared, lifting him. His aunt clapped her hand across his mouth.

"Okay," she said. "Lay low. They're outside and they're gonna hunt."

Her voice was a whine, high and thin, another child's. She touched his shoulder and Redford leaned over with her to look through a crack in the boards.

They were out there all right. Mary Fred saw them. One tribal police officer, a social worker, and Zelda Kashpaw. There had been no whistle, no dream, no voice to warn her that they were coming. There was only the crunching sound of cinders in the yard, the engine throbbing, the dust sifting off their car in a fine light-brownish cloud and settling around them.

"We'll wait, see what they do." She took Redford in her lap and pressed her soft arms around him. "Don't you worry," she whispered against his ear. "Mary Fred knows how to talk to them."

Redford didn't want to look at the car and the police. If he saw Grandma Zelda, he would feel like crying to her, even though Mary Fred had explained she was trying to steal him away. He'd heard the sisters talking, worrying late at night over Lyman's case. Suitcase. He thought it was a kind of carrying box. His aunt's heart beat so fast beside his ear that it seemed to push the satin roses in and out. He put his face to them carefully and breathed the deep, powdery air of her, and the lower smell, the yeast and ferment, the beer. Flower smells were in her little face cream bottles, in her brushes, and around the washbowl after she used it. The petals felt so smooth against his cheek that he had to press closer. She hugged him still tighter. Within the smells of her soft skin and her roses, he closed his eyes then, and took his breaths softly and quickly with her heart.

The three didn't dare get out of the car yet because of Mary Fred's big, ragged dogs loping up the dirt driveway. They were rangy, alert, and bounced up and down on their cushioned paws, like wolves, like they were dancing on hot tar. They didn't waste their energy barking, but quietly positioned themselves on every side of the car and in front of the bellied-out screen door to the Toose house. It was six in the morning, but the wind was up already, blowing dust, ruffling their heavy coyote coats. The big brownish dog on Zelda's side had unusual black and white markings, stripes almost, like a hyena, and he grinned at her, tongue out and teeth showing.

"Shoo!" Zelda opened her door with a quick jerk.

The brown dog sidestepped the door and jumped before her, tiptoeing. Its dirty white muzzle curled and its eyes crossed suddenly as if it was zeroing its crosshair sights in on the exact place it would bite her. She ducked back and slammed the door.

"It's mean," she told Officer Leo Pukwan, a slow man. The son of the son of tribal police, he was carrying on the family occupation. He sat solidly and now, with no change in expression, rolled down his window, unsnapped his holster, drew his pistol out, and pointed it at the dog's head. The dog smacked down, threw itself under the car, and was out and around the back of the house before Pukwan drew his gun back. The other dogs vanished, and from wherever they had disappeared to, they began to howl and the door to the low shoebox-style house slammed open.

"You've got no business here." Tammy was ready for them, tousled but calm, a wide short woman in a boxy haircut, man's sweatshirt and worn-out jeans. "You've got no warrant."

"We do have a warrant," said Pukwan evenly.

"And the court papers?"

"We've got those too," said Zelda.

Tammy's rough raw-looking features were bitter and belligerent. Her swollen eyes took Zelda in and she looked ready to spit with disgust. Standing outside the car, Officer Pukwan stood firm, but watched her warily.

"*Booshoo,* Tammy."

"Get the fuck out of here."

"We have *papers.*" Zelda spoke emphatically.

"We're doing this for the protection of your nephew," said the social worker, Vicki Koob, holding a manila envelope in the air.

"Protection from who? Where's Lyman? Scared to show his fat face?"

"Just let us take Redford and we'll go." Zelda stood firm, commanding.

"Redford loves me, loves us," Tammy said. "His mother's our fucking sister."

* * *

At first glance, Vicki Koob could see that Redford and Mary Fred were not in the house, but she pushed past Tammy and took out her notebook to describe it anyway, for the files, to back up this questionable action. The house consisted of just one rectangular room with whitewashed walls and a little gas stove in the middle. She had already come through the cooking lean-to with the other stove and a washstand and rusty refrigerator. That refrigerator contained nothing but some wrinkled potatoes and a package of turkey necks. Vicki Koob noted that fact in her bound notebook. The beds along the walls of the big room were covered with tattered quilts and cheap, pilled dime-store blankets bearing faded American Indian geometric designs. There was no one hiding underneath the beds. She felt the scored, brown, wooden chairs. Touched the top of the little aluminum dinette table covered with a yellowed oilcloth. One wall was filled with neatly stacked crates—old tools and springs and small half-dismantled appliances. Five or six television sets were arranged in a kind of pyramid. Their control panels spewed colored wires and on at least one the screen was cracked all the way across. Only the topmost set, with coat-hanger antenna angled sensitively to catch the bounding signals across the reservation, looked as though it could possibly work.

Not one detail escaped Vicki Koob's trained and cataloging gaze. She noticed the cupboard that held only commodity flour and coffee. The unsanitary tin oil-drum beneath the kitchen window, full of empty surplus pork cans and beer bottles, caught her eye, as did Tammy's serious physical and mental deteriorations. She quickly described these "benchmarks of alcoholic dependency within the extended family of Redford Toose" as she transferred the room to paper.

"Twice the maximum allowable space between door and threshold," she wrote. "Probably no insulation. 2–3 inch cracks in walls inadequately sealed with whitewashed mud." She made a mental note but could see no point in describing the burst reclining chair, the shadeless lamp with its plastic orchid in the bubble-glass base, or the three-dimensional picture of Jesus. When plugged in, lights rolled behind the water under the Lord so that He seemed to be strolling although he never actually went forward, of course, but only pushed the glowing waves behind Him forever, like a tame rat in a treadmill.

When Mary Fred saw Pukwan ambling across the yard with his big brown thumbs in his belt, his placid smile, his tiny black eyes moving back and forth, she put Redford under the cot. Pukwan stopped at the shed and stood quietly. He spread his arms wide to show her he hadn't drawn his revolver.

"Mon petite niece," he said in the mixed voyageur's language, in the soft way people used if they were relatives or sometimes if they needed gas or a couple of dollars. "Why don't you come out here and stop this foolishness?"

"I'm not your goddamn niece," yelled Mary Fred.

She bit her lip, pushed her permanent-burned hair off her face, and watched him through the cracks, circling, a big, tan punching dummy with his boots full of sand so he never stayed down once he fell. He was empty inside, all stale air. But he knew how to get to her. And now he was circling because he wasn't sure she didn't have a weapon, maybe a knife. Pukwan knew that Mary Fred was big and strong and would be hard to subdue if he got her mad. She had broad shoulders, dirty tricks, and stood solid like her father, the Toose who was killed threshing in Belle Prairie.

"I feel bad to have to do this," Pukwan called to Mary Fred. "But for god sakes let's nobody get hurt. Come on out with the boy, why don't you? I know you got him in there."

Mary Fred did not give herself away this time, but let him wonder. Slowly and quietly she pulled her belt through its loops and wrapped it around and around her hand until only the big oval buckle with fake turquoise chunks shaped into a butterfly stuck out over her knuckles. Pukwan was talking but she wasn't listening to what he said. She was listening to the pitch of his voice, the tone of it that would tighten or tremble at a certain moment when he decided to rush the shed. He kept talking slowly and reasonably, flexing the dialect from time to time, even mentioning her father.

"He was a damn good man. I don't care what they say, Mary Fred, I knew him."

Mary Fred looked at the stone butterfly that spread its wings across her fist. The wings were light and cool, not heavy. It was ready to fly. Pukwan wanted to get to Mary Fred through her father, but she would not think about him. Instead, she concentrated on the sky blue stone.

"He was a damn good man," Pukwan said again.

Mary Fred heard his starched uniform gathering before his boots hit the ground. Once, twice, three times. It took him four solid bounds to get right where she wanted him. She kicked the plank door open when he reached for the handle and the corner caught him on the jaw. He faltered, and Mary Fred hit him flat on the chin with the butterfly buckle. She hit him so hard the shock of it went up her arm like a string pulled taut. Her fist opened, numb, and she let the belt unloop before she closed her hand on the tip end of it and sent the stone butterfly swooping out in a wide circle around her as if it was on the end of a leash. Pukwan reeled backward as she walked toward him swinging the belt. She expected him to fall but he just stumbled. And then he took the gun from his hip.

Mary Fred let the belt go limp. She and Pukwan stood within feet of each other, breathing. Each heard the human sound of air going in and out of the other person's chest. Each read the face of the other. Mary Fred saw the patterns of tiny capillaries that age, drink, and hard living had blown to the corners of his eyes. She saw the spoked wheels of his iris and the arteries like tangled thread.

She took a quick shallow breath and did not move. She saw black trails, roads burned into a map, and then she was located somewhere in the net of veins and sinew that was the complexity of her world, so she did not see Zelda and Vicki Koob and her sister Tammy running toward her, but felt them instead like flies caught in the same web, rocking it.

"Mary Fred!" Zelda had stopped in the grass. Her voice was tight as a string. "It's better this way, Mary Fred. We're going to help you."

Mary Fred straightened, threw her shoulders back, then lifted into the air, and flew toward the others. The light, powerful feeling swept her up. She floated higher, seeing the grass below. Her arms opened for bullets but no bullets came. Pukwan did not shoot. Instead, he raised his fist and brought the gun down hard on her head.

Mary Fred did not fall immediately, but stood in his arms a moment. Perhaps she gazed still farther back behind the covering of his face. Perhaps she was completely stunned and did not think as she sagged and fell. Her head rolled forward and hair covered her features, so it was impossible for Pukwan to see with what particular expression she gazed into the headsplitting wheel of light, or blackness, that overcame her.

Pukwan turned the vehicle onto the gravel road that led back to town. Redford sat between Zelda and the social worker. Vicki Koob remembered the emergency chocolate bar she kept in her purse, fished it out, and offered it to Redford. He did not react, so she closed his fingers over the package and peeled the paper off one end.

The car accelerated. Redford felt the road and wheels pummeling each other and the rush of the heavy motor purring in high gear. He knew that what he'd seen in his mind that morning, the thing coming out of the sky with barbs and chains, had hooked him. Somehow he was caught and held in the bleak tin smell of the pale woman's armpit. Somehow he was pinned between their pounds of breathless flesh. He looked at the chocolate in his hand. He was squeezing the bar so hard that a thin brown trickle had melted down his arm. Automatically, he put the candy into his mouth.

As he bit down, he saw his aunt very clearly, just as she had been when they had carried him from the shed. She was stretched flat on the ground, on her stomach, and her arms were curled around her head as if in sleep. One leg was drawn up and it looked for all the world like she was running full tilt into the ground, as though she had been trying to pass into the earth, to bury herself.

There was no blood on Mary Fred, but Redford tasted blood now at the sight of her, for he bit down hard and cut his own lip. He ate the chocolate, every bit of it, tasting his aunt's blood. And when he had the chocolate down inside him and all licked off his hands, he opened his mouth to say thank you to the woman, as his mother had taught him. But instead of a thank you coming out, he was astonished to hear a great rattling scream, and then another, rip out like pieces of his own body and whirl onto the sharp things all around him.

CHAPTER SIXTEEN

SHAWNEE DANCING

An early morning rain freshened the grass and high winds blew off the clouds, but over and over that day the dust thickened, a slow haze that choked the dancers. A water truck bounced around the arena in low gear and a boy slouched on the back end, spraying slow arcs. Rainbows sprang from side to side as he gestured with the water, and Shawnee focused on the shifting colors, slowed her heart, tried to calm her mind during the endless memorial giveaway.

So many poplar branches wrapped in money! So many blankets, so many shawls, so many pillows and headscarves and kerchiefs and washcloths passed before her that she began to tire of objects and things. So much *stuff* in the world. She grew hungry, mentally counted her change, listened hopefully for another feast to be announced. So far, she'd been in every line of guests fed to honor every relative who'd died in the past year.

Corn soup, fry bread, Juneberry pie, and bangs with jelly. Tripe soup, boiled meat, plates of sliced cantaloupe and watermelon. Shawnee Ray remembered a heavy white bakery bun stowed in her canvas carryall. She reached in and removed it gratefully, ate standing so she wouldn't crush the jingles on the type of dress her father had called a snoose dress, because the shiny clackers were made from the tops of Copenhagen tins.

She brushed the crumbs carefully away from her hips, smoothed the fringes on her sleeves, and thought of Redford's thick hair. The jingle dress was original to Chippewas, given to a Mille Lacs man by women who appeared to him in a dream, moving to their own music. Shawnee loved dancing the jingle dress dance best because her father had so often helped her with the steps—hard to do because the skirt was straight and tight, but when she danced right, it was as though she were stepping down upon a springy cushion of air.

She had danced hard at each Grand Entry, earning every last point, and she'd been led by the hand by the judges and placed among the final four in the traditional women's and the shawl dance. Her chances for the last, the jingle dress, were good, and she had actually slept peacefully and deep in her bedroll the night before. She'd rubbed her feet raw in places, but she'd brought a roll of duct tape and a tiny scissors. Back in her tent, she'd cut pieces off and stuck them onto the places were she'd stepped hard on pebbles or blistered. Nothing hurt, nothing pained her anymore.

The last of her corn bread eaten, she watched the woman who sponsored the special memorial dance for her daughter. That young woman's staged portrait, head tipped, smiling in a pretty, dreamy way, was carried around the circle along with her dead brother's army photograph. The woman, who held both of the pictures, was solid and thick with muscle, but her feet tapped underneath her powerful body with a fastidious deer's grace. Shawnee watched her—a judge for these dances, she had laid a heavy pawlike hand on Shawnee's shoulder, choosing her, motioning her to the line, and Shawnee had smiled. But the woman, Ida, registered nothing and walked almost rudely away, slow, swaying, implacable in her long grief.

Shawnee was ashamed to realize she almost resented that slowness, for she was grateful for the sponsored prize and desperate to win it. The old woman had her own time and everybody else's too—sometimes when the sun shone hot she put up an umbrella, a white one bearing a portrait of Daffy Duck. Sometimes she set a giveaway washcloth upon her head. She spoke with only a few relatives, seemed mostly content to preside over all she saw like a monument or feature of the landscape.

A cool wind flowed down, reaching from the shadows of the low belt of olive-pale mountains to the north. Dusk fell for hours in violet bands. Over the encampment a great blue night cloud spread, slowly unfurling like a cape, and then, from underneath, as the announcer called in the dancers, a low barge of red fire moved.

Black light jabbed the stillness. The air came tremendously alive. As the jingle-dress dancers walked into the center of the grass arena, their clothing trembled sweetly. The women arranged themselves in a circle and stood composed, elbows tucked to their sides, chins set, eagle fans, macaw feathers, bead purses, and dream catchers held stiff. Shawnee Ray was positioned at the eastern door, facing the west, country of the spirits. Lifting her face to the band of red light, the cloud, as she waited for the first throb of the drum, the push up, for the long-winded announcer to cease, for her last chance, her vision suddenly focused on one incident from her childhood, snapshot clear: she saw her father, in her mind's eye, bent by the curved grille of their old gray car.

Wings of sweat, dark blue, spread across the back of his work shirt—he always wore washed-blue shirts the color of cloudy shade. His blackbird hair had grown out of its haircut and flopped over his forehead. When he stood up and turned away from the car, Shawnee Ray saw that he had a butterfly in his hands.

She must have been eight or nine, wearing one of the boys' T-shirts Mama bleached in Hilex water. Her father held in his toughened hands the butterfly, brittle and long dead, but still perfect. It was black and yellow-orange, all charred lines and fire. He put his hands out, told Shawnee Ray to stand still, and then, glancing once into her serious eyes, he smiled and rubbed the butterfly wings onto her collarbone and across her shoulders, down her arms, until the color and the powder of it were blended into her skin.

"Ask the butterfly," he whispered, "for help, for grace."

Shawnee had felt a strange lightening in her arms, in her chest, when he did this. The way he said it, she had understood everything about the butterfly. The sharp, delicate wings, the way it floated over grass, the way it seemed to breathe fanning in the sun, the wisdom of how it blended into flowers or changed into a leaf. In herself, Shawnee knew the same kind of possibilities and closed her eyes almost in shock, she was so light and powerful at that moment. Then her father caught her up and threw her high into the air. She could not remember landing in his arms or landing at all. She only remembered the last sun filling her eyes and the world tipping crazily behind her, out of sight.

GETTING NOWHERE FAST

I BELIEVE IN THE WANDERING SON, THE MISSING FATHER, AND the naked spirit of the Holy Ghost. I believe in the crush of night, the ragged holes in the feet of the plaster Jesus, through which you see the wires cross. I believe in the single malt whiskey if you're rich, the bottle of white port if you're broke. I believe in the peace of worms. I believe in the extension ladder and the angel with the torn mouth at the bottom, waiting to wrestle. I believe in the one on one, in the hands and voice of Jimi Hendrix, and that I will always love Shawnee Ray, even though I come to know a side to her that's fearful.

Before I go on out with Lyman to my vision fast I feel it is important for me to have just a word, a normal conversation, with Shawnee Ray Toose. After all, she is the one I hope will be there with the feasting food when we return. She is the reason I am going off on what seems, the more I think about it, a desperate and foolish mission. And I am worried, too, about the way Zelda Kashpaw and Lyman have managed to get Shawnee under their control although she did what she said, earned some money, made a college hunt.

Zelda took Redford from the Toose house, using the system, and now that Shawnee Ray is back from her nearly bigtime second-place jingle-dress finish, there is no sign of her. She lives again with Zelda. But no one sees her, no one hears what she's up to, no one reports on her the way they used to. She has dropped out of my line of vision, or maybe she is a prisoner fed scraps in Zelda's house. In Lyman's company, however, we will be admitted for a visit.

We swirl into Zelda's driveway, get out of the car, and immediately, looking so anxious and tense my heart cranks over, Shawnee Ray walks slowly down the steps with a cookie-smeared Redford in her arms. She hesitates. There is a sadness about the way she looks at us and her movements seem quiet and shocked. In a dazed way, she hands Redford over to his father, who holds him with a sort of neat authority and starts fussing with and dusting up the little boy right off. I think they look natural together, Lyman and his son, and in my heart I feel a plucked string.

"Hey," I greet Shawnee Ray.

She nods. I look very serious and searching into the unknowns of her face.

Suddenly Redford lets out a belly shriek at nothing in particular. To prove the efficiency of his fatherhood status, then, Lyman is forced to resist tossing him back to his mother, and begins to try all sorts of methods to divert the boy's attention. He jiggles, he prances, he hops and changes his voice to high, odd, coos, but nothing works. At last he turns away from me and Shawnee Ray and walks around the back of the house, where there is a little sandbox set up, and a couple plastic trucks.

I take my chance, turn to Shawnee Ray again, with urgent haste. There is an eager look in her face for me, I am sure of it. I think she is about to bloom toward me like the flowers in my dreams. In spite of knowing Lyman is just around the corner, my lips part and my whole face yearns for her face and I have to jerk my arms around my back to keep them from winding around her waist, from gliding down the fountains of her soft, thick hair, from holding the delicate seashell structure of her chin, her cheeks, from smoothing the lids of her eyes and the sweet, short eyebrows. I stand there with my mouth open, waiting for inspiration.

"Would you marry me?"

At first Shawnee Ray draws back like she is insulted at my request, as though she maybe thinks it is a joke. The edges of her mouth go down and she starts to turn away, and then, giving me one slight glance, she sees the something in my face. The ravaged something. The diet of Polish sausage and old cookies, the dreams, the anguish and the tea, the sacrifice of half my sanity, the religion. She stares hard at me, and I cleave tenderly toward what I anticipate as the equal longing in her look. I hold out my arms, but she bats at the air, leaning backwards, her face changing, moving.

"Get real." Her voice is high-pitched, strained, and her eyes are shining too bright.

"I am real."

I say these words so desperate that my knees buckle. I go down before her on my knees, and then I put out my arms and tenderly clasp the worn blue spots on the knees of her jeans. It is like I never saw a thing so beautiful as those two lovely pieces of fabric, rubbed smooth. She tries to move away but my arms tighten in spite of myself and she's hobbled. She almost loses her balance. She stands still a moment, and then she bends over and she pushes at me in a panic. I loosen my grip of her knees in surprise and then her foot plants itself under my chin with such force I go tumbling backwards.

"Get out of my way. . . ." Her voice is too even, too low, trembling underneath the tone with a kind of threat I've never heard. I scuttle backwards like a crab, out of reach of her hard leather toes, away from that scorching voice.

"What'd I do?"

"What'd he do?"

It is Lyman, returning with a now sand-over-cookie-caked Redford round the side of the yard. The two make their way evenly toward us, but Shawnee abruptly strides over to Lyman and grabs Redford from his arms. Too shocked to wail, Redford looks at us with big eyes, back and forth.

"What'd he do?" Shawnee's voice is a ripped screen. She is not my sweet Shawnee, not my tender airbrush picture. Suddenly she shows the undertone, the strokes of which she is created. Her hair flows like snakes, shaking down, and in her cornered anger she is jiggling Redford so fast that his cheeks bounce.

"He asked me to *marry* him!" She says these lovely words in an intense and awful voice of scorn.

"And I mean it," I say humbly, falling back onto my knees, dazed and addled as a sheep.

"Oh, shut up," says Shawnee Ray. "And you," she addresses Lyman as he starts for me, "stay away from him. I won't marry you either. Get that idea out of your bingo brain."

Lyman stands in paralyzed surprise like he was frozen with a laser gun.

"Shawnee Ray," he says gently. "You don't know what you're saying."

There is a silence, and then, taking one deep breath, she screams loudly—an incoherent, strange cry, like a baboon in the desert. The air vibrates. I put my hands over my ears. She does that same robbed and naked scream again, a sound that makes my neck crawl. Her face is working, witchy, so frightful that Redford buries his face in her shirt, hanging on like a frightened little monkey as she whirls. She seems to grow larger, her shirt billows, her hair is dark leaves in a storm.

"Get out of here! I won't marry either of you. Period. You . . ." she looks down at me, her mouth twisting, "you talk so big about your feelings and you can't even make it back to school."

Lyman steps toward her.

"Don't you come near me, don't you even try. If you ever go to court again, if you ever get in my way . . ."

"I'm Redford's father," says Lyman gently.

Shawnee turns. She walks back to the house with Redford,

talking to him in a soothing and familiar voice. She opens the door, goes inside, and we hear a cupboard slam. A short wail, more calm talk. Lyman shuffles around, and I back toward the car, both of us uncertain, hoping that the scene is over. But no, just as we are tentatively confident in our leave-taking Shawnee Ray comes back down the steps and stands in front of Lyman. She puts her hands on her waist. She is like that tough lady in "The Big Valley," hips thrust out in tight pants, heeled shoes, mouth held in a bold sneer.

"You're Redford's father? Says who? You weren't there when it counted. You're too late. I'm Redford's mother."

Her voice becomes musical and horrible, for it is falsely charming with a loathing current underneath. "Think back, Lyman," she warbles. "You weren't my only boyfriend, remember? I had three other guys and I only made a birth control mistake with one of them."

She leans close to Lyman, chin jutting, and pushes her face into his face.

"Want to take a blood test?"

Lyman is smiling foolishly now, with a look of glazed wonder. I put my hands on his shoulders, guide him backwards, open the car door, and put him in still with that amused and quizzical indulgent expression on his face. It's like an expression made of china, one that can easily shatter to its opposite, and I know it's time to get moving, get out of there.

The funny thing is that as we drive along no silence grows between us, and we have no reaction to what just happened. Not two miles onward, we begin to talk about inconsequential things. We wonder about the sky, if it looks rainy or the day will hold. We anticipate the road and what comes next. We have a lot to think about, but we can't talk. We can't make the past half hour real. It is as if neither one of us can take in the Shawnee Ray we both saw. We can't understand, can't absorb, can't admit, and will not let that woman be her.

* * *

We drive the small roads, the back roads, leading surely and slowly farther on toward the house that belongs to Xavier Toose. He lives at the edge of an allotment that blends into the land around Matchimanito, the land that belongs to Fleur Pillager. I can't figure Lyman here. We are nearing the very same rolling, sweet, wooded hills that he wants to use for the big casino that he plans, the luck place, the money-maker scheme that will build day cares, endow scholarships, cure the ills of addiction of which it is a cause. I know that Lyman has thought out the consequences and the big-time benefits, but I believe, now, that he hasn't really examined the personal. Maybe that's what his quest is about, the bigger picture of an operating genius. Or maybe Lyman Lamartine is deep down religious. And then again, maybe given what we've just been through, we have a lot of things to think about regarding Shawnee Ray.

We take a turnoff, and the brush closes. I am still stunned by Shawnee's knees so close, her ankles so perfect to grip. Luckily, by this time, Lyman is concentrating on the world beyond this one, and has let go of that final scene. As we bounce down the last, long drive, just wheel ruts, to Xavier's, he is trying to instruct me about a sweat lodge, the proper way you enter it and crawl around in it, but I am dizzy. There was a moment back there when I felt that Shawnee Ray wasn't really angry, that she was screaming hard to cover up the true feeling that she has for me. I try to recast the whole scene in my thoughts. I wonder if she wasn't putting on her tantrum for the benefit of Lyman, and planning to wink at me as we left. I never turned around! I never looked in the rearview! If I had, what would I have seen? If I had only stayed, I think now, ditched Lyman, let her rage herself into my arms, maybe she might have bent to my life. I fear I may have blown it, may have lost my narrow chance. I still can't admit that she really might be furious. For one thing, there is no reason, is there? How could she? I have done nothing but overadore her.

We come to a halt in the yard of Xavier Toose's place, and we get out of the car. Xavier walks lightly toward us, easily, like his joints were new oiled. He's wearing a light green shirt and blue jeans. He is a kind of medium-looking man all around. You wouldn't pick him out in any crowd as holy, that's for sure. He has no blessed airs about him, he is not like a priest, and not spooky like Fleur. He has no manner of the Touch Me and I'll Strike You Dead. He is sort of round, just tall enough, not fat in the face or thin, and cheerful. He is not like Russell Kashpaw, who works with him, a Mount Rushmore–looking Indian. No, Xavier has a kind of big, arched nose, extremely black and shining eyes, thin and surprised-looking eyebrows, and a humorous mouth. The one different thing besides his hand with the fingers gone is that he wears an earring, one little shell. We touch his arms and right away, from the warm current in his presence, I am reassured. Here is not a man who will allow me to waste away and die or be eaten by wild animals in either the spirit or the natural realm. I am encouraged by the kind gaze upon my face, the joking forbearance.

"I almost chickened out," I tell him.

His only answer is, "Some do."

He motions for us to walk out in back of his small, brown house and down a trail. I take deep breaths, for at any moment I expect a flash to hit, some kind of electric power to jolt on, a message to seep into my feet through this holy land that stretches from Xavier's backyard all the way to the shore I don't want to think about, the waters of Matchimanito Lake. I expect some unearthly voice to blare on with each footstep, worry that I might be smote from the days of old. What happens, however, is that Xavier Toose puts us to work.

"Heavy labor's good for body sculpting," says Lyman, an hour into what we're accomplishing.

"I thought we were coming here to get enlightened," I complain. It has turned into a muggy, hot, scratchy day and we are in deep and windless bush searching out nice-size and bendable willow poles, slogging through the steaming, spongy grass near a slough. I have a small hatchet, not near sharp enough, with which I am chipping at the base of a tough sapling. Lyman, lucking out as always, has a keen bow-shaped Swedish saw with which he dispatches three times as many trees.

When we have enough leaf-stripped poles, we drag them back, and then there is the careful twine-tying with tight lodge knots, the posthole digging, the gathering of the stones that pass muster. And for the last, standing at the shores of the lake I don't want to think about, there is a lot of argument over which kind of rock heats up the best. Not that I know enough to argue—it is just that by then I am in all respects pissed off at Lyman.

"Who cares?" I pick up one that I hope Fleur has cursed. "I mean, take this smooth black one here. Hot's hot."

"Hot's not just hot," he answers. "There's qualities of heat. Take this speckled one."

"That looks like an egg, like it would explode."

"Rocks don't blow up."

"If they get hot enough and if there's any water in their seams, they do." I make this up.

Lyman bites his lip, tries to control himself.

"I'm worried about this idea of superheating stones," I continue, annoyed he doesn't believe my scientific theories. "The physics of it sounds dangerous."

"I'm sick of babying you."

"Who asked you?"

Lyman sighs, and hefts another big rock in his weight lifter's arms. For him, the heavier the better-heating.

"Wouldn't a banana split taste good about now?"

Lyman kind of laughs.

"How hot could it really get?" I wonder after a few minutes.

"Real hot," Lyman answers in a relishing voice.

Later on, I find out. The lodge looks too little for us all to enter and I wish we'd made it three times as big. There is this person attending to the fire, a big Terminator-muscled convict type with a lot of tattoos—probably free, courtesy of Russell Kashpaw. The whites of his eyes show and he grins too much. A red bandanna is tied onto his head, and he is getting the instructions, too, even as he prepares the fire for us and then keeps heating up the rocks fiery red. They're placed in a little half circle next to an altar made of earth, sprinkled in a line with cedar. A bowl of tobacco, just a small wood bowl, is set to one side. When Xavier says he is ready, the guy, Joe, puts the rocks in the fire pit with a shovel. Xavier goes inside the sweat lodge. Lyman and I take our clothes off and get in too. The big guy closes the flap. Xavier throws a dipperful of water down on the stones, and then it starts getting hot.

Xavier prays and talks to us and instructs us. Out of the blue, Lyman comes up with a very insightful, long, and meaningful prayer that sounds like it could be used to open up a conference. I am worrying about what I'll say, since I don't believe exactly in who- or whatever I am talking to, but when the turn is mine I find that heat adds to my praying ability. My words flow, as if my syllables are thinned honey. Amazingly hot, surprisingly hot. So hot I can't take it. But then I do take it, and I get hotter yet. I try to cool off by talking faster, praying louder, as if my tongue is a little fan, but then I give up and fall quiet. Xavier has given us this teaching that the sweat lodge is female, like a womb, like our mother we have to crawl on the earth to re-enter. He has encouraged us to let ourselves feel that connection we must have forgot, and I think I do without trying, for as I am getting hot, as I am praying, I find myself slipping away from the present, into a dark dream that hasn't a forwards or a backwards. I stop talking, or thinking, or even feeling the blasting heat that sizzles out of the rocks every time Xavier splashes them with water. I just exist, float, my ears stopped, my mind doused. After a while the heat feels bearable, then it feels like the most perfect embrace there ever was. Then Lyman says he wants it hotter, and splashes more water on the stones.

I could kill Lyman. I'm a cooked steak. My breath feels cold on my hands, and I know that I'll never leave the place alive. Panic grabs me. I begin to pray in a maniac's voice, desperate and pure, until I slip from the present in which Xavier Toose's voice is wide and soothing as the sky. I don't get the gist of his instructions, but I feel the comfort. Again, I want to stay there, and stay, but it's all over. We emerge into the normal sunlight, the day which before had been low and humid but now seems fragile, fresh and cool. I should be a newborn baby but instead I feel strange, unrocked. A roar of disappointment builds inside my head.

I look around for June, through the trees, toward the road, as if I'd see the flash of the blue car speeding into the mint-conditioned day. But there's no sign of her, no return.

I mope around half listening to Xavier tell us what we must do, but I'm only there in the flesh. We walk down to the lake, dive in to wash ourselves entirely clean. The water doesn't thrill me, doesn't want me. I close my eyes against the darkness and get out as quickly as I can without looking either at the annoying perfection of Lyman's muscle-toned wrestling star's build, or at the beefy collisions of scars and tattoos of snakes and women in eventful positions that round the thighs of the helpful convict. Xavier douses himself, too, and he teases Joe about his snakes and women. But I can't get into the tone of the day, for sadness inhabits me.

"What's wrong?" Lyman whispers to me once, impatient, probably thinking I am hurt by Shawnee Ray.

I considered. What is wrong? What is my problem?

"I miss my mother," I say.

Lyman snorts, puts his hand before his face, and I know at that moment he is sorry that he ever asked me to go with him on this spiritual journey. I try to whip myself back into mental shape. I am hardly managing to do the least thing that is required, just go along with what is happening, truck off into the woods behind Xavier's house. In the long shadows of that afternoon I find myself wandering alone looking for a place where I can spend as long as it takes for a vision to come my way. The choices are numerous, but I am supposed to pick a personal spot to gather power.

I try, but I just stumble around for the longest time until I lose track of where I am, but nothing matters. By that time, being lost is a trivial detail.

I lower myself onto a hard, cold rock, and get depressed still worse when I look up and see that I am in eyeshot of the damn old lake where bad things happen, where I visited the old woman, where in deep fear I listened to her bear talk. In Matchimanito Fleur Pillager drowned and came back to life, and her cousin Moses haunts the island with the howls of cats. I don't care though. If the horned thing, the grappling black thing that lives down there, bellies after me, I won't run. What's the point? There is no good book to help me and once again I have no motive, no reason for staying alive.

"This is great," I say out loud, building myself a little nest out of pine needles and wood moss and leaves. "If I was feeling like myself, I'd be so fucking scared I'd never sleep."

I have only three pieces of equipment—my sleeping bag with the blue elks in rut pictured on the inside flannel, a plastic bottle of water, and a garbage bag. That last, my supposed tarp for rain, I fill with more leaves to make a mattress. That is probably cheating. Oh yes, I have some tobacco too, and a little cedar that Xavier pressed into my hand. Beyond that, nothing. Although it is still daytime, and the light is falling dappled through the twigs and leaves, I crawl into my sleeping bag.

I don't know what time it is when I wake. In sleep, my dragging down feeling vanished and is now replaced with the normal instinct for self-preservation, only crazed beyond sense. I can't believe I've gotten myself into this situation. The wind picks up, the dark is pure and intense, and I hear the terrible rustles of surrounding animals, and even the monster hoot of *Ko ko ko,* the owl, sounding in my ears.

From all sides, fears grab and shake me. I put my head in my hands, rock back and forth, wish at least I'd built a little place for myself up in the trees. Deer could step on me down here on the ground. I think of their pointed hooves. Then I think of teeth. Fangs, tusks, rabbit incisors. Jaws for tearing. Sharks. Forget sharks. Bears. Raccoons. In this overbearing dark, I won't see it coming. Slashing death. Of course, I know there have been no bear attacks, no packs of wolves descending on lone campers, no owl or squirrel flocks reported tearing up a human, not in all the time I have ever been around here, and yet, and yet there is always a first for a freak occurrence. That's what makes the news.

I groan out loud and curl into myself and for the rest of the night whenever some noise startles me I jump up, shout, then settle back again to wait for the next advance of nature. In this way, with frequent yells, I fend off the invisible intruders. I keep peering and staring into the faceless dark that is not even lit by the glow of wild eyes.

Morning. Morning. Night. Night. Morning. I go through two cycles and then I lose track. The first day I am hungry and all my visions consist of Big Macs. The next day nothing matters again. I drink water from the lake and wait to die of an old paralyzing curse, but nothing happens. Upon waking, sometime after, I begin to take an interest in my surroundings. I watch an ant kill a bug of some kind and saw it into pieces and carry it away. A small brown bird hops from one branch to another. Then it hops back to the first branch again. A weasel flashes through once, looks straight at me, curious, and vanishes. A blue jay lands, squawks, and disappears. I try to interpret these things as signs of something bigger, but I can't jack up their meanings.

I sleep, becoming weaker, and when I wake my head feels light and fat as a balloon. I fall into a dreamy and unpleasant mood and all of a sudden I am annoyed that I turned out as an Indian. If I were something else, maybe all French, maybe nothing, or say, a Norwegian, I'd be sitting in comfort, eating pancakes. Or Chinese. Longingly, I shut my eyes and imagine the snap of fried wontons between my teeth at Ho Wun's. I taste sweet-and-sour fried batter. Hot crispy noodles. No fair. I resent the lengths that I am driven by the blood. I take mental revenge, then, by imagining what would happen if all the Indians in the country suddenly disappeared, went back where they came from.

In my mind's eye I see us Chippewas jumping back into the big shell that spawned us, the Mandan sliding down their gourd vine, Navajos climbing underground and covering themselves up, the Earthmaker accepting Winnebagos back into primal clay, the Senecas hoisting themselves into the sky, the Hopis following their reed to the Underworld.

And then what? I study on that only for a moment before I know the answer. Lyman Lamartine would somehow wangle his way out of the great Native apocalypse. Lyman would finally, and entirely, be in charge. Policies and programs would flow from his desk, examining this problem. He'd issue directives with a calm born of disaster, marshal all his forces. Even if no Indian returned to this world, Lyman Lamartine's paperwork would live on, even flourish, for the types like him are snarled so deeply into the system that they can't be pulled without unraveling the bones and guts. Cabinets of files would shift priorities, regenerate in twice-as-thick reports.

Yet, in that same daydream, I get even with Lyman too. He sheds his turquoise and inlay rings, his Hush Puppies shoes, his go-to-Washington two-hundred-dollar suit and bolo tie, and he stands along with everybody else. I make Lyman run for the shell along with all the other Chippewas, but too late. The shell claps shut around me and Shawnee Ray and Redford and it sails off, leaving Lyman on the shore. He's left to watch until it's just a pearl in the distance, until it winks over the edge of the world.

Of course, this is just a dream. It won't be so easy to get rid of him.

By throwing my lot in with Lyman I've gotten to be part of something very big, very muddy, and very slow. A megalith of mediocrity, somebody said, but he was a dropout from the Bureau, fired, and Lyman and I have our fates intertwined, mixed up like the roots of two plants. I kept on seizing in my mind on that comfortable feeling we once had together, when Lyman said he remembered the day he and his brother Henry lay and dozed under the powwow trees, the pine arbor, listening to dancers pound dirt.

Nowadays, they put a rug of Astroturf down on the arena and there is no dust, no grit to chew on. Still, I fall asleep imagining those good food-filled days and more like them, before us, with the bingo money I've accumulated. I wake, wishing that I had a book to read, my Walkman. I play back all the Hendrix in my memory, then heavy metal and around the time the sun goes down I make a surprising discovery that I don't really need a stereo cassette. I am hooked up to my own brain. This is not a major vision, but it helps pass the time. Movies come back. Books. I rewatch all the *Godfather* series, then reread the *Dune* trilogy and my Kashpaw dad's favorite, *Moby-Dick.* I go on and on back below the surface of my mind. Of course, Shawnee Ray is there at each bend. The thought of her is so troubling, every time I look out toward the lake, especially, that I have to try and stow it. I imagine a little cardboard box, and then I wrap her up tenderly, even though she fights me, and I put her inside. I mail her to myself. Open on arrival. I feel better once she is temporarily contained.

I have gotten used to the rustlings and squeaks and calls by then. I have given up on getting scared. I am just bored, and now I realize I've never been that way before. Something was always happening in my real life, at every minute, compared to out here in the woods. What is so great, what is so wonderful, what is so outrageously fantastic about the woods? I ask this of myself as I sit there. There's not a goddamn thing to do but think. From time to time, I get disgusted. I start talking to myself, mutter a curse on all I see.

"Let Lyman build his old casino here, what's the difference? What does it matter where he puts the thing? At least there would be other human voices. I wouldn't mind a little slot machine right here, by this rock, with a big dollar lunch and free Pepsi. That would be fine with me."

For the purposes of his plan, this is a spot like none other: lake view, perfect for a large-scale resort. And now, as I sit here, my mind a blank for long hours, I have to agree.

Morning. Night. Night. Morning. I have no idea what is passing, time or space. I am still falling in and out of deep despairs, plus I am still not getting what I define as a vision. Where is it? I think that after I have dealt with the hunger, which gets so bad sometimes I put leaves in my mouth and chew them and spit them back out, some bright picture will approach me. I now settle into the frame of mind where nothing frightens me, or surprises me, where I would welcome a bear walking into my little camp and saying something conversational.

That's another thing: I am getting lonelier and lonelier. After a while, it is a toss-up between the loneliness and the hunger. Shawnee arrives during one of my periods of wakefulness, and I can't help untie the package and take out her memory. From then on, her face before she flew into the rage is on a line with the image of the hot dog I so regret not having eaten back at the Dairy Queen. I taste mustard, sweet relish, and most agonizingly, the light salt sweat on Shawnee's neck. How I regret the waste of all the ice cream that smashed on people and the floor. Towering concoctions rise in my mind. Walnut toppings. Shawnee Ray spoons large quantities of frozen slush into my open mouth, or drops in loaded nachos, one by one. I try to heighten this, to make it into something like a vision to light my path, but I know that it isn't the real thing. I get stubborn. I am positive that Lyman is having by-the-book visions right and left, and that I will be completely smoked if I don't have something deep and amazing to balance him off. But nothing happens, nothing happens, and still nothing more happens, until I began to call this my getting nowhere fast.

Then early in the morning something does occur. Not the thing that should have, of course. The light is gray in the trees when I wake, like old silver, and the sleeping bag feels snug, warmer than usual. I drift in and out of sleep twice more before I surface to the consciousness that there is *something else warming me up*. I feel the weight suddenly, the other presence, and as I uncover my head and peer out of the bag the smell hits me before the sight of the shaggy round ball of fur nestled at my hips. Black fur, white stripes. The mother of all skunks. I don't know why but I think it's a she. Maybe it's the self-assurance, the way she continues to sleep heavily on the most comfortable part of my body. I begin to ease myself back from her, carefully intending not to drop her or damage or even wake her with my movements, but of course, there is no hope of that. All of a sudden, her black eyes open gleaming bright, her mouth yawns, full of pointy teeth.

This ain't real estate.

I hear a crabby, drowsy voice in my head. Now is it the skunk who says this, or is it that my mind has finally sprung a leak? I panic at the thought that I've finally flipped, and scramble backwards, dumping her, rude and sudden. She rises on her tiptoes, this skunk. She stiffens. And then I swear, frozen as I am in place, that she pats down with her front paws, drumming a little tune. Then, just before she lifts her plumed tail, she glances over her shoulder at me and gives me a smile of satisfaction.

This ain't real estate, I think, and then I am surrounded

and inhabited by a thing so powerful I don't even recognize it as a smell.

There is no before, no after, no breathing or getting around the drastic moment that practically lifts me off my feet. I stand, drenched, but not alone, for the skunk odor is a kind of presence all of itself. It is a live cloud in which I move. It is a thing I can feel and touch—and then Xavier Toose appears. He is there so suddenly and looks so real that I just gape. I think at first he's been shot, had a heart attack, that he's finally bought it, for he collapses on the ground and begins to roll this way, that, over and over so quick it looks like he's in agony. But now, as I run to him, as I try to help, his arms flap helplessly, his face is screwed up but not with suffering. He's laughing, and laughing so hard there is no use talking to him, no use at all.

I walk back in silence, without my spiritual guide. I enter the area set up for us underneath a tarp near Xavier's house. Well ahead of me, Joe the convict dives for cover. I see that there is food underneath clean white and blue dish cloths, all centered on the picnic table. But the skunk has shut off all of my senses. I have to imagine from a long distance. Wild rice cooked with mushrooms, Juneberry jelly on fresh bannock and bangs. I have to imagine the taste of Kool-Aid and iced tea and picture steam rising in the sealed thermoses of coffee. Sliced melon and the cake. Angel cake. I dig in and no one stops me. The skunk smell rings in my head so loud I can't hear, can't face them. I just know they're somewhere else, around me, howling at the outcome. I swallow down a hot dish thick with hamburger and tomatoes. I chew jerky—beef and buffalo.

No one dares to approach me. They make a circle, call to me from the edges of Xavier's yard. But that's too far away and I don't answer, just keep eating, though I'm full sooner than I can believe. I see the smoke that rises from the little fire, but I don't go there to sit. They're all weeping with laughter now, heady with my story.

I am completely shamed out by Lyman.

Eventually, I creep close to the circle around the low flames.

"I was begging for a vision," Lyman begins quietly, his voice low but very pleased with what is coming. "I was begging for a vision." He sets his preface out again.

The drama of it! I look unhappily from side to side, and everyone's eyes are fixed with solemn satisfaction upon Lyman, even as they discreetly hold their noses because of me. Lyman it is, and will always be. Never Lipsha. I settle into the bones of my defeat, sit there quiet with my hands in my lap. In my heart, I hate Lyman, but on my face a look of expecting love is pressed.

CHAPTER EIGHTEEN

LYMAN DANCING

ON THE THIRD DAY HE ROSE AND IN THE CLEARING, WHERE the sun shone down, on the edge of the dried slough, in long sharp yellow-green spears of grass, Lyman began to dance. It was the first time since Henry had died that he had not danced in his brother's clothes. It was the first time, ever, that he didn't dance for money. The air was cool, the sun a mild radiance. In places the dried mud was baked into an even floor of shaley cracks, and although his bare feet made no impression, the packed silt was powdery and soft. Among the clumps of grass, he moved with the wind, side to side, swaying in the old northern style. He trembled with the grass, did the shake dance, shoulders loose as rags. He felt no hunger and no thirst, and he wasn't tired, although he'd hardly slept. As the wind came up, as he stepped and twirled, he began to hear the singing that had begun at dawn as a murmur and complaint in his head take shape and form.

The song advanced, grew round, came closer, closer, always in fours, slowing and then picking up, until just beyond the frame of thick scrub he knew that someone—he didn't recognize who—had set down a drum. That person was joined by the other voices—one deep as a frog's bark, another hollow, an owl's request, a woman with a hawk's *keer,* an old-style victory trill, high and shattering, and then he could not distinguish one from the next—there was a whole crowd out there, singing.

Everybody thought that when Lyman danced, he was dancing for Shawnee. But no, every dance, he was dancing for Henry. In younger days there had been times he resented dancing in the shadow of his brother, always hearing those words from the announcer. *We have here our most promising grass dancer, Henry Lamartine Junior. And his brother there, Lyman, he's pretty good too.* There were times he almost thought he wouldn't shake his brother's hand coming through the line to congratulate the winners, except that he never did succeed because Henry always reached out eagerly and hugged him to his chest.

As the sun rose, heating the ground, as he continued to dance, Lyman began to wish for that shadow. For Henry not only danced before him and blocked out the sun but the glare, too. He had absorbed it and folded his brother back into his friendly shade.

When you dance, Lyman Jr., you are dancing with my ghost.

That day, as the light went down in the hills and the breeze came up, cool, Lyman once more felt his brother's shadow fall. He kept on dancing as the shadow lengthened and spread into dusk. The sun vanished and then, very clearly, from just beyond the trees, he heard Henry tell him that he should put those old dance clothes to rest.

They look beat, man, and so do you.

Then they both laughed, for when Lyman danced in those clothes, it was to keep Henry alive, to give him heart, for his drowned ghost was restless and low in spirit. Now the song came up, the words strengthened, and Lyman bent with the reeds, back and forth, side to side. His dance was all about the dusk Henry had jumped into the river, went down with his boots full of cold spring runoff, drowned. Lyman danced the water closing over, running, going and running and running, and he danced his brother losing resistance, slumping, his body feeding into the current. Then Lyman danced his own rough struggle from the freezing muscle of water where he had jumped in to grab Henry back, and failed. Leaving the water, Lyman wiped his feet along the slough bed, along the grass, wiped the mud of that river bottom off over, over again, and once again, carefully, gracefully, with completeness, hour after hour, until finally, from the drum and with the singers just past the clearing, he heard Henry's voice ride the sky.

It is calm, so calm
In that place where I am
My little brother

CHAPTER NINETEEN

ALBERTINE'S LUCK

ALBERTINE WOKE DIZZILY IN THE SMALL ROOM THAT HER mother always kept for visitors, and turned over again, pushing her face into the animal-warm pillows. Browning toast, coffee, the scent of sizzling butter, juice of berries boiling down and thickening on the stove, drew her out of sleep. She pushed her hands over her face and kicked her mother's quilts down her knees, then stumbled across the cold linoleum and dragged on socks, jeans, a sweatshirt. She had a short vacation break and her car had died twice on the way home. Much later than she was expected, almost halfway through the night, she'd pulled into her mother's driveway. Now the buzz of exhaustion and spent adrenaline surged over her. Her ears burned from the cold wind and her temples pinched and throbbed.

"Want some?"

It was Shawnee, a mug in her hands lettered in red *Yes, there is a Kalamazoo!* Albertine accepted it in both hands and breathed lightly on the steaming coffee. The thin, acid stuff went down leaving a burn like a hot thread in her chest.

"Where's Mom?"

"She went to church."

"Where's Redford?"

"With her."

The two young women could have been sisters, though Albertine was older and tired-looking, her eyes circled in dark violet stains. Her hair, a shade lighter, fell in a long sweep and sun through the window picked out streaks of red blond. She glanced at Shawnee, dropped her eyes, wondered what to say and if she had the strength to say anything at all. Her own relationship with her mother was one of careful and mutually calibrated distance. They had faced off long ago and then reached an agreement. Albertine would reveal nothing troubling or damaging to the image that her mother wished to keep of her, and for her part, Zelda would not pry for details about Albertine's life. The unstated pact had made things so much easier between them that it was hard, almost impossible, to strike a deeper chord in their conversations now.

It was enough for Zelda to know that Albertine was in medical school. That fact relieved Albertine of every other explanation. It had been enough for Albertine to know her mother had a job. Their work had given them both safe topics and easy complaints. Even Shawnee's presence had been helpful at first, removing the pressure that Zelda had often brought to bear on Albertine in the past regarding marriage, a grandchild, a larger picture for Zelda to compose around herself, its center.

"Are things any better?" Albertine was slightly more alert, knowing that once Zelda returned they wouldn't have a chance for honesty. "Have you got any plans?"

Shawnee tucked a strand of hair behind her ear. She looked down at her knees, rubbed her hands across the faded material of her jeans. She was wearing a belt with a turquoise stone butterfly buckle.

"I'm leaving here," she said, into Albertine's silence.

"Really leaving," she said to Albertine, again.

Albertine felt herself sliding, tumbling, falling back into the soft-grained emotions of her childhood. She used to crawl beneath the quilts on the bed where her mother slept on her back—rigid, alone, untouchable, like a carved statue—and she used to breathe in her mother's warmth, the smoky human closeness, the coffee, and the stale spice of her clove gum and cigarettes.

Zelda had once entered and left rooms in drifting clouds and the mousy menthol vapor was part of the whole of Albertine's love. No matter that, now, she knew all about the effects of secondhand nicotine, no matter that she didn't smoke and helped counsel patients not to, she thought of the odor as safe. She never dared fold herself against her mother, never dared to grab her tight, but only swept her lips against the porous, fine skin of her cheek, touched her work-tough fingers. Even that hurt, and once, in bed with a man she hated, paralyzed with what she'd done, Albertine had realized that the desperation with which she gave in to his touch had been no more than a child's wish to crawl closer to the side of her mother. And never mind her father, a picture in a frame.

There would be no end to what she needed from a husband, a lover. Albertine knew this at the time and understood that the only answer to her need would be realized in healing others the exact way she herself needed to be helped. It was what she saw in so many doctors, even the best ones, the most obsessed—something missing at the core, something they filled in themselves, mysteriously, by giving it entirely away.

Now, in the tiny sun-struck room, with Shawnee Ray sitting in front of her, Albertine leaned back and tried to gather all of the strings. There seemed no way at first to break the sinew of her mother's need. The tighter you pulled the tighter it held.

There was an empty place sawed out of Albertine where a child should have fit, and when Redford ran into the house her arms shot open with an ache even though he was probably not going to greet her the way she hoped. It was true, as Shawnee had said, that he had become more suspicious and watchful since the incident with the tribal police. Zelda picked him up, let him down again, and he struck the floor with sturdy quickness. With only a lowered glance in Albertine's direction he ran to his mother and welded himself to her, crawled up her legs with his hands gripping her pockets, her belt loops, until she swung him to her chest. He wrapped his legs around her waist and hung there for several moments before he turned and only then, relief breaking from inside of him, he shouted hello to Albertine. He would go to her from Shawnee, swinging his arms to meet hers, but he had to assure himself first that his mother would stay in the same room. Once, when Shawnee walked into the entryway to put away his puffy red jacket, Redford clawed his way down and wrestled from Zelda's quick snatching grip to make sure that his mother returned.

All that day, as she watched the boy and the two women, Albertine saw patterns developing in the air. A cat's cradle. Twine pulled, relaxed, made telling shapes. Later on that night, falling into sleep, she remembered her uncle Eli's hands pulling and dropping the slender designs. Lightning. Frog. Bat. Twin stars. Turtle. Chicken foot. Arrow. Women's belt and butterfly. The figures moved against the dark like trails of light.

Zelda sewed everything too tight, pulled her thread until it broke, became impatient with the way her work turned out before she halfway finished, but when the three women were working together on Redford's dance outfit, Albertine could see that Shawnee Ray bent her strength like a bow to the older women's need, that there was force in the calm way she took the needle from Zelda and pulled out stitches while Zelda fumed, threw up her hands, and went to the stove. The food that Zelda loved to make was all contained in one pan— browned rice, butter, chicken gravy, and a box of frozen peas. Shawnee Ray turned to look at what Zelda was stirring and then caught Albertine's eye.

"You two think it's so funny," Zelda remarked. "So what if I can't sew—I can type for days. That's just the way I am."

"One-pot dinner?"

Zelda turned to the side, opened her mouth, and shifted her hip. She was in a good mood, ready to be teased, happy for all of the attention directed at her.

"You complaining? After hospital food, in that cafeteria?"

"It's just that you used to be so particular, get everything just so, like Grandma. It's just that I'm used to you being so particular."

"I don't do that anymore, not since our little boy."

Shawnee's lips stiffened and although she bent to the needle, quickly bit the end off a knotted thread, Albertine saw the design.

"What do you mean 'our boy,' Mom? What about when Shawnee decides she's ready to go back to school?"

"I'll be right here to keep Redford." Zelda's voice was too firm, her eyes opened too wide, fixed, her spoon banging down too hard in the pot. "He deserves full-time care."

Albertine looked at Shawnee, leaving her the opening and the silence. But the younger woman couldn't make the words fill her mouth. She kept biting the string, looking at her hands now, shaking one finger free of the prick of her needle.

"Whether Redford goes with her or not is really Shawnee's choice, isn't it?"

Albertine strove for a cheerful tone, a coaxing normalcy, an open-ended lightness.

"Not if she's going to fool with a no-good Morrissey."

Shawnee put down the cloth and almost tipped the little plastic tubs of beads over as she violently began to straighten and put away the project that they'd all been working on. Albertine pressed her fingers to her eyes, suddenly exhausted, as if she'd been reading reports through the night and morning and was now expected to make decisions on the basis of details she'd not quite absorbed. The practice seemed to have improved her ability to reason unstated futures quickly, because now, cutting through the mess of emotions and unknown facts, she was able to state the impossible quite clearly.

"Let me get this straight. You're talking about Lipsha?"

"Should be Lyman," Zelda said tersely, plunging her spoon into the stew. "He's around here all the time, asking for her, talking to me about it. He's always asking me how come Shawnee's so furious with him, asking me what's wrong with him, how come she's changed? After all, he's Redford's natural father."

Shawnee turned a yellow tub of beads over onto the floor and the sudden spill diverted all of them. Albertine crawled after the beads, and Redford and Shawnee did too. Chasing them back and forth across the floor, they made a game of capturing the tiny glass specks and brushing them off their fingers. Zelda continued to stand at the stove and at last, when Shawnee had left the room to wash Redford, she spoke to her daughter.

"You think I'm standing in her way."

"Maybe she feels something for Lipsha."

"She'll get over it."

Albertine paused, thought a moment, and then spoke of something that had never been raised between the two of them before.

"Did you? Ever get over it?"

Zelda stopped, poised the spoon, then turned slowly to regard Albertine.

"Did I ever get over who, your father?"

"No. Him. The one before."

Zelda gave a sharp, almost hysterical croak of laughter and then turned back to the stove and busied herself, salting, peppering, finding and tasting the ingredients to her stew. She made no acknowledgment of the question and spoke of nothing related to their conversation for the rest of the evening, but kept up a stream of talk that fell between the two of them, a mild rain of inconsequences that extinguished any topic of serious regard but also signaled to Albertine the extent of the blow she had dealt her mother, the shock of recognition.

A LITTLE VISION

MY COUSIN ALBERTINE, BACK FROM MED SCHOOL, USES A careful touch to divert me from the congregation around Lyman and leads me to her car. Each leaf springs clear to me as we leave Xavier's place, each blade of quack grass and each thorny stick. You ever seen a coyote pick his way across a field? He doesn't just walk, but wends himself careful among unseen menaces and small attractions that we have no way to sense from our dimmer world. That is how my thoughts move as we drift along the gravel that has been freshened by a sprinkling of rain. We get into the car, pull onto the pitted road, and I try not to brush too hard against my sorrows. Instead, I ask Albertine about hers. Not that she has many. Albertine is doing what she wants, and I can see that although she is tired she is also sure of her path.

The window is open and the air is rushing in, probably sweet with hay and pollens though I can't smell this air, the last breeze with any summer warmth left. From now on there will be all heavier and clouded evenings awash in rain, and then the snow, which will begin early in the year and drag on without end until we're all of us worn out and gray as foiled ghosts.

"I can't think ahead," I say to Albertine. "I don't want to live."

"Take a bath in tomato juice," she suggests.

"This ain't related to my getting sprayed," I tell her. "It's an emotional thing."

"To do with Shawnee Ray?"

"That's right."

There's a long and rushing silence, trees blurring, sloughs beside us.

"Let her go to school," Albertine says. "Leave her alone until you get your own self together, Lipsha."

Her voice is low, but it easily carries within the wind that fills the front seat of the car.

"You're a hard-ass like your mother," I tell her, but my voice doesn't penetrate like hers and slides right out into the breeze that booms and sings all around us.

I mean to at least thank Albertine for the ride and all she has done to support me, and also to tell her that I do not mean to give up on Shawnee Ray, not ever, even if my battle is useless. I intend to express my regret for letting down all of those who cared about me, by not coming up with a proper vision, and on, and on, but as I start to make this speech I find my tongue has rusted from lack of use. All that I can muster is a wave from my weakened hand, a gesture.

The day is quiet, and I creep around the back way to my room without seeing anyone, just sneak in and open the door and let myself in. I put my things down and without turning on a light, even, without doing anything besides shower long and uselessly, drinking nothing more than a glass of water, I fall into the comforting wash of my bed and drift into embarrassed sleep. I just go into it, boom, and I am out of commission.

Deep in the night, I wake.

With that waking, something happens to me which I attempt to resist. I try to go back to sleep, to let the green fuzz overtake me, but instead, my thoughts connect one onto the next and I begin to remember things I do not even want to think about. I remember back through the days of my youth and then my childhood until I reach the time when I was a baby. The feelings I had then are very clear to me. For the first time, I realize what happened the moment after I was placed onto my first cradle of water, after I sank down. A darkness like the darkness that now covers me swarms up, and I drift lower. I feel the hand from which I've fallen. I feel the cool shock. I rest on the mud bottom with the stones in the sack. I open my mouth to cry and water gushes into my chest.

Gone! Gone! I am alone, the same as dead, and then I am dead. The water crushes out my life.

I lie there on the bottom of the slough all the rest of the night and the next day too, crying. It is like my whole body has been filling all of these years with a secret aquifer, a sorrow. I remember the sensation I spent my whole life trying to forget. The quick tug, the stones that tumbled, the deep of dark. I hear my mother's voice, feel her touch, and by that I know the truth. I know that she did the same that was done to her—a young girl left out to live on the woods and survive on pine sap and leaves and buried roots.

Pain comes to us from deep back, from where it grew in the human body. Pain sucks more pain into it, we don't know why. It lives, and we harbor its weight. When the worst comes, we will not act the opposite. We will do what we were taught, we who learnt our lessons in the dead light. We pass them on. We hurt, and hurt others, in a circular motion.

I am weak and small, shut in my tiny room, but I am safe. No one to hinder, no one to find, no one remembering, even my buddy Titus, who thinks I am still at Xavier's house. No one calls for Lipsha, no one knocks. It is as if I stayed down at the bottom of that slough.

And I go into it, and I kept going, for I have no strength to pull myself out.

You heard what Zelda said to me from her barstool. *So why*

weren't you drowned? I never thought about it either, since, but a long ways into the night I realize one thing: no way I could have made it alone. I was saved. And not by Zelda, not at first, but by something else, something that was down there with me. I don't know who or how, and then sometime in the night I look up into dark air and see the face.

Darkened and drenched, coming toward me from the other side of drowning—it presses its mouth on mine and holds me with its fins and horns and rocks me with its long and shining plant arms. Its face is lion-jawed, a thing of beach foam, resembling the jack of clubs. Its face has the shock of the unburied goodness, the saving tones. Its face is the cloud fate that will some day surround me when I am ready to die. What it is I don't know, I can't tell. I never will. But I do know I am rocked and saved and cradled.

No wonder, as Zelda reports it, I smiled.

Now that I have unwillingly remembered all the past, I counsel myself that I should get up and live my life a new and normal person, but like I said, I am so weak that I just lie in my waterbed. The pictures and stories and sights do not relent. I go farther, see more. I unroll my whole childhood and go on into the present, until I pass myself up and I get the future. It is so ordinary and so demanding all at once that at first I can't understand it. There is no punch to it, no great convening dramas, and it makes me all dismayed, it is so small.

Here is the gist of what I see and hear. There is a voice all right, but it is coming out of that damn skunk. That creature is a nuisance! Even here, in my room, I am not safe from that animal. It putters over, slick and determined, and it jumps back onto my chest. I see it through the dark.

This ain't real estate, it nags at me.

I'm tired of waiting for a vision and just getting this unpleasant refrain, so I lash out.

"Go back where you came from," I order it. "Shut up and quit bothering me. I got enough to think about."

The animal blinks its brilliant black marble eyes at me, all curious.

"I'm not kidding," I threaten.

You're a slow learner like they all said, despite your A.C.T.s.

"You must have sneaked in the back way," I say. "Or did you get here in my sleeping bag?"

There's no answer.

"Okay." I finally give up. "Tell me something I don't know."

And that's when I get the vision.

The new casino starts out promising. I see the construction, the bulldozers scraping off wild growth from the land like a skin, raising mounds of dirt and twisted roots. Roads are built, trees shaved, tar laid onto the new and winding roads. Stones and cement blocks and wood are hauled into the woods, which is no longer a woods, as the building is set up and raised. It starts out as revenue falling out of the sky. I see clouds raining money into the open mouths of the tribal bank accounts. Easy money, easy flow. No sweat. No bother. I see money shining down like sunshine into Lyman Lamartine's life. It comes thick and fast and furious.

This ain't real estate, the skunk says again.

Of course, that skunk is right, for the complex is slated to develop Pillager land, partly Fleur's land and partly old allotments that the tribe holds in common, and which is fractionated through the dead and scattered holdouts who have never signed the treaties that gave away so much of what we called ours.

Where Fleur's cabin stands, a parking lot will be rolled out of asphalt. Over Pillager grave markers, sawed by wind and softened, blackjack tables. Where the trees that shelter brown birds rise, bright banks of slot machines. Out upon the lake that the lion man inhabits, where Pillagers drowned and lived, where black stones still roll round to the surface, the great gaming room will face with picture windows. Twenty-four-hour bingo. I see the large-scale beauty of it all, the thirty-foot screens on which a pleasant-voiced young girl reads the numbers of balls, day in and day out. Auditorium seats, catered coffee, free lunch. State-of-the-art markers, electronic boards. I see the peach and lime interior, the obedient lines of humans all intent on the letters and the numbers that flash on the twin screens telling how near, how far, how close to the perfect dreamstuff they're coming.

I try to be polite, then, even gentle.

"Excuse me," I say, "I got the wrong vision. Could you change the channel?"

To what?

"I don't know. Maybe to some horses who split the sky with their hooves. Or a bear, an eagle with a bald head and long brown wings to carry me a saying to mess with Lyman's mind."

There's more.

And I argue out loud.

"I see it another way!" I cry. "I see the casino dome, the rounded shape, maybe of a great stone turtle. I see it winking and glittering under all those lights! The old ones used to say you eat turtle heart, you win at cards. I hear the hush of bells, continual, a high and ringing money-mutter, and the slick sigh of bills changing hands. I feel the cash in my fingers. New twenties so fine they stick to one another. I hear the dinging and the silvery chatter of coins sliding down the chutes, quarters upon quarters upon tokens upon lovely silver dollars. And oh, here's best part. I see the dealer dealing me face up, and I am hitting on each hand, yes, hitting once and hitting twice, and the other customers are saying *Good hit, Lipsha,* putting their money down with mine, more and more of it in piles and drifts. Because I'm lucky, don't you get it, don't you see?"

And these words come next, and last.

Luck don't stick when you sell it.

"Mine does," I insist, but inside me, I know that damn skunk is right.

Then I sleep for a long while and when I wake it is bright, it is morning, and I am new and ready to begin the day that dawns. There is a small strip of field between the littered parking lot of the bar, which I must clean, and the housing area of small windblown trailers and prefabs where Lyman Lamartine lives. I walk out there and with a mind full of hard thoughts I stand by popple scrub, in tall grass, blown over and harsh, green and dry. From my low vantage, I consider the modest huddle of human development. The thing is, I already know the outcome, and it's more or less a gray area of tense negotiations. It's not completely one way or another, traditional against the bingo. You have to stay alive to keep your tradition alive and working. Everybody knows bingo money is not based on solid ground. The Mindemoya's took to Lyman, though, even appeared to him somehow in a dream, or so he said. People used to say she was waiting for me to visit in order to pass on her knowledge, but that's not true. Fleur Pillager is a poker sharp, along with her other medicines. She wants a bigger catch, a fish that knows how to steal the bait, a clever operator who can use the luck that temporary loopholes in the law bring to Indians for higher causes, steady advances.

And yet I can't help wonder, now that I know the high and the low of bingo life, if we're going in the wrong direction, arms flung wide, too eager. The money life has got no substance, there's nothing left when the day is done but a pack of receipts. Money gets money, but little else, nothing sensible to look at or touch or feel in yourself down to your bones. I can't help think that Fleur Pillager has made the best of what gives here by tapping Lyman for the long term. As for the short, what the skunk said is right. Our reservation is not real estate, luck fades when sold. Attraction has no staying power, no weight, no heart.

CHAPTER TWENTY-ONE

GERRY'S LUCK

MONTHS WENT BY AND HE LIVED ONLY FOR THE DREAMS—
bright, monotonous, unwinking dreams in which he led a
thoroughly boring everyday life. To sleep in a bed wider than
himself, to shit behind a closed door, to walk a curved road, a
straight road, a ditch, to make love, to make love, he would
never stop making love, eating steak, eating hash browned
potatoes. Fried potatoes. Bangs. Fry bread. To watch his last
wife, Dot, knit solemnly and fiercely, frowning at each stitch.
To see his children. To stand still as a doe detached from a
screen of brush, to put aside the rifle, forget venison with mustard, to watch the animal swivel her intelligent ears, watch
ducks land, watch light gather blue dark in the eyes of a
woman, his daughter, his son, to walk inside of a house, out,
in, to open a door with your own hands.

In solitary, he stared at his foot until it changed to a paw.
He chewed his paws and wept and let his hair grow long,
coursing down his back. He said the name of his wife a thousand times every morning. Dot, Dot, Dot. A mantra. Morse
code. She called him every week, even after the divorce.
Remarried, she kept on calling him but still, after a time, it was
another woman who began to obsess Gerry. He drew June's
face on notebook paper, a woman of leaves, rain, snow, clouds.
She was a storm in his dreams and her teeth were lightning.

She was a little brown mink stealing bait on his trapline, a curve in air, a comma, winking and unwinking. All day he stared at the crack beside the door and thought *windigo, windigo,* because he had a flu, a fever that made the cell bloom and collapse, and he remembered the stories of Old Man Nanapush.

In a voice like a wind-strummed reed, Nanapush spoke from his bed, where he sat all day that winter, falling over into sleep at night. He told of the ice giant shoving cracked floes between drifts of his lips, chewing ice bones with ice teeth, sinking frozen into view from frozen clouds. For two days Gerry's cell breathed to life, walls disappeared, and then the world shrunk back to itself again and his mind hid underneath a black cloth. His mind was deepest sky, dreamless and pure, his thoughts black earth. He smelled dirt and new rain. Prison smells were chemical, or sweat, milky disinfectant, piss, old piss, metallic breath, the aftershave on guards. His own smell was of a dog. The dog his mother kept—tick-bit, rangy and half feral.

His intuition told him there would be a low whistle when it happened, a warning, but there was nothing. Just papers. Tribal council papers with his mother's name obscure. The tribe had taken an interest, and under the Indian Religious Freedom Act brought him near his medicine advisors. Lulu Lamartine's name was merely set down with the rest of them but her forceful wrangling was behind every single other signature, he knew. Minnesota prisons were renting cells. There was one available in Minnesota's new maximum-security facility and he would be transferred there. Fine! Fine! Oh fuck! Something surged in him like true love at the prospect of being somewhere, anywhere else, and he looked forward to the ride like a child, impatient for the power of different clouds, the brush of a different wind.

He was issued a jacket, boots, a hat, army mittens. The hat had earflaps that tied on top like a lumberjack's. Not only would he have to wait in deep cold for the plane, but once there he'd have time to walk around outdoors. Minnesota, land of changing seasons! Land of 10,000 Lakes and happy Vikings. Land of Chippewas, land of Sioux, land of weak coffee and fiberglass walleyes. Kind and righteous Minnesota, land of weight machines, real eggs, deep-fried doughnuts, iced Long Johns, and for some reason birthday cakes galore. Why did he see, all night in his mind, big square sheets of pink-frosted birthday cakes, sugar heavy, lettered in white, dimpled, fluted. Land of 10,000 Birthday Cakes. Land of mushy sloughs, wheeling honkers, ranging wolves, and pleasant women, earnest Swedish women, staunch political support.

When he woke in the white blast of light at four thirty they did it all—packed his things into a duffel bag, locked his hands in front of him, walked him out to the federal marshals who politely asked him please to stand still as they attached leg irons and a transport belt. The cuff and chain hobble around his ankles allowed him to walk like a man with his pants down around his feet. His arms fit snugly, buckled to his waist. He hugged himself. And it was better, as the car moved, as the view began to change—so much view, so many trees—better than he could have fucking dreamed.

Fucking dreamed! His thoughts, on fire, wheeled in bright array. To see the trees in changing rows, fields, the curious white suburban ranches, farms, huddled trailers, too much going by all at once. Too much! And from the hangar, wanging like a cracked radiator, laughter and an argument he didn't catch the drift of, back and forth, between the marshals and the pilot.

As they lifted off and gravity pressed him back into the vinyl seat, he felt his luck coming back, floating down on him like a nylon net to drag him to the top. He shut his eyes. He could feel the weight of his body, smell burnt plastic, acid coffee. Pleasure wrapped him so suddenly that he thought his bones would crack. Then they were out of the steep ascent, leveling off, and he saw raw pink light, the sunrise twist and burn.

He knew from sitting in the still eye of chance that fate was not random. Chance was full of runs and soft noise, pardons and betrayals and double-backs. Chance was patterns of a stranger complexity than we could name, but predictable. There was no such thing as a complete lack of order, only a design so vast it seemed unrepetitive up close, that is, until you sat doing nothing for so long that your brain ached and, one day, just maybe, you caught a wider glimpse.

Some people, lightning struck twice. Some people attracted accidents. Fate bunched up and gathered like a blanket. Some people were born on the smooth parts and some got folded into the pucker. When the engine skipped and chattered and burped back into its drawl, Gerry opened his eyes, alert, and asked if there wasn't some way to remove the bar from his legs while airborne.

"Can't do it."

The marshals were firm, professional, both slim and tall, though with opposite coloring and a difference of twenty years or so in age. One was all shades of sand, tan hair and thick eyelashes too, and the other was black haired with pale green eyes and a lumped-out jutting chin. The sand-colored one leaned back into his seat to doze, and the dark one by agreement kept his eyes fixed upon the prisoner. They were well trained, confident, with nothing to prove, and Gerry felt safe with them.

The sky went dark again.

"We're moving through a storm system," the pilot called back into the cabin, then all they heard was the sound of his effort as he strove to guide the small craft into wind. There was a long period of turbulence, and several times the air seemed to have been yanked out from under them like a magic carpet, so that they quickly dropped altitude.

"Ah, shit."

It was the pilot. His voice registered a thrill of regret. Gerry looked out of the window and saw the white earth, the branches of bare trees, rush so quickly up from below that he scarcely had time in his surprise to roll into a cannonball. Crash position. But the landing wasn't so much a crash as a peculiar distortion of time and space in which things moved soundlessly, and afterward, what he remembered of it was an almost liquid passion of disruption and then silence. Quiet snow. One eye was banged shut like a cupboard. The sun was up all around him and the white world glowed like the inside of a giant coffee cup.

The sandy-haired marshal hung still. The other—he couldn't see the other, or the pilot. Smoke puffed from the mangled tail and Gerry squeezed himself tighter, rolled off the split seat and through a gap torn into the fabric of the cabin. Once outside the plane in a litter of wreckage, in falling snow, he knelt to recover his balance and slowly stood on his feet and then began to hobble-hop, the prisoner's two-step. He drove himself through crossed brush, skirted stands of cattails and reeds and kept hopping. And all the while, as he moved, not cold in the least because of the effort, his life kept surging up between his feet, his bound wrists, welling up like black water when you step on thin ice, spreading up through his arms, choking him, practically killing him with the accumulated joy.

CHAPTER TWENTY-TWO

ESCAPE

I TURN DEEP INTO MYSELF AFTER ALBERTINE'S ADVICE THAT I
should let Shawnee go while I retrieve myself and better my
position in life. As it turns out, I don't have any choice.
Shawnee leaves the reservation after gaining back the custody
of Redford, and for a while I hear nothing of her, then learn
she is enrolling at the university. "In the arts, in the arts," people say, with a rhythm in their voices that means although
dubious at least there is a name to her future. I put my hand
on the phone, draw it back, and then finally call information. I
carry Shawnee's number around in my shirt pocket like a lucky
sweepstakes and occasionally read it out fondly. Sometimes I
even dial, let the phone ring just once, and hang up. In that act
I see myself as her guardian angel, announcing my presence,
my faraway affections, but not demanding so much as the
complication of a friendly hello.

For my love is larger than it was before she blasted it with
fire. It was a single plant, a lovely pine, but now seeds,
released from their cones at high temperatures, are floating
everyplace and taking root on every scraped bare piece of
ground. My love before she got so mad was all about what
was best for Lipsha Morrissey. Since those endless moments
of truth and rage in Zelda's yard, I have reconsidered. If my
love is worth anything, it will be larger than myself. Which is

229

not to say I don't dream about motels, her body moving, and read sex books and thrillers and my Gideon's for more inspiration.

One night, I am at the dizzying bloody part, all of the ways in which King David smites right and left, and I am trying to get a handle on what lesson I might learn. All I keep seeing is a ninja dressed up in old-time robes. You read Samuel and see if you don't see the same. I page forward to Chapter 17 of Kings where Elijah lays himself over a child three times and prays for the kid's soul to return to its body. He finally brings this child to life, and then he delivers the revived boy back to his mother. This is more my type of scenery and I build up a picture of myself as Elijah, saving Shawnee Ray's son for her. The concept is so rewarding that I douse my light and lie down on my bed, in the dark, and I begin to project a career of doing this sort of savior work, which makes Shawnee Ray so grateful that she doesn't just apologize, she anoints my head with oil and washes my feet with her hair like those long-ago women did to show their appreciation for a kindness.

I can feel her hair coil around my feet, my ankles. I can feel her tears of regret and thankfulness upon my legs, her face gently touching my knee, and then leaning in her sorrow on my thighs and then by accident, just by sheer accident at first, losing her balance a slight bit and grasping at my belt loop and then trying to right herself but slipping on that water and oil and putting her warm face to me. Like magic, then, my robes part. God, how the Red Sea burns! I rewind the tape to play it again, go back to the beginning where I am just dragging Shawnee Ray's son from water, say, and using the CPR ability that I learned in high school, when I suddenly sit up in my bed in a dizzy rush.

I am sure she sees me, sure I see her, and I know that we will be together in the way most ultimate. We can't vision what the future harbors, and we are blind to our approaching fate. I have to hope that my long and faithful trudge toward heaven will not be ignored. I have to believe that surely we will be together in some subdivision of the higher ground.

Cheerfully, saving for the future, I go off to bingo. Though dark rumors abound, my winnings are now taken for granted. I am considered lucky, that simple. People envy, people grumble, but nobody challenges the assumption. I am the only one who can see the mounting figures in my joint account.

Night after night, I let the numbers accumulate until it just so happens that I go to the bank. There, I chance to find the actual amount in the book is zero, not closed by a stranger, but by Lyman Lamartine, joint account signer. I say nothing to him, although the steady pattern on the ground is tossed directly into focus: through my winnings, my uncle has paid up on loan moneys, questionable and necessary transactions. He has made the bottom line. I was the conduit, the easy mark, my name the temporary storage. I was the pool in an indoor-plumbed wishing well. Lyman kept his money going round and round, recycled his dollars through me. And yet, I don't get upset and I don't get overbearing or complain. I just stop going to the bingo.

For my luck has turned uncertain. My luck is pollen and chaff. Sprinkled onto me by Lyman's schemes, it was merely sucker's fortune.

Drifts of bright leaves collect around me, and then the driving snow. For the whole autumn season into winter, I do nothing but work at a slow driving pace. Christmas comes, I ignore the jolly caverns and parties, and New Year's Eve, too, with its blast of booze and sound. I don't want to make predictions, and have no reason for taking on any self-improving vows. I go into one of my mental hibernations to think and figure. I am laid up alone in January, then, staring at the ceiling above me when I hear the news. I don't even have a radio or television going in my room. I don't even have my phone hooked up after I ripped it from the plug one night spent willing it with reddened eyes to ring.

I am thinking of nothing in particular when the screen in my head goes all irrational, buzzes with noise and static, then blanks out.

What's happening? I wonder to myself.

And before you know it I am sleeping, and not only that but dreaming a bad dream that I am in a jail, in the night that never is a night but always full of sighs and noises and hollers, full of clanking and never wholly dark, either, so that confusion of the senses overtakes judgment. I resent the gray fuzz, that fake night, and know I'll wake meaner than when I slept.

This is my father's night, and all of a sudden I am beside him, there in the all-night workroom of the laundry where he washes and folds. I see him working with billows of clothes, of pillowcases and such, simple jumpsuits, underwear, socks. He is surrounded by heavy machinery and he keeps on folding, drying, dragging twisted wet laundry from big tumblers. I wake with that square of prison light still shining in my head. I have dreamed my father real on many occasions, but I never had a picture like this one, so authentic and full of the assurance of him, so perfect in its knowledge.

I wait, to find out what it means, and by noon of the next day word filters through the bar. People entering for quick lunches tell me of the startling event. I hear it first from Titus, who knows my blood connection with the escapee. In previous breakouts, Gerry Nanapush has foiled guards, shrunk himself through an opening no larger than a pie box, somehow managed to torque himself into the body of a truck that drives through the gates with him clinging underneath. He has hid in the trunk of June's car when I was at the wheel. He has climbed drainpipes and appeared within public spaces. This time, it seems, he flew. He was in transit—nobody knows where for sure, but the rumors congregate around the efforts of Grandma Lulu to get him transferred. Yes, that is Gerry No-shit-barn-built-can-hold-a-Chippewa Nanapush. Same as ever, running free.

I race back to my room, where the phone is still ripped from its little jack, and I reconnect myself back to the outside world. I hope a wavelength will now summon me. My number is in the book, the marked bone is in the left hand, the sinner's hand, the gambler's hand. I know I'll get a call.

Midnight.

"Hey."

"You."

"Yeah."

"Phone booth?"

"Fargo."

I want to ask where in Fargo and for a long moment I ponder how, in case the line is tapped. But he takes care of that for me and into the yawn of space between us says some words in the old-time language. The syllables bunch and go by fast, but I catch at them before the phone buzzes smooth. I memorize what I heard, but as I scope out his intention for the next hour, I become confused. My father is either playing Star Wars games at Art's Arcade, or he is holed up at the Fargo library, or he is hiding curled up in the lodge dumpster of the Sons of Norway.

Here's the thing. Except for that evening at Fleur Pillager's, when terror caused me to understand every word that came through, loud and clear, I don't know our traditional language all that well. Now the lack catches up with me. To my horror, I'm not sure what my father revealed to me on the phone. I work out each word with a pencil, then erase it. I fix on each syllable, slippery as a minnow. In the end, however, all I can make out are these three strange possibilities. It occurs to me, though, that I'd better get to Fargo before the library closes tomorrow or before Dad runs out of quarters or before the day of civic garbage pickup.

And so, tossing on my heaviest clothes, grabbing from the bar rack some bags of nuts and jerky, I make ready to take the van.

* * *

When you're driving the sweet empty roads between home and Fargo, endless and empty possibilities surround you. That's the view I like, all nothing particular. Sky, field, and the signs of human attempts to alter same so small and unimportant and forgettable as you whiz by. I like blending into the distance. Passing shelter belts and fields that divide the world into squares, I always think of the chaos underneath. The signs and boundaries and markers on the surface are laid out strict, so recent that they make me remember how little time has passed since everything was high grass, taller than we stand, thicker, with no end. Beasts covered it. Birds by the million. Buffalo. If you sat still in one place they would parade past you for three days, head to head. Goose flocks blotted the sun, their cries like great storms. Bears. No ditches. Sloughs, rivers, and over all the winds, the vast winds blowing and careening with nothing in the way to stop them—no buildings, fence lines to strum, no drive-in movie screens to bang against, not even trees.

I park outside Art's Arcade, a twenty-four-hour video gaming enterprise. No sign of Gerry, not yet. I walk inside and after I carefully scout the men's room, outskirts, the other players, I myself start playing, so as not to arouse suspicion. For about an hour, I play, then all of the drop-outs enter, the hooky-players. Beeps accelerate, mass destruction occurs, shifting futures. Blips of light dodge mad mummies and mine disasters, and street fighters groan and gripe at each other. From time to time, I am sure I feel Gerry's gaze rub through my jacket, hear his voice at my sleeve. But the minutes skim by into hours as the quarters flash off my fingers. I keep playing because I want him to see me winning when he enters. And so I spend quarter after quarter, save worlds without name, only to find when I turn around he has still not shown.

Morning floats by, dead on its feet, then afternoon.

I try to calculate what has happened. Outside, in the deep-ening cold, he might have stolen a car only to find that the bat-tery dies. There is probably corrosion on his spark plugs, a frosted gas line, cracked tires. One picture in my mind features Dad with a pair of jumper cables coiled in his arms. I see him patiently attach them to his terminals, and then step back while I press down the gas. Life roars into the engine. Still, he doesn't show. The afternoon drags out and in time another episode forms. This one has my dad bound and handcuffed, sitting tight in the backseat between two smokies, who are writing in their pocket notebooks.

Gerry Nanapush is wanted by the entire combined police force of North America, but no sooner do they catch him, he dissolves their shackles. He's not made of human stuff. Rain melts him. Snow turns him to clay. The sun revives him. He's a Chippewa. Yet in spite of his talents, he always does end up getting caught, and that is my fear, that is why I play hour after hour, until I have just one quarter remaining.

I turn around, sly, but Art himself catches me and points to the sign One Play Every Half Hour or Get Lost. He stands behind his register, cracking Russian peanuts and blowing the shells between his teeth. I pull my quarter out and hold it up for his approval. It is damp and sleek from touching, not just a piece of money, but a cool little circle of hope. I flip it once, and play an old-time classic.

A special current floats through me when the asteroids come whirling from all sides. Desperate concerns have tuned my reflexes razor fine. The controls warm to my hand, fuse flush to my nerves so I cannot miss. My mind pulls apart from my body, tugs off the screen, and hovers over me, impervious, in calm control. The watchers bunch around me, exploding their lips, punching air, urging me along. I don't need them. The score ticks high, higher. I go to the limit where there is no contest and the machine plays with me. I hit the edge. And then, I go further. I punch through all resistance into the white center of my mind.

Where I know he won't be waiting.

That's when the nerve cuts. My hands fly off the buttons. I turn, push my way out through the crowd, and another kid jumps into my place and starts firing. But he can't pull it out. The boulders keep falling and dividing until they crush his rocket in a flash of pulsing noise.

Outside, it's so far below zero that the wind stiffens my face to a paper mask. It's early dark, and I get right into the bingo van to start it warming. I put the key into the ignition. I turn the key. Something clicks. There is an instant in which I'm completely hollowed, then I revive. I push the gas down, let up. I turn the key again with confidence. A twanging click, this time. The worst sound in dead of winter. I wait, freezing, turn the key again. I'm frantic, but no matter how I sweat and beg nothing happens any different. I've left the headlights on all day and run the battery down to nothing. There's no one up the street, no one down. I don't even have a dime to call a tow truck.

I zip up my army jacket, pull down my Vikings face mask, stick my hands in my pockets, and start walking toward the library, the second possibility I heard or misheard on our telephone conversation. All I can bank on is that when I find Dad he'll know how to hot-wire the vehicle, how to get it going. At the very least, he's bound to have ideas on how to scare up some cash.

The wind barges against me and I draw my hands up into my sleeves. The air is dangerous, thin to breathe as a scaling knife. My footsteps crackle. No one is outdoors. I keep walking, watching from the eye holes of my mask for some bar, hotel lobby, garage, anyplace to stand for a moment out of the wind. But the spaces grow between the buildings. The streets turn longer, wider, and I cross the downtown mall. It is too cold for life-forms in downtown Fargo, too cold for even me. I am thinking that I might end up as a municipal lawn ornament, a parking meter, mouth froze open to receive the night's spare change, when among the leftover Christmas mangers and hydrants the lighted castle of a building draws me across the snowy street. And there it is.

There are great squares of glass, rectangles of golden warmth that stream onto the snow in a rich, full invitation. I walk up the stone steps, push through the doors with my elbows, stand there, a stunned animal. Forced hot air blows over me, gentle and from far away. The mask has shifted on my face so I can hardly see out, and my arms are still locked around my chest.

As long as I walk around pretending to browse for something to read, chances are no one will tell me to leave. Behind my face mask I'm not anyone special, not an Indian even, just another half-froze Vikings fan. I put my hands through the sleeves, through cylinders of trapped and frozen air, and hold my breath. Then I walk upstairs and down the carpet, down the narrow rows.

In my line of work as night watchman, I depend on books. I read terror for the purpose of staying alert, I seek out mysterious crime, scare myself so bad that each creak means doom at the hands of the Undead, or a psychopath, and only the rising sun brings guaranteed safety. In the library, here, I look for the terror, the crime adventure, the space wars or weird occurrence titles to keep my motivation. As I wander the rows searching for Gerry, I warm too quickly, and now suddenly I'm tired. My arms and legs are huge and heavy. My brain fills with star noise. I want to stretch out on the floor between the rows, drift into a blessed sleep. But I have to keep moving, up and down, grab books and pretend to scan the first page. I can't help stumbling from time to time and I'm afraid the authorities will think I'm drunk, kick me out. Snow is falling through my mind.

"Can I help you?"

It's a man's voice. I make like I don't hear him and walk quickly through the shelter of stacks of volumes.

Fateful coincidence. Things happen you can't deny. Good advice speaks from graves and love hints from the hearts of trees. Bags of light float through open windows on a summer night. Horses count with the knock of their hooves. Children are born who can add up unbelievable numbers. These things are possible.

I see the book through the gunner's vision of the eye holes in my face mask and my hands reach for it without any command of my conscious brain. Luckily, I know enough to brace myself before I read the title.

Fear and Trembling, it says, *and the Sickness unto Death.*

I shut my eyes and for a minute I sway in the mystery. I am staring down, off the railings of a bridge, into a river that is treacherous, full of suck holes and underground streams. I have looked into that river once, and thought I'd crossed it for good on my way back to reservation home ground. The title of that book drives back upon me like the current of that river, flowing north, certain in its course with no meandering, no pardon. I feel how fragile I've strung my own heart above that river, like a bridge of spiderwebs.

I open my eyes. It is a small dark volume with a covering like burnt skin. The title confronts me again, no letup. I stare straight back. I hold the book, careful, in my hands, and then I open it, random, to see my fate or pick a name out of it. I drop my finger on the words. *If, at the foundation of things, there lay only a wildly seething power* . . . I read. I consider. I think of the river in its misdirection, the fickle current, and the flood that washes out bridges and the porches of homes. I want to believe in the spirit, the order, the will, the blame. I want to believe in the blessed book where no stone can crumble, no arrow fall. But God won't be watching when they take my father up the hill.

* * *

The Sons of Norway lodge is large, as are the Sons of Norway who belong to it, strapping and bold. At the back of the building, I find the trash cans, covered by one large drift that has heavily swirled down and through which I try to dig with my hands. It is like trying to force a rock apart, and I fail as the snow is packed too tight. Dad has to be in there, I think in panic, Dad sealed alive.

I turn away from the snow-packed dumpster behind the lodge, and go looking for a shovel, but in all of the surrounding blocks there is nothing even useful or resembling one—just shut buildings. The great lights burn high on their poles and by counting their vague halos I keep track of where I am, know how to get back, and yet, though I continue to walk neat square upon neat expanding square I do not find what I am looking for. I only pass empty doorways, barred windows, lightless, empty, as if Fargo was all taped-up boxes and the people inside stunned and still as shoes.

And then, as I walk through a bleak alleyway, back toward the Sons of Norway, a gust of brash wind slings the giant Frisbee of an aluminum garbage-can lid right into my chest, knocking out my wind but giving me the proper tool. I barrel back, holding the lid hard to me against the wind. When I get to the place I dig into that drift with the top of the can and I pull snow, drag it, clear it. I manage to get down to the lid. I pry it open, lift it up, and then wait for my father to jump out like a spring-loaded child's toy.

Around me the wind swirls and blows and whistles through the lamps and roofs of the city like a flock of crazed swans. Nothing. I climb up, peer in. Not only is there nobody home in the dumpster but there is no scrap of garbage, not a cardboard box, a wisp of paper. Immediately, in my mind, expectations and pictures bloom. I see my father tumbled out of sleep into a big white Scandinavian garbage truck and hear those gears grind, those strong jaws champ. My thoughts reel shut on the possibilities, my mind is overstrained. I stumble along the lodge wall until I meet his open arms.

There, in the driving wind, Gerry Nanapush. Regular size and big as life.

Or not so big, maybe, for it looks to me that even covered in shelves of wool and parka hood and blanket though he is, my father is smaller, even diminished beneath. His face has contracted around the bones, and there are tired lines around his eyes, so deep that I can see them in the faint aura of the parking lot spotlights. We stand against the wall breathing hard. Neither of us speaks and for a while there is just the sound of the wind sighing and battering. He finally leans over and asks where our transportation is, and then I have to tell him that June's car is stolen and my van's frozen dead. When he understands this, he seems to lose his control. Whirling, he turns and slams his arms once against the building. Then he flips around and hops up and down to bring the blood back to his feet. He drags me down to a little side-cellar just next to the door, where a vent blows heat straight upon us, melting, at least, my strained lips so I can talk. We cut right through the greeting, through the where-the-hell-were-you's, and come immediately to the desperate business of what-the-hell-we-do-next.

CHAPTER TWENTY-THREE

ZELDA'S LUCK

ONE AFTERNOON DURING THE FIRST MONTHS AFTER SHAWNEE and Redford left her house, Zelda Kashpaw walked in the front door and found, lying on her spangled kitchen counter, the softly tanned and quilled bag containing her father's ceremonial pipe—an object she hadn't seen since well before his death. She knew it came from Marie through Lipsha, from him through the hands of Lyman Lamartine. She knew it was his way of reaching her and of conceding the unspoken failure of their truce. She walked around the pipe all that day, without touching or moving it, cooked her dinner, boiled her coffee the old way, in a blue enamel pot on top of the stove.

From a dark sleep that same night, her heart woke her, loudly drumming. The pounding in her chest was so sudden that she didn't recognize the sound as coming from her own body. A painful lightness bloomed beneath her ribs and her heart surged powerfully, gathering speed, galloping until she gasped and sat bolt upright in fear. She saw her heart explode from her chest and continue to dance, hot and fierce, alone along the snowy fields, the frozen sloughs, the staggered lines of fences. It twirled out of her and broke in the raving dusk. A pigeon in halves, a dove in threes, ripped velvet pillows.

Zelda shook her head, reached over and pressed the switch on her little bulldog lamp. In its soft glare she inhaled cautiously, trying to quiet the valves and pumps, but her breath squeezed in and out. Her chest muscles hurt, she gasped profusely, and it became clear at last that she was having a heart attack. When that fact sank in, she immediately became more calm. Death, she understood. She grew officious about herself, slammed pillows around to prop her back and then leaned into them, arranged herself to be found. She smoothed her hair along her shoulders, placed the lines in her quilt just so. She did not call for help because she did not want saving. No CPR. Preparing a serene pose, she brushed her face into a smile, threaded her rosary between her fingers, and said an act of perfect contrition.

She couldn't think of anything that she was sorry for, at first, and then the sight of Redford's stunned, chocolate-stained face, the sounds of his sudden night terrors, caused her to grip the beads tighter in her fist. Small things came back, losses of her temper, pieces of rage she could not control around her father and her mother. She made a devout penance, and then, right in the middle of her Hail Mary, the picture thudded. Zelda saw herself twisted in bedsheets, naked, lying with her arms around a man with long, dark hair, and she took her breath so harshly that the immediate pain made her cry out. The pictures kept on coming. The scenes she'd missed would not stop, not blur, and that is when she came to realize that, in her life, she was sorrier for the things she had not done than for the things that she had.

The wrong things! She was sorry for the wrong things!

Light shortened and built in the gray windows of her bedroom, and the breeze stirred. Far off in a neighbor's field she heard the groan of a cow, and although she knew what the sound was, she pictured something else. Her hands trembled, her breath again weakened. The sounds came closer and her whole body shook.

She was a house coming apart, the nails, each in turn, wrenched from the wood with a sob, the boards bounding off

like blows, wheeling end over end in a dark wind, punishing
the fields, the house in pieces gliding over dark snow, the inner
beams shouting *huhnh, huhnh, huhnh,* panting with the sound
of a woman giving birth.

She closed her eyes. A startling and painful radiance
flooded her. Ice shattered. Her heart thawed unbearably, an
unfrozen fist.

Another thing! She glared, thrashed her arms. In her mind
someone stood before her. Another thing! She'd heard this old
medicine could still be worked. Someone was trying to kill
her. Someone had scratched a bark drawing of her, detailed,
meticulous, all her insides etched out in empty strings. Into
those lines that person had rubbed red clay, ochre, rouge, an
owl's thick blood, until the color reached her heart's knob. So
let it burst! Her heart was an old hand-iron that clanged
against her ribs, hot and hissing. She wouldn't mind setting
down such a heavy weight.

Quit, she ordered. *Quit!*

But the grip of her own life continued so strong it amazed
and disgusted her. She braced herself, rose for a glass of water,
and her hair fanned, deep as rain, across her rigid shoulders.
She was afraid to look in the mirror, afraid to see an old
woman with her father's stern face, so instead she peered into
the dawn window. But her father was there, watching her with
her own eyes, the fire of the sunrise surrounding his features.

It was the same fire that bent behind him thirty years ago,
peculiar and sudden, the wall of bursting darts. Flames rose in
her eyes again, the brand and shame of Lulu Lamartine's
house, raging out of control. And she there to see it and see
her father, she the one who had to drag him back home to her
mother, while she let the witch burn. But she wouldn't burn.

That was the effect of passion on a life. Zelda nodded,
caught up in seeing it all happen again. She passed her hands
before Nector Kashpaw's features, pushed them back into the
frieze of leaping flames. He started the fire that bounded cat-

like through wastepaper and rags, up a gas line, and destroyed his lover's house. To get even with him, Zelda would unmake him inside of herself. She never would be subject to love, never would be overtaken. Able to choose, to use her head and starve her heart, that was Zelda. She was capable of hovering in a blanket, in a room where her own breath rose and fell, a plume of longing, all night. She could exist in the dark cell of her body. She was capable of denying herself everything tender, unspoken, sweet, generous, and desperate. She could do it because she willed it. She could live in the shell of her quilt as the cold night lengthened, and she could let a man's fires flash and burn, flash and burn, until they disappeared. Again, she watched Xavier waste his fingers to the stubs like candles, one by one.

Her heart strummed sickeningly, now, and she stumbled back to her bed. She was sure that she could hold in these emotions—she had done so all of her life! Instead, she cried out, as she never had allowed herself in birth, and her cry was the old desire, a groan deep as a tree pulled over in a storm. Roots surged from the dirt. Curved arms dragged boulders to light. When the taproot came, violent, she leaned over on her bed certain that she'd die, but something else happened.

She took one calm breath, another, and then her heart grew quiet. It tipped back and forth, a muted bell. In that stilled ring disturbing thoughts were forced upon her—faint pictures, portraits. She saw Xavier Toose, how his arms were wrapped like clubs for a solid year while they healed into a shape that would never hold her. She saw his face, the haunted starkness of that arrested smile. Hollowed, drained, she overheard him when they sang at the drum those years after. He left his hair loose, as if in mourning, and it flowed down his back, heavy, with an animal scent. She stood behind him, breathing in the darkness of his neck, his throat, the woodsmoke and the clean male sweat, the tannins of his hide shoes. She heard his voice—loose, low, raw—the spirit voice that came on him deep in song, like the voice in the shaking tent, unseen, a rejoicing howl. Her chest was hot, split open. Shame covered her as she recalled a time she had been sitting to one side and not quite listening as he talked to some younger men. They asked how he acquired so many women, what his secret could be, and he raised his one blunt hand.

"True," he said, "I don't have everything you guys have. And yet . . ." He gazed thoughtfully and fixedly down past his belt buckle, so that all of their eyes followed and witnessed the obedient and sudden alertness there.

She had turned furiously away from their laughter. Now, she fought the understanding that all of her grown life she had cared for him with a secret unkilled feeling stronger than acids, unquenched, a coal fire set inside of her and running through each vein with a steady heat. She loved Xavier Toose.

"And I always will, and I always will," she said out loud, beating a fist on her chest.

She struck herself like a person begging to be admitted to her own unworthy house. *Mea culpa, mea maxima culpa.* She hit her chest with unceasing regularity and monotony until her arm fell, the muscles spent, until the day came full on and she slept.

She woke slowly the next time and the thought of her father's pipe struck suddenly into her mind. She didn't need to see it, to hold it, but she pictured it there on her counter. Earth and heaven, connecting, the fire between that burned in everything alive. She lay straining for the familiar sounds of the day beginning, the small pleasurable noises of a woman caring for a child, and then she remembered that she was alone. A holy fire exists in all we touch, she thought, even in the flames that fed my father's heart. Framed and finished in the anguish, she felt her own face take on his depth.

It was too late for them to do anything but smoke the pipe together, she and Xavier. But that small thing was possible. She rose and showered in the little stall next to her room, calmer as the water coursed down, smoother as she soaped and rubbed. She wrapped a worn towel around her waist, her breasts. She dried her thick hair in which there was still so little gray, and she brushed her teeth twice. She wasn't hungry or anxious. Her heart was again docile in her chest, except when she thought directly of Xavier. Then, it yawned open like a greedy young bird, ready to be fed.

When she drove into his yard near Matchimanito and stopped, she was suddenly aware that her visit was strange and unnatural. Thirty years had passed. Between them there had been no word exchanged, and at the thought of what she possibly could say, she put her hand to her cheek, uneasy and afraid. Her actions would be unfathomable, the behavior of a crazy woman. Still, she did not turn the car around but sat for a long while, staring at the house, watching for a sign. The place was small, hand built, not a prefabricated government box but an old cabin like hers, shored up through the years. It was painted neatly and well shoveled, the snow heaped to each side of the walk. Zelda knew that Xavier had special tools built for his arms, that he could do anything, that he never believed or allowed himself to be treated like a man with something missing, but rather, it always seemed he had more than other people. The young came to him, sought him out, just the way she was seeking him now. He had simplified his heart.

She saw the window curtain drop, then Xavier appeared. Although they hadn't looked into each other's eyes since she refused him in the breath of horses, although they were more strange to one another than strangers, upon approaching her there was no hint of awkwardness in Xavier. He was wearing a heavy red and black hunting jacket, leather boots, an old billed hat. He leaned down to her window and Zelda's face bloomed toward his as though his features gave out warmth. Deep vertical gashes of age ran from the corners of his eyes to his chin and folded like a carved fan in symmetrical weavings. They held one another in long regard, and as their stillness remained unbroken a mysterious peace descended. Light dashed itself upon Zelda, but she wasn't shaken. Her hands floated off the steering wheel and gestured, but she wasn't helpless. She left the car, stood before Xavier, new as if naked, but she had no shame. They walked toward the house and left the pipe in its leather wrappings in the front seat, buckled carefully as a child.

I'M A MAD DOG BITING MYSELF FOR SYMPATHY

WE ARE AT METRO DRUG IN DOWNTOWN FARGO, PASSING TIME WAITing for the right moment. When the next train pulls into the Amtrak station two blocks north, we think a car might be left outside, idling, keys in the ignition. That's our hope, but we don't dare hang too near the tracks. I never stole a thing as big as a car before and I keep having to turn my mind off. I wander the aisles of the big drugstore just to hear the canned leftover carols over the loudspeaker, and Gerry frowns at the pages of a magazine.

"Maybe there's a Santa Claus," Gerry says. "Maybe we'll get lucky." I walk away from him and then, instead of lucky, I see the bird.

You think you know everything about yourself, how much money it would take, for instance, to make you take it. How you would react when caught. But then you find yourself in the middle of planning to steal a car walking out the door with a stuffed toucan. I can't explain this right, just why, though I put it all upon myself. Perhaps it is to warm up to grand larceny, to see if I'll get spotted, which I do. Or maybe it is just to distract the two of us, which also happens.

And too, there is Shawnee Ray. I think of Christmas, how this bird should have sat underneath her tree. The minute I see that toucan, I wish I'd won it for her at a county fair, though we never went to a fair. I see myself throwing a half dozen soft-balls and hitting every wooden milk jug, or maybe tossing rings. But then, you never win because those things are weighted or loaded wrong, and that's another excuse. I never would have snagged this toucan for Shawnee Ray because life's a cheat in general.

I lift the bird.

Outside in the street it is the tag end of this bleak day, unpleasant and gray. A light snow is letting up now, having dusted a few hard clumps, but covered nothing. Yellow grass from last year even shows on the boulevards. The temperature is up in the last few hours. I like the smell in the air, the dry dirt, even the threat of new snow, too, in the gloom of the gathering night sky.

The usual stiff-neck turns to look at me, at Gerry, who walks in front toward the train station and has not seen my petty theft. This bird is really huge and furry, with green underneath its floppy wings and fat stuffed orange feet. I don't know why they'd sell a strange thing like this in Metro. Maybe a big promotion, maybe some kind of come-on left over from the holiday season. And then the manager yells at me from the door. I am halfway down the street when I hear him. "Come back here!" Probably he points at me, too, though there is no reason since I stick out plenty, and still more as I begin to run.

I pass Gerry, looking over my shoulder, and he rises up like he was shot and springs high on the balls of his feet right next to me.

First I put the bird underneath my arm, but it throws me off my balance, so I clutch it to my ribs. That is no better. Thinking back now I should have ditched it, slipped off through the alleyways and disappeared. Of course, I don't—otherwise none of all that happens would have gone down. I sit the bird on my shoulders and hold the lumpy feet under my chin, then I bear down, like going for the gold. My legs churn beneath me. I leap curbs, dodge among old men in long gray coats and babies in strollers, shoot up and over car hoods until I come to the railroad depot, the new Quonset hut aluminum one just beside the old brick building. It is our destination, after all, so I slip in the door and look out the window just as the train sighs and breathes its way toward us along the tracks.

A gathering crowd follows with the manager. There's a policewoman, a few mall-sitters, passersby. They are bustling and talking together and making big circles of their arms, to illustrate the size of the toucan, and closing in.

That's when our stroke of luck, good or bad is no telling, occurs. Gerry stands beside me, breathing hard, looking wild. Then a white car drives into the parking lot, a solid plastic luggage rack strapped on its roof. A man jumps out, eager for a relative maybe, and he leaves the car running in neutral. We ease out of the depot and stand beside the car. At that moment, it seems as though events are carrying us. I open up the hinges on the plastic rack, stuff the bird under its restraints. No one notices. Encouraged, Gerry and I casually get in, him behind the wheel. He takes the car out of neutral and we start to roll, backing out of the lot. Gerry changes gears, then stops at the cross street and looks both ways.

There we are, in a car. It isn't ours but for the time being that doesn't matter. We get to the corner and we look up the street one way. It is clear. We look down the other, to where a bunch of people are still arguing and trying to describe us with their hands. Either way, the road will take us straight out of the town.

Gerry lets the car idle, looks at me, his expression asking which way to turn.

I know we shouldn't show up on the reservation, not with Gerry, with the toucan, much less the car, but then the truth is we don't have nowhere else to go. I think of the bird. In a way, Shawnee Ray got us into this, I tell myself, even though I know it is more my wish than a thought that makes any sense.

Maybe her bad sisters will take my dad in, hide him, get us over the border. So I nod north and Gerry makes the turn, and then another complexity, although at the time I don't realize, occurs when the man at the depot, the one who has left the car, appears very suddenly in the rearview mirror.

We have just started moving when I hear a thump from behind. It is so surprising. Just imagine. He is there on the trunk, hanging on as though by magnetics. The man reaches up and grabs the hitches on the rooftop luggage rack, gets a better grip, and sprawls across the back window. He is a small man, young. Through the side view, I see his boots, blue Dr. Martens, kicking in the air, and the edge of his black coat. I hear him shrieking in an inhuman desperate way that horrifies Gerry so much he floors the gas.

We must go by everyone fast, but the effect is dreamlike, so slow. I see the faces of the people, their mouths falling open, their arms stretching and grasping. As we turn the corner the man rolls off, over and over like a seal in water. He flies from the trunk and bowls the followers before in his rush so they heap on the ground beneath him. The man is in their laps, they are holding him. They lay him down as though he is a live torpedo and start running after us.

"Scandinavians," I say to Gerry, because Aunt Zelda was married to one. "They don't give up the ghost."

I want to yell out, to tell them, "Okay, so it's stolen. It's gone! It's a cheap stuffed bird anyhow and I will *park* the car. I promise."

"We'll check the oil in Devils Lake. No sweat, Dad." I talk as though we've got everything under control. I point out the scenic route, and we take it at a fast clip, but I know the view anyway. We are down near the river when the worst thing comes about, when all of a sudden I understand the man with his eyes rearing back in his skull, his thick heels kicking. I understand the changed faces of the people in the group, their blurting voices, ". . . baby."

As from the backseat, it wails.

I have my first reaction: I don't know what I'm hearing. I think it is an animal, car trouble, anything else but the obvious. Gerry pulls to the curb and I turn around in a frantic whirl. I still can't see that it's a baby because I am behind on the new equipment. He sits in something round and firm, shaped like a big football, strapped down at the chest and over the waist, held tight by a padded cushion. I guess he is a boy because he is dressed in blue. His blanket features flying baseball bats and hockey sticks. Above his face there is a little diamond attachment made of plastic, a bunch of keys and brilliant balls that dangle out of reach.

His face is small and dark, almost copper, and his fingers, splayed out against his cheeks, are tiny as the feet of a sparrow. There is a bottle of juice in a bag beside him. I reach back, put the nipple in the baby's mouth and the little guy sucks, but he can't hold the bottle by himself.

"Don't drop it!" I warn as the car sways and lurches.

Gerry pulls onto the road, gasping.

"Let's get the fuck out of here."

"We should leave off the baby," I say.

"No, keep him."

Gerry guns right out of there. The baby's cry begins again and I wish I knew how to stop him from suffering. I know he feels the confusion in the air, the strangeness, the whiff of threat. I feel like I should convince the baby that things will be all right, but I don't know how and also I don't know for sure. I would be lying if I said I did. Gerry has to slow down to get through traffic. Sirens rush ahead on their way to the interstate, passing in a squeal which surprises me. This car, this pack on top, it is so obvious. I say to Gerry that maybe we should ditch it at the old King Leo's, get out and run. But then we pass the place. Over us, the sky is bearing down and bearing down, so I think now maybe snow will really fall. A white Christmas like the music in my brain. I know Gerry must remember how to drive in snow and this car has decent tires, I can feel them. They never lose grip or plane above the road. They just keep rolling, humming, all four in this unified direction, so dull that after some time it all seems normal again.

The baby stops crying and drops off to sleep. He shouldn't be there. I have to realize the situation. There is no use in thinking back, in saying to myself, *You shouldn't have stole the damn bird in the first place,* because I did do that and then, well as you see, it is like I went along with the arrangement of things as they took shape.

Of course, a few miles farther on there is a smoky waiting, which we knew would happen, but not whether it would be before or behind us. So now our answer comes. The officer's car turns out of a dirt road and starts flashing, starts coming at us from the rear. We take it up to eighty and then a hundred and we move, *move,* so the frozen snow standing in the fields flashes by like scarves and the silver snow whirls out of nowhere to either side of us, and what rushes up before us is a heat of road and earth.

I am not all that afraid, but now I realize why I feel sure that they will not use their weapons. The baby. I can't believe that Gerry thought to keep him with us for that purpose, though, and I try to put that thought out of mind—but it keeps popping in. We keep driving and then, as we take a turn, as we bound across a railroad intersection, I hear the roof rack snap open with a cracking thump. I twist around and see the bird as it dives out of the sky, big and plush, a purple blur that plunges its yellow beak into the windshield of the police car and throws the state police off course so their cruiser skids, rolls over once, comes back with such force the car rights itself and sits quiet in shock.

We slow back to eighty. The pack blows off too, and I reason that now the car is not so easy to identify. I should have thought about that in the first place, but then the bird would not have hatched out and attacked. About this time, being as the toucan is gone, I begin to feel perhaps there is no point in traveling farther. I begin to think that we should just stop at the nearest farm, dump the car and the baby with someone else, and disappear into the fields. I start to feel positive that if I show up at Shawnee Ray's, even with nothing, even with a convict criminal, she will not throw me out. She'll have to take me in, let me sleep on the couch. I fast-forward. She will live with another man, someday, a guy of world experience. Soon she will visit restaurants and zoos, go camping in the wilderness, ski. She will know things and I will still be the same person that I was the day before I got this phone call from my dad. And I am glad about the toucan, then, which would have made me look ridiculous—me, showing up there like a kid in junior high school with a stuffed animal, when her tastes are becoming so enlarged. I should send her chocolates in a little red and green box. I wish I had. And then I look past the road in front of me and realize it is seriously snowing.

It isn't just like ordinary snow even from the first. It's like that rhyme or story in the second grade, the sky falling and let's go and tell the king. It comes down. I think to myself, Well, let it come down. Gerry keeps on driving. I know you'll say it, you'll wonder, you'll think what about the child in the backseat, that baby, not even one year old? Because he does have an age and all, but what could I know of that?

Gerry talks to the baby. He says, in a funny voice, "You little bastard you, what are you doing here?"

"Don't call him bastard."

My state of mind is lowering. I roll the passenger window open. Snow whites out the windshield and I can't see the road in front of us. I watch the margin, try to follow the white border before it is obscured by a twisting cyclone of snow. My attention vanishes when the baby bawls. My ears fill. He roars and I hear the wind screaming like his father on the trunk yelled, but there is something about that baby that is like a weight in me, heavier than a shrunk-down star, older than gravity. I don't mind the cries because they make a certain sense in this situation, and I understand him in a way, his misery, his wish for the tried and true. I can tell that he knows something is wrong, his world is fucked, some essential thing.

The sky grows darker, the snow is near solid in the air, and we are hitting zero-definition. The sky is in our face. The car's a hollow toy, and we're struggling for purchase when we chance in behind a snowplow. We almost run into it at first, but I see the faint glow of its lamps and flashers. Gerry whoops and he's pounding the wheel and the baby shrieks out still louder. Carefully, with sure belligerence, deliberate patience, the plow grumbles on in front of us, heading due north. Like a big, clumsy angel, like an ocean liner, clanking and mournful, the snowplow parts the waves and makes us our way.

We fall into the cleave of its wake and hang there, held fast, as it cruises into the boundless wastes beyond. We slow when it slows, stop when it pauses for breath, then go on into the deeper spaces of the night. It rumbles past the lights and past the farms and lighted elevators. We keep its tail in our sight, breathe easy. Gerry has me light a cigarette for him, in reprieve he takes a deep, slow, drag. It all seems simple now, for this one moment, it seems to me that we're saved. Never mind the fact we have stolen this car, not to mention the baby who needs rocking, feeding, never mind what comes next.

I reach back to joggle the plastic egg and reassure the baby that we're doing better, but I have to keep my hand there because I feel the car give on the road, shake and rattle, as another vehicle plunges alongside us. Out of nowhere, like a star, it rushes in a hollow of wind. This car gives off its own light, a flash of fire and deep blue, and it stays steady with us, almost glowing in the wall of snow. Running neck and neck to us, it breasts the impossible drifts, floats over them like a soundless ice blue skiff.

I suppose I should be more amazed than I am to see that it is June's car, and that she is driving. We see her silhouette, the barest outline of her, head high, hands resting on the wheel, one elbow on the open window ledge. Her hair is a black net, her back is held straight. We see her shrug her shoulders once, and smile through the clouds and frost.

My dad leans forward, grips the wheel, his voice ragged and amazed.

"June!"

He calls to her, begging her to stop although of course she can't hear. And then he starts to follow her car, turns out of the safety of the snowplow's salvation. He deviates. I lean over, wrench the wheel, try to take it from him in a struggle, and I manage to get him back into the tracks for a moment. I am all of a sudden shaking and cold with the dread. He strains to the windshield glass, looking after her, weaving for a glance of her through the sheets of irregular snow. He wants her so hard that the desire takes me over too and I can't catch him back because I'm caught up in the anxious necessity. He swerves into line behind the blue car's trail. He follows even when she pulls calmly from the plow's path and leaves the blacktop highway.

The snow is packed so hard underneath that we continue across the fields at a steady pace, following her red taillights, which shine and wink as we travel unbounded through the perfectly flat land that runs along the interstate. Of course, here and there, the ground falls away, hollow and uncertain. Each time we falter, I turn to Gerry and open my mouth, but each time, before I can prepare myself to argue, he hits my shoulder and cries out not to stop him. He's fascinated, gripped, won't talk to me now, and doesn't notice how the tracks narrow into one, and then widen, go from wheel tracks to no tracks to unbroken snow.

In a sudden clearing in the blizzard, her car stops before us. We see it calmly waiting there, no lights on, lounging still and dark. Just like in a cartoon, like Dumbo flying and he realizes that he isn't supposed to be up in the air, Gerry panics and we get stuck.

"Dad?"

There is silence. No answer. He just turns his head slow and looks at me with an air of sad puzzlement and hard choice. I want to ask him not to go, but my lips are frozen still and frosted shut. His eyes are deep and the shadows on his face roar in my ears, blue receding, flooding out of my life as if sucked back from creation. The blackened moon shocks out somewhere in back of the blizzard's violence. I take a deep breath of the stale smoke and desperation of my father, but already he's halfway out the door. Into the diamond swirl of radiance and chance, he vaults. He's drawn to June, lost in the surge of his own feelings.

The door slams. I sit waiting for a moment, hoping, watching. I see him slide into the passenger's side of the blue car and then, a small pause, and her headlamps go on. It isn't that he doesn't care for me, I know that, it's just that his own want is too deep to resist. June's beams trace the air, open spaces in the dark wind, and the car begins to move. I watch it until snow slams down over us, covering the windshield.

I am out in the middle of nothing, in a storm that can go on for three more minutes or three more days. And remember this: it is a white car we stole. Most difficult kind to spot. I can't recall what they say in the papers every fall, the advice about how to survive when a blizzard hits. Whether to stay on the road with the car, or to set out on foot for help. Plus, there's the baby. I know I shouldn't let the car run, use up the gas and the heater, but for a moment I do. I crawl into the back and unstrap the boy from the egg seat and I hold him in my arms. The heater roars, though I've got it on low, and in the breath of warmth I'm suddenly so very tired.

I think about my father and my mother, about how they have already taught me about the cold so I don't have to be afraid of it. And yet, this baby doesn't know. Cold sinks in, there to stay. And people, they'll leave you, sure. There's no return to what was and no way back. There's just emptiness all around, and you in it, like singing up from the bottom of a well, like nothing else, until you harm yourself, until you are a mad dog biting yourself for sympathy. Because there is no relenting. There is no hand that falls. There is no woman reaching down to take you in her arms.

My father taught me his last lesson in those hours, in that night. He and my mother, June, have always been inside of me, dark and shining, their absence about the size of a coin, something I have touched against and slipped. And when that happens, I call out in my bewilderment—"*What is this?*"—and the thing is I never knew until now it was a piece of thin ice they had put there.

Come what might when we are found, I stay curled around this baby. The heater snaps off, the motor dies down. I rummage in the seat for whatever I can find to keep us warm and find small blankets, baby size. I know it will be a long night that maybe will not end. But at least I can say, as I drift, as the cold begins to take me, as I pull the baby closer to me, zipping him inside of my jacket, here is one child who was never left behind. I bite my own hands like the dog, but already they are numb. The shooting star is in my mouth, cold fire blazing into nothing, but at least this baby never was alone. At least he always had someone, even if it was just a no-account like me, a waste, a reservation load.

As I fall away into my sleep, I'm almost happy things have turned out this way. I am not afraid. An unknown path opens up before us, an empty trail shuts behind. Snow closes over our tracks, and then keeps moving like the tide. There is no trace where we were. Nor any arrows pointing to the place we're headed. We are the trackless beat, the invisible light, the thought without a word to speak. Poured water, struck match. Before the nothing, we are the moment.

CHAPTER TWENTY-FIVE

LULU'S CAPTURE

THEY SAY THAT SHE WAS READY FOR THE FEDERAL MARSHALS when they drove up to the doors, though they were quiet, their tires hardly crunching snow. The rest of us had no wind and no warning, no inkling, but we were mostly awake anyway in the dark chill of a day that began with a plunging degree of cold. That below-zero chill burned our feet through the covers. We shivered, twisting deeper. Old bones need warm caves. From outside, in the insulated halls and behind the doors, we heard the shuffling, we heard the boot steps, the noise of their invasion, but most of us turned over into a sleep that would soon go on forever. We dreamed the young dreams, missed the beginning of what happened, missed Lulu's capture.

Of course, there was always Josette Bizhieu to tell us what occurred. There was Marie Kashpaw, who maintained calm and smiled past her questioners. There was Maurice Morris— man about town, he called himself—just returning to his apartment around the time the federals entered Lulu's door.

They did not knock, they did not give her a chance to form an answer, just busted their way into her apartment and discovered her sitting there, ready. And she was prepared. All was in perfect order for their arrival. No possible doubt about it, none at all. For who else was attired in her full regalia at that hour, dressed traditional, decked out in black velvet with flowers from the woodlands beaded into the shining nap—red rose, yellow heart, white leaves, and winking petals—who else was dressed like Lulu? She carried her fan of pure white eagle tailfeathers. Four of them, upright, in her hand of a sexy grandmother. On the wrist of the other arm, there dangled her beaded carrying pouch, full of cosmetics and papers and identity proof. Of that, they disarmed her as with drawn guns they searched rudely through her precious things.

Let's say they found a knife, they found a weapon, they found something besides that machinery and bundled newspaper and Congressional material that she quoted as she took our money while playing cards. Let's say they found an Illinois matchbook, a pair of sawed-apart handcuffs, some direct proof her son had been to see her. Or let's say they didn't find a thing, but that motherhood itself was more than enough.

Whatever the reasoning, they questioned her. At this, we have to laugh.

We hide our smiles back behind our hands, to be polite to our government, for which so many of our men have died and suffered, and our women too, but we can't help but say it was a useless cause for them to offer Lulu Lamartine her own coffee from her own pot on the stove, to ask her if she would like to sit down in her own chair and encourage her to make herself at home in her own home. It was useless to set up the tape recorders and take out the pens and papers. For what question were they going to ask her, after all, what question that would receive a reliable answer? A truth? When her son and her grandson were the ones at issue? What truth but Lulu's own truth? What other possible response?

Maybe they thought Indians dressed that way all the time. Maybe they thought Indians dressed that way to go to bed at night. No one commented on or noticed Lulu's outfit, ceremonial and bold, as if she was ready to be honored. Her moccasins, she always called them works of art: smoked deerhide, expertly tanned. Little roses were beaded on the toes, white rabbit fur sewed inside, and meanwhile the rest of us wore house slippers, thin quilted robes. Listening at doorways, we called softly between ourselves, and shuddered with cold. Underneath her powwow dress, Lulu wore a pair of red long johns, we were sure. Winter is not gentle with us old ones and she anticipated drafts, who wouldn't, during the entry and seizure.

They were very smart, these federals. No doubt they were wise. They had seen a lot of hard cases, chased a lot of criminals, solved a great many crimes that would stump us ordinary Chippewas. And yet, the fact is, they had never encountered Lulu. For that reason, they spent a long time questioning a fish in the river, they spent a longer time talking to a turtle in its shell, they tried to intimidate a female badger guarding the mouth of its den and then, to fool an old lady coyote who trotted wide of the marks her pups had left. They spent hours, in which they should have been tracking down their wary escapee, asking Lulu one question, in many different ways, until she seemed to break down, shaking her hands and fanning herself with feigned distress.

"Yes, yes," she whispered. "Something happened."

They got a story all right. One hour passed, then two, but then it's frustrating to question an old woman who is losing her memory. In shock, she gets the past mixed up into the present and cannot recall what age her son is now, or when, just precisely, these things occurred that all the clever and keen-eyed men describe to her, and then of course, when they bring in a woman, more sympathetic, there is a great deal of additional confusing material to relate, all of the normals and particulars of her son's habits and childhood behaviors that were so impressive at the time.

Heads are spinning and just then, when their tongues are sticking in their cheeks and their brows are going up, she remembers perfectly.

"Of course, of course he was here. He came home."

And at those words, of course, the ears perk and the recorders whir, but then the sense retreats, the poor old woman faints, slumps dead away, and must be revived with a strong fresh cup of coffee.

"Where else would he go?" she says when she wakes up, and hours later, it turns out that she has just returned from taking him up north across the border in her automobile. Where? That takes quite a while more to figure out. She tries to help but the world is going vague, losing its shape and everything is getting mashed around inside her stumbling brain, although she frowns helpfully and often hums to herself, annoyingly, in order to aid her memory.

"Where? Where?"

Dreamy, she smiles, in her own time and place perhaps, but maybe they are onto her at last. Maybe they have lost their patience, it is true, or have finally understood that they are playing with a cat whose claws are plump and sheathed. They have dusted everything for fingerprints. They have examined every surface for nail clips and hair. They have looked into each drawer and sounded walls. Gone over each of her possessions, in turn. Including the wanted poster, nicely framed.

We told her, we reminded her that she'd done wrong. We scolded Lulu Lamartine to read the warning, heed the label, pointed out that she harbored stolen government property upon her shelf. For that offense, they finally take her in, arrest her, cart her off but with a kind of ceremony that does not confuse a single one of us, for she has planned it. And all so perfectly! By this time, outside the door, in the hallway, so many popping lights of cameras, whining shutters. All of the North Dakota newspapers. By that time, the local tribal officials. The Chippewa police. Jurisdiction issues? Sure, plenty of them right there to worry over.

There goes Lulu Lamartine, powwow perfect, chained at the wrists but still clutching the eagle-feather fan. Lulu Lamartine surrounded, walked off by muscle-bound agents, as if she would escape, and so frail! Removed from an old people's home! Lulu Lamartine luring dogs away, diverting attention, making such a big statewide fracas, and with her story, sending agents on a new goose chase. It is perfect, it is sinful, and any one of us could have told them they were getting into something like a mazy woods when talking to that woman.

They should have backed out early. They should not have taken her into custody, brandishing her hooked wrists with simple dignity. They should not have let her do the thing that she does, the act that gets onto the six o'clock news, everywhere, all through the country.

Down the frosted squares of the sidewalk, Lulu Lamartine dances the old-lady traditional, a simple step, but complex in its quiet balance, striking. She dances with a tucked-in wildness, exactly like an old-time Pillager. And then, at the door to the official vehicle, just before they whisk her inside, she raises her fan. Noises stop, cameras roll. Out of her mouth comes the old-lady trill, the victory yell that runs up our necks. Microphones squeal. Children cry. Chills form at Lulu's call, fierce and tingling. What can we do? Drawing deep breaths, hearts shaking, we can't help join her.

CHAPTER TWENTY-SIX

SHAWNEE'S MORNING

STONES OR EARTH HAD SHIFTED DIRECTLY UNDERNEATH, OR maybe the university housing was like most new construction—cheap, uneven. Whatever the reason, Shawnee Ray woke cold every morning. Shivering as she prowled the apartment, a cup of coffee in one hand, a piece of clothing or a towel in the other, she usually managed to find the source of the draft before waking Redford. Cracks beside the windows where the frame and Sheetrock had separated away were stuffed with washcloths. All of her summer T-shirts insulated cold black squares through which tangled plumbing ran into the cinder-block bathroom. Most of her underwear was rolled under one broad sill with a northwest exposure. She was shedding herself slowly into the walls, pressing scarves and socks against thready fingers of wind.

And then one morning she woke, warm, from a dream. She must have finally managed to fill every one of the builder's mistakes. Her windows were frosted over in pale etchings of glittering and mysteriously detailed ferns. The dream still hung close, and she saw Lipsha.

There is so little time, just the warmth of a breath.

She touched her face, took a swallow of air. Dizzily, she pressed her hot fingers to the icy window and kept them there even though the frost burned. Peering through the melted spot on the glass, she saw that deep snow had fallen, an overnight blizzard. The world was thickly covered and arrested, a place of sudden peace.

On the radio, lists of cancellations. No classes, no day care. No milk. She turned the radio onto a station of generic musical sounds, heard that Gerry Nanapush had still not been apprehended. She and Redford ate handfuls of cereal, drank juice with slivers of slush frozen off the side of the bottle. Partway through the morning, there was more news. Gerry Nanapush still at large. A hostage found in good condition. She turned off the radio and when Lyman called she put Redford on the phone. He spoke seriously, thoughtfully, full of plans. The sun blazed through cottony clouds. After the call was over, they ate a lunch of more cereal and then Shawnee Ray fitted Redford into his quilted nylon snowsuit, pulled thickly knitted mittens onto his hands, stuffed his three-layer stockinged feet into boots. The two went outside and Shawnee began to shovel her car free of the enormous dolphin swoop of drift that covered the front end. This was work she liked, and as she bent and swung to it she grew excited, along with her son, and they moved snow until his feet pinched with cold.

Back inside, Redford fell asleep as Shawnee Ray carefully spread her patterns and materials and drawings across the kitchen table and began to work, first in the slowly failing light and then in the deep glow of the lamp. She was making a ribbon shirt for Lipsha, interest on his loan, the whole amount now stuffed into a sealed manila envelope. Brown calico, blue, cream, salmon trim—she was fitting collar to shoulders, figuring out the way she would join the ribbons at the yoke. At the end of one ribbon, she had thought of attaching a dime-store wedding ring. As a joke, except it wasn't. Lipsha's absence was a constant ache. Maybe she would buy two rings with that two hundred dollars.

Scraps of other projects—turquoise, black and yellow satin littered the floor and twirled as she kicked the table restlessly.

She had begun to paint and draw, and her tackle boxes full of materials were neatly stored upon the counter. As she worked out the design for Lipsha's shirt in her head, she found her thoughts drifting. A deeper part of her was listening. From time to time, the wind picked up outside, whirling a scythe, sifting snow down the shingles, sending clouds skittering into the frozen night. When the air boomed against the glass or scraped the splintered siding of the apartment house, Shawnee Ray raised her face and stared into the darkened window glass, as if to question the invisible presences.

In her dream, Lipsha had kissed her with a matter-of-fact joy, deep and long. The kiss still seemed so real that she could smell the smoke on his jacket. She closed her eyes—again his lips brushed hers once, twice, then carved a dark blossom.

CHAPTER TWENTY-SEVEN

PILLAGER BONES

IN THE DEAD COLD OF WINTER, FLEUR PILLAGER WENT OUT. It was said by those who came to call on her, who came to take her house away with signed papers, that to move at all the old woman had to oil her joints with a thin grease she kept by her door. They examined the details, deciphered what they could and imagined the rest. After rubbing her elbows and knees with the bear's fat, she burned a wand of sage, breathed the pure smoke, and let her eyes shut. She sat in the dim and fading warmth of her house until the sun struck the center of the roof, at its zenith. Then she smoothed her thin braids back underneath a white headscarf and stood, ravenous and stooped. She shifted her arms slowly into the husk of an elegantly cut black coat that smelled of burnt leaves and cedar. The smooth lining, blanket-heavy satin, draped her shoulders. The collar was a curled swale of fur. She paused a moment, frowning, her face pressed to the worn nap, then hooked a pair of Lulu's child moccasins off the wall and put them in her pocket. The small hide shoes were pierced with tiny holes so that if death approached Lulu her mother could always make an argument. *My daughter cannot come with you, see the holes in her shoes? The journey is too long for her. Now go.* Fleur's own moccasins, knee high and embroidered in a looping tangle of flowers, were lined with the snowy pelts of rabbits she'd

271

snared. Her hat was woven of owl feathers. Onto her hands, she pulled a pair of leather mittens.

She didn't take the written walls, she didn't take the storehouse facts. She didn't take the tangled scribe of her table or the headboard, the walls, the obscured and veiny writing on the tamped logs and her bed. She didn't take the yellow newspapers, brittle as the wings of butterflies, scrawled in the margins, or the bound railroad ledgers or the linen sheets or scribbled mats. No, all of the writing, the tracked-up old cabin, she left for the rest of us to find. Fleur Pillager only took those things she carried with her all of her life.

Outdoors, into a day of deep cold and brilliance that often succeeds a long disruptive blizzard, she went, thinking of the boy out there. Annoyed, she took his place. Snow stars caught light in the packed yard and the toboggan that she dragged from the shed, a simple wooden frame loaded with skin-wrapped packages, was dusted with glitter, too. Her earrings blazed, silver-green circles, at the jaw of her fiercely cut and unchangeable face. The wooden runners that slightly elevated the bed of the drag squeaked against the packed whiteness as her dark form moved, a hole in the dazzling air.

The shore of Matchimanito Lake was iced perfectly to its broad lip of stone, and the night's relentless wind had carved the snow on its surface into mock waves delicate as shells. The island in the center of the lake was another core of darkness toward which Fleur traveled, dragging her toboggan of bones.

All afternoon, on into the fast-falling dusk, she walked. Her step was brisk and driving at first, but then slowed, and she often had to rest. Her breath sawed in and out, the cold searing her lungs. On the island there was a cave and in that place her cousin sat grinning from his skull chair, waiting for her to settle into the whiteness and the raving dust along with all of their relatives. Steadily, slowly, her clean steps pressed down between the runner's trails. She stopped in the still breeze, she listened.

Her sisters bickered and argued, threw the marked pits of wild plum, gambled their rings and beads and copper bracelets back and forth. Her grandmother, Four Soul, who had given Fleur the burdensome gift of outliving nearly all of those whom she loved, sang quietly with her thin arms open, waiting. Nanapush was there to smooth her face and again he was a young man, straight as birch, rubbing his clever hands with pollen, and talking without cease. With the twig of a pine, her mother was combing her father's hair calm about his shoulders. The child she lost whimpered, rocked safe by the wind that swirled through and scoured clean the cave where Moses Pillager had slept with his child and his one love between him and the *windigo*. As she walked over the frozen waves she felt the lake bottom buckle far below her feet. The water trembled in its sleep. She waited to catch her halting breath and felt the years slide through her arms so that she braced herself, dizzy, almost weeping to see how far it was that she still had to travel.

It was then that the old strength that had served her in her hardest times seized her, lifted and set her again on the unmarked path. In later days, there would be some who claimed they found her tracks and followed to see where they changed, the pad broadened, the claw pressed into the snow. Others heard songs rise, eager, old songs that haven't been sung since that winter. There is enough we can't account for, however, we need no more. Her tracks should have been obscured. Her tracks should have filled with snow. They should have blown away with those rough songs from the wild dead we cannot hush. Somehow, we should have learned not to tamper with what's beyond us. And yet on clear and brilliant days and nights of black stars they are sometimes again left among us, Fleur's tracks, once more, so it is said that she still walks.

We understand that from her island, when the lake is hard and deep, she covers ground easily, skims back to watch us in our brilliant houses. We believe she follows our hands with her underwater eyes as we deal the cards on green baize, as we drown our past in love of chance, as our money collects, as we set fires and make personal wars over what to do with its weight, as we go forward into our own unsteady hopes.

She doesn't tap our panes of glass or leave her claw marks on eaves and doors. She only coughs, low, to make her presence known. You have heard the bear laugh—that is the chuffing noise we hear and it is unmistakable. Yet no matter how we strain to decipher the sound it never quite makes sense, never relieves our certainty or our suspicion that there is more to be told, more than we know, more than can be caught in the sieve of our thinking. For that day we heard the voices, the trills and resounding cries that greeted the old woman when she arrived on that pine-dark island, and all night our lesser hearts beat to the sound of the spirit's drum, through those anxious hours when we call our lives to question.